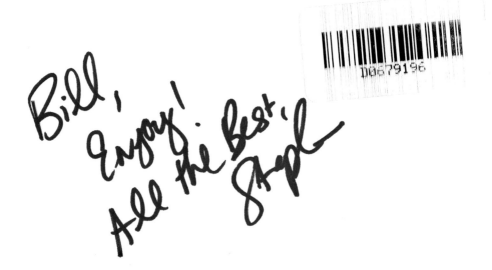

Bill,
Enjoy!
All the Best,
Steph

DRIVEN TO PERFORM

Risk-Aware Performance Management From Strategy Through Execution

Nenshad Bardoliwalla • Stephanie Buscemi • Denise Broady

Evolved
Technologist
Press
New York, NY

Driven to Perform
Risk-Aware Performance Management From Strategy Through Execution

Nenshad Bardoliwalla, Stephanie Buscemi, and Denise Broady

www.driventoperform.net

Published by Evolved Technologist Press, an imprint of Evolved Media, 242 West 30th Street, Suite 801, New York, New York 10001

This book may be purchased for educational, business, or sales promotional use. For more information contact:
Evolved Technologist Press
(646) 827-2196
info@EvolvedTechnologist.com
www.EvolvedTechnologist.com

Editors: Dan Woods, Deb Cameron
Writers: Dan Woods, Deb Cameron, James Buchanan, Sophie Jasson-Holt,
 D. Foy O'Brien, Kermit Pattison, David Penick, and Dan Safarik
Production Editor: Deb Gabriel
Cover and Interior Design: 1106 Design
Illustrator: Rob Romano
First Edition: April 2009

ISBN: 978-0-9789218-9-7

Contents

Part II: Automating Performance Management

Part III: Bringing Performance Management to You

Preface

When we three authors started out on the journey that created this book, we shared a common vision of writing a book that would help the business we serve become inspired about the potential of performance management. Throughout the course of our careers, we have worked at the pioneering vendors in the analytic applications, business intelligence, enterprise performance management, and governance, risk, and compliance spaces, as leaders helping to establish these market categories, defining the product vision and then building the products themselves, championing them to the market, and working with individual customers to make them successful in their own performance management initiatives. Our design for this book reflects this rich body of knowledge and experience, from which we were able to distill the key lessons of performance management and the way we teach it to others. However, whether we are successful teachers of performance management is up to the reader to decide.

In Part I, we attempt to clear the decks and explain from top to bottom the breadth of all the topics involved in performance management and the details of many issues that are often not sufficiently emphasized.

For example, we considered using the term "risk-aware performance management" throughout instead of just performance management because we feel that the biggest favor we can do for people who are starting on the road to improvement is call attention to the need to explicitly include analysis and management of risk and compliance factors. In the end, we felt that this would be overkill because we stress the role of risk and compliance in so many places in the book.

The critical role of performance management in orchestrating the business network is another rising trend that we emphasize in Part I. As companies become more global, have more partners, and come under increasing scrutiny from regulators and stakeholders, it is vital that the operational model grows. The work in progress, quality, and compliance of partners must be tracked. Environmental and sustainability indicators must receive close attention. The operational drivers for various performance outcomes, both within and beyond the four walls of the organization, must be understood so that results can be better predicted and problems found as early as possible.

Perhaps the biggest change that separates those who have performance management fever from the uninitiated is a detailed awareness of the performance management lifecycle. Once understood, it is a process that affects pretty much everything a person does in both their personal and professional lives. The idea of formulating a strategy, translating it into initiatives, tracking their implementation, finding the right metrics, looking for and managing risk, gathering the best data possible, modeling and optimizing the best new ways forward, and then using what you learned to improve your strategy is a closed loop, the scientific method brought to pragmatic life. Whether you are running a little league team or a multi-national corporation, the performance management lifecycle applies and will help. We have spent a lot of time trying to explain the lifecycle so that you too will catch the fever.

Part II expands to some larger issues that demand close attention. We cover the technology that can be used to support implementation of the lifecycle, the role of business intelligence as a platform for managing data and transforming it into information that fuels performance management, and the relationship between risk and compliance management processes and performance management. With the increasing focus on intertwining enterprise risk management with a company's strategy and compliance management needing to be linked with a company's risks, we felt compelled to truly fuse the performance, risk, and compliance management processes together in a holistic methodology. Needless to say, each of these chapters could have been books on their own.

Part III of the book is where we translate performance management into specific domains of business such as Finance, HR, IT, Sales, Marketing, Service, Supply Chain, Procurement, and Product Development to make it truly relevant to every reader who might pick it up. A unique angle that we explore that we have not found in other books on performance management is the exploration of the actual end-to-end execution processes that each business domain within companies uses to close the loop with their strategies and the implications this has for ensuring the synchronized collaboration necessary to get all the groups in the organization aligned. We attacked this problem with tremendous energy and designed a uniform structure for each of these chapters that presents how to apply performance management to that specific domain in concert with various business partners. We hope these chapters drive change in companies by connecting the dots between the generic potential of performance management and how to put the practices to work in a specific way.

To write any such book is a labor. While it might be too much to say that this has been entirely a labor of love, it is accurate to say that this has been a project driven by our obsession to share what we have learned in a comprehensive way. We hope that you find your own way to the passion we have for performance management and the results it can produce for your organization.

Nenshad Bardoliwalla
Stephanie Buscemi
Denise Vu Broady

Dedications

Nenshad Bardoliwalla: To my father, Dr. Dinshaw Framroze Bardoliwalla, who came to the United States with nothing yet found a way to give us everything, thus showing us by example what being *Driven to Perform* could accomplish.

Stephanie Buscemi: To Peter, who brought me into this profession and has mentored me throughout. Because of you, I am a better person professionally and personally.

Denise Vu Broady: To my loving and supportive Tsafi and our beautiful Leah for making every day even more special.

Acknowledgments

We would like to thank our colleagues who gave of their time in hours of interviews, including Dave Vonk, James Fisher, Kirk Anderson, Manish Jiandani, Ryan Leask, Ravi Mohan, Christian Gheorghe, Bryan Katis, Jennifer Maddox, Karol Bliznak, Dan Kearnan, Rob Davis, Brian Wood, Adrien Sirolli, Muthu Ranganathan, Mike Sherratt, Prakash Darji, Jason

Rose, Frederic Laluyaux, Stefan Karl, John Carter, Peter Rojas, James Thomas, Timo Elliott, Ranga Bodla, Lana Smith, Anthony Reynolds, Richard Barrett, Mark Crofton, David Ludlow, Michel Morel, Lothar Schubert, Carsten Hilker, Nicolas Sabatier, Stéphane Neufcourt, Narina Sippy, Jim Dunham, John Garrish, Charles Zedlewski, David Milam, Louise Stonehouse, Rebecca Adams, Adam Thier, Steve Barrett, Roman Bukary, Stefan Sigg, and Thomas Zurek.

We would also like to thank our reviewers, who carefully read through chapters and provided us with valuable feedback, including Dave Anderson, Padmini Ranganathan, Georg Kube, Carr Philips, Richard Howells, Vivek Bapat, Dawn Crew, and Bernard Chung.

No project as intense as this can occur without the support of executive sponsors who contributed both in their thought leadership and in interviews, including Sanjay Poonen, Jonathan Becher, Vishal Sikka, Marge Breya, Doug Merritt, Richard Campione, and the members of the SAP Executive Board.

Tom Greene, CIO of Colgate-Palmolive, graciously allowed us to interview him for this book. The model of governance and performance management that Tom drives is worth writing a book about itself.

A handful of industry analysts have had a significant impact on shaping the evolution of our thoughts on these topics over the years through their research and our discussions with them, and we would like to give special thanks to them, including Paul Hamerman at Forrester Research, Henry Morris and Kathy Wilhide at IDC, Nigel Rayner, John Van Decker, Gareth Herschel, and Bill Hostmann at Gartner Research, Mark Smith at Ventana Research, Howard Dresner at Dresner Advisory Services, and Michael Rasmussen at Corporate Integrity. We would like to give special thanks to John Hagerty, Vice President and Research Fellow at AMR, who not only helped shaped our thoughts over the years through his research and our discussions, but who spent time reading chapters and helping us make this a book that will reach the widest possible audience. His input was invaluable.

Professor Robert Kaplan of the Harvard Business School has had profound impact on the field of performance management and on us individually from his classic work on the Balanced Scorecard, strategy maps, and activity-based costing, as well as his most recent work on "Mastering the Management System." We have been privileged to work with Professor Kaplan directly over the years as students in his classes and frequent correspondents and could not fail to mention his influence on this book.

In addition to the individuals we've named, an important portion of research in this book was based on materials written by numerous other

SAP colleagues and the many discussions we've had with them over the years, including the fantastic members of our EPM, GRC, and BI teams, as well as numerous colleagues in Business Suite Solution Management and Solution Marketing. Your influence on this book was immeasurable, and we thank you for giving us the privilege of being your colleagues. We did everything we could to present your work accurately.

Finally, we wish to extend our deepest gratitude to Dan Woods and his entire team at Evolved Media for their support and professionalism throughout the process of writing this book. Special thanks are due to the writers who helped on this project, including James Buchanan, Sophie Jasson-Holt, D. Foy O'Brien, Kermit Pattison, David Penick, and Dan Safarik. In particular, we would like to express our sincerest appreciation to Deb Cameron, our managing editor, who worked tirelessly on the book with us through vacations, weekends, and all hours of the night to make it a success despite its massive and ever-increasing scope, and yet managed to maintain the highest professionalism throughout the project. We would also like to single out the efforts of Deb Gabriel, our project manager, who performed similarly heroic tasks to keep the book on schedule despite having to navigate the many obstacles that conspired to prevent us from doing so.

Chapter 1

Making Performance Management Work

If you had more information about your business, would you be able to run it better? For most people, the answer is yes. This book describes the modern practice of performance management, which is the task of getting more and better information about a business and using it effectively to improve results and manage risk.

The term "performance management" (PM) has had many meanings in the past 20 years. The term is used in the field of human resources to refer to reviewing and improving the performance of employees. That is a separate discipline from the one covered in this book.

If you work for the CFO or in the Finance department, the words "performance management" probably bring to mind the effort required to create accurate consolidated statements for reporting on the financial condition of the company. And for many years, performance management was limited in its focus to finance and accounting. It was the practice of efficiently tracking the flow of money around a company. Performance management can be narrowly defined as the task of defining, computing, and presenting metrics and key performance indicators. In its broadest sense, performance management encompasses the top-to-bottom management system.

In today's business world, performance management has become a way to align strategy and execution and then to monitor and optimize the work performed in an organization. Performance management creates views of a company from the broadest perspective to the most specific. Deciding on, capturing, and propagating a clear and detailed strategy is performance management. So is determining how to allocate shared costs over specific projects in order to better understand profitability. Performance management helps track the specific resources assigned to carrying out a strategic initiative and also seeks to understand, model, and monitor the risks involved in doing that work. In a general sense, performance management boils down to the following processes:

- Performance management is the way the broad outlines of strategy are translated into the specific actions of each staff member and partner
- Performance management is a continuous multi-directional flow of information into which plans and forecasts are made, actual results are monitored, and then everything is adjusted as the size of the divergence between expectations and reality is determined
- Performance management is how a company makes accurate promises and keeps them so all stakeholders can take comfort knowing what is happening
- Performance management is how risks are identified, monitored, and managed
- Performance management is how awareness is expanded so new opportunities and new challenges are proactively discovered instead of emerging in a crisis
- Performance management is the discipline that leverages data and capabilities of all previous generations of technology and business applications (from ERP, to legacy applications, to analytical tools) and distills and delivers information where it is needed

Performance management has become a key differentiating factor that separates the companies that thrive from those that struggle. This book is a guide to achieving that differentiation.

The Challenge of Performance Management

The challenge of performance management is that each company must discover on its own how best to understand and improve itself. Each company must discover the best ways to communicate its strategy, create detailed plans, track progress, and improve operations. The urgency and passion associated with this task is what separates the companies that consistently deliver the highest performance and are able to change rapidly from those that are constantly reacting to events that take them by surprise.

By attempting to improve performance management, most companies end up expanding their visibility and redirecting their focus from the past to the future. Financial reporting essentially looks backward at the money that was pumped out of the value-creating machine of a business. The best performance management practices gradually create models of an enterprise that unearth the metrics that are the best predictors of future results. This information creates a deeper understanding of how a company operates and allows problems to be indentified in time to take corrective action.

The enduring challenge of performance management is that the optimal model of the enterprise and flow of information is different at every company and changes over time. Performance management software applications provide a strong starting point, but the challenge is to create a lifecycle that carries a company through the management process, making sure that the information deemed relevant by a company's strategy and the chosen methods of execution are being collected and analyzed in each stage. Performance management replaces a world in which people run a business based primarily on hunches and instinct with one in which data turns the lights on and spurs new thinking. The ultimate, sustainable victory is the creation of a performance management culture, one in which the thirst for information and the desire to dig in and understand operations based on facts is the way everyone does their jobs.

What You Will Get From This Book

Meeting the performance management challenge is both an art and a science. This book tells you not only what performance management is, but also what's in it for you: how learning about and implementing a systemic practice of performance management can make a real difference in the bottom line of the company as a whole and in how you—whether you are a strategy-setting CEO or a business unit manager—can realize the benefits that accrue from an active, focused, and penetrating approach to measuring and managing performance effectively.

This book provides a big picture approach, designed to take into account the diverse and idiosyncratic nature of the people and organizations that compose the world of business.

Some companies are drowning in data from information overload, while not being able to effectively measure performance in ways that are meaningful for their business. Others use different metrics across departments and divisions, with the result that nothing is really comparable.

Most companies have more information tools than ever, but are not getting the maximum benefit in terms of financial and operational performance.

This book presents a comprehensive explanation of the performance management lifecycle along with detailed suggestions for improvement in each phase.

If you help craft strategy, this book explains how to:

- Take risk into account when evaluating new strategic initiatives
- Ensure that metrics are developed to measure implementation of strategy and determine the success of new approaches
- Cascade a strategy from high-level directives into specific instructions at the department level

If you are involved in planning, budgeting, and forecasting, this book explains how to:

- Gain increased visibility so you can tune your existing business processes to eliminate pains and inefficiencies
- Accurately and efficiently gain insight as to past, current, and future performance by implementing key operational and financial metrics
- Identify problems early enough to avoid unexpected disasters

If you are involved in monitoring and analyzing operations the book will help you to:

- Engage in a process of continuous learning with regard to the success of operations, and use the knowledge discovered to improve strategy and planning, thereby closing the loop
- Employ advanced analysis and modeling techniques to better understand profitability, spend, and marketing effectiveness, enabling the creation of predictive models

Unlike many other books on performance management, this book goes deeply into how to apply performance management in specific areas of a business like HR, IT, Finance, Sales, and so on. For example the chapters in Part III show how to use performance management to:

- Attract and keep employees in a connected culture where success is visible and where social networking provides new ways to connect with the knowledge and skills hidden in corners of the organization as well as outside, within the information cloud of the Web
- Analyze IT operations to determine their business value and find cost savings

• Extend performance management metrics into the wider business ecosystem, from customers to partners to supply chain

We have written this book to introduce the modern practice of performance management. Our goal is quite simple: after reading this book, you should know what performance management is, why it is important, and specific steps to take to improve both individual and institutional practice in the most important areas of your company. You will understand the impact that improved performance management has on individual business users and on each separate area of the business such as HR, Finance, IT, and Supply Chain. The remainder of this chapter clears the decks and explains the various areas collected underneath the umbrella of performance management, shows how they are connected, and outlines the benefits of evolving to higher levels of competence. The rest of the book provides more detail about exactly how to achieve those benefits.

The Scope of Performance Management

Because performance management is such a broad activity with many specialties, a simple and precise definition is elusive. For the purposes of this book, however, we define performance management as follows:

• **Performance management is communication.** Creating the organization's nervous system and cerebral cortex, ensuring that every person—executives down to line employees—has the trusted information and accurate data needed to maximize individual and organizational effectiveness

• **Performance management is optimization.** Defining a model of the enterprise and the extended business network based on reliable data and contextual information, enabling you to better describe, track, and optimize the behavior of the value-creating machine inside and beyond the bounds of the enterprise

• **Performance management is visibility.** Exploring the means and methods by which you can better understand, and, by extension, better manage the enterprise to sustain optimal performance throughout all of its operations and into its extended value chain

• **Performance management is technology.** Exploiting the way that all of the investment in technology, automated business processes, and communications systems come together to amplify productivity and effectiveness

- **Performance management is culture.** Transforming collective thinking, moving away from the practice of making decisions based on instinct to one in which decisions are based on trusted data, where outcomes are known and thoroughly aligned to the strategic objectives of the company. As such, it provides the means to move from a vague notion or summary understanding of the business to a more precise model based on broadly shared measures of actual performance

The Scope of Performance Management

Creating and communicating strategy

Managing a comprehensive and iterative planning and budgeting process

Increasing the efficiency of creating financial and operational reports

Improving the detail and accuracy of forecasts

Distributing information throughout the enterprise to support decision-making

Constructing an expanding and detailed model of the value-creating processes of a company

Optimizing both financial and operational results

Tracking performance against specific objectives

Rolling up detailed metrics into aggregate measures

Modeling and comparing strategic and tactical alternatives

Revealing and managing the risks inherent in a company's activities

Supporting compliance with laws, rules, and regulations

Offering embedded analytics to support specific roles in making better decisions in the midst of business processes

Combining both unstructured and structured forms of data to support analysis

Helping a company move iteratively through the performance management lifecycle of setting strategy, planning, monitoring operations, and optimizing and learning

Expanding the domain of performance management practices beyond Finance to other areas of the company such as Sales, Marketing, Service, Supply Chain, IT, HR, and Procurement

Performance management is about better managing a company with operations and partners all over the world. It is about going from a backward-looking and finance-centric view of performance to a more granular model of performance that can support early detection of problems and rapid responses to changing market conditions. It is about focusing on the business user and closing the loop, in order to take action based on the visibility you have gained. It is about linking what you want to do—strategy—with what is actually happening—execution. And it is about a continual lifecycle of measuring, monitoring, and optimizing strategy and performance in a holistic and structured system that enables a far greater degree of agility than would otherwise be possible.

Performance management has become a vastly more important activity because its scope has expanded from the practice of tracking money into a domain that encompasses all of the activities captured below.

In the not too distant past, many of these processes were not seen as related. They were often done separately by different departments, each requiring their own tools and technology. For example, most companies had, on average, three data warehouses, five ways of creating reports, countless spreadsheets, and a multitude of applications, each aimed at figuring out a specific process like planning, purchasing, forecasting, and so on.

In the modern vision of performance management, each of these activities is supported by a set of processes, tools, and technology, all built to accelerate the flow of information and the creation of knowledge. Performance management will never be as precisely defined as the standard processes that exist in CRM or in specific areas of ERP like accounting or inventory management. But the core processes, models, analytical tools, and data structures are well understood enough to be served by an integrated system. "The GPS Metaphor for Performance Management" shows that, however complex the practice of performance management may at first appear, it is actually a simple and straightforward part of achieving excellence in any endeavor. The fundamental message of the GPS metaphor is that performance management systems help executives decide where the business should go, not just watch where it happens to be going. Unlike ERP systems or CRM systems, often used by staff members but not consulted directly by executives, the best performance management systems are part of the daily process of steering a company toward success from the boardroom on down.

The GPS Metaphor for Performance Management

Modern performance management goes beyond past practices in the same way that GPS systems have enhanced the quality of information available to a driver.

A car dashboard tells you about the inner workings of a vehicle. It lets you know how fast you're going, how much gas is in the tank, and how hard the engine is working. It includes warning lights to mitigate the risk of running out of oil or gas.

Much of the history of performance management was about creating similar dashboards focused on the current state of the company. The typical performance management system provided finance-centric measurements, processes, and systems that told how the business did in the prior quarter and provided guidance about how it is currently running.

A GPS system provides an interactive map of where you want to go and how to get there. It describes the surrounding environment so that you know what roads to take. It provides context for your surroundings and options based on your preferences and needs, such as shortest route or freeways only.

In addition, GPS systems alert us when there are risks in the road ahead, such as an accident blocking a certain highway, traffic congestion, or a bridge closed for construction. Using this information, we can replot our route to make sure we still get to our destination.

Modern performance management does the same thing as a GPS system by helping companies define direction in a precise way, by providing the means to communicate and propagate a detailed understanding of the way forward, by looking ahead to what the likely outcomes are with predictive models, by looking into what is happening in the business network, and by expanding and deepening awareness of the direction of the employees, partners, and key stakeholders.

In terms of the analogy, our destination represents the strategic goals of the business. The roadblocks and weather alerts represent the risks we encounter while pursuing that strategy. Compliance is following the rules of the road, such as traffic signs or speed limits. Heeding these rules helps us get to our destination. If we ignore a red light, we're more likely to get into an accident; if we disobey the speed limit, we're more likely to get pulled over by a police officer. Compliance is also a matter of adhering to internal requirements such as keeping tires inflated to the optimal pressure or maintaining proper oil pressure. Needless to say, ignoring compliance has bad consequences: our travel time is slower and the costs are higher.

The task of performance management applications is to provide the traditional dashboard and to supplement that information with a model of where a company is going and how fast it is getting there. Performance management is both a dashboard and a GPS system for the modern enterprise, one that adds the dimensions of time, risk, and compliance while looking at what happened in the past, present, and future.

The Changing Shape of the Enterprise

Performance management has expanded so dramatically because the modern enterprise has become more complex and difficult to understand. To understand why the discipline of performance management has grown, we must have a firm grasp of how the enterprise has changed as well.

Core vs. Context in the Globally Distributed Enterprise

In the distant past, companies were one organization operating on one continent. The corporation owned and controlled everything needed to design, create, market, and distribute its products. One powerful economic driver motivating this consolidation was the notion of transaction costs. Trading goods across company boundaries incurred expense and delays, so to gain the most efficiencies, a large group of resources was assembled under one corporate umbrella. The effect of transaction costs is one of the most common explanations for the growth of mega-enterprises in the first 80 years of the 20th century. Since the beginning of the 1900s, the early incarnations of Ford Motor and General Motors brought every part of the production and distribution process under one corporate umbrella.

In the modern world, we are witnessing the effect of a dramatic decrease in transaction costs. Telecommunications technology, reduction in barriers to trade, increased sophistication in global logistics and the many faceted effects of the Internet have dramatically decreased the barriers that prevented specialization and distribution of tasks.

Many of today's companies are defined by the following characteristics:

- Global in scope, with operations in many countries
- A distributed value chain in which many partners and suppliers work together to create products or deliver services
- Accelerated outsourcing of context functions

These pressures have led to a change in the identity of the corporation, shown in Figure 1-1, that has been codified by Geoffrey Moore in *Living on*

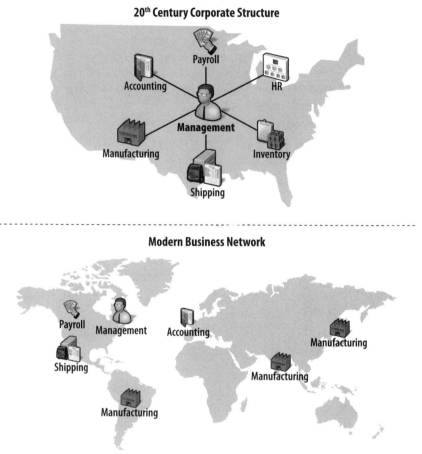

Figure 1-1. From Centralized Control to a Global Business Network

the Fault Line (Collins Business, 2000), in which he explains the tradeoff between core and context activities.

In *Living on the Fault Line*, Geoffrey Moore describes the choices facing the modern company in the era of the business network. Because of the Internet, automation technology, standardization, logistics, and improved communications technology of all kinds, the world has undergone a transformation. What used to be done under one corporate umbrella may now be done by partner companies under contract with an orchestrating company. While this phenomenon is called by many names—globalization, business process outsourcing, contract manufacturing—this book refers to the idea as the business network.

In his book, Moore recommends that companies organize the creation of their business network in a way to amplify their returns. Functions that the company performs itself, in which it has the most competence and creates the most competitive advantage, are core activities. These should be the focus of the operations controlled directly by the company and should be the focus of investment. Other activities that support the core are called context. Those activities should be outsourced to other companies for which they are a central focus. In other words, outsource activities that are context to your company to other companies for which those activities are the core.

The core vs. context analysis can be used to distinguish between different styles and strategies. For example, UPS and FedEx have transportation and logistics processes at their core and are used by many companies for which these processes are context. Disney could be considered a company with the customer experience at the core, while manufacturing products is a context activity. For Apple, product design is a core activity, while at Dell the customer experience and flexible manufacturing are central to the core.

Moore points out that some context activities are so vital to a company that they may need to stay under the corporate umbrella, but in general, he recommends pushing as many context activities to partners as possible.

Tracking the Core and Context

Performance management is vital to both core and context activities. Optimization of the core can only be performed with adequate instrumentation. The effective outsourcing of context activities requires tracking of activities that are carried out by partners for timeliness, compliance, and quality.

Performance management plays a key role in tracking activities and understanding operations with sufficient detail to define the boundaries between processes that may be hived off and handed to outsourcers. For outsourcing to work, the description of an activity must be clearly defined. Specifically, the following is needed:

- The information that is needed to start a process
- The information that comes back during a process
- The information that must come back when the process is finished

Once these definitions are in place, it matters less which organization handles that process. As long as metrics provide visibility into the progress of the process and the quality of the output, outsourcing can take place efficiently and with manageable levels of risk and accountability for proper performance.

For example, Nike creates its shoes using a global supply chain and a host of contract manufacturers. While Nike does not own these assets, it tracks the flow of materials between manufacturers and the work in progress at the factories. In this way Nike can keep a close eye on quality and the flow of shipments, and can optimize production to meet demand. Nike's core competence is product design, but it also is expert in running an extended business network for manufacturing.

The Rise of Business Networks

The structure that has replaced the mega-corporation that owns all of its operations is the business network in which one orchestrating company controls and directs the activities of a vast array of partners. Most large enterprises operate in this manner. Firms like Wal-Mart, Apple, Cisco, Hewlett Packard, Nike, Li & Fung, and others run massively complex value chains as well as centralized management functions that are outsourced more than ever. Participant companies may serve several different networks at once. These organizations are not run by luck or trust. The operational relationship between the orchestrator and partners is carefully designed and meticulously tracked through various forms of performance management.

The orchestrators are able to achieve efficiency, profitability, and agility because the key activities of all of the companies in the business network are closely monitored, as are the activities that are carried out by the central organization. Like Nike, these companies are expert at using performance management systems to create the brain of a business network that can coordinate hundreds or thousands of companies. If a shipment of raw materials must go from Singapore to Malaysia, the orchestrating company finds the right way. If products are flying out the door of the retail stores at Wal-Mart, alerts go off in one of two replicated data warehouses and send signals to the manufacturers of those products so that deliveries can be accelerated and stock outs can be avoided. At the best companies, performance management provides a massive model of the worldwide state of the business network, where problems can be detected early and operations continually optimized. Many of the most prominent catastrophes in business networks can be attributed to a lack of adequate visibility by the orchestrator.

In the central management processes of companies' business networks, performance management plays a key role in pushing responsibility down to the people best able to make decisions and providing granular information to allow business operations to be optimized. Teams can be empowered to make decisions that affect both operational and financial performance. Performance management allows profit to be calculated not just by division but also by customer, region, season, product, or any combination of these dimensions. This allows, for example, the shift workers at a factory

The Cost of Performance Management Complacency

In March 2000, lightning caused a fire at a Philips semiconductor plant which was a sole-source supplier of chips used in both Nokia's and Ericsson's handsets. Nokia was proactively monitoring the supply chain risks and key risk indicators across their supplier plants, and reacted quickly to this event by redesigning phones to accept other makers' chips and commandeering Philips' other available semiconductor manufacturing capacity. Nokia effectively managed the risk in their business network and was able to react and recover quickly as a result.

Ericsson was not proactively monitoring supply chain risks, and their delayed reaction severely disrupted production and postponed new product releases. Ericsson attributed the fire as a primary cause of its $1.6 billion loss during FY 2000. One year later, Ericsson announced a plan to spin off its handset division into a joint venture with Sony. Ericsson, which had seen steady growth rates in the two years leading up to 2000, suffered a drastic fall in revenue growth in the two years following the incident.

Both companies were affected by the event, but the firm that had a heightened awareness of the impact of the fire was able to navigate around the disruption. Such agility is the result of a pervasive performance management culture.

to see how much money was made during their time at work, based on the decisions they made that day. Performance management turns on the lights and supplies detailed analysis of costs and tracks the effect of marketing programs with microscopic precision.

AMR Research has defined the structure used by these leading companies as the Performance Driven Business Network, a business model focused on synchronizing business strategy, organizational principles, and enterprise architecture (the structure of processes and systems in a company) not just within a company, but also up and down the greater business network with suppliers, customers, and other partners to better compete in the new global economy. Like the shift workers in a plant, as the direct result of decisions become available faster because of performance management, companies become performance driven rather than project driven. As a result, the firms are able to react more predictably to business conditions, make better use of information, knowledge, technology, and human capital assets, and create a collaborative culture focused around the goals that matter, whether they be profit, risk management, compliance, or various forms of operational efficiency. Increased awareness of the acceptable limits set forth by regulations or other compliance standards, and how close a company is to exceeding those limits, can have an immediate positive effect on improving compliance.

Current trends indicate that the forces driving toward the business network as a form of organization show no signs of slowing down. For example, 89% of respondents to a recent survey conducted by CFO Research Services[1] said that partner relationships are an important aspect of their business strategy, and 51% said that they are going to increase their use of these relationships over the next few years. We can also point to the fact that these relationships have proven to be very effective at fostering co-innovation, improved customer experience, and faster market access (especially in emerging regions).

The number and complexity of the outsourced relationships in a business network has further increased the demand for the sophisticated application of performance management. Both orchestrators and partners in a business network gain significant advantages if they are ready to exchange large amounts of detailed information to track the operational activity as work is handed off from one company to another. The more relationships that can be effectively automated and managed, the more leverage both an orchestrator and a partner have.

External Pressures for Visibility and Predictability

Managing the complexity of the modern, global, distributed enterprise could not happen without sophisticated performance management. But other pressures are also at play in addition to the desire for competitive advantage that comes from gathering and analyzing information about profitability and operational performance.

Stakeholders of all stripes—investors, analysts, and regulators—are clamoring for businesses to be more predictable in terms of operational and financial performance, as well as for executives to demonstrate a greater degree of understanding of the drivers behind performance. Those executives whose companies are perceived as being unpredictable and who are unable to demonstrate that they are in control of their operations and processes are being punished by reduced shareholder price and, as the current fiscal crisis shows, by more dire consequences.

Almost every company, large or small, faces some combination of the following challenges:

---

[1] "Filling in the Information Gap: Finance's Role in Successful Business Collaborations," CFO Research Services in collaboration with SAP, August 22, 2008.

- **Limited insight.** Too much data, not enough information; too much defensive reaction, not enough proactive anticipation; few alerts in place to warn of potential problems
- **Limited transparency.** Information trapped in silos, fragmented instead of unified; lack of visibility into business process performance; minimal awareness of and information about risks across processes
- **Inefficiencies and costs.** Lack of automation for business process management; manual compliance, risk and reporting methodologies; lack of alignment to strategy and performance initiatives
- **Complex environments.** Expanding global business environment; increase in global regulatory requirements; lack of standardization in risk and control processes

In many of the areas identified above, performance management processes overlap with other management disciplines such as governance, risk, and compliance or the core functions of specific enterprise applications that report on business activity. This overlap highlights the complexity of sorting out what is a question of performance management; what is governance, risk, and compliance (GRC); and what is just a matter of carrying out a business process. Indeed performance management and GRC are often seen as two sides of the same coin, both concerned with tracking operations but with different goals in mind. In both performance management and GRC, the goal is not to have a separate process but to make the creation of metrics that reveal performance, help manage risk, or comply with regulatory reporting requirements part of everyday business processes. This dynamic means that the challenges of performance management, GRC, and the automation of business processes are most efficiently solved in an integrated fashion.

The Automation and Information Infrastructure

The maturity of the automation and information infrastructure in the corporations that have implemented a full suite of enterprise applications, along with tools for collaboration and data analysis, is one of the main reasons that performance management is able to produce such dramatic results. Performance management creates value by introducing an ever-more detailed model of the financial and operational processes in a company. The roots of the performance management models are the transactional systems of record that capture and store the basic business activity. The way that ERP records the flow of funds in and out of a company, or CRM records orders coming in and customer inquiries, provides a foundation to build higher-level forms of performance management to track financial and operational activity. Performance management starts to use the information gathered in new ways and can have a huge impact on a business.

Perhaps the most significant enabler of performance management is the suite of enterprise applications that have been implemented to automate common processes. The information captured by ERP, CRM, and SCM applications, as well as that gathered by the HR, IT, and Procurement departments, all represent raw materials for performance management analysis. With this, the story of the business and a more comprehensive and sophisticated understanding of the value-creating machine can be extracted in order for you to better engineer and optimize its performance.

The components of a modern automation and information infrastructure include:

- **Collaborative tools** help people communicate and collaborate in a variety of ways with varying amounts of structure and time-shifting
- **Performance management applications** use the capabilities of search, business intelligence, and the information in enterprise applications to support the processes of the performance management lifecycle
- **Governance, risk, and compliance applications** work to ensure that enterprise applications are complying with regulations and also add functionality for managing other processes such as risk, health and safety, and trade
- **Business intelligence** gathers information from enterprise applications into data warehouses so it can be consolidated and analyzed and reports can be created en masse or on an ad hoc basis. In many ways, BI provides the foundation on which performance management can build and grow
- **Search and knowledge management systems** organize and allow access to unstructured information inside and outside a company
- **Transactional systems of record** automate and track the core processes of the value-creating machine in a company

This rich collection of information, automation, general-purpose tools, and special-purpose applications and technology highlights the performance management challenge. The problem at most companies seeking to improve their performance management is not a lack of information or the absence of capabilities to analyze it. That was the challenge when performance management first began as a discipline in the Finance department. High-quality information was hard to come by and had to be painstakingly

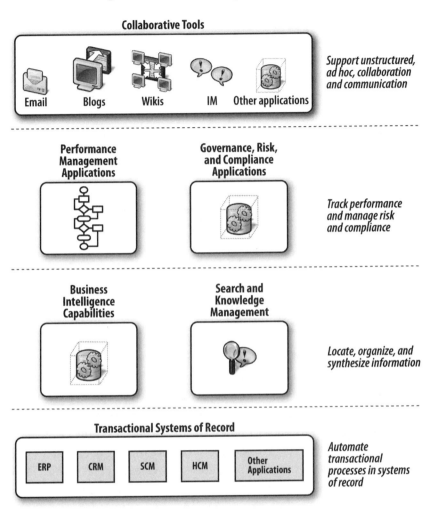

Figure 1-2. *The Components of a Modern Automation and Information Infrastructure*

gathered. Analysis tools and targeted applications were just emerging. In the modern company, the challenge is to select the right information to provide to each role in each process and to provide the tools to analyze that information and the capabilities to take action or to make adjustments to existing processes, plans, and strategies.

The Process-Centric Enterprise

The rise of business process management (BPM) as a focus in companies and business networks has had a tremendous impact on the way that performance management systems are designed and implemented.

BPM is the modern way to refer to the idea that a clear definition of the business process should be the primary focus when attempting to understand and optimize a business. The idea of a business process focus stretches back to the early 1900s when Frederick Winslow Taylor introduced the idea of scientific management and time and motion studies. In the 1990s, Michael Hammer and James Champy popularized the idea of business process reengineering, which recommended a focus on the business process as companies attempted to optimize operations in the face of competitive threats. Since the advent of the Internet, the rise of service-oriented architecture—the ability to access the data and functions of software based on standardized web services—and advances in modeling and various forms of visual software development, business process management has had a strong resurgence.

In BPM today, the goal is to transform a company into a process-centric enterprise in which activities are described in terms of business process models. Sometimes these models just have inputs and outputs because the processes are non-deterministic. Other processes are described in step-by-step fashion, using visual models to show how the process should be performed. The goal of the process-centric enterprise is not to trap people within a confined structure, but rather to capture and understand what actually makes a business process effective at creating value. While some people take an overly mechanistic view of the process-centric enterprise and imagine that every activity is described by a business process, the best practitioners quickly tend to find those processes that are core to value creation and then spend time mapping these processes in great detail. These key processes frequently start inside a company and then migrate in and out across company boundaries, through operations executed by partners.

Performance management provides the instrumentation for business process management. For non-deterministic processes, like recruiting new employees, performance management can track the inputs, outputs, and results. For processes with a more complete step-by-step model, like processing and paying an invoice, performance management systems can track inputs, outputs, and various intermediate metrics that indicate key aspects of the process. As time passes, performance management data can be used to determine relationships between inputs and outputs so that predictions can be made based on the value of the inputs to a process.

In a company that is implementing business process management, performance management systems provide the day-to-day means for managing and optimizing processes, as well as creating predictive models.

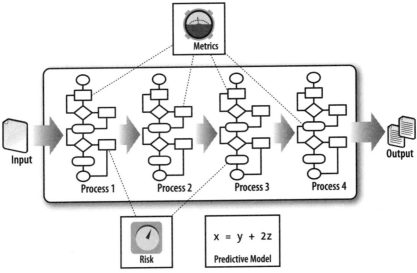

Figure 1-3. Process Instrumentation

Another way to think of business process management implemented in conjunction with performance management is as a way to construct a description of and then provide instrumentation for the important processes of a company, as shown in Figure 1-3.

With a detailed view of a process in hand, performance management allows a process to be adjusted and tweaked. Visibility leads to rapid response.

Do-It-Yourself Support

One of the lessons learned as the practice of performance management grew out of the core Finance department processes and the application of business intelligence tools was that it is easy to create bottlenecks. Common problems that occurred in the early days were the delays created because tools could only be configured by experts. New systems arrived, such as business intelligence environments for writing reports or portals for customizing views of enterprise applications. This configurability provided value but then became a problem because IT could not keep up with user demands.

The general solution to this problem has been found in the trend toward adding do-it-yourself capabilities to analytical tools and enterprise applications—that is, support for the business user. The goal is to replicate the dramatic expansion of self-service that was enabled by spreadsheets to all sorts of other environments. Spreadsheets were and still are the gold standard of business user empowerment. While presentation technology like Microsoft Power Point has created an explosion of slides used for do-it-yourself communication, when it comes to complicated tasks involving capturing and organizing information and creating models and analytical tools, spreadsheets are the method used by most business users.

By allowing a business user to create reports or to configure the design and flow of a business process, IT is no longer a bottleneck and users can respond more quickly to changes and create just the environment they need to do their jobs. The translation of requirements is no longer needed, which paves the way for an outpouring of user-driven innovation as described in the research of MIT professor Dr. Eric von Hippel.

Because performance management is primarily an activity involving business analysis, creating and expanding understanding of financial and operational activities, environments serving business users are tuned and created best by the users themselves. This direct access to tools avoids the need for requirements translation that gets in the way of providing useful systems. Systems that allow users to create their own reports, to assemble mashup applications from widgets or web services (those that provide data or invoke functions in other software), to adjust the flow of processes, to record events and notify people of risks and problems, and to make adjustments to forecasts and models of activity, all empower the business user and make the investment in all types of technology more valuable, especially with regard to performance management. When at its best, do-it-yourself environments for the business user provide the same pleasing experience at

---

Business User Defined

Business users tend to exist within the operational management band. They are the people running the day-to-day business and, in the decentralized enterprise, are far more responsible for managing the business than in the past when the command and control mentality predominated. They can no longer manage by walking around the office. Businesses are running 24/7 around the globe and require a system that supports the expanded complexities of globalization.

Their work tends to be composed of more of what McKinsey calls "tacit interactions"—unstructured processes—and in a decentralized business model requires a far more sophisticated system for gaining access and managing information to support strong decision-making processes. It is also important to properly support this group's ability to collaborate and follow iterative question paths as they seek answers to the issues that confront them as they manage their respective piece of the business.

work that people are used to as consumers when they use social interaction software and other consumer-oriented interfaces available on the Web.

This tour of the shape of the modern company has brought to light many of the dimensions that an effective program of performance management must address. We will now move from analysis of the key drivers shaping the need for performance management to an examination of exactly how performance management works and how to get started making it work for your company.

The Performance Management Lifecycle

You cannot wave a wand and improve performance management in some abstract way. The only way that benefit accrues from activities that fall under the umbrella of performance management is when specific changes are made in how a company does business. In practice, performance management is a set of specific improvements that are made to various processes and systems inside a company to provide people with more information, more ability to analyze that information, more ways to work together to deepen their understanding, and more ways to take action.

All companies, departments, and individuals go through a project management cycle when conducting their business—the extent to which they are conscious of and do so successfully varies greatly. A key point to this book is to demonstrate that you need *all* aspects of the process working to sustain performance. How good is a strategy if not connected to a plan? How good is a plan if you cannot monitor the execution? How can you optimize strategies without an understanding of your associated risks and the ability to model your possible course of action? The kinds of specific improvements that come under that umbrella of performance management fall into the following categories:

- **Strategy management.** Closing the gap between strategy and execution
- **Planning and budgeting.** Supporting top-down and bottom-up processes of determining the resources needed to carry out strategy
- **Monitoring and forecasting.** Keeping track of what is happening and what you expect to happen
- **Analysis and optimization.** Comparing alternative scenarios and inventing new ways of working
- **Identifying and managing risk and controls.** Finding and tracking specific risks and making sure every activity is evaluated and monitored with appropriate controls to manage risks

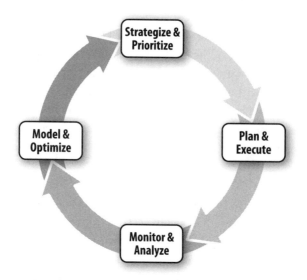

Figure 1-4. The Performance Management Lifecycle

- **Closing the loop.** Adjusting the larger plan as execution reveals more information

These categories of activities have a sequential flow and it is natural to think of them as a performance management lifecycle, as shown in Figure 1-4. This lifecycle represents the natural stages that most companies go through over and over again as they improve their performance management practice. Part of the science of performance management is determining which of the areas is in most need of attention. Chapter 3 takes a detailed look at this lifecycle and how you can examine your maturity at each stage. It is useful, however, to summarize the goals of each stage of the lifecycle, and the interdependencies to other stages, to better understand

Do we need to do all of this to make progress?

As we will discuss in more detail in Chapter 3, improving your game in performance management does not mean moving forward to the maximum extent possible. The most successful implementations of performance management are based on a deep understanding of where more information is needed and on a targeted program of improvement. The challenge of performance management is to understand what information is needed now and in the future and to invest in capabilities to make sure that the information is available at the right time in front of the right people so better decisions are made and better actions are taken.

> But in a sense, the idea of a lifecycle can be an impediment to making progress. It is not necessary to implement anything like a full performance management lifecycle to make dramatic progress. The following explanation will present a fully realized vision of what would happen if a company were executing at the highest standard in all areas of performance management. While that may be needed in some companies, the challenge of performance management is to determine where changes in your support for the lifecycle will have the most benefit.

the context in which mechanisms are described later in this chapter and in detail in Chapter 3.

Strategy Management

The first phase of the performance management lifecycle is strategy management, in which the high level goals for an organization are set forth along with the specific initiatives that will be carried out to meet those goals.

The challenge for strategy management is capturing the strategy and then communicating it with sufficient granularity to the rest of the organization. While this sounds simple, in practice it can be quite challenging. According to one study, between 60–80% of companies fall short of their desired goals, not because they have the wrong strategy, but because they never fully carried out what they planned to do.[2] This problem is known as the strategy-to-execution gap.

The gap between strategy and execution is the disconnect between what an executive says the company should do to succeed (strategy) and what the organization actually ends up doing (execution). Too often, strategy setting has been a yearly exercise that really is not connected to the daily work within the company. Lofty goals are declared but never translated into specifics that make it clear to an employee what needs to be done to meet them.

Poor communication is the main cause of the strategy-to-execution gap. At almost every company, the CEO and other senior executives spend a significant amount of time determining the right goals and then figuring out specific initiatives to reach those goals. The strategy may be captured in presentations and then expanded in further detail in documents and spreadsheets describing each initiative. The primary cause of the strategy-to-execution gap is that, at some point, the communication of the strategy stops. Only senior executives are aware of every initiative at any significant

---

[2] "Mastering the Management System," Robert S. Kaplan and David P. Norton, *Harvard Business Review,* January 2008.

Three Questions for You to Consider:

– How valuable would it be to you to have a systematic means to be sure the organization at large is actually working toward outcomes delineated by the strategy?

– How valuable would it be to your company to take the annual strategy exercise from a theoretical pursuit into one that improved two-way communication that is the foundation of continuous learning and rapid response?

– How valuable to your company would it be to ensure, down to the line employee, that the day-to-day work is aligned with and driving strategic objectives?

---

level of detail. The bulk of the employees know that a strategy was put in place and may know that specific initiatives are underway, but they don't know what they must do to make sure those initiatives succeed.

Performance management creates a systematic approach to strategy execution that provides the structure and processes to plan, communicate, execute, monitor, and optimize a strategy inside the four walls of a company and across the business network. Specifically, performance management applications focused on strategy management provide capabilities to:

- Define and capture strategy in detail
- Describe strategic initiatives related to the strategy
- Break initiatives into component parts that will be the basis for planning and budgeting
- Construct a hierarchy of metrics and specific targets for improvement
- Communicate the strategic initiatives and the hierarchy of metrics to employees at all levels to build and confirm consensus
- Identify risks that are inherent in the strategy and propose a method for monitoring and managing them
- Make sure that individuals are aware of the performance expected of them, how it fits into the larger strategy, and how it will be linked to specific metrics
- Make sure that all partner relationships are designed with the strategic initiatives in mind and that each partner is aware of the performance required of them to meet strategic goals in terms of specific metrics
- Drive greater accountability and empower employees to make better decisions by providing them context

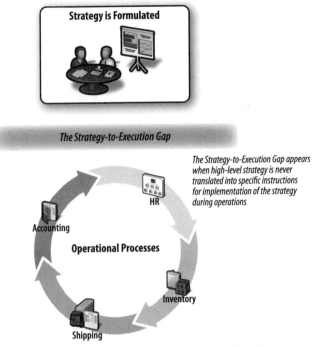

Figure 1-5. Closing the Strategy-to-Execution Gap

Modern strategy management applications provide a configurable process that allows strategy to be captured and communicated so that a clear consensus can be achieved about where a company is going and how it is going to get there. The applications allow the component parts of each initiative to become the basis for planning and budgeting activities. Unlike older approaches, modern strategy management applications allow strategy to be modified and adjusted in a continuous process, not an annual cycle. As they are recognized, adjustments to the original strategic plan flow downward through the performance management lifecycle without having to start from scratch. Similarly, changes to strategy that result from ideas gathered in execution can flow back upward from monitoring, to planning and budgeting, to strategy. Enabling a two-way flow of information that does not require starting from scratch is the essence of achieving a closed loop in the performance management lifecycle.

Planning and Budgeting

Planning and budgeting picks up from the strategy process by taking the component parts of a strategy and assigning resources to them. While the budget acts as an aggregate forecast of key measures, in the planning process, the initial forecasts for more detailed measures, and for those that are not budgeted, are also created. Planning and budgeting frequently is inefficient because the systems and processes used cannot handle the interplay between the top-down planning process and the bottom-up budgeting process.

The planning and budgeting cycle generally takes place in the following steps:

- Senior management sets forth a plan for a part of the organization or for executing a strategic initiative. That plan generally has some specific goals for key metrics such as revenue for various products, or improvements in key metrics such as customer satisfaction. Setting these goals out as specifically as possible is the first key task of the planning process. Detailed risks that must be monitored are also identified
- The second part of the planning process is setting forth estimates of the resources that management thinks are required to execute the plan. Communication of the specific targets and the resources complete the top-down planning cycle
- The budget process begins when the specific business units take the targets and budget estimates and attempt to create a detailed estimate of all the work that will have to be performed to meet the plan. Because the budgeting works from specific tasks and then rolls them up to show how the goals for the plan would be met, it is called a bottom-up process. It is not uncommon for the budgeting process to result in estimates for resource requirements that exceed those set forth in the plan
- Driver-based budgeting, creating budgets from predictions made by models of activity, and activity-based costing, accurately allocating costs for shared services, makes the process more accurate by creating a much more detailed operational model of what a business does so you can understand exactly how you will meet a plan, or how costs are consumed by specific types of customers or activities
- Reconciling the top-down plan and the bottom-up budgets is the key to an effective planning process and the best performance management systems have a way to capture and represent both and to allow information to flow easily back and forth between plans and budgets and to show the impact on the consolidated results of various changes to the plan

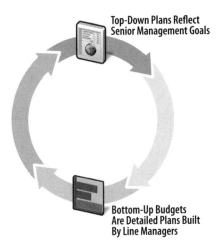

Figure 1-6. Top-down Planning and Bottom-up Budgeting

By enabling a structured negotiation between senior management and business unit executives, the planning and budgeting stage of the lifecycle completes the process begun in the strategy stage—expressing exactly what must be done—by setting forth a detailed description of how the strategic goals will be met. The planning and budgeting system is used to communicate the detailed goals to the entire enterprise and to the partners in a business network.

Sophisticated performance management systems of the type defined in Chapter 4 provide prescribed business process flows that guide users, allowing them to use a common tool, a spreadsheet, while ensuring the proper controls and alerts are embedded into the process to meet compliance requirements.

Monitor and Analyze

A plan and a budget are forecasts, predictions of what you intend to spend and accomplish, which means that the forecasting process begins in the planning and budgeting phase of the lifecycle. But, as Napoleon said, "no plan survives contact," and so it is in business.

The next stage of the lifecycle involves monitoring actual results, consolidating them, and then gradually adjusting forecasts of what you expect to achieve. The monitoring and analyzing phase of the lifecycle then involves all of the following steps:

- Harvesting data from enterprise systems, partners, and any other needed sources and putting it into a centralized form that allows all the needed metrics to be computed—metrics defined in the strategy phase and made more granular in the planning and budgeting phase

- Making sure that not only data is harvested but also qualitative information, such as notes on exceptional conditions or outliers, is collected to provide a more complete picture
- Creating consolidated reports of both financial and operational performance. The financial reports look backward at the money produced by core value-creating processes of a business. The operational or management reports look inside the value-creating machine at the drivers of future performance. By creating an understanding of drivers that are indicators of future performance, a business can spot problems early and make more accurate predictions
- Comparing the consolidated reports, the "actuals," to the forecasts to determine the variance. Based on the interim results, forecasts can then be adjusted, a process known as a rolling forecast
- Propagating the financial and operational metrics to everyone in the enterprise and the business network so they can see how well they are doing with respect to executing their component parts of the strategic initiatives
- Monitoring risks that were identified in earlier stages

The consolidation, monitoring, and forecasting phase of the performance management lifecycle allows the company to make adjustments based on an increased volume of data. Instead of finding out that things are not going as planned based on financial information at the end of a quarter, the company can see indications much earlier through forward-looking operational data. Because many more specific indicators are delivered to executives about specific initiatives and parts of initiatives, mid-course corrections to tactics can be made, as well as adjustments to strategy, which are the essence of the closed loop process.

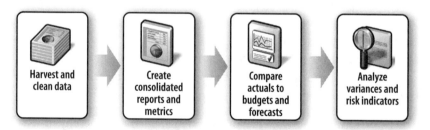

Figure 1-7. Consolidation, Monitoring, and Forecasting

Modeling and Optimization

As more is learned about how the initiatives are actually working, ideas for improving both tactics and strategy will emerge. A deeper understanding of the actual drivers of business activity and costs will also come to light, allowing improvement of those models to make them more accurate and predictive. New ways of meeting strategic goals will be conceived. In the modeling and optimization phase of the performance management lifecycle, the metrics computed and other data gathered are used to start comparing alternative suggestions for ways forward. The types of activity in this phase include the following:

- Creating models of proposed changes to business processes or tactics to determine the expected benefits
- Comparing the impact of alternative proposals for changes to business processes or tactics
- Based on information from actual performance, adjusting the models of the operational aspects of a business used for activity-based costing or driver-based budgeting
- Based on insights gained from the analysis, adjusting strategy, plans, and budgets to reflect the new understanding
- Suggesting new ways of managing risks or making sure newly identified risks are monitored and managed

In modern practice, analysis and optimization becomes far more forward-looking. In the past, analysis and optimization primarily used financial data to look backward. But the models of the value-creating machine for activity-based costing or driver-based budgeting provide a starting point for a forward-looking approach. Operational metrics are used to identify the key factors that will affect performance.

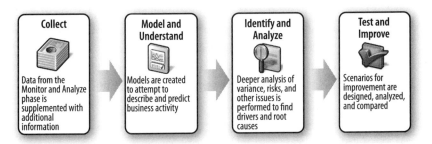

Figure 1-8. Model and Optimize

For example, imagine a driver-based budgeting model of the sales process. Direct marketing expense identifies 1,000 leads. Telemarketing qualifies them down to 100 that should be followed up with by a sales representative. Experience shows that 10 of those leads will close in the three months after the first contact and 10 more will close in the next three months. This relationship, 1000 leads to 10 sales in three months and 10 sales in the next three months, can then be used as a forward-looking predictor. As time goes on, the models can get better. For example, perhaps it is possible to find a faster and cheaper way of qualifying leads than telemarketing. Then perhaps even more leads can be pushed through the process, resulting in more sales. Problems can be found faster as well. If it turns out that a source of a great number of high-quality leads is found, it may be possible to predict that the sales force will be overwhelmed by the increased numbers and will not be able to follow up properly. Before this becomes an acute problem, the sales force can be expanded.

The expansion of operational models, those that describe key business activity, is one of the most fertile areas for the application of performance management techniques. Even though improved operational performance has been shown by the latest research to be strongly correlated with increased financial performance, only about 23% of companies establish a causal link, according to research published in *Harvard Business Review*.[3]

Operational metrics are also crucial to managing partner relationships. Operational metrics are an important means to not only better understand and manage a single partner's performance via service level agreements, but also to gain visibility into the partner's governance processes, supply chain, and distribution network in order to assess its stability. Risks with respect to quality and compliance can be monitored and mitigated while the impact is still small. In addition, these metrics allow executives and others to compare the metrics of all partners in order to know that their performance is adequate to support the strategic objectives of the company as well as its financial performance—for example, is it possible to correlate network performance to financial outcomes? This in turn will make the company more predictable to analysts and investors.

The insights in the model and optimize phase are used to make changes to all the other lifecycle phases. A strategy may be found not to be working,

---

[3] Christopher D. Ittner and David F. Larcker, "Coming Up Short on Nonfinancial Performance Measurement," *Harvard Business Review*, November 2003.

a model used for planning, may be faulty, or metrics may be missing. In a closed loop performance management system, these changes then flow back and forth, affecting how the business executes and how it is analyzed and tracked.

Identifying and Managing Risk

One of the most striking changes between the modern practice of performance management and that of previous generations is the increased awareness of risk as a dimension that must be addressed in all phases of the lifecycle. Leading performance management systems have embedded features to help manage risk integrated into the software and supported processes. This is in sharp contrast to historical practice in which compliance and risk initiatives are managed manually and viewed in isolation. To fully support its mission, performance management must not only identify new opportunities and optimize execution, but must also provide a way to identify, understand, and monitor risks. In this sense, performance management processes overlap with the risk management functions of GRC software that also help identify and monitor risks. The management of risk shows up in the following ways in the performance management lifecycle:

- Strategic alternatives must not only be compared with respect to the expected outcomes, but also in terms of the risks involved. Two strategies that promise the same returns can be differentiated through analyzing the risks involved
- Risks that are brought to light in planning and budgeting processes must be added to those identified in the formation of strategy. For example, if the capacity of a new supplier was identified in the strategy process, in the planning process it may be discovered that logistics could pose a problem. Both risks must be monitored
- Metrics to track risks and thresholds that indicate a need for escalation must be identified. These metrics must track not only risks within the company's operations but also those in the extended business network
- During execution, risks must be monitored and new risks must be identified. While much of this activity takes place in dedicated risk management applications through controls and alerts, the awareness of risk is always prevalent in performance management activities

The dimension of risk provides a new way to prioritize activities and focus attention. In a sense, risk metrics and controls are like the warning lights on a dashboard that indicate low tire-pressure or that a car is running out of gas. With the advent and increased reliance on business networks, many sources of risk may come from beyond the company's four walls. Outsourcing to partners offers cost savings and access to enhanced capabilities, but it comes with a greater risk because the processes and practices of partner organizations must be monitored in addition to your own. As the number of outsourced relationships grows, the same sort of automated monitoring mechanisms must be applied. For example, consider the numerous stories emanating out of production facilities in Asia. Not only do these represent a direct financial risk, but also a risk to reputation and brand. There is also the example of companies seeking to promote an environmentally friendly or socially conscious image only to find out that a partner's practices severely undercut that effort, damaging the company's reputation—not to mention the executives responsible for assessing and managing these relationships.

Closing the Loop

The final process in the performance management lifecycle is closing the loop, the practice of using the insights and information revealed to improve both strategy and execution. The most challenging aspect of understanding closing the loop is that there are two loops in play at most companies, a strategy loop and an execution loop. Closing the loop means something different depending on which loop you are referencing.

The strategy loop is the one we find in the performance management lifecycle. Closing this loop means being able to adjust strategy and propagate the changes throughout the lifecycle without having to start over. For example, if it turns out that a strategy for testing a new product in one local market is going spectacularly well, perhaps it makes sense to accelerate the rollout to every other market. To make this change in an integrated performance management system, you would go back to the definition of strategy, add the initiative, and then modify the existing plans, budgets, and metrics. You would not have to start over; you could add resources and potentially increase your forecast. As an example, you would be able to model the scenario in other regions and determine if regional-specific dynamics would help or hinder the success of the program. The loop is closed in the sense that new insights and directions find their way into a process of formulating and propagating strategy, of managing and monitoring execution, and of analyzing the results.

Closing the loop with respect to execution means something altogether different: namely enabling someone to take action after analysis has led to some insight about the right way to proceed. Performance management and analytic applications are frequently designed to support a specific role in a business process. For example, a credit analyst might be provided a set of tools to analyze the credit of a customer and the incoming order stream to make sure that credit limits aren't exceeded. Closing the execution loop, for a credit analyst, might mean providing the ability to override the denial of credit or to increase the credit limit of a customer temporarily so that a flow of orders is not interrupted. By providing the ability to close the loop between analysis and action, a company becomes more agile and speeds up its operations.

The Payoff

In practical terms, what all of the above leads to is the ability for the people at your organization to do more, to be more effective in their work, which in turn will create sustainable and considerable competitive advantage for the business as well as increased professional achievement for you and the other professionals at your organization. In later chapters we will look at the various domains of business in detail, but for now it is important to understand that progress toward supporting the performance management lifecycle will engender a number of benefits, which include:

- **Visibility.** By providing users with the ability to receive information promptly and in the context it is needed, a more accurate and timely representation of the performance of both company and important operational areas is created. Further, by pushing responsibility for managing and manipulating the systems to business users, you will aid in these people's productivity and free valuable IT resources for other strategic initiatives and innovation
- **Alignment.** Aligning execution to strategy, and then being able to optimize both, can provide significant gains in competitive advantage and profitability. Performance management, as we are describing it, will allow you to better link strategy to execution so that resources and people are used where they are most effective. In order to garner buy-in from employees, it is also important that they are able to see clearly how their key performance indicators (KPIs) and incentives are directly correlated to the established goals of the company

- **Agility.** Every stakeholder in the company will be able to identify issues and opportunities as they occur and take appropriate action. Organizations would also be able to adapt plans rapidly and reallocate resources to compete more effectively in global or local markets. In all, by empowering more users in the organization with access to trusted and meaningful information, and the capability to perform analysis and take action, you will be proactively supporting powerful decision-making processes and resource allocation
- **Protection.** By expanding the awareness of the specific risks that must be monitored and managed, and the boundaries that must be observed to stay in compliance, a company can become much more proactive in two areas that are frequently the source of significant negative surprises. Active monitoring and management of risk and compliance issues changes the culture and can make significant risks easier to take because management skills improve

In short, the payoff for better performance management is a company that is in conscious control of itself and has a culture that seeks to expand awareness and deepen understanding.

Expanding the Practice of Performance Management

So far, the discussion of the performance management lifecycle has focused on the process of managing an entire company and its business network. It is important to understand that performance management is not only applied at a high level, but is also a methodology that can be used in each of the domains of the business—HR, Finance, Procurement, Supply Chain, IT, Sales, Marketing, Product Development, and Service. Any of these organizations is a collection of people working with common purpose. The more each of the individuals is armed with the information they need and the tools to expand understanding, the more effective each will be. Each of these areas has a chapter in Part III that further explains the performance management lifecycle in the various business domains. The broad theme found in these chapters is that awareness of the big picture is vital to optimize any single part of a business. Managing a business or an organization as if it were an isolated silo will no longer work. The Part III chapters show, in each area covered, the benefits to expanding management practices by leveraging the knowledge and assets of other departments and of partners in the business network. Here is a preview of how performance management is applied in a few specific areas.

Finance

CFOs in particular, and the Finance department in general, are now concerned more than ever with maximizing business profitability, managing risk and compliance, and acting as a forward-thinking advisor to the business in order to aid optimization of the value-generating machine. To be able to engage in these activities successfully, the CFO must be supported by technologies beyond those for ensuring a smoother and more efficient consolidation and close process:

- **Business profitability** requires systems for addressing and optimizing profitability by measuring assets, profitability, costs, and capacity at as detailed and granular a level as is practical. CFOs must also be supported by systems that enable execution by aligning strategy with initiatives, objectives, metrics, people, and incentives. In addition, Finance must also be able to have visibility into the resources and exceptions that potentially would have the most impact on strategic objectives
- **Optimization of operational efficiency** requires effective communications to all employees with clearly defined accountability controls; aligned planning, budgeting, and forecasting that supports top-down and bottom-up collaboration in order to condense the budget cycle; and predictive analysis for risk-adjusted short, medium, and long-term planning
- **Governance, risk, and compliance** requires a cross-organization view of risks, ensuring data quality for internal management and external statutory reporting (such as integrated consolidation and aggregation models powered by Business Intelligence); fast and accurate quarterly and yearly close with a documented audit trail; and integration with solutions that support governance, risk, and compliance efforts

Human Resources

HR professionals have the ability to help drive value using tools that support competency management, goal and objective management, assessment management, and mentoring and coaching to improve employee effectiveness, as well as tools to help managers in other areas of the company do a better job of managing a diverse and decentralized workforce.

Performance management for HR provides access to new forms of information to expand the understanding of employee performance—going beyond traditional employee metrics such as MBOs and beginning to develop trends and patterns on employee behavior and interaction at a much more granular level. Performance management demonstrates a deeper view to the types of work conducted and therefore the skills required.

As James Holincheck notes in a report for Gartner Research,[4] HR professionals will be able to create a 365-day performance management program where managers and supervisors set performance expectations upfront, and then, throughout the year, as performance is continually monitored, records and comments can be stored in the system, regular feedback and coaching sessions can take place to help employees with their work, and regular and annual reviews to finalize compensation can be based on employee success as it is charted through the year. In all, it is a strategy to ensure that employees and managers have much better transparency into what they do, why they do it, and how it benefits the organization as a whole.

IT

In terms of the IT department, performance management means transitioning from a reactive, operationally focused caretaker of assets to a proactive strategically focused enabler of business value[5] via capabilities such as:

- Improving the granularity of information about the cost to serve various constituencies and support specific applications, assets, or business relationships
- IT project portfolio management and IT asset portfolio management, which can help better align IT investments with business objectives
- Asset rationalization,[6] which helps IT professionals identify opportunities for server/data consolidation, vendor optimization, infrastructure redeployment, and contract negotiation. As Anil Gupta writes in a report for Ventana Research, with more than 50% of IT spending going toward infrastructure assets, rationalization management capabilities allow IT executives to find savings that can be directed toward higher-value strategic objectives

---

[4] James Holincheck, "Employee Performance Management Software Marketscope," Gartner Research, June 10, 2004.

[5] Anil Gupta, "IT Performance Management—Aligning for Success," Ventana Research, August 10, 2004.

[6] Ibid

- Risk reduction, which will help professionals reduce internal risk factors by improving execution of projects, ensuring they are aligned with overall strategic objectives, and delivering them within budget and on time

Sales

In all, there is a rich array of performance management capabilities and tools that can be combined to match the particular needs of your organization to form a comprehensive solution. These include relationship management, forecasting and planning, referrals management, opportunity management, activity management, market intelligence, and monitoring and analysis. The CRM system, the repository for all customer-related interactions, is the fountain of data for sales. Performance management systems focused on sales sit on top of CRM, allow insights to be created based on the data, and then for sales-related processes to be changed to optimize performance.

Once in place as a comprehensive management solution for Sales, managers can expect to see a number of benefits that include:[7]

- Changing the focus from tactical to strategic, enabling executives to identify the larger, longer-term patterns that lead to successful outcomes instead of only focusing on closing deals for the current quarter
- Increased understanding of market characteristics and potential opportunities within geographic regions and accounts
- Improved account planning and strategies for selling to established clients
- Better aligned compensation plans
- Improved relationships with partners via more efficient compensation processes, shared sales target planning, and improved sharing of account and opportunity information, all of which serve to drive greater accountability
- Reduced inefficiencies from turnover, misallocation of resources, misdirected sales efforts, and overpayments
- More developed agility in terms of detecting and responding to market trends

---

[7] Michael Dunne, "Introducing the Concept of Sales Performance Management," Gartner Research, June 21, 2006.

"Successful implementation of Sales performance management practices and enabling technologies," notes Michael Dunne in a report for Gartner Research, "will produce a more informed, motivated, and competitive Sales organization that better exploits insights on market conditions and the self-interests of selling personnel."

Each of the Part III chapters describes the unique character of how performance management is applied to that domain and how the lifecycle is adapted to those concerns. For example, Chapter 13, on performance management for the supply chain, covers applying performance management to the extended business network.

A Guide to This Book

Throughout the remainder of this book we describe the methods, mechanisms, and culture of performance management in a manner that will allow you to begin a discussion of how performance management could benefit you, and your company. Further, our discussion is not intended to provide a rigidly prescriptive or dogmatic approach to what it means to achieve performance management maturity. Rather, as the elements of performance management—people, process, and technology—exist in one form or another at all companies, our intention is to help you better understand how to match performance management principles to the idiosyncratic nature of your company.

We do this in four parts:

- **Part I.** This section looks at the evolution of performance management from its beginnings as a way to monitor past performance through to the vision of performance management as a mature methodology and set of systems. Chapters include a discussion of its evolution and provide a vision of what modern performance management can be. Next is a detailed explanation of the performance management lifecycle, followed by a discussion of the frameworks available to you, as well as suggested methods for adapting and applying the elements of those frameworks that will best meet the needs of your organization.
- **Part II.** This section explains the mechanisms used to automate performance management, which include those central to the function of performance management, such as performance management applications as well as those in other domains such as GRC and business intelligence. Chapters here include a survey of

performance management applications; an analysis of how business intelligence is used as a platform for performance management; and an analysis of the relationship of GRC and performance management.

- **Part III.** This section explains how performance management can be applied and to what benefit within the domains of business. We start with Finance, since this is the birthplace for many of the methods and systems that have evolved to become performance management as we think of it today. The following chapters look at performance management in terms of the people, processes, and technologies that are adapted and used to support continuous improvement for Human Resources, IT, Sales, Marketing, Service, Supply Chain, Procurement, and Product Development.

Business conditions are in a constant state of evolution and change, making performance management more than ever a necessary component for the success of the modern enterprise. Executives who understand the importance of performance management and gain insight about implementing it in a timely, holistic, and cost effective manner will earn returns on their investments both for their companies and for themselves.

Chapter 2

The Evolution of Performance Management

Thinking about performance management is much easier than getting down to the hard work of transforming an organization. In this chapter, our analysis moves from the theoretical to the practical. We examine the processes and mechanisms that must be put to work to achieve the differentiation that performance management promises to deliver.

Every company will have a different starting point on the journey to better performance management, based on its culture, business processes, existing applications, information analysis tools, and other technology in place. The challenge of performance management is figuring out the right path forward for a specific company. Each company must figure out its own way of understanding and improving its performance management practices. Each company must also carefully choose which tactics will be of most benefit.

It is important to realize that the journey never ends. Performance management will never be implemented overnight, in one fell swoop that results in the perfect system. Performance management must be addressed as a process of continuous improvement that expands the practice within a company and at the same time responds as new processes, new relationships, and new risks must be monitored and analyzed.

Every company starts with a different set of strengths and weaknesses in its current performance management practices. In this chapter we outline the historical development of performance management, tracing the evolution from manually executed performance management, through the introduction of business intelligence, to systems for focused applications of performance management (like spend analytics). The end of the evolution is the current state of the art for performance management technology—the integrated performance management system—technology supporting the entire performance management lifecycle, from strategy, through planning and budgeting, to monitoring and analyzing results and the modeling and optimizing of new approaches. The chapter will explain the role that each generation of tools and processes played and how each successive generation solved the problems of its time. A clear understanding of this evolution will help readers chart a path toward greater maturity.

Most companies start with information that is in some senses trapped inside existing applications and systems and cannot be accessed or shared. Usually, other information is not collected or is not sent from suppliers. Not enough or too many tools may be in place.

For example, for some parts of your company, manual techniques may be the most cost effective solution, if the amount of information is modest, the manual workload is low, and significant value can be obtained. In other areas, analysis may not be possible without technology. The challenge then is to determine the payoff. Will it be possible to save a large amount of money by implementing a spend analytics system? For some companies that have made inroads into a broad application of performance management, it may be time to use an integrated performance management system to reach a higher level of adoption and reduce costs. These sorts of questions can only be answered in the context of a specific business, but this chapter will give you a clear idea of what choices are available and which may be most appropriate.

The key to success is starting with a precise idea of what you want to achieve as a first step toward a larger vision. For some companies, just putting more information in the hands of everyone will have a huge positive effect. Other firms that have the right information in place may benefit from more tools for automated analysis and modeling that can indicate where problems are so that staff and management can focus attention efficiently. Other firms may benefit most from incorporating partners into their models of the enterprise.

Whatever the current state of performance management is at a company, the most important thing is to start evolving. We now turn to the evolution of the field of performance management itself.

Manual Performance Management

The first generation of performance management techniques and technology were manual methods that were developed to bring together a consolidated view of activity in a company. The concern of performance management in this era was financial consolidation, budgeting, and planning, which, until recently, was the primary focus for performance management solution providers. The story of the evolution of performance management is primarily a description of how practices originally developed for financial performance management have been applied to different functional areas.

In the manual performance management era, spreadsheets and simple formatted reports were the dominant method of consolidating and aggregating information. Starting in the early 1970s until the emergence of comprehensive enterprise application suites in the 1990s, the fundamental problem remained the same: How do you extract data from all of the different systems of record in the enterprise, roll everything up to a consolidated view, and then analyze what's going on? Figure 2-1 shows the way that manual consolidation occurred through cascading levels of spreadsheets and formatted reports.

The pattern for most manual performance management was as follows:

- Extraction files or formatted reports were used to gather data from all of the various systems of record that contained the source information
- Spreadsheets and simple report writers were used to massage this information as automatically as possible into interim quantities that were used for aggregation
- The interim quantities were then combined to create a consolidated view of the enterprise

Manual consolidation had a few advantages that persist to this day. The spreadsheet is the ultimate tool for supporting the business user. Once the information was extracted from the source systems, business users could then take the process to fruition by themselves, without help from IT or anyone else. The do-it-yourself nature of spreadsheets is so attractive that it continues to appear in every generation of performance management systems, filling in the gaps in what the automated systems provide.

But in the manual era of performance management, spreadsheets were not just filling in the gaps; they were the entire performance management system, which had a variety of drawbacks. First of all, the manual massaging

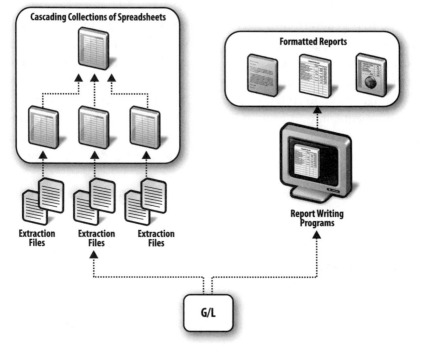

Figure 2-1. Performance Management Started with Reports and Spreadsheets

of reports and extraction files was error-prone. In a spreadsheet-dominated environment, it is very difficult to discover errors in calculations or spreadsheets, which then are passed from one layer to the next. Some people are far better than others at working with Excel, so there can be great variation in the quality of work.

Second, the data was on a one-way trip. If the numbers at the source of the consolidation changed, you had to go through the entire process to adjust the consolidated numbers. In a manual world, there is no ability to drill down and examine the detailed components of an aggregate number.

Third, the manual process took a long time. Closing the books was time-consuming, taking weeks, and delays could occur if Finance department members encountered issues regarding the reconciliation of all of the data flowing into the Finance department.

Fourth, and most obvious, the manual process by definition is labor intensive.

The next generation of performance management systems helped address some of these problems.

Business Users—The Management Layer

It is more than likely that you, the reader, are a business user, our name for the hands-on, managerial strata at most companies. If not, you may be a corporate executive seeking a better means to manage the company, and know intuitively that it is at this layer of the organization where key day-to-day management decisions are made. Business users run all of the individual components of the business, and in the decentralized enterprise they are far more responsible for managing the business than in the past when a command-and-control mentality predominated.

In order to perform their duties effectively, business users require the capabilities to slice and dice data into a variety of views and to model the data so that it can be used to support better decisions. These capabilities are important at the executive level as well.

Therefore, the work of business users cannot be automated, nor should it be. Rather, you need tools that allow you to bring in information from a number of sources and analyze it, to collaborate with others in the company and with partners and suppliers in business networks outside the company. The needed information is not just structured data, but also includes unstructured content. Everything must be presented in personalized dashboards that can be configured and adapted without requiring intermediation from IT.

When considering the massive investments made by most companies in their transactional systems and standardized processes, and the investment you have likely made in learning to use various personal productivity tools, there is great benefit to bridging the gap between tacit, unstructured processes, like analyzing risk in the supply chain or drafting a partner agreement that are managed outside of a single discipline with the repetitive task-oriented and data-rich processes found in ERP, CRM, SCM, and other systems of record. If your company is going to create and capture all of this data, you should also make it accessible in a way that supports the day-to-day decisions necessary to managing the business. And it must be done in a way that reduces any barriers to your ability to work and collaborate with the data.

An example of the power of proper support for the business user comes from a company that discovered $300 million in lost revenue in the first 18 months by tying initiatives to objectives. A top level goal to increase revenues by 30% was cascaded into specific goals and objectives for everyone in the organization tied to meeting this goal. In Marketing the specific goal was to increase the conversion of campaign leads into the sales pipeline. The ability to monitor both the call center telemarketing activities and the fulfillment center revealed that the agents were not extending offers consistently to inbound callers and the fulfillment center was not shipping to respondents in a timely fashion, both of which hurt the response rate and conversion to the sales pipeline. Based on this insight, adjustments were made to the call center modules in CRM and to the SCM application for fulfillment, which resulted in the company meeting its revenue target.

Business Intelligence

Throughout the 1970s and 1980s, the number of enterprise applications in use grew rapidly. At first, many of these functions were consolidated around a single database in large applications for financial, controlling, and a variety of other functions that became known as ERP. Then new applications such as CRM, SCM, PLM, and many others appeared in the late 1980s and 1990s, each collecting information in its own database. Further, it was common for many instances of these applications to be in use. The resulting situation is still with us today: the information that represents the state of the enterprise is spread out across many databases controlled by many applications.

The good news was that more and more information about the activity of the enterprise was being recorded. More processes were being automated. As time went on, the ability of the applications to present this data in useful forms became much better.

In 1989, the term "business intelligence" (BI) was coined by Howard Dresner, a leading technology analyst, to describe a collection of tools used in a number of areas of the company to extract, organize, and make useful the reams of data being collected in the organization's transactional

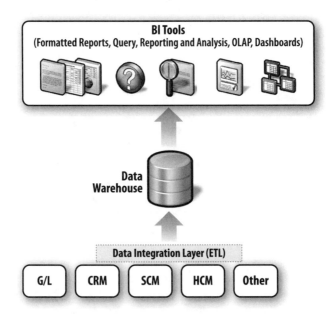

Figure 2-2. Performance Management Based on Business Intelligence

systems. The concept of business intelligence brought together many ideas that had been percolating under the general umbrella of decision support systems (DSS). The BI paradigm involved a new type of database, usually called a data warehouse. This database was the repository for all of the information that was transferred from the systems of record. The process of moving this data from the enterprise applications and other sources was known as extraction, transformation, and loading. Figure 2-2 shows how information flowed as business intelligence became adopted.

Business intelligence became a powerful way to gather and collect information and had a profound effect on performance management, which matured during the 1970s and 1980s. Performance management grew from its roots in financial consolidation to a more advanced model of the enterprise used for planning and budgeting. BI tools provided a rich foundation for companies' own solutions, and software vendors, inspired by the techniques and infrastructure of business intelligence, created a series of PM applications aimed at budgeting and planning and eventually many other areas.

Business intelligence had an impact on many other areas besides performance management. Entirely new areas of analysis such as online

ETL and Modern BI

It is important to note that ETL (extraction, transformation, and loading) capabilities played a major role in the emergence of modern business intelligence. The following capabilities are critical to the mission of BI:

- Extraction refers to pulling data from source systems (ERP, CRM, and so on)

- Transformation refers to ensuring the quality and reliability of the data as a trusted single version of the truth

- Loading refers to placing the data in a data warehouse or data mart

All three of these are critical components to business intelligence's ability to act as an integrated data management platform for performance management systems. The ETL layer is the automation of much of what was performed in the manual processing of spreadsheets.

The cleaned and normalized data then ends up in a data warehouse. A modern BI system then uses this data for production reporting, visualization, ad hoc reporting, and OLAP analysis.

analytical processing (OLAP) were created based on business intelligence. OLAP systems stored data in info cubes, a form that is optimized for rapid calculation and statistical analysis across a variety of dimensions of the data. Automated and ad hoc reporting tools dramatically widened the scope of information that could be presented to people at all levels of a company. Data marts were created to hold smaller amounts of data for special purposes. Companies like Wal-Mart created mega-data warehouses to hold all their transactions that were then used by the company and its partners to support performance management analysis and many other purposes. Business intelligence became one of the most active areas of investment.

From a performance management perspective, it is important to note three things. First of all, it is easy to conflate performance management and business intelligence. As the sidebar explains in more detail, business intelligence is a tool while performance management is an application of technology to automate a key analytical business process.

The second point to note about business intelligence is that PM applications usually mimic the structure of BI systems. In PM applications, there is a function similar to ETL in which data is gathered from many source systems and consolidated into a model used to aggregate the data, while preserving the ability to drill down to see more granularity. Performance management systems also provide reporting and analysis functionality so that issues can be identified and then the causes can be explored. Given the similarity of the structure of PM applications to business intelligence, it is no wonder that business intelligence comes to mind when attempting to understand and put these applications to use.

The third point to remember is that during the era of business intelligence, companies tended to have a proliferation of business intelligence tools and distinct PM applications. By 2005, most of the Global 2000 companies were running between 5 and 15 separate BI systems for extracting, reporting, and analyzing data, which created redundancy in terms of work and training as well as straining IT resources. Further, all of these varied and siloed systems were buzzing away without any coordination or integration and therefore were creating multiple—often competing—versions of the truth. The scope and frequency of the data collected and analyzed was also narrower than is required today. Analysis focused on internal operations and processes and rarely was extended to activities performed by partners in the extended business network. Inefficient methods for gathering data meant it was collected much less frequently.

Disentangling Business Intelligence and Performance Management

Even in 2004, as Keith Gile and Laurie M. Orlov indicate in their study titled "Business Intelligence and Performance Management Complement Each Other—But Serve Different Purposes," there was confusion in the market between business intelligence and performance management.[1] But as the report also makes clear, there are clear differences.

Business intelligence is a generalist while performance management is a specialist.

Business Intelligence

- Analyzes data with no preconceived notion of process requirement

- Reports historical data and information to users

- Discovers trends of business anomalies that could impact future growth

- Enables analysis used in strategy evaluation with an eye toward future decisions

Performance Management

- Monitors specific business activities and processes as they occur

- Alerts stakeholders when metrics and indicators are out of tolerance

- Links indicators to business processes (for example, operational metrics as well as financial measures)

Performance management is a methodology powered by business intelligence.

As Keith Gile, an analyst and expert on business intelligence, wrote in a 2005 report, "…most of these reporting and analysis solutions were either purchased at a departmental level to solve a single problem, such as brand analysis in CPG or customer churn in telco, or were included within enterprise applications like ERP, CRM, and financial budgeting and planning. This myopic approach to technology spending has created an overabundance

---

[1] Keith Gile and Laurie M. Orlov, "Business Intelligence and Performance Management Complement Each Other—But Serve Different Purposes," Forrester Research, June 23, 2004.

of redundancy that costs companies millions of dollars and often leads to inconsistency and frustration on the part of end users."[2]

The same proliferation was true of PM applications. Individual systems for planning, budgeting, strategy management, cost and spend analysis, and forecasting all sprang up, which we will describe in more detail in the next section.

The Bottleneck and the Platform

To understand more fully the way that PM applications developed, it is useful to further examine a major problem that developed with business intelligence and the response of the software industry.

One of the challenges that emerged with the rise of BI systems was that it reduced the do-it-yourself nature of the technology, as we pointed out in Chapter 1. In the manual era, at least the business user had control over the process, though it was admittedly fragmented and error-prone. As business intelligence systems were adopted, many of them were complex and required IT intermediation to create and modify reports. This in turn led to a bottleneck, as IT departments were unable to handle the backlog of reporting requests they received. IT was not needed for everything, but the amount that business users could do for themselves was reduced in the business intelligence era.

As the Internet boom of the mid to late 1990s unfolded, the need to better support business users fully emerged and became known as "business intelligence for the masses." The term was coined in 1997 by Microsoft and refers to the move by a handful of companies to provide reports and some basic data analysis capabilities to an ever-increasing number of business users. This was generally done in an organization-wide manner and, in some instances, was expanded to include partners and customers when applicable.[3]

The buildup behind extending business intelligence beyond the realm of the relatively small number of power users (such as the IT department) reached a tipping point as many companies began to adopt various easier-to-use BI tools throughout the organization in order to provide a broad array of users with access to data and some decision-support software. The

---

[2] Keith Gile, "Business Intelligence Driven By Compliance, Standardization, and Performance Initiatives," Forrester Research, April 5, 2005.

[3] Philip Russom and Keith Gile, "After the Bubble Burst: Business Intelligence for the Masses," Giga Information Group, Inc., September 23, 2002.

net result was that the IT department no longer had to play so much of an intermediate role between the applications and business users.

In the 2000s, the BI industry also started to address the issue of the proliferation of tools that operated as siloed processes and sapped valuable computing resources.

The vendors responded to evolving customer needs by introducing a number of solutions for business intelligence standardization as a means to better integrate different BI tools across the operational areas of the organization. And as the market moved toward a single BI platform approach, there was also the desire to place more functionality on top of the platform in order to gain more value—become smarter—from the data being collected. Increasingly a central data warehouse became the source from which data used for production reports, ad hoc reporting, OLAP analysis, modeling, and simulations all flowed.

What this concurrence of trends means is that business intelligence became a single data aggregation, transformation, management, and analysis platform—a single version of the truth—for all areas of a company from which other process-specific applications can pull data.

The reason for analyzing the growth and development of the BI industry in such detail is that there is a strong parallel in the growth and development of PM applications.

Performance Management Applications: The First Generation

The first generation of performance management apps started to appear in the late 1980s and rapidly accelerated in the 1990s. Each of these applications could be considered a special-purpose application of business intelligence, and, like business intelligence, there was a proliferation of tools for specific tasks.

The development of PM applications tended to follow the money. Applications for financial consolidation appeared first and matured fastest because they played a crucial role in rapidly assembling the financial statements used for statutory reporting to regulators and investors and operational reports used by management. Using such applications, the financial close process could happen in days rather than weeks. Large amounts of error-ridden manual work using spreadsheets was avoided, which cut costs and improved quality. Financial consolidation applications resembled BI systems in that they had component parts for loading data from many sources, cleaning and rationalizing the data into a common form, performing transformations of data like currency conversion, and creating a consolidated view of the financial reports that aggregated the data. In addition, the applications had capabilities for creating documents used in regulatory filings, reporting, and various forms of analysis, replacing the cascading pyramids of spreadsheets through which consolidation was performed manually. One of the most popular features of such applications was the ability to drill down into numbers on the top-level balance sheet and income statement and see the components from which key numbers such as gross sales or net income were computed.

Other early arrivals were PM applications for planning, budgeting and forecasting. These applications helped streamline another process that had previously been dominated by spreadsheets. The applications covered these processes and often were offered as an integrated suite.

Planning applications allowed companies to look at what they expected in terms of financial and operational performance for the next three to five years. A forward-looking model of the balance sheet, income statement, and various operational activities could be created, incorporating detailed descriptions of the resources needed and the financial performance expected from various operating units. Alternative scenarios could be compared and the impact of major events, such as mergers, could be modeled and analyzed.

Budgeting applications generally started when the plan for the year was set. This became the basis for the top-down communication of the financial performance that senior management was looking to achieve. The budgeting applications would allow the operating units to respond with budgets that attempted to meet the targets using estimates derived from detailed models of operating performance. Budgeting applications then supported the consolidation of the detailed budgets and the subsequent negotiation between senior management and line executives that may lead to several versions of the process that flow through many different cycles.

Forecasting applications started with the budget numbers and focused on managing the forecasted numbers that were usually computed on a rolling basis after each reporting period, sometimes more frequently. Planning, budgeting, and forecasting applications have sped up the process, cut costs, supported more advanced budgeting techniques like driver-based budgeting, and allowed much more time to be spent on analysis as opposed to manual manipulation of spreadsheets.

Another class of PM applications for monitoring and analysis of execution grew out of the financial consolidation applications. Just as the net income or revenue was calculated by aggregating the financial results of various components, aggregated operational statistics could be calculated in the same way. Many times using the BI capabilities as a foundation, monitoring and analysis applications automatically computed KPIs and metrics that described financial operational performance. The applications allowed definitions of KPIs to be standardized, and presented the results in cascading dashboards that highlighted which metrics were out of expected ranges. Applications for monitoring and analysis helped identify problems early, focused management attention on important areas, and put in KPIs to quantitatively manage many aspects of the business that previously had gone unattended, such as risk and compliance issues.

Another category of PM applications for modeling and optimization focused on specific types of analysis sprang up in the wake of the success of consolidation and planning applications. These applications provided detailed ways to model and analyze spending, sales activity, marketing, supply chain flows, and other specialized areas. Each of these applications came ready-made with models that provided a starting point to describe activity and the processes that took place. All of the data gathering, reporting, analysis, and drill-down capabilities of other PM applications were present in these special purpose applications. The payoff from these special purpose applications came from the money saved or from increases in productivity or effectiveness they helped achieve.

Oftentimes PM applications uncovered difficult problems that could only be solved through in-depth analysis. A new class of modeling and simulation applications was created to help understand business activity at a deeper level. Sometimes these applications helped implement specific ways of modeling business activity such as activity-based costing. Other times, the applications were powerful, general purpose environments for creating models or running simulations. These applications usually allowed assumptions to be adjusted so that many different scenarios could be compared. These applications often helped uncover deeper problems and root causes. Looking forward, modeling and simulation helped analyze risks and identify new opportunities.

The last to arrive were applications that tracked strategy and helped manage the development, communication, and translation of high-level strategic initiatives into specific goals for each operating unit. This category of application often implemented mechanisms to support a specific methodology for strategy such as the Balanced Scorecard, which recommends the use of various perspectives and the documentation of strategy using strategy maps and themes. Like budgeting applications, strategy applications helped cascade the strategy from its top-down expression into more detailed objectives for each division and department. Like monitoring and analysis applications, KPIs and metrics could be established to track the implementation of initiatives that must be carried out to execute a strategy and risks inherent in the strategy.

For all of these applications, following the pattern set by BI applications, the initial functionality was supplemented by advanced features for analysis that allowed more do-it-yourself support of the business user.

Figure 2-3 shows how the evolution of these applications supported every phase of the performance management lifecycle.

These applications were all effective in their own right and, as time passed, each of them matured, taking advantage of the Internet, service-oriented technology, and advanced technology for user interfaces.

It is in this era that performance management as a field really started to emerge. There was something similar about all of these applications that started to be recognized. Just as business intelligence first arrived as many individual tools that were eventually combined into an integrated system, it became clear that performance management could follow the same path. The domain of performance management came to encompass the way that these applications used models of corporate activity and collected

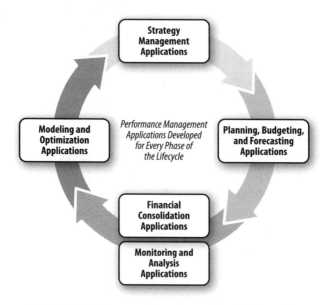

Figure 2-3. Performance Management Applications Were Developed for Every Phase of the Lifecycle

and aggregated data to fill those models, to support reporting, forecasting, scenario analysis, and simulations.

A cycle of performance management also started to be recognized. Sales and operations planning had always been a process in which revenue targets were set and then plans were made to meet them. But as more information was available about more parts of the enterprise, it became clear that a larger process for performance management could be explicitly supported with all of the PM applications that were now in use. Strategy could be formulated about more than just revenue targets. Strategic initiatives then could be devolved into specific budget items and targets for key measures that would indicate how well the implementation of the strategy was proceeding. These measures were both financial and operational, that is, tracking activity indicative of progress toward goals and the quality of processes. The goals for specific financial and operational measures could then be set for specific departments and individuals as part of the budgeting and planning process. As execution of the strategy went forward, consolidation and aggregation expanded beyond financial measures to include operational data. As information collection became easier, forecasts could be monitored and adjusted monthly instead of quarterly. Other operational measures could be tracked, especially those of a predictive nature, so that problems could be found before it was too late to take remedial action.

At leading companies, the possibilities for the future of performance management started to become clear. As David Kasabian and John Hagerty write, "As companies matured in their use of business intelligence and performance management technology, many started to connect the dots between disparate parts of the business. Yet many of those connections were tenuous; executives and analysts largely default to their original areas of specialty. The performance management spirit was willing, but the corporate flesh was weak."[4]

Integrated Performance Management Systems

The performance management situation today, at most companies, is complex because applications and practices from each era of performance management are in play. It is not uncommon for spreadsheets to be employed for certain performance management tasks, special-purpose reporting from

---

[4] David Kasabian and John Hagerty, "Pervasive Performance Management: What It Is and How To Prepare," AMR Research, July 2007.

business intelligence for others, even while special-purpose PM applications do the bulk of the work.

But just as the cost of multiple BI tools has led to greater consolidations on single platforms, so have a variety of forces lead to the creation of integrated performance management systems.

Pressures Leading Toward Integrated Performance Management

Here are the pressures leading companies to seek greater and greater integration of PM applications in order to optimize their performance and increase their ability to detect problems and react quickly.

The first pressure is that the performance management lifecycle has become recognized as an iterative and bidirectional process. At first glance, the performance management lifecycle seems to have a natural flow from strategy to planning and budgeting, monitoring and analysis, and modeling and optimization. But performance management is never only a top-down process. As goals are communicated and budget targets are set, a negotiation begins. Departments frequently either reject goals as too ambitious or only possible with increased resources. This back and forth leads to changes in budgets, plans, and forecasts and sometimes to changes in strategy. The information flows upstream and downstream. The models at all levels must be able to be adjusted and communicated in both directions. Making a change to the models in any PM application should not require the entire process to begin again, as it did when cascading levels of spreadsheets were used. Supporting such a back-and-forth iterative performance management process is what is referred to as closing the loop.

The second pressure is that the models used in PM applications are often duplicative. The model of a company's budget is frequently just a mirror image of the model used for consolidation and aggregation. The forecast is simply the same model projected into the future. While unique and highly granular models will always be needed for special tasks, the core model of the enterprise is something that can be defined and shared across the enterprise via PM applications, creating new levels of efficiency and supporting integration.

The third pressure comes from the need to close the loop in a different way by allowing action to be taken from performance management systems. The first generation of performance management systems was developed before the era of service-oriented architecture and mashups—simple applications created from services, often by business users. It was difficult for someone who noticed something problematic, such as a drop in a sales pipeline or a potential risk in the supply chain, to reach out into the enterprise applications and take action. Instead, emails were sent, but the power of the enterprise applications to make sure that these events were properly handled was not addressed. Integration between performance management and enterprise applications is something that is inefficient to do over and over again for each separate PM application.

The fourth pressure comes from a persistent and expanding need for companies to deliver more and more data both internally and externally. Modern performance management is about increasing the efficiency by which data is collected throughout the enterprise—whether financial or nonfinancial metrics—as well as ensuring that the data can be trusted, comes with an auditable pedigree, and provides a single version of the truth shared throughout the enterprise.

In order to provide this level of data quality, it is important that the various systems and models employed by the organization for financial consolidation and data aggregation are integrated and flexible enough to allow for multipurpose use of the data. This means creating a single data collection, transformation, and management platform from which multiple applications supporting multiple processes can find what they need.

Further, the system and process must be more than simply a flow of data into a single warehouse. It must include qualitative and unstructured information in order to provide as much context to the user as possible to support strong decision-making.

Mandates Are Leading the Way

We should also point out that standard-setting and regulatory agencies are moving toward data reporting models and financial standards that require you to adopt a new level of data management. We will discuss these in Chapter 7, but the fact is that the world is moving inexorably toward recognizing a single set of financial reporting rules termed the International Financial Reporting Standards (IFRS).

Concurrent with the acceptance of these standards is the growing acceptance of a technical standard known as XBRL (Extensible Business Reporting Language) for the electronic submission of financial statements using taxonomies in order to support a much richer set of data than has traditionally been used, including key nonfinancial value drivers.

The bottom line is that you must do more than simply collect and manage a bunch of numbers; you must collect and manage trusted data in as close to a single version of the truth as possible with relevant information, so that it is useful and actionable.

Additional Integration Demands

In addition to these pressures, a growing landscape of technology now surrounds every sort of application used for enterprise computing. Each of these capabilities must be addressed with an integration if an application is going to be as useful as possible.

As they have become more powerful, PM applications, like many BI tools, are able to create dashboards that bring together a large amount of information into one view and allow drill-down into details. These dashboard creation environments have started to resemble other environments that allow business users to create simple do-it-yourself applications. PM applications should be able to allow users to create mashups or to offer services or embeddable parts of user interfaces for use in other dashboards or mashups. Again, repeating this work for each PM application would be inefficient.

A variety of collaboration tools for broadcasting information (blogs), for supporting shared workspaces and content development (wikis), and for engaging in real-time collaboration (IM and telepresence) are becoming part of modern enterprise applications and should be part of PM applications. Enterprise applications were built to provide transactional records and to automate well-defined, step-by-step processes. The explosion of Web 2.0 has shown the power of less-structured collaboration, which is being used as a communication layer on top of enterprise applications. The combination of these unstructured and structured forms of technology is becoming the state of the art for enterprise applications.

Analysis and drilldown for more information in PM applications is not limited to the sort of structured information that is stored in databases. Qualitative information about the data collected must be stored and follow that information through the consolidation cycle. Frequently, deeper analysis of PM applications requires searching through unstructured information such as web pages, blogs, wikis, strategy papers, presentations, meeting minutes, regulatory filings, and other documents stored in internal and external repositories. The unstructured information provides additional contexts along with the performance management information to better support decision-making. Integration with such technology should be performed once and used by many applications in a performance management suite.

Analysis of performance management data can lead to the recognition of risks or compliance problems. When risks are identified, they must be tracked and monitored, which is essentially a performance management activity. The risks could be the performance of a supplier or the expected cost of transportation or the ability to perform a certain process within a defined time limit. Many of these risks may also be relevant to compliance. In addition, the monitoring of compliance by governance, risk, and compliance (GRC) applications may indicate the presence of risks or other operational problems. As GRC applications become more and more prevalent and important in the face of increasing demands for transparency from regulators and investors, increasing connections have been recognized between the two sorts of applications. To optimize the ability of both performance management systems and GRC applications to help each other, there should be a two-way street between them. As in many of the other forces mentioned so far, it doesn't make sense to perform such an integration for each PM application.

An integrated performance management system would have all of the aspects just mentioned.

Applying Integrated Performance Management

The arrival of integrated performance management systems, coupled with the growth of business process management methods and technology, has led to a new vision of how to think about running a business.

For a while, senior managers have realized that the key processes of their businesses have very little to do with the division of an organization into departments. Processes like order-to-cash or design-to-manufacture stretch across departments and involve many different enterprise applications. The arrival of BPM methods and technology allow these processes to be explicitly described and managed.

To arrive at the full vision of what is possible if integrated performance management is in place along with BPM and GRC, let's take a step back and think of each step in one of those end-to-end processes. From the point of view of the head of a department, each step in a process is either collaborative, meaning that it involves other departments, or it is contained within your department. If the process is internal to your department and doesn't involve others, then the head of the department truly owns that process and can do whatever he or she wants with it. However, if the process step is collaborative, then there are two cases. The department is responsible either for that process step, that is, the department is the driver, or the department is supporting the step, meaning it is a passenger. In these cases, the process must be carried out in communication with other parts of the business. Performance management helps transmit a description of the activity for a process step throughout the enterprise. GRC applications help monitor the risk and compliance issues for processes.

At this writing, no existing performance management suite is as completely integrated as just described, but the vision is now in place and such integrated suites are in active development.

Perhaps the main benefit of such an integrated suite is that the state of the enterprise is no longer a mystery. Decisions are made within the context of a single version of the truth and shared information. The process of setting strategy, planning and budgeting and forecasting, consolidation and aggregation, and monitoring and optimization are themselves automated and optimized. This means more time is spent on value-creating activities and less time is spent on the assembly of information and the care and maintenance of models.

But another benefit is that an integrated performance management suite is robust enough to allow the extension of performance management from the traditional realms into new areas. While financial consolidation, budgeting, planning and forecasting, have all been applied to the corporation at large, performance management is increasingly being applied to specific areas such as IT, Supply Chain, HR, Product Development, and Marketing. Integrated performance management can support the extension of performance management processes to these areas and keep them integrated with the larger corporate strategy and GRC processes, such as those designed to prevent segregation of duty violations. GRC applications help identify such violations, resolve them, and then make sure they do not reappear. Companies that have taken significant steps toward integrated performance management have achieved dramatic benefits. For example, a major theme park operator uses data from an integrated performance management system to actively make comparisons and predictions to determine how best to manage crowds. Data is made available to floor managers and ride managers. They can determine when and how to open up lines for a ride—or prepare for an influx of visitors into restaurants, shops, and other indoor amusements. From a control center that looks like mission control at Cape Canaveral, they send actionable information to managers throughout the park, via their mobile phones, enabling them to take the actions necessary to ensure visitors have the best experience possible in the park. Such coordinated action would not be possible without an integrated collection of information and appropriate analysis tools.

Realizing the Vision

The next steps for the modern vision of performance management will happen in two stages. First, imagine that the application-centric view of the enterprise is replaced by a process-centric view, and performance management is extended to each of the functional areas of the enterprise and also to the outsourced activities in the supply chain. What you have then is a situation like the one shown in Figure 2-4.

The performance management model can be adjusted to monitor and optimize the end-to-end processes in the company instead of the more narrowly defined processes that take place in one application. Regardless of how the processes are implemented in enterprise applications, the performance management layer becomes the place where the business process view of the company comes to life.

By integrating the process-centric performance management view with GRC, you will now be able to make decisions about tactical moves for

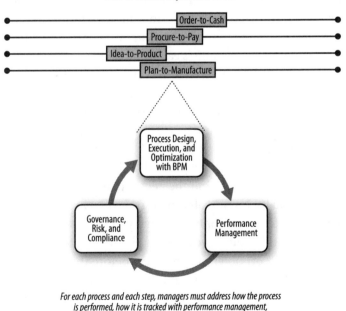

For each process and each step, managers must address how the process
is performed, how it is tracked with performance management,
and how it is monitored for risk and compliance with GRC

Figure 2-4. A Vision for Process-Centric Performance Management

optimizing processes that incorporate the performance considerations, but that also take into account the risk and compliance issues that are associated with each tactic. This risk- and compliance-adjusted view of performance and strategy is something that is only performed on an informal basis at leading companies. As the integrated performance suite develops, such a practice will become far more commonplace and will be explicitly supported by software.

The Implications of Performance Management

So far, this chapter has spent much time under the hood of performance management, looking at the ways that models work and how applications are structured and integrated. In the last section, the perspective changed to a higher level, examining the big picture vision for an integrated performance management system. For the rest of this chapter, the perspective will broaden further and we will examine some of the long-term implications of performance management.

Predictability

The increased predictability that can flow from well-implemented performance management processes is one of the most compelling areas driving adoption. Being a public company is a lot like undergoing a minute-by-minute referendum via the company's stock price—the ultimate metric, as it were, of the health of the company's operations. For those companies that do well, the perpetual referendum is easily won, but for companies that may hit a bump in the road, the referendum may become a losing proposition. As James Surowiecki writes in the September 29, 2008 edition of the *New Yorker*, "The perception of weakness exacerbates the reality of weakness."

One way to protect the company from losing when things take a turn for the worse is to be in the position to look predictable even when you are losing some money. Doing this requires showing that you understand the issues at hand, the drivers behind the performance, and that, due to your understanding, you have a workable plan. You will win a vote of confidence if you can give stakeholders confidence that you know what you are doing.

More importantly, though, you should be moving to a position where you are able to fend off potential problems before they occur or in their earliest stages. By getting better data more efficiently, as well as better understanding the drivers behind your business, the company will become more predictable and proactive. You will be able to find problems faster and in time to prevent them before they occur, implement a remedy at an early stage, or, when practicable, include a mitigation plan in external reports that indicates you truly understand the internal workings of the business and are in control of its processes and performance.

Understanding and then communicating the drivers behind performance, and how performance in seemingly nonfinancial areas impacts the bottom line, will increase the value of the company in the eyes of external stakeholders.

Enhanced Support for the Business User

As stated above, performance management and the technologies used to support it should be built not for experts only, but for everybody else. The most powerful PM applications empower business users and do not require intermediation by the IT department as they seek to understand, analyze, manipulate, model, and play with information in order to innovate, optimize, and generally manage the business. Technology supports decision-making and does not slow or hinder it.

As David Kasabian and John Hagerty write, business users must be engaged with the tools and need for performance management in a manner that addresses the "What's In It For Me?" question that lies at the heart of all adoption strategies: "Therefore, [engaging business users] requires a focus on process enablement, analysis, and visualization in context of role and process, as well as ease of use in order to facilitate user adoption and retention... Functionality must be walk-up and use, requiring little if any training [to establish] an environment that creates efficiencies in their day-to-day responsibilities and doesn't bog them down in complexity." [5]

The process must also include the ability to garner the wisdom of crowds; collaboration—externally and internally—should be not only supported, but also encouraged. In fact, effectively practicing performance management not only requires sophisticated support for collaboration—such as the use internally and externally of blogs, wikis, mashups, web-supported meetings and document creation, social networking technologies, and the like—but also drives user adoption of these new and powerful work techniques.

---

[5] David Kasabian and John Hagerty, "Pervasive Performance Management: What It Is and How To Prepare," AMR Research, July 2007.

Closing the Loop

Chapter 4 provides a deeper analysis of what is meant by closing the loop. The concept can be confusing because it has two meanings.

The first and most important concerns the way that PM applications are integrated in support of the lifecycle. Closing the loop means being able to send a strategy or a budget down from the top levels of the company and then react to what is heard from the bottom up, and adjust strategies and budgets and other aspects of the performance management models without having to start over. Without such closing of the loop, performance management systems are not able to support the two-way flow of information in the enterprise.

The second meaning of closing the loop concerns integration with the company's transactional systems. In a closed loop system between performance management and enterprise applications, a business user, after discovering an innovative approach or solution to a problem, should be able to take action and implement the solution in a timely fashion.

For example, suppose a production manager learns that production will be reduced at a plant in Asia due to an impending strike. That person should have the capacity to seek out and implement a solution, such as redirecting some percentage of capacity to one or more other facilities, without going through an extended process.

Where to Start

Those that are inspired by the possibilities of performance management have no doubt already started thinking about how to make progress toward adoption. Here is some initial guidance about how to bring performance management to your company.

Look internally at the efficiency of your performance management processes. How long does it takes to close the books? How much manual work is involved in getting answers to questions?

Look outside the organization and begin to benchmark against peers. Before moving forward, understand where you stand in terms of other companies in your industry.

Find burning performance management issues. For example, is your planning and budgeting falling short because you don't have good forward-looking visibility? Are the models you use to look at future performance able to support testing assumptions and create what-if scenarios? Is there a lack of granularity and dimensionality in cost and profitability, inhibiting the ability to understand and optimize pricing, costing, processes, and operations? Can you quickly and efficiently prepare external financial reports? Is performance management still singularly a role for Finance as opposed to being pushed out to the operational areas?

Reform budgeting practices. Consider the advantages of doing away with the annual budgeting cycle and begin managing by rolling monthly forecasts and quarterly strategic reviews.

End accountancy. Rather than considering the Finance department the domain of accountants, it should be the home for directors of performance management. These people should be aligned with operational areas, to act as business partners to support better decision making and value creation. The bottom line is that the ERP and consolidation systems are essentially automating the accounting role.

Change the culture. It is no longer a matter of whether line managers come in at or under budget, but rather how well they did at creating value or cutting costs. For example, bonuses and other incentives should be tied to constant improvement and then invested in resources to be able to achieve that mandate. For example, if the cost of handling a customer interaction is $10.00, the goal should be to get it down to $9.50 and then provide the resources for outsourcing, streamlining, or upgrading technology.

Bring IT into operations. The IT department should not just support transactional systems, but should have a real understanding of how best to support HR, Finance, Manufacturing, Sales, Marketing, and Service. IT

Three Myths of Performance Management

It is difficult—It is true that many IT projects require starting from scratch and undergoing a significant user adoption exercise. Performance management is about augmentation, not replacement, leveraging resources you already have to greater purpose and value.

It is also important to note that there is no specific starting point. It can be broadly or narrowly applied, which means that for most, taking an incremental approach and perhaps starting with even just a single project is the best place to begin.

It is only about Finance—Performance management is a discipline that exists well beyond Finance and reaches across all operational areas and into the distributed value chain. It is about laying bare the interconnected nature of all of the company's resources.

It is a "nice to have" as opposed to a "need to have"—In fact, performance management is the only way to effectively manage the modern enterprise within a model that emphasizes the need for continuous change and optimization.

should be specialized to deliver the right application and set of capabilities for each of these areas to achieve its strategic objectives.

Conclusion

As we move forward, this book will help you transform your organization by raising people's consciousness of the benefits and necessity of engaging in a systematic and holistic approach to performance management.

We will explain how to go from the complicated starting point that likely exists at nearly every company to an improved to-be state in which trusted data leads to more information and where more capability to publish and analyze that information leads to higher performance and profitability for the organization.

The next step is to understand in greater detail the end-to-end strategy and execution lifecycle as well as the measures of performance management maturity, which are the topics of Chapter 3.

Chapter 3

Performance Management Lifecycle and Maturity

Like any complex undertaking, setting out to improve performance management can quickly become a confounding task. The scope is so wide and deep that it is daunting to imagine even the smallest amount of progress. Transformation at scale is usually achieved through incremental steps; a series of smaller projects that improve skills, processes, and technology, gradually adding up to a massive transformation.

There are several key ingredients in such a transformation process. The first is an indication of how to organize your thinking about performance management. The second is a definition of the specific changes that must occur to improve each stage of the performance management lifecycle. The third is an idea of the major stages of the transformation. The final ingredient is a vision of where the company wants to go to make the most of performance management and provide the most value.

This chapter provides three of the four ingredients:

- The first section provides an overview of the various methodologies and frameworks that are used when implementing performance management
- The second section is a detailed description of each phase of the performance management lifecycle

- The third section contains an overview of the stages that different observers have identified in a journey toward performance management maturity. These stages provide a roadmap of the way that transformation takes place

The remaining ingredient is a vision for where your company wants to end up in its performance management capabilities. The right vision depends on each company's particular circumstances and priorities. Crafting this vision is the primary challenge of performance management identified in Chapter 1. This chapter presents a guided tour of the essential processes that must be carried out at each stage of the performance management lifecycle. In doing so, we aim to provide enough information to support the creation of a clear vision for performance management.

Performance Management-Related Methodologies

Performance management has been studied for many years by leading researchers at business schools and universities around the world. In addition, a variety of other management and quality methodologies stress that measurement is a prerequisite to management. So there is no shortage of theories about performance management and any discussion of the topic is peppered with phrases that come from methodologies like the Balanced Scorecard, Six Sigma, total quality management, and several others. The following overview is a summary of these theories. They have influenced many of the processes in the lifecycle and the software systems described in Chapter 4.

Specifically, this chapter will review:

- The Balanced Scorecard
- Six Sigma
- Total Quality Management
- European Foundation for Quality Management
- The Baldridge Award
- ISO

The Balanced Scorecard

Invented in 1992 by Robert S. Kaplan, a long-time Harvard Business School professor, and David P. Norton, a researcher and writer who founded several performance management consulting organizations, the Balanced Scorecard provides an excellent way to understand the performance management lifecycle from the top down.

The method began as a way to measure and track performance beyond financial measures and used four perspectives: Financial, Internal Business Processes, Learning and Growth, and Customer (shown in Figure 3-1). To design a Balanced Scorecard, four or five measures are selected in each perspective and then tied to company objectives.

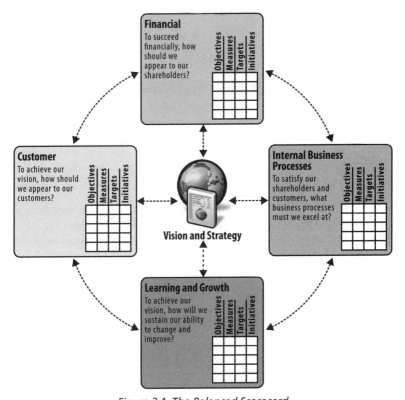

Figure 3-1. The Balanced Scorecard
(Source: Balanced Scorecard Institute, http://www.jiscinfonet.ac.uk/tools/balanced-scorecard © Paul Arveson, 1998)

But as this tool was used, it became clear that it was vital to understand why each objective and measure was being chosen and how they all fit together. As the Balanced Scorecard evolved, it became the name for a variety of practices for the creation, management, and execution of business strategy. Figure 3-2 gives an indication of this bigger process.

The Balanced Scorecard has become a management system that begins with the clear definition of the mission and values of a company and then moves on to create a future vision, and includes various hypotheses on how to achieve that vision. The strategy spells out specific actions that will lead to desired results.

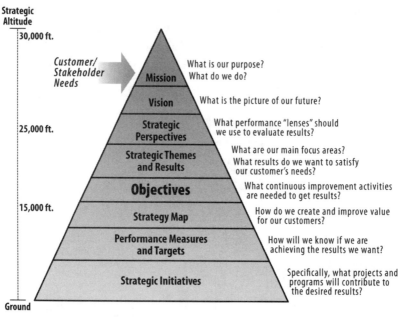

Figure 3-2. The Logic of Balanced Scorecard Strategic Planning
(Source:Balanced Scorecard Institute, http://www.jiscinfonet.ac.uk/tools/balanced-scorecard
© Paul Arveson, 1998)

The four perspectives—financial, customer, internal business processes, learning and growth—help organize thinking around the objectives that are going to be pursued to execute a strategy. Categorizing the objectives into specific themes helps boil down the essence of a strategy. Figure 3-3 shows how objectives in the various perspectives (the rows of this diagram) are categorized into themes (the column headings).

Another aspect of the practices surrounding the Balanced Scorecard is a strategy map that connects objectives and shows the logic of how lower level, more specific objectives are related to and help achieve those at a higher and broader level.

The objectives are related in a cause and effect manner. If an objective at a lower level is achieved, it should, in turn, help achieve an objective at a higher level. Notice also how the strategy map shows the objectives categorized in each row by the perspectives.

The Balanced Scorecard presents a strategy that devolves each hypothesis into a set of objectives of cascading levels for transforming different parts of the organization. The next step is to create performance measures and targets that can be tracked to determine the progress. These measures and targets may also help to create strategies for business units or departments.

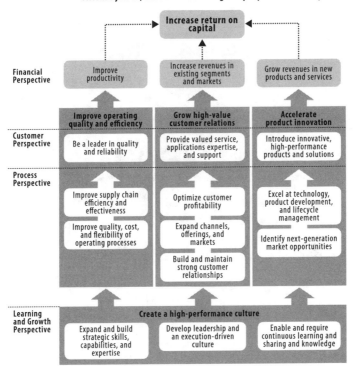

Figure 3-3. How Objectives are Organized into Themes
(Reprinted by permission of *Harvard Business Rreview*. From: "Mastering the Management System" by Robert S. Kaplan and David P. Norton. Copyright © 2008 by the Harvard Business School Publishing Corporation, all rights reserved.)

The Balanced Scorecard Institute has a nine-step process, shown in Figure 3-4, that illustrates how the formulation of strategy, and the tracking of that strategy through performance management, form a continuous lifecycle.

A closer look at the "Nine Steps to Success"™ shows how they can easily be mapped to the lifecycle stages we presented in previous chapters and will examine further in this chapter.

Six Sigma

The Six Sigma management practices for reducing defects by locating causes of variation in a process is another technique that often is related to performance management. Six Sigma involves analyzing manufacturing or business processes to determine and reduce causes of variation.

If performance management leads business to an understanding of which processes are crucial to success, Six Sigma can then be employed

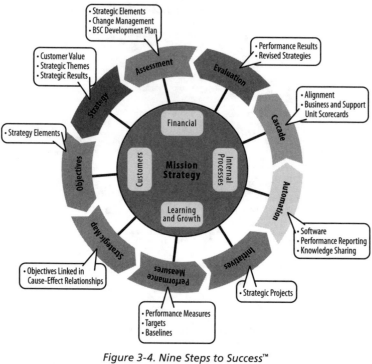

Figure 3-4. Nine Steps to Success™
(Source: Balanced Scorecard Institute, http://balancedscorecard.org/BSCResources/
TheNineStepstoSuccess/tabid/58/Default.aspx)

as a method to understand and improve those processes. Data gathered and models created then can become part of the information available for performance management.

Total Quality Management

Total Quality Management is a well-known performance management concept that began in the early '50s and gained wider recognition beginning in the early '80s. The term "Total Quality" refers to the attitude, culture, and organization of a corporation that works toward providing its clients with the right services and products that they need in order to achieve success. The idea is that, by requiring quality in all aspects of a company's structure, things will get done right the first time around and there will be less waste in the overall process.

Total Quality Management is comprised of eight key elements:

- Ethics
- Integrity

- Trust
- Training
- Teamwork
- Leadership
- Recognition
- Communication

These elements are grouped under four headings, which resemble the process of building a house.

These four headings, with their respective key elements, are:

- **Foundation.** Ethics, integrity, and trust. Every successful business is built upon a foundation composed of these elements, according to the tenets of Total Quality Management. If any elements are weak, the "building," that is, the organization, should analyze the weaknesses and make corrections to ensure that the foundation is solid
- **Building bricks.** Training, teamwork, and leadership. The next step in the construction process would be adding the bricks to the foundation. With proper training, followed by organized and collaborative teamwork and strong leadership, an organization can ensure that its "structure" is sound
- **Binding mortar.** Communication. In order to bind the bricks together, quality binding mortar should be used. This mortar takes the form of effective communication
- **Roof.** Recognition. The last area that completes a solid and quality structure is the roof, or recognition. When employees receive recognition for their efforts toward a company's success, this helps foster trust and further motivates them

European Foundation for Quality Management

The European Foundation for Quality Management (EFQM) is a not-for-profit member organization that was established by a group of European businessmen in October 1989. As the practice of quality assurance gained prominence in Europe in the 1950s, it was recognized that elements of Total Quality Management should be incorporated into it. Out of this came the EFQM, which has approximately 700 large and small member companies. One of its main services is bringing members together to do a Mutual Assessment of an organization, a discovery process that helps lead to strategic recommendations.

In early 1992, EFQM introduced the Excellence Model, which is the framework for assessing companies for the European Quality Award. The basic premise of the model is this: "Excellent results with respect to performance, customers, people, and society are achieved through leadership driving policy and strategy, that is delivered through people, partnerships and resources, and processes."

The Excellence Model can be used in a number of ways: as an assessment tool, as a benchmarking tool, to guide an organization toward needed improvement, to establish a basic common vocabulary and way of thinking, and as a structure for a company's management system.

The Baldridge Award

The Malcolm Baldridge National Quality Award (or Baldridge Award), established by the U.S. Congress in 1987, recognizes U.S. organizations for their achievements in quality and performance, and raises awareness about the importance of performance and quality as a competitive edge. It is named for Malcolm Baldridge, Secretary of Commerce under President Reagan from 1981 until his death in 1987. Three Baldridge Awards may be given annually in the following categories: education, healthcare, manufacturing, nonprofit, service, and small business.

The Baldridge Award was established when government and industry leaders recognized that simply having a renewed emphasis on quality was not enough; American companies had to improve standards and quality in an increasingly global marketplace.

There are seven criteria that companies are judged on when applying for a Baldridge Award: leadership; strategic planning; customer and market focus; measurement, analysis and knowledge management; human resources focus; process management; and business results.

Any organization with headquarters in the U.S. may apply for the award, including U.S. subunits of foreign companies. An independent board of examiners judges applicants on achievements in each category. The aim is to enhance U.S. competitiveness.

ISO

ISO (International Organization for Standardization) is the world's largest developer and publisher of international standards. Conceived in 1946 in London by delegates from 25 countries, the goal of the organization is to "facilitate the international coordination and unification of industrial standards."

ISO is composed of national standards institutes of 160 countries, with one member per country. The organization maintains that when products, devices, and technology work well it is because they meet international standards. Consumers often don't notice except when something doesn't work properly.

Another area where having international standards is useful is in technology. Technological "language" standards allow computers to talk to each other.

ISO currently has approximately 17,500 international standards and other nominative documents. While these standards are not legally binding, many have made their way into legislation around the globe.

ISO 9001 and ISO 14001

The majority of international standards apply to specific materials, products or processes. But ISO 9001 (quality) and ISO 14001 (environment) are generic management systems standards. According to ISO, "This means that the same standard can be applied to any organization, large or small, whatever its product or service, in any sector of activity, whether it is a business enterprise, a public administration, or a government department. ISO 9001 contains a generic set of requirements for implementing a quality management system and ISO 14001 for an environmental management system."

The Contribution of Frameworks

Companies around the world adopt these frameworks, in whole or in part, for quality and performance. Each provides valuable insights to improving management processes at a business. When learning about performance management it is important to be aware of such frameworks and methodologies because programs of improvement are often organized using these ideas. In the end though, a fundamental principle of these methodologies is that organizations benefit from more information about how they are performing. In essence, each of these methodologies leads to the doorstep of performance management.

The Phases of the Performance Management Lifecycle

With the big picture in mind, this chapter looks in detail at each phase of the performance management lifecycle: strategize and prioritize, plan and execute, monitor and analyze, and model and optimize. The narrative examines the people and processes at play in each. The depiction of the various activities at each stage of the lifecycle should been seen as a menu of specific ways that performance management processes can be improved.

Strategize and Prioritize

The strategize and prioritize phase of the performance management lifecycle represents the broadest umbrella. Strategy records what a company should be doing and why, and performance management should be able to indicate the progress toward full implementation and the achieved results.

The relationship of strategy and performance management is both simple and complex. This ambiguity stems from the word "strategy," which is seemingly easy to understand but in practice means many different things. For the sake of clarity, we will use the terms as they are defined by the Balanced Scorecard.

What is Strategy?

Strategy flows from the mission of a company and its vision for the future. A company forms an identity through its mission statement and the principles that it holds to be true. The vision expresses what a company believes it can become and the forces that are shaping the evolution of the customers and markets that it serves.

At the most fundamental level, a specific strategy is a hypothesis, a proposition that says, "If we take certain actions then we suspect we will get a specific set of results." The goal of a specific strategy is to help a company fulfill its mission of serving all of its stakeholders including its customers, investors, employees, suppliers, and regulators. A complete strategy is like a story: it tells what must be done to move a company to success and provides an analysis of the risks along the way.

Most companies set their strategy for the long term. It is not uncommon for strategic plans to stretch out over many years, although the definition of the long-term changes based on the nature of a company. A decade may be the long term for a large industrial firm, while a year may represent the long term for a start up.

The scope of activity and processes affected by strategy is unlimited. Strategy can involve both changing existing operations and creating new ones. It can take action on a bold level, such as seeking out an acquisition or setting up operations in a new country, or at a detailed level, such as addressing the way that employees greet customers. Ideally, everyone on all levels is aware of what they need to do to make a strategy successful.

Ensuring that awareness of strategy is pervasive and examining how well that strategy is working is the goal of strategy management.

As the pace of change has increased in most industries, continuous improvement is a necessity. Often the expenses for making improvements are linked to strategy and strategic initiatives. Accordingly, StratEx, standing for strategic expenditures, has become a new category of spending, alongside CapEx, capital expenditures, and OpEx, operational expenditures.

During the formulation of strategy, the expense and potential revenue, or other impact of an initiative should not be the only factors used to evaluate alternatives. The risks that are expected to arise when executing a strategy are key ingredients in determining the correct path. The goal is not to eliminate risk, but to be aware of it and put appropriate monitoring mechanisms in place. The same holds true of compliance that is associated with each strategy, which must be accounted for during formulation.

Theories of Strategy

While there is abundant guidance about how to formulate strategy, each company tends to do the process its own way, even when following guidance offered by a defined method. Strategy formulation is one of the most studied aspects of business. Here is a sampling of the leading approaches:

- **Competitive strategy** is a doctrine invented by Michael E. Porter that suggests that a firm's relative position in its industry is key to its success. Firms should focus on identifying and defending a sustainable, competitive advantage either as a niche player, a strongly differentiated offer, or as a low cost provider.
- **Resource-based strategy** suggests that each firm is unique and the right approach is to understand the unique core competencies in a company and then craft a strategy that makes the best use of them.
- **Emergent strategy** is strategy that is not just the result of a top-down formulation by management but is also influenced by individual decisions at all levels and interaction between the company and the marketplace. The goal is to create an organization that understands that strategy evolves. The organization then learns to react quickly to adjust strategy and speed the path to higher performance.
- **Blue-ocean strategy,** invented by W. Chan Kim and Renée Mauborgne, suggests business should seek to avoid markets rife

with competition and instead create new markets, blue oceans, which they can have all to themselves.

- **Disruptive strategy,** created by Clayton Christensen, describes how new entrants into a market can overcome established players through products that have simple functionality that sets new expectations.

Each of these types of strategies finds a home in different business situations. The first three generally help companies leverage existing positions while the last two help in the search for new ways of succeeding. None of these approaches will do any good if they just sit on a shelf.

Once the strategy is formulated, it must be captured in a structured way and then communicated, cascaded, and translated into specific goals for each level of the organization. At this stage, the process becomes less mysterious and more amenable to practical recommendations.

Closing the Strategy-to-Execution Gap

No strategy has a chance of success unless it is instilled in the hearts and minds of employees and is monitored and improved based on experience. That is the core of strategy execution.

The problem that we have pointed out in both chapters 1 and 2 is that, too often, strategy gets stuck in the boardroom or at the top levels of a company, creating a gap between what the company intends to do and what it actually does. Such gaps mean that higher-level executives understand the strategy, but the company as a whole doesn't. Departmental and line staff may know a strategy was formulated and its general outlines, but they don't know how it should change what they do every day. Nobody can tell how well the strategy is going or even how completely it has been implemented. These are the essential characteristics of the strategy-to-execution gap. This gap has a variety of causes:

- The strategy is only formulated at a broad level and never communicated outside senior management
- The strategy is never translated into specific objectives
- Metrics to track the completeness of implementation and the impact of strategy are never designed
- Objectives at a high level are not cascaded downward into specific objectives for departments and individuals
- The effectiveness of the strategy is never analyzed so the strategy can be adjusted

- The associated risks with the strategy are never uncovered and therefore the plan and execution do not mitigate the risks
- Suggestions for adjustments from departments and individuals are never considered

Consider a typical example of a company that decides to execute a strategy to dominate a certain market. In the absence of metrics and definitions for growth in market share, how will anyone know if they are succeeding? Unless the incentive plans for individual workers are connected to indicators of progress with respect to growth in the market, why will anyone care if the strategy is implemented? Unless the information about how well the implementation is going is available on a timely basis, how will anyone be able to take action in time to affect results? Unless the skills, capabilities, and technology are in place to execute the strategy, how can it succeed? Unless senior management is listening to ideas and knowledge garnered in implementing the strategy, how can it ever be improved?

The strategy-to-execution gap can be avoided by ensuring that planning and communication take place to address all of these problems. Strategy management is a disciplined and methodical approach to such communication.

Four Steps of Strategy Management

Strategy is not just a top-down process that stops at high levels. It is a cyclical flow of information, with technology acting to enable more effective strategy development and communication throughout the company. Strategy management can be a bottom-up or even middle-out process where people, who work to achieve success in their particular area, collaborate with other parts of the organization to cascade strategy up.

The four steps of strategy management, which are sub-phases in the larger strategy phase of the performance management lifecycle, represent a linear process with a defined beginning and a clear path to a defined end. These four steps—plan, identify and communicate, manage (for exceptions, interpretations, priorities, and so forth), and report and monitor—are shown in Figure 3-5.

The ultimate goal is to use performance management processes and technology to close the loop so that strategy and all phases of the lifecycle are informing and responding to each other. Ideally, everyone, up and down the organization, plays a role in the strategy process. Effective strategy management means not only aligning strategy more tightly to

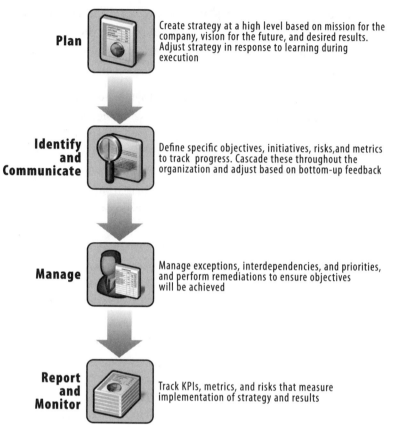

Plan — Create strategy at a high level based on mission for the company, vision for the future, and desired results. Adjust strategy in response to learning during execution

Identify and Communicate — Define specific objectives, initiatives, risks,and metrics to track progress. Cascade these throughout the organization and adjust based on bottom-up feedback

Manage — Manage exceptions, interdependencies, and priorities, and perform remediations to ensure objectives will be achieved

Report and Monitor — Track KPIs, metrics, and risks that measure implementation of strategy and results

Figure 3-5. The Four Steps of Strategy Management

what people do, but enables those people to become involved and a part of the strategy process.

Strategy Planning

The strategy planning step is a process of formulating questions and answers about where the company wants to go and how it is going to get there:

- Which *customers* or *markets* will we target?[1]
- What is the *value proposition* that distinguishes us?
- What *key processes* give us competitive advantage?

---

[1] First six questions come from Robert S. Kaplan and David P. Norton, "Mastering the Management System," *Harvard Business Review*, February 2008. The last two were added by the authors.

The Tangible Value of Strategy Management

While strategy management seems like a relatively obscure process, improving the formulation and communication of strategy can have significant impact. Here are some of the real world results:

- A high-tech manufacturer reduced the cost of its monthly reporting cycle by more than 66% while adding weekly and daily information

- A healthcare company was able to reduce administrative overhead by 25%, achieving the leanest operating margins of all of its competitors

- A life sciences company was able to achieve third-party verified 889% ROI, primarily based on productivity enhancements from better alignment

- A beverage manufacturer was able to better prioritize its sustainability initiatives and get national recognition

- A local government was able to drive consistency and improve its reporting of performance to executive management

- What are the *human capital* capabilities required to excel at these key processes?
- What are the *technology enablers* of the strategy?
- What are the *organizational enablers* required for the strategy?
- What are the *inherent risks* in the strategy?
- What *compliance burdens* are implied by the strategy?

The process of creating strategy will vary from company to company, and reflect the organization's personality. Some companies will create and adjust strategy in offsite meetings once every year while others will methodically strategize every quarter, or even monthly, as part of their routine.

Using Perspectives to Organize a Strategy

One of the hallmarks of the complete strategy is that it addresses all aspects that will influence a company's success, which can be quite confusing. The Balanced Scorecard attempts to address this by sorting strategy into layers of perspectives, financial, customer, process, and skills and learning. For most companies the layers are as follows:

- The objectives of the financial perspective represent the way a company maintains its health and ability to continue operating and providing rewards to investors, employees, and other stakeholders

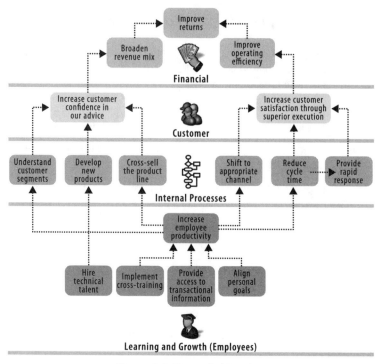

Figure 3-6. Strategic Mapping
(Source: "A Balancing Act," by Howard Rohm, Perform, Volume 2, Issue 2, p. 4,
Balanced Scorecard Institute, 2002)

- The customer perspective contains objectives that will make customers happy in a way that leads them to interact with a company to achieve the financial results
- The process perspective contains objectives for changing the way the company operates to make customers happier
- The skills and learning perspective contains objectives for what will enable the company to perform the processes in improved ways

These perspectives help sort out the maze and make the relationships between strategy objectives a bit clearer. Each organization may have its own set of perspectives or may use the layers in different orders. For example, public sector organizations frequently put the customer or stakeholder perspective at the top level, because providing benefits is the key mission, not achieving financial results.

Once the objectives have been prioritized in all the layers it is possible to show the dependencies. For example, a financial strategy for a retailer may be to increase revenue through expansions into new markets. Customers in those markets may have different expectations. New customer service processes may need to be created and new skills may be needed for the new processes. As shown earlier in this chapter, a strategy map can be used to depict these dependencies.

It is important to know that the Balanced Scorecard approach is just one example of how to sort a strategy into layers. It is a popular way, but not the only way.

Turning the Lights On

Another aspect of creating and managing strategy is ensuring that the process starts with a complete and accurate picture of the status quo. The need for data that represents a view of the organization as a whole, yet also can be drilled into for more detail, is one way that the strategy management process has the same requirements as the monitor and analyze phase of the lifecycle.

In both phases, a consolidated model of the company is used that must be rolled up from more detailed sources. For strategy management, the goal is to understand the nature of the operations, to perform analysis related to strategic questions, to evaluate risks, and to help set realistic targets. For the monitor and analyze phase, the consolidated model is used to track the results of operations against budgeted numbers and targets related to strategic initiatives.

Chapter 4 describes more about the technology infrastructure that collects and presents the consolidated view. Such applications, whether fully integrated suites or collections of best-of-breed technology, gather data from across various sources, which includes those for GRC (as we will see below), and then feed it into the strategy management system.

Top-Down and Bottom-Up

Strategy formed at the senior levels should represent the beginning of the process, not the end. Just as top-down budgets are presented to departments who then respond with bottom-up estimates, a similar process should be used for strategy. And just as the bottom-up estimates of what can be achieved may induce changes in top-down budgets, so it is with strategy.

A leading automotive company, for example, went through an intensive exercise with a consultant to generate 75 ideas to increase demand. After whittling those down to three or four, the company then brought in a group of dealers to help them analyze how to make those ideas work. The dealers despised one of the ideas, saying it would never work and would have a profoundly negative impact. By including a larger group of people who had never been part of strategic discussions, an idea that was unlikely to succeed was quashed early, saving large amounts of time, money, embarrassment, and brand equity. Including a larger group also increases buy-in when the strategy is finally adopted.

Assessing Risk

Incorporating risk analysis into strategy formulation represents a new level of integration between performance and risk management, which is usually associated with governance, risk, and compliance (GRC) processes. You will see problems much earlier and have time to make adjustments by analyzing the risk inherent in a strategy and putting in metrics and KPIs to monitor it. These risk-oriented metrics and KPIs, and the thresholds set for them, also act as controls in the GRC sense of the word. Controls are procedures, either automated or manual, that are put in place to test for problems. In the case of risk-oriented metrics and KPIs, you want to find whatever is going wrong as early as possible.

Every strategy involves some degree of risk. Perhaps the strategy depends on new skills that may not be easy to learn, or new technology that is not yet implemented, or the need to create new kinds of relationships. Also, a new strategy may cause unforeseen effects that are potentially problematic. Executing a new strategy could risk a negative perception or reduce market demand for other products. Risks in the supply chain could jeopardize adequate flows of parts or raw materials in the face of increased growth.

The bottom line is that risk related to strategy must be monitored. The process of creating metrics and KPIs and gathering data for those KPIs represents a large overlap between performance and risk management. Usually risk management is under the purview of a Chief Risk Officer who reports to the CFO, but operates in a silo, while the job of executing a strategy is under the business unit managers. Obviously it is of vital interest that both parties monitor and manage risk, but it sometimes can be difficult to sort out these overlapping duties when managed in silos.

Another concept is the idea of risk weighing each strategy and the tactics used for execution. Here are questions that must be asked when comparing alternative strategies and tactics:

- Which alternatives have more risks?
- Do the riskier alternatives have a higher return?
- Can the risks identified be managed and contained?

Sometimes higher risks lead to greater rewards. Sometimes they are just higher risks. Asking the questions above does not mean that strategies should be cast aside because of the possibility of risk. For example, if the company sees real opportunities to market products in Africa, but is aware of possible compliance risks, the company should not automatically table its strategy. What should be taken into account are the tactics used to achieve the strategy. For example, you may want to enter a market in Africa, but decide that it would make more sense to manufacture that product in Eastern Europe, where compliance may be less of a challenge. In this way you are factoring risk into the choices you are making to pursue a strategy.

Identifying risks at the strategic level also affects later parts of the performance management lifecycle. The specific risks will create challenges for strategic planners related to risk and compliance. For example, if part of the strategy is international expansion, the company will need a wide range of approvals and must determine financial risks in terms of currency. The company will then have a better understanding of any new regulations regarding everything from sustainability, environmental concerns, potential operational failures, supplier compliance, to financial reporting.

With methodical risk management connected to strategy, risks do not disappear, but they are managed better. This means that the organization can comfortably take on a fairly aggressive strategy and yet reduce the risks to achieve greater reward. Chapter 6 explores this issue and the relationship of performance management to GRC in far greater detail.

Identify and Communicate

Once a strategy is set at a high level it must be transformed into specifics. The objectives must be transformed into initiatives that will lead to the intended results. Metrics, measures, and KPIs must track progress of both implementation of the strategy and the improved results. Key risk indicators (KRIs) must also be set to track the risks so that appropriate action can be taken in case things go wrong. When done properly, a high-level map of the strategy, objectives, and initiatives can act as a standard or template to be used across divisions and business units. It can include traditional financial measures as well as operational measures such as cost of goods sold, customer satisfaction, order to fill rates, or whatever would hold relevance.

One of the most important mechanisms to avoid the strategy-to-execution gap is to involve all areas of the company in translating the strategy into specific initiatives and metrics. In addition, the strategy must be analyzed to surface interdependencies between initiatives in separate organizational silos.

While defining the highest-level objectives is a top-down process, setting initiatives, especially those further down the hierarchy, should be viewed more as a bottom-up or middle-out process. Communication goes down to include the team level so that they understand their relevant piece of the strategy's goals, the objectives they will be trying to hit, the broad metrics (KPIs) that will be used to measure execution against the goals, and the risks involved.

It can be challenging to translate high-level objectives into specifics at the departmental or individual level. The Balanced Scorecard methodology has developed the concept of strategic themes, which are groups of related objectives. Cascading a strategy can be easier when departments and workgroups are asked to translate a theme into something that is meaningful to their work, rather than attempting to achieve an objective that may not seem relevant at their level of the organization. For example, if several initiatives at a high level are grouped under the theme "Increase Customer Satisfaction," a department can translate that theme into specific measures, such as improving the response time on a web site or reducing the wait time in a call center, that fit into the theme but were not specified directly by the strategy.

The high-level metrics (KPIs), used to measure corporate-wide execution of initiatives against the strategic goals and objectives, act as the connecting tissue between the goals and objectives and the initiatives to achieve them. The measures set during strategy may get even more detailed during the planning phase of the lifecycle.

Regardless of where initiatives and metrics are defined, it is vital to have up-to-date information. The staff needs to extract, consolidate, and aggregate data from source enterprise systems as well as communicate the broad strategic goals to the proper levels and then work collaboratively.

To do this, the company will need the technological capability to manage the consolidated and aggregated data collected during the strategy planning stage, to provide a level of granularity necessary to gain multiple views along a number of dimensions. This capability can better support the process of defining the goals, objectives, and initiatives via visualization tools—strategy maps, balanced scorecards, graphical visualizations, integrated screens, and a centralized KPI repository to hold defined sets of KPI templates (such as, delineate the meaning of net sales according to U.S. GAAP and/or IFRS, how the cost of goods sold is calculated, criteria for customer satisfaction, and so on). All of these will be discussed in more detail in Chapter 4.

One feature of modern performance management applications, the KPI repository, has proven quite valuable in propagating strategy. This centralized KPI template repository provides each layer of an organization with a harmonized set of KPIs from which they start contextualizing their particular activities and needs. Modern applications can cascade these measures and the strategy down to the relevant role, business, and ownership piece of the organizational strategy.

It is during the identify and communicate step that the power of technology becomes clear. At higher strategy levels, general-purpose tools for creating content and representing strategy are sufficient. But when hundreds or thousands of people become involved, each in a different part of a process that is connected from top down by a web of mutually supporting objectives, measured by metrics and KPIs, the technology must be able to form a powerful nervous system that ensures proper alignment and communication.

Manage the Strategy

In the manage step of strategy management, executives and staff at all levels must stay on top of the actions being taken to execute the initiatives. While performance management systems are used to track progress and provide visibility, from a strategy management point of view, the goal is to make sure that the projects are on track and the results expected from new strategies are being achieved.

It is vital to see on a daily, weekly, monthly basis how well you and the organization around you are progressing on initiatives that are being executed both separately and together. Technology plays an essential role in this process by creating personalized dashboards that provide visibility into the KPIs, KRIs, metrics and other information that represent progress. In most companies, the amount of information is large. Strategy management systems alert executives and staff to what is not going well so time can be focused on those issues. When a process or activity affects strategy execution and performance, the user receives a notice of an exception or a risk that has passed a key threshold. This could be a color-coded indicator on the personalized homepage flashing red. When exceptions to expectations occur, that is when projects do not go as planned or results are below or above expectations, it is important to find out why.

For example, once an exception has been detected, the executive or division leader can see that an objective has exceeded budget and is also behind schedule, and then jump to a detailed report. The report could then provide information on the specific initiatives that are trending below expectations and the KPIs related to the initiatives that are underperforming.

Another possibility would be a high-level scorecard where the user is able to scan down to detect where there may be alerts and then click down through to gain visibility into the related initiatives and KPIs that may be underperforming. Granularity and multidimensionality of data collected and stored should allow drill down by region, detailed product type, channel, and so forth. Such visibility is empowering to staff who can make better decisions based on data right away, instead of having to wait around for management to tell them their next step.

The system should also be able to notice if another person has enhanced data related to an objective or initiative, changes the status from a positive to a negative value (e.g. green to red), and/or enters a comment into the system that may be important.

In all, the managing of strategy should flow directly into the next piece of the strategy management process, which is reporting and monitoring.

Report and Monitor

The report and monitor step of strategy management represents the preparation of detailed information that will support ongoing monitoring and management of strategic initiatives. The preparation of structured reports is tightly coupled with the manage step, in which such information is consumed. It is also vital that staff at all levels can create their own reports to track information as they see fit. In the past, creating such reports was a time-consuming burden. The modern strategy management applications described in Chapter 4 automate this process.

These reports could take the form of a briefing book with content tables, cover pages, and contextual information from other sources. The information needed will likely be highly granular, such as profitability in a number of dimensions for a single product, project, and region, or even a range of products, projects and regions.

In addition, these reports serve as historical references that tell the larger story over a number of months or years of how the strategy has been carried out, the exceptions that emerged, and the steps taken to correct or mitigate these issues. The reports also would highlight areas that were successful beyond expectations so those lessons can be applied to future strategy.

The knowledge in these reports is used to create a finer-grained model of the value-generating machine to inform the next cycle of strategy development by better identifying methods for optimizing operational performance that may be lagging or making the decision to refocus resources to areas that are performing well but need a small push to achieve better results.

From Execution to Refinement

Ultimately, the strategy management process results in information about what is working and which strategic hypotheses were off the mark. At some point in the cycle, the team that created the strategy must look at the data in relation to the progress of implementing the initiatives and the results. When the team makes adjustments to the strategy, the cycle begins again, which is referred to as closing the loop. What was learned in execution is used to refine and improve the strategy.

But in business, something almost always goes differently than expected. The challenge then is to determine what happened: Was the initiative properly implemented? Were the expected risks manageable or excessive? Perhaps the strategy was right and the execution was poor. Or was the execution done properly, but the hypothesis at the root of the strategy was wrong?

In most cases, it is too early to tell. In the absence of data, a void can provoke blame and bad decisions. This is when information gleaned from a well-implemented performance management system really earns its keep. With the right information, it is possible to determine what is wrong with a strategy, fix it, and get the company back on track. The essence of closing the loop is to make an honest assessment and then move forward with a new hypothesis.

Plan and Execute

If the strategy explains the destination, the plan and execute phase of the performance management lifecycle describes how a company will get there and how long it will take. In this phase of the lifecycle the desires expressed in the strategy are translated into specific actions, actions that require resources and produce results that then become inputs to other actions. By the end of this phase, the marching orders at all levels should be crystal clear. But as anyone who has been through this process knows, the journey to clarity is often hard fought.

The Three Core Planning Activities

There are three primary activities in the planning and budgeting phase of the performance management lifecycle—planning, budgeting, and forecasting. The challenge in explaining this phase of the lifecycle is that, while everyone has a general understanding of what each of these activities entails, the process varies widely by industry and by the maturity and size of the company. The explanation below attempts to summarize the essence of what takes place.

Planning

In the abstract, planning is the process of creating a model of the inputs and resources needed by various parts of the value creating machine, determining the likely outputs, and then making adjustments to ensure that the desired goals are met. The planning horizon generally matches that of the strategy, for many companies three to five years, for some shorter and for others longer. Plans are more detailed in the shorter term. Generally, planning is broken down into specific plans for any of the following items.

- Capital costs
- Plant costs
- Workforce planning
- Administrative expenses
- Finance
- Sales forecasting
- Marketing campaign planning

Planning can mean many things. A strategic or long-term plan is usually a high-level description of the major financial and operational characteristics of an organization over the next three to five years. Sometimes these plans start with a base case determined for current performance and then adjust numbers up and down. On the other hand, plans can build a model of results from the bottom up by estimating detailed performance in many areas, based on the business drivers. Generally, these long-term plans are used to assess the impact of pursuing various strategies under consideration.

Initiative-based strategic plans include detailed sections that map out the resources required and revenue needed for major initiatives such as launching a new product or expanding into a new market.

A financial plan can be another name for a budget, that is, a financial description of a company's expected performance over the next 12 months. Financial plans go into a much higher level of detail than long-term plans.

An operational plan is a description of what one part of the business expects to do, usually over the next year, expressed not merely in financial terms but also in terms of units sold, activities performed, and other non-financial drivers that affect financial results. For example, a sales department may be told it has a certain amount of money to spend to get a certain number of sales. The operational plan would describe the activities that would take place, the number of units sold, the prices of the units, and other factors that are under the control of the sales department.

The planning process is generally iterative, starting with high-level expectations for results that are then translated into specifics. When contradictions are found and expectations cannot be met, or new possibilities occur, then the plan is adjusted.

Budgeting

Budgeting proceeds to a more granular level of detail from the plan. Budgets are most often created for a fiscal year and include detailed descriptions of expenses and expected results. A budget is essentially a financially oriented plan that shows the items in the general ledger (revenue, operating expenses, aggregated profit and loss, and so on) in a tabular, month-by-month format. Strategy is not generally represented in the budget, except perhaps, if there is a separate line item for the expense of a major strategic initiative. The budget is the financial scorecard for the company, the one the CFO uses to understand the drivers of cost and revenue.

Budgets are most frequently created starting with top-down expectations that are then analyzed by each specific department. Then the bottom-up view of each department is expressed and a negotiation occurs that results in the final budget for the year. This may happen in many iterations.

Forecasting

Forecasting is the process of refining and adjusting the predictions made in budgets to get a more accurate view of future results. Forecasting may use statistical techniques, predictive modeling, or optimization algorithms to better understand how the value-creating machine produces results. Forecasting almost always means financial forecasting, and most often takes place using a rolling, one-year horizon. That is, each month or quarter the forecast for the next twelve months is analyzed and updated.

Usually in a forecasting process the expected results, that is the amount in the budget, are compared with the actual results for a period. The causes of the variance are analyzed and then the forecast for future periods is adjusted. In the future periods, the actual numbers are compared against the budget and the forecast. In the beginning of the year, the budget and forecast are the same. As the year proceeds, the forecast becomes the number that represents the expectations rather than the budget.

In all of these activities, the goal is to seek the drivers that predict future outcomes and needs for resources. A clear understanding of the drivers of costs and results along with a model of all parts of the value-creating machine is a recipe for increased predictability and early warning of major problems.

The Evolution of Planning

Before the 1990s, planning was conducted within a spreadsheet dominated way that involved a considerable number of manual processes. While effective at improving annual budgeting cycles, this method was time-consuming and error-prone due to a lack of automation. Imagine thousands of numbers being transferred from gray bar reports into spreadsheets to get the idea of the potential for error in the process of this era.

By the 1990s, the large-scale adoption of ERP meant that the amount of transactional data available to companies had increased, which allowed for more timely and detailed reporting and accounting practices. These in turn allowed the planning process to occur more frequently and gain a bit more depth. Paper reports were gone. In their place were many different files or digital versions of reports that were used to extract information from ERP systems and load them into spreadsheets. Past performance was recorded and, after some analysis, a forecast of financial performance was established as a percentage increase broadly applied across the organization.

From Spreadsheets to Integrated Models

As the 2000s dawned, it became apparent that to facilitate a more detailed planning process that could drive profitability, planners had to build as detailed a model as possible to enable planning across the multiple dimensions of the business. This required having not just transactional technologies to capture data, but also technologies that could support modeling capabilities that followed a set of best practices. In the end, the model was generally implemented as a special purpose database, frequently located in a data warehouse, but sometimes residing in a SQL-based storage mechanism.

As these technologies developed they have enabled a planning process that is:

- Cyclical in nature via annual planning and budgeting followed by quarterly rolling forecasts
- Based on driver-based models of the business built on assumptions provided by business users as well as transactional data
- Collaborative in that it operates beyond finance and the executive suite down into the operational layers of the organization
- Predictive via analytics using statistical techniques

Modern models used for planning have many levels of depth and are rolled up automatically. Each division or department may have its own planning model that enters data used to compute the key numbers that are used in the rollup to higher levels. Depending on the approach, the models can be financial or operational, or a combination of both. In general, it is easy to extract information from these models into reporting, forecasting, and visualization tools, and, of course, into spreadsheets.

In some ways, modern environments for planning may be too powerful. A common mistake is to create a model that is ornate and has a lot of levels of detail that aren't necessarily useful in the planning and forecasting process. The best way to build a planning model, regardless of the form in which it is kept, is incrementally over time. At first the model starts out simple, and then as the key drivers are discovered, they are added. This approach ensures that relevant data is used in the model.

Another challenge in creating planning models is to believe in them too much. Models are tools to enhance the judgment of the people and insight in a business, not to replace it. Human judgment and experience should not be removed from the model or interpreting the results of the modeling process. Modeling tools are not an incarnation of Big Brother—people must use their judgment based on personal experience, because without that human element the company could make major mistakes.

The Planning, Budgeting, and Forecasting Cycle

The three core planning activities result in three types of deliverables: plans of the long-term variety, budgets that focus on the financial outlook done in a yearly time frame, and forecasts that attempt to keep a rolling prediction of financial performance.

While there is wide variation in how exactly each of these deliverables is created, there are broad patterns that are followed. The planning and budgeting phase of the lifecycle takes place in four steps shown in Figure 3-7.

Communicate   **Collect**   **Analyze**   **Report**

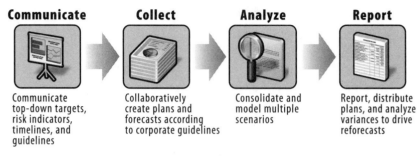

| Communicate top-down targets, risk indicators, timelines, and guidelines | Collaboratively create plans and forecasts according to corporate guidelines | Consolidate and model multiple scenarios | Report, distribute plans, and analyze variances to drive reforecasts |

Figure 3-7. Steps in a Typical Planning, Budgeting, and Forecasting Process

Preparing for Planning and Budgeting

Planning starts in general after the strategy is set, but frequently in the context of plans that have been made in years past. Generally, most strategies and the plans that flow from them are attempts to preserve existing business and expand into new markets or introduce new products. Management typically wants to balance the need to maintain momentum in existing markets with the need for new investment in strategic initiatives.

As a result, planning activity frequently starts with the assembly of all the information needed to define trends, such as past years' volumes by dimensions such as product category, sales channel, region, business unit, and so on. It is also important to include seasonality (such as micro trends), which refers to specific time periods during the year where sales tend to peak or ebb.

The teams assembled to do planning and budgeting are generally led by the CFO and include senior representation from sales operations, financial planning and analysis departments, VPs of the business lines, VPs of brand management, product managers, and specialists involved in executing strategic initiatives.

Planning Communication

The four steps involved in planning start with the initial top-down communication, that is, a specific declaration from senior management of the desired end state for a plan or budget. One way to think of this is as setting "guard rails" for the process. Usually a time frame for the completion of the planning and budget process is also set. Of course, the whole process is predicated on the fact that detailed planning will need to take place in order to determine if the initial expectations can be met.

The initial top-down definition is more a wish list than anything else. It generally expresses a plan or a budget that would be ideal, not one that takes into account any analysis of how to achieve the balance between spending on existing markets and new initiatives. These high-level goals are then cascaded down by the leadership at each level until each line manager has a description of what results are expected, both in terms of keeping the momentum of existing business and of executing strategic initiatives. At this point the top-down process is complete and the bottom-up process begins.

Each line manager then makes a detailed plan to make best use of the resources allocated to achieve goals. Sometimes, not often, the amount of resources and the results expected fall precisely in line and a plan or budget is created that reflects that. Most often, however, something is not in alignment. Usually, the amount of resources that is allocated cannot support the results desired. In this case, the tradeoffs that could be made are described in a series of alternative plans.

Collecting Planning Information

In the next stage of planning and budgeting, the bottom-up ideas are discussed and analyzed. If many different scenarios were created, perhaps one is picked and then all of the bottom-up plans and budgets are rolled up into a first version of a master model that incorporates detailed planning from everyone. It is this first rolled-up version that really represents a complete plan, one that reflects both the desires of senior management and the estimates of what line managers think is possible.

This stage also highlights the importance of having some sort of unified and integrated planning system. Everyone only has so much time. If creating the plan or budget and then allowing it to be rolled up is a tedious, manual process, then the quality of the planning process will suffer.

Analyzing the Plan

Once the cycle proceeds through one iteration from top down to bottom up and a comprehensive plan is in place, the difficult work begins. Senior management and business unit and departmental executives dig in to figure out how to make the tough tradeoffs. People are pushed to do more with less. New risks are discovered.

The more this phase can be supported by detailed analysis of what is possible, the more discussions are focused on how to do things differently. The worst-case scenario occurs when two parties disagree about how many resources a task may take but have no data to inform the analysis.

Once the comprehensive plan is understood and analyzed, then adjustments are made and the top-down process starts again in the first version of the model. The bottom-up process is then repeated and a new comprehensive model is rolled up. Then another analysis is performed.

It is not uncommon for many such iterations of a plan to take place before it is completed and agreed upon.

Reporting on the Plan

The last step in most planning and budgeting processes is to capture the final form and propagate it to everyone who is going to use it in their hands-on management.

This general planning and budgeting cycle takes place every year at most companies. But there are many techniques to address various weaknesses that can occur in this generic process. The next section explains some of them in detail.

Planning Techniques

Bodies of knowledge and specific practices have been developed about planning, budgeting, and forecasting to address common failings and to improve quality. Some of these techniques are elaborate while others offer simple, general guidance that put forth important points to keep in mind during the planning process.

Driver-Based Budgeting

Driver-based budgeting seeks to eliminate guessing and ballpark estimates from budgets. The goal of driver-based budgeting is to create a model that explains how you will achieve your goal and how the fundamental inputs, the drivers, lead to the desired result. For example, in budgeting for a sales department, often the results are determined by guessing about the level of sales based on last year's sales and hunches about the performance of the sales staff and market forces. A driver-based budget would estimate how many leads would come in, how many meetings would be set up based on those leads, and how many sales would come from those meetings.

A driver-based budget has the huge advantage of explaining how you are going to get the results you are seeking. In addition, at the end of a given period, the actual performance can be examined and the model used in the driver-based budget can be improved.

Implementing the models for a driver-based budget in software allows you to explore alternate scenarios and determine the most effective way to achieve results with the minimum resources. Modeling software for driver-based budgeting may include analytic capabilities that perform statistical calculations to help you understand how changing an assumption or adding a new driver will affect the outcome.

Risk-Adjusted Planning

Risk-adjusted planning attempts to infuse a range of possibilities into a plan. Every plan has risks, but most plans are expressed as single numbers. A risk-adjusted plan attempts to identify the key risks that would affect the results achieved. Then the results may be expressed as a range, or as two or three scenarios, based on how the risks were managed.

For example, imagine a company was working with a new celebrity spokesperson that had not been used with its products before. If the promotions based on the spokesperson were a failure, sales might be in the low range. If the promotion were extremely effective, then sales might be much higher. A risk-adjusted plan expresses the ranges of possibilities based on the varying risks.

Event-Based Planning

Most planning happens on a yearly cycle. Event-based planning suggests that events both expected and unexpected affect the planning cycle. An unexpected event such as a hurricane could be the trigger for adjusting the supply chain and fulfillment planning for a chain of retail stores. In this way, event-based planning can be linked to specific risks. If a downside or upside risk occurs, then an event-based planning cycle can adapt the plan to the needs.

Event-based planning can be used for expected events when it makes sense to plan closer to the event when more is known about the nature of it and how it will affect the plan. In this type of event-based planning, a planning cycle kicks off at a predetermined time.

Beyond Budgeting

Beyond Budgeting is a general management philosophy that has particular relevance to planning and budgeting. Beyond Budgeting has many ideas (listed in Table 3-1) that are oriented toward focusing an organization on improving performance through decentralization, open sharing of information, and transparency.

From a planning and budgeting perspective, thinking related to Beyond Budgeting can change practices in many ways. For example, the principles suggest that when you are allocating budget money, it makes more sense

Table 3-1. Principles of Beyond Budgeting
(Source: Beyond Budgeting Round Table–BBRT:
http://www.bbrt.org/beyond-budgeting/bbprinc.html)

Leadership Actions	
1. Customers	Focus everyone on their customers, *not on hierarchical relationships*
2. Processes	Organize as a lean network of accountable teams, *not as centralized functions*
3. Autonomy	Give teams the freedom and capability to act, *don't micro-manage them*
4. Responsibility	Create a high-responsibility culture at every level, *not just at the center*
5. Transparency	Promote open information for self-management, *don't restrict it hierarchically*
6. Governance	Adopt a few clear values, goals, and boundaries, *not fixed targets*
Aligning management processes with leadership actions	
1. Goals	Set relative goals for continuous improvement, *don't negotiate fixed contracts*
2. Rewards	Reward shared success based on relative performance, *not fixed reports*
3. Planning	Make planning a continuous and inclusive process, *not a top-down annual event*
4. Controls	Base controls on relative indicators and trends, *not variances against a plan*
5. Resources	Make resources available as needed, *not through annual budget allocations*
6. Coordination	Coordinate interactions dynamically, *not through annual planning cycles*

to look at internal and external benchmarks. Instead of handing everyone a 10% increase, reward only the departments that are performing better. When examining expectations for operational efficiency, base the targets or the direction on analysis of other companies' performance.

In Beyond Budgeting, the focus and direction of the results are as important as the specific plans. Planning happens continuously as feedback confirms or contradicts the strategy of the company and the effectiveness of operations.

Planning, budgeting, and forecasting provide the framework for tracking how operations are proceeding. Forecasting, especially, is a part of continuing operations, given that most forecasts are adjusted at the end of monthly or quarterly reporting periods. The planning and budgeting process may also be revisited in response to traumatic events.

Just as the planning, budgeting, and forecasting process started from the goals and initiatives that were set forth in the strategy phase of the performance management lifecycle, a company's operations begin with the plans and budgets.

Monitor and Analyze

Execution begins in the monitor and analyze phase of the performance management lifecycle. All of the hypothetical propositions embedded in the strategy and the specific plans and budgets are tested against reality. This phase takes place in the context of metrics that have been set forth to measure various aspects of performance, risk, and compliance and the projections made by the budget and by forecasts.

The essence of this phase is captured in these questions:

- How can we ensure we have high quality data about our performance?
- How well does our operational performance match our expectations?
- What accounts for the variance?
- To what extent are metrics showing success or failure in the implementation of strategic initiatives?
- How many of the expected risks and operational problems measured by metrics are appearing?

In the monitor and analyze phase, problems are discovered and described in as much detail as possible. A deeper analysis of causes and what to do is performed in the next phase, model and optimize.

Consolidating Data and Computing Metrics

The foundation of the monitor and analyze phase is accurate, detailed data, which is not easy to come by. The first task of the monitor and analyze phase is known as consolidation. Chapter 7 goes into this process in detail and explains how an efficient consolidation process provides accurate numbers describing performance ("actuals") that can be compared against the budget and the predictions made by forecasts. The consolidation process also creates information that is used to produce statutory and regulatory filings. In addition, consolidation is also used to compute various operational metrics that may have been set up to track risks, the progress of implementing strategic initiatives, or indicators of performance and quality.

Generally, not all important metrics come out of the financial consolidation process. It is quite common for business intelligence capabilities to be used to compute metrics that track various types of operational performance or risk. In addition, an increasing amount of information about performance management comes in from the extended business network.

The process of computing metrics may be continuous or it may take place on a weekly, monthly, quarterly, or annual cycle. The goal is to create a set of data that can be used to understand how to manage and optimize a business and to identify risks and operational problems as soon as possible.

Metrics by themselves are far more useful when some indication is given for how to interpret them. The data is ready for analysis after the metrics and KPIs have been calculated and then paired with the expectations for them set in the strategy, planning, and budgeting process. In addition, if historical data for each metric is available, it is much easier to understand what the current value for the metric is revealing.

Dashboards for Monitoring and Reporting

In most companies that are making serious efforts toward implementing performance management, the amount of data that is collected quickly overwhelms a person's ability to keep track of it. This flood of data is a phenomenon not only for senior management but also at the line level, especially as the technology related to performance management increases the availability of high-quality data.

The challenge for any manager or staff person then becomes understanding what the data is telling you and spending time on the right issues. The generally accepted method of solving these problems involves using dashboards that efficiently present large amounts of metrics. Usually, the dashboards show a collection of aggregated high-level metrics or KPIs. The metrics are displayed along with alerts, often in the form of red, yellow, and green indicators that indicate if the numbers are in the expected range. While the whole idea of monitoring brings to mind a vision of dials indicating the levels of a certain metric, what executives really want in practice is an indication of when exceptions have occurred.

Once an exception has occurred, it is important to be able find out the cause. High-level, aggregated metrics then lead to pages where components used to calculate the aggregated metrics are shown. This sort of drill down may be possible several levels deep. Once the issue is clear, more detailed data about specific issues may then be consulted or analyzed. This general dashboard structure is supplemented by traditional reports and environments for ad-hoc analysis.

Applying Analytical Tools

As the value of such deeper analysis has been recognized, a variety of special-purpose applications have been developed that allow specific areas to be analyzed in great detail. Applications for spend analytics, for profitability analysis, for sales analytics, and for supply-chain analytics are among the most commonly used performance management applications.

These environments come ready made with cascading structures of KPIs and metrics that are designed to track business activity at an extremely detailed level. In addition, the environments have special-purpose visualization and analytical functionality that are used for many different types of analytics including trend and event analysis. It is common for special-purpose applications to have predictive models that are used in the model and optimize phase to help determine root causes and also for forecasting and scenario analysis.

The availability of high-quality data from a variety of sources in real time has opened the door to even more advanced forms of automated tracking and analysis of business activity. Systems created according to the principles of business activity monitoring (BAM) take the dashboard concept to a new level and present a real-time view of important business activity. These systems may also include the ability to correlate information to immediately identify trends and recognize events, possibly using methods derived from the field of complex event processing.

Model and Optimize

The monitor and analyze phase is complete once executives feel they really know what is happening in key areas and have at least an initial understanding of the factors involved. The next step is to understand the nature of the problems more deeply and to figure out what to do about them. This is the essence of the model and optimize phase of the performance management lifecycle.

The model and optimize phase is perhaps one of the most complex, given that it occurs in the context of what has been done in the previous three stages. The strategy, plans and budgets, and the metrics and KPIs describing the results of operation have set the stage; now the analysis must go deeper. By using advanced modeling techniques, simulations, and other analytical tools, the underlying causes are searched for. Once found, the question becomes how should current practice or strategy be altered, which leads to the need to construct and compare various scenarios. Once the right path is clear, then the challenge may be to pursue it in the most productive and efficient form, which leads to various techniques of optimization. It is at this phase of the performance management lifecycle that the most advanced forms of statistical analysis and probabilistic and predictive modeling occur.

Modeling for Understanding

The idea of modeling permeates the practice of performance management, so it is important to sort out exactly what we mean by modeling in the model and optimize phase. Budgets and plans can be considered descriptive models of corporate performance and expectations. Forecasting takes this a step further and constructs some sort of model that is used to project future performance based on current data. When some important event is being considered, such as a merger or acquisition, various scenarios are analyzed and compared. This sort of modeling enters the ballpark of the type of modeling that occurs in the model and optimize phase.

The purpose of the models created in this phase of the performance management lifecycle is to deepen understanding of what is happening at a business and why. The modeling techniques used range from advanced models implemented in spreadsheets, to special purpose models that are applied to a functional area like profitability, spending, sales, or supply chain. Generally, regardless of the modeling technique used, some sort of starting point is defined, one or more scenarios for future growth are created, the assumptions used in the scenarios can be tweaked and adjusted, and the results produced in the various scenarios can be visualized in aggregate or in varying levels of detail. These models can be constructed based on the concerns of a specific business problem or by using a defined methodology such as activity-based costing.

As models become more and more complex and detailed and have the capability to replicate the flow of events and information, they enter the realm of simulation. Advanced statistical techniques such as Monte Carlo simulations can be used to understand the likely range of outcomes. Computer simulations can be used to understand the flow of information, identify potential bottlenecks in processes, and determine the sensitivity of business results to specific sorts of changes.

Scenarios and Simulations

The modeling in this model and optimize phase is sharply focused on understanding how to get better business results. A typical problem in marketing involved figuring out how to optimize the money spent in each marketing channel to get the best results. Each channel has different ways of sending messages or offering product promotions to create demand. In a market with multiple channels, the optimal mix of advertising, direct marketing, discounts, and other methods can be fiendishly difficult to determine. Modeling plays a role by allowing many different scenarios to be constructed and then compared so a deeper understanding of the right thing to do emerges.

Modeling also looks backward and attempts to determine what actually has been happening at a business. Activity-based costing, described in more detail later, attempts to create a detailed model of the resources that are used by different types of products and customers. This allows the shared costs to be more precisely allocated so a true picture of profitability can be created.

Simulations bring a process alive and allow the flow of information and work to be observed. Contradictions in processes can be identified. For example, if the service level for a response to a request must be sent in 24 hours, but alerts are not raised until a request has aged for two days, a change in procedure may be needed. Simulations can bring such problems to light and suggest new ways of organizing work.

In general, the sort of modeling just described helps demystify and prepare for the future. You can ask many questions and see what the results would be. What will happen if interest rates rise? If a product sells much less or much more than last year? If a process could be performed more cheaply through outsourcing? Even if a model is not perfectly correct, and they never are, the process of thinking things through speeds reaction times when an event does occur.

Modeling and scenario comparison must always take into account the risks involved. A small amount of savings from outsourcing a process may not be sufficient to compensate for losses that could occur due to a supply disruption.

There are two techniques that are often applied in the model and optimize phase that should be described in more detail: activity-based costing and economic value added.

Activity-Based Costing

Activity-based costing is a methodology for creating a deeper understanding of cost allocation that can be a crucial part of a program of the model and optimize phase. Activity-based costing (ABC) was developed to address the challenge of accurately allocating indirect costs to products or activities. ABC analysis can be useful in many stages of performance management, so it is important to explain the technique early on in this narrative.

A classic example of the application of ABC goes like this. A company sells three products, Widget X, Widget Y, and Widget Z, each of which is serviced after the sale by a customer service center. In the past, the indirect costs of the customer service center may have been allocated equally across each product. An ABC analysis might show that this equal split was not correct. Perhaps 70% of customer service calls are generated by Widget X, 10% by Widget Y, and 20% by Widget Z. Such an analysis could reveal that Widget X is actually an unprofitable product and that Widget Y is far more profitable than realized.

The actual implementation of ABC can be quite complex and involve definition of cost pools and activity centers representing the indirect costs and cost drivers (usually products and services) that consume resources. Because implementing ABC can involve a significant amount of research including lengthy surveys of employees and other time consuming information gathering methods, the method has been criticized as being perhaps too much work for the benefit.

Robert Kaplan, promoter of the Balanced Scorecard, developed a streamlined approach that simplifies the analysis of resource usage by allocating costs based on time spent supporting business activities. This approach, called time-driven ABC, allows the costs to be estimated and allocated much faster based on management estimates of cost per unit of time and how much time is spent on each activity.

Kaplan points out that once such cost models are in place, they can then be used in a new way: to predict costs and resource requirements when analyzing new scenarios for optimizing business processes or launching new products. This point holds with respect to not only ABC, but also all forms of modeling used for performance management. Models that start out as ways to understand and track business processes can be used, once they are proven to be accurate, to predict future costs and results when basic assumptions have changed. The rise in the ability to better predict future results is a major benefit of improved performance management practices.

Economic Value Added (EVA)

EVA is a widely used performance calculation method to help organizations calculate their true economic profit, and in this sense it shares a purpose with ABC. It can be used to calculate net-operating after-tax profit minus a charge for the opportunity cost of the capital invested. EVA is essentially an estimate of the amount by which earnings exceed or fall short of the minimum required rate of return for shareholders at comparable risk.

EVA can be used for the following purposes:

- Setting organizational goals
- Performance measurement
- To determine bonuses
- To communicate with shareholders and investors
- To motivate managers
- Capital budgeting
- Corporate valuation

Both economic value-added and activity-based costing are often mentioned in discussions of performance management.

Innovation and Strategy

The opportunity for innovation and the connection to strategy are important aspects of the model and optimize phase. What is often forgotten is that the act of modeling and comparing scenarios often leads to new insights that then can be used to improve processes or to suggest adjustments to strategy.

The model and optimize phase is a venue in which the hypotheses set for the strategy can finally be tested based on actual results. When strategies are implemented according to plan, models then can be created to analyze current performance and project future impact. If the analysis shows that the strategy isn't working or needs to be adjusted, then the insights can be delivered to senior management who can start the performance management lifecycle all over again by adjusting the strategy in place.

The essence of a closed-loop performance management system is that insights can flow from any phase to any other and then have a positive effect on the system. The model and optimize phase can influence strategy. The monitor and analyze phase can have impact on budgets and plans. The planning process can expose contradictions and flawed assumptions in strategy. The faster such insights and information flow and the easier it is to incorporate changes all along the line, the more mature the performance management practices are. The next section offers up some insights about how to evaluate and judge performance management maturity.

Evaluating Performance Management Maturity

A maturity model is like a benchmark or a framework that sets forth specific characteristics against which a process can be evaluated. By comparing a process at your company to a maturity model, it is possible to see where the process is more and less mature, which can be an indicator of the areas that will yield the greatest benefits if improved.

Perhaps the most famous maturity model is the Capability Maturity Model Integration that was developed at the Software Engineering Institute of Carnegie-Mellon University. This maturity model sets forth a series of levels, shown in Figure 3-8, that describe how software development moves from an unorganized, chaotic process into one that is predictable, closely monitored, and continuously improved. Although CMMI was developed for software, it applies to many types of processes.

CMMI, Six Sigma, and ISO standards for quality have all been influential in propagating the idea of maturity models. Most of them take a similar shape to the CMMI and define levels of increasing sophistication that build on each other. Each level describes in general how a process is performed. For example, in CMMI, level 1, where most companies start, is where processes

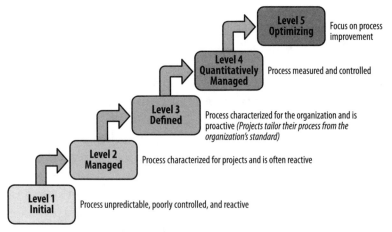

Characteristics of the Maturity Levels

Figure 3-8. The Levels of the Capability Maturity Model Integration for Software Development
(Source: Software Engineering Institute, Carnegie-Mellon University)

are not formally defined. This level is characterized by "heroics," that is, individuals doing their best to do a good job. In CMMI level 2, processes are defined for project management, in level 3 the processes for creating software are defined and standardized, in level 4 they are instrumented, and in level 5 there is a process for improving the processes based on the instrumentation.

One common mistake people make when thinking about maturity models is imagining that two companies at any individual level have the same processes in place. Maturity models do not say specifically how you should do something. Rather, maturity models recommend ways of thinking, defining, and improving processes that you invent to help you do your work. In other words, using a maturity model does not remove the primary challenge of performance management, that is, crafting a program that fits the needs of your business. Instead, a maturity model can be a guide to where you should pay attention and the order in which you should improve your processes.

This point is important because sometimes people take maturity models too literally and instead of using them as a guide to invention and continuous improvement, they attempt to imitate specific stages of a maturity model in the levels set forth. As we shall see in the discussion below, usually companies have some processes at every level of maturity and are working to move forward in a complex way that is unique to their circumstances. In general, companies should seek most maturity in areas that are differentiating and can tolerate less maturity in performance management processes in areas that are not as central to creating value.

The AMR Research Model for Performance Management Maturity

AMR Research has been a leader in the analysis and research of performance management. In a paper published in January 2007, John Hagerty describes a maturity model for performance management that is useful for companies seeking to improve their processes.

The AMR maturity model for performance management, summarized in Figure 3-9, has four levels that are similar in spirit to maturity models from other fields.

The levels of the AMR maturity model map a progression from departmental maturity to a state in which a performance management culture is established throughout an entire company. In this way, the AMR model

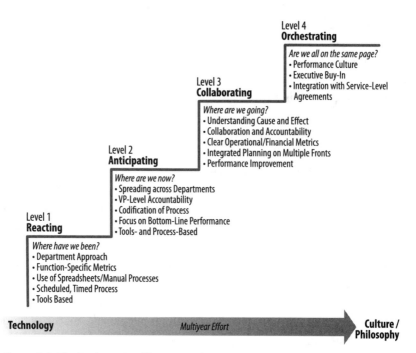

Figure 3-9. The Business Intelligence/Performance Management Maturity Model
(Source: AMR Research, 2007, "A Maturity Model for Enterprise Performance Management")

describes how performance management frequently emerges from the bottom up and gradually spreads throughout a company.

Level 1 of the AMR model is called reacting. Analysis focuses on understanding what happened in the past. At this level, departments and narrow units of organization below the scope of entire business units are using simple tools to improve access to business data, reduce reporting cycle time, and increase visibility into a specific department's performance. The scope of performance management data and the focus of the analysis are the tactical issues faced by the department rather than larger strategic initiatives. Spreadsheets and simple BI and reporting technology are often used to realize benefits quickly.

Level 2 of the AMR maturity model is called anticipating. Analysis focuses on understanding what is happening at the current moment. At this level companies use the information, techniques, and technology implemented in level 1 to build a larger picture of the value-creating processes in a company. The need for a common data infrastructure becomes evident as analysis attempts to depict events that cross the lines of departments and business units. Technology that may create a reusable platform for performance management may be acquired and formal programs for spreading competence in performance management may be initiated, but the action is not yet at a company-wide level. Even though VP-level executives may now be aware of the growing competence in performance management, the activity still remains in silos of the organization and has a tactical focus on business needs and operational performance, not strategy. Technology investments may be expanded to include data integration, event monitoring, and data mining capabilities used to create dashboards, which are the primary vehicle for performance management. Information starts to become part of the day-to-day activities. The more companies prepare at this level for systems that could actually create a larger integrated model that includes strategic objectives and advanced analytics, the faster they will move to a higher level of maturity. Choosing solutions to meet specific tactical needs rather than constructing a platform for performance management will retard progress.

Level 3 of the AMR maturity model is called collaborating. Analysis focuses on understanding the direction an organization is headed. At this level, one or several business units reach an optimal state of performance management and a larger view of the performance of the enterprise is created, expanding beyond the silos. A few clear operational and financial performance metrics are used to keep score and drive the business forward. The departmental metrics created in levels 1 and 2 are mapped back to corporate goals, giving visibility into the health and future prospects of the business. At this stage, planning takes place in terms of the broader performance management measures in use. Dashboards and scorecards align activity and promote communication across boundaries. Information about the performance in each cycle starts to influence planning, creating a closed-loop process.

Level 4 of the AMR maturity model is called orchestrating. At level 4, performance management is a cultural philosophy that guides how the company does business at all levels. Strategy, planning, and execution are linked from the top down through carefully crafted metrics that track both strategic and operational goals. Top management pays close attention to monitoring and accepting accountability for performance. A company is run according to the view of reality present in the performance management model. Important events are sensed early and response is rapid. The few companies that have reached this level translate strategy into a cascading series of specific objectives so that each person in the company knows how their individual actions are linked to higher-level strategic and operational goals. Companies at level 4 have a unified, consistent, streamlined view of the enterprise. The investments in technology and the scale of the improvement projects executed by level 4 companies are massive and can stretch over many years, as new processes and technology are introduced to make performance management information, processes, and techniques pervasive.

In some ways the AMR maturity model provides less specific guidance for how to implement performance management than the Balanced Scorecard-based approaches and related techniques such as activity-based costing and Six Sigma. But the AMR model has the virtue of explaining the process based on real-world observations for how performance management takes hold and gradually grows in an organization. If you are a CEO, perhaps you can change the direction of an entire company. But most of us are not, and the AMR model shows how anyone at any level can get started and make better performance management part of his or her job. Then, if the benefits of the technique are noticed, the rest of the organization can gradually get the idea.

Assessing Your Performance Management Maturity

The primary challenge of performance management is determining in which areas maturity matters most to your business. For some this will be improving consolidation and reporting systems and methodologies. For others it will be integrating predictive modeling tools with their strategy and planning management systems. Others will need to improve their ability to extract, transform, and manage data from transactional systems in order to perform as close to real-time monitoring of processes and activities as possible.

In order to gain this understanding, it is important to ask some of the following pointed questions about the current performance management processes and capabilities across people, processes, and technologies.

- How good are you at extracting data from transactional systems and how reliable is that data?
- Does it seem to take a long time to reconcile data from multiple systems because you lack an integrated data management platform?
- Do you fully understand where your company derives wealth and incurs costs?
- Can you delineate costs and profitability by multiple dimensions such as product, channel, customer, project, region, and business unit?
- Is consolidation and reporting a seamless and timely operation?

- If necessary, could you quickly and easily create a real-time operational snapshot of the company?
- Are you fully realizing the potential of your strategies or are they getting lost in an operational cloud?
- Do you have a solid understanding of the associated strategic, financial, and operational risks to your business and a risk response for each in order to successfully execute on your key objectives?
- Do you have a solid understanding of the business and the necessary tools so that you can engage in predictive analysis?

Of course, this list could be easily expanded to hundreds of questions. It is vital to be courageous and look for areas where your company is the weakest—where the burning performance management issues are.

Most companies divide the analysis into two stages.

Stage 1: Prepare an adequate self-benchmark of current capabilities. It is important to remember that this benchmarking activity should not be overwhelming in scope. Often, benchmarking data is not available and the only way to get a sense of practices in an industry is to do some reporting and interview other companies. The goal is not to write the final word on benchmarking for your industry, but rather to get a general idea of what companies of a similar size in the same or similar industries are doing with respect to performance management. Of course, sometimes data is available and it will be possible to compare current practice to metrics about best practices for performance management and related processes. For example, if most of your industry can close its books in 5 days that is an important indicator of performance management maturity. Other measures could be the variance between predicted and actual sales.

Stage 2: Prioritize and execute on a to-do list. In this case, improving performance management becomes one or more objectives of the sort described above in the Balanced Scorecard section. The logic relating the objectives may be described in a strategy map. Metrics and measures must be developed to track progress, and specific projects must be created, executed, and monitored.

Usually items that are mandatory (such as regulatory compliance) or fundamental (such as speeding time to close) dominate the first cycle of improvement. Then performance management improvement starts to focus on the unique aspects of a business and specific business processes. This is where activity-based costing and Six Sigma are often applied.

Programs for performance improvement vary immensely depending on the span of control that is exerted across the organization. For those with a diffuse span of control there is a far more pronounced need for performance management, whereas in a highly centralized organization, achieving a high level of maturity may not be necessary.

One could think of this as the difference between McDonalds and GE. McDonalds is fairly hierarchical in that every French fry in every restaurant should taste the same no matter if it is in Singapore or Idaho. This model necessitates a high degree of top-down control. By contrast, a company such as GE, where control is very decentralized among a number of operating units, would require performance management at a general level, probably focusing on financial performance. Inside each division, higher levels of performance management improvement would no doubt be required.

In other words, performance management becomes more important as the scope of activity that is relevant to the business increases, but the amount of control exerted from the executive level decreases. The implication of this relationship is a rise in the importance of performance management as globalization, distributed management and business decision making, and decentralized value chains take hold.

The flow of the performance management lifecycle and the way that organizations grow in maturity to higher levels of practice should now be clear. But it should also be clear that, in order to make significant progress with performance management, technology will play a significant role. This chapter has focused on the processes and practices, but the next chapter will provide a tour of the technology that is applicable to each phase of the performance management lifecycle, which is an important part of understanding how to move forward.

Chapter 4

Performance Management Applications

Whitile it is conceivable to improve performance management practices to some extent through changing processes and work practices, in practice implementing various forms of technology is a requirement. The first three chapters covered the general context and concepts surrounding performance management, as well as the performance management lifecycle. This chapter will describe the functions across the range of available performance management applications and provide guidance about how to select and apply them appropriately. The discussion of the functions of each type of application will be organized around the phases in the performance management lifecycle described in Chapter 3. Think of it as a "wish list" of applications that could be used to transform your business.

Typically, these applications have been developed to address one or more of the phases of the performance management lifecycle, and in some cases, they have been developed for a specific business function, such as IT or HR. This chapter will review the most critical "need to have" features of the applications as they apply to a point on the lifecycle, but will not delve in any great detail into the requirements of each business function—that information is presented in Part III.

To provide an idea of the progress that is possible when PM applications are implemented successfully, this chapter begins with a vision of how a collection of applications might work together in harmony as an integrated performance management suite. While it may sound like science fiction to some, the integrated performance management suite—the applications able to synchronize across all business units, catalog all of the risks and manage them with controls, incorporate unstructured data, and leverage all of the data points that your business generates every day to the best possible level of performance management improvement—is ready to make its appearance.

Strategize and Prioritize

Chapter 3 explained a number of methodologies for strategy formulation that can help generate hypotheses about how to better run your business. This section walks through the applications that help create and manage an organization's strategic direction.

Strategy management applications provide a packaged approach to support strategic planning, modeling, and monitoring to improve corporate performance, accelerate management decision-making, and facilitate collaboration. These solutions are usually tied to strategy maps or methodologies, such as the Balanced Scorecard. Strategy management applications usually support some or all of the following functions:

- **Strategic planning.** Strategic planning capabilities support creating high-level business plans to evaluate the impact of different strategic alternatives. They enable creating strategic plans on a "base case plus" or using an initiative-based approach, along with scenario modeling to compare the financial outcomes of various strategies. Strategic planning includes long-term financial planning, which creates a high-level perspective of revenue, expenses, balance sheet items, and cash flows to show the financial impact of different strategic alternatives. Strategic planning is usually offered as part of a planning application not as part of a strategy management application. For this reason, we cover strategic planning in the section on planning applications
- **Dashboards.** Dashboards aggregate and display metrics and key performance indicators, enabling them to be examined at a glance before further exploration via additional BI tools. Performance management suites should, at the very least, provide dashboard capabilities to help display performance information in a way that is easily understood by users. However, more sophisticated organizations are implementing strategy maps (linked frameworks

of KPIs) using scorecard software to link strategy management to other aspects of performance management. Strategy management is becoming an increasingly important aspect of performance management suites

- **Scorecards and strategy maps.** These tools record strategies, objectives, and tasks; measure performance; and provide a collaborative environment for effective, enterprise-wide communication
- **Initiative management.** These project-management-like tools enable responsible managers to execute specific tasks related to a strategy

Strategy management applications help you translate your general strategy into specifics, which can then become part of the plan and can be tracked throughout the lifecycle. These applications need to be able to model organizational goals and decompose them into individual goals. As we have indicated, the best way to motivate individuals to perform against organizational goals is to show them "what's in it for them." To drive behavior, you must understand the consequences of that behavior. The best strategy management applications will cascade organizational goals to individuals and demonstrate the direct impact of positive performance on their compensation. Strategy management applications can leverage the definition of your organization and its hierarchy from the underlying HR or HCM system of record.

Strategy Maps and Scorecards

A strategy map links the long-term game plan or competitive strategy of a business with its operational activities. It illustrates the cause-and-effect relationships between different key performance indicators (KPIs) and key risk indicators (KRIs) that are included in the underlying score-cards. Leading-edge strategy mapping applications allow users to choose any visualization of their strategy that makes sense to the organization by important visual diagrams and then map the KPIs and KRIs of the application to the relevant graphical locations in the diagram. An example of such a visualization is shown in Figure 4-1.

There are numerous methodologies and approaches for constructing scorecards, some of which are touched upon in Chapter 3. Kaplan and Norton's Balanced Scorecard is one of the best-known templates for visualizing how metrics management works, separating the measurement and KPIs for different perspectives, processes, or people in the organization.

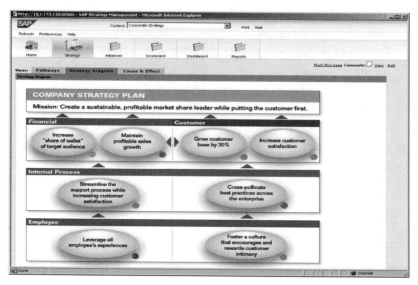

Figure 4-1. Example of a Strategy Map in SAP BusinessObjects Strategy Management

For example, a strategy management application should be able to relate the three metrics that talk about employee satisfaction to the five relevant internal business process metrics, on layer two of the balanced scorecard. Those five internal business process metrics in turn correlate to five customer metrics in the customer layer of the balanced scorecard, which ultimately impact the financial bottom line. The strategy management application should help answer a question such as, "If I increase my net dollars spent on training, how does it increase my business process efficiency?"

At a more detailed level, in addition to the perspective and KPIs or KRIs, a scorecard should display the trend (up, down, or no change), the status (traffic lights or other indicators configurable by how your business likes to discuss status), the actual values, target (planned) values, a score (weighted index or treatment of the KPIs or KRIs), as well as comparisons to previous values. The data should be capable of being sourced from any of your transactional or analytical applications (for example, the "targets" should be able to be populated from your planning system while the "actuals" directly from your supply chain system), as well as provide facilities for workflow-driven compliant data entry, since strategy data is often not necessarily housed in any existing system.

Unlike the snapshot in time represented by the dashboard, a scorecard represents more of a forward-looking view, and it shows your KPIs and

KRIs in relation to targets and results. It also displays the direction your KPIs and KRIs are moving in. A scorecard is generally more strategic, while a dashboard is generally more tactical.

Initiative Management

Strategy management software also contains initiative management capabilities that allow you to set up and control initiatives generated by your strategy. Think of these as lightweight project management applications.

For example, your initiative might be "improve customer satisfaction." It might have milestones and sub-milestones to achieve that initiative. One of those milestones might be the completion of X number of customer surveys or call center interviews querying about customer satisfaction with support-call quality. The initiative management application would track the hiring of the consultant to do the survey, the distribution of the survey, and the status of survey completion and analysis of the survey results. Each of these steps would have a KPI set against it that would show you if you were making progress toward completing the initiative as well as KRIs that indicate the likelihood of risks that may derail the initiative along the way.

The "cascading" we were talking about earlier happens within the boundaries of this application—the KPIs that track progress are decomposed in initiative management and farmed out to the appropriate parties or divisions, who see the KPIs in their own contextual lens: a CEO sees the goal as "increase revenue;" a sales manager sees that same goal as "convert a higher percentage of leads that we get from marketing." A visualization of a set of cascading projects using a fishbone diagram is shown in Figure 4-2. Cascading takes the high-level goals and connects them to contextual goals and metrics that people should have at the next level of the organization.

Initiative management applications can do the same cascading with KRIs that it does with KPIs, so that you can see risk and reward right next to each other on the screen. You want to be able to correlate risk and reward in as direct and immediate a manner as possible.

Initiative management capabilities must be robust. You use these capabilities to define initiatives and then enforce them. By "enforcement," we mean that you should be able to construct business processes on the fly, based upon your understanding of what must be done in order to achieve the strategy. Typically, the interface will be a visual modeling tool that allows a business user to construct and alter the initiatives. Leading-edge initiative management

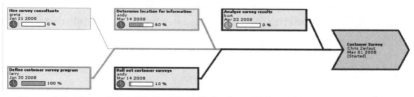

Figure 4-2. Managing Initiatives in SAP BusinessObjects Strategy Management

systems can tie strategic initiatives to operational business processes through business process management (BPM) technology to close the loop between strategy and execution. For example, in an initiative step to "hire survey consultants," it should be possible to directly map this step in the initiative management module to the HR hire-to-retire process in your HCM system via processes modeled in your BPM environment so that the parameters of who to hire, what skill set is needed, and so forth, can be passed as context to the HR business processes from the initiative. Then once this business process is triggered, the initiative progress can be monitored via direct monitoring of the underlying HCM business processes from the transactional system or from a data warehouse built off of the transactional system.

In a similar manner, initiatives created in the initiative management module should be capable of being used as one of the dimensions in the financial and operational planning modules or in a risk and controls module and the opposite should be true as well. Thus, a single initiative can span and bind the entire performance management lifecycle.

Given the large portfolio of initiatives in any one organization, prioritization matrixes should be available that allow users to plot the importance versus the status of the various initiatives to allow users to see those initiatives that are both important and behind schedule. These can then be focused on immediately and then drilled into directly from the prioritization matrix.

Metrics Management

A strategy management application should also have the capability to define metrics, watch their progression over time, and to look at their relationship to each other in order to determine the outcomes. Ideally, the application should be able to set up a model where metrics A, B, and C drive metric D, which then in turn subsequently influences metric C. It is ideal to be able to see metrics in their proper hierarchy from the top to the bottom of the organization, to know how they are statistically correlated, and to have the capability to alter those correlations.

It is also exceptionally helpful to be able not only to define but also to intuitively visualize relationships between metrics in order to understand the impact of one set of metrics on another. Figure 4-3 shows an example of such a visualization.

Strategy management applications should also be able to decompose the strategy into specific component pieces in the planning phase. In other words, if your strategy is, "increase margin by 20%," the application should be able to instruct planning and resource allocation applications (which we will get to shortly) to assign resources and implement a plan that directly reflects the strategy. There should also be bidirectional dialogue between these applications; in other words, the planning application should be able to inform the strategy management application that there are not enough resources to execute the strategy as defined—perhaps new staff need to be hired, or the strategy needs to be scaled down. These options should be clearly displayed to the user.

Essentially, a strategy management application is helping to model goals against the constraints of reality. The state of the art strategy management system would alert you that initiative C will consume a certain percentage of resources, which were already assigned to initiatives A and B. The planning system must be made aware of the initiative that generates the instructions. It does not make sense to create goals or initiatives that are completely unachievable.

Strategy management applications provide strategic planning capabilities to model the specific effects of strategic initiatives in combination with each other or against an overall "base case" scenario that represents ongoing operations. This means that the management team now has the tools to perform "proper" strategic planning, rather than relying on spreadsheets. If these applications are used, the outcome of strategy planning can be

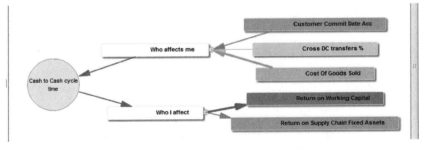

Figure 4-3. SAP BusinessObjects Supply Chain
Performance Management Metrics Impact Diagram

expressed as a financial budget, which can be used to reconcile individual operational budgets to the corporate goals and objectives.

A high-level enterprise strategy needs to be linked to lower-level goals and objectives, which is where the concept of a strategy map discussed earlier is very powerful. Many applications provide this functionality and increasingly offer strategy management capabilities for tracking and implementing strategic initiatives. In a true closed-loop performance management approach, this provides the framework to link the strategic plan to the financial budget and the individual operational budgets and plans.[1]

Dashboards for Performance Monitoring

Dashboards are probably the most commonly discussed and presented feature of strategy management applications. Some vendors will describe these as if they represent a total strategy management application, but in fact, they are only one part of the total. Think of dashboards as containers for displaying metrics. They are like the speedometer on your car. They allow you to conduct performance monitoring—but it is a one-way, at-a-glance, tactical system. You can see what's happening, but you need performance management to be able to link the KPIs together in a meaningful way and to represent them from different perspectives.

That being said, dashboards are an extremely intuitive way to visualize metrics and get "at a glance" visibility into your business. State of the art dashboarding solutions are highly interactive with sliders and toggles and visually compelling with beautiful user interfaces. Figure 4-4 has an example of a modern dashboard that combines different styles of visual elements. Visual panache captures the interest of business users and drives system usage, which is a very important goal in making performance management propagate throughout your organization. They can also be highly effective for monitoring processes "in flight," using an underlying technology called business activity monitoring or BAM, which allows users to track events as they are happening in real-time to allow them to take corrective action on mission-critical, time-sensitive business processes.

---

[1] Gartner Research, "Using Corporate Performance Management to Understand the Drivers of Profitability and Deliver on Strategy," presentation by Nigel Rayner, October 14, 2008.

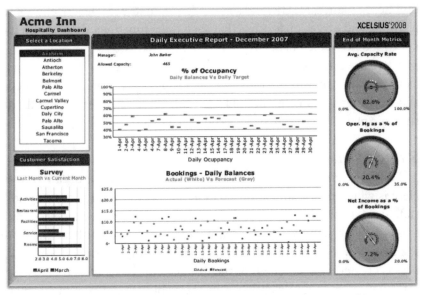

Figure 4-4. A Sample Dashboard from SAP BusinessObjects Xcelsius

Combining Strategy Management and Risk Management

As we articulate throughout this book, we believe performance and risk management are completely intertwined. As such, a leading-edge strategy management solution will allow a completely flexible use of both KPIs and KRIs with strategy maps, scorecards, initiatives, metrics management, and dashboards. Risk heat maps can be embedded directly within the application, and clicking on any cell in the map can take you to the corresponding risk in the risk management module.

Similarly, within a strategy diagram, it is just as easy to link to KPIs like profit, revenue, and market share as it is to link to risk exposure.

Plan and Execute

Planning applications help you decide how to allocate resources within your department to support the strategies you have created. Strategic planning generally takes a 3- to 5-year view of where the company should be going. In this phase, companies try to decide how to go about expanding their market reach, through mergers and acquisitions, through strategic investments, or through divestitures. When it comes time to convert that plan into something executable, you enter the realm of financial and operational planning software. Typically, the software is configured for each business function: Finance, IT, HR, and so on. We will first speak generically about planning and execution features that span these functions, delving into the key differences when necessary.

There are three basic categories of planning: strategic planning, financial planning, and nonfinancial or operational planning. The financial and operational plans should fold up into and directly correlate with the strategic plan. The software helps you make that happen.

Strategic Planning

The strategic plan resides at the highest level of the organization. Here is where the organization sets forth its 3- to 5-year profit-and-loss statement. In this application, different scenarios can be modeled: what happens if we acquire this company at this price? What happens if we shed this division at this price? In essence, a single model of the business is created into which all of the financial and operational plans feed information and subsequently derive their objectives. The strategic planning application should have the capability to allow cross-pollination and alignment between the three planning categories. It aggregates the information across the entire organization.

A strategic planning application should be able to model a balance sheet, cash flow statement, and the impact on these from major changes in business direction. A plan puts into motion and allocates resources appropriately to support the initiatives created in the strategy phase.

Financial Planning

In the Finance function of the business, planning is essentially the determination of resource allocations across the company. Typically, the activity called "planning" in the Finance function implies a top-down directive from the C-suite. The plan influences and informs the "budget," which is more of a bottom-up process of negotiation under the aegis of the business unit managers. Those business unit managers then describe what they need to achieve their goals from a financial perspective. Financial planning software needs to be able to support this kind of top-to-bottom reconciliation, allowing managers to go through multiple iterations of the plan and find a healthy balance between what they are trying to achieve and what the company is trying to achieve. The line managers should be able to engage in a back-and-forth setting of terms with upper management through the vehicle of these applications, which will lead to adjustments in the plan and the re-initiation of the cycle.

Typically the financial planning software will look at objectives and budgets in a one-year time frame, which rolls forward one month at a time. The key aspect to look for when selecting financial planning software is the ability to tie financial targets to broader objectives, and to understand the need for resources to execute that strategy.

One of the keys to user adoption is providing them with an environment they are familiar with. The best planning solutions provide both rich web-based experiences as well as the environment most Finance users spend the majority of their day in—the spreadsheet. Over the years, it has become possible for vendors to offer their planning functionality completely through a spreadsheet metaphor, allowing the end-user to use all of the functionality of the spreadsheet application they are comfortable with, like formatting, forms, and formulas, while still accessing the back-end power and centralized environment of a professional planning application. From a web perspective, the best solutions allow the use of much of the same interactivity a spreadsheet provides, including sorting, formulas, graphical allocations, and spread functions directly from the web page.

From the perspective of the end-user, leading-edge planning applications greatly minimize plan errors and the need for significant amounts of training by leveraging a capability called process flows. These process flows package the best-practice sequence of steps users need to take to conduct their planning process along with all of the underlying application artifacts like the dimensionality, business rules, and data entry templates. Business processes that should be provided out of the box include strategic planning, budgeting (including multi-currency budgeting processes), sales and revenue planning, capital expenditure planning, workforce planning, expense budgeting, line item detail budgeting, financial statement budgeting, and forecasting. It should be possible to compose performance management processes from individual process flows. For example, the annual budget is really a composite of the individual target setting, revenue, HR, expense, capital expenditure, and balance sheet and cash flow processes.

Leading-edge planning applications also offer another important usability feature, a context-sensitive action pane. The action pane is a unifying metaphor throughout the application that lets the user know where they are in the application in terms of what slice of the multidimensional cube (which entities, accounts, time periods, and measures they are working on) and what actions they can take next (such as submit budget, or ask for approval). As the user navigates through the application, the action pane changes to reflect the right options to provide to the user based on what is appropriate to the process they are executing.

Another great time saver in planning applications is packaged report templates. Over the years, Finance professionals have standardized on typical planning report patterns that are used over and over again. The best solutions provide a rich set of these templates, for comparative and year-to-date variance analyses, trend analyses, consolidation, and nested reports. It is also critical that the solution offer the exact same metaphor for both reporting and data entry. The system should not require the user to build reports any differently than they would for building a data entry template.

Another key area where a planning solution must be highly proficient is having built-in financial intelligence. The solution needs to provide pre-configured accounts, rate, and currency dimensions to support standard financial processes. For example, the accounts dimension should have preconfigured intelligence for different account types such as expense, income, asset, liabilities, or equity accounts along with the business rules that define their relationships to each other. The ability to track openings, additions, deletions, transfers, and closing balances, especially for asset/ liability accounts, should also be provided out of the box. The ability to support multiple currencies as well as translate between currencies is critical, especially given the multi-national nature of most organizations, and different exchange rate types should be supported for different accounts. Finally, predefined ratio analysis functions built as rules, such as profitability analysis, liquidity analysis, activity and efficiency analysis, and capital structure analysis ratios all need to be available for financial analysts to get the most out of the application.

Leading-edge planning products use statistical analysis to determine the relationship between KPIs. This is not a time trend of the KPI, but a mathematical analysis of the data to determine what relationships "drive" the KPI. In this way, for example, product quality might contribute to the analysis of the customer satisfaction KPI. These models can be used in two different analyses: when making predictions, and when analyzing root causes. To be competitive, planning solutions need to include linear and nonlinear regression as well as multiple linear regression.

Finally, end-users need powerful drill-down capabilities. It should be seamless for them to drill down into the hierarchy of application or slice of their application cube, with formulas preserved as the users drill down. Users need to be able to view both summary and detail views on the same page and drill down directly to the transactional details. Reuse of the same report input schedules should allow one report to be automatically contextualized for different levels in the organization.

Of course, while end-users are a key constituent of planning applications, they are not the only constituents. Leading-edge planning applications provide very robust application modeling facilities to build complex applications quickly for administrators. A unified design-time environment that is built for business users, not IT staff, with wizard-driven interfaces for application design is essential.

Visual facilities for building simple, reusable business rules, along with a flexible underlying business rules language for more complex scenarios, support the full spectrum of formula authoring needed to fuel a wide variety of planning applications. Context-sensitive action panes that provide a guided, flexible environment where administrators can build their applications are also highly valuable both in reducing training time and in helping to ease the error-prone nature of the application development process. It should also be simple for non-IT staff to be able to administer the application for even traditionally IT-intensive functions such as security administration. As in all financial applications, a robust automated audit trail capability is absolutely mandatory. It should also be possible for business users to define data flows and transformations from existing source systems like the general ledger, as well as flat files and spreadsheets. Finally, a packaged dimension library with the key financial planning dimensions, such as accounts, categories, entities, and so forth, should be provided out of the box so that they do not have to be built from scratch every time.

We advocate a fully unified approach to planning and consolidation. The exact same end-user and administrative metaphors, dimensions, and business rules that fuel planning solutions should also appear in planning and consolidation solutions.

Driver-Based Planning: The Bridge between Financial and Operational Planning

The state-of-the-art planning solutions today typically are driver-based systems. In a driver-based plan, operational metrics are linked with relevant financial outcomes. For example, if the call center takes 15 minutes per call on average, and a marketing plan will result in the sale of 400 more products per month, it will be possible to figure out how many more call center agents would be needed to handle that increased load and hence how much more money would be needed to pay for that increase in call center staff.

Additionally, a call center manager does not typically think in terms of budget, but rather in terms of operational levers he or she controls. If the strategic directive from corporate is, "reduce the budget," this may be expressed to employees by the directive, "Reduce the amount of time that your reps spend on the phone by 40%," or "Increase your customer service value by 30%." Then a cost must be assigned to those things. Driver-based budgeting, and the software that supports it, allows you to set up a common language for the dialogue—effectively, a translation mechanism between the financial world and the operational world.

Note that this is the state-of-the-art condition. Many organizations have not reached this stage on their journey to performance management maturity, and still have considerable gaps between their strategic, financial, and operational plans. Many organizations still look at their business like this: "I started with these resources and I ended up with this profit," but they can't effectively link the two. Driver-based planning capabilities allow you to look at the beginning state, which is, "I am going to do X activity, and I want to make Y amount of profit or absorb Z amount of cost conducting that activity. If I implement these four activities at the beginning of my process, how is that then going to result in a cascading set of metrics that eventually get me to that profit?" It is optimal to be able to work backward from the profit or forward from the drivers, just as it is useful to be able to go up from budgeting and down from the plan.

When costs and revenues are associated with activities, it is possible to understand how many activities need to be carried out in order to achieve certain goals and estimate the related costs. Then based on data, it is possible to determine whether or not a plan is realistic. Driver-based planning can help you do exactly that.

Operational Planning

To make the two previous plans work, operational planning software steps in to assist in planning the objectives and processes that will return the desired results. Operational planning refers to all nonfinancial, nonstrategic planning—in other words, the planning undertaken by each business unit to accomplish its goals.

Sales & Operations Planning (S&OP)

Sales and operations planning allows people in Sales and Supply Chain to input data about projected sales and production, and matches those two categories iteratively. A sales and operations planning software solution typically has more functionality and granularity than a financial planning solution. S&OP software allows you to model bills of sale at the product level, for instance, or to model detailed demand patterns. Whereas a financial planning solution is ultimately only concerned with expenses and revenues, an S&OP solution is concerned with bills of lading and order configuration. The key to making the lifecycle work is to connect these pieces where it matters—whenever money is allocated, changes hands, or is predicted to change hands.

A leading S&OP solution needs to support linking product and supply plans to cost and margin, and linking plan to actuals (detailed orders, supply, pipeline), while supporting rough-cut planning of demand, revenue, and capacity. The solution should be able to model new product introductions, provide bill of materials support with attach rate for promotion planning purposes, and conduct top down and bottom up scenario modeling in real-time with minimal latency. Since forecasting is such a core component of a robust S&OP process, a statistical forecasting engine with a rich library of forecasting algorithms is essential. Given the level of detail of a sales and operations plan as well as the nature of the entities being modeled, flexibility in hierarchies and attributes to change with the business is needed. From an integration perspective, leading-edge S&OP solutions provide tight integration with operational systems and translation of rough cut plans into detailed demand plans, with the ability to link customer demand across supply sites.

The business process of S&OP is covered in further detail in Chapter 13.

Marketing Planning Applications

Marketing planning applications are usually packaged by vendors to represent metrics in several categories, including product, price, offers and promotions, channels, and segments. A marketing planning application helps create campaigns to reach target audiences, customizing those campaigns as market conditions change or the strategic plan from upstairs changes. The application also helps plan and execute promotional vehicles and lead-generation schemes against branding activity.

The business process of marketing planning is covered in further detail in Chapter 11.

Workforce Planning

Workforce planning applications allow you to plan for workforce-related expenses, such as bonuses, fringe benefits, overtime, merit increases, and so on. These applications help you manage head count, salary, and match organizational skills to the strategic plan. Workforce planning is used, mainly in the HR department, to answer questions such as, "how many people do we need who have the ability to fix routers, versus those who know HDTV inside and out?"

The best workforce planning applications will successfully relate the individual needs of your HR department to the planning applications in Finance. Some workforce planning applications even have a separate line of logic for particularly detailed or specialized business functions, such as oilfield services, medicine or electrical engineering.

The business process of workforce planning is covered in further detail in Chapter 8.

Tying Risk to Planning

As we have seen in the economy recently, not accounting for risks can lead to some pretty serious damage pretty quickly. It is irresponsible to set forth a plan without any accounting for risk. If you project earnings of a certain amount, it is important to know what level of risk would destabilize the possibility of hitting that target. Fortunately, today's planning software allows making those adjustments with a degree of confidence. Of course, it is not necessary to broadcast the output of the software directly. The prediction can be tempered in a way that adds credibility and manages reputational risk. Instead of predicting, "I'm going to make $5 million in sales this year," a risk-adjusted plan, budget, or forecast would say, "We believe the range is $2 million to $6 million, depending on these factors."

If multiple possible risks are identified, different scenarios must be present in a plan that compensates for those risks. So, just as different versions of a plan are created, different scenarios would be implemented that account for various combinations of the risks occurring.

Essentially, the software needs to account for risk in such a fashion to support statements like the following: "If this risk materializes, here's what we're going to do," or "here's how many widgets we should create" or "here's how many people we should hire."

As mentioned earlier in the chapter, leading-edge planning applications contain the ability to orchestrate processes via the notion of a process flow, and it is possible to use this capability to link the planning and risk management processes and include a "risk adjustment" process step in the planning process. Through the process flow, users are guided to update plans to include identified risk impacts and mitigations from the risk management system, to review and reforecast plans upon changes in risks, and to quantify the impact of risks on quarterly trends such as the all-important forecast to obtain a "risk-adjusted forecast," which we stress throughout the book. The end result of the risk-adjusted planning process is a review of the risk-adjusted P&L against the initial budget.

When evaluating planning applications be sure that any application considered supports the planning techniques that will truly enable your company to differentiate itself as a high-performing organization through driver-based budgeting, risk-adjusted planning, event-based planning, and Beyond Budgeting in the most important areas of your business. See Chapter 3 for more details on these methodologies.

Monitor and Analyze

Monitoring and analysis applications consolidate data, provide analytic tools, and compute metrics to create visibility into key aspects of a business, making it possible to drill down to the root causes of deviations from the past trends and expected outcomes. From this analysis, it is possible to develop models that will establish better efficiency, profitability, and growth.

Consolidation

Financial monitoring applications must include specialized functionality to consolidate the various values of the underlying business units' performance in financial terms, apply currency and other statutory laws, and ultimately produce the final measures of financial value: the balance sheet, the profit and loss statement, and the cash flow statement. The consolidation parts of monitor and analysis applications take all of the raw financial data in an organization from the general ledger system and transform the data with a series of currency rules, ownership rules, time period rules, and so on, so that at the end of that process, these three "cleansed and blessed" financial statements are produced.

This "primitive" data produced by the consolidation solution can then be used to report actual performance in the strategic or financial plan, or in the operational plan, or it might be used in public financial statements. The consolidation system is essential to informing the metrics measured by other business functions, such as capital expenditure, IT resource planning, and cost of sale, for example. However, there is really no analogous application for other business units. It is really the province of Finance.

Secondarily, a consolidation application can compute KPIs and KRIs. These metrics will not be reported correctly if the constituent data is not of superior quality. These two functions combine to form an audit trail and statutory reports that extend from the data source to the disclosure of financial information to the public.

In terms of state-of-the-art consolidation solutions, the first distinguishing characteristic to look for is speed. The close, that is closing the books, is traditionally one of the slower financial processes, and being able to close in minutes rather than days can give an organization a significant competitive advantage. Solutions that can support incremental consolidations, instead of having to recalculate the entire matrix, can dramatically improve close times. Solutions that run consolidations in parallel can also dramatically speed up the close process. These operations should all be possible with thousands of concurrent users on the system.

The next thing to look for in a leading-edge consolidation application is unification of statutory and management reporting views. Most consolidation applications run separate statutory and management consolidations that must then be stitched together by hand. On the other hand, what is desirable is that a single task consolidates both views in parallel, including actual, budget, and forecast data, and then consolidates them into a single matrix to ensure both views are 100% reconciled to each other.

A critical element of leading consolidation solutions is their auditability, which is so crucial given the increasing regulations that govern the production of financial statements. The solution should provide detailed audit trails to ensure full traceability, but this must be possible without crippling the system's performance or impeding other ongoing tasks to ensure fast close initiatives are both successful and fully compliant. In order to support the full breadth of worldwide compliance needs, having multiple, dedicated dimensions in the product for audit is essential. Also, the auditing capability should be automatic and mandatory. There should be no way for someone to perform undesirable actions on the consolidation system without it being captured for further investigation.

The flexibility and extensibility of the data model is also critical to covering the full spectrum of consolidation requirements worldwide. Best-in-class solutions provide for up to 40 dimensions, with more than half being user defined. These dimensional models should support both unlimited characteristics as well as unlimited properties for maximum flexibility, which is especially critical for multi-national consolidation implementations with multiple regional sub-configurations.

As with leading-edge planning applications, consolidation applications must support very powerful financial intelligence. Automated currency conversions and equity eliminations should be provided out of the box, along with the ability to apply these to different charts of accounts and account flows. Even as the system changes, it is critical that past reporting frameworks are retained and history is not restated. It should not be necessary to destroy or rebuild previous reporting scenarios in order for users to always see the correct data.

A strong set of controls for compliance is also essential to a leading-edge consolidation solution. The system should provide intelligent controls and validations that are both automatically part of the system as well as configurable controls to ensure data accuracy and quality. Controls should be highly configurable with a set of properties for the full range of capabilities necessary in a system that produces such important numbers for the organization. Controls should be able to be set on imports and logs, manual journal entries, manual input controls, and every other aspect of the data collection process. Full transparency with time stamps and user names must be provided along with a real audit trail from source to disclosure and detailed workflow information. It must be possible to view all actions traced through logs and event viewers.

Another key capability of leading-edge consolidation solutions is the ability to have pre-configured starter kits that deliver best practices in statutory reporting and compliance. Your vendor should be able to provide you a fully packaged consolidation application capable of generating IFRS and U.S. GAAP compliant financial statements with the chart of accounts, consolidation rules, controls, and calculations, and the ability to generate the final publishable financial statements in XBRL with minimal configuration.

As stressed in the section on planning solutions, unification between planning and consolidation solutions (as well the rest of the extended performance management suite) is rapidly becoming mandatory. Thus, all of the same criteria around end-user and administrator empowerment and flexibility and minimizing the involvement of IT apply equally to consolidation solutions.

It has not required much effort, when reading the financial news on any given day in the last ten years, to find a report on a company that had to restate earnings or liquidate because of an error in financial reporting or a serious oversight in performance management.

That's why consolidation is an essential part of the performance management application toolkit.

Packaged Analytics

Packaged analytic applications help model, analyze, and understand business activity. Analytics applications are able to drill down and figure out why certain metrics look the way they do. The superior packaged analytics programs will also have some pre-built, best-practice macros that help anticipate problems and find warning signs, such as, "These are the typical root causes of people overspending." When determining the effectiveness of any business function, it is vital to see any variances or deviations from expected trends that would indicate potential problems.

Spend Analytics

To meet strategic business goals, procurement organizations drive sourcing strategies that impact the bottom-line, supplier relationships that enhance the business value network, and compliance across the company's policies, as well as compliance to contracts.

Such strategic sourcing initiatives begin with visibility into spend information. Information enables strategic sourcing professionals to answer questions about what they are buying, from whom, and how much they are spending. With this information, sourcing professionals can identify cost-savings opportunities, rationalize suppliers, monitor compliance, track progress toward meeting goals, and manage their overall spend performance.

Spend information needs to be complete, across multiple dimensions, accurate, and trustworthy. Therefore, there is a need for spend to be classified according to a market taxonomy that facilitates procurement in a global economy, with normalized supplier data for negotiation leverage and the ability to link to external market data for benchmarks.

All of this information needs to be at the fingertips of the business user for better informed strategic decisions, such as when to buy, what and from whom, with insight into impact on strategic plans and initiatives, earnings, and impact to supply chain. And ultimately, the business user should be able to close the loop between insight and action and take action upon what they learn in the spend analysis solution in an operational procurement system.

This is best achieved with an effective spend analytics solution. Spend analytics applications are a subset of packaged analytics that present metrics relevant to analyzing and understanding how a company spends money for goods and services. Vendors will typically produce a spend analytics platform for each business function. For example, in the supply chain and procurement area, spend analytics focuses on determining the best suppliers and sources for raw materials and parts.

A leading-edge spend analytics application needs to support numerous use cases. It should provide spend-related insight across multiple dimensions—categories, suppliers, geography, business units/organizations, cost-centers, GL Accounts, and so on. Figure 4-5 shows a report that breaks down spending by category. In terms of KPIs, the out-of-the-box KPIs should support spend volume measures and spend trends. The solution should also allow for the comparison of actual spend to planned/budgeted spend. The solution should have native support for price variance measures such as invoice price variance (IPV) and purchase price variance (PPV). This is critical because PPV, for example, has an impact on inventory valuation and therefore the supply chain and balance sheet. The solution should also provide price optimization measures—such as supplier price optimization—to help determine parts purchased from different suppliers at different prices and what the effect is of consolidating quantity, say by geography or even across the company and applying a minimum price or even market price. Finally, a leading-edge spend analytics application should have risk and compliance built-in, with contract compliance measures such as leakage, utilization, and off-contract visibility provided out-of-the-box.

Another key area where innovative spend analytics solutions distinguish themselves is in their evolution to more fully packaged spend performance management solutions. These spend analytics solutions provide the ability for business users to establish goals and indicate the measures that would be used to track performance to the goals, monitor key contributors to the lag on any of the performance indicators, and apply external data feeds

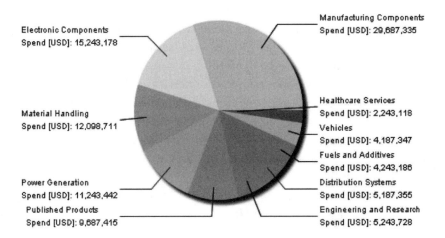

Figure 4-5. SAP BusinessObjects Spend Analytics Top Spend by Category Analysis

such as price indices or benchmark information, to compare how you are doing in the market.

Finally, spend analytics solutions are only as good as the data they rely on. Spend data and supplier data can be enormously fragmented and dirty, making it extremely challenging to conduct effective analysis. Leading-edge spend analytics solutions provide automated spend classification capabilities, resulting in over 95% accuracy and thoroughness levels. These solutions can also provide a supplier business compendium with millions of supplier records sourced globally, including ownership, credit, risk, and diversity information from both public and private data sources. These solutions also provide large knowledge bases for classifying spend based on the examination of trillions of dollars of spend using advanced statistical techniques such as neural networks.

Supply Chain Analytics

Supply chain analytics provide end-to-end visibility into all supply chain functions and perform root-cause analysis. Key to a leading-edge supply chain analytic application is a rich set of packaged supply chain metrics in key areas that measure supply chain effectiveness, including Perfect Order Fulfillment (Reliability Focus), Cash-to-Cash Cycle Time (Assets Focus), Return on Working Capital (Inventory/cost focus), Supply Chain Management Costs (Overall SC costs), Order Fulfillment Cycle Time (Quick Responsiveness), Return on Supply Chain Fixed Assets, and Cost of Goods Sold (Cost focus: manufacturing to other operations). Figure 4-6 shows a user interface that presents a collection of such metrics.

Supply chain analytics provide visibility across the entire supply chain network and allow users to perform root-cause analysis to uncover issues. The best solutions come with out-of-the-box, role-based content across the entire application—packaged scorecards, metrics, dashboards, and reports for all the major roles in the supply chain. Of course, packaged content is just a start, and end users need the ability to author content themselves, such as being able to create reports and dashboards on the fly. Finally, performing ad-hoc analysis such as drill-down and slice and dice should be native capabilities for the application.

Risk and Compliance Analytics

Analytics play an extremely important role in a full-fledged set of risk and compliance capabilities. From a risk quantification perspective, leading-edge risk and compliance analytics solutions provide inherent

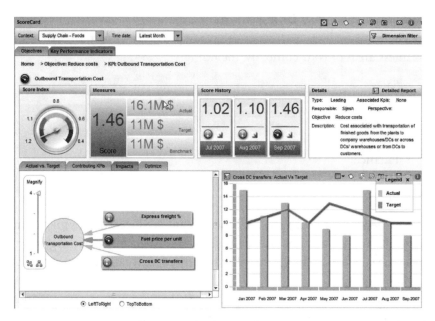

Figure 4-6. SAP BusinessObjects Supply Chain Performance Management Dashboard

risk and planned residual risk analysis using qualitative and quantitative measures. This information should be managed through comprehensive reports, heat maps, dashboards and visualizations. From a compliance reporting capabilities perspective, the solution should assess and monitor control design and effectiveness to manage compliance with internal policy and external regulatory requirements, and monitor the effectiveness of mitigation responses and overall risk exposure from noncompliance. From a scenario modeling capabilities perspective, the solution should provide comprehensive scenario modeling capabilities, including Monte Carlo simulations, to support what-if scenarios. Controls should be able to be modeled for their effects on processes. Scenario analysis models the impact across risk categories. From a reporting capabilities perspective, the solution should provide unified risk and control analytics, management and reporting by organization unit, level, process, and geography. Process, activity, risk, and control metrics should be shared across organizational structure and by role-based access. Finally, from a dashboarding capabilities perspective, leading-edge solutions provide full reporting, dashboarding, and visualization capabilities. KRI information should be defined against business processes and should be integrated with KPI content to align and manage the impact of risks against performance indicators.

Analytics for Every Department

There are analytic applications that can provide a view into most of the business areas of your company, including:

- Sales
- Marketing
- Service
- Product Development
- Finance
- HR
- IT

Key benefits of packaged analytics include reduced deployment time (configuration is minimal since the software targets needs of the group in question) and ease of use, since it is already contextualized for that group of business users.

The details about analytic applications that support specific business units are discussed in relevant chapters in Part III.

Predictive Analytics

Predictive analytics encompasses a variety of techniques from statistics and data mining that analyze current and historical data to making predictions about future events. This crystal ball is powered by an extensive library of statistical algorithms that scours a company's BI foundation for root causes, then extrapolates these factors forward and attempts to show how a business function will perform under a given set of assumptions.

Predictive analytics applications are generally more sophisticated than packaged analytics and require more IT support in the setup. These applications use advanced algorithms to make predictions or otherwise examine the data in a mathematical as opposed to human manner. Predictive analytics can help forecasting, for example, by determining how historical sales, costs, and key performance metrics translate to future performance and how the predicted values compare to plan. Predictive analytics can also identify key influencers, for example, to determine what are the main influencers of customer satisfaction, customer churn, or employee turnover that impact success. Predictive analytics can also uncover historical/emerging, sudden step changes, or unusual numeric values that impact the business. They are exceptionally powerful for helping you to understand the correlations between business data and events to determine which variables relate to each other and how they do so. Finally, predictive analytics allows you to focus on the anomalies that might exist and conversely what groupings or clusters might exist for specific analysis.

For example, instead of hiring somebody to filter through a lot of reports to try to find the root cause of why sales are decreasing, data mining technology can be put to use to examine the data set, and return a conclusion and the specific causes of declines in business activity or quality. Predictive analytics applications use data mining to extrapolate trends and forecast what the same set of elements would look like in three months. This can add new layers of sophistication to functions such as budgeting forecasts. A simplistic approach to budgeting is to take the results of the first quarter, multiply it by three, and consider the result as your expected performance for the year. A more sophisticated predictive analytic platform would take into account trends and variations such as seasonality, market shocks, and other events.

Predictive analytics are also used in individual business functions, such as Marketing, where the composite calculations that go into determining segment analysis, churn analysis, or customer lifetime value (CLTV) often use very advanced predictive techniques.

In terms of capabilities, predictive analytic platforms need to support the import and export of a large number of data sources: relational and multidimensional databases, text files with fixed or variable length fields, and spreadsheets, as well as supporting direct user input.

From a modeling perspective, leading predictive analytic platforms support a broad range of classification models: linear regression, binary classifiers, QUEST, CHAID, decision lists, factor analysis/principle components analysis, neural networks, support vector machines, discriminant analysis, logistic regression, generalized linear models, Bayesian networks, Cox regression, self-learning response models, and ARIMA are all used in different business applications.

Segmentation models are also very important to a leading-edge predictive analytics platform. The platform should support K-Means, Kohonen, two-step clustering, and anomaly detection algorithms at a minimum.

Leading-edge predictive analytics platforms also have a rich library of association models, including generalized rule induction, a priori, CARMA, and sequence models.

Finally, these platforms provide a rich library of graphics and visualizations such as plots, multiplots, distributions, histograms, collections, webs, evaluations, and time plots for displaying the model data in the optimal way.

Model and Optimize

The applications used in the monitor and analyze phase unearth the first layer of information about the basic factors that are contributing to the performance of your organization. In the model and optimize phase, the applications perform analysis that delves deeper into the root causes, helps create models based on those root causes, and proposes and evaluates optimizations to increase performance.

Modeling and optimization software proposes how best to optimize a company's resources and determines whether there is a need to increase or decrease the resources to meet current goals. It helps construct business models and scenarios that will provide guidance about forward-looking decisions.

Revenue, Cost, and Profitability Modeling

Cost-management software analyzes all of the costs that go into creating revenue. Cost-management applications basically act as super-powerful allocation engines. These applications explore the direct as well as the indirect costs of pursuing a customer or revenue strategy, and they also attribute the overhead costs to their sources.

One of the most common and useful approaches to cost management is activity-based costing (ABC). ABC is the methodology that allows you to assign cost to different activities, each of which is attached to resources that are consumed in the pursuit of that activity. Processes in the enterprise, or things in the enterprise like customers, consume a certain number of resources, and those resources use activities. ABC gives you a model of the resource consumption of each one of those activities of the sort summarized in Figure 4-7. Using ABC, you can determine how profitable it is to serve each of your customers.

Organizations are under scrutiny on many aspects of their operations. One of the things managers want to clarify is the direct labor cost, the direct material cost for something, and overhead or indirect cost for performing a task or pursuing a strategy. It's typical to try to estimate the overhead cost by simply taking a ratio of the fixed cost proportional to the amount of revenue being generated by a line item instead of really understanding what the cost of that overhead is.

Take this example: Imagine trying to generate a profit and loss statement by customer, in order to determine how much revenue comes from each customer, and from there, the true cost of each sale. If the revenue is $10,000 and it costs $7,000 to sell to this customer, the contribution margin for that sale is $3,000. Without ABC, the analysis practically stops there. Organizations usually factor in the overhead cost of shared services that are necessary to support that customer—order processing, IT, electricity, administration, and so on.

When ABC is not used and standard costing methodologies are employed that overhead is assumed to be a fixed ratio of the cost of sales. ABC presents a much more accurate picture of the overhead and creates much more precise profit and loss statements per customer, which in turn represents the profitability of the customer much more accurately. ABC catches the variability in the consumption of operational resources that the company uses to service that customer or that product.

Leading-edge ABC modules provide extremely rich model-building capabilities. The application should be built with pre-defined dimensionality specifically optimized for ABC. This means quick and easy model building as all the multi-dimensionality is provided straight out of the box. The application should also provide complete flexibility with

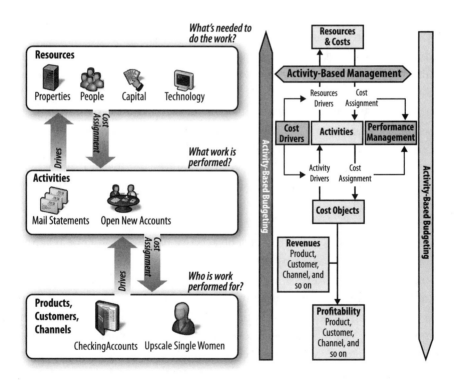

Figure 4-7. Activity-Based Costing

costing methodologies. Specifically, it should support time-driven ABC by providing a wizard to help the model builder write time equations for the handful of responsibility centers that carry out a high number of repetitious activities such as pick and pack operations and contact centers. The application should also support time splits for business units such as Marketing, Legal, and Finance. Like planning and consolidation applications, leading-edge ABC applications should support models that have multiple versions, periods, and currencies. Especially important is the ability to have attributes on the dimensional hierarchies for unlimited grouping and alternate hierarchies.

For costing of specific business processes that involve cross-charging, leading-edge ABC applications provide a specific revenue dimension and services dimension for cross charging and other shared services. The solution should support flexible methodologies for costing, pricing, and cross-charging IT and other support services, and provide the ability to generate detailed invoices that provide transparency into cross-charging and information for an informed discussion between business users and service providers. Unique to these scenarios is the need for reiterative allocation. This takes into account the fact that shared services units provide services that are consumed by other shared business units as well as the business unit providing the shared services. When costs are assigned to business units, they should be reiteratively reallocated between shared service units until they become insignificant. It is critical that, regardless of the usage of reiterative allocation, full traceback be maintained at all times.

In ideal scenarios, model building should be possible via point and click assignments across multiple dimensions. It should be possible to assign activity costs, service costs, or line items by responsibility center, and rather than use the default assignment, vary the assignment methodology used by both version and period. You should then be able to select the assignment methodology, cascading costs across cost objects in a particular order or assigning it multi-dimensionally in a single pass rather than "cascading" activity cost to each cost object in turn. If the driver data is available, it can be assigned to the exact intersection. The activity driver from the drop-down list again should provide the ability to vary the assignment by responsibility center. The model builder should be able to select the cost objects either individually or simply assign to all. Model maintenance should also be minimized to make application development simple. Any new member detected in a hierarchy should automatically inherit the assignments of its siblings.

The application must also support comprehensive traceback, that is, the ability to trace back all assigned costs to line items and responsibility centers. Inevitably, as soon you produce reports showing that someone's long-time favorite customer is barely profitable, they will want to challenge the figure. Having the ability to trace back all assigned costs through the activity layer and right back to the line-item expenses in the GL is thus vitally important.

While point and click model-building capabilities are state of the art, the fact is that there is always a need to customize models, and rich rule-building capabilities are thus necessary. Leading-edge solutions provide flexible rules engines for custom model building with a front-end wizard for easy and rapid modeling of more complex business rules for calculating "derived drivers." Given users' familiarity with Microsoft Excel, it is especially useful to be able to author business rules in VBScript, and there are solutions on the market that allow just that.

Like planning and consolidation solutions, leading-edge profitability solutions need to provide sophisticated security models, with comprehensive security and access rights, by group, by role, and by individual, right down to cell level with an optional audit trail with date and time stamps. Also like planning and consolidation solutions, the application should support context-aware views so that users can see only their data. Thus, a single report caters for many, minimizing deployment time. End users also need to be able to view screens in their local language and terminology and be able to enter financial amounts in their local currency, enabling cross border deployments.

Another area where leading-edge profitability management solutions are innovating is in the area of high-volume costing. This is accomplished via the application choosing either a relational or multidimensional data structure to calculate the costs depending on the data volumes. Modeling costs in a multidimensional data structure allows for the more sophisticated modeling of real life situations—giving more accurate costs. However, when calculating profitability on millions of individual transactions down to the account, SKU, or sales order line level, applying calculated costs to high volumes of transactions is much more efficient in a relational data structure. Hence, both scenarios must be supported.

No matter how much data is electronically imported, there is always some driver data that is not in any system, such as time splits or cycle times, that must be collected from managers in the organization. User-friendly web books and workflow tools need to be provided that allow users to expedite the collection of non-system driver data. Using the workflow capabilities, users can receive automated alerts and reminders to enter critical data.

Finally, a key capability of all modeling applications is the ability to conduct "what-if" analysis. Users should be able to slice and dice the data themselves with consolidated results being calculated on-demand with their web book automatically refreshed. Using this functionality they can test out the impact of changes before committing to them.

Activity-based management (ABM) applications represent an evolution beyond pure ABC. ABM systems provide modeling capabilities that enable users to model the effect on profitability of different cost and resource allocation strategies. More sophisticated applications have moved beyond the traditional ABC focus to allow revenue to be allocated for some industries with complex sales models (such as those selling through intermediaries) that can be as complex as the costing model. This approach can help model optimal product and service offerings in terms of packaging, bundling, and pricing, as well as optimize channel strategies.

A word of warning—applying ABC might lead to discoveries that the customers or suppliers considered very profitable might turn out not to be profitable at all—especially when the opportunity cost of ignoring other potential customers or suppliers is factored in.

Generic Simulation Modeling and Optimization

There is also a class of simulation modeling and optimizing software that tends to be heavily used by certain industry sectors. Simple scenario modeling can include creating a base case and then high and low cases based on changes made to input variables, such as market growth rates or inflation rates. This technique is often used in modeling market and business opportunities and creating business plans and is frequently used in strategic financial applications. Simulation modeling is a more advanced modeling technique that includes Monte Carlo simulation. Monte Carlo simulation supports creating a broad range of scenarios based on multiple iterations of input assumptions and combinations. With this technique, probabilities can be assigned to various outcomes. These techniques allow the uncertainty associated with a given forecast to be estimated and to reduce risk by applying sensitivity analysis, correlation, and trend extrapolation. Of course, as a recurring theme throughout the book, it should be noted that simulation capabilities should be equally possible for both KPIs and KRIs and any combination of the two.

Optimization applications allow you to take data inputs, constraints, and the end goal, and use algorithms to solve for the best means of achieving that goal. For example, profitability optimization applications are emerging that use advanced constraint-based algorithmic modeling to enable executives to see the effect of different strategies on profitability. These types of applications provide a link to business process improvement, because they focus on activities and process-oriented views of the business. This helps identify which business processes have the highest effect on profitability and, therefore, the greatest potential benefits for improvement. However, very few organizations are at the maturity level to implement this concept, and the applications are still nascent.

Managing Risk and Ensuring Control

No performance management initiative is complete without effective risk and compliance management capabilities. In this section, we discuss the state-of-the-art capabilities you should be looking for in these solutions.

Managing Risk

Leading-edge risk management solutions need to be able to support the entire lifecycle of the risk management process: from planning, to identification and analysis, to response and monitoring.

Risk Planning

From a risk planning perspective, the first step the solution needs to support is the ability to define organizational structure across the extended enterprise and align organization goals and objectives. Also key is an organizational unit hierarchy that allows flexible modeling of your organization and the ability to define users and their roles as they intersect with the risk management process.

Next, you identify types of risks to track and align risks to business processes, assets, and goals of the organization. The risk management application needs to allow users to set up the risk and activity catalogs for the enterprise based on the top risks that could affect your business and be able to import and export these catalogs from industry expert sources. The next step is identifying the key risk indicators (KRI) for each of the top risks. It should be possible to set KRI thresholds using configurable business rules. Some typical examples are when a KRI crosses a particular level (more than 3 injuries per month organization-wide), on a percentage increase/decrease basis (5% increase in unplanned manufacturing downtime), or percentage of volume (customer complaints of more than .005% of products shipped). Additionally, multiple KRIs could be defined for monitoring a risk if needed. Leading-edge solutions will provide pre-defined KRIs for continuous monitoring whereby the KRIs can monitor risk drivers directly in operational systems like ERP, CRM, or SCM. The ability to react to the KRIs is also crucial by flexibly defining actions such as alerts, risk reassessments, or changing the exposure when key tolerances are exceeded.

Finally, the risk-bearing appetite for each business unit and the enterprise as a whole needs to be documented. Depending on how much loss the business can absorb based on current capitalization, you may want to take more risks in some areas—in one product line, for example—while managing other product lines (the revenue-generating "cash cows") more conservatively. The software solution needs to support being able to break higher-level risks down by organizational unit, or geography, for example.

A key challenge that many solutions do not address effectively is the ability to not only roll-up all of the risk individually, but also to provide risk exposure for a small set of "what-if" scenarios. Solutions that provide scenario-based risk planning capabilities allow users to build business events and link them to the primary risks that would be affected, regardless of what organizational units these risks belong to. They also provide the capability to analyze how one risk influences one or more existing risks, thus building a cluster of risks moving together (positive or negative influence factors). Finally, a leading-edge risk management solution should provide the ability to change expected losses for these primary risks and see the results on correlated risks and for the entire scenario.

Risk Identification and Analysis

From a risk identification and analysis perspective, it is important to identify risk with the various business units in your organization using automated risk assessment and surveys. The goal is to identify all key risks, regardless of where they exist—internally or externally—and analyze them based on qualitative or quantitative methods. For as many risks as possible, it is preferred to automatically identify the risks based upon the KRIs set in your business operational systems. Of course, not all risks can be automatically identified, and a risk management system needs to support this as well. Providing user-friendly self-assessments as well as collaborative survey capabilities that can be used to gather information on risk type, impact, probability, timeframe, and mitigation strategy/costs is critical for these situations. It is also critical to be able to generate documentation of your risks, including risk ownership at multiple levels within your organization. The capability to do organizational unit-dependant calculations of risk levels and expected losses is also critical.

A key capability to look for in a risk management solution is the ability to do cumulative risk analyses. This stems from the need to be able to consolidate common or similar risks at higher levels of the organization and adjust the aggregate exposure to represent the overall risk portfolio appropriately. Solutions that support this can define "virtual"/aggregate risks of higher-level organizations while pointing to risks from lower-level/ different organizational units, substitute risk analysis from lower-level risks with higher-level risk analysis in reporting, and allow you to define the cross functional or horizontal visibility of risks.

Finally, after identifying the risks, the solution should allow you to prioritize your risks for response investment using the standard risk "heat map" approach. The heat map should be customizable to match your specific company definitions and categories and should allow you to identify shifts in risk profile and alert you to those risks in need of response.

Risk Response Strategies

Once you've identified critical risks, you need to have a risk response strategy (watch, research, transfer, delegate, mitigate). Any risk management solution you consider should allow a completely customizable set of response strategies tailored to your organization. The solution should allow a single risk to have multiple responses, with every response documented having a cost, owner, status, and workflow reminder set at a certain frequency for updates on progress. You should be able to view aggregate risks by category, process, and asset. As articulated multiple times in the book, addressing single risks may not always resolve the highest-priority problems. Instead, crucial issues are often the result of not being able to correctly identify what happens when multiple risks occur simultaneously and interact, combining into a severe risk, and any software solution should make it easy to surface these interdependencies. Also, the individual departments need the tools to effectively mitigate risks. Often, they already have the tools in place to operationally mitigate the risks, specifically the transactional applications for operative processes. Leading-edge risk management solutions can close the gap between strategy and execution by tying risk responses directly to the operative processes in your underlying ERP, CRM, and SCM systems without requiring you to manually switch between the various systems to stitch the holistic view together. With an effective response-tracking capability within your solution, you can monitor the status of responses (such as draft, committed, on track, completed), track the costs of the response, and even have multiple responses for a single risk.

It should also be possible to tie risk responses directly to business process controls since controls are one of the most effective mitigation techniques. Without this linkage, it is often difficult to know if regulatory-related risks are being adequately mitigated and what the true exposure of regulatory risks is. By mitigating risks with process controls, you can document corrective and preventative responses/controls and then monitor those controls to track their effectiveness and calculate the residual risk value.

Risk Monitoring

From a risk monitoring perspective, one key aspect of monitoring is dashboarding, as dashboards provide insight for more informed business management by answering key questions: What and where are your top risks? How have risk levels changed for key activities/opportunities? Have incidents/losses occurred? Are we assessing our risks in accordance with company policy? Another key value proposition of leading-edge risk management solutions is the ability to automatically monitor KRIs. By embedding these KRIs directly into key business processes, you have the ability to take proactive measures to prevent a risk from becoming an incident. A workflow capability is necessary to deliver reassessments to experts when thresholds are crossed. Finally, while effective risk management can dramatically reduce their likelihood, incidents and events are impossible to completely prevent. An effective risk management system should be able to document "occurred risks" or "external events," even if they weren't being tracked as risks in the system yet, along with causes, related costs, and owners. This information can then be used to close the risk management loop, leveraging this information to better estimate risk probability of occurrence as well as tune risk response playbooks.

Business Process Controls

The challenge with business process controls in most companies today is that, too often, controls are managed using inadequate tools that require too much manual tracking and updating: individual point solutions, document repositories, spreadsheets, documents, and emails. Even companies that have invested in some of the best-rated previous generation GRC software find that they are still spending too much time and effort testing controls, as this is still a manual process. They do not properly manage risk and track fraud as the related controls are only tested periodically, whereas they should be continuously monitored. The tests are too limited in terms of sample size, and they struggle to consolidate all the pieces of information on a timely basis to provide management complete, real-time visibility and reliable information for better decisions and confident certification.

Thus, there is clearly a need for more robust solutions to solve these problems, and also allow them to have fully transparent, controlled, auditable business processes, which in the end means better performance and better decisions to support long-term profitability and growth. A leading-edge business process control solution should have the capabilities described in the following sections.

Central Documentation of Controls

The solution should allow you to centrally document your complete control framework and all attached test and remediation information, in a single, transparent system of record. This framework should be centralized, secured, and comprehensive to document processes, control objectives, risks, and assertions. It is critical that the organization and process hierarchy are both extremely flexible as well as support time dependency. This ensures that you can see a picture of your organization as it existed. Finally, the application should be structured in a way that is laid out sensibly for the roles that will interact with it. For an internal control manager, seamless navigation between the organization hierarchy, account groups/ assertions, process hierarchy, control objective catalog, and entity-level controls hierarchy should be facilitated. For the audit manager, seamless navigation between assessment surveys, manual tests, automated tests, and scheduling processes should be facilitated.

Evaluation and Testing of Controls

A robust business process control application should also provide robust capabilities to evaluate and test the controls. Manual tests and assessments should be able to be performed flexibly, using user-defined multi-step test plans and flexible assessment surveys, and assigned to responsible users through a scheduling facility. Automated control tests should also be scheduled, and the system should allow continuous monitoring of the most critical controls. It is very helpful to have pre-delivered scripts for automated control testing delivered out of the box, along with the ability to monitor these controls across many different applications. Finally, it is critical for users of the system to be able to schedule the workflow of tests and assessments and send out email notifications.

Exception Monitoring and Remediation

Another key area of leading-edge business process control solutions is the ability to monitor exceptions and remediate issues. Testing and monitoring generate issues when control failures are detected. They can be raised by the user, but most of the time, since testing should be automated as much as possible, the system does that automatically and notifies control owners. Workflow-based notifications alert users on failed tests, design issues, and potential risks such as fraud. The monitoring of key controls allows quick detection of deficiencies, and helps manage risk. Issue remediation should be supported by a powerful workflow capability, ensuring action items are assigned, performed, and ultimately validated for complete resolution of the issue. Effective monitoring of exceptions and remediation also requires the capability to document, rate, and track issues and remediation action items. Finally, all the steps taken in the application need to be recorded to ensure complete auditability of the monitoring process.

Reporting and Certification

Finally, a business process control solution should provide complete visibility on real-time control and issue/remediation information to executives and compliance managers, through a comprehensive set of reports and compliance dashboards. For example, leading-edge solutions can use heat maps that track compliance status with traffic-lighting across geographies. It is critical that the information is real-time and not after the fact. In other words, it reflects the information as it is in the system and aggregates data automatically for all controls. There should be no unnecessary intermediary steps or painful manual consolidation of fragmented data required by the user. The system should enable companies to perform complete reviews and, when required, full certification for each of their entities in scope. This can be done in a hierarchical pattern, for each entity, region, or business unit, for example, starting from the lower level of the organization structure all the way up to corporate headquarters. Certification and sign-off need to be supported by comprehensive workflow so that the completion of certification for all entities of a region, for example, can trigger notification at the regional level to start the certification at that level. This should then be possible to continue to the company level. Finally, it should be possible to freeze data to ensure historical reporting accuracy. It is very important that, once sign-off has been performed, no information for the period can be altered. All the information obviously remains available for reporting and is fully auditable.

In terms of closing the loop, you should look for leading-edge business process control solutions that are tied tightly with risk management systems, allowing both risks and mitigating controls to be orchestrated together and not fragmented as has traditionally been the case. Furthermore, look for business process control solutions that provide a large library of packaged controls for both your existing transactional applications as well as your analytical applications. For example, a process control module should be able to manage control activities around highly sensitive financial processes like the close.

The End Stage

The performance management lifecycle can become a closed loop by unifying the processes we discussed in chapters 1 through 3 and using the software we have discussed in this chapter.

The goal we are working toward is a completely unified system where strategies, goals, metrics, plans, forecasts, analytics, cost modeling, risk, and controls are seamlessly integrated and inform each other. In the future, there will be a system where strategy, plans, actuals, and modeling are all part of one integrated system.

The Vision of the Integrated Performance Management Suite

The integrated performance management suite will allow you to "close the loop" with confidence that your strategy and execution are aligned and working off the same set of goals and metrics.

Here is how the loop is typically applied to software. There are six key components: strategy, plans, actuals (the results of the implemented plan), modeling, risk, and controls. In an integrated performance management suite you should be able to stop and restart the loop at any point, and transfer your emphasis from one component to the other, with the result being that each component will have a correlated effect from the change in the other components.

Here is an example: the strategy calls for increasing overall profitability and one tactic calls for increasing net sales in a certain region. A goal could be created in the system that says, "Increase profitability by X percentage." Then an initiative (a time-bound entity with a set beginning and end date) would be created to which activities and steps would be assigned that take the initiative from strategy to execution. The initiative in this scenario would be, "create a new incentive for the Western region," or "create new sales training and collateral to push the product line." A control would be created to ensure that the incentives and sales training were being administered in accordance with company procedures. That initiative would then be monitored to track its risks as well as its progress toward success, and changes could be made to it without restarting the process. This system allows corrections to be made to the initiative in case a problem is encountered or change of plan is required and the rest of the system will adjust accordingly.

For example, if a plan is created that shows that, as currently designed, the company will not be able to make the forecast for the end of the quarter due to a suddenly increased liquidity risk that has severely reduced working capital, there are several possible responses. Resources can be reallocated in the plan, salespeople or more product incentives can be added to the region, or, you could return to the strategy module and create a new initiative entirely. At any step along the way, you have the ability to intervene and either remand (back-step) or propagate (step-forward) the impact of the strategic decision. You can see how you got to where you are, and you can back up and change the plan, or you can see where the plan is going, and make adjustments to future milestones and resource allocations.

Planning, budgeting, and financial consolidation can now happen on a single platform. There are already products in the marketplace that are approaching this level of fusion natively, combining strategy management (typically isolated in the strategist's realm), planning, analytics, profitability modeling, risk, and controls. Combinations like this are allowing organizations to create and dynamically adjust forecasts in a way that was never before possible.

There are more significant implications: the middle-management shell game known as "budgeting" may soon sing its swan song. Traditional project management may be turned on its ear as well. Here's why: with a top-down project management system that moves only in one direction, managers get allotted a certain amount of money to accomplish a certain project in a certain amount of time. They immediately begin padding their time in excess of what it actually takes to accomplish the project, and if they finish early, they simply bill for whatever's left in the pool. They spend the amount of time the C-suite *thinks* it should take to execute the project, rather than the time it *actually* does take. That time is wasted time. But within an integrated performance management suite, a new level of transparency enters the scene: because the loop is immediately infused with timely analytics, time is wasted no more, and the only padding time-wasting managers will get is the pillow they'll need to protect their backsides from the slamming door.

In this near-future state, profit is linked directly to the plan by way of the actual results, each of which exists in a financial category for consolidation and in a planning category. As "actuals" are collected, we can see whether they actually fit into our plan at a very detailed level, not only at the profit level, but also at the driver level. By doing this, we can also test our models for accuracy and improve them if need be, mid-process.

Public companies that give earnings guidance six weeks into the quarter might discover one week before the earnings call that conditions have changed, and the anticipated revenue will be significantly off the advertised. If their financial model is optimized as we described, and changes can immediately be made to the forecast, they will be able to soften the blow by pre-warning the Street, and by giving management time to come up with a new proposal. By closing the loop with performance management software and meshing your planning with your real-time, actual results, your company will become a finely tuned expectation machine. You might not be able to be profitable every quarter, but if you can manage your shareholders' expectations, you can increase the value of your corporation to your shareholders.

The Integrated Performance Management Suite Orchestrates the Business Network

What we describe in the previous section occurs within the four virtual walls of your organization. Imagine a world where you can actively monitor and engage with the processes that affect your business across your entire business network, including those of your channel and supply chain partners. This is business network transformation. In order for you to have profitable relationships with your ecosystem, you need to establish value between you and your partner network. If, as a company, you are willing to outsource a certain non-core function, you need to know with some degree of detail that you are contracted under a service level agreement that will allow you to continue to maximize your performance. The first step is to link models within the enterprise; between Sales and Finance; between Supply Chain and Finance and between Sales and Marketing.

The next step is to link those models to the corresponding models where there is a handoff of value between your company and the companies in your partner network. The Supply Chain performance management initiative you have in your organization needs to be tied into the Procurement performance management initiative of an organization to which you outsource some portion of your supply chain. In the next generation of performance management, you will use advanced software to link business processes that not only span the enterprise, but also span across multiple companies and allow you to manage the service-level agreements between the hand-offs.

Closing the Loop—Unifying Strategy and Execution Systems to Enable Strategy-Driven Execution

It's important to understand that when we talk about "closing the loop," in essence, we are really talking about two loops, one superimposed above the other. In the upper loop, the performance management lifecycle, all of the modules are connected and each one has a material effect on the other. The second, lower loop is an operations loop, which is connected to the PM lifecycle loop at critical touch points—the points where you actually collect the data and manage the day-to-day processes. On the upper level, the adjustments you make are largely strategic and have long-term time-scales. On the lower level, you are intervening in daily operations, because something in the upper loop tells you the process is not working or needs to be changed.

Today, it is already possible to embed analytics in a sales order screen, empowering someone in the call center to have the same granularity into their effect on strategic execution as a manager today, looking at reports compiled from a quarter's data. This gives them an immediate understanding of their impact on organizational goals and motivates them to take more ownership of their sales or service initiatives.

Soon, these barriers will fall, and you will not have to process what one application is telling you, then set a response in another. The applications that were formerly separate will morph into capabilities that can be completely integrated and will give you a range of options for action. For example, as a manager, you might need to patrol for the over-spenders in your organization. Imagine how much easier it would be to enforce this if your spend analytics capabilities were completely intertwined with your e-sourcing application, and you could directly make the needed changes based on what you learned in the analysis.

In the strategy-driven execution suite we see arriving shortly, the management of your strategy is directly enmeshed with your execution processes. For example, if your goal is that you want to get a 20% net margin increase, then that goal should ultimately physically limit someone engaged in the order-to-cash process from completing a sales transaction with a massive discount that thwarts the attainment of that goal. If you have established that it is a significant risk to have a single supplier for your direct procurement needs and you need to diversify, the possibility of this risk should be surfaced to the Procurement professional engaged within the procure-to-pay process before they make the next purchase from that supplier. Or, the system can leave open the option to override the goal or risk and push the transaction through, but then immediately subject it to analysis against the goal or risk to learn what the impact of that decision is on the ultimate outcome. You can think of these next-generation transactions as "strategy-driven transactions" of the sort summarized in Figure 4-8. The entire behavior of the system is being driven directly by the goals of the organization.

We are already seeing the signs of an integrated strategy-driven execution platform, with a highly flexible mix and match of performance, risk, and transactional components fusing into a business process. Recent advances in BPM technology allow the flexible composition and orchestration of processes from a library of business services instead of the traditional hard-coded processes found in enterprise applications. Just as the building blocks of the core ERP, CRM, and SCM applications that fuel today's execution processes are being decomposed and made available in business service repositories, so too will this occur for the strategy management, planning, profitability, risk, and control applications that form the core subject matter

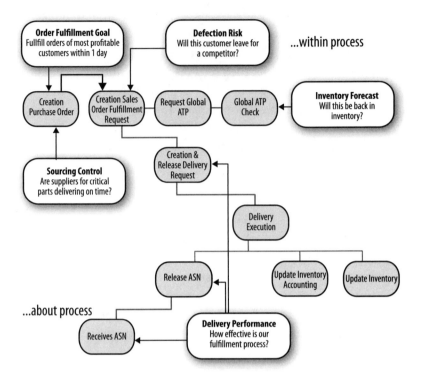

Figure 4-8. Strategy-Driven Execution: The Complete Fusion of Goals, Initiatives, Plans, Forecasts, Risks, Controls, Performance Monitoring, and Optimization with Transactional Processes

of this book. It is from this rich library of business services, orchestrated via BPM technologies, that the next-generation execution and management processes will be coalesced and united to give rise to the vision of strategy-driven execution.

Chapter 5

Leveraging Business Intelligence

In Chapter 2, we explained that as companies put newer and more powerful enterprise applications in place, they found that they were capturing volumes of relevant data that—if properly managed—could be of benefit to the company. In response to this opportunity, software vendors created early iterations of business intelligence (BI) in order to help customers extract, aggregate, manage, and then make use of the data they were generating.

While BI addressed some of the burning issues of data management, its early forms fell far short of becoming a comprehensive performance management solution. In order to understand and optimize a business in a sophisticated fashion, it is necessary to go beyond simple reports produced from a system of record. These and other rudimentary mechanisms of BI do not provide the necessary depth of understanding nor the functionality to analyze and model business processes. A system and methodology must be applied to the data in order to make it useful in helping manage and create value for the modern enterprise.

Performance management has the systems and methodologies, but these while valuable, are not enough on their own. Data must be converted to information. Information must be analyzed in many ways and delivered where needed in many forms. To effectively engage in the successful application of performance management, all of the capabilities of a modern BI platform must be leveraged. BI is a key building block that provides a single platform for data management as well as enhanced functionality such as scorecards, dashboards, and analytics.

In this chapter we will describe how BI can be leveraged as the data infrastructure used to power PM applications in order to enable the vision of modern and pervasive performance management we advocate for.

Unpacking BI, PM, and Analytic Applications

For a number of reasons, not the least of which is the concurrent evolution of BI and performance management and their reliance on data drawn from source systems, there is considerable confusion as to the difference between these two technologies, as well as how they work together to create a unified solution. Simply stated, where does BI end and performance management begin?

In Chapter 2, we briefly answered that question by defining BI as a general-purpose data infrastructure used to enable special-purpose PM applications and methodologies. In many ways, PM applications developed as small, special-purpose reflections of the structure of BI platforms. However, this brief description is incomplete as it is important to understand how these two entities play supporting yet distinct roles within a performance management solution. In addition, it is important to explain how analytic applications are factored into this mix.

What is BI?

Our explanation will start from scratch. Essentially, BI can be defined as the technology capabilities to transform data into information. BI is a general-purpose toolkit that operates independently of any single business application. Its sole mission is to extract raw data from source systems, place it into various data structures such as data marts and data warehouses, and then allow users to perform some query and analysis functions as well as create and distribute enterprise reports.

However, as noted in Chapter 2, BI on its own requires users to possess a relatively high degree of technical skill, necessitating costly and time-consuming intermediation by the IT department between the system and business users. In response, the vendor market developed special-purpose tools, generally referred to as "analytics," to allow business users to manage and manipulate the data held within BI systems in order to support specific business needs.

User Benefits of BI

Throughout this chapter we will describe BI as beneficial to and supportive of performance management. However, on its own BI can provide significant benefits to the company as well as to individual business users.

First, BI provides the tools to create a link between individual KPIs and strategy as well as to demonstrate to employees that their individual work and contributions toward the company's strategy are recognized by management. For example, imagine the benefit of being able to provide each employee with a regular and updated scorecard that shows how the work they are doing is affecting their incentive package?

Second, BI lessens the need for individual employees to reconcile data held in a number of spreadsheets and then integrate that information into the system. Instead, these people have a cleansed pool of information they are able to easily access. In addition, the data is held in a multi-dimensional repository where the business user, not just the IT department, is able to gain the view they need when they need it.

What Are Analytics?

Analytics represent the deployment of BI tooling to specific business processes or sets of business problems in a manner that increases the value of the data held in these systems and removes the need for IT intermediation between the system and business user. Analytics are do-it-yourself mechanisms for increasing understanding.

For example, a sales analytics application can take sales-related data from the BI environment and provide a packaged set of reports, dashboards, and metrics, as well as analysis that provides the business user with a consolidated view into sales processes. This in turn leads to data-driven business decisions rather than operating by gut instinct.

Highlighting the specialized nature of these applications is that they are usually named for the business process they support such as sales analytics, financial analytics, spend analytics, supply chain analytics, and so on.

Performance Management

PM applications are related to, but distinct from BI inspired analytics. Like analytics they perform process specific functions, though for the purposes of performance management methodology these functions can be used across general process flows that cut across the organization. Unlike analytics, PM applications have, out of necessity, relied on their own unique data extraction and consolidation models. This is a legacy of the concurrent yet separate development of these applications from BI and related analytic applications. Simply stated, they could not take advantage of the ETL (extraction, transformation, and loading) capabilities held within BI solutions.

Therefore, PM applications on their own represent localized silos of information and functionality used to optimize specific processes and activities. Because they have to date remained within their relatively process-specific silos it has been difficult to gain a broad view of end-to-end process flows that cut across a number of processes and activities.

Table 5-1. BI, PM, and Integrated BI and PM

BI Alone	Integrated BI and PM	PM Alone
Extraction of raw materials from different data sources into a multi-dimensional repository	Leverages extraction capabilities of BI to link PM functionality and processes such as KPIs and strategy	Provides key processes such as KPIs and strategy, but only for the specific function and siloed application
No processes, just a repository of data	Extends visibility of end-to-end processes by using BI as a platform to consolidate PM applications	Provides visibility to the specific processes for the single PM application
Lack of PM lifecycle or methodology of strategy, monitor, model and optimize	Creates a consistent PM lifecycle across the PM applications	The PM lifecycle varies across the different PM applications

BI and PM Converged

As these technologies have matured and there has been consolidation within the vendor market, a single BI data management platform can be created and integrated with performance management functionality. Essentially, PM applications can be built on top of the BI infrastructure, allowing them to take advantage of data consolidation and aggregation, enterprise reporting, and process-specific analytic functionality. Further, PM applications can be integrated into a system and methodology to provide visibility into end-to-end process flows allowing you to broaden your ability to manage the organization.

By being built on top of the BI infrastructure, PM applications can be much simpler in their design and therefore more powerful in their functionality.

This functionality can then be placed within the PM lifecycle of strategy, plan, monitor, model and optimize.

Performance Management and BI: The Intersection of People, Process, and Technology

Perhaps more than any other management solution, performance management represents the intersection between people, process, and technology. It is the means and foundation upon which corporate leaders can begin to understand the intricate relationships between these three areas and how they can best be optimized to better work as a unified whole to support continuous improvement.

The glue, though, that is able to link people, process, and technology together as well as integrate them, is BI. It is therefore important to describe how BI relates to performance management in these three areas.

People: Supporting a Culture of Performance Management

In terms of decision-making ability and quality, most companies could be described as existing within an opinion-based as opposed to a fact-based environment. For example, according to a survey by *The Economist* magazine,[1] more than 60% of respondents indicated they follow gut instinct more than 50% of the time when making decisions; only 22% said they have the right amount of information to make informed business decisions; and 77% believe they make bad business decisions because they don't have sufficient information.

One of the key elements acting to propel this rather frail decision-making culture is the failure to provide a trusted and integrated information management platform in an enterprise-wide manner.

The Business User

Historically, many of the larger systems used by business today have been extremely complex and, therefore, out of necessity have been owned by the IT department. One of the central tenets of performance management is the emphasis on business user–friendly systems that remove the need for constant intermediation from the IT department.

---

[1] *The Economist* Intelligence Unit, "In Search of Clarity: Unraveling the Complexities of Executive Decision-Making," 2007.

For example, as business users have sought different types of data and different views into transactional data, they have often had to submit a ticket, or some other message requesting support from IT for one of the central enterprise systems, in order to get what they needed. As a result, the IT department would often have a large queue of requests from all of the business units. Often, IT would then have to estimate the type and timeframe of the work being requested and send it back for another person to validate and approve the expense before actually working on it.

Worst of all, the resulting change to the system or report would sometimes not conform to the initial needs of the user, causing even more of a delay as it is reworked. To say the least, from the business user's perspective, as well as that of the IT department, this model has a number of flaws, which have led to a go-by-the-gut culture of decision-making at many companies.

However, one of the fundamental aspects of BI—as an information management platform and via its core components—is the ability to deliver information to business users in the way that they want it, in a

---

Business User Personae

Business users have different personae and varying interactions with the BI system, even though each is directly connected to the practice of performance management. Understanding these personae can help you see how BI can flexibly support their needs.

Information Professionals—People who actively use and work with BI tools, between 10–15% of the business user population.

Information Consumers—People who don't directly interact with the BI tools, but who consume the information generated by these tools, representing 50–60% of the business user population.

Information Prosumers—People who work with ideas and need to find facts quickly, which means that they are not only generating information, but consuming it as well. For example, in the Web 2.0 world, people not only consume content on wikis and blogs, but they also generate content. Prosumers represent about 30% of the business user population.

Advanced Power Users—A small group of people who use highly specialized and complex tools such as OLAP (Online Analytical Processing) and other advanced analytics and predictive applications. Essentially, they take historical data and apply algorithms to model future results.

A New Role for IT

Despite being somewhat removed as an intermediating layer between business users and the systems they use, the IT department still has two important roles to play.

The first is to act as the systems administrator—performing system maintenance, installations, and applying various support packages.

The second, and arguably the most important to the success of the organization, is to move from being the designer and creator of solutions to something more like a chemistry teacher with a lab full of students. In this model, IT delivers software to users and then steps back and observes the results. The experiments that work should be replicated and leveraged to improve the overall performance of the organization.

timely fashion, that's relevant to their business unit, and in a familiar or easy-to-use interface, so that they can make meaningful decisions during their day-to-day work. Further, the core components of BI, such as dashboards, KPI monitoring, reports, and analytics, should be designed in such a manner that business users are almost able to use them intuitively. They should also be capable of being embedded in the applications, including personal productivity tools,that these people use. For example, why shouldn't a sales manager have access to a meaningful and relevant dashboard on a handheld device?

BI, as a platform and its core components, allows mere mortals to gain timely access to the information they need to make decisions and do their jobs better.

Changing the Culture

The most important aspect of any kind of performance management system is the people that interact with it. It is critical for them to understand the drive for performance management so that they then can become hungry for improved performance on an individual basis.

So, when a company considers leveraging BI in order to sustain and support a performance management system, understanding the cultural change that must take place and getting the change management process right is vitally important. Consider for a moment the *Economist* statistics about how most business decisions are made by instinct—going from an opinion-based environment to a fact-based environment is an important cultural change. It is not enough to simply adopt the technology; leadership must also engage in an appropriate change management exercise in order to ensure that people are properly using the system to create accurate information, and then use that information as the basis of their business decisions.

Table 5-2. Types of Users and Decisions in a Typical Organization

Type of Decision	Decision-Making Timeline	Value of Any One Decision	Decisions and Data Needs	Sourcing	Tolerance for Latency
Strategic	Weeks / Months	Months / Quarters	Few in Number; Cross-Domain	Data Marts / Cubes	High
Tactical	Days / Hours	Days / Weeks	20x; Cross-and-Single-Domain	Data Warehouse / Enterprise Apps	Medium to Low
Operational	Seconds / Minutes	Minutes / Hours	100x; Single-Domain	Enterprise Apps / ODS	Very Low

Process: Feeding the Model with Trusted Data

All of the processes related to performance management require trusted data, and BI is the tool that provides that data.

Linking Strategy and Operations

BI supports creation of an information management platform that can act as a central repository for transactional data as well as the KPIs and other measures that will be used to monitor and then model and optimize processes to better support strategy. BI is able to do this by extracting data from a number of different and heterogeneous sources and then reconciling that data into a single version of the truth. And it is able to ensure data consistency in a timely fashion.

By centrally storing KPIs on a single platform, you ensure their consistency, from strategy to plan to financial consolidation to profitability and cost. You use the same information and definitions for KPIs throughout the process and across the enterprise, ensuring that you are comparing apples to apples. Such comparability can never be achieved with confidence using spreadsheets.

A central information management platform and repository also ensures greater efficiency across the various performance management processes built on top of the platform, which in turn reduces the total cost of ownership. As the data platform for performance management, BI eliminates or reduces the need to manage a number of siloed systems and processes. In turn, the amount of hardware and other infrastructure is reduced because the PM applications no longer require their own distinct data consolidation and aggregation models. Everything can be run and installed on one BI environment.

Collaboration

As with nearly every other activity, strong collaboration relies on the use of trusted and reliable information in order to ensure that quality inputs will lead to quality outputs. Therefore, BI—as well as performance management—capabilities should be embedded within the collaborative environment via the tools that people use to connect and communicate with each other such as IM, wikis, and web browsers, for example.

Once BI is embedded within these other tools, they can be used to bring reliable third-party information from the Web. As such, this further exemplifies the ability to mesh quantitative information with qualitative information to provide contextual information along with transactional data—the ability to tell the story behind the numbers.

The BI platform also provides the infrastructure to create alerts, interactive forums, and many other ways to inform a wide array of people of the need for more information or to engage in a process to address an anomaly. In addition, since data will have a high degree of granularity as well as contextual information, users will be able to drill down into the alert to get a deeper insight into what is behind it.

In all, performance management naturally leads to the desire and drive to collaborate. In order to get the biggest payoff from the company's efforts, it's important to have a mature means for collaboration and gathering information, of which BI plays an important part.

Be More Predictive

We mentioned that the system is better able to alert a wider array of people and then feed a strong collaborative process with reliable inputs. BI is also able to help users act more proactively by supporting predictive analysis of information and alerts.

In the past, companies were able to generate a lot of reports, but the problem was that analysts were then tasked with taking all of those reports and trying to determine what they said about the business. They looked for variances and any other trends hidden in the data that could provide visibility into underlying issues. If they noticed anything, they would then have to sift through even more data in order to try and determine the nature of the issue.

This could be done in a general sense—we are selling less of a certain product—but there were barriers to doing this in a more specific sense— we are selling less of a product because a regional network has lost some functionality.

However, BI integrated with performance management creates a system where users are alerted to variances and then are able to drill down through the alert to find the source of the problem.

For example, with a BI platform, business users have the ability to be notified when there is a variance in a key indicator they are responsible for keeping an eye on, and then they can drill down to find the root cause of the variance. Once the variation has been identified, it is then possible to take action outside of the BI platform to resolve the issue before the impact is more severe.

It is also possible to use predictive analytics with historical data to gain a better view of how best to optimize a strategy or operational activity. Rather than have someone take whatever information may be available and try to manually work out the best strategy, the system can provide the information and perform the analysis to support the business user's decision-making process, leading to better outcomes. And since the KPIs live in the BI system where they can be consistent across the organization, the view gained by the business user is likely better aligned with strategy. And as this capability matures, the integrated analytic capabilities will be able to provide recommendations as well.

Enhanced Usability of Unstructured Data

In previous incarnations, BI was not able to incorporate unstructured data in a meaningful way, which made searching difficult.

However, BI is moving toward a vision where users will be able to search for unstructured data and mine it to provide additional context.

The benefit to this capability is that as companies create volumes of data—structured and unstructured—the BI system will be able to perform broad searches and combine the results with analytic software to enhance the usefulness of search results. This means that users of any stripe will be able to seamlessly search documents and other text fields held in corporate wikis, blogs, and email to gain an understanding of the drivers behind specific issues, activities, and processes.

Further, the means by which unstructured data is used to provide context to quantitative data can also be greatly improved as the BI market matures. For example, consider a customer call center where the primary metrics for how they are managed revolve around issues such as customer wait times, throughput, successful close of a ticket, and so on. They are easy to measure on a dashboard or through some other BI component, but these measures don't provide insight about customer sentiment in any kind of automated way. The call may have closed with the successful resolution of the customer's issue, but was the customer happy about the experience? Were they using certain phrases to indicate overall satisfaction with the process, product, and company? Or were they saying thanks for fixing a bad product or that they felt the company was providing inferior support as compared to a competitor?

Being able to capture these sentiments in an automated way is key. Functionality contained in the BI platform is able to understand linguistics associated with the interaction, such as the kinds of adjectives used in conjunction with certain nouns. Therefore, the platform could capture and aggregate not just the quantitative analysis of calls—using metrics such as wait time—but also the qualitative aspects of calls—customer satisfaction with the experience.

What this represents, in a sense, is the right brain (structured data) comporting with the left brain (unstructured data) within the context of BI and performance management to help provide the ability to analyze and manage this one very important aspect of the modern enterprise.

Technology: Tying It All Together

The story of performance management and BI is one of integration. Initially, performance management systems—such as those for managing strategy, risk, profitability, financial consolidation, planning, and others—operated as siloed and self-sufficient applications not only in terms of the functionality provided to the company, but also in the manner by which they extracted data from source systems. For example, a strategy management system would have what could be described as "connectors" to the source transactional applications in order to extract and aggregate the data required to properly perform its strategy management duties. As such, each of the performance management systems contained its own siloed extraction and aggregation model.

This duplication of processes among these systems—as well as weaknesses in data reconciliation—meant that not only were they disconnected in terms of leveraging their functionality into a performance management system, but also they were highly inefficient and could be unreliable. This led to issues such as questionable data integrity; multiple data versions being used for separate, but linked processes; inability to easily share data across operational areas; lack of data lineage; and inefficiencies as multiple systems pull from transactional systems.

For example, it is common for companies to have separate tools for financial consolidation and planning, and while these two logically link, there is generally a lack of integration between them. Essentially, the planning tool is extracting transactional data as a basis upon which to build a forecast of the company's future performance. Meanwhile, the financial consolidation system is extracting what is fundamentally the same data in order to feed it into a reporting system for statutory and some management reporting. However, though each relies on what is basically the same data, there isn't any integration between the two to share the data. And if data from one is placed in the other, it is usually done manually. Therefore, the company has one system that consolidates data on profit, another that creates a forecast on future profit, and another system that provides relatively detailed reporting on profits, and all are using, albeit separately, what is functionally the same data.

The primary issue, though, is that, in a spreadsheet-dominated environment supported by multiple consolidation models, there will be significant inconsistencies in the underlying data that emerges from each system. This means that trying to reconcile all of these numbers is immensely time-consuming, not to mention trying to trace back to the source of the numbers for auditing and related purposes.

The Architecture of BI

BI has been around long enough that it has been divided and subdivided into numerous specialized areas, each of which is literally the subject of academic dissertations. While those interested in improving their performance management practices do not have to delve deeply into all of these areas, it is quite helpful to understand the breadth of the functionality that is included under the umbrella of BI.

One of the fastest ways to get up to speed in the many areas of specialization in BI is shown in Figure 5-1, which summarizes the BI stack.

The rest of this chapter will describe the elements of this stack that are most relevant to performance management.

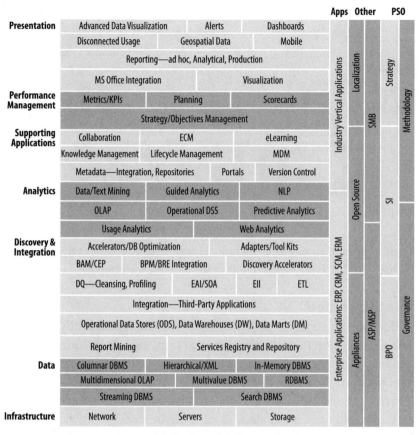

Figure 5-1. Business Intelligence Stack
(Source: Forrester Research, *Forrester Wave™*—Enterprise Business Intelligence Platforms, Q3 2008)

The Data Layer: Building the Foundation with Enterprise Information Management

Without data there is no performance management. One of the most important functions that BI plays with respect to PM applications is to assemble a clean and consistent set of data from many sources. Figure 5-2 provides an outline of the various components involved in that process.

Data exists all over the enterprise in a myriad of formats, types, and shapes. The purpose of the BI platform's data layer is to obtain data from all of the various places it sits and place it into a data warehouse or data mart after transforming and harmonizing it from various sources so that it can then be used by BI tools, analytic applications, and PM applications. The

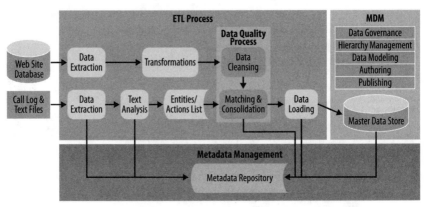

Figure 5-2. The Data Layer

specific types of capabilities include data integration, text extraction, data quality, master data management, and the data warehouse.

Data Integration

Most organizations do not have access to a single, beautifully integrated transactional system, but instead many point systems (accounts payable, accounts receivable, and treasury are examples), or multiple ERP, CRM, and SCM systems. Data integration technology enables a process called ETL, or extract, transform, and load. The data is extracted from the various systems, moved into a central place where it can be transformed via matching, duplication, or by having rules applied to it, and then loaded into the data warehouse. Typically data integration technology works with structured data such as database tables that power business applications, but it has become increasingly better at accommodating semi-structured information such as XML, a common data interchange format that web services are based on, and even text in documents, emails, PDFs, and so forth.

Text Extraction

The vast majority of information in the enterprise is unstructured, such as the text in documents, email, or PDFs, but until fairly recently, there has been little technology to mine the wealth of information in that data and combine it for analysis in BI paradigms. Text extraction technologies can convert the unstructured text data in documents into structured data that can then be tied to the structured data from other enterprise applications to gain much deeper insight. For example, with only structured data, typically extracted from standard data integration technologies, it is possible to extract the reason codes that call center agents choose from a drop-down list in a CRM system when customers call to complain, and put these codes into a data warehouse where they can be analyzed by BI tools. This might give us information such as how many customers called because of a "warranty issue" or because of a "billing dispute." With text extraction, it would be possible to extract the notes from the call center agent's conversation with the customer, as well as the customer's own inquiry submitted to the web channel, and analyze the root causes for why they called and even their sentiment toward your company! For example, one could learn that the number one phrase that kept occurring in the customer's submitted web requests was "unhappy because handle is broken," which would then spur an investigation into the quality of the most recent shipment of the product from the warehouse.

Data Quality

Ensuring data quality is a task that is never completed. It is always possible to invest more to improve the quality of data. The tough question is how good is good enough? Figure 5-3 shows the various processes that are involved in ensuring data quality.

The quality of data in the myriad systems in the enterprise is often quite poor. Customer addresses may not be completed correctly, financial account names may be misspelled, and product names may be unnecessarily duplicated, and this makes it impossible to obtain a consistent view of what is going on in the enterprise. Data quality capabilities in a BI platform provide built-in features for validating data against business rules and auditing the execution of data movement. According to Forrester Research,[2] the criteria for a leading data quality solution include:

- Data hygiene to cleanse and standardize data
- Data matching to establish relationships between data
- Data merging to consolidate data
- Data profiling to gain insight into what data you actually have
- Third-party data enrichment for more complete data

---

[2] *Forrester Research, Information Managers: Deliver Trusted Data With A Focus On Data Quality,* January 3, 2008

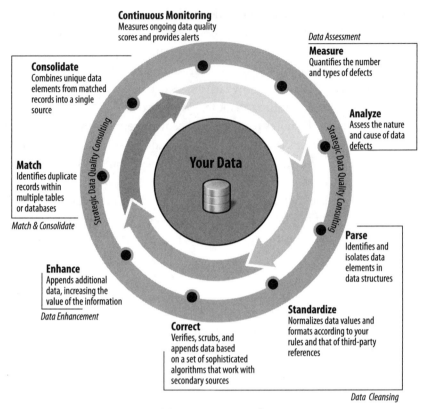

Figure 5-3. Data Quality

Master Data Management

Master data management (MDM) ensures the consistency, accuracy, stewardship, and accountability of the enterprise's core information, thus enabling organizations to eliminate endless debates about "whose data is right." Master data is characterized by being enduring in nature, and is typically associated with real world entities: customers, products, vendors, parts, assets, employee information, general ledger, cost centers, plant information, and equipment records. BI platforms allow for creating not only standard definitions of how the enterprise wants to define customers or contracts or products, but also standard definitions of the individual customers or contracts or products themselves that ensure their uniqueness. For example, an MDM solution can ensure that the chart of accounts in an ERP system (one of the key pieces of master data in Finance) is synchronized with the chart of accounts in a financial consolidation system. An MDM solution also puts a governance process in place that determines who is allowed to change what master data. For example, it's not a good idea for any user of an ERP system to be able to change the chart of accounts master data, but when they do, it should not be finalized until approved by someone who has the authority to make those changes.

The Data Warehouse

Ultimately, regardless of where data originates, once it has been transformed, cleansed, and harmonized by the aforementioned technologies, it needs a home, a safe container in which to reside. This is often the data warehouse or data mart. In the data warehouse or data mart, the information from the various systems is structured in a standardized way that is optimized for analytical purposes. All of the BI tools, analytic applications, and PM applications then draw from the data in the data warehouse to give a single, consistent view of the information from across the business. Data warehouses are exploding in size in every organization, and as they do so, the amount of time it takes to retrieve data often becomes correspondingly longer. Recent advances with in-memory technology allow the entire data set to be loaded into main memory, instead of in disk-based storage, where it can be accessed many hundreds of times faster.

The Business Logic Layer

Once you have a foundation of high-quality data, it is possible to build layers of meaning on top of this data and attempt to draw inferences and recognize events and trends of importance. The business logic layer of the BI stack has various mechanisms that each play this role in different ways.

Semantic Layers

On its journey toward becoming information and reaching the end consumer, data needs to be ascribed the appropriate semantics, or meaning. Technologies referred to as semantic layers provide this translation layer between that which is understandable by a database administrator (table XYZ.row 123) into something that is understandable by the end-user (customer address). In a semantic layer, a model of the business's key objects of analysis, such as customers, products, and accounts, are mapped against the correct data warehouse or data mart data structures and then arranged hierarchically and related to one another. For example, in the semantic layer, one can define that a customer has a name, address, zip code, and telephone number, and that these attributes are arranged hierarchically with cities belonging to states, states belonging to countries, and countries belonging to continents. The semantic layer also defines the key business metrics of the organization and how these map to the underlying data structures, as well as prescribes how metrics relate to each other. This is where the establishment of an enterprise-wide metrics framework, a crucial facet to enabling enterprise-wide performance management, becomes possible. Semantic layers provide the ability to model calculations, either through an easy-to-understand language for business users or through visual metaphors, compose calculations from existing calculations (such as Profit = Revenue − Cost), and provide the ability to search, discover, reuse, and improve these calculations.

Metadata Management

Metadata is literally "data about data," that is, data that describes other data. It describes and ties together all of the various facets of a software system. In a BI platform, a metadata management system connects all the various components of the platform, from the source systems, to the data integration and data quality repositories, to the data warehouse, to the semantic layer, and all the way to the end-user reporting tools and PM applications. One capability this provides is to understand the lineage of data as it flows through the system. For example, a user can right click on a field in one of their reports and then see where this data came from, tracing it all the way back to the source screen in their CRM system so they know exactly what they are looking at. Another capability metadata management systems provide is the ability to assess change impacts when some part of the system changes. For example, a business user can see that if he changes the chart of accounts in his source ERP system, then it will impact these data integration mappings, these semantic layer objects, and ultimately the specific reports he receives every day.

Business Process Management

Business process management suites are not necessarily part of a BI platform, but are increasingly being linked with them. BPM suites support the entire process improvement cycle, from definition to implementation, monitoring, analysis, and ongoing optimization. BPM suites enable intelligent information to be injected into processes, as well as provide intelligent information about processes in a very flexible fashion. Steps in the process can be simulated, optimized, and rearranged to provide a very agile balance between efficiency and effectiveness. Reports, dashboards, and analytics can be seamlessly embedded into every step of a business process to empower the user, so they have the most timely and relevant information with which to make a decision within the process. For example, infusing BI into BPM can provide an environment where, as part of an existing warranty renewal business process, an intelligent analytic that calculates the customer's profitability and lifetime value can be executed at a crucial step in the process to determine if they should be offered an automatic warranty extension or not. With a BPM system infused with BI, when conditions change, it is not a difficult task to change the process very quickly by rearranging the process steps visually, unlike more traditional business software applications whose processes are coded directly in the software. Tying to business activity monitoring and the events captured there, events can also activate a business process so that the business event can be followed up and acted upon.

Business Rules

Business rules engines are highly useful in BI environments for automating high-volume operational decisions that need to be made in real time. The beauty of the rules approach, much like the BPM approach, is that the rules themselves are externalized from the application, allowing them to be changed much more easily, and quite often by the business users themselves, without deep IT involvement or coding. Business rules systems facilitate complex rule-based decisions (such as making automatic pricing or credit decisions) and can be used for responsibility determination (if this occurs, assign it to this person), recognition of business events (if this occurs then do this), routing (if this occurs, send it along this path), and parameter thresholds and tolerance (constraint rules).

Business Activity Monitoring

Given the dynamic and rapidly changing pace of so many variables in the enterprise, it has become crucial for business applications to both produce and respond to events—signals sent from a system whenever a key criteria changes. For example, in a supply chain system, it might be necessary to send an event every time the stock threshold reaches a certain value to alert the appropriate party. BAM provides real-time access to key business metrics that are updated from captured events as they arrive, not after the fact. The reasons for deploying BAM are to monitor key business objectives, anticipate operational risks, and reduce the time between a material event and taking effective action.[3] It can be especially useful for observing the patterns that are taking place in the enterprise so that swift action can be taken. For example, a BAM system monitoring events from a call center switch can display very clearly that a massive queue has suddenly developed and there aren't enough call center agents on staff to handle the load, allowing the call center manager to react by rerouting some of the calls to another call center, thus averting a serious customer satisfaction crisis.

Data Mining and Predictive Analytics

Data mining identifies patterns in data to estimate the likely outcome based on prior instances. Data mining capabilities provide a rich toolset of algorithms that facilitate a whole host of analyses, including correlation analysis, regression analysis, cluster analysis, factor analysis, and many others. Data mining can be very powerful for finding previously unexplored relationships between data sets or finding the root cause of the relationship between data sets. For example, an analyst looking at millions of records of aggregated data may not be looking for the unintuitive relationship between home prices and credit score fluctuations, and data mining techniques could show that home prices are related to credit score fluctuations through mortgage applications. On the other hand, the same rich library of algorithms could also be used to actually predict future trends based on the existing data at hand. For example, predictive analytics can be used to look at the existing data for a retail store in terms of the number of visitors it gets per day and predict how this volume will change over the course of the year using techniques that can decipher the seasonality of the relationships between variables.

The User Layer

There are many different styles of reporting, as well as other types of capabilities in the user layer, that are useful for different types of users and different end goals.

Formatted reporting. Formatted reporting tools provide an incredibly high degree of control and flexibility regarding the final product. It is possible to produce finished, publication-quality reports using these tools that can be distributed to a very large numbers of users in short periods of time. For example, pixel-perfect formatted reporting is often used for reports

---

[3] *Gartner Research Business Intelligence Summit 2008, Processing Events Into Real-Time Awareness With Business Activity Monitoring*

that will be made available external to the company that are of significant importance, such as a profit and loss statement.

Query and analysis. Query and analysis tools allow end users to easily build or personalize existing queries from databases, and the reports build off of those queries to answer their own business questions. Users can interact and analyze their data to gain more clarity, for example by ranking, sorting, or even applying advanced formulas. For example, a supply chain manager can use a query and analysis tool to look for the right data in the data warehouse and query it, pull it onto his screen, and start manipulating it to understand how quickly the inventory is turning over by warehouse or what the capacity is of each work center.

Dashboards and visualization. Forrester Research defines dashboards as "one style of interactive user interface, designed to deliver historical, current, and predictive information typically represented by key performance indicators (KPIs) using visual cues to focus user attention on important conditions, trends, and exceptions" (from *Forrester Research, Dashboards, Turning Information into Decisions*). They are often very popular with managers and senior executives as a one-stop shop window into the performance of their business. Dashboarding products often have a rich library of pre-built components, skins, maps, charts, gauges, and selectors. They may also have specific visualizations relevant to people working in specific departments. For example, salespeople often use the metaphor of a pipeline to represent the funnel of opportunities as they progress toward close, and pipeline visualizations can be very effective in communicating this information.

OLAP. OLAP, or Online Analytical Processing, provides analysts with a very comprehensive set of capabilities to slice and dice data along many different dimensions. Because these tools are geared toward analysts, they provide a comprehensive range of business and time calculations well suited for this type of user. OLAP tools have long been used by financial analysts to slice and dice financial data, for example by drilling down from high-level profit and loss statements to individual business units to understand the root cause of the increase in a company's margins.

Alerting. Events captured and filtered in the business logic layer through BAM or BPM or business rules need to be expressed to the end-user through some type of alerting mechanism. Alerts are typically triggered by a data condition, such as a low safety stock threshold, which is then visualized for the user or sent to their email or mobile device. Alerts can be especially powerful when they inform the user of events that are relevant to them but are in a part of the business they normally don't have visibility to. For example, for a CFO, an alerting infrastructure can provide the ability to gather a wide range of non-financial information from event sources like Supply Chain Management systems for order fulfillment and logistics management, and from other operational areas of the business that may have a material impact on the company's stock price, along with external sources like credit ratings, stock market changes, key bond market ratios, and so forth. When key criteria are met, for example if the inventory levels reach a point where the company is in danger of having too little working capital, alerts proactively inform the CFO so she can take action, for example by freeing up cash from other parts of the business.

Search. The runaway success and simplicity of Google have inspired users of BI systems to ask why they too cannot get information from their business applications so easily. With search capabilities being natively integrated into BI platforms, users are able to find reports that they, or others within the organization, ran previously by searching on the titles, rows, and columns which can save them time from having to write the report themselves. More sophisticated search capabilities allow users to type free text questions like "What are the top 10 sales opportunities for this quarter?" and have the system automatically run a query for them and return an answer in the form of a report. Finally, search can also couple the analyses that a user might be currently looking at with a list of relevant other information that a user might be interested in seeing. For example, if the user highlights "Procter & Gamble" on their report, systems can automatically search and display in a sidebar all the other related reports relevant to "Procter & Gamble."

Collaborative decision spaces. Leading edge BI vendors are starting to build capabilities into their software that deliver on the original vision of BI, which was to facilitate decision making for everyone. Combining technologies such as wikis and portals with social networking tools and other collaboration tools, as well as the rich content in their BI tools, analytic applications, and PM applications, vendors are starting to deliver collaborative decision-making platforms that enable business users to find or create information, coordinate people, and monitor activities to make better fact-based decisions and take action. These platforms allow users to find relevant and related information quickly (internal and external, structured and unstructured, transactional and analytical) to:

- Solve problems, decide, and act on those decisions, all using linked and related factual information
- Monitor all activities, problems, and information

- Collaborate with others to make decisions, collect opinions and information, and resolve problems
- Share and communicate problems, actions, and decisions via email and portals in any work environment

For example, selecting a new supplier for a given part often requires the involvement of multiple parties to provide different perspectives on the value of each potential supplier. Using collaborative decision spaces, these users can now collaborate in a single space; add key information; review activities, comments, recommendations and decisions; and ultimately act on their collective insight to sign up the best new supplier and publish both their thinking and research for others.

All of these user-layer capabilities should be available in any environment the user prefers to interact in, be it portals, Microsoft Office, mobile devices, rich Internet applications, or others, and should be able to be flexibly combined into end-user mash-ups that allow the user to meet their information needs without the involvement of IT.

The Promise of BI Integration with PM

While siloed systems represent disunity, the vision of performance management integrated with BI is one of unity. Essentially, think of BI as an intermediating data management platform between the transactional applications and the performance management systems. In this model, BI acts to extract, aggregate, and transform data to create a repository of trusted information with a number of capabilities surrounding it. The PM applications maintain their individual aggregation models for their own unique purposes, but pull from a trusted BI platform.

Further, BI, if designed correctly, should also support users as they seek to carve and pare information in order to support related capabilities such as reporting, dashboards, and scorecards, not to mention the ability to manipulate the data into nearly any view the user needs. This latter capability reflects a point made earlier in this book that, in order to fully support performance management, it is necessary to create a multidimensional repository of trusted data.

In all, these capabilities mean that the PM applications are able to focus on core competencies while BI does the heavy lifting of extraction and ensuring data quality and usability. Further, as they move forward with their efforts, companies are able to build out their performance management capabilities in an integrated fashion by using BI as the core data model.

BI Capabilities

The capabilities of BI can be placed into two broad categories: Information Discovery and Delivery, and Information Management.

Information Discovery and Delivery provides a set of functions that includes query, reporting and analysis, search, and advanced analytics. The net benefits to the company include, but are not limited to:

- Reduced dependency on IT by providing business users with more information in a far more intuitive manner

- Ad hoc query and reporting that can be shared across the organization

- Integrated analysis tools that can be broadly used by the various user personae defined above

- Collaboration on data analysis

- Drilling through data lineage to its source

- Multidimensional views of the data

- Support for monitoring, modeling, and optimization

- Embedding in the personal productivity tools that most of the company's employees are using, such as Microsoft Office and handheld devices

- Ability to seek answers to spontaneous questions and follow iterative interrogatory paths

Information Management provides functions to support data integration, federation, data quality, text and sentiment analysis, metadata management, master data management, and data mart solutions. Benefits to the company include:

- Greater agility in terms of faster time to market and collaboration

- Universal access to trusted information via improved data governance and end-to-end metadata management

- Improved operational performance via a single repository and platform

- Accelerated consolidation and ability to derive value from mergers and acquisitions

These capabilities then lead to a number of benefits beyond efficiency and data quality:

- Creating an audit trail
- Knowledge of who is using the data

- Repurposing of data and information as it is generated throughout the enterprise
- Easy sharing of data across operational boundaries because it is managed in a single BI environment

Importantly from the CFO's perspective, data consistency also ensures a faster close as well as a heightened control environment.

As we noted above, the former model is about disconnected systems performing redundant data-related operations. With an integrated BI data management platform, the company is now able to unify the various PM applications in a manner that supports a vision of a systemic and structured model of continuous optimization and improvement. Ultimately, users performing functions related to planning and consolidation, for example, will have a system that does the planning, the consolidation, and performs the analysis and reporting seamlessly and within a single user environment.

As performance management and BI continue to evolve, albeit as distinct yet unified systems, the lines between transactional and analytic applications will be blurred to the point where a seamless user experience is created.

A Few Recommendations

- In the short term, when performing data integration, ensure that it is being done in the BI system and then transferred to the PM applications

- Mid term, seek out good BI standardization and integration solutions

- Long term, bring in solutions that provide tight integration between PM applications and the BI platform so that the applications are utilizing key components of the platform

Chapter 6

Managing Risk and Ensuring Compliance

Performance Management is characterized by integration, a holistic view of the enterprise and a collective instrumentation of the enterprise. This approach is especially relevant to the topic of governance, risk, and compliance (GRC). You can't effectively manage and optimize your business without visibility on the risks associated with your strategy.

Governance, risk, and compliance form a three-legged stool. Each one plays an essential role in supporting the organization. Ultimately, good governance is the result of good risk and compliance management (along with a few other factors such as performance management and strategic planning).

Let's establish some basic definitions:

- **Governance.** The culture, policies, processes, laws, and institutions that define the structure by which companies are directed and managed. Corporate governance includes the relationships among stakeholders and the goals for which the corporation is governed
- **Risk.** The effect of uncertainty on organizational objectives. Risk management is the coordinated activities to direct and control an organization to realize opportunities while mitigating the negative consequences of events

- **Compliance.** The act of adhering to, and demonstrating adherence to, external laws and regulations as well as corporate policies and procedures. Compliance management is the coordinated activities to stay within internally and externally mandated boundaries

We can think of Performance Management as a GPS system in your car. It alerts us when there are risks in the road ahead, such as an accident blocking a certain highway, traffic congestion, or a bridge closed for construction. Using this information, we can replot our route to make sure we still get to our destination.

In this analogy, our destination represents the strategic goals of the business. The roadblocks and weather alerts represent the risks we encounter while pursuing that strategy. Compliance is following the rules of the road, such as traffic signs or speed limits. Heeding these rules helps us get to our destination. If we ignore a red light, we're more likely to get into an accident; if we disobey the speed limit we're more likely to get pulled over by a police officer. Compliance is also a matter of adhering to internal requirements such as keeping tires inflated to the proper pressure or maintaining proper oil pressure. Needless to say, ignoring compliance has bad consequences: our travel time is slower and the costs are higher.

While compliance to external regulations has been a necessity of business practice for as long as commerce has existed, it took center stage as a strategic topic in the corporate boardroom with the passage of the Sarbanes-Oxley Act of 2002. Sarbanes-Oxley, often abbreviated SOX, was a landmark U.S. law enacted to restore public trust in corporate accountability and auditor independence in the wake of a series of scandals which severely damaged public trust in corporate governance practices. It includes two key sections: section 302, which requires that the CEO and CFO of public companies certify financial reports, and section 404, which requires companies to report on the adequacy of internal controls. Since that time, the rate of increase in regulations across the world has picked up significantly, but many individuals still associate compliance with SOX and financial reporting.

Similarly, risk management practices have also existed for many years, being especially prevalent in small corners of every organization such as treasury, and in certain industries such as insurance and banking. Like compliance, risk management practices have evolved to their greatest maturity in financial domains. Credit risk is the risk of economic loss suffered due to the default of a borrower or counterparty and deals with how far an organization extends itself in the accounting world. Market risk refers to exposure to potential loss that would result from changes in market prices or rates and focuses on the risk of loss surrounding products, services, and stakeholder value in the markets the organization competes in. Both credit risk and market risk have been clearly established as formal disciplines for some time.

In the past, organizations often took a narrow view of GRC. They viewed GRC only in financial terms and exiled it to a pocket of the organization. They also tended to view the risk portion of GRC only in terms of non-compliance, for example, the risk of someone violating a legal regulation. This "silo" approach failed to take a comprehensive look at the organization or integrate risk and compliance with day-to-day operations and strategy. Instead, companies approached risk and compliance as a set of chores to be checked off rather than as inherently strategic concerns.

This "checklist" approach to managing GRC is myopic, dangerous, and no longer viable in today's dynamic, turbulent business environment. Risk exposure is increasing significantly for businesses. The complexity of

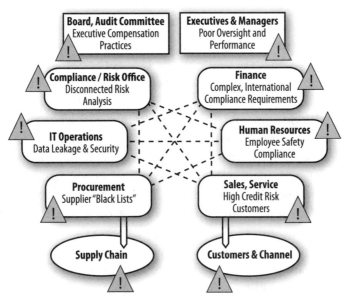

*Figure 6-1. Fragmented Alignment between Strategy,
Corporate Policy, and Operations*

compliance has increased considerably. Meanwhile, the readiness of most organizations has flattened out. Ask about risk and compliance and you may get a response such as, "You mean SOX? Yes, we did that a few years back." Such an approach completely misses the myriad ways that the wide variety of risk and compliance concerns impact today's businesses and how an integrated approach to managing GRC can help drive success.

In this chapter, we discuss the evolution of the risk and compliance islands into a modern, holistic view of GRC. We make the case for how GRC must be woven into the fabric of the performance management lifecycle in order for you to truly be able to optimize your business performance.

Dollars and Sense: The Business Case for GRC

Many pressures and market forces are driving businesses to take a more integrated approach to GRC. Many organizations are developing comprehensive compliance schemes that go far beyond both government mandates and basic risk management. Why? Because it makes good business sense. "Frankly and unabashedly, they are doing so because it is good for business," Gartner Research stated in one 2007 report. "Risk management not only can reduce the cost of compliance, but also can improve decision making."

Let's look at some of the reasons why GRC means good business.

Regulation

Governments around the world are taking a more active regulatory role. The best-known measure in the U.S. is the Sarbanes-Oxley Act (SOX), alluded to earlier. SOX was enacted in 2002 in response to a series of corporate and accounting scandals at companies such as Enron, Arthur Andersen, WorldCom, and Tyco International. The law, also known as the Public Company Accounting Reform and Investor Protection Act, imposed more stringently enhanced standards for public company boards, management, and public accounting firms and prison terms of up to 20 years for people who distort or conceal financial reporting information. It has been called the most far-reaching reform in corporate regulation since the Great Depression.

Yet SOX is not the only regulation at play, and in a global economy where a single company's business extends into far-reaching business networks, U.S. regulations are just one facet of a far more complicated challenge in terms of compliance. Government agencies are aggressively combating fraud and other financial crimes. Since 1981, the U.S. federal government alone has introduced more than 100,000 new rules and regulations.

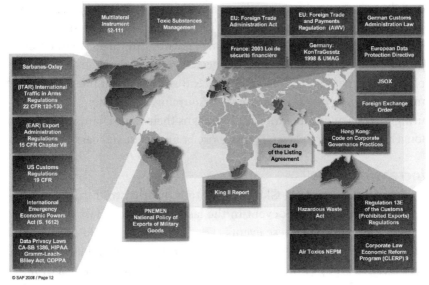

Figure 6-2. Increasing Regulatory Requirements Worldwide

The rising tide of regulations has substantially increased the cost and complexity of compliance.

Market Demands

Financial markets are applying more scrutiny to corporate management and accounting. Listing exchanges and rating agencies now take a hard look at risk management practices within organizations, such as how a risk management culture is inculcated in the organization, how risks and strategies are aligned, how risk management activities are standardized and communicated, and what processes are put in place to enable all of these elements to function effectively. For example, the New York Stock Exchange requires that a board's audit committee evaluate the organization's risk assessment and risk management processes. The enterprise risk management practices and capabilities of an organization are now being included as a key criteria in ratings by organizations such as Fitch, Moody's, and Standard & Poor's.

Globalization

As we described earlier in the book, for business, all the world's a stage. Globalism has knocked down barriers and made the business playing field increasingly flat. Business is growing more complex and dynamic and distributed over wide geographical areas and government jurisdictions. This far-flung environment comes with a Pandora's box of risks: political instability, terrorism, natural disasters, pandemics, or threats to intellectual property. Operating in this interconnected environment adds to the complexity of managing risk and compliance. Businesses are pursuing multiple markets, forging new partnerships, outsourcing, specializing, and distributing their business operations. This means their value chains have grown longer, involve more players, cross more boundaries, and carry more risk.

Increasing Risks

According to the IBM Global CFO Study, nearly two thirds of respondents experienced a risk event in the last three years. Half admitted to being unprepared for these events. The implications could not be more serious. The impacts of being unprepared for risk can often be devastating. As a Deloitte study of the risks that contributed to the 100 largest drops in value showed,[1] companies that experienced a catastrophic risk that they were unprepared for lost immense value that they were unable to recover.

More Stakeholders

In the old days, companies answered primarily to one stakeholder—their shareholders. They operated with a bottom line attitude in which profit was the ultimate driving force. Now, however, companies operate in a complex ecosystem where they are accountable to multiple stakeholders. These include:

- Customers
- Employees
- Regulators
- Partners
- Media
- Investors
- Non Governmental Organizations
- Competition

These trends mean that the three-legged stool of GRC must support more weight. For governance, it requires better alignment, performance accountability and cross functionality. For risk, this requires a broader approach that takes into account factors well beyond traditional financial ones, such as strategic, operational, and geopolitical risks, and applies

---

[1] Deloitte, "Disarming the Value Killers: A Risk Management Study," 2005.

them to every part of the organization. For compliance, this new world means that business must adhere to an array of regulations from local, state, and national governments, with each region having its own unique regulatory framework. At the same time, business must also identify and make the most of the opportunities afforded by these frameworks.

In order to reap the maximum returns from risk-aware performance management, we must view the imperative for GRC not as a drag on business but as tools for more principled and balanced management.

Core GRC Applications

Software applications can be invaluable in managing the challenges of orchestrating your governance, risk, and compliance initiatives in a holistic way. A unified GRC platform has several core applications. Of course, the specifics of these platforms will differ from organization to organization. Here are some of the most important potential uses:

- **Policy, procedure, and control documentation.** This allows for definition, approval, maintenance and communication of corporate procedures, policies, and business practices. Such documentation provides a central repository of information as well as procedures for automating review and approvals of documentation as well as information about testing and workflow related to controls
- **Risk and control assessment.** These features manage and survey various areas of the business to assess risk, compliance, and the effectiveness of controls in the environment. This allows for the establishment of a risk management context, risk identification, analysis, evaluation, and remediation as well as the ability to document, test, monitor, and certify controls
- **GRC analytics.** These features use the mandates laid forth in policy and control documentation combined with data gathered in risk and control assessments to quantify and model risks to the business. This empowers the enterprise to aggregate, visualize, analyze, and report on governance, risk, and compliance across the entire organization so that GRC information can be placed in context to facilitate decision-making through comparison and correlation and ultimately be distributed to the board, top management, business units, and department managers
- **Loss, event, and investigations management.** These features collect records for tracking organization losses, transaction and operational

events, gaps in controls, and audit findings while facilitating the investigation and response process. It allows for monitoring and managing corporate investigations, regulatory interactions, whistle-blower complaints, and corporate losses

In this chapter, we will explore how performance management can be intermeshed with GRC. This approach not only reduces the cost and complexity of GRC, but also enhances strategy, execution and the ability to respond proactively. Ultimately, that enhances the bottom line too.

Performance Management and Risk Management

Managing risks is a fundamental aspect of business. Investments in new products, research into new technologies, acquisitions, divestitures, and new business processes all involve taking chances. Risk in itself is not undesirable. To the contrary, risk taking is an essential part of creating value and competitive differentiation. As Peter Bernstein wrote in *Against the Gods—The Remarkable Story of Risk* (John Wiley & Sons 1996), "The capacity to manage risk, and with it the appetite to take risk and make forward-looking choices, are key elements of the energy that drives the economic system forward."

According to the very well-known COSO enterprise risk management framework, enterprise risk management (ERM) is a "process, effected by an entity's board of directors, management, and other personnel, applied in strategy setting, and across the enterprise, designed to identify potential events that may affect the entity, and manage risk to be within its risk appetite, to provide reasonable assurance regarding the achievement of entity objectives."[2] Organizations, especially those that are publicly held or regulated, must be able to inform their stakeholders about risks and document their risk reporting.

While the furthest evolution of risk management techniques has taken place in financial disciplines, risk is about far more than just financial risks. Risks can be strategic, operational, related to brand reputation, and so on. Every decision and every key process in your business carries associated risks. Risk has many meanings among different audiences. It overlaps with IT governance, financial risk, strategic risk, operational risk, IT risk, corporate compliance, SOX compliance, employment/labor compliance,

---

[2] "Enterprise Risk Management—Integrated Framework: Executive Summary," *Committee of Sponsoring Organizations of the Treadway Commission,* September 2004.

and privacy compliance. Figure 6-3 delineates various types of risk. A key point here is the tie between risk and compliance: compliance risk is just one type of risk and is typically driven by regulation. Although compliance risk is extremely important, it is only one type of risk that an organization must manage, and, as Figure 6-3 shows, it comprises only 8% of the material risk events encountered by CFOs in the last three years, according to IBM's 2008 Global CFO study.

From the descriptions in Figure 6-3, something should become clear. Risk management and performance management have much in common. Both demand the clear articulation of strategy mapped onto an operating model through its objectives. Both require the firm to manage and operate in unison. Both rely on key indicators to give ongoing feedback on performance. Both provide information so that companies can make decisions based on facts and the latest information. We might even say performance management and risk management are two sides of the same coin.

A company that uses performance management tools to continuously monitor key initiatives can rapidly identify opportunities and threats—and, when necessary, quickly change tactics. Such agility distinguishes high-performing organizations. IBM's 2008 CFO Study also found that high performing enterprises spent 21% more time on risk management and

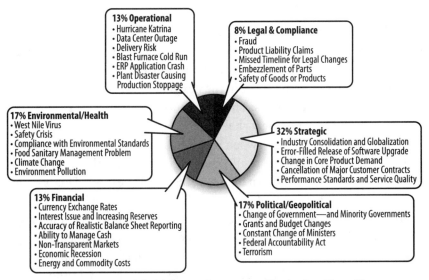

Figure 6-3. Material Risk Events Encountered in the Past Three Years
(For Enterprises Over U.S.$5 Billion in Revenue)
(Source: IBM Global Business Services, "The Global CFO Study," 2008)

decision support than their lower-performing peers. The most effective organizations, known as Integrated Finance Organizations (IFO), followed more formal risk management activities such as monitoring, reporting, historical comparisons, evaluation tools, predictive analytics, risk-adjusted forecasts, and process controls. Their stock price also appreciated by 22% over five years, compared to 17% for their non-IFO peers.

By integrating risk management methodologies into your performance management practices, you can more accurately predict the future—and better prepare yourself for eventualities that you can't predict. Decomposing this in terms of how it affects day-to-day business operations and decision making, when key objectives are understood and their progress is measured using key performance indicators, and the key risks to reaching those objectives are measured via key risk indicators, management can become a truly exception-based process where the added value of human judgment is leveraged to its greatest effect. Instead of surveying managers about performance and risk—a process that is ripe for biased reporting— combining performance management and risk management provides you with "telemetry" from your organization that you can use to monitor the ongoing health of the business.

Multiplying Risks

Organizations operate in an increasingly complex and volatile environment. They must grapple with a maelstrom of forces: globalization, more intense competition, the financial meltdown, and greater regulatory demands. In this choppy sea, they must stay true to the course charted in their strategy. At the same time, they must retain the flexibility to steer around obstacles and react to unforeseen events. The simultaneous execution of strategy and risk management is extremely challenging—yet necessary.

In the most extreme case, when strategy and risk management remain isolated from each other, the results can be disastrous for the organization. Witness the financial meltdown following the subprime crisis. This is a good example of what happens when an aggressive, growth-oriented strategy is executed either oblivious to the risks, or worse, ignoring known risks. The result: billions of dollars in losses, one in four risky home mortgages going into default and some of the most vaunted names in global finance going out of business. While outcomes this extreme are rare (although not as rare as one would hope), they serve as a clear backdrop to how high the stakes can get.

Yet amid this disaster we can find positive lessons from those who did it right. Some firms identified the sources of significant risk as early as 2006. They were wary of rating agency assessments and assessed credit quality within house expertise. Some even tested their assessments by selling limited portions of their assets to obtain pricing points. These firms took proactive action when the risk became apparent to them. They were the ones left standing when the meltdown occurred.

Risks may threaten more than the company's immediate financial performance. An enterprise may also face risks in areas such as strategy, operations, geopolitical instability, or brand reputation. In one study, Deloitte surveyed companies about the types of risks that contributed to the 100 largest drops in value and found that non-financial risks such as strategic risks, operational risks and external risks factored into about two-thirds of all cases. By comparison, financial risk played a role in only about one-third of the cases. In another survey of CFOs by IBM Global Business Services, 87% of risk events reported by executives were non-financial.

Eventually most forms of risk do hit the bottom line. In the report "Orchestrating Risk-Adjusted Performance Management," IBM Global Services noted that "for publicly traded companies, it seems all risks come home to roost in the stock price. Therefore, virtually all risks ultimately have a financial impact." Deloitte's research concurs with this conclusion.

These various forms of risk often have a compounding effect. After all, risks don't occur in isolation. Value losses often are caused by the confluence of several risks that produce a cumulative loss in value. This is not just a function of the company's own risks; it also involves those of the company's partners, suppliers, and customers.

Organizations often recognize risk too late to intervene. Most business catastrophes don't happen because one domino fell. They happen because events trigger a succession of dominos falling and triggering catastrophic failure. Risk management provides the methodology and processes to identify particular events or circumstances relevant to the organization's objectives (risks and opportunities), assess them in terms of likelihood and magnitude of impact, determine a response strategy, and monitor progress so that when one domino falls, you immediately see where the problem lies and can respond appropriately to prevent a cascade of failure.

Understanding how each risk might interact with others allows a company to develop a more complex risk portfolio and plan for a variety of possible scenarios. As Deloitte noted, "Risk management strategies should include an analysis of how responses to one type of risk might trigger other types of risks." While many firms have invested in enterprise risk management, few adequately manage risk interdependencies. Few enterprises plan for the compound effect of multiple risks. Indeed, most firms take a compartmentalized approach—and blind themselves to the interplay between risks. In a 2003 survey by the Global Association of Risk Professionals, more than half of financial services executives said their firm used disparate systems for operational risk and credit risk. Only 10% said that they had integrated technology that covered both sets of risks.

Risk management strategies should include an analysis of how responses to one type of risk might trigger other types of risks. Understanding the interdependencies between risks and how the response to one set of risks can impact another set of risks is essential. For example, sometimes you might be willing to accept increased exposure on risk B, based on the response to risk A. You might have an increased tolerance for risk B because of other mitigations that are in place. The key is understanding the context of how one response impacts other risks and how you can manage that impact. Similarly, enterprises should understand how the risk profiles of partners fit into the company's own overall risk profile.

Where do you begin to integrate risk and performance management? Quite simply, it happens in the first step, in your strategic planning process, where you identify your various categories of risk, standardize your risk taxonomy, and identify the key risk indicators while setting your strategic objectives. This explicit linkage and standardization process sets the stage for being able to intelligently integrate the silos of information about risk and performance throughout your organization. This allows managers to understand the connections and develop a broad strategy. The Bank of America integrates risk management into the process of planning business strategies rather than approaching risk as an afterthought. This approach yields two benefits: it reduces overall risk and lowers the costs of risk management. In another example, Honeywell formerly purchased product liability, property, and foreign exchange insurance policies separately. It now purchases a more comprehensive insurance contract that combines several types of policies—an approach that yielded a 15% savings.

Flying Blind

Companies that fail to manage their risk are flying blind. Not surprisingly, many eventually crash.

Unfortunately, the old model of risk management is not up to challenges of the modern business world. In many cases, risk management falls victim to organizational silos, lacking consistent taxonomies, measurement, and reporting, which obscures visibility. Valuable information is trapped in pockets of the organization and is not aggregated with information from other silos. As a result, managers lack a true picture of the overall enterprise.

Imagine your marketing group develops a new advertising campaign to counter the launch of a new product by a competitor. Unbeknownst to marketing, however, one of the company's backup suppliers had gone out of business. In the meantime, the main supplier could meet the current demand so the purchasing department felt no sense of urgency in looking for another backup supplier.

The marketing campaign turned out to be a great success and demand soared but the main supplier could not meet the demand and the company had no backup supplier in place. As a result, the company could not keep up with the demand and shelves went empty—and consumers turned to the competitor's new product. In this case, the company had been poised to out-maneuver its competitor but had been blind to risks and ultimately saw defeat.

Unfortunately, this scenario is fairly common. Most organizations have yet to meet the challenge of modern risk management. The IBM Global CFO Study surveyed 1,230 executives and found a huge gap in performance. Some 66% of the executives said that supporting, managing, and mitigating risk is important but only 45% rated themselves as effective at it. Similarly, 62% of executives rated integration as important but only 30% said their organization is good at it.

Most management processes are predicated on certainty and accuracy— both flawed assumptions. Budgets provide a specific profit number; forecasts offer a single, and often very detailed, view of the future. This leads to a dangerously excessive degree of confidence in the future. In reality, there is only one thing that is certain about any plan or forecast: some part of it will be wrong.

When performance and risk management are not aligned, the effects show up in unpleasant ways. Strategy can become unrealistic and the organization is unable to meet its goals or deliver on expectations. Conversely, the strategy can be so conservative because of an unwillingness to take smart risks that the company's competitive position erodes. It loses the ability to adapt to a changing operating environment. In sum, it sacrifices enterprise value that the company spent years building.

The integration of performance management and risk management often presents a cultural challenge. In many organizations, the people familiar with performance management come from different parts of the organization than those familiar with risk management. In banking, for example, risk management frequently emerges from treasury management or currency management. In manufacturing, risk management often grew out of procurement. In contrast, performance management was born in a different part of finance. These pockets contributed to the narrow view and siloed approach. In these organizations, the only person who may have a broad, integrated view of risk might be the CFO who supervises all these teams.

What are the warning signs of bad alignment? Here are some indicators that performance and risk management are not properly linked:[3]

- Lack of linkage of risk to enterprise value
- Periodic risk assessments rarely impact business plans
- Management typically embraces a single point of view of the future and does not anticipate risk scenarios that could derail execution of the strategy
- Poor alignment of risk responses with strategy
- Unacceptable risk taking or risk adverse activity, e.g., risk taking and risk appetite are not in alignment
- Performance management focuses on financial metrics and efficiency, but ignores risk

Too often, companies approach risk management with a narrow perspective. For example, they might regard it as merely a matter of data security and loss prevention. In some cases, they view risk management as a cost and an inhibitor to business. Such a myopic view ignores its potential value as an *enhancement* to business.

How Risk Management Enhances Strategy and Performance

Enterprises should seek a new approach to risk management. This approach is intimately intertwined with the company's overall strategy, integrated with other enterprise systems, provides constant feedback, and is actionable.

Three processes should be going on continuously:

---

[3] "Performance/Risk Integration Management Model: The Convergence of Enterprise Performance Management and Risk Management," Protiviti white paper.

- Assessing risks
- Choosing risk responses
- Monitoring the status of the risks to decide if a response is needed

This monitoring should not be the exclusive privilege of top management or the board. Instead, the entire organization should have access to these instruments to give them the full spectrum of factors that need to influence their decision-making. The key is to have risk management available to business unit managers so they can see risks within the context of higher-level corporate goals and act upon information right away.

Let's examine how this approach can benefit people throughout the organization.

Executives

Risk should be considered in the process of setting corporate strategies such as mergers and acquisitions, investments in new products, and so on. After setting strategy, executives need to consider risks for meeting each objective and then set key risk indicators to monitor those risks. However, it should be clear that, just as with any lifecycle, this is a continuous process. It is not enough to identify risks up front and be done with it. Executives must monitor the risks and adjust their actions going forward based on responses, impacts, and new mitigations. This involves ongoing monitoring of KRIs associated with KPIs to ensure that strategies stay on course.

Risk Managers

An integrated platform leverages the data currently in their enterprise systems so that risks can be automatically identified, analyzed, and monitored. This approach provides a single platform to automate risk management processes across the disparate systems within their enterprise. This means a reduction in time-consuming manual tasks, such as toggling between applications such as spreadsheets, email and word processing. Risk managers can spend less time collecting data and more time as strategic advisors.

Business Owners

Business leaders can use these tools to drive performance and mitigate their top risks to help them achieve their MBOs. Managers can be provided with guides that help them identify risks, apply mitigation strategies, and establish risk-monitoring processes. Companies can learn from their experiences and avoid repeating mistakes. Because they have a record of the mitigations other business owners have tried, they can benefit from the experience of others in similar situations, whether they personally know the colleagues in question. In this way, they can choose a more effective response based on the collective learning of the organization. Managers can own and drive risk management in their areas.

How Risk Management and Performance Management Dovetail

It should be clear from the previous discussion that we strongly advocate combining risk management and performance management approaches because they strengthen each other. This begins with the integration of risk management into an enterprise's strategy. By embedding risk management in a business unit's planning and control cycles, we make the line manager both aware of risks and accountable for managing them, which promotes common ERM processes.

Benefits of Linking Risk and Performance Management

- Enhanced strategic execution

- Reductions in risk-related losses

- Cost savings through eliminating duplicated processes and removing complexity

- Better quality and actionability of information

- Potential to reduce regulatory capital and the cost of capital

- Fewer operational surprises and losses

- Identifying and managing multiple and cross-enterprise risks

- Better ability to seize opportunities

- Improved deployment of capital

- Real-time transparency into operations of the enterprise

- Ability to proactively identify and mitigate risks inherent in strategy

- Enhanced ability to communicate and deploy strategy across the enterprise

- Integration of strategic plans, risk management, and performance management in the execution of the strategy

Risk management is the flip side of performance management. Even so, risk management and performance management programs often remain separate and parallel initiatives in many enterprises—an approach that falls prey to the "silos" discussed earlier. Fortunately, this may be changing. AMR Research predicts these two management systems will ultimately "fuse into one governance system to strategically guide an organization to its next level of business performance."

Performance Management and Compliance

Simply put, compliance means adhering to the rules of the road. It means interpreting what a given regulation requires, understanding how it applies to your organization, and documenting a plan for meeting its requirements. It means executing that plan, keeping measures that show how you've performed, and maintaining an evidence layer that can prove that you have met your compliance requirements.

In the U.S., corporate compliance has often been synonymous with the Sarbanes-Oxley Act of 2002. SOX requires that an organization show how it generated its financial statements and why auditors should trust them. The impact that SOX has had from a corporate psyche, business process modification, as well as a sheer cost perspective cannot be understated. However, it's a common misperception that compliance equals SOX, and nothing could be further from the truth. Compliance pressures also arise from many other regulations. In the U.S., a financial services organization may have to comply with a myriad of other requirements such as—just to name a few—Gramm-Leach-Bliley, the Health Insurance Portability and Accountability Act, the USA PATRIOT Act, California Senate Bill 1386, Basel II, or NASD. Companies with global operations may face additional requirements abroad such as Canada's PIPEDA, the EU Data Protection Directive, and so on. And the fines for violating compliance requirements can be very steep indeed: ITT had to pay a fine of $100 million for violating the U.S. Arms Export Control Act by selling night-vision technology to China in 2001.

Compliance is not only a matter of conducting business in accordance with external laws and regulations. Compliance also means heeding the internal policies and procedures of the enterprise, such as policies for ensuring equitable treatment for employees, data security, or privacy. These policies and their associated procedures set the standards as well as the means to implement the standards for conducting business ethically.

Ignoring compliance represents a substantial risk in its own right. To return to our driving analogy, if you flout the rules of the road, you run the risk of getting into an accident or getting pulled over by police and getting a ticket—and this only increases the cost and time of getting to your destination. Thus, managing compliance and performance together is a matter of predictability. If you choose to ignore the compliance aspects, you expose yourself to unforeseen costs such as fines or bad publicity. If you work within the bounds of your compliance initiatives, you may get where you want to go faster.

If you approach compliance as just a chore of filling out government forms, you fail to reap the full benefits of it. Companies have found that implementing sound compliance practices actually has many positive effects in terms of driving better business performance because these practices allow you to automate the ability to gain visibility into business processes to ensure that they are operating as designed. Compliance can actually prime a company to use "best practices" that enhance business performance by optimizing business processes. Thus, the information gathered by these compliance processes represents a goldmine for performance management.

Standardized, rationalized controls lead to process improvements and greater efficiency. Process consistency leads to more efficiency and reusable information. A "compliance culture" encourages more integrity and accountability.

In short, the infrastructure for gathering compliance-related information can be a launching pad for better management and even create a competitive advantage. For example, a study performed by America's SAP User Group (ASUG)[4] showed that organizations that have a greater number of automated controls can close their monthly books more quickly. Those with the highest proportion of automated controls can close in just four days, compared with 12 days for companies with the lowest number of automated controls, demonstrating an overall performance improvement when coupling compliance and controls.

Getting Started

First we can boil down compliance into a few key elements:

- **Accountability.** Executive management and the board are ultimately accountable for compliance

---

[4] Dan Fagan, "Compliance: How Is Everyone Else Doing It?" ASUG Annual Conference, May 2008.

- **Governance.** Establishing a culture of compliance in the organization
- **Responsibility.** Ensuring that business owners take charge of managing compliance for their areas
- **Understanding.** Identifying what the regulators are looking for
- **Architecture.** Developing a compliance control architecture
- **Validation.** Verifying that controls are in place and functioning properly

Now let's establish some basic terms. A "process" refers to a set of activities relating to a specific function in an organization's operations. These activities produce the desired output or process result. It includes the flow of material, information, and the business decisions involved in the various steps in the process. One example might be a sales process that begins with a sales order and ends with receiving payment from the customer.

A subprocess is a subset of the activities within a process. In our example, a subprocess might be processing the sales order or shipping the goods.

Controls are used to ensure that the processes and subprocesses are performed in accordance with the company's requirements and policies. These activities are designed to address control objectives and mitigate risks in the company's internal control environment. Controls may include approvals, authorizations, verifications, reconciliations, reviews of operating performance, configurations, security of assets, and segregation of duties. In our example, one risk is a lack of visibility to the credit exposure. A control objective involves applying company rules, for example that the credit exposure does not exceed organizational norms. A control activity looks backward, reviewing all system records and reporting on any company's credit exposure that has exceeded preset limits.

We can divide controls into two basic types:

- **Operational controls.** Operational controls consist of management and operational procedures that must be followed for compliance
- **Technical controls.** Technical controls involve the elements of policy and operational controls that can be technically automated and/or enforced

Controls are tied to compliance risk, but can also be used to great effect to address other types of risks. Controls provide mechanisms that ensure

Segregation of Duties

Segregation of duties for key information assets is one of the key concepts of internal control. SoD came to prominence due to the enactment of the landmark Sarbanes-Oxley Act in 2002. In essence, SoD puts an appropriate level of checks and balances on the activities of individuals. SoD has as its primary objective the prevention of fraud (intentional activities) and errors (accidental activities). This objective is achieved by disseminating the tasks and associated privileges for a specific business process among multiple users. For example, it is critical not to combine roles such as receiving checks (payment on account) and approving write-offs, depositing cash and reconciling bank statements, or approving time cards and having custody of pay checks. In a perfect system, no one person should handle more than one type of any such function. It is one of the most effective safeguards against fraud and mistakes and a prerequisite for sound corporate oversight. It is also one of the most difficult and sometimes the most costly type of control to achieve given the thousands of users, roles, and processes that require access and authorization evaluation, testing, and remediation.

SoD solutions need to support an effective and efficient initial cleanup, during which existing access risk and violations are uncovered and remediated. They also need to support a process to ensure continuous compliance through a comprehensive set of capabilities to prevent future violations, such as centralized role definition and simulation functionality, and superuser functionality that enables users to perform activities outside their ordinary role in a way that is controlled and auditable. Finally, these solutions need to allow reporting on current system status and SoD status, enabling the management team and role owners to have oversight and ultimately the ability to sign off on compliance certifications with confidence.

that risks are addressed and mitigated appropriately. A system of controls requires periodic reevaluation based on changing risks, business objectives, the external environment, and other business conditions. Effective compliance and risk management depends on good controls. The ASUG study also shows that automating the testing of business process controls enables many more controls to be implemented for less money. Companies with 70% of their IT process controls automated paid an average of $3 per control whereas companies with less than 20% of their controls automated paid almost 10 times that much per control.

So how does an enterprise design and implement effective controls? Gartner Research suggests that controls should be:

- **Measurable.** Controls include reliable metrics for reporting and analysis. These measurements help companies judge the effectiveness of controls and alert them to risk exposure
- **Testable.** Controls should include formal testing procedures and timelines to ensure they are functioning properly
- **Auditable.** Controls, especially financial ones, should generate sound audit trails with individual accountability
- **Enforceable.** Controls should prevent circumvention. This may require the use of multiple controls to ensure that nobody does an "end run" around one risk mitigation

Compliance architecture will vary by organization. But there are several common elements:

- **Compliance framework.** Establishes the compliance system for the whole company. It includes the processes and responsibilities for continuously fulfilling the compliance requirements and provides ongoing oversight to the various compliance programs. Most companies adapt a framework such as COSO or COBIT that prescribes control sets and a compliance architecture
- **Continuous controls monitoring.** Keeps tabs on adherence to policy, ideally in real time or close to it. It should automatically detect errors and alert managers so they can take action
- **Risk management framework.** A system that evaluates key risks to the business and organizes priorities based on potential exposure

While there are undoubtedly similarities in technology requirements, the unique capabilities of performance management applications and business intelligence (BI) platforms can also enhance GRC by providing insights about matters such as data quality, performance, or governance. This is because performance management and BI platforms provide important capabilities that are both synergistic with and supplementary to the GRC infrastructure. In fact, many of the underlying technology components of the business intelligence platform provide the infrastructure links between governance, risk, and compliance and performance management. By connecting governance, risk, and compliance capabilities with performance management capabilities through business intelligence, you can significantly improve visibility, control, communication, risk management, and fraud prevention over what you could achieve deploying any one of these capabilities in isolation. You can also leverage business intelligence to push end users to proactively monitor risks and quickly take action.

AMR's Active Compliance Architecture

Compliance needs dictate an underlying technology architecture to implement them effectively. AMR's Active Compliance Framework articulates nine primary technology components necessary to support the full breadth of compliance requirements.

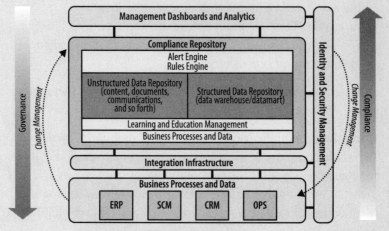

Figure 6-4. Active Compliance Architecture

- Integration infrastructure—A mechanism for sharing data among several applications and databases
- Business process management and workflow—Manages process flows and coordinates internal cross-application processes
- Learning and education management—Delivers key information and training for compliance-related matters
- Content, document, and records management—Administers and stores the large amounts of unstructured data that support documentation, governance, and internal and external communications
- Data warehouse/data mart—Stores the structured data needed to support compliance requirements
- Rules engine—Stores all compliance-related business rules
- Alert engine—Informs individuals and applications when a concern arises
- Identity and security management—Protects privacy and prevents unauthorized access
- Management dashboards and analytics—Delivers key performance data as well as analysis and reporting capabilities

These technical components also fuel modern performance management applications (see Chapter 4).

(Source: AMR Research, 2004, "Planning for a Sustainable Active Compliance Architecture")

From Risk and Compliance to Unified GRC

In this chapter, we've learned about the importance of risk management and how it relates to performance. We've learned about the importance of compliance and how it relates to performance. Now it's time to put it all together. To return to our driving analogy, it's time to put together the elements that make up our on-board GPS navigation system.

Performance management and GRC are likely to continue to become more intertwined in the years ahead. Solutions will become more proactive. The GRC market will evolve from a compliance-oriented approach—essentially a reactive stance—toward a more integrated synthesis of risk management, corporate governance, and technology.

Similarly, enterprises will move from a compliance focus to a risk focus. According to AMR, risk management is the number one driver for GRC investments. SOX and financial needs accounted for 15% of GRC investment.

Enterprises are beginning to look at real options, such as scenario planning, contingency planning, and rolling forecasts that all recognize the crucial importance of understanding risk in performance management. At the best companies, these tools are being combined with enterprise risk management. These companies have elevated what used to be a narrow "audit-like" approach to a more comprehensive approach that integrates risk management into the overall management process.

In terms of maturity, GRC follows an identical path to the performance management maturity of an organization, making it possible for organizations to navigate both areas in tandem. AMR Research's GRC maturity model describes the following four stages, which directly correspond to their performance management maturity model:

- **Step 1: Reacting.** In this step, the organization responds with a general attitude of "You want me to do *what?*" It struggles to find out what is required and how fast changes must be made. Such GRC projects become focused on the single task of compliance with whatever requirement has been set before it, even if they have widespread implications. Organizations may initially spend a long time at this step, but once they have been through this process once, the next time they will take a more mature approach based on lessons learned
- **Step 2: Anticipating.** This organization sees that GRC is part of running the organization effectively. Efficient handling of

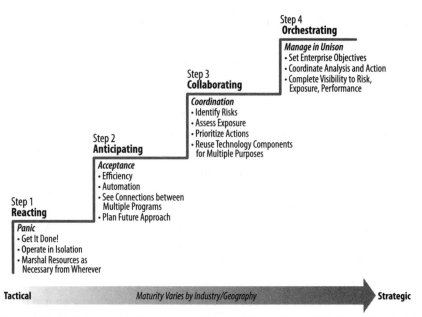

Figure 6-5. AMR Research's Governance, Risk, and Compliance (GRC) Maturity Model
(Source: AMR Research, "The Governance, Risk Management, and Compliance (GRC) Landscape,
Part 1: A Segmented Marketplace With Distinct Buyers", 2008)

GRC activities is a hallmark of this stage, with automation, repeatability, sustainability, and cost-effectiveness coming into play at this level

- **Step 3: Collaborating.** At this level, a more holistic view of risk is embraced. Risk management becomes not just about following the letter of the law (compliance risk) but takes into account the risks in the larger business environment (business risk). Discussions include the level of risk the organization is willing to take in various areas. Although the right questions are being asked, risk management is not being coordinated across the organization at this level but takes the form of isolated efforts

- **Step 4: Orchestrating.** This highest stage of maturity involves coordinating risk management efforts across the enterprise, referred to as enterprise risk management (ERM). All types of risk are managed in a formal way that includes identification, categorization, assessment, and prioritization. At this stage, risk management and performance management are effectively intertwined

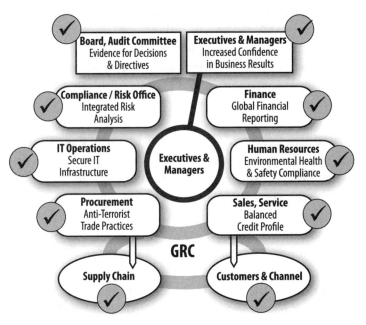

Figure 6-6. The Impact of Unified GRC on the Enterprise

As a result of the fusion of GRC with performance management, the enterprise will become more interconnected. As Michael Rasmussen of Corporate Integrity observed, "GRC is moving from the 'past' of individual silos working autonomously, to the 'present' where GRC is becoming collaborative and focused on aligning with business performance." In the future, Rasmussen predicts that GRC will merge with corporate social responsibility—an idea that we will explore more fully later in this chapter.

All Together Now: Weaving Risk and Compliance into the Performance Management Lifecycle

One of the greatest benefits of modern performance management is enhancing how we address risk across all aspects of the business and in all phases of the lifecycle. Here we will show how risk can be plugged into our model of the performance management lifecycle.

Strategize and Prioritize

In the process of setting business strategy, the development of strategic and operational plans should include the identification and assessment of risks to short- and long-term objectives and plans. Interfacing strategy with risk management to assess the vulnerability and impact of risks inherent in alternative strategies is integral to scenario analysis. Additionally, prioritizing inherent risks may demand risk mitigation tactics that will need to be factored into the annual plan and budgeted for during the planning process.

Understand the Corporate and Departmental Contexts

Review the corporate strategic goals, strategic plans, initiatives, and metrics. Contextualize them to the implications they have for the departments and use this context to drive the PM lifecycle.

Develop and Set the Strategy

First, review the environment. To get a holistic picture of risk, understand where you currently stand and assess the internal environment and properly define and prioritize the most important risks with the greatest impact and likelihood of occurrence (risk type, impact, probability, timeframe, and mitigation strategy/costs). Be sure to assess external as well as internal risks. External risks include capital availability, competitors, shifting customer needs, economic downturns, legal or regulatory actions, shareholder relationships, disruptive technologies, and political unrest. Internal risks relate to process, management information, human capital, integrity, and technology, as well as financial concerns.

Next, get a holistic picture of the full set of compliance initiatives you will intersect with, such as SOX, OSHA, data privacy laws, and global trade regulations.

The next step is to set the mission, values, and vision:

- **Define mission (the fundamental purpose of the entity, especially what it provides to customers and clients).** Make every information asset in the company add value to every business process
- **Define core values (the attitude, behavior, and character of the organization).** An example of a core value is willingness to do whatever it takes to help customers succeed
- **Define the vision.** A vision is a concise statement that defines the 3- to 5-year goals of the organization. For example, by 2012, be consistently ranked in the top 10% of customer satisfaction as a value-added partner for every business unit in the company

Next, set the goals. Define a strategy and set business objectives using risks as a key variable for deciding which strategies to pursue. With all that contextual information in hand, set a strategy to follow.

Consider using a strategy map to display the cause and effect relationships among the objectives that make up a strategy. A good strategy map tells the story of how value is created for the business.

Assign KPIs to Goals and Set the Right Targets

Define KPIs and targets that translate strategy into performance expectations. Identify value drivers (those elements that contribute to the value in your organization). Value drivers and related performance tolerances (KPIs) have risks associated with their achievement. Identify these risks and establish tolerance levels (KRIs). This connectivity between a value driver and a relevant KPI and KRI is an important bridge from a strategic view of risk—which can have a time horizon of three or more years—to a more focused budgetary view of risk, which is often applied to a single year.

Perform Additional Risk Analysis and Set KRIs

Now look again at risks to see what could keep you from meeting your goals. For each risk, decide what your risk appetite is. Can you afford to take that risk? What's the worst-case scenario? What is the contingency plan? Set a response strategy for the risk (treat, tolerate, transfer, or terminate). Decide whether you can afford the worst-case scenario presented by that risk from a performance management perspective. Could it bring down some critical value-generating mechanism for the company?

Define KRIs and risk thresholds and tolerances for those risks. Key risk indicators, like KPIs, are the early warning signals that define the threshold at which a risk could occur.

Perform Additional Compliance Analysis

Define your compliance requirements. Define policies, procedures, and controls that must be in place to ensure that you can meet the compliance requirements. Make sure that this applies not only at the main business process level but also to all subprocesses including and perhaps especially those related to partners. Define control targets that translate compliance expectations into performance.

Work on the Strategic Action Plan and Initiatives

The strategic initiatives help define the exact methodology (the roadmap) for achieving the various goals. The results of this planning may require revisiting the strategy.

First, develop the roadmap (sequence of actions) for achieving performance, risk, and compliance expectations.

Next, define critical success and failure factors for all initiatives. Every project or investment must, in addition to defining the critical factors for its success, also define its critical "failure factors," that is, those circumstances under which the project or investment is no longer likely to be successful. These failure factors can then be translated into metrics that serve as an early warning mechanism, allowing the organization to restructure or cancel a project before good resources and money are thrown after bad.

Finally, develop different risk-adjusted scenarios with contingency plans should risks to achieving plans materialize.

Cascade Accountability

Each KPI, KRI, and control and its target should be owned by some department or group. Cascade accountability of KPIs, KRIs, and controls throughout the organization and ultimately into individual MBOs for alignment. The MBOs of the staff must reflect the KPIs, KRIs, and controls you set. This sounds obvious, but frequently performance is measured at an individual level in a way that does not in fact relate directly to corporate goals and strategies.

Plan and Execute

In the strategize and prioritize phase of the PM lifecycle, we put together strategic action plans and initiatives. The planning phase gets into the details of planning the strategic initiatives both from a financial and operational standpoint.

Align Corporate Budget to Departmental Budget and Link Corporate and Departmental Initiatives

The budgeting process takes each of the outcomes or actions from the planning process and aligns revenues and expenses against them. Decisions regarding investment priorities and resource allocations define how the company will operate and set the bar for measuring performance.

To create risk-adjusted budgets, incorporate the range of possible revenues and costs of each action into the budget at the appropriate organizational level. A risk-adjusted budget is one that responds to changing circumstances, providing the financial capability to react to events in a planned, proactive manner. Align risk-adjusted budgets with contingency plans should risk events occur, or if risks exceed the acceptable threshold to achieving budgets.

Align Departmental Budget to Departmental Operational Plans

The operational planning process links the financial budget to specific operational factors. Plan out each step of each initiative. Consider what risks you have in each area of the operational plan. For example, in a risk-adjusted operational plan, for every decision to allocate resources to one set of operational activities versus another, you determine the impact and probability of the highest priority operational risks on those individual line items and use this to set a range of expected and forecasted values instead of fixed values. If the risk materializes, you would want a contingency plan in place that showed the performance and risk implications if we moved the budget from one initiative to another.

Forecast Performance and Risks

Create rolling, risk-adjusted forecasts of the budget (revenues and costs) and operational plan (including number, capacity, and cost of resources necessary to achieve plan) so that you can see trends over a rolling time horizon for those risks whose probability, consequence, and resiliency change over time. That way if you have to make adjustments, you can see where you've been and the direction in which things are likely to go. Predictive analytic techniques can be a particularly powerful tool for building risk-adjusted forecasts by modeling the impact previous risks had on previous forecasts.

Execute Plans

This step is essential but obvious; put the plan into action. Be prepared to execute on the type of risk associated with the plan once the threshold or tolerance is exceeded.

Monitor and Analyze

In the monitor and analyze phase of the risk-adjusted PM lifecycle, you monitor to understand what is happening in the business, analyze to understand why it is happening, and for those things not on track, adjust to improve the situation relative to your goals.

Monitor

The presentation of information to be monitored is crucial in order to facilitate decision-making. Risk monitoring is aligned directly to KRIs across the source systems that provide transactional data for the KRI. Dashboards linked with risks should help identify and manage key risks versus overall risks that are being prioritized based on exposure through quantitative/qualitative assessment. Dashboards are effective ways of combining the events, trends, and intelligence monitoring patterns across all of the major facets of the business to be monitored, including the key business dimensions like customers, products, projects, and employees and the related KPIs, KRIs, controls, and incidents and losses.

Monitor performance. You can evaluate the KPIs you've set to identify progress made toward achievement of objectives and trends.

Monitor initiatives. You can also evaluate which initiatives are failing or behind schedule.

Monitor risk. You can then evaluate important key risk indicators to identify:

- What and where are our top risks?
- What are the changes to the risk levels for key activities and opportunities?
- Are risks being assessed in accordance with company policy or according to industry best practices?
- Are our mitigation strategies effective in reducing the likelihood or impact of a risk?

Monitor internal controls. Report key control deficiencies, approvals, verifications, and reconciliations to mitigate risk. For example, how clean is our access control? Have there been major organizational shifts that require that we reexamine our roles? Do we need to add another layer of sign-offs?

Monitor any incidents and losses. What incidents or losses have occurred? If risks or losses have occurred, or external events are affecting the department, document this information, even if you haven't been tracking it in the system yet.

No matter how diligent you are, manual monitoring can be very inefficient. Automated monitoring can proactively identify out-of-tolerance conditions, associated with a KPI, KRI, or a control, and then alert the responsible party. This should take into account forecasting, trending, and modeling capabilities so that if a metric falls out of range of a trend or budget/plan, then the appropriate alert is raised, along with the workflow process to get the investigation under way.

Analyze

Analysis is a key step in which you not only look at where you are, but what is happening (or what has happened) and why. The techniques for analysis can range from highly manual and simple to fairly automated and complex in terms of the usage of statistical techniques.

Analyze performance. For KPIs, perform analysis to understand why they are increasing or decreasing.

Analyze initiatives. To evaluate initiatives, perform analysis on the initiative to understand why it is succeeding or failing.

Analyze risk. For KRIs, perform analysis to understand why they are increasing or decreasing.

Analyze controls. When analyzing internal controls, you perform analysis on their effectiveness. For example, you notice that a control seems to generate a lot of incidents and find that the thresholds are set too low, creating false positives. You conclude that your controls have lost their effectiveness and analyze why.

Analyze root causes of incidents or losses. If incidents or losses occur, perform analysis on the root causes and trends.

In all of these cases, analysis was done with human intervention. However, it is important to note that this does not necessarily have to be the case. With the volume and complexity of data in the enterprise today, it is becoming increasingly difficult for humans to mine through the data and come to intelligent conclusions. Using data mining techniques, it is possible to have software determine the likely root causes and even suggest recommended actions to remediate.

Adjust

After monitoring to know what has happened and analyzing to understand why it happened, for those things not going according to plan, it is time to set the business back on course by taking what you've learned and using that information to adjust the settings across the enterprise. However, you must always consider the impact of your goals, risks, and compliance concerns when making decisions to adjust your actions.

Adjust performance. If you see KPIs trending in the wrong direction, once you have analyzed the root causes, it should be clear what actions to take to set things back on course. However, it is critical to remember that KPIs are interlinked, and you must optimize your performance goals in the context of risk objectives without violating your compliance objectives.

Adjust initiatives. For initiatives that are not going as planned, it becomes essential to rapidly take remedial action or cancel them. For example, if an initiative is failing and you determine the root cause to be the MBOs for the key employees staffing the initiative, the simplest thing is to change the MBOs to see if this gets the initiative back on target.

Adjust risk. For KRIs trending in the wrong direction, once you have analyzed the root causes, it should be clear what actions to take to set things back on course, often by putting the appropriate mitigating controls in place to stabilize them. The following types of actions can be performed to adjust risk: treat it (mitigation), tolerate it (accept it), transfer it (to another entity), or terminate it (closing down the activity that is exposing the plan to risk). However, it is critical to remember that KRIs are interlinked, and you must optimize your risk goals in the context of performance objectives without violating your compliance objectives.

Adjust controls. For controls violations, adjustment takes the form of remediation and certification.

Adjust after incidents or losses. For incidents and losses, the correct adjustments typically involve reexamining if we are tracking the right risks and have put the appropriate controls in place to mitigate them. Keep in mind that not every risk can be adjusted or mitigated; in some cases, you must simply accept the risk based on the established controls.

Model and Optimize

In this phase, the goal is improvement.

Model

Modeling falls into three categories.

Revenue, Cost, and Profitability Modeling. Modeling the costs, revenue, and profitability implications of performance management, risk management, and compliance management activities and their drivers can be achieved at a very detailed level using activity-based costing and associated methodologies.

Scenario Modeling. Scenario modeling can be applied to financial and operational modeling and focuses on creating different business scenarios. Simple scenario modeling can include creating a base case and then high and low cases based on changes made to input variables, such as market growth rates or inflation rates. This technique is often used in modeling market and business opportunities and creating business plans.

Simulation Modeling. More advanced modeling including Monte Carlo simulation supports creating a broad range of scenarios based on multiple iterations of input assumptions and combinations. With this technique, probabilities can be assigned to the various outcomes. These techniques allow the uncertainty associated with a given forecast to be estimated and to reduce risk by applying sensitivity analysis, correlation, and trend extrapolation. By simulating the effect of uncertainty, it becomes possible to answer questions such as, "How certain are we that a given project (or group of projects) will result in a minimum outcome of x?" Or, conversely, "What's the minimum outcome that we can be, for example, 90% certain of achieving?" Simulation also makes it possible to identify and rank the various contributors to overall uncertainty.

Optimize

The goal at this phase of the PM lifecycle is to determine the optimal way to achieve objectives by taking into account the entire context of the problem, including all relevant constraints and assessments (costs, benefits, risk, labor and time), as well as business strategies, objectives, risks, and compliance factors. Optimization can be done both through human evaluation as well as through advanced algorithmic techniques.

Wrapping Up

From a process unification perspective, risk and compliance management operating in tandem with performance management will become differentiating capabilities in the management of an organization. By effectively communicating and deploying strategy across the enterprise, proactively identifying and mitigating risks and integrating them with goals and plans, and doing so in a fashion compliant with external regulations and internal policies, the enterprise can be confident that it is maximizing performance in the context of its risks while adroitly responding to a dynamic market.

From a technology unification perspective, business intelligence can be conceptualized as the base of the pyramid upon which performance management and governance, risk, and compliance are built, since it provides the basic technology capabilities and infrastructure that serve as a foundation for the higher layers of the pyramid. Connecting governance, risk and compliance capabilities with performance management capabilities through a common business intelligence platform establishes a single, unified, cleansed repository of information and common semantics on top of that information, which is critical to enabling risk-aware performance management business processes. Without this common foundation, it is impossible to obtain any synergies that extend beyond deploying any one of these capabilities in isolation.

Performance Management and GRC as the Basis for Sustainability

Earlier in this chapter, we showed how integrating GRC and performance maximizes performance in terms of shareholder value. That's all well and good—but not enough. Nowadays, the world judges our performance as more than our ability to crank out money. They want to know if we treat employees well, protect the environment, and are good corporate citizens.

Sustainability, long a domain of environmentalists, has firmly entered the business world. Simply put, sustainability means meeting the needs of the present without compromising the needs of the future. Corporate social responsibility (CSR) is the response of businesses to the challenges of sustainability. It integrates social and environmental concerns into business operations. This is often called "triple bottom line performance." The World Business Council for Sustainable Development defines Corporate Social Responsibility as "the continuing commitment by business to behave ethically and contribute to economic development while improving the quality of life of the workforce and their families as well as of the local community and society at large."

Sustainability became a boardroom topic because it became a factor in driving shareholder value. Now leading companies include it in their overall strategy. Because sustainability has become a key building block in corporate strategy, it requires management tools. Thus was born Corporate Sustainability Management, or CSM. The Global Reporting Initiative (GRI) is the de facto standard in sustainability reporting used by organizations in more than 60 countries. The market has recognized this ethic with new indexes such as the Dow Jones Sustainability Index and FTSE4Good.

Figure 6-7. Corporate Social Responsibility
(Source: "The Fundamentals of CSR," 2009 GRC Fundamentals, Trends, & Market Directions,
Corporate Integrity LLC, February 2009)

Sustainability is not only about doing the right thing. It's also about profit. According to a survey by the Economist Intelligence Unit, 36% of North American companies that implemented sustainability programs saw the biggest benefit as attracting or retaining customers. The second most popular reason was increased profitability (28%) and the ability to identify and manage risks to the company's reputation (27%). According to AMR, 27% of companies have business relationships dependent on their own environmental stance. But this appears to be scratching the surface: 57% expect such relationships to be dependent on their stance within the next two years.

Sustainability and CSR represent another layer in the performance management pyramid. Sustainability resembles performance management and risk management in viewing the organization's operations in a holistic way. It encourages efficiency, good planning, automated reporting, transparency, and actionability. It offers the capability to better manage the organization. Sound familiar? Earlier in this chapter, we saw how performance management could be used to optimize financial performance. Similarly, performance management and CSM offer the potential to optimize the triple bottom line performance. As such, sustainability may be the next great frontier in performance management.

Top Sustainability Issues of the Global 100
(Source: "The Fundamentals of CSR", 2009 GRC Fundamentals,
Trends, & Market Directions, Corporate Integrity LLC, February 2009)

- Third-Party/Supply-Chain Management

- Environmental, Health, & Safety

- Equal Opportunity & Diversity

- Ethics/Integrity/Code of Conduct

- Fair Labor Practices

- Product Safety

- Transparency

Performance Management and GRC as the Orchestrator of the Business Network

There are profound implications for your company as it becomes an integral part of the business network that makes risk-aware performance management a necessity not only to survive, but to thrive. But it is worth taking a moment to conceptualize what risk-aware performance management might look like beyond the four walls. AMR Research introduced the concept of performance-driven business networks to describe this concept.[5]

From a business strategy perspective, one of the key tenets of business strategy in a performance-driven business network is that closed-loop execution is a must. As much as the proposed strategy must be analyzed to predict its benefits, it must also be instrumented to give quick confirmation that the analysis is correct. This means designing metrics that will let the business and partners see a single source of the truth of how well it is working and adjust it in an ongoing, closed-loop fashion. Also, compliance and risk management constraints must be designed into the strategy and measured as a matter of course. This capability lets companies continuously balance risk and opportunity in their business planning.

From an organizational point of view, performance-driven business networks need continuous change capability, that is, the organization needs to be able to change on short notice, potentially shifting work, processes,

---

[5] AMR Research, "Performance-Driven Business Networks: Taking Competitive Capability to the Next Level," January 08, 2008.

reporting relationships, and incentives midyear. Employees and partners need constant feedback to clarify the current goals, results, and benefits of the ongoing change.

From a technology perspective, performance-driven business networks rely on a pervasive performance platform. Since performance-driven business networks are based on shared risk and a virtual business environment, the companies and individuals need a common view of performance and risk. Performance must be aggregated across the company, its partners, and its service providers, requiring a federated approach to sharing data and analysis.

A performance-driven business network is not just one network, but a set of networks as shown in Figure 6-8. Extended business processes are deployed on a federated platform to enable the various companies to work together to serve the customer or execute a process. A core concept for performance-driven business networks is that performance management and risk management are designed into the business process and not added on later. When implemented, these networks have parallel, federated performance management and risk management platforms monitoring the business processes.

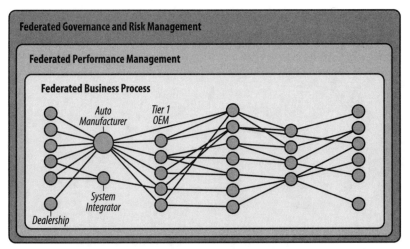

Figure 6-8. The Platform for Performance-driven Business Networks
Embeds Federated Performance and Risk Management
(Source: AMR Research, 2008, "Performance-Driven Business Networks:
Taking Competitive Capability to the Next Level")

Chapter 7

Performance Management for Finance

Modern financial departments are changing profoundly. Formerly known as the company's "bean counters," Finance is increasingly expected to act as a strategic advisor to the organization to deliver financial and operational success.

These are big shoes to fill and yet you are probably lacking even the most elemental information required. For example, can you quickly determine the profitability of your company by customer, product, channel, project, or any other dimension? Can you quickly—within a few days rather than weeks—close and create reports for statutory and management reporting? Are you able to track strategy and say with any reliability that the processes and activities occurring across the organization are actually aligned to that strategy? At a time when your company's value chain is literally spread across the world and is reliant on a number of complex relationships, how confident are you that the guidance you provide the company's stakeholders is as accurate as it needs to be? Are you able to rest easy, assured that governance is being followed and risks are being taken into account and mitigated?

You probably could not answer yes to all of these questions. Why? Because the world has changed and the demands of this new world call for a modern management solution that is designed to overcome the challenges of the

---

PM for Finance or Financial PM?

It is no accident that this chapter is titled "Performance Management for Finance." We are not simply talking about planning and reporting. We are instead saying that Finance and performance management are becoming far more operational in scope. It is not just about efficiency, but about better understanding the story behind the numbers and communicating that to the company in a meaningful way to help grow value and improve overall performance.

---

decentralized enterprise with a highly distributed value chain. Companies that try to operate with a 1984, 1994, or even 2004 mindset will be overtaken by companies that understand the need to manage performance.

This chapter will provide you with the techniques and methods that will help you to establish a comprehensive practice of performance management in Finance.

Looking Back: How Your World Has Changed in Finance

Today, companies are organizationally and globally dispersed. They need a laser-like focus on the core of their value proposition—what differentiates them, what they specialize in, what provides and sustains competitive advantage, and the sources of wealth.

Those aspects of the business that are not core value propositions are being outsourced to partners, suppliers, and in some cases customers. The possibilities are great, but so too are the challenges to your work in Finance. You are no longer just orchestrating, monitoring, and reporting on the movement of value within your company but now you must create value across the entire business network.

Consider the need to be predictable in terms of the forecasts you provide external stakeholders. Accuracy is critical, but how can you be confident in the accuracy of a forecast when you operate within a very complex web of interdependencies? All these interdependent entities—partners, customers, and suppliers—must not only be predictable to you, but you must also be predictable to them. If you cannot manage the performance for what these other people provide to your company as part of an extended value chain (web actually), then you cannot confidently predict your own performance. In turn, your partners need to be able to predict their own performance for their extended value chains.

The Evolution of Performance Management

Not long ago, performance management meant working with a spreadsheet and a single chart of accounts—fact, there are still multi-billion dollar companies that handle planning this way.

Because the business world is not a static place, it requires a new methodology to manage this concurrent evolution of the modern enterprise and the role that Finance plays within it. Supporting this progression has been the development of multidimensional databases; customer P&Ls, which were formerly only possible via manual and data-intensive processes; and general ledger values that in a modernized model flow into consolidation systems for a far faster close than was previously possible.

In moving to a performance management model, there are methods and tools to help you collect and manage the volume of newly created data. Leverage these tools and place them within a model of continuous measurement, modeling, and optimization. No longer will you and others throughout the company be managing by gut instinct. Instead you will be managing based on actionable data and with a far greater understanding of the value-creating machine.

Why You Must Do This Now

As a direct result of business network transformation, globalization, and other realities of the modern business world, to successfully compete, companies must demonstrate a high degree of agility. These new realities demand the management of risk, profitability, and operational effectiveness not only across international boundaries, but also across organizational boundaries. This means a mind-numbing degree of collaboration, data-driven decision-making, and the ability to juggle a

---

Does This Sound Familiar?

- "It takes three weeks to close our books. By the time that happens, it's too late to make adjustments or decisions based on timely information."

- "Our plans are never up to date, and all of the managers game them anyway, so part way through the year they become meaningless."

- "We have no idea if we are going to make the quarter even two days before the quarter closes. In addition, we can't quickly identify why we may succeed or fail in achieving our forecasts until well after the close."

number of moving parts—the value generating machine—in as close to real-time as possible.

If you are unable to gain visibility across this widely distributed system with its multiple interdependencies, and to do so within a framework for continuous monitoring and optimization, you simply will not be competitive in the near- or long-term. The flip side is that if you quickly can begin to leverage assets that you likely already have and start the performance management journey (remember, it doesn't have to be hard or expensive,

---

Managing a Financial Downturn

As of the writing of this book the world economy has slumped into recession. It remains to be seen how deep and long the recession will go, but it is clearly having profound impacts on consumers, the financial sector, world markets, and the regulatory environment. As companies take measures to deal with these conditions, Finance professionals will be at the forefront of efforts to reduce negative impacts and lead the way when recovery begins.

In particular, Forrester Research[1] has identified a number of trends that underline the importance of performance management practices:

- Performance management will garner increasing prominence as Finance organizations increasingly focus on measuring and aligning business performance. However, organizations without a well-designed framework will have difficulties delivering results

- Finance professionals will seek expert services to address needs in performance management, financial reporting, compliance, risk management, treasury, tax, and financial process efficiency to address the economic climate and evolving regulatory requirements

- Companies will seek to upgrade planning, budgeting, and forecasting technologies in order to expand and include more detail. In addition, improved forecasting capabilities will be used to provide better corporate predictability for future results

- Financial compliance and controls will encompass a significant level of corporate investments in order to expand and optimize governance and risk management efforts

---

[1] Paul D. Hamerman and Scott Tiazkun, "Trends 2009: Financial Performance Management: Macroeconomic Conditions Present Challenges and Opportunities," Forrester Research, November 21, 2008.

but rather an iterative process), you will have implemented a practice that can lead you on a path of continuous improvement.

The Business Process Angle

Performance management bridges the gap between strategy and execution by aligning the two. Therefore, in order to understand how to make performance management truly work for you, it is critical to understand the execution processes within your business and how they generate value for your organization. The process that is most important to your company will ultimately be what differentiates it—for example, the quality of your product or service, the speed of your supply networks, or your excellent customer service.

Finance plays a part in every business process that crosses the business units—everything a business does ultimately costs or generates money. Examples of these processes include collaborative demand and supply planning, continuous product innovation, integrated sourcing and procurement, and optimizing sales and marketing investments.

In many companies, Finance takes the lead in orchestrating the key end-to-end business processes that form the core subject of this book:

- **Driving strategy and growth.** In order to better manage the business, executives and managers need critical insight into financial reporting, more effective management of key revenue sources, improved financial planning and forecasting, and the ability to link strategy to execution
- **Managing risk and compliance.** Businesses are required to manage several classes of financial and operational risk and comply with regulatory mandates. From access control, complying with global trade mandates, to mitigating financial risks, companies must ensure they have adequate controls in place

In addition to the business processes that cut across the organization, other processes exist primarily within Finance itself, such as:

- **Optimizing working capital.** Cash is the lifeblood of all businesses. They must take steps to ensure they have enough liquidity to fund normal business operations. This requires rigorous management of receivables and collections, customer credit risk, and cash and liquidity management

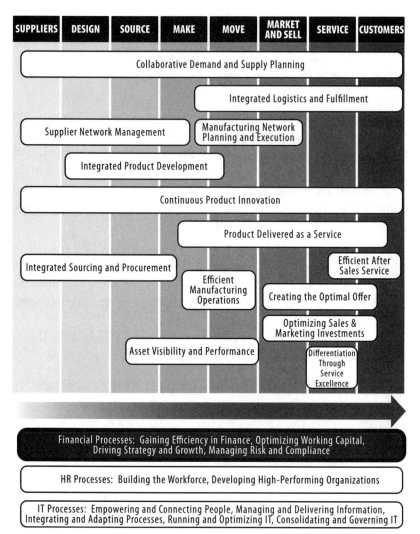

Figure 7-1. Finance Underlies All the Business Processes in the Company

- **Gaining efficiency in Finance.** Finance departments themselves are characterized by labor-intensive and manual processes that consume resources, drive up operating costs, and detract from overall company profitability

The detailed activities of these within finance processes are depicted in Table 7-1.

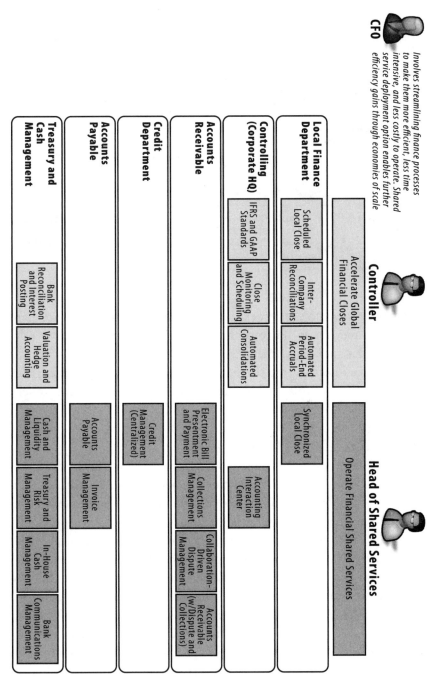

Figure 7-2. Gaining Efficiency in Finance

Table 7-1. Examples of Business Processes within Finance

Financial Supply Chain Management	Electronic Bill Presentment and Payment; Collections Management; Compliance Management; Dispute Management
Treasury	Treasury and Risk Management; Cash and Liquidity Management; In-House Cash; Bank Communication Management
Financial Accounting	General Ledger; Accounts Receivable; Accounts Payable; Contract Accounting; Fixed Assets Accounting; Bank Accounting; Cash Journal Accounting; Inventory Accounting; Tax Accounting; Accrual Accounting; Local Close; Financial Statements
Management Accounting	Profit Center Accounting; Cost Center and Internal Order Accounting; Project Accounting; Investment Management; Product Cost Accounting; Profitability Accounting; Transfer Pricing

Key Roles in Finance

Before getting into a more detailed description of the performance management framework for Finance, first it is important to explain the roles within the Finance department and the pressures they currently operate under. These roles fall into three broad categories: strategic (the CFO), tactical (director of financial planning and analysis and the controller), and operational (financial analysts).

Strategic Roles: The CFO

As a CFO, you know that more is being expected of you and yet the tools and processes you've always relied upon may not be up to the demands. This is the perfect opportunity to embrace performance management techniques to help you gain visibility and insight along with predictability.

Perhaps your single most important measure is captured in the forecasts and guidance that you provide the company's stakeholders on a regular basis. Inaccuracy can carry stern repercussions not only for the company, but also for you professionally. However, working within a spreadsheet-dominated environment with numerous source systems and reporting units means questionable data quality. Further, most likely you cannot gain visibility into operational issues that could impact your forecast, as well as numerous other risk and compliance factors. In this context, gaining control of the sources of variability within your forecast is all but impossible. You're going forward on gut instincts as much as on ambiguous data.

As the complexity of your tasks increases, you are likely to be asked to help drive profitability and ensure strategic alignment within the operational areas of the company.

Companies no longer want you to simply generate backward-looking reports for external consumption. Rather, the CEO is expecting you to do more gathering and reporting of information on operational performance, with an eye toward developing and employing key strategies for increased growth and profitability. A 2007 report from CFO Research Services notes that nearly 75% of CFOs said that compared to five years ago they are spending far more time contributing to strategy. The majority also said they spend far more time on regulatory compliance and financial planning and analysis.[2]

According to an analysis from the Corporate Executive Board, a leading provider of financial best practices, accounting and auditing, which used to account for 83% of the finance skill set in 2003, make up only 21% of the

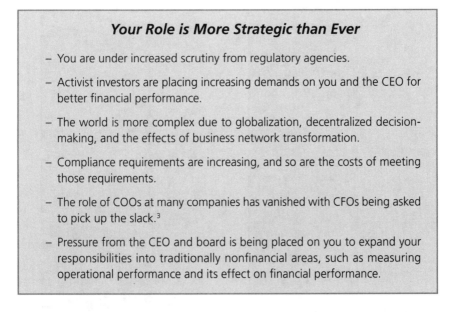

Your Role is More Strategic than Ever

- You are under increased scrutiny from regulatory agencies.

- Activist investors are placing increasing demands on you and the CEO for better financial performance.

- The world is more complex due to globalization, decentralized decision-making, and the effects of business network transformation.

- Compliance requirements are increasing, and so are the costs of meeting those requirements.

- The role of COOs at many companies has vanished with CFOs being asked to pick up the slack.[3]

- Pressure from the CEO and board is being placed on you to expand your responsibilities into traditionally nonfinancial areas, such as measuring operational performance and its effect on financial performance.

---

[2] Mary Driscoll, "The Office of the CFO in 2007–2008: Understanding the 'Pressure Cooker' Context Before Selling a Solution," CFO Research Services.

[3] Marshall Krantz, "Who Needs A COO?" CFO.com, August 1, 2008, at: http://www.cfo.com/article.cfm/11871792?f/.

optimal skill set for today's Finance professionals. Leadership, which didn't figure into the 2003 skill set, accounts for 38% of the current optimal skill set (a share that will increase). Statistics and modeling are also on the rise, from 4% in 2003 to 17% in 2008.

Why are management skills so important? Partly because you need to manage the infrastructure of the various business functions that have moved out of house and partly because you need to be able to evaluate whether what appeared to be good ideas really panned out. Are the business partners really helping the company financially? How can you best manage those

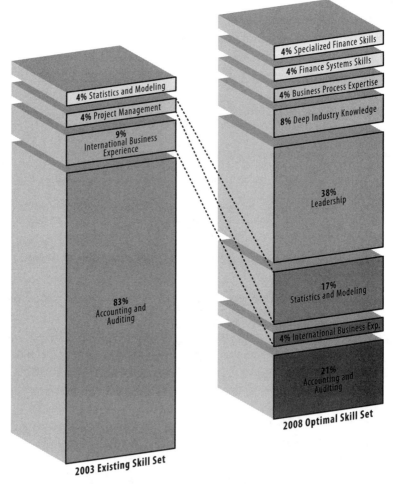

Figure 7-3. Skillset Composition of Global Finance Staff
(Source: CFO Executive Board, a division of the Corporate Executive Board Company;
The Vision of the Future for Finance, 2004)

relationships? Are you getting what you need to do your reporting in an accurate and timely fashion? What changes will make the most sense and bring the best value? The more you can cut the cost of managing those activities that are not your core business, the more money you help free up to support the company's revenue-generating mechanism. Now that's supporting the bottom line.

To meet the obligations placed on you effectively, you need visibility across business units, regions, projects, products, initiatives, and processes in order to generate accurate external statutory reports. As the company's financial services leader, you are for all intents and purposes being forced to also don the title of Chief Performance Officer. You not only must do a better job of making processes more efficient and effective within the finance department, but also improve predictability, incorporate a complete analysis of risk, support corporate decision-making about strategic alternatives, and help optimize operations to produce improved financial results.

Tactical Roles: The Director of Financial Planning and Analysis

As the director of financial planning and analysis, you need performance management because your plans have to be aligned with corporate strategy to ensure correct resource allocation. By linking business drivers to the financials, you can help translate between Operations and Finance.

The primary tool to help you achieve your goals is a far more detailed and granular model of the business than you currently have. The model should be able to support planning and budgeting processes by providing information on profitability by business unit, product, customer, project, or any other dimension, to show where resources could most effectively be allocated. The model should also support the ability to monitor performance against the company's strategic goals so that variances can be noted and actions taken to optimize areas that are falling short.

Tactical Roles: The Controller

As the controller you have to provide both timely and, in many cases, detailed regulatory and management reporting. You need performance management because it's going to help provide you with fast and accurate financial information at the level of detail required to support not only statutory but also management reporting from a single data source. You also need a performance management system that can comfortably operate within the GAAP and emerging IFRS accounting frameworks, including support for the transition from GAAP to IFRS.

Operational Roles: Financial Analyst

As a financial analyst you might think that performance management is only for those higher up in the organization and may make your responsibilities more difficult. However, performance management is not simply an executive or leadership tool, but a systematic approach to increasing everyone's efficiency.

For example, it is a huge pain to track down the inventory clerk, the shipping agents, and the procurement staff to accurately calculate cost of goods sold (COGS) for the P&L, considering that this information typically resides in multiple ERP or accounting systems. However, if all of those operational areas had an integrated performance management system, you could do the forecasting in real-time throughout the quarter and see the effects that variable inventory and category spend is having on the P&L.

Real-time forecasting would also benefit the supply chain management team as well—instead of reacting at the last minute to a shortfall at the end of the quarter, visibility into the forecast helps the supply chain manager react to what is happening in real-time and look for ways to reduce inventory, for example, in time to make a difference in the bottom line. Typically, current management techniques mean that by the time the operational staff gets word from Finance about what's happening, it's too late to prevent it.

Key KPIs That Matter for Your Success

To effectively practice performance management, KPIs must be established in a hierarchy of strategic, tactical, and operational, mapped to the roles in the Finance department from the CFO on down.

One of the more critical high-level KPIs for the finance department that is watched by analysts and investors is the amount of time it takes to close the books. According to a report by the Paragon Consulting Group,[4] the faster and more efficient your close is, the better. "Our hypothesis is that those who have the fastest external reporting close cycles will typically also have some of the most effective and efficient Finance processes and systems."

---

[4] "Close Cycle Rankings 2008: U.K. Top 100 League Table and European Trends," Paragon Consulting Group, July 2008, at: http://www.paragonbpm.com/Assets/ Downloadablefile/Close-Cycle-FTSE-100-League-Table-White-Paper-2008— FINAL-15750.pdf.

The KPI Hierarchy

The following is a sampling of KPIs to give you some ideas of what to look for depending on your role within the department.

Strategic:

- Profitability—gross, operating, and net margin
- Liquidity—current ratio, DSO, DPO
- Efficiency—inventory turns, ROI, ROA, RAROC
- Market/shareholder value—price/earnings ratio and EPS
- Peer benchmarks (cost of finance, speed of closing cycles, cost of audits)

Tactical:

- AP/AR metrics

Operational:

- Close cycle time
- Forecast Accuracy
- OpEx/CapEx

Given the clear correlation between fast close and competitive advantage, look at how you compare in terms of the speed of your quarterly and annual close. Improving your ability to close the books is more than just an efficiency exercise; it's about developing a consolidation model that provides accurate measures, creating a detailed picture of the business and how it is operating.

Leading and Lagging Measures of Performance

One of the more compelling ways performance management can help you develop and sustain competitive advantage is by comparing past operational performance with current performance as an indicator of directionality. Are we heading toward our goals and directives and what do these trends suggest our future performance will be if we keep to the current course?

As noted above, finance-centric measures do not go far enough in telling you the story behind the numbers to provide a glimpse into future performance. For example, a statement of receipts tells you what is coming in, but measuring and trending customer habits can help assess directionality as well as suggest new products and services.

Examples of Quantitative and Qualitative Measures

You may be familiar with traditional financial measures such as:

- **Valuation**—Enterprise value, trailing price/earnings, forward price/earnings, and earnings before interest, taxes, depreciation and amortization (EBITDA)

- **Financials**—Profitability, return on assets, revenue, revenue growth, net income, and total debt

- **Trading Information**—Share price, stock price history, shares outstanding, and dividends

However, to gain the visibility that we advocate, these traditionally finance-centric measures should be mixed and matched with operational ones as well. It is up to you, based on the idiosyncratic nature of your company, to develop a set of metrics that hold value (there are hundreds of potential candidates), but the following examples of metrics by industry should help begin the discussion:

- **Banking**—Loan loss, fee-based revenue growth, customer retention, customer penetration, assets under management, and brand equity

- **Insurance**—Customer retention, capital adequacy, employee satisfaction, market risk exposure, asset quality, and IT expenditures

- **Chemicals**—Product quality, utilization of facilities, customer loyalty, manufacturing costs, and strategic direction

- **Consumer Goods**—Sales volume, quality of strategy, sales and gross margins by product category, growth of strategy, customer service, and percentage of new product sales

Nonfinancial metrics can be viewed as leading indicators of the value-creating machine. Once you define and embed the metrics that hold value, you will gain the visibility to understand what is driving the machine's performance.

Measure the Right Things

After identifying the need to expand your measures to include non-financial metrics, the next trick is to prioritize the measures that will work best in your industry and business. Develop a laser-like focus on those measures that hold the most meaning to your company and its approach to business network transformation. Focusing adeptly on your specific value proposition will ensure strategic alignment as well as hone in on those core capabilities that deliver wealth to the company.

You will also be able to avoid metrics overload. Measuring things simply for the sake of measurement is not a principle of performance management because this will ultimately lead to too much data, much of it beside the point. Metrics for the sake of metrics quickly become just numbers, obscuring the ability to see the overall picture.

No one-size-fits-all solution can help companies determine which measures mean the most to their performance. Finding the right measures that hold value is a mix of methodology and trial-and-error, though some best practices exist.

Further, as you begin to define a proper framework for your company, it is important to develop an idea for how these metrics can cascade up. Various taxonomy schemes can provide granularity to the metrics as they are rolled-up in a hierarchical manner, which in turn allows users to drill down through the various metrics as well as create an audit trail.

What's In It for Me?

Let's just recap what performance management can provide you:

- Faster close
- More accurate information ahead of time so you can make decisions that prevent risk and enhance processes and activities
- Visibility into the drivers behind the numbers
- Trusted data and information at your finger tips to make your job easier and more productive
- Insight into how you can achieve your MBOs and enhance your position with the company

While this list enumerates important benefits for the individual, there are also real benefits that can be gained by the department and organization as a whole, including:

- **Greater automation.** One of the biggest benefits to you as a member of the Finance team is changes to the workload and type of work that you are doing. According to research conducted by BPM International, companies move from an average 29 days in the U.S. and U.K. and 50 days in the E.U. to about 10 to 14 days when the close is automated
- **Data you can trust.** As transactional and consolidation systems become more integrated and efficient, the data quality will be much improved, thus increasing confidence, providing drill-down

capabilities, and reducing the risk of noncompliance. Further, the data can be tagged to provide more granularity and different views for external and management reporting

- **Enterprise alignment.** Linking overall financial goals to specific KPIs, such as customer satisfaction, allows people to see how their day-to-day tasks are connected to financial performance. Likewise, people in Finance gain visibility into drivers behind financial performance
- **Deeper Finance connection to value creation leading to greater performance and profitability.** As the role of the CFO and Finance continues to expand and become more strategic, and as automation speeds up routine tasks, Finance can spend more time identifying and evaluating opportunities to improve operational performance
- **Timely and improved internal and external reporting.** Producing faster reports for internal and external consumption enables you to reduce time spent collecting and reconciling data. The outcome is lower costs, important information in the hands of management, and increased predictability and market confidence

Effective Collaboration

The fact is, even if Finance elevates the discipline of performance management to the level of an Olympic athlete, it's not really going to drive change in the long run. Finance is still reliant on nonfinancial metrics from other departments, and the drivers for those metrics are outside the realm of Finance.

All the other business units—HR, IT, Supply Chain, Manufacturing, Procurement, Sales, Marketing, and Service—must understand the value of integrating not only the methodologies and technologies, but also a culture of performance management into their day-to-day work and processes. Finance must become a partner to the business units and demonstrate how performance management represents an opportunity for everyone.

Collaboration with HR

The relationship between HR and Finance is fraught with tension. Here's a typical scenario. Finance posts guidance—the expected earnings for the next period—as part of a strategic plan. Built into that guidance are certain expectations about the margin the company will be making. The tension arises when Finance is trying to bring external best practice and benchmarking data into the conversation, and HR tries to claim the high road by saying, "You're tying one hand behind my back by giving me a salary number arbitrarily; that won't allow us to attract top talent." HR will try to back this up by demonstrating that its benchmarking software shows that the optimal salary raise is 6%, when your guidance calls for 1% raises this year.

Another tension arises from the commonplace occurrence that HR is always last in line at the till. HR has to fight to live up to the company's "we care about our people" slogan. The department must constantly argue for perks like tuition reimbursement programs and training for management-track personnel. You want to see results from HR, proving that their training programs are effective, that they are hiring the right people, and that their salary estimates are correct for this market. You want to see it proven in cold, hard cash, and the people people are telling you it's not so easy.

Collaboration with IT

Most of the conversations you will have with IT involve security and compliance. But IT speaks its own language. When you talk about segregation of duties, IT thinks "access control." You're interested in who gets access rights and authorization to information—firstly, to maintain security within the organization, and, secondly, to ensure that you have a proper audit trail for compliance purposes.

You also want to make sure that usage of your IT assets isn't driving up costs. If the database can only have 100 simultaneous users, ask IT to monitor that database's use so that licensing costs do not increase.

A typical question from IT to you would be, "What are your security requirements?" You might have to ask them to rephrase that to be a little less open-ended. What you really want to do is express which access rights and authorizations you want to see tied to financials among employees, what regulatory requirements they need to meet, and what audit trails you need to demonstrate that compliance.

Collaboration with Sales

The relationship between Sales and Finance is a bit of a political football. Salespeople are about as excited sitting in your office as the kid in the principal's office. They just want to get paid, and they don't want to hear about rules. It's worth reminding yourself that you have the power in this situation.

It's your job to measure salespeople's productivity. To so, you study metrics such as sales per representative and the total cost of a sale. You will see salespeople most often when they turn in their travel and expense reports, holding their breath and crossing their fingers. Your eagle eye is what comes between them and their reimbursement check. A little proactive maintenance—maybe a short online tutorial on filling out reimbursement slips and sales records—might save you quite a bit of teeth-gnashing when it's time for commission checks to go out or when the numbers come in to your system. Proper recordkeeping, hopefully aided by a crisp, clean BI foundation, can keep things relatively painless between Finance and Sales. The collaboration should begin well before expenses start piling up. You should take the time to educate Sales about the metrics Finance is looking at.

The other major conflict with Sales can occur when salespeople attempt to get revenue recognition, determining who gets credit for what part of the sale. If a product's sales are lagging, you will be in charge of coming up with some motivating incentives for salespeople to hit the pavement. A healthy part of your dialogue should be an effort to make sure the quotas are realistic.

Many companies are now trending toward withholding sales commission payouts until the first customer payment arrives. Relaying this information may not make you the most popular kid on the playground, but you will save yourself a lot of trouble if you proactively notify Sales staff that they will need to hound their new customers and remind them that reminding their customers to pay is a form of customer service. It may take awhile, but eventually, they'll care, because you care.

One way to limit sour notes is to get on the same page with Sales. In the integrated performance organization, Sales will be providing valuable information to Finance that will set the future roadmap of your company and inform revenue goals. Your integrated view of Sales' performance has a direct implication for the overall bottom line, and you can see this relationship propagating in real time if you have the right software links. If the overall goal of Sales is to meet and forecast revenue targets while maintaining a competitive pricing structure for the company, and the goal of the CFO is to effectively manage profitability, performance management will support Sales by providing a consolidated view of Sales' activities against relevant metrics. You, too, will have a window into Sales' analytical tools, allowing you to forecast revenue and meet pipeline targets. When the PM lifecycle comes full circle, there is payoff.

Collaboration with Marketing

There is valuable information to be gained through your collaboration with Marketing.

You are Marketing's partner in trying to determine the efficacy of your product strategy. To determine product ROI, Marketing needs historical information of expenses and sales receipts. You can help each other answer:

- What was the average cost of this product?
- What was the actual cost-of-sale associated with it?
- What was the fully loaded cost to the company once the product was on the market?
- What was the profitability of the product?
- What was the profitability of all 20 flavors of the product in a particular region?

You then feed the results of these dialogues back to Marketing, who packages the information for Product Development, whose work then informs the next Marketing strategy. This information will help Marketing to develop pricing models, a go-to-market strategy, and sales training programs.

Your reward: accountability from the team that sets the strategy for your company in the marketplace.

Collaboration with Procurement

Finance is typically happy to engage with Procurement because it is the one group that has a maniacal focus on reducing costs and driving efficiency. The Procurement group serves as a layer of protection from rogue spending and provides Finance with a consolidated view of spending by department. Further, Procurement mitigates compliance risks for the organization by ensuring that all parties follow a consistent and compliant process for acquiring assets and services.

Finance relies on Procurement to acquire goods and/or services at the best possible total cost of ownership, in the right quantity and quality, at the right time, in the right place, and from the right source for the direct benefit or use of the company. Simple procurement may involve nothing more than repeat purchasing. Complex procurement could involve finding long-term partners or even co-destiny suppliers. The latter has heightened levels of risk that Finance counts on Procurement to manage.

Procurement needs access to all spending data in every division of the company, whether or not they manage that spending directly. Only in this way can Procurement figure out how to save the company real money. Finance expects Procurement to drive cost efficiencies throughout the business so Procurement needs to demonstrate its value by showing the savings generated. Finance also requires Procurement to put the appropriate policies and controls in place to ensure that purchasing is handled according to corporate policy—for example, competitive bids for purchases above a certain amount.

Collaboration with Supply Chain

Finance recognizes that the supply chain is extremely complex, and anything complex typically has high associated costs and risks. Finance interacts with the head of Supply Chain to ensure that the supply chain is operating efficiently and is compliant. Costs and compliance are the two most important aspects for Finance. As a global company, the number of regulations and documentation required by country is significant and cannot be managed ad-hoc. Ad-hoc steps create additional costs and Finance will not tolerate this from Supply Chain.

Finance expects to get visibility into Supply Chain processes, workflow, and automation to gain confidence in their cost effectiveness and compliance. Specifically, Finance expects the Supply Chain department to provide full documentation of adherence to regulations for accurate corporate and legal reporting. They also expect that Supply Chain, in concert with Procurement, will ensure that suppliers manage their businesses in accordance with company standards and policies.

Collaboration with the Business Network

You cannot ignore the performance of partners, suppliers, and even customers. The complex interdependencies in this network can have profound effects on the operational and financial performance of the company. Your company, partners, suppliers, and customers must be as predictable as possible so that you can manage their performance and impact on your company. Working collaboratively should be a shared goal, supported by technologies capable of pulling data from any source system to create as complete a model of operational and financial performance as possible.

Stakeholders with an interest in the company's financial prospects want to know more than just how well the company performed yesterday. They want visibility into the drivers behind the guidance you are providing relative to future results, which demonstrates that you are in control of, and understand the value-generating machine as well as its direction. This in turn drives future investment decisions. Finance professionals that put performance management capabilities in place, to manage the execution of strategy and provide the agility to deliver on financial goals in an unpredictable economy, are the ones that will be rewarded.

Predictability is also a goal for the business network. If you are not as predictable as possible to your partners, they will start looking for other companies that can provide more stability. On the flip side, if one source of variability in your forecast is a partner, you will want to engage in performance management measures to ensure that the partner's performance does not affect the predictability of the organization unduly. Good visibility into the value a partner adds can helps determine if the relationship is working.

Establishing Your BI Foundation

Performance management is powered by business intelligence (BI). BI provides critical capabilities that can be used across the organization to support a common data management platform that the various analytic and performance management applications can use to pull consolidated and cleansed data. In particular, Finance needs the following features from BI:

- **Precise control over data.** Most Finance professionals are very particular about rich spreadsheet-based formatting and want very precise control over what appears and at what level of detail
- **Relevant event-capture and alerting.** The ability to gather nonfinancial information from event sources like SCM for order fulfillment and logistics management, and from other operational areas of the business that may have a material impact, along with external sources like credit ratings, stock market changes, and key bond market ratios. Finance also needs the ability to define alerts for critical events (a top competitor just announced earnings and the value of our stock plummeted 15%) and inform the right person to take action
- **A unified semantic layer, data integration, and data quality across departmental and application silos.** BI allows Finance to bridge the siloed systems if they do not have access to an integrated transactional system, but instead to many point systems (accounts payable, accounts receivable, treasury) or multiple ERP systems
- **Trusted, cleansed master data.** BI provides Finance standardized definitions of how accounts are defined (in fact, many companies today are moving to a single, global worldwide chart of accounts) as well as key attributes for those accounts (debit or credit, asset or liability, and so on)

- **Structured and unstructured data.** BI platforms can provide insights into structured and unstructured data. Tremendous insight is available in internal management reports as well as in unstructured data like the 10-K and 10-Q filings of competitors (for example, all of our top competitors mention supply chain risk in their filings)
- **Reports.** These include publication quality reports for internal and external distribution, dashboards to visualize Finance information such as budget spend by department or cost center allocation by department, and query and analysis reports. An example of a query and analysis report is commissions paid to sales reps this quarter or number of contracts closed this quarter. Multidimensional OLAP analysis can slice and dice financial data for the analyst. You see this when you analyze data to determine company margins or review historical product data to assign sales budget by product line

Assessing Performance Management Maturity and Setting Your Course

Where you are in terms of performance management maturity depends on the idiosyncratic nature of the organization and its capabilities, as well as on a number of related factors. Chapter 3 describes a maturity model for performance management that is applicable to Finance. There are also a few questions to consider as you begin to think about where various processes and activities are in terms of maturity:

- Do we have a BI-powered data management platform?
- Is our close less than 10 days or are we closer to the average of 29 days for the U.S. and U.K. and 50 for the E.U.?
- Do we have confidence in the forecasts and guidance we provide stakeholders?
- Are our budgets relevant throughout the year or are they outdated by changing conditions?
- Do we have a broad understanding of the operational drivers behind financial performance? Do we have visibility into them?
- Do we have visibility into cost and profitability by customer, product, channel, business unit, and region?
- Can we firmly link strategy to operational processes and activities?
- Do we engage in frameworks such as Beyond Budgeting, activity-based costing, and driver-based budgeting?
- Do we have clear visibility into risks and appropriate controls to ensure compliance with internal and external mandates?

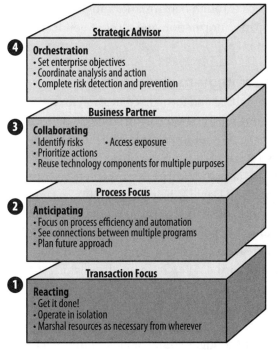

Figure 7-4. The Performance Management Maturity Model

- Are we actively collaborating with all the business units to fully understand their needs and the value they add to the organization?

The PM Lifecycle for Finance

As the CFO, you have a seat at the table as the organization goes through its strategy cycle—creating strategic goals and initiatives, creating a plan and budget to achieve those goals, monitoring the effectiveness of the company at achieving its goals, creating a model of performance in order to understand the best methods to optimize performance, and then feeding that learning back into the strategy cycle. With the CEO and the other executive-level leaders, you determine the direction of the company as well as monitor its success at achieving its most fundamental objectives. You are being asked to provide insight about where performance variances are occurring within operations as well as the best means to optimize operational performance.

However, your job is not done. Finance must also ensure that its own strategic goals, processes, and activities are properly aligned with the overall strategy of the company. You must ensure that planning is being done properly and that you are monitoring and measuring your own performance through benchmarks and personal improvement. You must also feed this information and all that you learn back into the PM lifecycle for Finance.

Closing the Strategy-to-Execution Gap

Without a structured and formalized method for continually developing, planning, monitoring, and optimizing strategic performance, companies will fail to achieve the full impact of the strategies they set. The primary reason most strategies fail is not because they are bad or wrong (though some are), but because they are poorly executed. According to research by Robert S. Kaplan and David P. Norton,[5] 60–80% of companies fall short of predicted outcomes of their strategies. In addition, they report that most companies realize only about 60% of a strategy's potential value because of defects and breakdowns in planning and execution.

As Kaplan and Norton note, Gresham's Law, which states that bad money drives out good, applies in analyzing why strategies fail. "Discussions about bad operations inevitably drive out discussions about good strategy implementation. When companies fall into this trap, they soon find themselves limping along, making or closely missing their numbers each quarter, but never examining how to modify their strategy to generate better growth opportunities or how to break the pattern of short-term financial shortfalls."

The gap between strategy and execution underscores the need for the PM lifecycle. Performance management involves the routine, and sometimes non-routine, measurement of key aspects of financial performance, and making this information available to decision-makers. In this section, we will walk you through the PM lifecycle, highlighting the factors and evaluation methods that your peers have found useful.

Strategize and Prioritize

As you work with corporate leaders to develop strategy and set priorities, your job is to provide critical analysis on cost, profit, and the drivers behind both to help the leadership team analyze and articulate what the strategy should be. You drive this analysis by examining finance-centric measures of past performance coupled with a rich mix of nonfinancial

---

[5] Robert S. Kaplan and David P. Norton, "Mastering the Management System," *Harvard Business Review,* January 2008.

data and measures that directly correlate to overall financial performance, supplemented with market data and competitor information.

Next, we'll look at the basic steps you'll follow in developing and prioritizing your strategies.

Understand the Context

Review the corporate strategic goals, strategic plans, initiatives, and metrics that track progress against them and understand them. Contextualize them with the implications they have for Finance and use this context to drive the Finance PM lifecycle.

Develop and Set the Strategy

Within the PM lifecycle, you are a catalyst. You set strategy and define measures to see if the organization is achieving its objectives. You provide key insights to help define initiatives to achieve goals and then define how the various pieces of the company will be measured through financial and operational metrics. To accomplish this, you need visibility into how operational performance can affect financial performance so that you can drive strategy and operational alignment. However, none of this will make any difference if it can't be cascaded throughout the organization in a meaningful and actionable way so that each business unit can see what its objectives are, what its metrics are, and how both align to the overall strategy of the organization.

Review the Environment

What are you well-positioned for? What are the main problems you face? What risks do you have? What compliance requirements must you meet?

One of your key capabilities as an organization might be the ability to forecast revenues and costs accurately. Your risks might include lacking access to lines of credit and low capital reserves. Your compliance challenges certainly include complying with regulations such as Sarbanes-Oxley, as well as statutory financial compliance objectives around U.S.-GAAP or IFRS.

Set the Mission, Values, and Vision

Define the mission, which is the fundamental purpose of the entity, especially what it provides to customers and clients.

Define the core values—the attitude, behavior, and character of the organization. As an example, we put integrity above all else because our organization and profession demands it.

Define the vision, which is a concise statement that defines the 3- to 5-year goals of the organization. For instance, by 2012, be involved in every strategic decision made by the CEO and top executives of the company.

Set the Goals

With all that contextual information in hand, set the strategies to follow (of course, you'll collaborate with the CEO and other top execs). Here are some sample strategies:

- Increase the efficiency of the Finance organization
- Increase overall profitability of the company
- Facilitate best practice business processes

Consider using a strategy map to display the cause and effect relationships among the objectives that make up a strategy. A good strategy map tells a story of how value is created for the business.

Assign KPIs to Goals and Set the Right Targets

Define KPIs and targets that translate strategy into performance expectations. Identify value drivers (those elements that contribute to the value in your organization). First, value drivers and the related performance tolerances (KPIs) have risks associated with their achievement. Second, these risks should be identified and tolerance levels defined, from which a KRI can

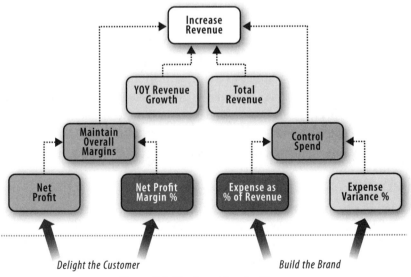

Figure 7-5. Strategy Map for Finance

be established. This connectivity between a value driver and a relevant KPI and KRI is an important bridge from a strategic view of risk—which can have a time horizon of three or more years—to a more focused budgetary view of risk, which is often applied to a single year.

For example, for the goal of "increasing the efficiency of the Finance organization" outlined above, you might choose KPIs for close cycle time and cost of finance versus industry benchmark along with targets to reduce both from their current values by 3% this year and 5% in 3 years. For the goal of "increase overall profitability of the company," you might choose the KPIs of net margin and net price/earnings along with targets to increase both by 1% this year and 3% over 3 years.

Perform Additional Risk Analysis and Set KRIs

Now look again at risks to see what could keep you from meeting your goals. For each risk, decide what your risk appetite is. Can you afford to take that risk? What's the worst-case scenario? Does taking the risk have the potential to wipe out important projects?

For example, if you are exposed to liquidity risk because you currently do not have strong cash reserves and suddenly credit becomes much more difficult to obtain, you may find it necessary to make fairly dramatic changes to free up working capital, including stopping critical new product development initiatives and laying off key staff.

Set a response strategy for the risk (watch, research, transfer, delegate, mitigate). You could decide that having low cash reserves and exposing

---

Examples of Risks for Finance

Planning & Forecasting. Budget overrun compared to plan, actual versus planned revenue, liquidity forecast by currency/day, days sales outstanding

Financial Reporting. Number of failed controls, number of postings in already closed period

Fraud. Segregation of Duties Risks

Accounts Payable. Overdue payments

Market Risks. Currency exchange fluctuations, equity value fluctuations, commodity price fluctuations

Credit Risks. Credit limit breaches, unsecured exposure and expected loss, credit concentration, collateral obligations, number of disputed charges

yourself to liquidity risk might be an appropriate risk to take given an unbeatable opportunity to acquire another competitor. You could mitigate this risk by starting a number of initiatives to free up working capital in other ways, including inventory reduction and supplier rationalization initiatives, as well as being much more judicious in your extension of credit to customers. This means being proactive instead of having to make dramatic cuts when it is too late.

Decide whether you can afford the worst-case scenario presented by that risk from a performance management perspective. Could it bring down some critical value-generating mechanism for the company? For example, clearly, without adequate cash reserves on hand, any business is at very serious risk. You should think very carefully before making an acquisition or a major capital expenditure that will significantly reduce your cash reserves. In the worst-case scenario, you may find the company significantly impaired without cash on hand, and this is not a risk any business can afford to take.

Define KRIs and thresholds for those risks. Key risk indicators, like KPIs, are the early warning signals that define the threshold at which a risk could occur. For the risk described above, liquidity forecast by day is a very good early warning sign. Once this forecast gets too low, it is time to set remediation plans in place to begin freeing up working capital.

Perform Additional Compliance Analysis and Set Controls

Define your compliance requirements. Compliance defines the boundaries within which companies must operate when achieving their strategies. For example, a large number of compliance mandates impact Finance, including SOX, SEC, U.S.-GAAP, and IFRS regulations among many others, notably industry-specific regulations.

Define policies, procedures, and controls that must be in place to ensure that you can meet the compliance requirements. Make sure that this applies not only at the main business process level, but also to all subprocesses including and perhaps especially those related to partners. Establishing a policy to review customer's credit histories to mitigate the organizational exposure to huge credit risk and lack of visibility to credit exposure in the market is an example of this. A control would put a procedure in place to ensure that the risk response is effectively carried out, that proactive monitoring of all system records to indicates the sum of credit exposure is being assessed in both an effective and compliant way.

Define control targets that translate compliance expectations into performance expectations. One example would be to set a target of a credit

Controls That Are Relevant for Finance

Finance Period Closing. Posting period control, logistics period cutoff, Prior period posting entries, Period control—company level changes, Recurring entries schedule changes, Analysis of recurring entries, Intercompany transactions

Procure to Pay. Accuracy of Invoice Tolerances, GR/IR posting accuracies and validity, Org Level Duplicate Payment Control, Vendor Eligibility for Duplicate Payments, Payments without Goods Receipt, Material Value Changes at standard and Moving Average Price, Inventory Postings other than system date, Duplicate Vendor Invoices, Overpaid Purchase Orders

Order to Cash. Changes to Billing Documents, Sales Returns by Customer, Credit Exposure for Customer Risk Category, Sales through one time customers, Sales Order Aging Analysis, Open Sales Orders, Customer Pricing Procedures, Company-wise Credit Exposure, Changes to Automatic Credit Check, Payment Terms—Higher Cash Discount, Payment Terms—Higher Credit, Credit Check—Sales Order Entry

Maintain and Manage General Ledger. GL Postings—account level, GL Postings—account Item level, GL Postings—document level, GL Postings—Document item level, Chart of Accounts—GL Changes, Company code—GL Changes, Changes to accounting document—Occurrence, Accounting posting changes, Monitoring material price changes in Financial Accounting, Analysis of manual invoices by user, Monitoring exchange rate changes (Workflow-based approval of journals prior to posting)

exposure of $100,00 after which it would not be sensible to close a sale with that customer.

Work on the Strategic Action Plan and Initiatives

The strategic initiatives help define the exact methodology (the roadmap) for achieving the various goals. The results of this planning may require revisiting the strategy.

The steps to working through strategic planning go something like this:

- Develop the roadmap (sequence of actions) for achieving Finance's piece of the strategic plan. Include risk and control management, specifically automating the process, workflow, and guidance for conducting risk and control assessments. For example, in order to achieve finance efficiency goals, you might begin an initiative to implement a finance shared services hub in an offshore location
- For each initiative, define critical success and failure factors for all initiatives. Critical success factors might include approval of various

international works councils that may object to the necessary Finance staff downsizing in high-cost locations. Failure factors might be any of the dominos along the way in an initiative's roadmap that could derail it. These failure factors can then be translated into key risk indicators that serve as an early warning system so that the project can be gotten back on track in time or alternatives can be found

- Develop different risk-adjusted scenarios with contingency plans should risks to achieving plans materialize. For example, if works councils do not approve of redistributing Finance staff in high-cost locations, you might consider offering training programs to allow affected staff to be retrained in different areas of the business like Marketing or Product Development

Strategic plans should therefore be risk-adjusted, with contingency plans for as many risk scenarios as you can reasonably imagine based on past experience and the current environment. You then want to come up with risk response plans that help you address how you will handle the risks if monitoring those risks provides an alert of risks materializing.

Cascade Accountability

Each KPI, KRI, and control and its target should be owned by some department or group.

The MBOs of the staff in those groups must reflect the KPIs, KRIs, and controls you set. This sounds obvious, but frequently performance is measured at an individual level in a way that does not in fact relate directly to corporate goals and strategies.

If Finance organizational efficiency is a key metric, make sure the people on that team benefit and receive appropriate personal goals and targets as well as incentives to streamline the processes they are engaged in.

Plan and Execute

In the strategize and prioritize phase of the PM lifecycle, we put together strategic action plans and initiatives. The planning phase gets into the details of planning the strategic initiatives from a financial and operational standpoint.

Build Your Strategic Financial Plan

Strategic financial plans are used by executives to represent a high-level and long-term (3- to 5-year) perspective of revenue, expenses, balance sheet items, and cash flows and to provide the ability to estimate the impact of alternative strategies (such as how merger and acquisition activity will affect your organization based on the timing of the transactions). Long-term cash flow and balance sheet forecasting are critical elements in any planning environment that are not handled well in generic planning applications. Strategic financial planning provides the ability to link the various aspects of your organization's financial performance, from earnings potential through working capital management to capital expenditures, taxes, and the capital structure that supports your business. This allows you to address the complex nature of funding, the impact of strategies on your credit ratings, capital structure optimization, and strategic treasury planning, which can reduce a company's cost of capital and create value. These solutions also allow for a variety of methods for specifying the way cash surpluses and deficits are treated in models such as debt borrowing and repayments, dividend payments, and share issues or repurchases. You can create fixed- or variable-rate debt instruments and generate accurate calculations of the current debt and accrued interest, as well as the amortization of bond premiums, discounts, and issuance expenses.

Orchestrate the Corporate Budget

Think for a moment about how your company handles the planning and budgeting process. Is it a yearly exercise where strategic goals are broadly discussed and a few extra resources allocated to certain areas? Would you describe your process as efficient and effective? Is it captured in multiple source documents and templates? Is it highly detailed with numerous line items along a number of cost centers? And lastly, does it often feel like such a lengthy and painful process that, once the budget is completed, is essentially out-of-date?

If so, your planning and budgeting cycle is like many companies that exist within a spreadsheet-dominated world where planning and budgeting ignore the drivers behind performance, where documents produced reflect past problems rather than future needs, and where your forecasts—the primary measure of your performance—are as apt to be off target as on.

You need to transition from the old process to one where you are able to quickly gain a consolidated view of where and how the company incurs costs. This means engaging in a planning approach based on operational drivers or running simulations in an activity-based costing model when the resource requirements needed to meet fluctuations in demand can be quickly assessed. It may be a vast oversimplification, but the intent is to develop as detailed as possible an understanding of the drivers behind past performance in order to constructively compare what will drive future performance. This will then allow you to focus resources on those processes and activities that will garner the most benefit to the company as well as help create a more precise model from which to prepare forecasts.

By better understanding where to target efforts (by customer, product, project, market, channel, process, activity, and so forth), you can better allocate resources using operating and capital budgeting.

The budgeting process takes each of the outcomes or actions from the planning process and aligns revenues and expenses against them. Decisions regarding investment priorities and resource allocations define how the company will operate and set the bar for measuring performance. Take each of the steps in the initiatives you've defined and put in revenues and expenses for them.

To create risk-adjusted budgets, incorporate the range of possible revenues and costs of each action into the budget at the appropriate organizational level. A risk-adjusted budget is one that responds to changing circumstances, providing the financial capability to react to events in a planned, proactive

Create Clear and Well-Defined End Product/Output of Financial Plan

From	To	Rationale
Financial plan is documented in multiple sources and templates	Creation of clear and tangible end product of financial planning comprising premises and input parameters	Premises and KPI values must be transparent and accessible with output format equal to monthly management report

Adjust Planning Detail

From	To		Rationale
Detailed financial planning on subcategory level with many line items along many cost centers and multi-dimensional KPI planning	Aggregated planning with few clearly structured P&L positions and definition of few business unit positions	Breakdown of strategic targets along only a few dimensions with relevant levers	Misleading accuracy on detailed level and high planning effort

Improve Process and Efficiency

From	To	Rationale
Loops and duration of overall process perceived as painful by participants and disproportionate to benefits caused by multiple loops	Loops reduced through lean process, and easy top-down discussion of interfaces between businesses, starting with strategic target setting for top-level KPIs	Initial target-setting through strategy workshop and performance management provides clear guidance for financial planning process

Figure 7-6. Planning Simplified

manner. Develop different risk-adjusted budgets with contingency plans should risk events occur.

For example, in a traditional budget, you list the individual line items (revenues from direct sales and channel partners selling products and services along with operating expenses for research and development, sales and marketing, and general and administrative) in each row with the actuals, budgeted amounts, forecast, and actual/budget comparisons and forecast versus budget comparisons going across in the columns. In a risk-adjusted budget, for every decision to allocate revenue to one line item versus another (for example, to allocate more budget to product development versus marketing), you determine the impact and probability of the highest priority risks (like not having enough demand generated in the market for all of the products you plan to develop) on those individual line items and use this to set a range of expected budget and forecasted values instead of fixed values. In this case, if the risk materializes and you have a product about to be released that does not have appropriate marketing support, you would want a contingency plan in place that shows the performance and risk implications of suddenly reallocating budget to marketing, which may jeopardize other products in the innovation pipeline.

Align Budget to Operational Plans

The operational planning process links the budget to operational factors. Plan out each step of each initiative in terms of what will be required in terms of technology, time, and resources. Consider what risks you have in each area of the operational plan. The operational plan is largely relevant to the other business units, but there are still areas where Finance owns operational activities such as managing payments, collections, and disputes and needs to have plans in place for them.

In a risk-adjusted operational plan, for every decision to allocate resources to one set of operational activities versus another (vendor invoice processing versus sales order processing), you determine the impact and probability of the highest-priority operational risks (like the risk of a spike in vendor invoicing due to the lack of working capital of those vendors) on those individual line items and use this to set a range of expected and forecasted values instead of fixed values. In this case, if the risk materializes and incoming invoice volume suddenly spikes, you need a contingency plan that shows the performance (the goal to process invoices and orders efficiently) and risk implications of removing resources from sales order processing and putting them into vendor invoicing.

Taking these factors into account, adjust your plans with a range of operational outcomes (instead of 10,000 invoices per month processed, use 6,000–14,000) and probabilities (likelihood 80% accurate) rather than an absolute number based on the various contingencies.

Capital Asset Planning

Capital asset planning is a complex process that typically involves high levels of expenditure and substantial exposure to risk. Organizations must correctly categorize every major component of their capital asset plan as complex projects develop, so that they're treated appropriately in the financial forecasts. For example, each component of an asset (such as equipment, property, or plants) whose cost is significant in relation to the total cost of the asset must be depreciated separately. Systems for managing capital asset planning tasks, such as categorization of assets, depreciation calculations, funding, and cash flow options over the duration of a project, have become available in recent years to manage this process. Some packages also let users plan for capital asset-related expenses such as maintenance costs, repairs, and insurance.

One of the key values of this technology is the guided workflow governing the approval process for capital asset spending. Automating and documenting the approval chain accelerates the process while maintaining a full audit trail of changes, which provides appropriate controls. Closing the loop between operational systems like ERP, existing assets can be brought into capital asset planning where partial additions and disposals can be recorded and depreciated or revalued as required after taking into account impairments.

Forecast Performance and Risks

Create rolling, risk-adjusted forecasts of the budget (revenues and costs) and operational plan (including number, capacity, and cost of resources necessary to achieve plan) so that you can see trends over a rolling time horizon for those risks whose probability, consequence, and/or resiliency change over time. That way if you have to make adjustments, you can see where you've been and the direction in which things are likely to go. Predictive analytical techniques can be a particularly powerful tool for building risk-adjusted forecasts by modeling the impact previous risks had on previous forecasts.

In a risk-adjusted forecast, you create a rolling forecast over a six month to one year window of a range of expected costs (the line items in your budget like product development, sales and marketing, and so forth), a range of expected revenues (line items for products and services), and an associated range of expected activity outputs from the business units (for example, number of products produced or marketing campaigns launched) that is dependent on the key risks in the environment. When the probability or impact of a risk changes, such as the risk of not having enough working capital to run the business, you adjust the financial or operational forecast revenues, costs, or activities accordingly. Using predictive techniques, you can learn from the impact of previous risks on previous actuals to predict the impact of your current risks on your current revenue, cost, or activity forecasts.

Capabilities: Financial Planning, Budgeting and Forecasting

Generally speaking, capabilities for planning, budgeting, and forecasting for Finance tend to be the most mature and widely deployed. These capabilities support processes that strike to the core of what the Finance department does.

Although these capabilities tend to be more mature, it still does not mean that most companies—including yours—have given up on operating within an array of source systems and spreadsheets, leading to complex, time-consuming, and ineffective processes. A performance management framework, however, promotes the integration of these capabilities so that you gain visibility and compare, for example, planned sales figures versus actual sales and then use the variance to understand what the trend will likely be.

These capabilities should also link to cost and profitability software to allow planners working with the director of financial planning and analysis to create what-if scenarios to examine how, for example, hiring 10 new sales representatives would affect costs and profitability. For planners and others in the Finance department, this capability provides a powerful planning and visualization tool. In addition, according to Gartner,[6] budgeting, planning and forecasting software should:

- Provide a financial modeling engine with an integrated profit and loss, balance sheet, and cash flow forecasting capability
- Support the complete budget creation and approval process that enables users to define and control the flow of budgets and plans and forecasts for review and approval as well as maintain a complete audit trail

---

[6] Nigel Rayner, "Understanding CPM Applications," Gartner Research, August 24, 2007.

- Support short-term financial budgeting and long-term financial planning
- Enable forecasting and modeling as well as the ability to run what-if scenarios for analysis
- Support the ability to model the effects of initiatives in combination with each other

Examine Repercussions for Execution Problems

In a tight economy, another look is in order before beginning to execute. Planning and execution must be based in strategy and be aligned to the strategies that have been set down. If Finance delays a key initiative that is not aligned with corporate strategy, its impact across the company can be profound. Given that Finance holds the keys to the kingdom in terms of ultimate resource allocations (it all costs money!), coordination across and with all the business units is critical so that there are no surprises. The key to excellence in execution is visibility.

Execute

Turn strategy into action by translating initiatives and activating corporate transactive business processes in the value chain based on the resource assignments made during planning. For example, once the plan is understood, we can begin building new products, procuring new materials, running marketing campaigns, and providing customer service outside of Finance and closing the books and managing disputes within Finance in line with the plan.

Monitor and Analyze

In the monitor and analyze phase of the PM lifecycle, you monitor to understand what is happening in the business, analyze to understand why it is happening, and for those things not on track, adjust to improve the situation relative to your goals.

Financial Consolidation and Reporting

For many, rolling up the numbers at the end of a quarter or year is handled by one-off databases and/or spreadsheets that cascade upward from multiple source systems and reporting units to division CFOs and then on to the corporate CFO. This process requires quite a bit of manual work—uploading, consolidating and reconciling data from transactional systems and preparing it primarily for external statutory reporting with some limited internal management reporting.

However, with modern ERP systems, additional technology supporting close and consolidation processes, and the use of BI, you can flow data upward far more efficiently and seamlessly. For example, it is no longer necessary to manually upload intermediate files between the source ledger systems and consolidation systems. Instead, data can be integrated between these two systems by reading it from a source ledger, mapping it, transforming it, and loading it into the consolidation system in an entirely automated process.

You can, and should, move from a consolidation system that is spreadsheet-driven to a formal model that collects financial and nonfinancial data from multiple sources, transforms it, and then consolidates the data for statutory and management reporting purposes. Rather than a separate set of spreadsheets containing non-integrated data of questionable pedigree and quality, a BI-powered consolidation system can remove uncertainty

Multidimensionality

The modern enterprise typically has very little use for one-dimensional management reports that only provide a glance at the state of the company in the past quarter. Rather, managers need the capability to be supported in gaining any one of a number of views into the data, which includes, but is not limited to:

- The ability to quickly slice and dice the data in order to perform ad hoc reporting on the current performance of the business

- The ability to easily view the data from a statutory reporting standpoint in order to, for example, review the plan for the following year and be able to use historical markers in order to anticipate the numbers that could be reported if the plan succeeds

- The ability to use the multidimensional capabilities of the system to support long-term strategic planning by incorporating what-if scenarios into their analysis

Modern consolidation systems are able to support these capabilities by tagging data with each dimension or attribute that holds value as it cascades up from localized reporting units. After data enters the consolidation system, it is then fed into a multidimensional database where the tags—such as by total revenue, by revenue split across reporting units, by region, by product, by project, by initiative, and so on—are able to support multiple views.

from data collection and reporting responsibilities not to mention make this one process far more efficient.

Further, these systems can incorporate a range of industry reporting standards such as IFRS and U.S. GAAP—not to mention XBRL, the emerging

XBRL—Technology Supporting Enhanced Reporting

The move toward IFRS as a global accounting standard is gaining momentum. Accompanying this shift is a similar move toward an electronic reporting software standard called Extensible Business Reporting Language (XBRL).

XBRL is designed for the electronic submission of financial reports using taxonomies. Rather than simply placing data into a printed report and submitting that to stakeholders, companies would use XBRL, a financial reporting data format, to tag the data with various attributes, which could then be fed in report form into any computer system in the world. The tagging allows the computer system to know what the individual pieces of data are. For example, the computer would know if it is a profit statement for the first quarter, the division it is related to, and the fiscal year.

The XBRL standard also supports inclusion of additional qualitative data to provide users with a much richer and contextualized data set that includes not only the numbers, but also the drivers behind those numbers. This means that analysts and other stakeholders will have greater transparency into the drivers behind performance, which in turn gives insight into predictability.

Using XBRL will mean that within hours of receiving reports, regulatory bodies will be able to build an entire library of all the financial statements received, and compare and contrast them using standardized taxonomies.

XBRL can also be used to leverage the data of other companies—which was formerly difficult to find and capture in the data cloud of the Web—for benchmarking purposes. The taxonomy functionality allows users to perform analysis and drill into profit as well as information on the drivers behind the performance of peer and competitor companies in order to allow a much deeper and immediate benchmarking exercise. In this way, XBRL creates a wealth of highly organized information that can be focused on internal purposes, such as helping define better metrics and optimizing processes and operations.

Further, XBRL, while still an emerging standard, is gaining wide acceptance. In the U.S., the Securities and Exchange Commission is driving adoption and has received approximately $2 trillion in financial reporting filed via XBRL. Globally, XBRL is gaining wider acceptance as the UK is mandating XBRL for company tax filings beginning in 2010; China is mandating that all public companies file in XBRL; and the Spanish Stock Exchange is using XBRL for receiving and distributing public reports from more than 3,000 listed companies.

software standard for electronic reporting—in order to meet the relevant reporting requirements and norms of the governing entities where your company operates.

Monitor

It is important to distinguish the different categories of monitoring in evaluating business performance.

- **Event monitoring** looks for a single, discrete activity or exposure event, like changes to an important exchange rate
- **Trend monitoring** is similar to event monitoring, but looks at events over time to determine patterns. For example, regular monitoring of the relative stock prices of key competitors and fluctuations
- **Intelligence monitoring** collects information from a variety of external sources, such as major stock exchanges abroad, that are of interest to the company and may indicate a risk exposure

The presentation of information to be monitored is also crucial in order to facilitate decision-making. Dashboards bring together all the relevant pieces of information in all the major domain areas of business that need to be monitored in role-based, contextual views to get a status at a glance. Typical dashboards for monitoring might be organized as follows:

- Payables dashboard
- Receivables dashboard
- Profitability dashboard
- Liquidity dashboard
- Shareholder value dashboard

Dashboards combine events, trends, and intelligence monitoring patterns across all of the major facets of the business to be monitored, including the key business dimensions like customers, products, projects, and employees, and the related KPI, KRIs, controls, and incidents and losses. From the dashboard, it is then possible to do many things.

Evaluate performance. You can evaluate KPIs to identify progress made toward achievement of objectives and trends. Is the critical KPI of net margin on target? Is it trending in the right direction?

Evaluate initiatives. Are they failing or behind schedule? For example, is the critical initiative to roll out the new Finance shared services center on target?

Evaluate risk. Data is monitored from source systems that provide transactional data for the KRIs. Dashboards can help identify and manage key risks versus overall risks (being able to prioritize based on exposure through quantitative/qualitative assessment to thresholds). Look at the KRIs to identify the top risks. For example, are you at risk for organizational exposure to huge discounts for customers via payment terms? Evaluate changes to the risk levels for key activities. Are more salespeople trying to push through orders with higher discounts than previously? Are risks being assessed in accordance with company policy or according to industry best practices? For example, are credit checks on customers being performed on every transaction in excess of $100,000 as prescribed by company policy? Are mitigation strategies effective in reducing the likelihood or impact of a risk? For example, is the new program to train salespeople on the appropriate legal discounting procedures reducing the risk of huge discounts?

Evaluate internal controls. Report key control deficiencies, approvals, verifications, and reconciliations to mitigate risk. For example, are we reporting and ultimately remediating control deficiencies on the policies we have put in place to check cash discount value, configured in customer payment terms, and provide details of cash discounts?

Evaluate incidents and losses. If incidents or losses have occurred due to the failure or absence of controls, such as not being able to recover the value of goods shipped to a customer who could not pay for them, this information needs to be documented.

No matter how proactive you are, manual monitoring can be very inefficient. Automated monitoring can proactively identify out-of-tolerance conditions, highlighting key areas for analysis of a KPI, KRI, or control, and then alerting the responsible party. This should take into account forecasting, trending, and modeling capabilities so that if a metric falls out of range of a trend, budget, or plan, the appropriate alert is raised, along with the workflow process to get the investigation under way.

Analyze

Analysis is a key step in which you look at not only where you are, but also at what is happening (or what has happened) and why. The techniques for analysis can range from highly manual and simple to fairly automated and complex in terms of the usage of statistical techniques.

Perform analysis on KPIs to understand why they are increasing or decreasing. For example, you find that the critical KPI of net margin on the profitability dashboard is trending downward and drill down to find out that it is because the costs of the Supply Chain department have gone way up due to the price of fuel increasing.

Perform analysis on an initiative to understand why it is succeeding or failing. For example, you analyze that the initiatives to roll out the new Finance shared services centers are heading down the wrong direction and determine that this is due to a sudden lack of IT capacity due to a competing initiative to build HR shared services centers.

Perform analysis on KRIs to understand why they are increasing or decreasing. As an example, you conduct a correlation analyses to identify the process deficiencies or other trends that are the most significant in increasing your organizational exposure to huge discounts for customers via payment terms risk before it reaches critical levels.

Perform analysis on the effectiveness of internal controls. You may, for example, notice that a control to test for cash discount values seems to generate a lot of incidents and analyze that the thresholds are set too low, creating a false positive. You conclude from your analysis that your controls have lost their effectiveness due to changing business conditions or organizational structures and need to analyze why.

Perform analysis on the root causes and trends of incidents and losses. You might notice a significant uptick in losses due to customer defaults and determine the root cause of these losses was a failure to follow the appropriate procedures for an established credit verification policy.

In all of these cases, analysis was done with human intervention, but this does not have to be the case. With the volume and complexity of data in the enterprise today, it is becoming increasingly difficult for humans to mine through the data and come to intelligent conclusions. Using data mining techniques, it is possible to have software determine the likely root causes for you, and even suggest recommended actions to remediate, often much quicker than you could on your own.

For example, you observe that a KRI for the liquidity forecast is increasing. Without any manual intervention, the system does a series of correlations or more sophisticated statistical analyses in the background. When you highlight the KRI, a popup shows that the number one factor associated with the sudden decrease in liquidity is the sudden increase in customer defaults.

Kaplan and Norton stress how statistical analysis can bring insight into how well the current strategy is working. "Companies, especially those with large numbers of similar operating units, can use statistical analysis to estimate correlations among strategy performance numbers. Such analysis will usually validate and quantify the links between investments in, for example, employee skills or IT support systems, and customer loyalty and financial performance. Occasionally, however, the analysis can reveal that assumed linkages are not occurring, which should cause the executive team to question or reject at least part of the existing strategy. Companies that consistently measure strategy performance through tools such as the strategy map and balanced scorecard have ready access to the data needed for strategy validation and testing."

Adjust

After monitoring to find out what has happened and analyzing to understand why it happened, for those things not going according to plan, it becomes time to set the business back on course by taking what you've learned and using that information to adjust the settings across the enterprise. However, you must always consider the impact of your goals, risks, and compliance concerns when making decisions to adjust your actions.

For KPIs trending in the wrong direction, once you have analyzed the root causes, it should be clear what actions to take to set things back on course. However, it is critical to remember that KPIs are interlinked, and you must optimize your performance goals in the context of risk objectives without violating your compliance objectives.

As an example, if it is only the Supply Chain team driving up costs due to an unexpected fuel hike that is affecting the net margin KPI, you can try to make up the difference by asking the Sales team to put an incentive in place to grow the top line to make up for the increased costs. However, this can only be done if it does not increase the risk of not delivering on other key sales initiatives (for example, the launch of a new product whose early market success is critical) and if it doesn't violate any compliance objectives like revenue recognition rules as salespeople attempt to maximize on incentives.

For initiatives that are not going as planned, it becomes essential to rapidly take remedial action or cancel them. If it's clear that the initiative is not going to work, either make changes that can help save the project or cancel the project altogether, if it is not critical, so you can reallocate those resources. You could, for example, find out that the initiatives to roll out the new Finance shared services centers are failing and determine that it is because of a sudden lack of IT capacity due to a competing initiative to build HR shared services centers. Depending on the economic environment as well as the internal political landscape, you may be able to convince the CEO that the Finance shared services initiative should take precedence.

For KRIs trending in the wrong direction, once you have analyzed root causes, it should be clear what actions to take to set things back on course, often by putting appropriate mitigating controls in place to stabilize them. For each risk, you can decide to treat it, tolerate it (perhaps because a mitigating control is in place), transfer it, or terminate the activity that is producing the risk.

However, KRIs are interlinked, and you must optimize your risks in the context of performance objectives without violating compliance objectives. For example, say you conducted a correlation analysis to identify process deficiencies or other trends that are most significant in increasing your organizational exposure to huge discounts for customers via payment terms risk. You put a mitigating control in place to have the Finance team manually spot check all new contracts being signed to ensure that discount levels are not being set improperly. However, this can only be done if it does not decrease the likelihood of delivering on the goal of turning around purchase invoices in a timely manner (since now your team is investing time in manually checking discounts) and if it doesn't violate any compliance objectives like having employees working longer than they are allowed to by law to cope with the increased workload.

For control violations, adjustment takes the form of remediation and certification. After the payment terms and higher cash discount control is repeatedly violated, you set up a remediation plan to create a more stringent set of discounting policies for all of the salespeople and make compliance with this policy part of their bonus plan.

For incidents and losses, the correct adjustments typically involve re-examining whether we are tracking the right risks and have put the appropriate controls in place to mitigate them. For example, after determining that the uptick in credit defaults is due to a failure to follow the appropriate procedures for checking customer credit, it would be appropriate to put an automated risk monitoring process in place that alerts you if credit checks are bypassed.

Model and Optimize

Modeling and optimization is the ability to take a very big thing, such as a mandate to reduce overhead by $10 million, and break it down into smaller pieces—and decide which piece or pieces can be fixed or made to work better. For example, it may be that the Sales team spends a lot of time traveling to clients for calls that don't require them to go on site. You could optimize this process by setting up rules about travel and then providing remote video conferencing tools so that you don't impact sales momentum and customer contacts.

Kaplan and Norton advocate the use of cost and profitability reports for assessing performance. "Any time a company reviews its strategy, it should first understand the current economics of its existing strategy by examining activity-based costing reports that show the profit and loss of each product line, customer, market segment, channel, and region. Executives will then see where the existing strategy has succeeded and failed, and can formulate approaches to turning around loss operations and expanding the scope and scale of profitable operations."[7]

Model

Financial modeling takes several forms, including revenue, cost, and profitability modeling, scenario modeling, and simulation modeling.

Revenue, Cost, and Profitability Modeling

Modeling the costs, revenue, and profitability implications of performance management, risk management, and compliance management activities and their drivers can be achieved at a very detailed level using activity-based costing and associated methodologies.

As described in Chapter 3, activity-based costing means not only tying your financial plan to operations but also gathering far more granular data directly related to the drivers behind the financial numbers. In the past, if your overhead for a particular activity was $10 million, you didn't really have a reliable way to determine how you arrived at that number. You were left with the inadequate data at hand and gut instincts about what was behind the number. With performance management systems and techniques, however, you are able to quickly drill down through overhead costs to pinpoint the source and cause. With this information, you can proactively make necessary adjustments.

Capabilities in this area include the ability to understand in a highly granular manner—by product, region, business unit, project, and customer—the exact nature of the associated costs and their relative ability to drive value.

---

[7] Robert S. Kaplan and David P. Norton, "Mastering the Management System," *Harvard Business Review*, January 2008.

Scenario Modeling

Scenario modeling can be applied to financial and operational modeling and focuses on creating different business scenarios. Simple scenario modeling can include creating a base case and then high and low cases based on changes made to input variables, such as market growth rates or inflation rates. This technique is often used in modeling market and business opportunities and creating business plans. For example, you might build a set of scenario models in Finance to understand how critical macro variables, such as market growth rate, will impact your profitability strategies.

Simulation Modeling

More advanced modeling, including Monte Carlo simulation, supports creating a broad range of scenarios based on multiple iterations of input assumptions and combinations. With this technique, probabilities can be assigned to the various outcomes. These techniques allow the uncertainty associated with a given forecast to be estimated and to reduce risk by applying sensitivity analysis, correlation, and trend extrapolation. By simulating the effect of uncertainty, it becomes possible to answer questions such as, "How certain are we that our cost-saving initiatives will result in a minimum increase in profitability of 3%?" Or, conversely, "What's the minimum profitability increase that we can be, for example, 90% certain of achieving?" Simulation also makes it possible to identify and rank the various contributors to overall uncertainty, which makes it an excellent candidate for tying goals to risks.

Optimize

The goal at this phase of the PM lifecycle is to determine the optimal way to achieve objectives by taking into account the entire context of the problem, including all relevant constraints and assessments (costs, benefits, risk, labor, and time), as well as business strategies, objectives, risks, and compliance factors. Optimization can be done both through human evaluation as well as through advanced algorithmic techniques.

As Nigel Rayner, senior analyst with Gartner, writes, "Increasingly, profitability modeling applications are focusing on profit optimization capabilities that enable executives to see the impact of different strategies on profitability from different perspectives, such as customer or product."[8] Leading-edge products now offer the ability to build very sophisticated

---

[8] Nigel Rayner, "Understanding CPM Applications," Gartner Research, August 24, 2007.

models that incorporate activity-based costing, constraint-oriented process modeling, and comprehensive financial modeling to provide a single model for operational and financial metrics that ultimately results in seeking out the best solution to a given problem for a given set of business constraints. These systems have the ability to quickly change assumptions, variables, and the interdependencies between them, which make for much more dynamic models. Ultimately, these solutions can identify the best strategic and tactical actions to take for a given scenario, using financial and operational metrics as the objective function. For example, with such an integrated financial and operational model, the system can optimize and tell you what the right product mix should be to achieve a certain net margin, or what the right pricing strategy should be to keep the lowest inventory levels.

Case Study: Performance Management in Action

Virtual Gates is a fictional cutting-edge computer manufacturer with retail outlets. This section provides an analysis of how the Finance department's team at Virtual Gates closes its loop during the process of increasing the company's profitability while optimizing its liquidity.

Setting the Context

Asha Madon, the CFO at Virtual Gates, has just left CEO Clint Hobbs' office with a new set of directives. Clint wants Asha to increase the company's profitability while optimizing its liquidity. Because Finance orchestrates the company's value, Asha must also guarantee that her strategies and plans align with the larger corporate objective, which requires all growth to be measured against Virtual Gates' net income and earnings per share growth, especially as they compare to VG's competitors, Hypercell and Packingflash.

Given the current economic downturn, Asha might have had reason for concern, but when Clint told her that she and her team would be introducing a new line of powerful netbooks, Asha knew they could meet his expectations. She was especially heartened when she learned about the recent studies conducted by her colleague Samantha Curtin, Chief Marketing Officer. Samantha's research suggests that 21.5 million netbooks are expected to be sold in 2009 (a growth of 189% from 2008), and that by 2012, sales are projected to increase up to 50 million. When Asha read the netbook's specs, she became totally confident: not only is it smaller and faster than VG's competitors, but its look and feel is customizable.

To accomplish her goals, Asha and her team must consider how facilitating cost-cutting initiatives in each of the business units can reduce overall expenditures. This reduction frees up working capital for the immediate term while leaving room for longer-term investments for growth.

Understand the Collaborative Impact

Asha's department plays a crucial role in all the business processes in the company. After all, Finance is the ultimate arbiter of the value generated by each department. In addition to its continual effort to gain financial efficiency, Finance often assumes control of additional business processes, including driving strategy and growth, managing risk and compliance, and optimizing working capital.

No matter what her choices, Asha must never fail to consider their impact on the Finance department or on related business units, both within and beyond the company's four walls, including lending banks that share potential risks and rewards. She knows that just because a decision makes financial sense does not mean it is automatically justified in other contexts.

For example, to achieve her aim of increasing the company's profitability while optimizing its liquidity, Asha may suggest reducing the budget for all of the company's departments by 10% and a 15% reduction in headcount. Before she does this, she considers the impact on the entire company. If employee motivation is dampened, will it affect the release of the new netbook? Will we meet the launch date? Will Marketing be able to prime the funnel for lead generation or drive sales? Will cuts in Service weaken customer loyalty? Asha weighs alternatives. On the other hand, if she could reduce the budget across the board without impeding the business units, she can almost certainly hand Clint Hobbs an optimistic report at the end of each quarter.

Establish KPIs and KRIs

Every successful business unit efficiently and accurately gauges its progress toward goals by selecting and implementing relevant KPIs and KRIs. Before Asha and her team begin, they must identify the main KPIs as well as KRIs reflecting the primary risks to which they might be exposed. They must also monitor the major interfaces between their partners and their processes and identify the drivers behind the KPIs and KRIs, along with their relationships. Lastly, they need leading indicators of performance.

Asha monitors net income growth and earnings per share growth to optimize the company's cash position by decreasing expenditures as a function of revenue. She must convey the influence of these metrics to all of her partners. For the supply chain to meet the KPI of net income growth,

George Martin, the VP of Supply Chain, must reduce inventory levels. CMO Samantha Curtin must reduce her overall campaign spend by running fewer marketing campaigns. To increase revenue per sales rep and profitability per employee, CSO Leah Broder must reduce the comp plans or increase the sales quota of her sales reps as well lower the departmental headcount.

Establish the BI Foundation

As you know, KPIs and KRIs are not selected randomly. Asha and her team must gather data from source systems, including ERP systems and individual AP, AR, treasury, and credit management systems. These are also the systems Asha's team will need to consolidate as they execute their Finance-related business processes.

The team must transform the raw data, then align it and load it into a data mart or data warehouse. This master data will provide a single source of truth from which they can select KPIs and KRIs to guide them toward a successful launch of the new netbook while lowering overall expenditures. Data from other key systems such as PLM, CRM, and SCM must be integrated into the semantic layer if they want to see the effects of their activities on all key stakeholders.

Strategize and Prioritize

After reviewing the collected information, Asha's confidence that VG's new netbook will generate both significant brand recognition and value and increased profit margins is the chief rationale for authorizing a reduction in overall expenditures. After much discussion, she and her colleagues from Product Development, Marketing, Sales, and Service conclude that the best way to cut costs is to eliminate as many unprofitable products as possible. Now her team must create a scorecard for monitoring the development of her strategy and plan.

The scorecard must reflect the risks of such an approach. The risk in reducing the product portfolio is that cuts could upset customers still using those products, and their dissatisfaction could injure VG's brand equity. The reduction in funding could impact product, customer, and operational effectiveness by shifting the focus to short-term goals, jeopardizing existing business processes.

To address such risks, Asha must implement a number of KRIs, establishing thresholds that cannot be crossed without taking immediate mitigating action. She sets KRIs for alerts to a 10% decrease in employee satisfaction, a 10% decrease in customer satisfaction, and a 20% decrease in the pipeline for new products, all from previous baselines. Responses to these KRIs include sustaining the product innovation lifecycle while making more aggressive reductions in areas like Marketing. Before implementing controls, Asha's team must first document, test, monitor, and certify them to ensure that her expense reduction process won't be blocked or stalled, especially in areas such as labor practices for HR, contractual and legal agreements with suppliers and customers, and quality criteria for products.

Plan and Execute

Once Asha knows which VG products and customers are most profitable, she and her team can facilitate a dialogue with each department to help them optimize. In her overall financial plan for VG, Asha set targets for how much available cash she needs as well as expenses to cut to increase profitable growth. Now she needs to break down her high-level plan so that each department can budget effectively. Funds that have been blocked from further spending on customers, products, suppliers, and employees will provide the capital needed for the strategic initiatives to launch the new netbook. Asha must also link her budget to the operational factors of all the departments. For instance, in HR, employee count drives training and shared services costs while in Service, the number of customers drives the number of service representatives and IT resources.

No matter how well Asha uses her detailed cost analyses to reduce expenditures across the organization, she will encounter risks, such as reduced customer satisfaction from having fewer call center representatives. Other departments might not be immediately aware of complications in other business units, but Finance can often foresee them and help align the organization.

Monitor and Analyze

Now each department has begun to execute its plans, Asha and her team monitor the results from transactional systems to see whether funds are freeing up. She must also ensure collaborative visibility by monitoring KPIs for each department. For example, are affected departments showing process inefficiencies or other bottlenecks as a result of staff reductions? Are raw materials accumulating for products being retired? Is Service receiving increased complaints? Is the expected increase in net income materializing or not?

If the results are unsatisfactory, Asha must find out why. Perhaps highly paid employees are not performing well, so staff reductions have less impact than planned. VG's profitable products may be too low volume to make up for lower margin but higher volume products. Maybe customers are frustrated by stockouts from reduced inventory levels. Whatever the case, Asha must ensure that any solution is aligned with other departments as well as with larger corporate goals.

Model and Optimize

A detailed operational cost model can help Asha and her team understand which products are profitable. She must know where and how resources are being leveraged in VG's manufacturing process. She needs a resource consumption model that enables her to see which people, time, and materials can help in achieving the strategy. Working with various departments will help her make intelligent decisions about cutting costs while keeping the most profitable products and customers in the portfolio.

Asha can simulate different scenarios—"what-if" analyses to determine which customers and products VG should keep—by changing key assumptions in her model, such as the amount of overhead for individual products, or by removing constraints such as the need to maintain historical pricing levels. Once Asha and her team know that their strategy and resources are sound, they can deploy a variety of optimization techniques to achieve their goals.

Closing the Loop in an Integrated System

While current technology can manage the scenario described to this point, it is continually evolving. Holistic, closed-loop systems will soon enable most organizational departments to consistently align execution with strategy. This is Asha's ultimate goal. When she can create a strategy management process that captures goals, initiatives, and metrics that can be linked to her driver-based financial and operational planning process, as well as to her monitoring and analysis, modeling and optimization, and risk and control processes, a whole new set of scenarios will emerge. She can then push the desired behavior out to transactional processes using goals, initiatives, plans, and risks and controls. In other words, the transactional systems enforce compliance.

Fortunately for Asha and her team, they have a closed-loop, financial close solution in place. With it, they can integrate and control their entire process—from individual AP and AR transactions, to reconciliation in the general ledger, to local close in the ERP system, to group close in the financial consolidation system, to generating the final P&L, balance sheet, cash flow reports, and forward-looking forecasts, and, finally, to submitting these reports electronically in the format required by various regulatory bodies such as the U.S. SEC.

The application's performance management capabilities enable her team to compare planned versus actual versus forecast weekly. Should they see a sudden change in the forecast, they can drill down to find out why the change occurred (for example, because the pipeline and close rate are suddenly much lower than the historical norm, resulting in an inability to make forecasted quarterly results). Asha can also model different scenarios to calculate what her expense reduction initiatives must be to match the revenue decline and still make the forecast. Moreover, she can start an initiative to more aggressively manage customer credit and receivables directly from the system. In turn, this will enable her to observe the effects of these changes in her PM application, and, hopefully, see that the actuals are trending back toward the original forecast. Thus, the strategy to launch the new netbook while simultaneously improving the company's profitability and liquidity during an economic crisis, the initiative to reduce expenses across departments and more aggressively manage receivables, and the real act of removing the budget from the various operational systems are seamlessly integrated. At the same time, both efficiency—doing things right—and effectiveness—doing the right things—are greatly enhanced.

Align the Workforce

Asha wants to link all of the previously mentioned activities with her teams' objectives and compensation. This will strengthen desired behaviors, both in product and resource development across all departments. Any time an accountant is shown that he'll be nicely rewarded with a bonus for his contribution to the successful achievement of the department's initiatives per corporate strategy, he will take pains to meet his personal objectives, and this is true for other areas in the company. All departments strive that much harder when they know that their bonuses are tied to the goals. Asha's success is based on the success of her fellow departments. She knows that the minute she presents CEO Clint Hobbs with a report that features a 5% growth in Finance's overall profit as measured by Virtual Gates' net income and earnings per share growth, including a 20% increase in netbook market share capture (leaving Hypercell and Packingflash in the far distance), she can count on a sweet bonus of her own.

Action Items

The following is a list of concrete steps you can take now to see real improvements via performance management.

Advice and Best Practices

- Benchmark against other top performing Finance organizations in companies that are similar to yours with excellent performance characteristics
- Pick the key levers you want to measure and stick to those. Nobody can track more than 7 KPIs at any one time, so pick the ones that make the most difference and get them under control before you move to others
- Use technology systems to move away from spreadsheet-based systems
- Leverage leading-edge technologies to get end users to collaborate about their performance: wikis, blogs, and tagging are all useful
- Think of leading indicators that predict performance instead of lagging indicators that reconcile the past
- Translate the key objectives the other business units care about (service requests, number of new product introduced, and so on) into key financial objectives that ultimately measure shareholder value
- Make sure that employee incentives align with corporate strategy

Chapter 8

Performance Management for HR

Every company has at one time or another said, "Our people are our most important asset." It is ironic, then, that most organizations are poorly equipped to measure the performance of their employees, and to measure the processes supporting the entire employee lifecycle, from hire through termination, in a way that links these measurements with the overall strategic goals of the organization.

In this chapter, we will summarize and explain how leading organizations are working to understand the value of the workforce as a whole and evaluate the success of their human resources policies and processes.

Looking Back: How Life Has Changed HR

When you understand the context within which you practice performance management for human resources, you'll be able to align the goals of your operations with your organization's high-level objectives, and the talent pool, far more effectively.

How the World Has Changed

Your company has changed. The marketplace is now global, and companies are increasingly global, too. That ultimately means that your human resources processes and policies will span languages, cultures, and geography, and the concept of "employee diversity" now encompasses a broader range of backgrounds than ever before. You must craft HR processes that make sense on a regional and local level, while still tying these processes back to the overall strategic goals.

In difficult economic times, you are being asked to make decisions about whether to eliminate positions or outsource some functions. In order to do this, you will need to have accurate and timely information in order to make the right decisions. You are under pressure to acquire, maintain, and develop the best performers, who will understand and commit themselves to the strategic vision and continue to perform as the economy improves. Across-the-board cuts will eliminate some of your best performers. Now more than ever, you want to be able to identify with confidence the people who will truly drive performance in your organization, whether they are already in your organization or need to be recruited.

The "Organization Man" is disappearing—few expect to rise in an organization solely on the basis of sticking around. We are now in an age of extreme volatility, and high performers move frequently between organizations in search of better opportunities. Yet organizations are still largely saddled with a 1950s model of human capital management,[1] which was based on assumptions of business predictability that today we find laughable.

Performance management for HR, when applied in a manner consistent with the vision promoted in this book, should intersect with the end-to-end processes across all of the functional silos as the means to manage the modern enterprise.

How Technology Has Changed

HR technology was once limited to employee recordkeeping systems. Gradually the vendors of these systems, as well as new vendors, developed technology for benefits administration, managing personnel files, and tracking time and attendance. These systems were typically isolated in the HR department itself, partially out of the need to protect private information.

Now, there are two technology revolutions underway. One major trend is the advent of collaboration and online networking. The second is an expansion of the vendor-provided technology to include performance management, succession planning, and employee development, a trend

---

[1] Peter Cappelli, "Talent Management for the Twenty-First Century," *Harvard Business Review,* March 2008.

that has also meant greater integration with enterprise planning and corporate strategy. You will need to understand and embrace both of these trends to build a fully effective HR performance management strategy in the coming years.

As we have mentioned previously, we are no longer in the command-and-control paradigm of corporate governance. The new enterprise is fundamentally collaborative, open-ended, and strategically aligned across all departments. We now live in a Web 2.0 world. Social networks such as LinkedIn and Facebook probably know more about your employees than you do. Many companies have a difficult time producing a simple report such as a headcount tally or a demographic trend. Mergers, acquisitions, and global expansions have marooned HR departments with multiple systems of record housing employee data.[2]

In the near future, we can expect organizations to begin to exploit Web 2.0 technologies to get a handle on their HR data and begin to engage employees on a much more iterative, interactive, and frequent basis, compiling and centralizing the data they garner in a far deeper and more consistent approach than is the practice today. Gartner Group estimates that by 2012, 30% of HR departments will approve the use of social network analysis to measure and reward collaborative behavior.[3] Social networking tools can help identify capabilities that were formerly very difficult to measure, such as the ability to collaborate and build a team. These tools will also help organizations to reward individual behaviors based on their alignment to strategic goals, rather than try to implement a top-down collaborative culture—the sort of strategy that is redolent of the 1950s Organization Man way of doing things.

In the meantime, a plethora of tools is now available to assist in human capital management (HCM). These include:

- Administrative applications, such as personnel, payroll, and benefits management—the original core of HCM software
- Talent management applications, including workforce planning, e-recruitment, employee performance management, succession planning, and learning and compensation management

---

[2] Paul D. Hamerman and Zach Thomas, "Trends 2009: Human Resource Management," Forrester Research, Inc., November 21, 2008.

[3] Jackie Fenn, Tyson Harmon, Stephen Prentice, Mark Raskino, and David W. Cearly, "Predicts 2008: Emerging Trends Expand Collaboration and Human Performance." Gartner, Inc. Research ID G00153366, January 8, 2008.

- Workforce management applications also date from the early days of HR software and include labor scheduling, time and attendance, and task/activity management

These groups of applications are at varying levels of maturity in HR departments. Some form of integrated human resource management system (HRMS) has been around for more than 30 years. But until the late 1990s, these systems were limited in scope by the limitations of mainframe and client/server computing technology. It was difficult to distribute these systems companywide, let alone to external job applicants and recruiters. The advent of the Web changed that, and HRMS applications expanded to reach users more effectively. Still, the focus to date has largely been on automating tasks such as benefits administration, time tracking, and processing employment applications. These are not necessarily investments that help the company move forward on strategic goals. To fill this gap, new workforce planning and analytic tools are beginning to emerge. These applications, when wedded with social networking tools and talent- and workforce-management applications, will provide HR organizations with unprecedented depth and understanding about their employees and the relationship between those employees and the overall goals of the company, and facilitate informed decision-making.

The Evolution of Performance Management for HR

Performance management for human resources used to be a fairly simple proposition, if a limited one. Excel spreadsheets were updated once a year per employee, making for sketchy data at best. This was fine for updating basic metrics, such as on-time performance and compensation history, but information could not be effectively tracked, trended, or reported. As new management techniques materialized, the reliance on spreadsheets held back the organization's ability to record and analyze nonfinancial feedback from multiparty peer (360-degree) reviews or correlate succession planning with corporate goals. This highly manual process was time-consuming and provided little true insight into employee productivity or satisfaction. There was no real way to consider overseas staff or to manage employees under different regulatory requirements.

Today, HR is harnessing performance management in new ways. Evaluations no longer consist of simple one-to-ten rankings. Vendors in the HCM and ERP spaces are now offering the ability to cascade performance management applications down to the employee level. This means that managers at the board level, who set the overall corporate strategy, can set strategic goals that can influence, or be influenced by, operational goals at the employee level. Upper management and department managers can also tap into these systems, which can effectively link compensation and evaluations to corporate profitability.

Cascading strategy in a way that is aligned and makes sense means that financial goals can be linked to operational and individual goals in unprecedented ways.

HR's purpose is to manage human capital and to minimize financial risk related to workforce investments. That risk can come from poorly

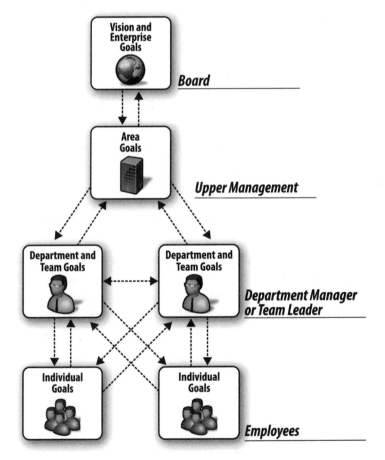

Figure 8-1. Performance Management: Cascading Goals

performing employees who are kept on staff because no one is aware of their effect on performance, poorly structured compensation schemes that reward nonstrategic efforts and punish performance-boosting work, or terminating employees without sufficient performance documentation.

HR must manage these risks through the key areas of training, performance management, compensation, talent management (recruiting), and succession planning. You need to understand clearly how the cost and time spent training an employee impacts the bottom line—do you know how many employees stay with the company more than a year after they complete your training process? Do you know how much that will cost you if they don't? What kind of skills will your top management need in two, five, or ten years? How are you going about grooming successors, or recruiting to fill gaps? You will need to know all of this and more to lead a successful HR department in the future.

Why You Must Do This Now

The competitive landscape is only becoming more intense. Your customers are international, Web-savvy, and information-hungry. Your employees need to embody these characteristics. Whatever your company's competitive edge might be in terms of products or services, in the end, people are the only source of long-term competitive advantage.[4] Companies that fail to invest in their employees jeopardize their very survival. Only about 3% of executives in a recent Deloitte survey believed that their HR department was world-class in terms of managing the workforce; only 23% felt that HR played a crucial role in strategy formulation and operational success.[5]

Next-generation enterprises stake their survival upon transparency. That means that HR must break through two walls—the wall between HR and corporate strategy and the walls between siloed applications within HR that prevent useful analysis. Analytics provide a framework for business decisions; in order to provide them, you must take

---

[4] Laurie Bassi and Daniel McMurrer, "Maximizing Your Return on People," *Harvard Business Review*, March 2007.

[5] Deloitte, Press Release, "C-suite and human resources (HR) executives 'bash heads' on addressing 'people issues'—reveals Deloitte research," http://www.deloitte.com/dtt/press_release/0,1014,sid%253D3566%2526cid%253D158847,00.htm.

steps to improve your processes and technology to foster collaboration and goal-sharing within and without your department. A linked-up system of dashboards, available to all critical management personnel, containing analytics, will help to serve this goal of transparency and begin to cement your role as an influential voice at the table when it comes to the future of your company.

To be well respected and effective as a strategic partner in the business, the HR organization needs to:

- Prioritize and focus on strategic levers such as aligning talent management and rewards with organizational needs
- Have a structure and roles that help speed transformation
- Have the skills to deliver on high value-added activities
- Use technology and outsourcing to improve the efficiency of HR processes and focus resources on value-added activities
- Have a realistic understanding of how you are viewed by the organization and what the business needs from you[6]

Does This Sound Familiar?

- Upper management complains, "You guys have a stranglehold on us with all your regulations. Why can't we hire who we want, when we need to hire them?"

- You have a high turnover rate and you don't have enough data from exit interviews to understand why.

- Despite using recruiters, you have difficulty attracting highly skilled employees, even in a down market.

- You hire people based on "gut feel" and don't seem to be getting any positive recognition from upstairs.

- You have no idea how employee performance is affecting the bottom line—but your superiors are asking.

- You don't comprehend the needs of customers and how they relate to your employees' performance and satisfaction with their jobs.

---

[6] Jim Kochanski. "How 100 Leading HR Organizations Are Improving Their Strategic Effectiveness," Wellesley Information Services, March 2007.

The Business Process Angle

HR is foundational to all the business processes in the company, but as shown in Figure 8-2, it is particularly responsible for:

- **Building the workforce.** Faced with talent shortages, mergers and acquisitions, restructuring, entering new markets or adding new product lines, companies must improve time-to-productivity of new permanent and temporary employees in order for the business to achieve its strategic objectives

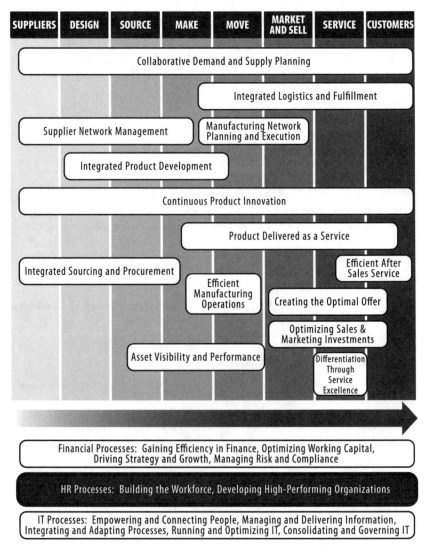

Figure 8-2. HR is Foundational to All the Business Processes

- **Developing high-performing organizations.** High-performing organizations must effectively identify, develop, and retain critical talent in order to develop the leaders who will manage and drive key aspects of the business. Figure 8-3 shows the details of this business process

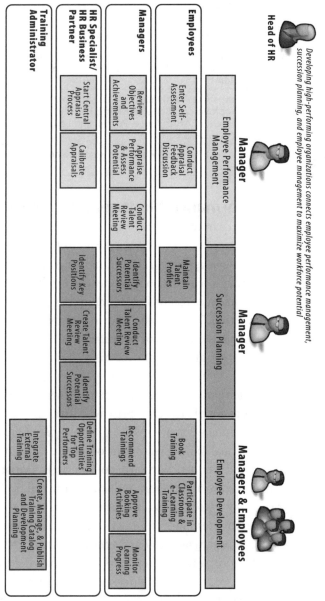

Figure 8-3. An Example of a Cross-Organizational Business Process in HR: Developing High Performing Organizations

Figure 8-3 shows collaboration with other departments during the employee lifecycle. The relationship between HR and managers is ongoing, and we will discuss this relationship in this chapter in considerable detail.

In addition to this business process, which crosses departmental lines, you may want to undertake performance management initiatives for any of the areas for which HR is responsible, as outlined in Table 8-1.

Table 8-1. Business Processes Within HR Department

Talent Management	Recruiting; Career Mgmt; Succession Mgmt; Enterprise Learning; Employee Performance Mgmt; Compensation Mgmt
Workforce Process Management	Employee Administration; Organizational Mgmt; Global Employment; Benefits Mgmt; Healthcare Cost Mgmt; Time and Attendance; Payroll and Legal Reporting; HCM Processes & Forms
Workforce Deployment	Project Resource Planning; Resource and Program Mgmt

Key Roles in Performance Management for HR

The object of the advice in this section is to help you become more than a marshal for the employees of your company and to transform you into an active participant in developing and communicating corporate strategy.

The advice and information in this book is intended for the various executives, managers, and employees responsible for delivering human resources services to the organization. Much of the information below is tailored to the vice president of human resources or a similar high-level manager with a considerable level of strategic control over his or her department. Your role is to provide basic human resources services (payroll, benefits administration, talent management, compensation management) and cooperate with all business units to supply the enterprise with an adaptive workforce that meets the skill and talent demands driven by the type of business you are in. However, it is critical to understand the other roles within the organization and their interdependency in terms of the goals, initiatives, and metrics they are managed by in order to understand the full performance implications for running a world class HR organization.

Recruiting managers are responsible for delivering all facets of recruiting success throughout the organization. This is achieved through the development of local and national recruiting plans and employing traditional sourcing strategies and resources as well as developing new, creative recruiting ideas. Recruiters play a critical role in ensuring the enterprise is hiring the best possible talent.

Training managers are responsible for the overall learning programs within a company. They arrange on-the-job training for new employees, help rank-and-file workers maintain and improve their job skills, and possibly prepare for jobs requiring greater skill. They also help supervisors improve their interpersonal skills in order to deal effectively with employees. They may be responsible for setting up individualized training plans to strengthen an employee's existing skills or teach new ones.

HR administrators are responsible for managing compensation by devising ways to ensure fair and equitable pay rates, and for handling the company's employee benefits program, notably its health insurance and pension plans.

HR today needs to organize its department around new strategic competencies: technical/professional skills and behavioral skills, as outlined in Figure 8-4.

KPIs for Success in HR

Based on best practices and experience, the following distilled metrics have proven to be effective in assessing HR health:

- **Strategic.** Profit per Employee, Total Workforce Productivity, Total Workforce Diversity
- **Tactical.** Employee and Manager Satisfaction and Retention, Learning and Growth Opportunities per Employee, Percentage of

Figure 8-4. How 100 Leading HR Organizations Are Improving Their Strategic Effectiveness

(Source: Jim Kochanski. "How 100 Leading HR Organizations Are Improving Their Strategic Effectiveness," Wellesley Information Services, March 2007)

Employees with Established Career Paths, Comparison of Employee Compensation versus Market, Average Lead Time to Develop Strategic Competencies

- **Operational.** Hours of Training per Employee Annually, Time and Cost to Hire, Average Length of Service, Number of Applications and Applicants for New Positions

Aside from the metrics themselves, it is important to understand the information gap that currently exists between metrics and analytics. Metrics measure "what is" and "what was." Analytics answer "what if." Most HR departments, if they are tracking data at all, look at metrics such as cost per

Report Title	Output	System of Record	Analytics	Metrics
Cost Per Hire	Total cost involved in hiring one person for a single position	Recruiting		✔
Course Enrollment	Number of people who are registered for a learning course	Learning Management		✔
Goal Progression	Progress either an individual employee or aggregate employees have made against their goals	Performance Management		✔
Headcount	Total employee headcount	Human Resources Management System		✔
Learning Efficacy	Workforce productivity (revenue per employee) based on learning initiatives	Performance Management and Learning Management	✔	
Performance Review Compliance	Number of employees who have finished a performance review on their current status	Performance Management		✔
Quality of Hire	Objective assessment of the quality of new hires	Recruiting and Performance Management	✔	
Time-To-Fill	Total time taken to fill a single position	Recruiting		✔
Time-To-Productivity	Amount of time elapsed from when a person starts in a position until he is considered productive	Recruiting, Performance Management, and Learning Management	✔	
Training Cost Tracking	Training budgets and expenditures	Learning Management		✔
Workforce Modeling	Readiness or gaps within the workforce based on different scenarios	Recruiting, Performance Management, and Learning Management	✔	

Figure 8-5. Metrics Answer 'What Was,' Analytics Answer 'What If'
(Source: "HR Analytics Become A Must," Forrester Research, Inc., November 2008)

hire, course enrollment, and headcount. What they lack is analytics, such as learning efficacy—what is the level of productivity that is attributable to learning initiatives? HR departments need to understand that knowing time-to-fill—the total time taken to fill a single position—is an isolated metric that is fairly meaningless unless it is correlated with time-to-productivity—how long it takes before a recent hire is considered productive. Can you predict with any confidence the readiness of your workforce to adapt to different market scenarios, and do you know how you would go about filling those gaps? These scenarios embody the difference between metrics and analytics, and this is a gap you must close in order to be a strategic partner in a competitive business.

What's in It for Me?

Performance management can vastly transform your department and elevate your position to a strategic echelon role at your company. Let's start with the basics of what performance management can do for HR.

Who wouldn't like to see less paperwork on their desk? The amount of information HR must maintain is mountainous. You track attendance, work schedules, benefits, compensation, learning, and myriad other factors. With an integrated system for performance management, you can centralize this information electronically and manage it rationally, sharing appropriate metrics and analysis with the enterprise-level management at more frequent junctures, with less paper flying around, and fewer opportunities for introducing mistakes or losing records.

Think about it—if you could track employee performance quarterly, so that it synchronized with your company's quarterly reporting needs, instead of annually, you would gain a greater sense of control over productivity and performance.

You're probably used to making hiring and other personnel decisions on gut instinct. This valuable talent is one of the core skills of an HR manager. But the decisions you need to make should be validated with data. You may also have the tendency to advocate for your employees, as you should—but not when it betrays a misunderstanding of broad strategic goals. This advocacy should not be based solely on gut feel and without the context of broader strategy close in mind.

Effective Collaboration

Human Resources is one of the departments that touches every single department—after all, they all have employees. That means that you, the

HR manager, will be responsible for initiating a good deal of dialogue with managers to determine what KPIs are important to them, all while keeping overall strategic goals in mind. A rationalized, standard data model and standardized HR policies across the enterprise will go a long way toward making collaboration effective. The rest is all about those fabulous "people skills" that made you an HR manager in the first place.

Your role is absolutely critical to overall collaboration. Your department drives performance assessments. As mentioned earlier, strategies must be tied to individual objectives in order for strategy to be executed. Only people can turn strategy into action, but mixed messages and nontransparent objectives and compensation policies reduce motivation and performance. In fact, they often motivate exactly the wrong thing. The more you know the corporate strategy, the more you can influence managers in incorporating objectives that directly connect to that strategy.

Despite this critical role, HR, for better or worse, has a certain reputation for following processes and procedures no matter what. Formal processes are given priority over future performance planning. This is not just an HR problem, however; performance management is often given short shrift despite its importance.

HR sometimes has a reputation for rigidity. Rigid approaches are not conducive to rapidly changing tasks and responsibilities. However, as the employee advocate, HR has a mandate to ensure that everything is fair and above board. The pace of business today requires some flexibility, however, and some additional give and take. Some areas are nonnegotiable (compliance). Other procedures may have been created for a reason—to ensure that everything is done in a consistent way—but there are times where exceptions can and should be made to those procedures. Rather than having an automatic response to requests (fill out form 37A in triplicate and submit it), see if you can work with hiring managers in a flexible way when needed. Bending where you can and compromising on points that are truly negotiable can go a long way in changing the perception of HR in the organization.

The needs of the HR department are changing. If you don't know much about workforce analytics, find someone who does. It may be that in tight times, an analyst in Marketing can help you with a proof of concept project or provide mentoring to an HR analyst who needs guidance in conducting such analysis.

Collaborating with Finance

You need to make fast friends with Finance if you want the flexibility to make your department the best it can be. Unfortunately, the relationship between HR and Finance is fraught with tension.

Here's a typical scenario. Finance posts guidance—the expected earnings for the next period—as part of a strategic plan. Built into that guidance are certain expectations about the margin the company will be making. The tension arises when Finance tries to bring external best practice and benchmarking data into the conversation, and HR tries to claim the high road by saying, "You're tying one hand behind my back by giving me a salary number arbitrarily; that won't allow us to attract top talent." You may try to back this up by demonstrating that the benchmarking information shows that the optimal salary raise is 6%, when Finance's guidance calls for 1% raises this year.

Another tension arises from the commonplace occurrence that HR is last in line at the till. HR has to fight to live up to the company's "we care about our people" slogan. The department must constantly argue for perks like tuition reimbursement programs, special training for management-track personnel, and domain and soft skills training. Of course, the difficulty in measuring the efficacy of HR programs does not help. Workforce analytics can go a long way to arming you with hard numbers that Finance will find much more compelling.

Collaborating with Sales

HR is a process-driven organization. Let's face it: you have to process a lot of forms, and people don't like to fill out forms. Especially salespeople. They can seem a little ungrateful when you just spent a large sum of money on a training program and they did not bother to fill out any of the online surveys. Consult IT to see if you can design a widget, a poll, or another easily integrated collaborative element to streamline your processes and make it easier for forms-phobic salespeople to comply with policies. Just as Procurement should design its internal buying infrastructure to help employees buy from vendors under contract, so HR can make it easier to file expense reports and the like. Employee self-service came into vogue with corporate portals and intranets, but new technologies like widgets and web services are easily integrated and can make it easier for salespeople to do the right thing in a timely fashion.

Sales also has tension with HR about sales compensation. HR should capture external benchmark data and provide Sales with market guidelines to ensure that Sales is competitive with the market and can attract top salespeople.

Collaborating with Marketing

HR is the conduit for providing good people with both creative and analytical skills to the Marketing organization. Both Sales and Marketing have tension with HR over recruiting. At many larger organizations, HR has a standardized protocol for examining resumes electronically for key words that correlate with certain skill sets and job descriptions. But if this process becomes too rote, or out of date quickly, HR will be circumvented by Sales and Marketing managers, who will write outlandishly inflated job descriptions so that HR's calculators will return an appropriately competitive salary.

Collaborating with Procurement

HR collaborates with Procurement, like other departments, in the area of human capital management. This means optimizing the hiring, recruitment, compensation and benefits, performance training, and development of employees. For procurement, specific skills are required and HR interacts with Procurement to ensure hiring of people who have these skills and to provide training programs to further refine those skills. Specifically, good Procurement professionals are extremely savvy at negotiations; their single biggest goal is to secure products and services for their organization at the best possible price. Because Procurement professionals deal with highly sensitive information such as pricing, credit, and contracts, it is also important these individuals have a flawless record. HR gets involved to ensure the appropriate background review of these individuals by conducting reference checks and police reports.

Collaborating with the Supply Chain

Talent is a key part of an effective supply chain. Supply Chain executives recognize that there is a direct influence of human resource management on supply chain performance. HR plays a critical role in enabling talent management for the supply chain. Today more than ever with globalization, supply chains have intense pressure to look to BRIC countries for not only cheap sources of labor but also for highly qualified labor. According to *Supply Chain Management Review,* "Outward foreign direct investment from emerging economies already accounts for 17% of the world total. There are now 33 million university-educated young professionals in the developing world compared to 14 million in the developed world." This fact highlights the need for HR to provide global talent management programs to help the Supply Chain organization maintain a competitive edge.

Collaborating with Product Development

As Product Development is focused on the process of managing the entire lifecycle of a product from its conception through design and manufacture to service, this is a people-intensive area of the organization that requires a high level of collaboration. HR supports the interaction model between Product Development and the wider organization. Product Development has tools in its product lifecycle management (PLM) solution to manage these processes, but these tools require an investment of time and effort to gain the necessary skills. PLM is typically not used by the wider organization and therefore HR needs to work with Product Development to identify collaboration points. In short, Product Development has its own language and processes around the mission-critical job of developing and bringing products to market. Their role requires tighter interaction with the organization, and HR can help facilitate that collaboration.

Collaborating with IT

HR helps IT hire and retain top talent. Given the technical skills required of IT professionals, the hiring profile and understanding of skills required by HR to properly recruit is much higher than it is for other departments.

HR also interacts with IT beyond recruiting. HR actually sees IT as a business partner for effectively managing employee productivity and compliance across the organization. The intersection point typically centers on employee access rights. HR relies heavily on IT to ensure that appropriate access rights are applied to each employee across all systems in the organization.

Collaborating with Service

Service can be a revolving door, particularly in the call center. Call center representatives often perform redundant tasks that do not require complex thinking. The rate of burnout is high in a call center and represents ever-increasing hiring and retention costs for HR. Average tenure is typically less than 18 months. Given that it takes, on average, 60 to 90 days to get an agent productive after investing in their training, organizations struggle when agents leave after just one year. HR also needs to help the Service team with aggressive compensation plans in order to stave off the competition. Since a call center role is much the same from one organization to the next, call center representatives tend to hop from one call center to the next based on where they can command the best possible pay.

Collaborating with Everyone

The rigidity and process orientation that can be endemic to HR departments actually can create tensions with all departments, particularly as we move into an era when recruitment activities on electronic platforms such as LinkedIn largely circumvent the dialogue between HR and headhunters.

HR plays a central role in database management and in changes to the company's organization chart. HR typically controls the master database, covering employee changes in roles, compensation, and registration in performance improvement plans. Process leaders in every department must interact with HR to ensure that the right people have the access to the right things; likewise, HR must be vigilant that someone who changed roles has the right permissions in terms of budget authorization, account access, limits on supply orders, and the like.

Establishing Your BI Foundation

In order to make progress in your HR performance management efforts, you'll need data that is aligned and integrated in a business intelligence platform. Figure 8-6 shows how the siloed applications that are so typically part of HR departments make the type of comprehensive analytics that you will need to do nearly impossible.

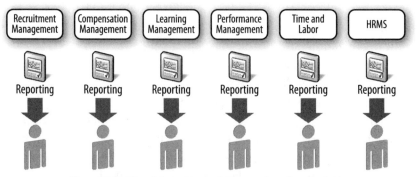

Figure 8-6. Siloed Apps Prevent Comprehensive Analytics
(Source: "HR Analytics Become A Must," Forrester Research, Inc., November 2008)

A BI system can incorporate and normalize data from all of these solutions, forming the basis for the fact-based workforce analytics that HR desperately needs, especially in times of economic downturns. For HR, the Business Intelligence foundation should provide:

- **Relevant visualizations.** BI is relevant to HR to the extent that product-specific visualizations are available to supplement the standard tables and graphs. Most HR professionals are much more comfortable with looking at employees and their organizational structure in the form of an organizational chart along with other key HR-related information
- **Relevant event-capture and alerting.** The ability to gather information from event sources, such as from internal chat rooms, along with external sources like competitor hiring announcements and recruiters, as well as the ability to define alerts for critical events (10% of our top talent has resigned since we paid out the annual bonus) and inform the right person in the HR organization to take action
- **A unified semantic layer, data integration, and data quality across departmental and application silos.** BI lets HR users bridge the silos when they do not have access to a single integrated transactional system, but instead many point systems, as in Figure 8-6, or multiple HCM systems. Use BI to establish common definitions and business rules of the key dimensions in HR (how we define employees, roles, profit centers, cost centers) and metrics (how we define the key metrics and their relationship to one another)
- **Trusted, cleansed master data.** BI allows HR to consolidate on standard definitions of roles. Leveling within an organization and driving consistency across levels is always a challenge for HR to monitor. BI provides standard definitions of individual roles and allows HR to make apples-to-apples comparisons among internal employees and groups as well as against third-party benchmarking data, such as Radford compensation data
- **Structured and unstructured data.** BI can generate insights from both structured and unstructured data. Unstructured data can provide tremendous additional value to HR. Insight is available in performance review systems (all of that VP's direct reports say he is arrogant), benefits administration systems, succession management systems, and employee manuals, not to mention newer unstructured

data such as employee chat, blogs, and email. Exit interviews are a potentially rich source of unstructured data, if employees are guaranteed confidentiality of the information they provide

- **Reporting capabilities,** including:
  - ○ Publication-quality reports to distribute to managers, such as overhead allocation by cost center
  - ○ Dashboarding for visualizing HR information such as headcount forecast compared with headcount hires in the last 5 years, HR organizational structure, and turnover rate by division
  - ○ Query and analysis to provide simple, intuitive analytics capabilities for end users such as vacation days remaining by employee or benefit cost by division

Assessing Performance Management Maturity and Setting Your Course

Where are you and where do you want to go in terms of HR performance management? HR has traditionally played a transactional role, but the ultimate goal is to become an influencer and business partner, using the information you have about your company's most important resource—people—to align with corporate strategy and help achieve that strategy. Figure 8-7 shows the stages of maturity that HR goes through on the way to achieving that highest level.

Stages				
1	**2**	**3**	**4**	**5**
Transactional	**Protective**	**Productive**	**Enabling**	**Influencing**
Doing things for managers and employees	Preventing bad things Providing good things	Improving efficiency of service	Improving abilities of employees and leaders	Causing improvements in business results

Figure 8-7. Transformation Stages in HR
(Source: Jim Kochanski. "How 100 Leading HR Organizations Are Improving Their Strategic Effectiveness," Wellesley Information Services, March 2007)

Your task then becomes to evaluate where you are in the PM maturity model in human resources and determine where you want to go, which naturally depends on how much you are willing to invest.

Of course, it is difficult to figure out where you need to go if you don't know where you are. Fortunately, IDC offers a model for assessing the maturity level of your HR PM program (as shown in Figure 8-8).

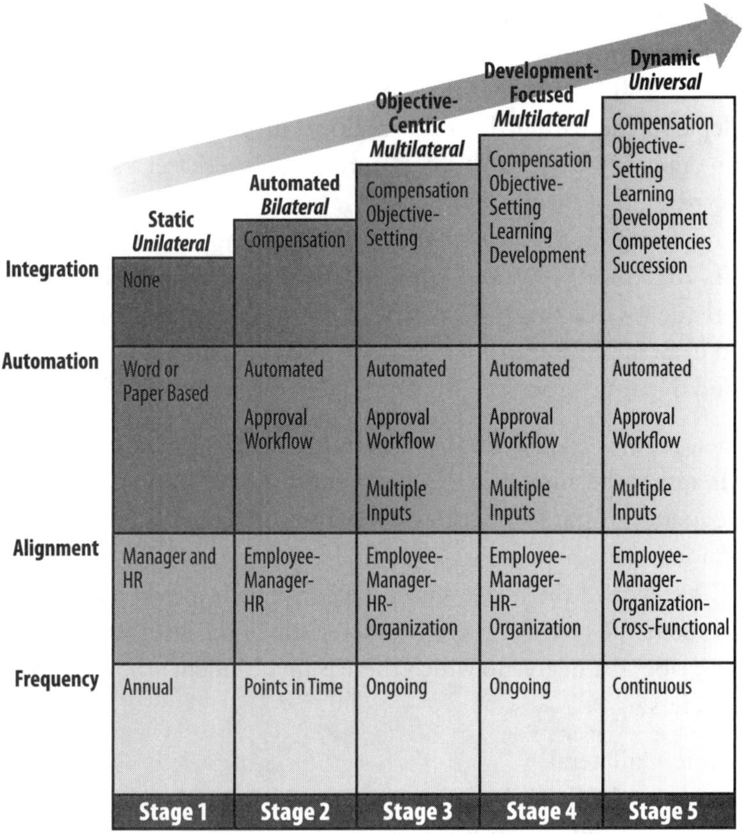

	Stage 1 Static Unilateral	Stage 2 Automated Bilateral	Stage 3 Objective-Centric Multilateral	Stage 4 Development-Focused Multilateral	Stage 5 Dynamic Universal
Integration	None	Compensation	Compensation Objective-Setting	Compensation Objective-Setting Learning Development	Compensation Objective-Setting Learning Development Competencies Succession
Automation	Word or Paper Based	Automated Approval Workflow	Automated Approval Workflow Multiple Inputs	Automated Approval Workflow Multiple Inputs	Automated Approval Workflow Multiple Inputs
Alignment	Manager and HR	Employee-Manager-HR	Employee-Manager-HR-Organization	Employee-Manager-HR-Organization	Employee-Manager-Organization-Cross-Functional
Frequency	Annual	Points in Time	Ongoing	Ongoing	Continuous

Figure 8-8. HR Maturity Model
(Source: IDC, Worldwide Workforce Performance Management 2008–2012 Forecast: Still a Hot Market, Doc # 211971, May 2008)

Although the characteristics are distinct from one another, there is a tendency for growth in several areas as maturity is achieved. The four major characteristics are:

- **Integration.** Workforce performance management (WPM, also called employee performance management [EPM]) must interact with other talent management processes to be effective, and the more mature an enterprise's use of WPM, the more interaction and process integration will exist among these functions
- **Automation.** Many firms still have little if any technical automation of WPM. The more mature the WPM, the more automation will be deployed. Rudimentary automation includes an electronic data collection mechanism, and more mature WPM enables workflow and integration with other systems

- **Alignment.** Immature WPM is characterized by a lack of communication among the major stakeholders. Frequently, less mature WPM occurs entirely between the manager and the HR department, with little or no employee involvement or input. As an enterprise's use of WPM matures, employees feel a sense of ownership of the process
- **Frequency.** In most cases, the performance appraisal process is the key driver for WPM and is largely an annual point-in-time event. Frequently, managers have little in the way of records from which to draw appraisals. A mature WPM program should be an ongoing and dynamic process, with appraisals being only one of its goals

When regular feedback loops are in place, the appraisal is not a surprise to either the employee or the manager. As WPM processes mature, the frequency of the feedback evolves from being periodic to becoming continuous.

IDC has named the five levels of maturity, each in two parts. The first part of the name refers to a key characteristic of the level, and the second part describes the degree to which there is involvement among the various stakeholders:

- Static/Unilateral
- Automated/Bilateral
- Objective-centric/Multilateral
- Development focused/Multilateral
- Dynamic/Universal

When you determine your location on the maturity model, it gives you a starting point to discuss with your managers.

The PM Lifecycle for HR

In this section we will define and examine best practices and options for executing the performance management lifecycle for Human Resources. By the end of this section, you should have a basic working knowledge of the critical elements of a performance management strategy for human resources.

Strategize and Prioritize

In this section we will help you set priorities and determine the best KPIs to measure. Here are the basic steps you'll follow in developing and prioritizing your strategies.

Understand the Context

Review the corporate strategic goals, strategic plans, initiatives, and metrics that track progress against them and understand them. Contextualize them to the implications they have for HR and use this context to drive the HR PM lifecycle.

To begin, you want to make sure you have good communication with the members of the C-suite who can clearly define corporate goals for you. They will be your advocates when it is time to ask for the money to improve your department and start making changes. You will probably also spend time with the Finance department, which owns many of the KPIs with which HR will need to align.

This very important high-level discussion needs to happen before you embark on any projects. Too often, HR does not provide the information C-level executives need to make strategic decisions about human capital.[7] Focus on the facts—anecdotes are not helpful here. And if you don't have facts, the following process can help you discover them.

Develop and Set the Strategy

After these discussions with the C-suite and Finance take place, you can start defining strategy. You are now at the point where you must identify the strategic goals for your HR organization and set in motion the plan to execute on those goals.

Review the environment

What does your department excel at? What are the main problems you face? What risks do you have? Take into account categories of risk factors, including risks for employment, occupational health and safety, working conditions, job satisfaction, recruiting, and skills development. What compliance requirements must you meet? Compliance challenges might include complying with medical privacy laws like HIPAA.

Set the Mission, Values, and Vision

Define the mission (the fundamental purpose of the entity, especially what it provides to customers and clients). For example, to serve as a strategic partner in managing the organization's most important asset alongside all of the organization's business units in supporting the mission of the company.

---

[7] James Holincheck, "Will HR Ever Be Strategic?" BlogERP: Jim Holincheck's HCM Software Blog, June 2007.

Define core values (the attitude, behavior, and character of the organization), such as respect, fairness, and tolerance.

Define the vision (a concise statement that defines the 3- to 5-year goals of the organization): By 2012, implement 5 best practices in HR as defined by industry benchmarks.

Set the Goals

With all that contextual information in hand, define goals and set business objectives using risks as a key variable for deciding which strategies to pursue. Sample strategies include:

- Increasing HR efficiency
- Increasing business-HR alignment
- Facilitating best-practice business processes

Consider using a strategy map (see Figure 8-9 for an example) to display the cause and effect relationships among the objectives that make up a strategy.

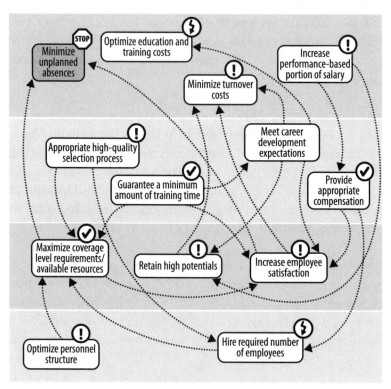

Figure 8-9. Example of an HR Strategy Map

Assign KPIs to Goals and Set the Right Targets

Define KPIs and targets that translate strategy into performance expectations. You are now on the hunt for key KPIs you want to get under control. See "KPIs for Success in HR" earlier in this chapter for a list of KPIs to consider. Identify value drivers (those elements that contribute to the value in your organization).

Value drivers and related performance tolerances (that is, KPIs) have risks associated with their achievement. Identify these risks and establish tolerance levels, from which a KRI can be defined. This connectivity between a value driver and a relevant KPI and KRI is an important bridge from a strategic view of risk—which can have a time horizon of three or more years—to a more focused budgetary view of risk, which is often applied to a single year.

Various components of HR performance can be measured. And determining the most important metrics would be a good place to start. Certain questions may be asked of the corporate sponsors in an introductory conversation, such as:

- Is the company basing its operating metrics on a recently created HR shared service center?
- Is the company's new ERP software providing an adequate range of HR analytics that the company feels obligated to use?

Once these questions are answered, a determination can be made as to the kinds of measures that will be required, such as operating efficiency measures or corporate metrics. There may actually be more than one layer of metrics, so it would be best to not bunch all the relevant measures into one scorecard. A typical HR scorecard metrics hierarchy is composed of some of the following: HR outcome measures that look at business outcomes; operational HR metrics that focus on efficiencies; and HR analytics that look at workforce data.

When the reasons for creating the HR scorecard are determined, it would be helpful to recognize the business context within which HR operates. This can be done by asking questions such as:

- What is HR's value proposition to the business?
- What human capital metrics are included in general business reporting?

From the answers to those questions, an understanding of what type of metrics framework would be possible can be determined.

It is important to note that obtaining HR metrics that relate to outcomes or contribute to value creation are of much greater significance than efficiency metrics. HR value (or contribution to business value) can be measured from several different perspectives, such as HR's value to the business as a whole and the quantification of people value to the organization, and their input to strategic decision-making.

Now the touch points where HR involvement has an effect on business performance can be mapped. Such a map will help provide the base for developing a link between HR metrics and business metrics, such as financial, process and customer metrics. The end result of this work will be a draft framework scorecard.

Perform Additional Risk Analysis and Set Key Risk Indicators (KRIs)

Now look again at risks to see what could keep you from meeting the goals you set. For each risk, decide what your risk appetite is. Can you afford to take that risk? Does taking the risk have the potential to wipe out important projects or a high-flying reputation? For example, if in an effort to drive HR efficiency, you decide to reduce employee benefits packages next year, it could dramatically impact employee satisfaction and lead to an increased departure rate, especially among top talent who value those benefits highly. Can you afford the departure of key talent even if it saves costs?

Set a response strategy for the risk (watch, research, transfer, delegate, mitigate). For example, you may come to the conclusion that cutting benefits is the least offensive option among many to cut costs. To mitigate the risk of increased employee departures, especially among top talent, you implement regular employee surveys to gauge sentiment toward the cost cutting. This allows you to watch the risk for now and see if it becomes enough of a threat to warrant future action.

Decide whether you can afford the worst-case scenario presented by that risk from a performance management perspective. If you are implementing a change in benefits packages for the employees in all of your operations, you risk fundamentally changing the character and morale of your company, and the results could spiral out of control—mass defections, unionization efforts, or protests could materialize. If it is legal to do so, it might make sense to try this approach in individual states or countries to test the effects before doing a large-scale rollout.

Define KRIs and tolerances for those risks. KRIs, like KPIs, are the early warning signals that define the threshold at which a risk could occur. A

KRIs for HR

Employment:
- Training costs per employee
- Departure rate
- Average age of employee
- Promotion to higher job classification

Occupational Health & Safety:
- Number of accidents with persons involved
- Number of injuries
- Number of OSHA-recordable incidents per month

Working conditions:
- Overtime rate
- Employee utilization

Job satisfaction:
- Departure rate
- Employee initiated leaving rate due to resignation
- Illness rate
- Average length of service

Recruiting:
- Offer vs. acceptance rate
- Time to fill open positions
- Talent ratio
- Comparison of salary structure against market

Skills Development:
- Training hours per employee
- Training costs per employee
- Rate of training course bookings over time

relevant KRI in the scenario we are discussing is the employee departure rate. Once this rate passes a certain threshold, it signals a risk that you may not have the right talent in place to execute on other critical initiatives.

Perform Additional Compliance Analysis and Set Controls

Define your compliance requirements. Compliance defines the boundaries within which companies must operate when achieving their strategies. HR faces a wide array of compliance requirements, as shown in Figure 8-10.

COSO* Framework—The HR COSO Cube

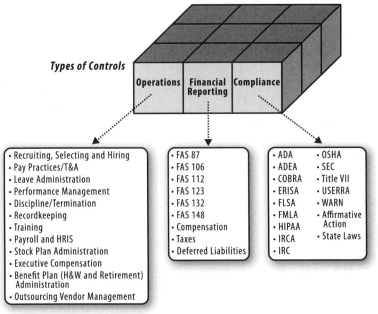

Types of Controls

| Operations | Financial Reporting | Compliance |

| • Recruiting, Selecting and Hiring
• Pay Practices/T&A
• Leave Administration
• Performance Management
• Discipline/Termination
• Recordkeeping
• Training
• Payroll and HRIS
• Stock Plan Administration
• Executive Compensation
• Benefit Plan (H&W and Retirement) Administration
• Outsourcing Vendor Management | • FAS 87
• FAS 106
• FAS 112
• FAS 123
• FAS 132
• FAS 148
• Compensation
• Taxes
• Deferred Liabilities | • ADA   • OSHA
• ADEA   • SEC
• COBRA   • Title VII
• ERISA   • USERRA
• FLSA   • WARN
• FMLA   • Affirmative Action
• HIPAA
• IRCA   • State Laws
• IRC |

*Committee of Sponsoring Organizations

Figure 8-10. HR COSO Cube

Define policies, procedures, and controls that must be in place to ensure that you can meet compliance requirements. Make sure that this applies not only at the main business process level but also to all sub-processes, including and perhaps especially those related to partners. Many countries have laws about the number of hours people can work during the week and what constitutes overtime, and violating them poses a compliance risk. In addition, tired workers are not the most effective and have more injuries at work, so preventing overwork is also sound corporate policy. A control would put a procedure in place to ensure that proactive monitoring of employee's time at work is happening in both an effective and compliant way.

Work on the Strategic Action Plan and Initiatives

The strategic plan helps define the exact methodology (the roadmap) for achieving the goals of the various initiatives. The results of this planning may require revisiting the strategy. HR should have a supporting role in the strategic plans of the organization, which are broken down into strategic initiatives.

The steps to working through strategic planning go something like this:

- Develop the HR roadmap (sequence of actions) for achieving HR's piece of the strategic plan. Include achievement of goals, and management of risk, and compliance (control activities, policies, and procedures) factors in the roadmap. For example, for the coming year, your most important initiative might be an onboarding initiative to bring in an influx of talent with the skills necessary to launch a product in a new market
- For each initiative, define critical success and failure factors. Critical success factors might include having all the new employees that are hired in the onboarding initiative being at full productivity six months from their start date. Failure factors might be anything in the roadmap that derails the initiative. These "failure factors" can then be translated into metrics that serve as an early warning system so that the initiative can be gotten back on track in time or alternatives can be found
- Develop different risk-adjusted scenarios with contingency plans at the ready, should risks to achieving plans materialize. For example, if your onboarding initiative is at risk, you should be prepared to secure an appropriate talent pool through an outsourcing arrangement

Cascade Ownership

Each KPI, KRI, and control should be owned by some department or group. The MBOs of the staff in those groups must reflect the KPIs, KRIs, and controls you set. This sounds obvious, but frequently performance is measured at an individual level in a way that does not in fact relate directly to corporate goals and strategies. For example, if cutting overtime is a critical objective, put a reward system in place for individuals who contribute to achieving this goal (obviously, choosing a system that splits the difference in terms of cost between offering no incentives and an amount equivalent to the amount of overtime you want to eliminate is a prudent choice). If their individual goals do not relate to limiting overtime, employees will not have the incentive to work more efficiently.

Incentives Should Match Strategies

It is critical to match employee compensation to overall incentives. This way, both the employees and the managers understand clearly that employee performance has a direct and measurable impact on corporate performance. Furthermore, it is absolutely critical that managers consider how strategy devolves into corporate incentives. If there are bonuses, employees will work to get them. It is surprising how often, however, that employees are compensated for doing something that is not strategic at all or even counterstrategic. Aligning incentives to strategy might seem obvious, but research from the Balanced Scorecard Collaborative (now Palladium) shows us that trends are quite to the contrary:

- Only 5% of the workforce understands the strategy
- 85% of executive teams spend less than an hour per month discussing strategy
- Only 25% of management has incentives linked to strategy
- 60% of organizations do not link budgets to strategy

You can help drive this point home to managers, which will ultimately make them more effective in achieving their own goals.

Aligning Performance Assessments

Performance assessments should be done as part of a continuous improvement process, reported in real-time and baked into company financials, accessible to managers' dashboards. The more meaningfully and deeply you connect financial goals with the outcomes of performance assessments, the more significant your contribution will be to the company's strategic direction and the more your role as ambassador between corporate strategy and the employees will be valued.

It's vital to develop a collaborative relationship with managers, and a meaningful process for sharing information, so that your benchmarks and managers' benchmarks are one and the same.

Implement 360-Degree Assessments

Consider introducing newer performance evaluation techniques, such as the 360-degree assessment. 360-degree reviews allow an individual to receive feedback from her superiors, subordinates, peers, and even customers and vendors.[8] This comprehensive process helps validate the employee's performance in the eyes of more people than just her direct supervisor and reinforces that the employee is valuable to the company in multiple aspects, some of which may not have been obvious. For the HR manager, it is a great opportunity to validate or invalidate "gut feel."

---

[8] Eric Karofsky, Judy Sweeney, and Will McNeill, "Employee Performance Management Landscape," AMR Research, November 2004.

For example, suppose a Sales organization wants to grow revenue by 10%. It conducts a 360-degree assessment and correlates the assessment data with sales contribution data. This organization finds that, despite a belief that salespeople must rise through the ranks, the effectiveness of the sales force does not correlate with length of tenure but with specific behaviors. New salespeople who exhibit these behaviors quickly become top performers. This is an example of hard data challenging organizational assumptions.

Plan and Execute

In the planning phase, the exact financial and operational resource allocations for achieving the goals of the projects defined in the strategy phase are set. The results of this planning may require revisiting the strategy if you don't have the operational resources necessary to execute the strategy. Although the performance management lifecycle is pictured as circular, the steps interact based on the findings of any of the other phases of the lifecycle.

The goal for this phase is to set forth a methodology for implementing the culture, processes, and software infrastructure to help you create an appropriate planning, budgeting, and forecasting facility in the HR department.

Align Corporate Budget to HR Budget

The budgeting process takes each of the outcomes or actions from the planning process and aligns revenues and expenses against them. Decisions regarding investment priorities and resource allocations define how the company will operate and set the bar for measuring performance. Take each of the steps in the HR initiatives you've defined and put in revenues and expenses for them.

To create risk-adjusted budgets, incorporate the range of possible revenues and costs of each action into the budget at the appropriate organizational level. A risk-adjusted budget is one that responds to changing circumstances, providing the financial capability to react to events in a planned, proactive manner. Develop different risk-adjusted budgets with contingency plans should risks to achieving budgets materialize. For example, in a traditional HR budget, you list individual line items (salaries, benefits, training costs, recruiting costs, shared services center costs) in each row with actuals, budgeted amounts, forecast, and actual/budget comparisons and forecast versus budget comparisons going across in columns. In a risk-adjusted HR budget, for every decision to allocate revenue to one line item versus another (like investing in new training programs for existing employees instead of recruiting new employees), you determine the impact and probability of the highest priority HR risks (not having sufficient skilled workers for key initiatives) on those individual line items and use this to set a range of expected budget and forecasted values instead of fixed values. In this case, if the risk materializes and you no longer have enough skilled employees who could be trained, you need a contingency plan that shows performance and risk implications if budget must be removed from training programs and put it into hiring.

Align HR Budget to Operational Plans

The operational planning process links the budget for the HR department to operational factors that HR manages (training activities, recruiting activities, and succession planning activities) and the costs and capacity for providing them. It is important to plan out each step of each initiative in terms of what will be required in terms of technology, time, and resources and consider what risks you have in each area of the operational plan.

For example, in a risk-adjusted HR operational plan, for every decision to allocate resources to one set of operational activities versus another (from running 10 courses to running 10 recruiting sessions), you determine the impact and probability of the highest priority HR operational risks (like the risk of launching a new product without adequate sales staff training) on individual line items and set a range of expected and forecasted values instead of fixed values. In this case, if the risk materializes and not enough training courses are available for salespeople, you need a contingency plan that shows the performance (the goal of recruiting sufficient staff for the coming year) and risk implications of removing budget from recruiting activities and putting it into training salespeople.

Workforce Planning and Budgeting

A category of software known as workforce planning solutions allow you to investigate the financial and operational implications of strategic workforce planning decisions. From a financial perspective, they allow you to quantify the financial impact of human capital decisions. For example, you can model budgeting scenarios and see costs and savings for each one. You can also forecast critical financial KPIs related to HR such as employee productivity, salary, benefits, and bonus expenses, cost of turnover, and recruitment expenses. Workforce planning solutions can also incorporate external benchmark data to compare your compensation strategies with publicly available data like annual mean wages of various salary categories from the U.S. Bureau of Labor Statistics.

From an operational perspective, workforce planning solutions are particularly valuable because they allow you to model the skills and competencies needed in the future. For example, these solutions provide the ability to forecast career progression by job categories (such as service workers, sales workers, professionals, and technicians) and analyze the impact on the future workforce. Workforce planning solutions also allow you to do workforce supply and demand balancing. From a demand perspective, you need to be able to accurately estimate the number and type of employees you will need for each scenario, business unit, and job type. From a supply perspective, you need to be able to accurately assess and forecast how many and what type of employees you will have for each scenario, business unit, and job type. You also need to be able to model vacancies, changes in workforce attrition rates, and organizational structure changes.

Forecast Performance and Risks

Create rolling, risk-adjusted forecasts of the budget (revenues and costs) and the operational plan (including number, capacity, and cost of resources necessary to achieve the plan) so that you can see trends over a rolling time horizon for those risks whose probability, consequences, or resiliency change over time. That way if you have to make adjustments, you can see where you've been and the direction in which things are likely to go. Predictive analytic techniques can be a particularly powerful tool for building risk-adjusted forecasts by modeling the impact previous risks had on previous forecasts.

For example, in a risk-adjusted HR forecast, you create a rolling forecast over a six month to one year window of a range of expected costs (the line items in your budget like payroll, benefits, training, and recruiting) and an associated range of expected activity outputs (training activities and recruiting activities) that are dependent on the key risks in the environment. When the probability or impact of a risk changes, you adjust the financial or operational forecast costs or activities accordingly. Using predictive techniques, you can learn from the impact of previous risks on previous actuals (the number of products sold with the number of salespeople you had trained) to predict the impact of your current risks on your current cost or activity forecasts.

Execute Plans

In the Execute phase, the goals, risks, and compliance objectives you have set in your strategy and the resources you have allocated in your plans now drive the end-to-end business processes discussed earlier in "The Business Process Angle."

Once the plan is understood, we can execute the business processes according to plan: set up new training courses, recruit new employees, or change compensation and benefits.

Examine Repercussions for Execution Problems

In an economic downturn, you will surely be asked to assess and reassess your hiring and retention policies as times get tough and executives look for places to cut. HR planning and execution must be aligned with corporate and departmental strategies. Coordination across all business units is critical so that there are no surprises.

Monitor and Analyze

In the monitor and analyze phase of the PM lifecycle, you watch what is happening (monitor) and then analyze why it happened and what, perhaps, could be done differently to improve the situation relative to your goals.

Monitor

It is important to distinguish the different categories of monitoring in evaluating business performance.

- **Event monitoring** looks for a single, discrete activity or exposure event, such as the detection of a manager violating the company's equal opportunity clauses in its hiring policies by discriminating
- **Trend monitoring** is similar to event monitoring, but examines events over time to determine patterns, for example, looking at employee satisfaction trends from monthly surveys
- **Intelligence monitoring** collects information from a variety of external sources that are of interest to the company, such as benchmarks for salaries for your industry

The presentation of information to be monitored is also crucial in order to facilitate decision-making. Dashboards bring together relevant information for status at a glance. From dashboards, it is possible to monitor performance, initiatives, risks, controls, and incidents and losses.

Evaluate performance. Look at the KPIs to identify progress made toward achievement of objectives and trends. Is the critical KPI of new employees being productive within six months on target according to plan? What is the trend? Has it changed since the last time you checked?

Evaluate initiatives. Are any failing or behind schedule? Is the initiative to increase employee self-service on target? What is the trend?

Evaluate risk. Look at the KRIs to identify:

- **Top risks.** What will the impact of changing compensation plans be on the departure rate of top employees?
- **Changes to risk levels.** Is there an upswing in the departure rates of key employees since the new compensation plan was rolled out?
- **Assessment procedures.** Are risks being assessed in accordance with company policy or according to industry best practices? Are employee complaints related to sexual harassment or other workplace issues being handled according to corporate policy?
- **Effectiveness of mitigation.** Are mitigation strategies effective in reducing the likelihood or impact of a risk? Is the new program to provide vouchers for continuing education mitigating the risk of top employees leaving due to the change in compensation plans?

Evaluate internal controls. Report key control deficiencies, approvals, verifications, and reconciliations to mitigate risk. Are we reporting and ultimately remediating control deficiencies on the policies we have put in place to ensure affirmative action compliance is ongoing?

Evaluate incidents and losses. If incidents or losses have occurred due to the failure or absence of controls, such as safety incidents in the warehouse due to not following the appropriate procedures, this information needs to be documented.

No matter how proactive you are, manual monitoring can be very inefficient. Automated monitoring can proactively identify out-of-tolerance conditions, highlighting when a KPI, KRI, or control goes over or under defined tolerances and then alerting the responsible party. This should take into account forecasting, trending, and modeling capabilities so that if a metric falls out of range of a trend or budget/plan, the appropriate alert is raised, along with a workflow process to get the investigation under way.

Analyze

Analysis is a key step in which you not only look at where you are, but what is happening (or what has happened) and why. The techniques for analysis can range from highly manual and simple to fairly automated and complex in terms of the usage of statistical techniques.

Workforce analytics is an important emerging discipline for HR. Marketing is the leading edge field today for analytics. HR remains relatively soft in this area, going with intuitive gut feelings rather than hard data. Workforce analytics helps bring rigor to this area of the business.

Hard data is needed to support hard decisions. For example, do you know what it will mean for productivity if staff is forced to move to a four-day workweek? Will layoffs impact succession planning? If you lose top salespeople, what will happen to the sales forecast? These decisions are frequently being made today without data.

All of these questions highlight important risks for the organization, so knowing the answers and providing risk-adjusted reporting is key to helping companies weather difficult times. The better that reporting can help sense risk and alert appropriate managers within the organization, the faster the organization can respond to and manage the risk event to reduce its negative effects.

In terms of what to analyze, look at what you have been monitoring: KPIs, initiatives, KRIs, controls, and incidents and losses.

Analyze KPIs to understand why they are increasing or decreasing. You find that the KPI of new employees being productive within six months on the dashboard is trending downward. Drilling down, you learn that this is because the new employees in Product Development are way behind compared to other employees.

Analyze initiatives to understand why they are succeeding or failing. All the employee self-service initiatives are heading in the wrong direction. You determine that this is due to the new HR self-service system being dramatically behind schedule.

Analyze KRIs to understand why they are increasing or decreasing. You identify the process deficiencies or other trends that are the most significant in increasing the employee departure rate before it reaches critical levels.

Analyze the effectiveness of internal controls. You notice that a control to test for timely OSHA reporting seems to generate a lot of incidents and realize that the threshold that defines timely is set unrealistically low, creating false positives. You then analyze why controls have lost their effectiveness.

Analyze incidents and losses to determine root causes and trends. You notice a significant uptick in warehouse safety incidents and determine the root cause of the incident was a failure to follow the appropriate safety procedures on the new loading platform.

In all of the cases above, analysis was done with human intervention, but this does not have to be the case. The volume and complexity of data in the enterprise today makes it increasingly difficult to mine through data and arrive at intelligent conclusions. Using data mining techniques, software can determine likely root causes and suggest recommended actions. For example, a key risk indicator for employee departure rate is increasing. Without any manual intervention, the system does a series of correlations. When you highlight the KRI, a popup shows that the number one factor associated with the employee departure rate risk is the employee survey indicating dissatisfaction with the company's new compensation policy.

HR Performance Management in Practice: A Case Study

Programs such as mentoring can be very important. According to a Gartner case study, Sun Microsystems demonstrated that mentoring can be highly effective, and, although it is one of the 'softest' metrics in HR, the impact of mentoring can be measured with the proper application of workforce analytics. In Sun's case, some counterintuitive results materialized: counter to what was expected, 8.5% of the lower-level administrative employees participating in the program saw positive changes in their salaries, while 6.2% of higher-skilled engineers saw salary raises.[9] Also, using the scientific approach of measuring a control group against a test group, it was determined that mentors were promoted six times as often as those not in the test group, and mentees (those taking the mentoring courses) were promoted five times as often as nonparticipants. Sun worked closely with analytics firm Capital Analytics, looking at 78 different spreadsheets, and measuring 68 variables, to find correlation with various metrics.

Sun found that mentoring was much more effective with some groups of employees than others. Those whose performance prior to mentoring was low benefited the most. Furthermore, those whose skill level was high (engineers) benefited little compared with administrative personnel, who benefited the most from mentoring.

Rather than analyzing HR initiatives across the entire employee base, learn from this example and drill down to analyze who really benefits and why. It might be that you can scale back an effective program so that it targets those who will benefit most.

---

[9] James Holincheck, "Case Study: Workforce Analytics at Sun." Gartner, Inc. Research ID G00142776. 27 October 2006.

Adjust

After monitoring to know what has happened and analyzing to understand why it happened, for those things not going accordingly to plan, it becomes time to set the business back on course by taking what you've learned and using that information to adjust settings. However, you must always consider the impact of your goals, risks, and compliance concerns when adjusting KPIs, initiatives, KRIs, controls, or as a result of incidents and losses.

Adjust KPIs. For KPIs trending in the wrong direction, once you have analyzed the root causes, it should be clear what actions will set things back on course. However, remember that KPIs are interlinked, and you must optimize performance goals in the context of risk objectives and without violating compliance objectives. If only one department is responsible for the poor showing on the employee productivity within six months KPI, you can assign more resources such as trainers from other projects or increase funding, but only if it does not increase the risk of not delivering on other key initiatives or violate any compliance objectives like mandatory harassment training for all new employees.

Adjust initiatives. For initiatives that are not going as planned, rapidly take remedial action or cancel them. If it's clear that the initiative is not going to work, either make changes that can help save it or cancel it, if possible, so that you can reallocate resources. For example, you determine the employee self service initiative is failing because the HR systems initiative is behind schedule. The simplest adjustment might be to reset expectations on the employee self-service initiative or work with IT to see if additional or different resources could expedite the rollout.

Adjust KRIs. For KRIs trending in the wrong direction, once you have analyzed the root causes, put mitigating controls in place to stabilize them. However, it is critical to remember that KRIs are interlinked, and you must optimize risk goals in the context of performance objectives without violating your compliance objectives. For example, a sensitivity analysis identifies process deficiencies or other trends that are most significant in increasing the employee departure rate before it reaches critical levels. You put a mitigating control in place to have the HR team increase the number of personal meetings with disgruntled employees to give them a voice to change the organization. However, do this only if it does not decrease the likelihood of delivering on other HR goals, such as delivering training or recruiting programs on time (since now your team is investing in numerous meetings) and if it doesn't violate any compliance objectives. Further, it's important to consider your options: for each risk, you can decide to treat it, tolerate it (since a mitigating control is in place), transfer it, or terminate the activity that is producing the risk.

Adjust controls. For control violations, adjustment takes the form of remediation and certification. After the affirmative action control is violated repeatedly, set up a remediation plan to create a more stringent set of training programs and stricter set of punitive actions for corporate policy violations.

Adjust incidents and losses. For incidents and losses, the correct adjustments typically involve reexamining whether you are tracking the right risks and have put the appropriate controls in place to mitigate them. For example, after determining that the uptick in warehouse safety incidents is due to failure to follow appropriate safety procedures on the new loading platform, put an automated risk monitoring process in place that alerts you to the first sign of increased injury activity.

Model and Optimize

In this phase, you find out what works and what doesn't. You will have collected enough information to create models that demonstrate forthcoming opportunities for optimizing the processes and practices you have selected for study.

Revenue, Cost, and Profitability Modeling

Modeling the costs, revenue, and profitability implications of performance management, risk management, and compliance management activities and their drivers can be achieved at a very detailed level using activity-based costing and associated methodologies. For HR applications, ABC can be very useful for breaking down the costs of the individual activities people perform to get a much more detailed sense of where employee time is being spent. For example, using ABC, you can model the amount of time HR specialists spend on the phone with employees, researching their issues, making changes in the underlying benefits systems, and so on to help you see how much time employee self-service could free up for them.

Scenario Modeling

Scenario modeling can be applied to financial and operational modeling and focuses on creating different business scenarios. Simple scenario modeling can include creating a base case and then high and low cases based on changes made to input variables, such as market growth rates or inflation rates. This technique is often used in modeling market and business opportunities and creating business plans. For example, you might build a set of scenario models in HR to understand how critical macro variables such as the rate of workforce retirement for skilled workers and the availability of new talent will impact your talent management strategies in a growth market.

Simulation Modeling

More-advanced modeling including Monte Carlo simulation supports creating a broad range of scenarios based on multiple iterations of input assumptions and combinations. With this technique, probabilities can be assigned to the various outcomes. These techniques allow uncertainty associated with a given outcome to be estimated and to reduce risk by applying sensitivity analysis, correlation, and trend extrapolation. By simulating the effect of uncertainty, it becomes possible to answer questions such as, "How certain are we that a given project (such as a series of recruiting drives) will result in a minimum number of highly skilled employees joining the company?" Or, conversely, "What's the minimum outcome that we can be, for example, 90% certain of achieving?" Simulation also makes it possible to identify and rank the various contributors to overall uncertainty, which makes it an excellent candidate for associating goals with relevant risks.

Other HR Models

Modeling helps you get a picture of where your workforce is today. Compensation modeling is one type of modeling that organizations often use to analyze their compensation plans. Other types of modeling are also highly relevant for HR. In a study of 100 leading HR organizations, Jim Kochanski, SVP, Organization and Talent Practice Co-Leader at Sibson Consulting, modeled employee engagement. Employee engagement was defined as a workforce that knows what to do (vision) and that wants to do it (commitment). In this model, respondents categorized employees into one of four categories:

- **Engaged.** Employees who know what to do and want to do it (52% of respondents)
- **Renegades.** Employees who know what to do and don't want to do it (11% of respondents)

- **Anchors.** Employees who don't know what to do and wouldn't do it if they did (33% of respondents)
- **Enthusiasts.** Employees who are committed but don't know what to do (5% of respondents)

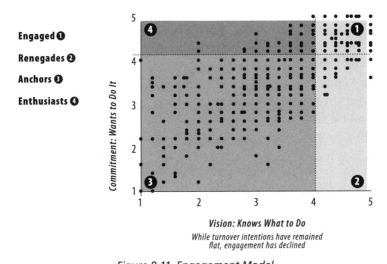

Engaged ❶

Renegades ❷

Anchors ❸

Enthusiasts ❹

Vision: Knows What to Do
While turnover intentions have remained flat, engagement has declined

Figure 8-11. Engagement Model
(Source: Jim Kochanski, "How 100 Leading HR Organizations Are Improving Their Strategic Effectiveness," Wellesley Information Services, March 2007)

A similar type of model could be created to help drive decisions regarding staff reductions or reorganizations. Mentoring, as described in "HR Performance Management in Practice: A Case Study" earlier in this chapter, proved highly effective with the company's lowest performers, so if your in-house results parallel those in this study, you might consider mentoring.

Optimize

The goal at this phase of the PM lifecycle is to determine the best way to achieve objectives by taking into account the entire context of the problem, including all relevant constraints and assessments (costs, benefits, risk, labor and time) as well as business strategies, objectives, risks, and compliance factors. Optimization can be done both through human evaluation as well as through advanced algorithmic techniques.

Becca Goren, Worldwide Marketing Manager of Strategy and Capital Management at SAS, has written an excellent article on workforce optimization."[10] This section draws heavily on her work. According to Goren,

---

[10] Becca Goren, "Optimizing Human Capital," B-Eye Network, (b-eye-network.com), November 3, 2008.

optimization is designing a system or process to perform as well as possible in some defined sense. And this definition is very much specific to your organization. What's optimal for you—with your goals and values—could very well be suboptimal for the next organization. Every performance management paradigm, every mission statement, could point to a different definition of success—and therefore to a different way to optimally allocate resources.

Effective resource optimization requires a certain rigor, consistency and agreement on processes. Whether you are explicitly developing a mathematical model or just trying to drive more effective and efficient resource use across the organization, all resource optimization models should be based on objectives, decision variables, and constraints that are relevant for your organization. You will first select a key performance metric that you want to optimize. The advantage of optimization is that it delivers a solution that will work within your constraints and the decisions you can reasonably make. Goren identifies the following five steps to guide you through this optimization framework and apply to any resource optimization scenario.

- **Step 1: Define the objective to reflect organizational mission and strategy.** For example, you might optimize workforce productivity by distributing existing employees to the most appropriate tasks internally to reduce or eliminate the need to hire
- **Step 2: Get buy-in and foster accountability.** Ensure that managers are willing to relocate personnel to different sites or departments in order to support overall organization-wide goals
- **Step 3: Define the conceptual resource optimization model.** Gather historical data from employment data sources to account for required skills, position, salary, experience and location. If possible, seek out ways to gather qualitative, subjective data from surveys to help identify variables (such as willingness to relocate, family and desired salary considerations). Identify decisions that can be made (such as, how many people at which salary/position can be allocated, for what cost, at which locations?)
- **Step 4: Formulate the resource optimization model.** This step is the translation of your conceptual model into an analytic model, which necessarily must embody more rigor and detail, represented in mathematical terms. In this step you begin to formally code the

key elements of the optimization model—objectives, constraints and decision variables (see Figure 8-12). There is no single right way to use mathematical expressions to represent the elements of a decision problem. Every formulation represents a compromise because no mathematical representation can (or should) reflect every detail of a real-world scenario. Good modeling balances realism and workability

- **Step 5: Implement and update the analytical model.** Analytical models must be validated and continually updated. Best practices for resource optimization are tied to performance management by answering questions such as: "Were recommended decisions put into action?" and "Were those decisions effective for driving improved alignment with organizational goals?" If the results were not what you would expect, revisit the model to determine whether the identified objectives, decisions, constraints, resources and other elements reflect your current reality. Make changes and updates as needed, according to the available data. For example, you could add relocation costs to an existing model to better account for their influence on cost-oriented decisions

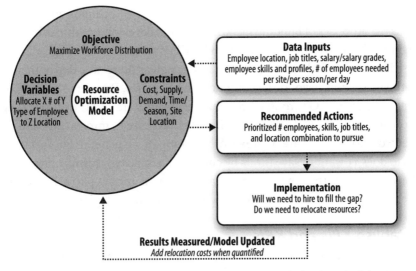

Figure 8-12. Sample Workforce Distribution Optimization Model

Case Study: Performance Management in Action

Virtual Gates is a fictional cutting-edge computer manufacturer with retail outlets. This section describes how the HR department at Virtual Gates closes its loop during the process of optimizing its value to the organization by reducing its workforce.

Setting the Context

Chad Fuller, the VP of HR, has just left the office of Clint Hobbs, VG's CEO, with instructions to decrease HR's overall spend as a function of profit by implementing a 15% staff reduction. Not good news, in Chad's opinion, though he sees that the cuts are necessary to the company's survival. Maybe if it goes well enough, Chad will see some of those who are cut come back on board after performance improves.

No matter what decisions Chad makes, he must align them with VG's larger goal of driving profitable growth as measured by the company's net income and earnings per share growth, particularly in comparison with competitors Hypercell and Packingflash. Chad must implement the reductions in the context of a drive to release a new netbook while retiring products that are no longer profitable.

Understand the Collaborative Impact

Because HR provides resources for every one of VG's business processes, it owns the processes of building the workforce and developing high-performing organizations. Another consideration for Chad when making tough choices is the impact on stakeholders within HR as well as on related departments, both within and beyond the company's boundaries. Partners that are co-innovating with VG through technology exchanges are certainly not among those whom VG can afford to lose. It makes no sense to implement changes that work for HR but are negative for the company in general. For instance, Chad doesn't want to save funds by cutting all employee-training programs if it also impacts the top performers' motivation or annoys partners because the reduction was not coordinated with their own strategies.

Establish KPIs and KRIs

The selection and implementation of relevant KPIs and KRIs is the way every successful organization gauges its progress toward goals. Prior to taking any action, Chad and his team must select KPIs and KRIs, the chief risks to which their choices may expose them, and the principle lines between their partners and their processes that they must closely watch. It's vital, too, that they note the drivers behind their KPIs and KRIs, as well as the relationships between them. Finally, the leading indicators of performance need to be identified.

Decreasing overall HR spend as a function of revenue, measuring employee performance, workforce productivity, and bench strength against top companies are the metrics relevant to Chad as he monitors progress. While these criteria are clear to HR, Chad must also ensure that their implications are just as clear to HR's partners. Increasing the profit per employee by reducing headcount, for instance, can severely impact the effectiveness of numerous other business processes such as production, quality, product management, just as increasing workforce productivity can produce opposite effects.

Establish the BI Foundation

Metrics for KPIs or KRIs do not just appear. Chad and his team must gather data from the various source systems, including HCM systems as well as individual recruitment, learning, employee performance, compensation, and ERP systems. Chad's team will need to consolidate all this information as they execute HR business processes. Of course, to see the effects of their choices on their partners, the team must also harvest data from systems such as CRM, ERP, and SCM as well as external web sites and unstructured information.

With the raw data in hand, Chad and his team cleanse it and load it into a data mart or warehouse. They will use this information to obtain the single source of truth that will help them to reduce the workforce during the process of developing and launching VG's latest netbook.

Strategize and Prioritize

Chad's department is not working alone. While his directive from Clint Hobbs is to adjust staffing levels to increase overall profit per employee, he knows that Product Development is simultaneously engaged in an initiative not just to produce a new netbook but also to eliminate as many unprofitable products from the VG portfolio as possible. This elimination has a manifold effect. Though it will certainly free up budget, it will also reveal the soft spots in the staff of the Product Development, Marketing, Sales, Service, Finance, and IT departments, to name a few. Those employees who have not been making the grade will become apparent, making the difficult job of choosing who stays at least a little easier.

Chad needs a scorecard by which to monitor his team's progress toward its targets. A key component is a list of the risks inherent in HR's initiative, foremost among them the real possibility that decreased employee morale and motivation be reflected in reduced productivity across departments. To account for such a risk, Chad must introduce KRIs and related contingency measures. For example, if the employee satisfaction level for any department drops by 10% or more, significant training programs for the remaining employees would be implemented to reflect the company's investment in them. Any move Chad makes must be compliant with VG's overall strategy, particularly in the areas of regional labor practices.

Plan and Execute

Chad's team will deploy employee performance management systems to identify employees who excel in each department to ensure retention of those with critical skills and competencies for the highest priority initiatives. Fewer employees mean reduced costs and fewer resources consumed across the entire HR value chain. Chad and his team can now reallocate funds to those training courses, recruitment services, and shared services (such as payroll and benefits) that will be needed to maintain effective operations.

Reducing the workforce carries obvious risks. The potential for a failed launch of the new netbook is the chief risk, followed by risks such as increased customer dissatisfaction in the face of fewer service representatives in the call center. It's critical that Chad contextualize these against the big picture. The leg bone, as they say, is always connected to the shinbone—any time one part of an organization suffers, another will soon follow. Once HR has determined how the choices could affect all the departments, Chad and his team must remain in close contact so that problems can be solved quickly. The KRIs and contingency measures mentioned in earlier sections are vital in this phase of the initiative's development.

Monitor and Analyze

At this stage, Chad's main concern is whether HR's costs as a percentage of profit are matching the forecast. To find out, he keeps a close eye on KPIs and KRIs. For example, with the 15% reduction in workforce, are affected departments showing process inefficiencies or other bottlenecks? Has the reduction actually liquidated more resources for the business and increased the value of HR relative to the costs? How is the reduced workforce impacting the performance of VG's suppliers and customers? Chad's team must also monitor both employee morale and the risks associated with compliance, which is crucial to effective HR management.

The team must immediately discover the source of any discrepancy between the anticipated and actual result of his department's initiative. Could it be that because the highest paid employees are not performing as anticipated, the staff reductions are less effective than predicted? Perhaps employee dissatisfaction has resulted in growing job security fears and spurred the best employees to leave. Regardless of the issue, Chad's number one priority after arriving at a potential solution is to ascertain that it is aligned with all partners, as well as with corporate's greater goals.

Model and Optimize

Chad's department can't comprehend the true costs of the services that it provides or which groups are absorbing those services without an operational cost model. A costing analysis can help Chad and his team to see the ratio between HR services (such as help desk resources, training, employee, and recruiters) and the value returned.

Frequently such analyses reveal unexpected results. For instance, they show whether HR services that appear to generate the highest ROI are actually less profitable. Chad's model could change assumptions to simulate different "what-if" scenarios to determine which services HR should keep. The number of HR centers that can be made into shared service centers is one such assumption that could change in the model, as is the minimum number of employees in each country. Chad's team can also use incentive compensation management to understand the impact on payroll of various compensation scenarios and then, depending on the results, set targets accordingly.

The team can deploy a variety of optimization techniques to achieve its goals once it confirms that their strategy and resources are solid.

Closing the Loop in an Integrated System

Today's technology can manage the scenario described so far. Soon, holistic, closed-loop systems will enable most organizational departments to align their execution and strategy with strong consistency. Chad's ability to build a strategy management process that captures goals, initiatives, and metrics that can be linked to his driver-based financial and operational planning process, as well as to his monitoring and analysis, modeling and optimization, and risk and control processes, will result in a game-changing set of scenarios. Most importantly, he and his team will be able to use their goals, initiatives, plans, and risks and controls to drive the desired behavior out to their transactional processes.

Such a system is now available to HR departments. It allows users instant visibility into employee's skill sets, project reallocation, appraisals, and goal achievement. It also enables HR and other department managers to model the impact of salary and benefits and to implement final payouts in payroll runs. For example, from the analytical views in the application, Chad's team can see that the future payout for a group of salespeople is likely to be much higher than budgeted. They can then model different scenarios and change compensation plans directly in the transactional compensation systems. Their data comes from a variety of integrated systems, including HR, supply chain management, procurement, resource management, service execution, and any other system that monitors employee productivity. As a result, the strategy to improve workforce productivity by increasing the profit per employee, the initiatives to reduce the workforce, and the act of removing people from payroll and benefits are integrated such that both efficiency—doing things right—and effectiveness—doing the right things—are significantly enhanced. Chad hopes that the netbook is so successful that some of the valued employees he had to let go can come back to work again soon.

Action Items

Although this is not strictly your responsibility, before embarking on a performance management implementation process, you should make sure that financial benchmarks are standardized across the company. Be especially mindful of interregional and linguistic differences regarding data points.

Advice and Best Practices

The following is a list of concrete steps you can take now to see real improvements via performance management.

- Base your decisions on data rather than gut feel or organizational assumptions
- Craft HR processes that make sense on a regional and local level, while still tying these processes back to the overall strategic goals
- Develop a clear understanding of how the cost and time spent training an employee impacts the bottom line

- Break through two walls—the wall between HR and corporate strategy and the walls between siloed applications within HR that prevent useful analysis
- Effectively identify, develop and retain critical talent in order to develop the leaders who will manage and drive key aspects of the business
- Develop an understanding of the other roles within the organization and their interdependency in terms of goals, initiatives, and metrics they are managed by, in order to understand the full performance implications for running a world class HR organization
- If you don't know much about workforce analytics, learn about it or find someone who does
- Consider introducing newer performance evaluation techniques, such as the 360-degree assessment. 360-degree reviews allow an individual to receive feedback from her superiors, subordinates, peers, and even customers and vendors

Chapter 9

Performance Management for IT

Y ou've probably heard the axiom, "IT people need to think more like businesspeople." It's true that in today's enterprise, IT has become more and more essential to business operations—but it is still treated, and sometimes behaves like, the proverbial redheaded stepchild. IT departments typically do not know how to demonstrate their value; they need to implement performance management—now.

Performance management is actively and proactively managing an organization to ensure that it achieves predetermined levels of performance while mitigating risk. It is the opposite of "damage control," which is what many IT managers end up doing.

Looking Back: How Has Life Changed in IT?

When you understand the context within which you practice IT performance management, you'll be able to align the goals of your operations with your organization's high-level objectives far more effectively.

Globalization has distributed the value chain and decentralized decision-making from a command-and-control model to a paradigm where business users, more than ever, are making the day-to-day decisions that run the company. This sounds like a good thing, and it is—partially. Placing more power in the hands of the people who carry out the day-to-day work of the company is definitely positive and transformative. But here's the catch—very quickly, your company begins to look more like a loose confederation than a unified republic. People begin to take this empowerment as a signal that they can operate in a vacuum and use customized technology solutions that appear to work for them but that are neither aligned with the strategic goals of the enterprise nor provide a holistic view. (In other words, they don't know what they don't know.)

End-to-end processes span the functional silos of the company, which makes measuring company-wide IT performance that much more difficult. In this context, performance management should help you effectively manage and monitor these end-to-end processes across all of the functional silos.

Here's why this needs to happen. You as a CIO or IT manager, probably feel like a firefighter. You are principally concerned with supervising existing systems, and every so often, you get tossed a pet project with very little lead time or direction. The bulk of your time is probably spent rushing from workstation to workstation, performing service requests or supervising those who do. Your job mainly consists of explaining why the system is slow today and why there's no budget to add more servers so that the system won't experience these periods of latency. Meanwhile, your boss up in the C-suite is calling you, asking, "How are we performing against our strategic goals? Why can't I run predictive modeling on my supply chain? Why can't I see the impact of a maintenance shutdown on next quarter's profits?" How can you find the time to put out these fires and answer those burning questions? How much of your time is spent on motherboards versus in the boardroom?

You must run IT as a strategic participant in the business and to be invited into that role (and into the boardroom where strategic decisions are made), you must measure and report your organization's performance in language that is meaningful to business executives.

How Business Network Transformation Affects IT

Technology has been perhaps the single most significant transformational force in changing the way we do business, especially in the last ten years or so. Because of the ubiquity of the Internet and collaborative technologies like Web 2.0, business processes can span multiple facilities, business entities, and even nations. IT is essentially the backbone of most companies, but may be properly valued only if the company can measure the success that IT brings. With that type of success comes responsibility, accountability, and opportunity.

That means that IT is now expected to support the transformed business networks and to open doors, linking business partners seamlessly and securely. IT is expected not simply to service the requests of the business side, but to proactively move forward, and even lead the business in finding new opportunities and improving business processes and helping the business meet its KPIs through the adoption of technology.

How Technology Has Changed

A significant shift has occurred in how IT perceives its role and the way businesses use technology. During the early days of the Internet, the role of corporate IT, whose roots were in automating internal operations, was defensive. The object was to allow very limited interaction with the outside world in order to keep the fortress safe. But now, with the Web serving as a major sales and marketing channel, service-oriented architecture enabling the creation of new internal and external applications and processes, and the incorporation of mobile devices in workflows, IT is now about facilitating collaboration on the edge while protecting internal transactional systems.

For an IT traditionalist, this is a scary new world, and it doesn't come with a roadmap. But for an IT professional with a view to future possibilities, these changes represent a chance for IT to do far more than ever before. However, to enable this transition, IT must incorporate agility as a standard practice, which imposes pressure on IT staffers who may have been used to the prior, more reactive stance.

All of this must be done at a time when budgets are being cut and business strategies are far more dynamic than in the past.

Now more than ever, IT must operate like a business with an understanding of strategy and execution and must link its processes and systems to business objectives and metrics in order to justify its activities and initiatives. Whiz-bang tools for their own sake are gone. You must learn to generate a business case and comprehend, serve, and even anticipate the needs of each department in order to be a partner in value creation. And the best way to understand whether any of this is working is to implement a performance management framework.

The Evolution of Performance Management for IT

IT performance management has not kept pace with technology's ever-expanding role, but there is increasing pressure for IT to actively measure its financial impact. The majority of IT reporting is cost-centered. Actual-to-budget is the most common approach, with "internal customer satisfaction"

(ICS) coming in at a close second. Both approaches are narrow in scope. Actual-to-budget does not incorporate the business impact upon IT or vice versa. It looks only at IT's performance against its own budget. ICS is basically determined by infrequent surveys with low responses. These methods create a scorecard for IT, but they are simplistic and do not effectively capture the true value of the IT organization to the business.

Service-level agreements (SLAs) are a common metric for inter-company agreements, but only about a third of enterprises use them for evaluating their own IT departments. SLAs are a more useful measure for IT organizations because they place the operational value of IT at the center of the discussion and engage business users directly—the level of service is agreed upon in advance, and it is measured objectively. But SLAs still leave out the direct impact on the business and its objectives. A useful tool for quantifying the value of IT—versus the cost—is IT chargeback, in which each department is responsible for its share of costs for IT initiatives. This topic will be explored later in this chapter.

Another effective approach to measuring the business value of IT is the Balanced Scorecard, described in detail in Chapter 3. The Balanced Scorecard is a comprehensive measurement along four metrics that directly relate the value of IT to strategic and corporate performance. However, few IT leaders use this approach.

IT performance management is still in its infancy; organizations are not even measuring the same types of things, making benchmarking your performance against others in the industry virtually impossible. In 2005, AMR Research began a project in which it sought to create a top 10 list of the most common metrics used by IT organizations to measure and predict performance. Researchers found little commonality across the organizations surveyed. As of this writing, there is scant evidence to indicate that IT organizations have begun to coalesce around a standard set of performance-based metrics.

Why You Must Do This Now

IT organizations need to measure and report performance, lest they be cast as a "cost center." IT needs to help implement projects to reduce operational cost and continue to innovate with automation and tightening of more processes by maximizing technology and information. The role of IT leadership is moving from a pure focus on technology to a focus on business processes and relationships. Business leaders need to understand clearly what technology can do for them. It is essential to articulate, execute, and monitor IT's value proposition. An IT organization should:

- Deliver high-value IT operations and services
- Understand the company's goals and objectives
- Provide strategic insight and leadership, based on an understanding of technology and its relationship to the connected economy

It's common for IT departments to excel at the first two points and fall short on the third. That can no longer be the case. In order to break the mold of "cost center"—and the risk of being viewed as a cost to be outsourced—IT leaders must transform themselves from tactical utility providers into entrepreneurs who can actively participate in strategy and business network transformation.

With business network transformation in full swing at your company, how are you managing outsourcing relationships? How do you connect the performance of partners and suppliers at a granular level with the company's performance? You need to have a handle on your internal systems, but you also have to deal with the systems and data of outside trading partners. You need to be able to implement systems that support secure collaboration. You are managing SLAs of systems that you may not actually own. You must be able to obtain and properly integrate the data of all your trading partners and customers. As the supply chain becomes increasingly distributed, performance management is that much more essential.

Does This Sound Familiar?

- You spend 80% of your time putting out fires and less than 15% of the time planning strategically.

- The CEO comes to you and says, "Here's what we need to get done; you figure out how to get it done," but rarely asks, "Where do you see our company in three years?"

- Other managers question IT's value because of cost overruns and lack of linkage to the business.

- Senior management can't determine if they have the best IT options for decision-making.

- Your projects are underfunded and behind schedule.

What Kind of Company Are You?

The type of business your company conducts should strongly affect the strategic choices you make. If the CEO says, "I need a 10% cut in IT spending," what do you do? If you universally cut everyone's IT budget, you could potentially be impairing far more than 10% of your department's capability to play a strategic growth role. You must be intimately familiar with the company's core business. Don't wait until your hands are tied, and don't expect all good ideas to come from the top.

For example, if you're a shipping and logistics company that is heavily dependent on its call centers, it might not be wise to cut call center support staff or their IT infrastructure. If a customer who's used to getting an agent suddenly has to wait twice as long, she may not be a repeat customer. Perhaps you don't need the latest version of the desktop operating system this year. Be strategic in everything you add and in everything you eliminate.

What part of your company is really driving revenue growth? That's where you should strategically align your department. You want to put resources behind projects that support your business' strategic objectives and deemphasize projects that don't serve that goal.

The Business Process Angle

Every activity and process in your company has an IT component. Historically, IT has viewed its role as a provider of point solutions for specific entities in the business: "I need a contacts database for marketing," or "the web site needs to support live chat." But in fact, IT can, and should, act more synergistically.

IT is very good at implementing standardized business processes. But running an IT department is not just about implementing an ERP system or integrating a CRM system as the result of an acquisition. It's increasingly about understanding how processes run within the organization. You can optimize those processes by understanding the business needs and applying the right technology to support those needs.

Think of packaged applications for ERP, CRM, and SCM. Your role is to act as a tailor and as an ambassador. Your role as a tailor is configuring solutions for specific department's tastes. As an ambassador, you take what you have learned from building solutions and apply that knowledge to proactively guide business process improvement across the company.

Think of IT not as a catchall service organization, but as a privileged and respected intermediary between fiefdoms that may not fully understand each other. Since you have worked under the hood at all the departments and divisions and seen their similarities, you can apprise each department of opportunities to optimize its business processes.

At the risk of introducing too many metaphors, it's sort of like being a mechanic and realizing that a gasket from a Honda works perfectly well in a Mercedes. How pleased would that Mercedes owner be to find that they don't always have to buy the "genuine" part? With that realization, they have cemented their role as your genuine customer and will probably proactively ask you to investigate problems or improve efficiencies that they might have neglected to do anything about previously.

It is not enough for IT to participate in business processes. IT must act as the enabler to make all the end-to-end processes work smoothly (see Figure 9-1).

To be good at this, you need to ensure that your systems are flexible. And this new, ambassadorial role means you not only understand the "macro needs" of the end-to-end processes but get intimately involved in the "micro needs" of each business area. You can improve your value to the organization by walking over to Sales and saying something like, "Well, I am working on a project for the shipping department, and this is how we got drilldowns on inventory. Let's take a look at your lead-generation software and see what we need to do—perhaps we can reuse some of the same web services. And then we can explore which customers cancel the most orders and create inventory, and populate your lead-generation software with information about the true cost per lead by factoring returns into the cost-per-lead calculation."

Another example: the CEO wants to reduce margin by two basis points, and that means selling more product profitably. Costs need to be cut. IT enables these things to happen. IT can be the critical difference between making swinging cuts across the board and implementing a cost-saving solution that drives future growth. You can use your knowledge of Sales' business process to create a customer profitability application. Of course, in order to create an application that really speaks to the Sales department and the CEO's needs, you need an understanding that comes from having been an active participant, not a reactive errand-runner, in both of these divisions.

Effectively, IT can:

- **Empower and connect people.** IT organizations can empower people to be more productive. With applications that support multichannel access, IT organizations can help enable teamwork
- **Manage and deliver information.** IT organizations can manage and deliver business information effectively. In particular, they

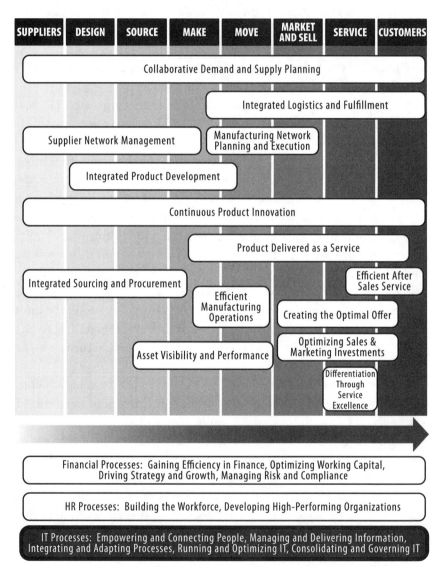

Figure 9-1. IT is Foundational to All Business Processes

can consolidate structured, unstructured, and master data to establish a single version of truth; accelerate access to information using enterprise search and analytics; manage information across its lifecycle with built-in retention management and archiving capabilities; and enable performance management to improve business insight

- **Integrate and adapt business processes.** IT organizations can implement a technology infrastructure based on SOA to enable greater flexibility. In addition, IT organizations can integrate applications to support end-to-end processes and manage those processes across the business network
- **Consolidate and govern.** IT organizations can optimize the strategic, operational, and tactical aspects of IT. They can align and manage IT projects to meet business needs, design an enterprise architecture to enable flexibility, manage the lifecycle of applications to ensure high availability, and consolidate heterogeneous solutions on a unified technology platform that simplifies the IT landscape and its management
- **Run and optimize IT.** IT organizations can be run like a business. They can execute IT projects on time and within budget and ensure no disruption of business systems and users

Key Roles in IT

Key roles in IT performance management include the CIO, the director of IT operations, the director of application development, the IT portfolio management team, and IT analysts.

The CIO

The senior-most leadership position in the IT organization has responsibility to interact with the other members of the C-suite as well as provide leadership on both the demand side (demonstrating what IT can do for the business) and on the supply side (providing IT services that effectively support the organization's key mission). At some companies, the CIO handles the demand side issues (how the company can use IT to business advantage) and the CTO, who might report either to the CIO or to the COO, handles supply side issues.

Director of IT

The director of IT plans and manages internal operations of an organization and coordinates and prioritizes the IT projects. The director of IT is the execution arm for the CIO for program coordination in his or her absence. The director of IT also supervises and manages the IT staff for application support along with new projects.

Director of Application Development

The director of application development oversees multiple teams of software engineers responsible for design, development, enhancement, and support of numerous products. The director of application development needs to ensure that applications meet quality and functional requirements.

IT Portfolio Manager

IT portfolio managers are responsible for helping to prioritize projects, allocate resources, and secure approvals for projects for the IT portfolio as a whole. By helping the company decide which projects to execute and who to assign to those projects, the IT portfolio manager helps determine whether the company meets its objectives.

IT Analyst

IT analysts design and support IT solutions to improve business processes. IT analysts work with the business to translate the requirements into IT solutions that help with both efficiency and productivity.

PMO Director

In general, the motive for establishing a project management office (PMO) is to ensure that IT projects are delivered on time and managed consistently. In the context of this chapter, the PMO director manages the PMO, and project managers in that group help coordinate all the projects in the IT portfolio.

KPIs That Matter for Success in IT

KPIs vary depending on the level of the organization in question, as shown in AMR's hierarchy of IT metrics in Figure 9-2.

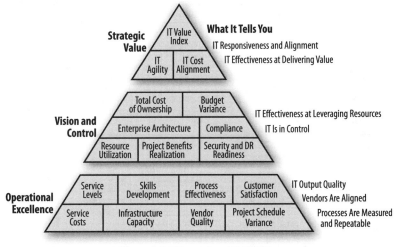

Figure 9-2. Hierarchy of IT Metrics
(Source: AMR Research, 2006, "Product Launch Dashboards,
Part 1: The Hierarchy of Product Metrics")

Marrying AMR's metrics hierarchy with the roles described earlier, we get something like what is shown in Table 9-1.

KPIs can also be aligned by functional area, as illustrated in Figure 9-3.

Table 9-1. IT Metrics by Role

Level / Role	Metric
Strategic / CIO	IT Value Index; IT Agility; IT Cost Alignment
Vision and Control / Director of IT; Director of Application Development; IT Portfolio Manager	Total Cost of Ownership; Budget Variance; Enterprise Architecture; Compliance; Resource Utilization; Project Benefits Realization; Security and DR Readiness
Operational Excellence / IT Analyst; PMO Manager	Service Levels; Skills Development; Process Effectiveness; Customer Satisfaction; Service Costs; Infrastructure Capacity; Vendor Quality; Project Schedule Variance

What's In It for Me?

By implementing performance management in your IT department, you will be able to explicitly draw the connection between the strategic objectives of the organization and the strategic objectives that you're driving with IT. You will be able to do that when you are able to run IT like a business. You will be able to show them plans and an understanding of the cost structure of your business, pinpointing where you're spending most of your time well, and where you are spending it on inefficient activities. Performance

	Objectives	Example Metrics
System Operations 	• Reliability • Efficiency • Scalability	• Systems Uptime • Production Controls • CPU Utilization • Help Desk Calls Per User
Project Delivery 	• On-Schedule • On-Scope • On-Budget	• On-Time Projects (Due vs. Done) • SDLC Compliance (Glide Plane) • Backing of Enhancements
Quality 	• More Testing • Fewer Defects • Better Code Structure	• Backlog of Defects • Defect Ratios • Testing Coverage • Code Complexity
Organization 	• Staff Development • Lower Turnover • Differentiation	• Staffing vs. Targets (Hires and Terms) • Salary and Bonus Distribution • Performance Feedback
Business Value 	• Lower Cost Per Unit • Time-to-Delivery • Better Service	• Cost of System Downtime • Back-Office Efficiencies (such as Units Per FTE) • Enhancements Time-to-Delivery • Call Center Metrics
Financials 	• Controlled Spending • Lower "Lights On" • Transparency	• Budget vs. Actuals • Maintenance % of Spending • Processing ("Lights On") Costs • Shared Cost Allocations

Figure 9-3. Six Metrics for IT Operations and Services

management increases your ability to demonstrate your ability to add value to other business units.

The challenging role in which you are placed puts you in a position of expertise. The majority of sea change in the business world is predicated on changes and improvements in technology. You can be an expert about that change and how it applies to the core competencies of your company.

The vast majority of spending in IT is focused not on innovation but on maintaining the status quo, 85% or more of current budgets. By finding ways to make current operations more efficient and effective, you can begin to implement self-funding IT initiatives that demonstrate payback and ultimately allow you to move from a stance of maintaining what you've got to providing what you know you need to enable the organization to reach its strategic goals.

Effective Collaboration

Improving communication skills. It is likely that some of the people in your department have trouble communicating with those who are not technology savvy. They may even view people who don't know as much about technology as they do with a measure of disdain. For effective collaboration, you need effective communication. As a CIO, you likely have this skill; people who can't communicate well don't usually make it to the CIO level. In fact research from Gartner shows that at lower levels of the IT organization, priorities are 90% functional and 10% relationship-oriented.[1] At the CIO level, this proportion is reversed. If the people in the IT organization want to ascend the career ladder, improved communication skills and emotional intelligence must be part of their growth.

The emerging role of the business process expert, as well as a great deal of other literature is aimed at helping to bridge the business-IT divide. This needs to be part of an active initiative on your part to help the IT department, which supports the entire company, learn more about all the business processes across the company.

Avoid Vague Questions: Become a Business Student

"What are your usability needs?" the IT person asks, clipboard in hand. This is a well-meaning question, but it blindsides the person on the receiving end of that question.

To find out where users are having problems, take a different approach. Ask them if you can sit and watch them work for half an hour. Watch them interact with the applications. Watch how frequently they switch from one application to another to get their tasks done (you may see an opportunity to create a mashup for them). Ask them what they hate most about the applications. That is a question that is likely to get a productive answer, if not five productive answers.

Designate an IT Emissary for Each Department

It's not realistic for everyone in the IT department to learn about every process in the business. But it could well work to have IT staff serve as the liaisons between IT and a particular business unit, especially if they have expertise in that area.

In the next few sections, we outline the collaborative intersections between IT and other business units. One of the problems with collaboration is that each department speaks its own language. If you know what questions to ask, you can get much farther.

---

[1] Ellen Kitzis and Barbara Gomolski, "IT Leaders Must Think Like Business Leaders," Gartner, 2006.

IT and Finance

Big concerns for Finance include security and compliance. When Finance talks about segregation of duties, think access control. Finance is extremely interested in who gets access rights and authorization to information—one, to maintain security within the organization, and, two, to ensure that they have a proper audit trail for compliance purposes.

Another concern of Finance is ensuring that usage levels don't drive up costs. If the database can only have 25 simultaneous users, Finance will want IT to monitor that so that licensing or maintenance costs do not increase.

From an IT perspective, it makes perfect sense to ask Finance, "What are your security requirements?" For a Finance person, however, it's much more productive to ask about what access rights and authorizations they would like to see tied to financials among employees, what regulatory requirements they need to meet, and what audit trails they will need to demonstrate that compliance.

IT and Marketing

IT and Marketing can be like two storm systems. While Marketing in the past consisted mainly of the creative department, today's Marketing departments house analysts whose mathematical prowess likely exceeds the training of most computer science departments. In other words, quantitative marketing people need access to data so that they can slice and dice it and find the best way forward to make the right offer to the right customer and thereby get the business that will keep the company going.

IT may have a perception that business and marketing were relatively easy degrees to come by and that marketing people are not as intelligent as they are.

Marketing needs access to data and needs it now. In part, they need data to analyze what data they need. If the database folks say, put in your request and in a month we'll give you back the data file and Marketing unknowingly set its pull criteria too narrow, the result may be only 14 leads. If Marketing now has to wait another month, this delay is unacceptable.

Another big concern for Marketing is data quality, which for Marketing means data consistency. From an IT perspective, the data in various systems may be relatively clean, but Marketing needs to identify customers uniquely. Marketing doesn't want to send separate offers to John Public and John Q. Public if that's really the same person. Marketing needs to build a profile for each customer and as they aggregate the data from various databases, it must be consistent.

Data dictionaries are often low on the priority for the IT department. Such projects are critical for the marketing department to understand not only what all those data fields mean but also the context for that information.

IT and Service

The Customer Service department and call center need several things from IT, including:

- **Dynamic call routing.** Service needs to be able to reroute calls dynamically based on any number of criteria, from product expertise to maternity leave. The more flexible the call routing system, the easier for business users to make the changes without IT's help. Furthermore, they may need to change this on the fly, based on who is making a lot of sales that day
- **Visibility into order processing.** The customer asks, "Where is my order?" The call center should not have to respond with, "I don't know." Where is the order, exactly? Is it in another system? In the warehouse? Has it shipped? If a customer sends in an item for repair, similar tracking capabilities are needed. Make sure that status messages are clear in terms of the exact location of the product at any given time. This optimally means visibility into logistics provider systems as well so that you can track the product on behalf of the customer (rather than asking the customer to make that extra call or inquiry)
- **Employee access to data.** Service needs the ability to annotate the call record with information from the current call. They may also need to change data about that customer (address, phone number, credit card number or expiration date) on the customer's behalf

IT and Procurement

Procurement needs several things from the IT department:

- **The ability to track spending.** Procurement needs detailed data on spending from across the organization, whether or not it currently manages that spending. In this way, Procurement can try to get better deals for the company

- **The ability to ensure segregation of duties.** Like Finance, Procurement wants to ensure that employees can't funnel corporate money toward themselves. They need strong access control to ensure that:
  - Only the right people can approve vendors
  - Only the right people can approve spending levels
  - Only the right people pay vendors
  - The people who write the RFP do not also approve the vendor
  - Spending is handled according to corporate policy (for example, purchases above a certain amount require competitive bids)
- **Clean consistent supplier data.** Similar to Marketing's need for a clean customer profile, the Procurement department needs a clean supplier list so that they don't have IBM on record as three suppliers (IBM, I.B.M., and International Business Machines). Only in this way can Procurement properly analyze corporate supplier data

IT and the Supply Chain

The Supply Chain department has an extremely complicated job. Shipments from around the world have to get from point A to point B in a given timeframe. In one industry we studied, it took on average 38 steps from the time the product leaves one distribution center for it to reach its destination.

Helping the supply chain get visibility into where everything is all the time is a difficult IT problem indeed.

Supply Chain needs:

- Automation of all its shipments
- Help with its compliance activities related to those shipments. Regulations and documents differ from one country to another and one industry to another
- Visibility into this complex process. Every single touch, the bill of lading, the signoffs, customs, border control, and more must be automated so that supply chain executives can look from end to end. Customers or suppliers will call and ask if something has shipped. But if Supply Chain does not have adequate visibility, even though it was shipped, it could be anywhere along the way and there could be additional charges, such as penalties or fees, associated with getting the shipment to the customer

- Help with managing (and preventing) supply chain horror stories. What if a truck gets turned around at customs and it's got to go back to the warehouse? Then there's the cost of that return trip, the driver, and the implication for the other shipments it throws off, the cost to check everything back into inventory and finally the cost of reprocessing the order

If you were to ask the supply chain manager what her IT requirements are, she wouldn't know how to answer that question succinctly. Given the complex problems outlined above, it's easy to see why that is.

Collaboration KPIs

Earlier we looked at end-to-end business processes. When we talked about KPIs earlier in this chapter, we didn't discuss that there should also be collaborative KPIs that measure how well one department hands work to another and how well that department takes it up again.

Exploring Your Relationship with the Business Units

IT plays as deep a role within organization-wide processes as Finance and HR. Financial processes underlie the entire value chain—design, source, manufacture, sell, deliver, and service. The same is true of HR, in that the organization will require the right people with the right skills performing necessary functions and who are motivated via personal KPIs that align their activities with strategy. IT is also an essential component, because in order to be effective and efficient, the company will need IT to help automate and optimize these processes and activities.

The business units require close coordination, as they are seen as customers of IT. Your department needs to be better able to understand these individual needs, which means collaborating with them and developing domain-specific expertise.

As you build the business network, in the same way that IT is integrating with other business units in order to support strategic alignment, as well as engage in the end-to-end processes that cut across operational boundaries, IT must be cognizant of the fact that its model needs to also include the linkages—technical and otherwise—where there is an interchange between the company and its partner organizations.

In fact, IT is the enabler for all of the business network transformation capabilities, which relies heavily on SOA as the means to expose key assets to external entities—customers and partners—in a such a way that these assets can act as services without causing significant security and integrity concerns.

Managing an SOA will comprise a major portion of the heavy lifting IT managers can expect in the next few years. Just as outsourcing saves money but does not make administrative and technical issues go away, SOAs do not magically transform business processes into intuitive applications. SOA administration will require a new kind of thinking in IT. Where traditional IT has been vertical, hierarchical and locked-down, SOAs and the business networks they support are collaborative and associative. As SOA and business network transformation become more significant fixtures in the IT administrator's world, you will be asked to evaluate their cost-effectiveness. The extensible, collaborative nature of these networks means that you will need to collect and evaluate data from outside your own firewall.

Thus, the burning questions you will be facing in the coming years indicate the wide scope that performance management will need to encompass:

- How is IT going to manage the need for its systems to interface with the systems of partner companies and customers?
- How can this be done in a manner that best supports the value aspect of the relationship, as well as reduces or eliminates the need for IT intermediation between business users and systems?
- How can IT assure system integrity and security (in particular, how can transactional systems be securely interfaced)?
- How can IT ensure that a partner system will not inhibit the customer experience, thereby undermining customer responsiveness, brand and reputation, when interacting with the company in a web-based application or mobile collaborative application?
- How can IT ensure that risks are accounted for, as well as compliance with internal policies and external regulations?

The mission for IT has expanded. You must provide an infrastructure for people—customers and partners—to collaborate with the company, which can be very difficult considering the complexity of interconnections, the pressure of managing the SLAs, ensuring security and enforcing compliance.

For you, the downside of this transition is significant and the upside is very difficult to achieve. In order to come out on top, you must have methodologies and metrics in place to constantly monitor performance—you need consolidated visibility into the things that really matter to you as an IT professional.

Establish Your BI Foundation

Business intelligence (BI) is an important IT performance management technology. If you can normalize the data you are collecting and organize it in a rational way that aligns with your business' strategic goals, you are many steps ahead of the game in the pursuit of developing a comprehensive performance management framework for IT.

BI allows business users to be more self-reliant while simultaneously providing IT with visibility across the organization into IT-specific data. If reporting has been a key responsibility of IT, enabling ad-hoc reporting via BI can lighten IT's load, not to mention saving trees or bandwidth (many paper reports move directly from desktops to recycling bins without ever being read; even reports that are emailed are never opened by most reporting stakeholders).

Establishing your BI foundation is a key step in implementing performance management for IT. When applied to IT, the BI foundation should provide:

- **Relevant visualizations.** The ability to view project-specific visualizations that supplement standard tables and graphs. For example, many IT professionals are comfortable viewing project data in Gantt charts that show interdependencies of critical milestones
- **Relevant event-capture and alerting.** The ability to gather information from event sources, such as from server monitoring agents, along with external sources like key infrastructure providers such as telecom or network providers, and the ability to define alerts for critical events (the cost of our server capacity from our outsourced application hosting center has doubled in the last 3 months) and inform the right person to take action
- **A unified semantic layer and data integration and data quality across departmental and application silos.** BI allows IT users to bridge point systems (such as application management, help desk,

> IT often helps all the business units implement performance management. Although this chapter primarily focuses on how you can use performance management to improve your game in IT, sections like this one also touch on your role in helping the entire company improve its performance management.

and policy management) when they do not have access to an integrated transactional system. You can use BI to establish common definitions and business rules for key dimensions (how we define services, cost centers, assets) and metrics

- **Trusted, cleansed master data.** BI functionality has enterprisewide implications that IT will appreciate. For use in the IT department itself, BI platforms allow you to standardize definitions of assets to the individual asset level (instead of having five people refer to the same system in five different ways). It also provides a framework to incorporate key attributes such as how long we've owned the asset, who it is leased from, and its likely useful life
- **Structured and unstructured data.** BI platforms can generate insights from both structured as well as unstructured data. Unstructured data can provide tremendous additional value to IT. Fresh insight is available through mining application monitoring logs, help desk interaction notes (all the new laptops have flimsy screen attachments), emails, instant messaging sessions, and the like
- **Reports.** The reporting capabilities of BI relevant for IT include:
  - Publication quality reports for strategy meetings with the C-suite
  - Dashboarding and visualization for IT information such as project portfolio status and project dependencies
  - Query and analysis to provide intuitive analytics capabilities for end users. Example of IT queries and analysis include resource dependency per project and IT assets per employee

Establishing a BI foundation for IT means going through the process of leveraging existing BI infrastructure into a BI data management platform. This means you must:

- Extract and aggregate data from multiple sources as well as provide a whole host of data management capabilities, such as data integration, data quality, metadata management, master data management, data warehousing and data mart solutions
- Establish a "cleansed pool," of validated data, within which you can manage data extracted from transactional systems. Performance management applications can pull data from this pool
- Enable the inclusion of unstructured data as well as data from external sources, such as the Web and partner systems

Incorporating IT relevant data represents a significant data integration challenge. Data must be brought in from project systems, application management systems, trouble-ticket tracking systems, quality systems, and more. It is likely that this will be a custom project—the marketplace currently doesn't have one holistic software package for managing all the systems that IT needs to monitor and gather data from. Such a project will make your operations smoother and more transparent.

Assessing Performance Management Maturity and Setting Your Course

There is a wide range of maturity levels across the spectrum of IT organizations. To give you a sense of where the bulk of businesses find themselves today, see Table 9-2.

Table 9-2. Investment Maturity Levels and IT Status Reporting Used
(Source: AMR Research, 2007, How Leading Companies Unite IT with the Business)

	Activity Measured		Value Measured	
	Chaos	Operational	Collaborative	Immersed
Characteristics	Siloed applications: no centralized IT governance or tech standards	Corporate standards for technology and investments in ERP for standard processes	Corporate analytic data models, business process management and integration	Business strategy shapes IT initiatives; IT capabilities can dictate business strategy
Estimated percentage of Global 2000	18%	55%	25%	2%
Focus	Survival	Producing consistent information and cost reduction	More effective decision making, harvesting the value of IT investments	Optimizing business capabilities created through technology
Reporting	If done at all, very cursory and little attention is paid beyond cost	Report on the work being done	Report on the results being achieved	Integrated into business-unit reporting

In Table 9-2, the levels of investment maturity range from chaos to immersed. The chart moves from left to right. A plurality of major corporations falls solidly in the operational camp. They are producing consistent information and they can present solid evidence on how to reduce cost. But they are not strategically aligned and are probably at risk for a paring-down of their workforce or assets. The table gives you an idea of the range of performance management maturity.

Here is another tool to help you gauge the maturity of IT performance management at your organization. The following questions provide a quick take on assessing your performance management maturity:

- Do you spend significant amounts of time on projects only to find that requirements have changed?
- Do the other departments tend to view your work as not being aligned to their individual business needs?
- Can you draw a concrete line between the work you are doing right now and your IT objectives, and can you succinctly state how both are aligned with corporate strategy and objectives?
- Are you a full partner to the business in terms of helping drive value and can you document your value to the company?

If you answered "yes" to the first two questions and "no" to the second two, your organization's performance management capability level is still somewhat immature.

What role does IT play when at its most mature? AMR Research has also developed a maturity model for IT that reflects how leading companies unite IT with business.

Table 9-3. AMR's IT Maturity Model
(Source: Ian Finley, Bill Swanton and David Brown,
"How Leading Companies Unite IT with Business," AMR Research, September 2007)

Level	Characteristics	IT Relationship to Business
Process Leader	Sees job as leading ongoing process improvement Focused on supporting transformation and driving continuous improvement Enterprise architecture is about process measurement and agility	Facilitator of business improvement Finds and promotes opportunities to use IT to improve business processes
Process Enabler	Sees job as helping business improve processes and implement strategies Focused on supporting transformation projects as part of team Enterprise architecture is about agility to respond to change	Team member on broader business initiatives Brings solutions to the table

Technology provider is the least mature while process leader is optimal. Again, this is not hard-and-fast but is a helpful guidepost to assessing performance management maturity.

The PM Lifecycle for IT

Ask an average IT director about performance and he will likely describe the technical performance of machines and networks, using procedures such as configuration and fault management. While technical performance is absolutely critical to the success of your business applications and the IT backbone, when senior management asks about performance, they are not really interested in throughput. They want to know that IT projects and activities are progressing as planned. They want to know if you can see any telltale signs of future performance problems or scope creep. They want to know if troubled projects require upper-management intervention. And they want to know that actions already taken to correct problems have actually worked.

Performance management involves the routine, and sometimes non-routine, measurement of key aspects of IT project and activity performance, and making this information available to decision-makers.

In this section, we will walk you through the IT performance management lifecycle, highlighting the factors and evaluation methods that your peers have found useful.

Strategize and Prioritize

Here are the basic steps you'll follow in developing and prioritizing your strategies.

Understand the Context

Review the corporate strategic goals, strategic plans, initiatives, and metrics that track progress against them and understand them. Contextualize them to the implications they have for IT and use this context to drive the IT PM lifecycle.

Develop and Set the Strategy

First, review the environment. What are your strengths? What are the main problems you face? You might have a state-of-the-art and highly efficient data center, capable of providing additional service to business partners.

Key Point for IT Strategy: Business-IT Alignment

Discussions of business and IT alignment are ongoing in many arenas, but let's detail what kind of alignment we're looking for when we talk about this topic. Business-IT alignment includes aligning the following.

IT initiatives to business strategy. Even if your current IT infrastructure is in the dark ages, in your opinion, the way to move it into the 21st century should be tightly aligned to support business strategy. IT initiatives need to support the core competency of the organization and the key strategies that it is pursuing. Joint IT and business councils should meet on a monthly or quarterly basis as part of the governance model to ensure alignment.

The IT organizational structure to the business units. For example, the business units should know their "go-to" person in the IT department. Having members from the IT organization from the various business units transition to becoming IT staff creates credibility for the IT organization.

IT initiatives with business processes. Analyzing the end-to-end core business processes and taking a hard look at their current effectiveness and efficiency can highlight which IT initiatives are essential.

The CIO with business peers. As the CIO, you should be aligned with the CEO, CFO, and other top executives. You need to absorb the direction they are planning to take and to contribute your knowledge of how technology can help meet strategic objectives. Further, you may recognize new strategic objectives before they do, helping to monetize expertise that you have that might lead to a new business model. Consider the case of Amazon.com, which leveraged its massive experience in running data centers to begin to offer cloud-computing services—something completely out of the scope of running an e-commerce store but completely aligned with the experience gained in that process.

What risks do you have? Your risks might include security risks, risks relating to project completion, and risks relating to data protection.

What compliance requirements must you meet? Your compliance challenges might include complying with data privacy laws, particularly for certain geographies. They may also include helping your supply chain deal with the myriad documents needed for cross-border shipments to different countries.

Next set the mission, values, and vision. Define the mission, the fundamental purpose of the entity, especially what it provides to customers and clients. For example, make every information asset in the company add value to every business process.

Define the core values—the attitude, behavior, and character of the organization. For example, we are willing to do whatever it takes to help our customers succeed.

Define the vision—a concise statement that defines the 3- to 5-year goals of the organization. For example, by 2012, be consistently ranked in the top 10% of customer satisfaction as a value added partner for every business unit in the company.

Set the goals. With all that contextual information in hand, set a strategy or strategies to follow (of course, you'll collaborate with the CEO and other top execs). Here are some sample strategies:

- Increase IT efficiency
- Increase business-IT alignment
- Facilitate best practice business processes

Consider using a strategy map to display the cause-and-effect relationships among the objectives that make up a strategy. A good strategy map tells a story of how value is created for the business.

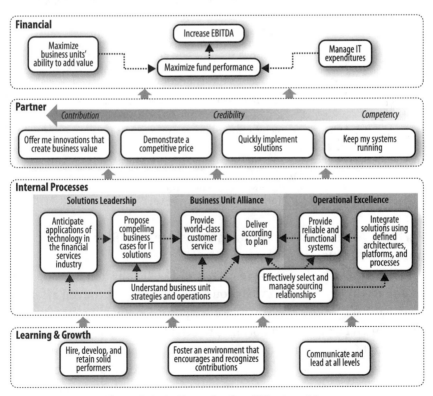

Figure 9-4. An Example of an IT Strategy Map

Assign KPIs to Goals and Set the Right Targets

Define KPIs and targets associated with your strategy. See "KPIs That Matter for Success in IT" earlier in this chapter to select relevant KPIs. Few IT organizations know how to assess IT's business value. As you look at developing your strategies, you should consider how, in practical terms, you could measure your progress toward your goals. As one example, Forrester Research has outlined a sample PMO effectiveness scorecard that helps IT executives in measuring their goals against performance metrics.

Table 9-4. Sample PMO Effectiveness Scorecard
(Source: "Measuring the Effectiveness of Your PMO," Forrester Research, Inc., October 2008)

GOAL	Measurements
Focus 75% of IT project investments on defined business strategies	Performance: • Distribution of approved projects around different investment categories—compliance, enhancement, business strategy No. 1, business strategy No. 2 • Time between business proposal, project approval, and project initiation Value: • Percentage of IT investment spend tied to defined business strategies
Maximize business value of IT investments	Performance: • Percentage of approved projects with business case, executive sponsor, and defined business outcomes • Percentage of completed projects with benefits audit Value: • Cumulative ROI of approved projects
Make project approval and prioritization flexible and transparent	Performance: • Distribution of project proposals across prioritization criteria • Participation of business execs in governance process Value: • Business exec satisfaction with process and communications as measured by surveys

Perform Additional Risk Analysis and Set Key Risk Indicators (KRIs)

Now look again at risks to see what could keep you from meeting your goals. For each risk, decide what your risk appetite is. Can you afford to take that risk? What's the worst-case scenario? Does taking the risk have the potential to wipe out important projects? For example, if you put your best team to work on installing a new system to support a Lean manufacturing initiative, what will happen to the other projects? Can you afford to put all five of your best people on that team or should you seed the new

---

Risks That Are Relevant for IT

Numerous risks apply to IT, but here is a sample to stimulate your own risk inventory:

- **Project Management.** Project scope management (percent of completion for revenue recognition), project cost management (budget overrun, compared to plan), project risk management (high risk initiatives)

- **Security.** Confidentiality, data loss, intellectual property loss, denial-of-service attacks, brand compromise, network attacks

- **Business Disruption.** Disaster recovery measures, backups, data recovery, application recovery

- **Compliance.** Customer's private data compromised (various laws around this that vary by jurisdiction), data breach reporting laws, SOX reporting requirements, email retention laws

---

project with one or two key people and let the rest stay with the projects that have a higher priority?

Set a response strategy for the risk (watch, research, transfer, delegate, mitigate). Here's an example. You could decide that installing the new system to support the Lean initiative has such great potential that you want to put the key team all on that initiative to help it gain traction. This would mean closely watching the projects along with the people who would be transferred so that if the main projects in the portfolio fall behind, you can move some people back to those projects in time to make a difference. You are deciding to watch the risk for now, followed by a mitigation strategy if you see indications that the risk has materialized.

Decide whether you can afford the worst-case scenario presented by that risk from a performance management perspective. Could it bring down some critical value-generating mechanism for the company? If you are implementing this new system with your best people, can you afford to let all of the other critical projects they are on fall apart without them?

Define KRIs and thresholds for those risks. Key risk indicators, like key performance indicators, are the early warning signals that define the threshold at which a risk could occur. One KRI could be percentage of IT high performers per project. Once this percentage gets too high for any one project, it signals a risk to the quality and likelihood of completion for the other projects.

Perform Additional Compliance Analysis and Set Controls

Define your compliance requirements. Compliance defines the boundaries within which companies must operate when achieving their strategies. A large number of compliance mandates impact the IT organization, including SOX and HIPAA, as well as industry-specific regulations.

Define policies, procedures, and controls that must be in place to ensure that you can meet the compliance requirements. Make sure that this applies not only at the main business process level but also to all subprocesses including and perhaps especially those related to partners. One example is establishing a password aging policy to ensure that system vulnerabilities are minimized or implementing a method of strong authentication.

Define controls that translate compliance expectations into performance expectations.

Work on the Strategic Action Plan and Initiatives

The strategic initiatives help define the exact methodology (the roadmap) for achieving various goals. The results of this planning may require revisiting the strategy.

Strategic Planning for IT: Strategic Portfolio Management

IT generally deals with a portfolio of projects, typically broken down into categories linked to the business unit and then broken down again into individual projects. Each portfolio (such as "sales transformation") may include five to ten projects (such as "implement sales territory mapping system"), each of which has its own goals and initiatives that should align with the overall portfolio goal.

Controls That Are Relevant for IT

Application Controls. Access control (to manage segregation of duties and security risks)

Infrastructure Controls. Monitoring system profile parameters, database profile parameters, developer access, system settings, system administration oversight (superuser access), physical access to servers and network equipment, laptop security

Asset Controls. Physical assets (servers, desktops, mobile infrastructure), information assets (email, databases, file shares)

Service Level Agreement Controls. This is not a control per se but can be measured in a similar way

The unfortunate truth about IT portfolio management is that it is often not conducted with an eye to the strategic objectives of the overall organization. In the new paradigm of business transformation, you will need to understand key metrics and the business value of all the projects undertaken by IT. You will need to use performance management to align the strategy with your work plan. If you are planning to assign 30 people to a project, and spend X dollars out of the capital budget and X dollars out of the operational budget, management will need to see a direct correlation between those expenditures and the overall strategic goals of the company.

The all-too-often-seen worst-case scenario is an IT department that has just finished up a sizable project portfolio, only to find that the business has moved on to different goals. These days, strategy changes on a dime, and the IT infrastructure and development team need to be agile enough to absorb those changes—ideally, it would have a hand in directing them. Implementing a balanced scorecard or any other performance management system will help to do this. At the very least, if strategy changes, you will at least be able to document that your project was aligned with strategy at the time it was implemented.

This is why it's essential that IT and corporate goals be aligned. This can be achieved through a process known as strategy management. Strategy management helps identify and communicate the high-level KPIs used to measure IT's progress against strategic goals. It's also essential that you understand the metrics behind each project—the overall business value, not just localized IT target numbers.

The steps to working through strategic planning go something like this:

- Develop the IT roadmap (sequence of actions) for achieving IT's piece of the strategic plan. Include risk and control management, specifically automating the process, workflow, and guidance for conducting risk and control assessments
- For each initiative, define critical success and failure factors for all initiatives. Critical success factors might include having the new call center up and running in time to train support staff before the major new project launch in June. Failure factors might be any of the dominos along the way in that initiative's roadmap that could derail the on-time delivery of the project. These "failure factors" can then be translated into key risk indicators with alerts so that the project can be gotten back on track

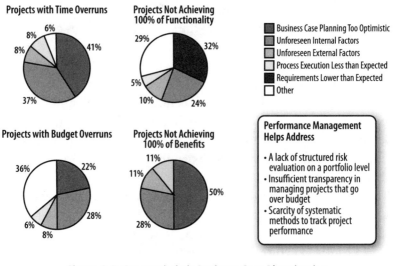

*Figure 9-5. Overoptimistic Business Case Planning is a
Major Factor in Many IT Projects*
(Source: IBM Institute for Business Value Analysis)

- Develop different risk adjusted scenarios with contingency plans should risks to achieving plans materialize. The IT roadmap must be sequential, but, as shown in the charts in Figure 9-5, optimism is not your friend in planning IT initiatives

Strategic plans should be risk-adjusted, with contingency plans for as many risk scenarios as you can reasonably imagine based on past experience and the current environment. You then develop risk response plans that address how to handle the risks if risks are materializing. These should be included in your contingency plans.

Focus on Quick Wins

Strategic plans should include a focus on the benefit payback period. In a tight economy, projects that are deemed to be "quick wins" trump projects with perhaps a greater benefit but with a payback period that stretches into years. For example, strategic sourcing, covered in more detail in Chapter 14, seeks to produce reductions in spend of at least 3% year after year. This is a better plan than attempting to reduce spend by 50% in one year. In the same way, an IT project that can reduce maintenance costs by a certain percentage year after year can free up resources for new IT initiatives that support business strategy. However, the payback for these initiatives should have a short window rather than stretching into years wherever possible.

Prioritize Based on Benefit Type

Projects should also be vetted according to the types of benefits they provide. Projects related to compliance must be done. But when it comes to other projects, cost-cutting projects often trump projects that might produce revenue. Again, if cost-cutting can be accelerated, resources can be freed up for additional revenue production.

Take a Phased Approach

The size of the investment is also critical. If you have to "bet the farm," so to speak, on an IT project, the risk is accordingly extremely high—losing the farm. Smaller, incremental projects that provide quick wins not only can support larger initiatives, but also represent best practices for most IT initiatives (a pilot followed by a phased implementation is better than a corporate rip-and-replace initiative, both from an economic standpoint as well as from a change management standpoint).

Cascade Accountability

Each KPI, KRI, and control should be owned by some department or group. The MBOs of the staff must reflect the KPIs, KRIs, and controls you set. This sounds obvious, but frequently performance is measured at an individual level in a way that does not in fact relate directly to corporate goals and strategies. For example, if on-time delivery of a key project is critical, make sure the people on that team benefit from putting in nights and weekends to make the deadline. If their individual goals do not relate to on-time delivery, they will not have the incentive to work hard to make the date.

Plan and Execute

In the strategize and prioritize phase of the PM lifecycle, we put together strategic action plans and initiatives. The planning phase gets into the details of planning the strategic initiatives both from a financial and operational standpoint.

Align Corporate Budget to IT Budget and Link Corporate and IT Initiatives

The budgeting process takes each of the outcomes or actions from the planning process and aligns revenues and expenses against them. Decisions regarding investment priorities and resource allocations define how the company will operate and set the bar for measuring performance. Take

In Practice: Linking Strategic Goals to IT Performance to Employee Performance

Even the most sprawling corporation can find a way to synchronize IT performance with overall strategic goals. Let's look at the case study of Colgate-Palmolive, a global consumer-products company with $15 billion in revenue and 36,000 employees.

First of all, the company has made a **C-level commitment to IT.** The IT steering committee is made up of the most senior people in the company, including the CEO, the CFO, COO, and all functional (head of supply chain, head of research and development, etc.) and product division heads. This committee meets three times a year, first in August, when the steering committee presents to IT their desires for the next year. Then, IT spends the next quarter determining if management's requests can be met. By December, at the second meeting, IT gets approval to proceed with certain projects. In April, another check-in happens, and changes are made to the plan.

Second, there is a **very clear relationship between IT governance and strategic goals,** and this is a two-way street. Under the CIO, there are six departments, each of which has a staffer called a "governance lead" who, with the other governance leads, builds a "grid" of projects aligned with goals. The grid is informed by the content of the steering committee meetings. These leads drive project management and accountability in the organization. They make sure that their IT staff is managing projects consistently, but they also defend the IT department from new, off-mission demands by management. If the project is not "on the grid," it's not happening.

Third, there is a **direct translation of strategic goals into incentives** for the IT department. At Colgate, bonuses of IT employees are directly correlated with the team hitting its group KPIs. To determine this, each project on the grid is rated by the steering committee for its success in project execution and its success in staying on budget.

each of the steps in the IT initiatives you've defined and put in revenues and expenses for them.

To create risk-adjusted budgets, incorporate the range of possible revenues and costs of each action into the budget at the appropriate organizational level. A risk-adjusted budget responds to changing circumstances, providing the financial capability to react to events in a planned, proactive manner. Develop different risk-adjusted budgets with contingency plans should risks to achieving budgets materialize.

In a traditional IT budget, you list the individual line items (software, facilities, servers, etc.) in each row with the actuals, budgeted amounts,

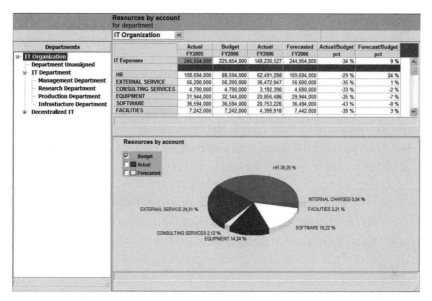

*Figure 9-6. An Example of the IT Financial Budget With
Major Categories of IT Expenses*

forecast, and actual/budget comparisons and forecast versus budget comparisons going across in the columns. In a risk-adjusted IT budget, for every decision to allocate revenue to one line item versus another (like purchasing new software instead of new equipment), you determine the impact and probability of the highest priority IT risks (like running out of server capacity) on those individual line items and use this to set a range of expected budget and forecasted values instead of fixed values. In this case, if the risk materializes and you run out of server capacity, you need a contingency plan in place that shows the performance and risk implications (the risk of our software prices increasing) if we then remove the budget from purchasing new software and had to put it into quickly buying new servers.

Align IT Budgets with Business Units

Few IT departments effectively charge expenses to the business units, but it's important to see where the highest costs are coming from. If the highest costs stem from an activity that doesn't differentiate your company, it's time to take a hard look at what that means in terms of cost-cutting or strategic outsourcing. Effectively charging back enterprise applications can be difficult, but it is nonetheless critical to assess the source of maintenance costs, which consume the vast majority of all IT budgets.

Align IT Budget to IT Operational Plans

The operational planning process links the financial budget for the IT department to operational factors that IT manages (servers, services, and applications) specific to running the IT organization and the costs and capacity for providing them. Plan each step of each initiative in terms of what will be required in terms of technology, time, and resources. Consider what risks you have in each area of the operational plan.

For example, in a risk-adjusted IT operational plan, for every decision to allocate resources to one set of operational activities versus another (from maintaining an application to upgrading an application), you determine the impact and probability of the highest priority IT operational risks (like application production downtime) on those individual line items and use this to set a range of expected and forecasted values instead of fixed values. In this case, if the risk materializes and the application goes down, you would want a contingency plan in place that shows the performance (the goal to release new versions of our applications would not be met) and risk implications if we then remove the budget from upgrading the application and put it into maintaining the application.

Taking these factors into account, adjust your plans with a range of operational outcomes and probabilities rather than an absolute number based on the various contingencies.

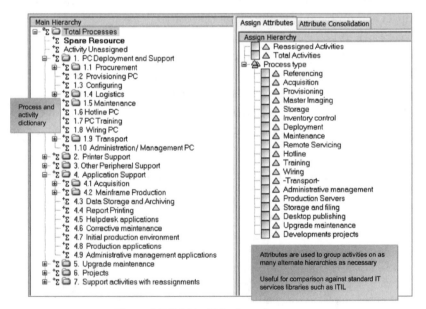

Figure 9-7. Within-IT Business Processes

Forecast Performance and Risks

Create rolling, risk-adjusted forecasts of the budget (revenues and costs) and operational plan (including number, capacity, and cost of resources necessary to achieve plan) so that you can see trends over a rolling time horizon for those risks whose probability, consequence, and/or resiliency change over time. That way if you have to make adjustments, you can see where you've been and the direction in which things are likely to go. Predictive analytical techniques can be a particularly powerful tool for building risk-adjusted forecasts by modeling the impact previous risks had on previous forecasts.

In a risk-adjusted IT forecast, you create a rolling forecast over a six month to one year window of a range of expected costs (the line items in your budget like software and equipment) and an associated range of expected activity outputs (upgrade activities and maintenance activities) that is dependent on the key risks in the environment. When the probability or impact of a risk changes, you adjust the financial or operational forecast costs or activities accordingly. Using predictive techniques, you can learn from the impact of previous risks on previous actuals (the number of upgrades that you were actually able to perform last year when applications unexpectedly needed to be maintained) to predict the impact of your current risks on your current cost or activity forecasts.

Examine Repercussions for Execution Problems

In a tight economy, take another look at the IT project portfolio before beginning to execute it. Planning and execution must be based in strategy and be aligned to the strategies that have been set down. If IT delays a project that is properly aligned with corporate strategy, its impact across the company can be profound. If the goal for this year is to enable more transparent and electronic collaboration with key suppliers to tighten delivery cycles and IT says it just can't meet the portion of the project for which it is responsible, the projected revenues from that initiative will obviously be impacted, having negative repercussions all across the organization. Coordination across and with all the lines of business is critical so that there are no surprises.

The key to excellence in execution is visibility. How is the project going? What is its current status? This visibility needs to extend far beyond the IT department since IT is providing the business infrastructure for the entire organization. Early warning of project delays can help business units to adjust appropriately in time to adapt to those delays or to provide additional resources, if possible, to accelerate progress toward strategic goals.

To minimize risk on the execution side, the project should be well documented so that any changes in resources and requirements are accompanied with documentation.

Execute

In the execute phase, the goals, risks, and compliance objectives you have set in your strategy and the resources you have allocated in your plans now drive the end-to-end business processes discussed earlier in "The Business Process Angle."

For example, once the plan is understood, we can provision the servers we procured or retire old ones, open new data centers and close the old ones down, develop or retire applications, and start or stop projects based on the transactive business processes we have established.

Monitor and Analyze

In the monitor and analyze phase of the PM lifecycle, you monitor to understand what is happening in the business, analyze to understand why it is happening, and for those things not on track, adjust to improve the situation relative to your goals.

Monitor

It is important to distinguish the different categories of monitoring in evaluating business performance.

- Event monitoring looks for a single, discrete activity or exposure event. An example of an event might be the detection of a single breach of a company's firewall
- Trend monitoring is similar to event monitoring, but looks at events over time to determine patterns, for example, how frequently that event occurred, and if that frequency was more or less common than in the past. An example of trend monitoring might be monitoring the number of times in a day external hackers attempt to breach the company firewall
- Intelligence monitoring collects information from a variety of external sources that are of interest to the company and may indicate a risk exposure. An example of intelligence monitoring might be monitoring the highest risk software viruses that are affecting peer companies

The presentation of information to be monitored is also crucial in order to facilitate decision-making. Dashboards bring together all the relevant pieces of business information in all the areas of that need to be monitored in a role-based, contextual view to provide status at a glance. For IT, typical dashboards for monitoring might include:

- Portfolio dashboards
- Project dashboards
- Asset dashboards
- Resource dashboards
- Service dashboards

Dashboards are effective ways of combining the events, trends, and intelligence monitoring patterns across all of the major facets of the business to be monitored, including the key business dimensions like customers, products, projects, and employees, and the related KPI, KRIs, controls, and incidents and losses.

From the dashboard, it is then possible to evaluate all the facets you are monitoring.

Evaluate performance. Look at the KPIs to identify progress made toward achievement of objectives and trends. Is the KPI of on-time IT project delivery on target? Is it trending in the right direction? Has the trend changed?

Evaluate initiatives. Are any failing or behind schedule? Is the initiative to roll out the new ERP system on target? What is the trend?

Evaluate risk. Data is monitored from source systems that provide transactional data for the KRI. Dashboards can help identify and manage key risks versus overall risks (being able to prioritize based on exposure through quantitative and qualitative assessment of thresholds). Look at KRIs to identify:

- **Top risks.** Are you having staffing issues (lost key staff, key people are too busy, new people not up to speed yet)?
- **Changes to risk levels for key activities.** Is there an upswing in security risks? Are certain types of projects sliding?
- **Assessment procedures.** Are risks being assessed in accordance with company policy or industry best practices? Do we need to have a third-party audit of our network if confidential data has been compromised?
- **Effectiveness of mitigation.** Are the mitigation strategies reducing the likelihood or impact of a risk? Are daily antivirus updates mitigating the potential of system downtime?

Evaluate internal controls. Report key control deficiencies, approvals, verifications, and reconciliations to mitigate risk. How clean is our access control? Do major organizational shifts require that we reexamine our roles?

Evaluate incidents and losses. If incidents or losses have occurred or external events are affecting the IT department (rolling blackouts, for example), document this information, even if you haven't been tracking it in the system yet.

No matter how proactive you are, manual monitoring can be very inefficient. Automated monitoring can proactively identify out-of-tolerance conditions, highlighting when a KPI, KRI, or control goes over or under defined tolerances and then alerting the responsible party. This should take into account forecasting, trending, and modeling capabilities so that if a metric falls out of the range of a trend, budget, or plan, the appropriate alert is raised, along with a workflow process to get the investigation under way.

Analyze

Analysis is a key step in which you not only look at where you are, but what is happening (or what has happened) and why. The techniques for analysis can range from highly manual and simple to fairly automated and complex in terms of the usage of statistical techniques.

Analyze KPIs to understand why they are increasing or decreasing. The dashboard shows that the on-time delivery KPI is trending downward. Drilling down, you find out that one of the projects is way behind schedule compared to the others.

Analyze initiatives to understand why they are succeeding or failing. You could find that all the application development initiatives are heading down the wrong direction and determine that this is due to the unintended effects of the new "application development efficiency" KPI you assigned in this year's MBOs.

Analyze KRIs to understand why they are increasing or decreasing. You might conduct a correlation analyses to identify the process deficiencies or other trends that are the most significant in increasing your system uptime risk before it reaches critical levels.

Analyze controls to see if they are effective. For example, you notice that a control to test for identity theft generates a lot of incidents and find that the thresholds are set too low, creating false positives. You conclude that your controls have lost their effectiveness due to changing business conditions or organizational structures and need to analyze why.

Analyze incidents and losses to determine root causes or trends. Perhaps you notice a significant uptick in firewall security breaches and determine the root cause of the incident was a failure to follow the appropriate network security policy.

In all of these cases, analysis was done with human intervention, but this does not have to be the case. The volume and complexity of data in the enterprise today makes it increasingly difficult to mine through data and come to intelligent conclusions. Using data mining techniques, software can determine the most likely root causes and even suggest recommended actions. For example, a key risk indicator for service delivery is increasing. Without any manual intervention, the system does a series of correlations. When you highlight the KRI, a popup shows that the number one factor associated with the service delivery risk is the sudden decrease in capacity due to reorganization.

Adjust

After monitoring to see what has happened and analyzing to understand why it happened, for those things not going accordingly to plan, set things back on course by taking what you've learned and using that information to adjust the settings. Always consider the impact of your goals, risks, and compliance concerns on other business units.

Adjust KPIs. For KPIs trending in the wrong direction, once you have analyzed the root causes, it should be clear what actions to take to set things back on course. However, remember that KPIs are interlinked, and you must optimize your performance goals in the context of risk objectives and without violating compliance objectives. If only one of the projects is the root cause for the poor showing on the project delivery KPI, you can assign more resources from other projects or increase the funding. However, this can be done only if it does not increase the risk of not delivering on other key projects and if it doesn't violate any compliance objectives such as having employees working longer than they are allowed to by law.

Adjust initiatives. For initiatives that are not going as planned, rapidly take remedial action or cancel them. If it's clear that the initiative is not going to work, either make changes to save the project or cancel it if it is not critical so that you can reallocate those resources. For example, you observe that a key initiative is failing and determine the root cause to be the MBOs for the key employees staffing the initiative. The simplest thing to do would be to change the MBOs to see if this sets the initiative back on target.

Adjust risk settings. For each risk, you can decide to treat it, tolerate it (since a mitigating control is in place), transfer it, or terminate the activity that is producing the risk. For KRIs trending in the wrong direction, once you have analyzed the root causes, put mitigating controls in place to stabilize them. However, it is critical to remember that KRIs are interlinked, and you must optimize risk goals in the context of performance objectives and without violating your compliance objectives. For example, a correlation analysis identifies process deficiencies that are most significant in increasing your system uptime risk before it reaches critical levels. You put a mitigating control in place to have the security team manually test server loads to ensure system uptime is not in jeopardy at high volumes. However, do this only if it does not decrease the likelihood of delivering on the goal of finishing projects on time (since now your team is investing time in manually testing servers) and if it doesn't violate any compliance objectives like having employees working longer than law allows them to.

Adjust controls. For controls violations, adjustment takes the form of remediation and certification. For example, after the identity theft control is violated, you set up a remediation plan to create a more stringent set of security policies for all of your internal applications.

Adjust after incidents or losses. For incidents and losses, the correct adjustments typically involve reexamining whether you are tracking the right risks and have put the appropriate controls in place to mitigate them. For example, after determining that the uptick in firewall security breaches is due to a failure to follow an established network security policy, it would be appropriate to put an automated risk monitoring process in place that alerts you to the first sign of increased firewall activity.

The Problem of IT Analytics: A Lack of Integrated Tools

Many resources can be used to monitor actual performance against planned performance, but in particular, a handful of capabilities targeted to IT processes should be contained within an IT-specific analytic application. And, ironically, for the most part, no one application fits this bill. While other business domains have a number of packaged analytic applications to choose from—sales analytics, spend analytics, and marketing analytics, for example—IT analytics—from a business perspective—is lacking, primarily because the concept of running IT as a business is still fairly new. To use BI for this purpose, IT will have to do a lot of heavy lifting, which will require developing an expertise in data analytics. Data must be integrated from project systems, application management systems, trouble-ticket tracking, and quality management systems. The marketplace lacks catchall applications for doing this, so this is likely to become a custom project, but it is a worthwhile endeavor.

The bane and boon of IT is the fact that it touches nearly every business process and business unit in the enterprise. So in order to provide actionable business intelligence for IT, data gathering must extend to the business unit databases, which relate to applications that IT has either created or is charged with maintaining, in addition to IT's own domain, including accounting, time management, and project tracking.

You want to search for and identify variances between actual and planned performance. You can use this knowledge of ongoing performance to optimize activities that are falling short, or to replicate those that are succeeding beyond expectations, because you will have learned the story behind the numbers.

Analysis can move beyond just tracking KPIs to more sophisticated types of analysis, such as:

- **Simulation.** This technique is used to see how changes in one area might affect others. It is actually a form of modeling that enables what-if analysis. For example, how will moving the timeline of a project 30 days impact the start of other projects in terms of resource allocations?
- **Trend analysis.** This type of monitoring takes a longer view. If you find a problem when monitoring, it's helpful to review trends in that particular area. Is the current problem an anomaly or indicative of a need for a more serious process improvement? For example, if projects are always late by several months, what is the underlying issue? Are schedules unrealistic? Where are the delays occurring?
- **Performance audits or reviews.** Are the resources currently allocated adequate to achieve the business goals? How often do servers fail and essentially stop whole groups of staff from working? Does slow response time introduce unacceptable delays in serving customers in the call center or in processing orders? Again, this can point out areas for potential improvement

Model and Optimize

When you are creating a model of your IT operations, the goal is to be predictive—you will base your model on past and current performance, as a means to forecast future performance—in terms of creating a model of the organization's IT resources utilization and related IT projects.

You can simulate the entire IT project portfolio to cancel or move the priority of one project over the next. This is modeling and optimizing the IT project portfolio to minimize the risk of the projects by looking at "what-if" scenarios.

Model

Types of modeling include revenue, cost and profitability modeling, scenario modeling, and simulation modeling.

Revenue, Cost, and Profitability Modeling

Modeling the costs, revenue, and profitability implications of performance management, risk management, and compliance management activities and their drivers can be achieved at a very detailed level using activity-based costing and associated methodologies.

Other tools that have been primarily used in the world of finance can also be adapted for use in modeling IT projects. For example, Geert Jan Beekman of Atos Consulting spoke on the use of CAPM (Capital Asset Pricing Model) to determine the real cost of IT projects at EQUITY 2007, the IEEE International Conference on Exploring Quantitative IT Yields. Beekman has adapted CAPM with IT-relevant parameters, including chance of failure, cost overruns, requirements creep, and time compression. In this way, IT risks can be more realistically assessed. Said Beekman, "Some 300 billion dollars are spent annually on IT projects that fail. The world spends as much on beer in a year."[2]

Another type of modeling with relevance for IT is business process modeling, which can be combined with activity-based costing. Modeling key business processes and their costs can highlight areas where processes can be effectively changed. Furthermore, this modeling technique can be used to help analyze the changes that will occur as a result of adopting a new technology system.

Scenario Modeling

Scenario modeling can be applied to financial and operational modeling and focuses on creating different business scenarios. Simple scenario modeling can include creating a base case and then high and low cases based on changes made to input variables, such as market growth rates or inflation rates. This technique is often used in modeling market and business opportunities and creating business plans.

---

[2] Quoted in Equity 2007 report, online at http://www.cs.vu.nl/equity2007/equity-report.php.

Simulation Modeling

More advanced modeling, including Monte Carlo simulation, supports creating a broad range of scenarios based on multiple iterations of input assumptions and combinations. With this technique, probabilities can be assigned to the various outcomes. These techniques allow the uncertainty associated with a given forecast to be estimated and to reduce risk by applying sensitivity analysis, correlation, and trend extrapolation. By simulating the effect of uncertainty, it becomes possible to answer questions such as, "How certain are we that a given project (or group of projects) will result in a minimum outcome of x?" Or, conversely, "What's the minimum outcome that we can be, for example, 90% certain of achieving?" Simulation also makes it possible to identify and rank the various contributors to overall uncertainty.

Peter Kampstra, an IT researcher at the Vrije Universiteit in Amsterdam, is researching computer simulations of outsourcing software projects. Modeling the outsourcing process can pinpoint inefficiencies in the process itself and allow IT departments to conduct what-if analysis prior to outsourcing coding projects. Kampstra has also analyzed how code reviews impact the efficiency of programmers. If code reviews are too strict, programmer productivity is severely impacted, according to Kampstra. However, since the resulting code may need to be validated for compliance, it may not be possible to loosen restrictions on code reviews.

Optimize

The goal at this phase of the PM lifecycle is to determine the optimal way to achieve objectives by taking into account the entire context of the problem, including all relevant constraints and assessments (costs, benefits, risk, labor and time), as well as business strategies, objectives, risks, and compliance factors. Optimization can be done both through human evaluation as well as through advanced algorithmic techniques.

An example of a good IT-relevant optimization is chargeback optimization, which leads to better IT cost control. In a chargeback scheme, the IT department acts like an external contractor and a "market cost" is determined for its services. Basically, the business is invoiced internally for itemized services, so that transparency is improved and, frankly, the business can assess whether it needs to outsource certain aspects of the IT organization's task. This is also a good example of how the IT department can do a better job of operating like a business, by accounting for services rendered in a fairly granular way and then consolidating the data, modeling

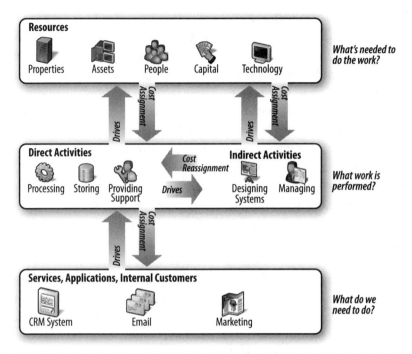

Figure 9-8. Activity-Based Costing is the Key for IT Services Costing Optimization

it, and optimizing the processes and activities that produce the data.[3] It also pinpoints usage levels in the business, as well as demand discrepancies and mismatches—perhaps a high-value server is not being used as expected by the financial analysts because half of them have been laid off. A chargeback scheme would identify such a discrepancy and that would prompt you to decide whether to reassign that equipment. In the hybrid internal-external IT sourcing model many companies use today, it's easier to account for services consumed by the various units of the company, as well as outsourced services used by the company.

With chargeback, IT can better assess the accuracy of billing from outsourcing organizations as well as understand which units in the company are using these services, the volume of the services, and whether the usage is consistent with strategic goals.

In addition, a good chargeback optimization program and tools will document usage, creating an audit trail that could be used for dispute

---

[3] Kurt Potter, "IT Chargeback as a Tool for Cost Optimization," Gartner Research, November 26, 2008.

resolution. It is also possible to automate approvals of chargeback statements and dispute resolution processes.

Case Study: Performance Management in Action

Virtual Gates is a fictional cutting-edge computer manufacturer with retail outlets. This section provides an analysis of how the IT department's team at Virtual Gates closes its loop during the process of decreasing overall IT spend as a function of revenue.

Setting the Context

Virtual Gates' CEO, Clint Hobbs, has just sent his CIO, Jason Barsoomian, back to his office with a list of tasks. Jason's top priority is to optimize IT's value to VG by decreasing overall spend as a function of revenue. But it must align with Clint's larger goals, which require all growth to be measured against VG's net income and earnings per share growth, especially as they compare to competitors Hypercell and Packingflash. Jason must implement his reductions in the context of HR's effort to reduce VG's workforce by 15% and Product Development's drive to release a new netbook while retiring products that are no longer profitable.

To accomplish his objective, Jason works on an IT services rationalization initiative to reduce investment in low-value IT services while enhancing those services with the highest business value. This is a tough call. IT cannot simply stop rendering services. His decisions must be made collaboratively with other departments and reflect a consensus on smart and effective cost reduction steps. The chief metrics that Jason and his team must optimize are IT as a percentage of revenue and IT's total cost of ownership (TCO).

Understand the Collaborative Impact

The IT department plays a key role in almost every one of the company's end-to-end business processes since technology connects them all. As such, Jason knows that IT must forcefully own such processes as empowering and connecting people, managing and delivering information, and integrating and adapting processes.

Jason's next consideration is the impact on stakeholders within IT itself and on other departments as well as business partners outside the company's boundaries. For instance, the last thing VG needs is to lose partners with whom it is co-innovating because they are unfavorably affected by IT's initiatives. Whatever Jason and his team do, they cannot implement changes that work for IT but harm the company at large. For instance, it would do no good for Jason to reduce the number of IT services he delivers to stakeholders if that reduction also shrinks process efficiency. At every turn, he and his team must fully appreciate how the internal and external business processes it supports may be impacted.

Establish KPIs and KRIs

Next, Jason must select *relevant* KPIs and KRIs as a means of accurately measuring his progress while taking into account risks and interfaces between partners and processes—all before embarking on any course of action. He must identify the drivers behind KPIs and KRIs, along with their relationships as well as leading performance indicators.

As we mentioned, the key metrics Jason needs to monitor are IT spend as a percentage of revenue and IT's TCO. He and his team are well aware of these criteria, but he cannot assume that their implications are evident to the rest of VG's departments. Although they will all be happy to know that a decrease in IT's TCO could well enrich the value of their processes, they might not so cheerfully embrace the possibility that decreasing IT spend as a percentage of revenue could result in a reduction of service levels to some or all departments.

Establish the BI Foundation

Getting the data for the KPIs and KRIs is not so easy. It must be gathered from the numerous systems, including portfolio management, asset management, help desk, and ERP systems. Moreover, to see the effects of their choices on partners, the team must also harvest data from systems such as CRM and SCM among many others. Information from all of these systems must be consolidated as the team executes its IT business processes.

Before anything meaningful can be done with their raw data, Jason's team must first align it into and load it into a data mart or warehouse. Once these tasks have been accomplished, the team can use the information to obtain the single source of truth they can use to help decrease overall IT spend as a function of revenue.

Strategize and Prioritize

We opened this section by noting the context within which Jason and his team must implement their IT reductions: while Chad Fuller, VP of HR, has announced a mandate to reduce VG's headcount across all departments by 15%, the VP of Product Development, Paul Burton, is working to release a new netbook while retiring those products that are no longer profitable.

These efforts will have several effects. First, the elimination of low-profit products will open the way to reduce headcounts in a variety of sectors. In turn, the employee reduction in all departments, including IT, will ease the pressure for IT services, thus supporting Jason's move to trim down selected services. On the other hand, the drive to release an important product, the new netbook, demands that IT maintain excellent system uptime and network throughput, not to mention security from the prying eyes of their competitors.

To meet these requirements, Jason needs a scorecard to monitor progress. The scorecard shows the risks IT faces by reducing its service level in specified areas. First, it could significantly decrease the satisfaction of affected departments. Second, the dissatisfaction could jeopardize the ability to enable new business processes in the future and achieve quantifiable growth. Jason must meet these risks by introducing KRIs and correlative mitigating actions. If the satisfaction level for any department drops by 10% or more, for example, Jason must renegotiate with them in an effort to adjust their behavior so that their service consumption becomes more reasonable. Jason must ensure that the action he takes is compliant with VG's overall strategy, particularly in the areas of security, audit, and recovery.

Plan and Execute

One thing Jason knows with certainty is that IT cannot retire a service that is essential to a core business process, regardless of how low its ROI. What he can do, however, is prioritize new projects according to those whose ROI-to-NPV (net present value) ratio is highest.

Once he has established priorities, Jason can reallocate significant funds from low value to high value services. He'll also need to link his budget to IT operational factors. His chief variable now is the number of IT support staff, servers, applications, and the like that the newly freed funds have made available. These resources will enable Jason's team to significantly increase the time to productive service delivery for both developing projects, such as the new netbook, as well as support for the remaining products in VG's portfolio. Jason must keep a watchful eye on KRIs and rapidly initiate contingency plans if they signal emerging problems.

Monitor and Analyze

Now that the IT support staff, application developers, and systems managers have begun to execute their plans, Jason must monitor their work to see whether costs as a percentage of revenue and overall ROI are falling in line with strategy. Jason must also watch the KPIs to ensure that his initiative remains aligned with those in VG's other departments, particularly Finance and Product Development. For instance, Jason does not want to hear from Paul Burton in Product Development that reduced or ineptly delivered IT services have caused process inefficiencies and bottlenecks that are preventing his teams from hitting their deadlines in the drive to launch the new netbook. Marketing could be affected, as well as Supply Chain, Sales, and Service. No sooner would Samantha Curtin, George Martin, Leah Broder, Madison Rice, and Asha Madon (the heads of Marketing, Supply Chain, Sales, Service, and Finance, respectively) leave his office in consternation than CEO Clint Hobbs would enter it with the demand to know what on earth Jason's team has been doing!

This, of course, is a worst-case scenario. To avoid it, Jason and his team engage in preventative maintenance starting with shrewd and unflinching analysis. At a certain point, if they realize that their execution plan isn't working, they compare their anticipated results with actuals. Doing so reveals whether they can decrease their selected IT service costs enough to free up the required funds or whether their threshold for customer dissatisfaction has been exceeded because of reduced services. Again, no matter what issues arise, Jason's chief concern is to ensure that his response aligns with his partners' activities and with corporate's greater goals.

Model and Optimize

Without an operational cost model, it would be impossible for Jason to verify the costs of IT services or see which groups are absorbing those services. Using such a model, IT can see which services (such as the help desk, servers, and applications) provide the most value per resources consumed. It often happens that those services that had been presumed to generate the highest ROI actually include costs that were hidden prior to examination with the operational cost model.

To determine which services IT should reduce or enhance, Jason can alter the assumptions or remove constraints in his model to simulate a variety of "what-if" scenarios. For example, he could question the value ratio between dedicated servers versus virtualization. If the number of data centers allocated to various IT services has been a restraint, Jason can remove it to see what the model produces in its absence. Regardless of what the model shows, all changes to services must be decided in collaboration with affected departments. Once Jason confirms that his strategy and resources are sound, he can select an optimization technique to achieve his goals.

Closing the Loop in an Integrated System

The scenario as it stands has been manageable with current technology, and yet because technology is continually developing, holistic, closed-loop systems will soon enable the consistent alignment of execution and strategy for most departments. A new set of scenarios will emerge once users can build a strategy management process that captures goals, initiatives, and metrics that can be linked to their driver-based financial and operational planning process, as well as to their monitoring and analysis, modeling and optimization, and risk and control processes. At that point, users can drive the desired behavior out to their transactional processes via their goals, initiatives, plans, and risks and controls.

As for Jason and his IT team, they are excited because they have just such a system. For example, integrated IT portfolio management and performance management solutions provide them with immediate insight into project status. Consequently, to investigate and analyze problems, they can drill into a central project repository at any level or project step tailored to individual reporting requirements. The PM application enables Jason and his team to see whether a portfolio of projects or services is behind schedule or trending the wrong way. To rectify a situation, the team can move directly from the screen to the execution processes and send the appropriate context into the system, whether it involves changing the number of individuals assigned to the project or increasing the number of virtual servers allocated to a project, thus closing the loop. In other words, the strategy to modify and reallocate IT services to prioritize support for the highest value business processes, the initiative to rationalize these service modifications, and the real act of reducing these services are now seamlessly integrated to improve both efficiency—doing things right—and effectiveness—doing the right things.

Align the Workforce

Connecting all of these activities with his team's objectives and compensation is Jason's final goal. Any time Jason can demonstrate to a system administrator that he will receive a bonus for his contribution to the successful execution of Jason's service alteration initiative as per corporate strategy, that sys admin will put in the extra time to get the job done. Other functional areas of the organization follow this logic, too. When the personnel in other departments see that their bonuses are also connected with successful attainment of IT goals, they will help out too. Success for Jason's partners is success for Jason. After he reports a 5% growth in IT's overall profit as measured by Virtual Gates' net income and earnings per share growth, Jason stands to receive a bonus package of his own from CEO Clint Hobbs.

Action Items

Here are some action items to consider:

- Run IT like a business
- Link all activities to the strategy of the organization, both via applications and in a meaningful way by taking an active interest in business strategy, which probably means going to more meetings
- Gain an in-depth understanding of the business processes that add value
- Ensure high quality data that is clean not only from a data perspective but consistent and consolidated

Performance measurement initiatives often falter for one or several of the following reasons:

- Those charged with planning and implementing the initiative had little or no prior experience with performance management and measurement. Often, with the best of intentions, they repeat common, predictable, and sometimes fatal mistakes
- Management's information needs were not identified in advance, and a well-thought-out conceptual framework and implementation plan was not developed. In one case, after a year's work, the first performance report was submitted to senior management two months late, and the designers were told, "This is not the information we need to see"
- Too much performance information can materialize too soon. Your organization's capacity to assimilate, interpret, and react to the information could be overwhelmed

To avoid these pitfalls:

- Fully understand management's information needs
- Have a clear picture of what you are trying to achieve and how you will do it
- Involve people who have established and managed performance management systems

- Study what other organizations are doing; learn what works and what doesn't
- Manage expectations. Make sure all key participants understand and agree on what will be accomplished and when
- Use a limited pilot to gain experience. Confine your mistakes to a small area so that you can fix them quickly and demonstrate early results

Chapter 10

Performance Management for Sales

Sales teams need to reliably forecast and meet revenue goals. It's a high reward and high stakes game. The company is counting on the sales team to deliver revenue; after all it is the lifeblood of a company. Performance management can provide the kind of rigor required to overcome today's increasingly complex and competitive sales environment.

Looking Back: How Life Has Changed in Sales

Changes in the world and in technology are inevitably leading to a shift in focus for sales organizations. Sales executives must address a new set of challenges and opportunities in the sales process. Taking stock of world events, technology milestones, and performance management pressures can provide the necessary insight for Sales organizations to benefit from performance management.

In the past as a Sales organization leader, you had to meet strategic sales goals, product or professional services sales quotas, and revenue targets. Your Sales organization was required to generate a sales pipeline with enough potential customers to meet your revenue targets along with developing competitive pricing strategies and accurately forecasting sales revenue. Your Sales organization had limited resources so you also had to execute your sales strategy within budget. You had to sell and you had to support your company's profitability.

In today's sales landscape, your core mission remains unchanged. So what in Sales is different today? In the last three to five years, the profile and behavior of your repeat and loyal customers and potentially new customers has shifted. Potential sales revenue for your products and services requires you to develop a sales strategy that encompasses the challenges of both a domestic and international sales market. You also have a more sophisticated customer who lives in different time zones and speaks different languages. It has become much more difficult to understand the customers and their needs, because the world is much more complicated. And because your market isn't just who is down the street from you, the cost of sale and bringing a product to market has increased. Consumers have access to so much information and this increases price pressure and makes pricing more competitive.

Salespeople are no longer the main source of information during a sale. Because people can buy online, the salesperson's role has diminished and the sales channel has changed.

The world of technology has also evolved and transformed the nature of sales. Technology has unleashed consumer's access to company, product and pricing information, and this has changed the rules of the game. Sales organizations are encountering a savvy and empowered consumer. As a result, sales methodologies need to respond to how user-generated content has empowered the consumer.

Additionally, the added layer of mitigating risks and managing increased regulation such as revenue recognition policies builds in an inherent tension for sales staff. Salespeople need to spend more time with customers but also need to spend time documenting their interactions with customers to comply with regulations.

Your sales methodologies and the business processes you design need to change entirely because the consumer is empowered. Today you need to include the customer perspective and experience when you define and optimize your business processes. And this starts with your Sales organization and other front-office business units. It also reaches all the way through to the backend, including enterprise resource planning, order management, supply chain management, as well as partners, channel partners, dealers, distributors, and third-party service contractors.

You need your Sales organization to keep up with a sophisticated, educated and connected consumer. You need to know more about your customers, their motivations, their desires, and their requirements. You also need to understand the cost associated with a sale so that you can measure profitability by customer. And your company needs to provide you with the process, tools, and people to track, analyze, learn, predict and achieve revenue targets so you can compete.

How Business Network Transformation Affects Sales

The success of your Sales organization depends on accurately forecasting revenue and delivering a robust pipeline, a pipeline that will convert the kind of sales numbers that align sales and corporate goals. You need to collaborate, control, and orchestrate sales activities with the key partners of your sales business network. Key players in the business network who affect sales include:

- Sales channels
- Sales partners

You can bring in the big whale of a deal but you need to collaborate with another company to pitch the business and deliver a complete solution. You need to extend yourself beyond the organizational boundaries of your company to craft and execute the deal so you can win.

Salespeople are increasingly called upon to move beyond being simply relationship managers, but also becoming general managers and bringing

---

As a consumer who wants to purchase a car, I can find the information I need on the Internet. I can access and read dealership reviews developed and published by other consumers, evaluate and compare ratings, and filter through a variety of reliable and anecdotal information sources. I no longer rely only on a salesperson to sell me a car. Before I ever go into the dealership, I have full transparency into the price of the car I want to purchase.

Think about the car dealerships and their sales techniques and sales methodologies, with the outdated price negotiations they still try to do today. Consumers come into the dealership and many already know exactly what kind of car they want, they know everything about the product, and they know everything about the prices. Consumers even know about the dealer margin and how far the dealer can actually go down with his price.

to bear the full capabilities and resources of their organization to serve the needs of their customers.

How Technology Has Changed in Sales

In 1989 the pre-sales technology era, your Sales organization worked with a combination of three ringed-binders, index cards and sticky notes to capture sales activities. A heavy dependency on administrative resources existed to support your sales efforts. And you had no central data repository to track sales leads, quotas, cross-sell/up-sell opportunities, and win/loss ratios.

As technology evolved, sales activity tools became available to you. In the '90s customer relationship management (CRM) systems began to flood the marketplace. CRM systems allowed you to input and capture your sales data and activities into a single repository. You could now automate the sales process.

In today's sales environment, you need to become more knowledgeable about your sales resources and your customers. The balance of power has shifted and consumers have the advantage because of the Web. And with performance management sitting on top of the CRM system you can get a new level of visibility and view about each salesperson and their individual productivity, and then you can orchestrate incentives, compensation and training.

So companies ran out and purchased CRM systems and captured data but what are Sales organizations doing with the data and how can the data be leveraged to feed business intelligence (BI), which can then support performance management activities.

As a result of business network transformation and technology changes the need for sales teams and executives will require an intensification of performance-focused activities.

Sales teams will need business processes and data to meet the burgeoning customer, service, and compliance requirements. In particular, Sales will be pressed to:

- Understand customer behavior and expanding customer requirements
- Deliver value and service to customers
- Comply with and document revenue recognition and other regulations

And as these pressures mount, sales leaders are being forced to increase their focus on activities such as:

- Training and educating sales professionals to understand expanding customer requirements
- Develop compensation plans that incent correct sales behavior
- Understand the impact cost of sales on profitability

The Evolution of Performance Management for Sales

So, what performance management challenges have resulted from a shift in power to the buyer? Sales teams need to consider price optimization because your potential buyer is informed and will use that leverage to drive your prices down. As a response to these trends, you require robust customer intelligence, an understanding of your product mix, and an effective distribution strategy. Due to the emergence of new markets, you are also facing a litany of compliance risks and requirements.

Your Sales organization needs greater transparency and visibility into sales activities. Managing the sales team based on instinct isn't enough to build a predictable sales practice. Performance management can enable sales managers to make strategic shifts and capitalize on opportunities or avoid potential market barriers.

Sales organizations must also develop and distribute activity metrics, along with performance metrics so that salespeople understand not only

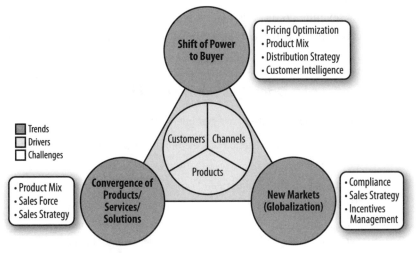

Figure 10-1. Trends and Challenges for Sales

what their sales results are, but also why they are occurring. Companies must also make sure the process that salespeople perform to capture activity data is simple. Once activity data has been captured, sales analytics can be used to correlate it with financial results to provide analytical insight into sales performance.

The Sales organization that can adapt, that can embrace the mantra of performance management, will be stronger, and consequently able to deliver revenue with greater predictably and higher profits. And to attain a competitive advantage, the role of performance management in sales will need to revisit and assimilate additional key performance management activities to drive greater visibility into the Sales organization. Some key activities include:

- Establishing management processes for improving Sales
- Providing financial visibility to sales compensation and forecasts
- Examining best practices for technology adoption for sales planning

Your Sales organization will also need to adopt a suite of human resource and business intelligence performance methods which:

- Embrace sales coaching and performance systems
- Leverage market and business intelligence to improve sales results
- Adopt best practices for compensation and incentives

Sales organizations will also need to maximize the potential of sales operations. How you incentivize your sales staff is a key component to hitting your revenue goals. The fastest way to change sales behavior is to change incentives for your sales staff. Location and customer intelligence

---

Does This Sound Familiar?

– We pursue sales leads that have not been accurately qualified.

– We have a rigorous qualification process but not all sales agents understand or use the process.

– We would like to better understand our win/loss ratios so we can adjust our market targets.

– Our sales forecast continues to be inaccurate and we either have tools that are hard to use and update or we have sales directors who are under-pricing to meet quotas.

access to design quota and territory plans can further drive to revenue goals and adopting methods to off-board the management of sales assets from the internal organization can influence profit margins.

Why You Must Do This Now

Sorry Boss, I missed the deal. If you have too many "I missed the deal" statements, the Sales team will miss its revenue targets. If the Sales team misses revenue targets, the company will miss its revenue targets. In today's complex sales environment, selling and managing predictable revenue requires visibility, agility, and collaboration. You need to begin considering an increased focus in sales performance management to attain sales visibility and predictability.

Some of the issues that plague Sales organizations and limit forecast accuracy, which influences sales visibility include:

- Inaccurate or missing sales data
- Sandbagging or holding back sales data
- Mismatched corporate goals with available sales resources

Pipeline accuracy and coverage are a critical component for delivering an accurate sales forecast. Pipeline activities need to be clearly defined and understood within your Sales organization and inside your company. Without a rigorous training process in place about how the sales pipeline operates, what the various stages in your pipeline indicate about the probability of closing a deal, or reliable metrics that provide an accurate picture of your pipeline's health, you have limited visibility.

Some of the issues that affect pipeline coverage include:

- Effective lead generation and lead qualification
- Incomplete or dated sales information
- Lack of training on sales pipeline processes
- Lack of formalized sales practices

> A service technician is out on a customer site and sees a lot of old equipment, which probably needs to be replaced. If he could share this information with the sales organization, this is an opportunity for sales. The service tech knows the equipment is about 10 years old. This information should go to the sales team so they can contact the customer and come up with an offer to replace this outdated equipment. Companies miss out on sales opportunities if they don't have this type of integrated and holistic view.

With performance management, you not only start to collect data but you also have increased visibility to identify trends and patterns. You can understand at an individual level how salespeople do deals and what type of deals. You get a level of granularity you didn't have before. Performance management can make your life as a sales professional better by helping you to:

- Align corporate goals and strategies with sales execution
- Understand key business drivers to hit revenue numbers
- Dramatically increase forecast accuracy
- Optimize incentives to match your sales strategy
- Reduce wasted time with spreadsheets so you can sell
- Optimize opportunities you want to pursue and which pricing strategy you should use
- Conduct collaborative demand/supply planning and matching so sales and service teams can collaborate more effectively to increase sales

Issues That Sales Currently Faces

Absent Analyses
- Lack of historical data about promotion effectiveness
- Lack of KPIs to measure past and current promotion effectiveness

Poor Coordination
- Misaligned sales promotion planning with consumer marketing
- Misaligned sales promotion execution with consumer marketing

Ineffective Planning
- Promotion plans out of sync with product supply
- Excessive out of stock at retail

Flawed Execution
- Repeat pricing errors
- Unplanned and random price deductions
- Unable to assign full costs to promotions

Table 10-1. Sales Pain Points

Area	Pain Points
Sales/Marketing	• Lack of integration with sales and marketing systems due to different systems and processes makes it difficult to have a full view of the customer acquisition process from cradle to close
Supply Chain/Operations	• Lack of visibility into supply chain leads to misaligned promotions and out of stock for customers in retail stores
Finance	• Lack of integration leads to misaligned deduction balances • Inaccurate cost assignments • Poor visibility into promotion and program costs
Partner/Channels	• Lack of visibility into Partner/Channel performance and their requirements to improve performance (i.e. sales education, better incentives, marketing promotions) • Lack of joint account planning processes to ensure effective sales coverage by channel • Lack of insight into customer satisfaction as the partner/channel keeps you a layer or two removed from the customer
Call Center	• Lack of a consistent hand off process between the call center and sales from initial lead qualification to pipeline opportunity. Lack of customer information sharing between the call center and sales

What Kind of Company Are You?

How to maximize sales effectiveness depends largely on aligning your type of company with your goals. Companies that focus on superior customer value as a value generation model are especially interested in long term relationships that are profitable and deliver strong customer experiences. You can think of big name brands that have built their entire value around superior customer relations as an example, names like Nordstrom, Four Seasons, and IBM Global Services. For these Sales organizations, customer profitability will be critical.

If you're a product company, then your value generation model is going to differ. Product companies want to crank out cool and innovative products to a large market whereas those focused on customer value spend effort nurturing their customer relationships, and don't necessarily have the best products or the most differentiated products on the market.

For both types of companies, you still need revenue but how you get that revenue is going to vary quite dramatically. Your sales cycles, sales teams and sales culture are going to behave and look different. Some sales cycles will involve teams of people going to the customer site over a series of months, while other sales will occur with a "call this toll-free number and then you to can have this for $19.95." So the way you treat the sale, the way you approach the deal, the methodology you practice vis-à-vis the customer in terms of a sale will vary.

If you're in a product and service company, don't propose to add 500 direct salespeople in your sales force if your strategy is to continue building on your existing business model, because you will definitely drive down profitability. So, if you're a Hershey's or a Nestle that's not going to help you, whereas if you're a software company, adding more salespeople may work. Basically you have two models:

- Volume business
- Tailored one to one business

There will probably be 50% of things that a head of Sales in any company will care about, no matter what company you're in, anywhere in the world, but there's probably upward of 50% variance in the things that each Sales executive will care about that are unique to their industry or to their company's value proposition. A conversation with the head of Sales for a consumer products company or the head of Sales for a professional services company is completely different.

If you're the head of Sales, you've got to forecast. You've got to make money. You have a forecast, a budget, a territory, quota, and goals, but your strategy, which drives your plans, which drives what you're going to optimize, is very, very different.

The Business Process Angle

Sales organizations play a role in many cross-functional business processes, as illustrated in Figure 10-2. Performance management offers the methodology and tools to pull back the covers of the organization to provide visibility into the interconnected nature of these end-to-end processes.

"Today, 30–35% of a salesperson's face time is spent with the customer. Salespeople spend too much time on administrating, expediting orders, arguing over receivables, and finding late shipments."

—Jack Welch, former CEO, General Electric Company

Broadly speaking, these processes include collaborative demand and supply planning, integrated logistics and fulfillment, supplier network management, integrated product development, and delivering products as a service. Sales takes the lead with marketing in owning optimization of sales and marketing investments, optimal offer, and streamlined order fulfillment business processes as described next.

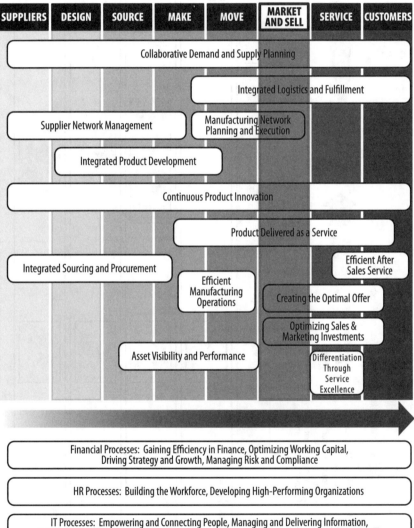

Figure 10-2. Business Processes That Involve Sales

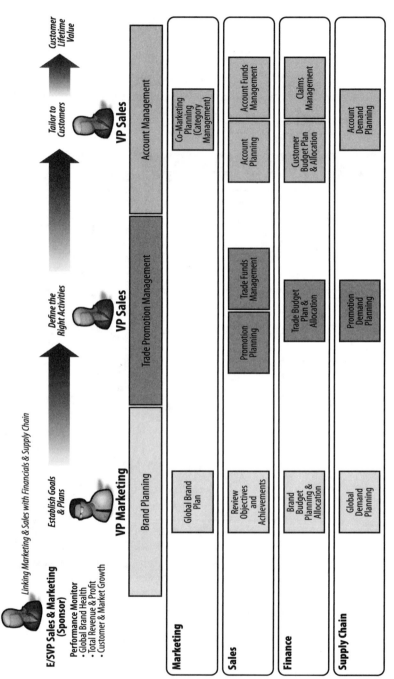

Figure 10-3. Optimizing Sales and Marketing Investments

Optimizing sales and marketing investments. This process has essentially four main activities. First, align marketing plans with trade promotions and sales execution plans. Second, integrate with demand planning teams for ongoing production, inventory, and logistics planning. Third, integrate with financials to ensure accurate budgeting and timely settlements and claims processing (for both direct and indirect channels). Fourth, use analysis to develop a 360-degree view of the customer and evaluate profitability of marketing programs.

Sales teams must collaborate effectively with marketing to leverage marketing intelligence so that gains can be realized from brand planning activities. Sales staff in trade management should be getting visibility from the brand planning side on the number of demand generation activities that are taking place so sales managers can use that as a driver for figuring out how many salespeople will be needed to hit sales forecasts.

When the trade management team is working across the functional boundaries with the Marketing team, then planned promotions are coordinated with marketing campaigns.

Collaborating not only feels good but also maximizes incremental revenue and sales value from promotions.

Table 10-2. Best Practice Process: Trade Management in Action

Process	Benefit
Track planned versus actual spend real-time for promotions and marketing campaigns	Minimize over/under spend v. plan; enable budget adjustments as needed
Pinpoint promotions and programs most likely to achieve revenue and volume targets	Coordinate marketing and promotion activity to maximize overall spend efficiency
Measure post-promotion effectiveness to assess ROI and inform future plans	Identify most effective promotions and programs; eliminate wasted spend

Creating the optimal offer. Leverage a true 360-degree view of the customer to create the optimal offer based on customer information and aligned with business goals. Maximize revenues and profits at every selling opportunity through leveraging advanced price and margin management. Come up with the best recommendations to offer the customers in any channel they choose to contact you. We discuss this process further in Chapter 11.

Streamlined order fulfillment. Perfect orders are generated with accurate product configurations, pricing, and due dates determined through availability checks done in real time. Orders are quickly converted to cash through automated and streamlined fulfillment processes across multiple channels. Orders are shipped with accuracy, speed, reliability, and at low cost, with the goal of increasing customer satisfaction.

The streamlined order fulfillment business process is often referred to as the order to cash transactional process.

For the Sales organization, order entry and processing can be tedious and error prone. How do you ensure that orders are properly and appropriately processed and that somebody can't just enter 500 of something when they meant five, and what sort of controls do you have in place to ensure data accuracy and compliance with assigned policies?

In today's business climate, with an increasing need for complete visibility and the requirement to provide full disclosure of your financial practices, order management is crucial to corporate success as the demand for perfection increases and flexibility and tolerance for errors decreases.

Superior order management can be a competitive edge across the board, improving customer satisfaction and retention as well as your bottom line and top line. What does it take to achieve superior order management performance? To move ever closer to order perfection and a truly happy customer base, you must cost-effectively develop, automate, and maintain a systematic set of processes that proactively account for potential risks with the appropriate controls and alerts.

This involves every process including planning and forecasting, acquiring and creating accurate orders and contracts, handling order changes, and resolving fulfillment and post-delivery problems.

The path toward the perfect order equates to taking customer-centric steps toward end-to-end order management, which requires operational excellence, cross-enterprise integration of processes and IT, and accessible enterprise intelligence about customers, products, services, and orders.

So it's critical to have a highly functioning order to cash process. If your order to cash process is not integrated and not aligned, you could sell more products than you have available.

In summary, from the perspective of collaborative business processes, sales and operations and marketing need to be aligned since all three business units are involved in the process. Marketing may have budgeted for 100,000 units while Sales may have sold 50,000 units and operations can only manufacture 10,000. With performance management you can collaborate with marketing and operations to sell the perfect order.

Finally, it's important to understand the processes that exist within sales. All sales organizations need to be effective at strategizing, planning, monitoring, and optimizing their account and contact management processes, quotation and order management processes, pricing and contract processes, and so on.

Table 10-3. Examples of Business Processes within Sales

Territory Management	Market Segmentation; Territory Assignment & Scheduling; Territory/Organizational Mapping; Rule-Based Synchronization for Mobile Devices; Sales Analysis by Territory; Interface to Third-Party Territory Planning Tools
Accounts and Contacts	Visit Planning; Fact Sheet; Interaction History; Activity Mgmt; Email & Fax Integration; Relationship Mgmt; Marketing Attributes; Customer-Specific Pricing; Account Planning; Customer Analysis; Account Classification
Opportunity Management	Opportunity Planning; Team Selling; Competitive Information; Account-specific Sales Processes; Automatic Business Partner Assignment; Pricing; Activities; Follow-Up Transactions; Product Configuration; Anticipated Revenue; Buying Center; Sales Project Mgmt; Opportunity Hierarchies; Sales Process & Selling Methodologies; Opportunity Analysis
Quotation and Order Management	Quotations; Package Quotation; Order Capture; Automatic Business Partner Assignment; Order Status Tracking; Pricing; Price Change Approval; Order Validation Check; Credit Mgmt & Credit Check; Payment Card Processing; Automated Follow-Up Processes; Product Authorization & Restriction; Product Configuration; Bill of Material; Availability Check; Rebates; Billing; Fulfillment Synchronization; Quotation and Order Analysis
Pricing and Contracts	Value & Quantity Contracts; Sales Agreements; Authorized Customers; Contract Completion Rules; Collaborative Contract Negotiation; Release Order Processing; Cancellation Handling; Fulfillment Synchronization; Automatic Business Partner Assignment; Product Configuration; Contract Status Tracking; Credit Mgmt & Credit Check; Pricing; Customer-specific Pricing; Promotional Pricing; Contract Analysis
Incentive and Commission Management	Direct & Indirect Sales Compensation; Incentive Plan Modeling; Configuration Templates; Roll Up Hierarchies/Indirect Participants; Contracts and Agreements Handling; Individual Plan Exceptions; Target Agreement; Adjustments; Posting and Settlement; Commission Simulation; Commission Status Mgmt
Time and Travel	Time Reporting; Receipt Itemization; Track Receipts, Mileage, Deductions & Border Crossings; Integration with Activity Mgmt; Cost Assignment

Key Roles in Sales Performance Management

Understanding the people and the roles within the sales department can benefit other business units such as Marketing, Service, partners, channels and Finance that must collaborate with the Sales department to truly understand various aspects of performance management. While many assume all of Sales is solely focused on closing deals, key groups within Sales have varying objectives for how to optimize the process of revenue generation. As an example, a strategic account executive with only one or two accounts is focused on building the relationship with the customer and on long-term revenue gains. A telesales rep who may be motivated and compensated on volume sales of a small add-on moves from one account to another quickly and the strategies they need to employ are much different. Familiarity with the motivations and roles of sales staff supports effective collaboration. How should other business units think about the challenges and responsibilities of the sales team? Having a common language as well as empathy for and insight into your colleagues' day-to-day responsibilities often enhance collaboration.

Sales Executive

A sales executive doesn't have time to hunt through data to find answers to key business questions. The data needs to be reliable, with answers to direct questions, such as year-to-date forecast rolled up by region or, in the future, by customer, channel, or product/promotion segments. As executives attempt to understand the reported data, they will ask why certain results were achieved or not. In this environment, custom analyses that respond to these queries are done for the executive. The results are then presented in a way so that they can be digested in a short time period, typically in a printed or "canned" report or via an electronic dashboard with KPIs and charts. The key predictive capabilities that a Sales executive is interested in are market growth and scenario planning—for example, reorganizing a sales channel structure to reduce costs for a particular market because that market is likely to become commoditized, or planning for growth based on demand forecasting.

Sales executives need to focus attention on the right opportunities and people as well as the appropriate KPIs and pipeline stages. They need to evaluate sales team performance at a macro level as well as to quickly drill down to the detailed level to understand peaks and valleys in performance. As an example, Sales executives are obsessed with accurate forecasting to satisfy internal and external stakeholder requirements and meet performance goals and sales targets. The health of the pipeline keeps Sales executives awake at night as the level of scrutiny applied to the forecast and the need for predictability is now greater than ever before. Companies that cannot demonstrate both profitability and predictability about how they will get there with their forecasts are severely penalized and this typically reflects in their stock valuation. Additionally Sales executives must work closely with Marketing to achieve demand consensus and ensure that the Sales team is effectively trained and well versed on issues and pain points of the market.

Further, Sales executives need the ability to roll up forecasts and to keep track of key performance indicators (KPIs) at a tactical level, such as sales calls made, leads converted, product and promotion success, or proposals generated. Once these basic needs are covered, sales organizations can move to provide a better understanding of the reported data by correlating performance data with activity data for win/loss reporting on sales cycles, promotions, and new product launches. Sales analytics can also enable Sales managers to mine data to profile the successful sales activities of their best salespeople, identifying key market/segment opportunities and best-practice processes. Predictive analysis can help sales managers determine customer lifetime value to help focus their resources on those accounts, sales influencers, field marketing campaigns and product portfolios that will yield the most benefit.

Account Executive

An account executive needs help prioritizing and managing opportunities and tracking pipeline performance as well as constantly maintaining a solid grasp of his or her portfolio offerings through education and training. Understanding customer relationships and having access to historical data such as contacts, customer interactions, and previous opportunities are beneficial to an account executive. Service and Marketing organizations should share key customer insights with Sales organizations to drive sales opportunities. Account managers also need to track and collect commissions and must reduce time spent on maintaining sales data. Less time spent managing internal processes leads to more time spent with customers. Account managers can't be successful without nurturing and growing customer relationships.

Account executives are often the overlooked individuals in the sales organization when sales analytics are deployed. While they are repeatedly tasked with providing information about the customers via data entry in the CRM system, they all too often do not get views into reports produced from an aggregated view of the data. This is unfortunate since they have the most capability to positively influence the customer relationship using the insight that sales analytics provides. Insight into up-sell or cross-sell data based on historical success across the sales organization helps salespeople increase deals without sacrificing margins. Competitive intelligence, such as pricing and bundling alternatives, provides salespeople with immediate information to adjust quotations to improve win rates. As we move up the hierarchy, more sophisticated queries and technologies will help salespeople prioritize sales opportunities based on parameters such as competition, available budget, customer need, customer loyalty, and potential sales commissions. The result is that a salesperson will work on opportunities that have the best chance of closing. Salespeople can leverage predictive analysis to help project account growth potential and future customer product preferences. Scenario planning, or "what if" analysis, can aid ongoing account planning and refinement. This will lead to more winning account management plans.

KPIs for Success in Sales

Selecting metrics that matter to benchmark your sales activities requires a disciplined approach. And within the sales organization, different KPIs apply to different roles. Sales goals will influence the KPIs you emphasize. You need to establish a causal link between a set of KPIs and financial outcomes. Select a KPI that you believe links to your role, a strategic goal, and a financial outcome. Then validate your KPI assumptions. As you iterate through your KPI selection and validation process, you are moving away from sales à la instinct to a fact-based sales organization.

Table 10-4. Sales Roles and KPIs

KPI Type / Sales Roles	Sales KPIs
Strategic / Chief Sales Office; SVP and VP of Service	Account Churn; Amount of New Revenue; Amount of Recurring Revenue; Cost of Sale; Days Sales Outstanding; Forecast vs. Budget/Quota; Margin; Number of New Customers; Number of Prospects; Number of Retained Customers; Per Head Productivity; Profit by Customer; Wallet Share
Operational / Sales Manager; Sales Support Manager; Account Manager	Average Discount %; Close Rate; Competitive Knockouts; Deal Margin; New Opportunities Within Customer Base; New vs. Existing Customer Bookings (expansion sales); Number of Cross-Sells; Number of Upsells; Renewal Rate; Revenue by Channel; Sales Cycle Duration; Sales Stage Duration; Time to Close by Channel; Win/Loss
Tactical / Sales Associate; Sales Support	Average Age by Stage; Average Opportunity Size; Number of Open Opportunities; Number of Proposals Given; Number of Sales Call per Opportunity; Number of Sales Calls; Number of Sales Calls Made; Per Headcount Productivity; Pipeline Coverage to Forecast

What's In It for Me?

You want to drive the right kind of sales behavior to meet your revenue goals.

> The quickest way to change sales behavior is to change the incentives. If you give somebody a $5,000 bonus for selling the worst product in your portfolio, guess what? Every customer suddenly loves that product, because that's what salespeople do.

It doesn't matter where you are in the sales hierarchy; you are always managing your activities to a specific revenue number. For you, it's all about retaining revenue and so at the end of the day you are measured on your ability to meet your revenue targets. So if you and your entire Sales organization have greater visibility into revenue forecasting and pipeline accuracy and you have the levers to help increase the likelihood of meeting your revenue objectives, you're going to find performance management to be highly appealing. At each level of the Sales organization, you want to have an understanding of how the revenue is going to come in and when. If you can get that information accurately and quickly, you have a much higher chance of succeeding.

Effective Collaboration

A good salesperson must collaborate to be successful. Selling products or services has become increasingly complex. A sales rep is a master orchestrator who needs visibility into supporting functions and other business units.

Collaboration with Finance

The overall goal of Sales is to meet and forecast revenue targets while maintaining a competitive pricing structure for the company. Finance relies on Sales to accurately forecast revenue and meet pipeline targets. Sales analytical tools can provide greater visibility for both Sales and Finance.

Collaboration with Marketing

The main input before an order comes from leads which demonstrates the connection between Marketing and Sales. Presales inputs include demand creation and demand management, which in turn drive opportunity management. Sales staff needs to understand demand creation investments to align sales goals and initiatives.

One key intersection between Sales and Marketing is the go-to-market (GTM) strategy. Sales and Marketing are two sides of the same coin and cannot exist without one another. Marketing develops the GTM strategy based on market research and generates demand. Salespeople then execute by selling, resulting in closed deals and revenue. Marketing is responsible for enabling the salespeople to sell, beyond just providing direction about the most prolific markets. Sales expects Marketing to provide them with account data and segmentation, compelling messaging and positioning, pricing and promotional offers, and competitive differentiation and selling strategies.

Collaboration with Service

Salespeople are constantly trying to balance driving revenue with developing strong relationships with their customers, and service staff can help with both. Service has a wealth of information about customers. Any good sales executive makes it a regular practice to engage with service reps. The service rep provides insight into possible new opportunities in the account by sharing pain points customers have revealed. Service reps can act as an early warning system for salespeople by informing sales staff of customer implementation issues, giving sales reps a chance to proactively identify remedies to resolve conflicts that could impact customer satisfaction and repurchase.

Sales teams can integrate customer satisfaction and customer reference-ability into sales compensation plans to ensure that salespeople are meeting customer needs.

Collaboration with Supply Chain

A key element to a successful sale is being able to fulfill the order and the supply chain plays a vital role in making sure this happens. Sales teams rely on the supply chain to keep them abreast of the availability of products. Sales teams do not want to actively promote a product that is not in inventory. Further, Sales expects Supply Chain to notify them of any potential quality issues. For example, let's say Supply Chain has a breakdown with its primary plastics provider in manufacturing a top-selling toy. As a result, Supply Chain must secure an alternate plastics provider, and in doing so must use a lower quality plastic. As a result, the toy might break more easily when firm pressure is applied. If sales reps know this up front, they can determine what audiences will accept this compromise. If sales reps don't know and sell the toys anyway, they will end up with unhappy customers and product returns.

Collaboration with Procurement

Sales organizations interact with Procurement in two ways. First, sales reps must work with Procurement to secure assets (laptops, training guides, software) and services (training courses, incentives) at the best possible price and the best quality. Since the major expense associated with Sales is head count and travel and entertainment (T&E), the relationship between the Sales and the Procurement department is limited. The same cannot be said for Sales reps and the interactions with Procurement at customer accounts. Quite often Procurement interaction with the client is the nemesis of the salesperson and the feeling is often mutual. Simply put, the two groups have conflicting agendas. Sales reps want to command the greatest price for their offering and the customer's Procurement department wants to negotiate the lowest possible price and the highest quality. The two go around in circles when it comes to the request for proposal process and contract negotiations because sales reps always want to circumvent the procurement process and get an exception and the procurement process is built on the notion of fairness and standard processes.

Collaboration with Product Development

Sales is the truth serum for Product Development. While months and years can be spent developing a product, Sales is the reality check on whether the market adopts the product. Sales staff typically interact with Product Development as a second line of defense. They most often work with Marketing, which plays a bidirectional role between the Product Development and Sales organization. When sales reps rely on Product Development directly, it is typically in a highly technical sales cycle where the expertise of the product engineers is required to communicate some of the more detailed technical capabilities. In addition, sales reps collaborate with Product Development as a voice of the customer. As Sales team members spend their day interacting with customers, they are well poised to give Product Development direct feedback on the most useful features and capabilities of the products to customers. Product Development typically welcomes this feedback since sales reps can often bring them a surprise or two about the most used or most interesting capability from the customer perspective.

Collaboration with IT

Managing the sales pipeline and ensuring forecast accuracy is mission critical and IT is at the helm of enabling these processes for sales. If the company does not have visibility into the sales pipeline, which is the life-blood of the organization, then it is essentially flying blind and at serious risk of eroding the company's margin and decreasing shareholder value. Sales organizations need IT to help automatically record all the stages in a sales process. Specifically, IT needs to provide a sales force management system to help automate sales functions. Such systems are frequently combined with a marketing information system, and referred to as CRM systems. Sales teams are looking for these systems to give them visibility across the following areas:

- Contact management for tracking all contacts with a given customer, the purpose of the contact, and any follow up that might be required. Eliminates duplication of sales efforts
- Lead tracking with lists of potential customers
- Sales forecasting, a prediction of future sales, based mainly on past sales performance. Given the volume of data, detail, and changes, it is essential that IT automate the sales forecasting task
- Order management, which facilitates order entry, whether online or through an application (for orders received via phone and mail). Order management captures customer proprietary information and account level information
- Sales data management, which is provided by IT to ensure appropriate access to data. IT provides segregation of duties in the sales force automation system to ensure that sales teams are compliant with company data privacy and access policies

Collaboration with HR

Sales organizations rely on HR for effective talent management method-ologies and tools. Most important to the sales practice is for HR to secure top talent in the market via financially aggressive sales compensation plans. HR provides Sales insight into market benchmark data on compensation to help Sales devise the most attractive compensation plans. Once hired, sales staff also looks to HR to provide a culture of training and personal development. HR can conduct needs analysis about training gaps to develop a training curriculum. When working together on this, the two organiza-tions also collaborate on the sales methodologies being used. Because the sales methodology is a sequence of steps or predefined processes put in place by management that is meant to increase the sales effectiveness, it is therefore an integral part of a sales training plan.

Establishing Your BI Foundation

Bad sales data is worse than no data at all. The purpose of establishing your BI foundation is to ensure that your data is clean and in order.

Sales staff resist entering sales forecast information into a web screen. The BI or technology platform for sales teams needs to be much more conducive to mobile data entry.

A lot of companies today are standardizing on CRM systems so that the main BI linkage is to get clean data from your CRM system. And for CRM there is also the problem of customer master data management. Sales teams have a huge problem with multiple customer identifiers for the same customer. So you may end up with the same sales rep pursuing two conflicting strategies for the same customer.

When applied to the sales organization, the BI foundation should provide the following features.

Relevant visualizations. BI should supplement standard tables and graphs with sales-specific visualizations. For example, salespeople often use the metaphor of a pipeline to represent the funnel of opportunities as they progress toward close, and pipeline visualizations can be very effective communication tools. Visualization or trending of performance such as sales per product line per quarter for 3 to 5 consecutive years can help companies predict upcoming sales forecast per product area and set budget and quota for sales representatives.

Relevant event-capture and alerting. BI should provide the ability to gather information from event sources, like RSS feeds with press announcements from competitors or from potential and existing customers and the ability to define alerts for critical events and inform the right person in the Sales organization to take action.

A unified semantic layer, data integration, and data quality across departmental and application silos. Sales users need to bridge silos when they don't have access to an integrated transactional system, but instead have many point systems (territory management systems, account management systems, opportunity management systems), or multiple CRM systems. Use BI to establish common definitions and business rules of the key dimensions in sales (customers, territories, accounts, leads) and metrics. For example, a sales rep can look at product failure rates and defects to identify the risk of positioning the product to a customer and leverage the information to appropriately educate the customer.

Data quality is a particularly thorny challenge for customer-facing business processes like sales as well as for marketing and service. Data quality tools can profile vast quantities of disparate customer data and parse it and standardize it either through generalized cleansing algorithms or through matching techniques, and ultimately proactively monitor ongoing conformance to data quality rules. When combined with master data management capabilities, it is possible to proactively ensure a single definition of customers and customer-related attributes in all of your systems as they change, which makes it much easier to share information across various systems and ultimately ensure that customer interactions are based on reliable data.

Trusted, cleansed master data. Master data management (MDM) for customers, often called customer data integration, is a crucial capability for managing customer master data and their hierarchies and taxonomies. A solid BI foundation with MDM enables you to consolidate on standard definitions of a customer, but also standardize definitions of the individual customers (for example, AT&T, ATT, and AT and T are the same customer) and their key attributes like their addresses. The automatic cleansing of customers, vendors, and materials enables sales teams to match important information. For example, for a retailer if Coke and Coca Cola have the same material codes, then sales information and inventory should cross check to ensure that the summary information for these two product numbers have the same material code.

We recommend looking for the following capabilities in a customer data integration solution to serve as the backbone of your performance management needs. First, look for a centralized repository. The solution should enable a flexible repository schema, complete with taxonomy editing; the ability to manage rich customer data, customer relationships, and addresses; and the ability to search single-style and seamlessly—with a simple search, a partial string search, and searches by dimension. Features specific to customer master data such as matching, standardization, and survivorship are important and can be supplemented by a data quality engine. It's also important that you can support both business-to-business (B2B) and business-to-consumer (B2C) customer definitions that rely on a generic business partner object in your transactional applications. The checklist should also include the ability to aggregate and normalize data coming from different sources. You must be able to syndicate and synchronize your information, as well as have high-performance workflows and a validation engine through which you can define valid data types stored within your master data management application.

Structured and unstructured data. BI platforms can generate insights from both structured as well as unstructured data. Copious amounts of unstructured data are available and can provide tremendous value to the sales organization. Insight is available in social media (these consumers hate our new product for this reason), but also in documents such as RFPs (for example, in the last four months, every RFP has mentioned a new feature that only our competitor offers).

Reports. Ad-hoc reporting capabilities should provide:

- Publication quality reports to distribute to large numbers of users such as a weekly forecast report
- Dashboards for visualizing sales information such as how many new accounts were added last week, the regional sales segmentation on a monthly vs. quarterly basis, the best selling product line, and the breakdown of revenue forecast vs. booking vs. deferrals
- Query and analysis to provide simple, intuitive analytics capabilities for end users. For example, as a sales manager, what are the closed deals by representative on a weekly basis? As a sales rep, I need a contact list of all customers within the sales rep's territory that have outstanding invoices over 10 days

Assessing Performance Management Maturity

It's daunting for most to consider how to assess performance management maturity. Is the garden soil ready for planting? Do you need to till the soil and add more minerals or can you just start watering and hope for a warm and sunny summer to grow your garden? Like any new gardening project, you should start small and plant just a few flower varieties. To assess performance management, select an issue and run it through the PM lifecycle.

Once you understand the cost of meeting your sales quotas, you can modify your cost activities. Then you can move on to the next question. The process of assessing your approach to performance management will provide you with insight and will also drive improvements in your organization.

The PM Lifecycle for Sales

All companies and sales groups go through some form of strategy setting. However, as we have noted in Chapter 3, there is often a yawning gap

---

Questions to Run through the PM Lifecycle.

Do you know how much you're spending to meet your sales quotas?

Do you collaborate effectively with marketing initiatives such as demand planning?

How reliable is your revenue forecast?

Do you have defined stages for your sales pipeline?

Are you learning from your win/loss's sales ratios and using the knowledge to modify your sales strategy?

Do you know how satisfied your customers are with your sales process?

What is the sales plan vs. actual revenue, cost, activity, or contribution margin variance?

What is the current pipeline by phase and region?

What is the number of win/loss opportunities?

What is the expected sales revenue vs. actual?

What is the expected revenue of all opportunities?

What opportunities are likely to close by sales stage?

---

between the strategy that is set and its execution at the operational level. And while there is a need for the company to adopt a lifecycle at a high level, it is also important for the Sales organization to adopt one specific to its role in the company.

And while there may be unique capabilities required to create and engage in a PM lifecycle, they fall under the need to manage strategy, engage in business planning, analyze data in order to monitor execution, and then perform some form of modeling and optimization of the various activities that may be falling short of planned strategic goals to determine the best way to achieve them.

Performance management involves the routine, and sometimes non-routine, measurement of key aspects of performance across your collaborative and within-sales business processes and making this information available to decision-makers. In this section, we will walk you through the PM lifecycle, highlighting information that your peers have found useful.

Strategize and Prioritize

In this portion of the lifecycle, the development of strategic and operational plans must include the identification and assessment of risks to short- and long-term objectives and plans. Sales is not exempt from this process. In fact, because it is so closely tied to revenue generation, it acts as the central nervous system in the body and needs to be intricately tied into the strategy setting process. The best-developed plans can fail without an execution plan. Sales is the execution arm and therefore requires a thoughtful and efficient execution plan that considers all of the key touch points to the customer since these touch points both create and influence revenue. Sales needs to have a 360-degree view of the touchpoints and have a strategy for engaging customers. Some key strategies and priorities to address as part of the 360-degree view include:

- Customer service strategy
- Customer satisfaction and support management conduct
- Go to market model/strategy
- Sales channel
- Partner strategy
- Sales and customer segmentation strategy
- Customer improvement targets

As an example, the Sales organization is told to increase margin, which for Sales means bringing in more revenue. With performance management, you begin tweaking your strategies to meet the increased revenue targets. This may involve launching product promotions as part of your go to market strategy. It may include modifying sales quotas and distribution channels (the online-offline mix) as part of your sales channel strategy and revisiting your partner ecosystem to ensure you have the right mix of partners to support your offering. This brings us to the importance of understanding the role and expectations of your internal and external stakeholders.

Understand the Context

Start by reviewing the corporate strategic goals, strategic plans, initiatives, and metrics that track progress against them and understand them. From there, contextualize them to the implications they have for sales and use this context to drive your sales PM lifecycle.

In doing so, ensure you have a 360-degree view of your company as a whole and are clear on the company's strengths and the drivers of the business. For example, are you a product company where every investment centers on the product? Or are you a customer-focused company, in which everything centers on customer interaction and customer experience? It is critical that you understand the overall strengths of the organization and align your sales strategy to capitalize on this, enhancing your strengths and not resisting them. For example, if the company has a plan in place to cut order fulfillment staffing by 30% this year, and you need to factor into your plan the potential implications for both your customer's satisfaction levels and your lead time to see recognized revenue on the books given the potentially added time to complete an order.

In addition, while Sales lives and dies by the quarter, Sales still needs to understand the strategic long-term direction of the company. As an example, your company currently has plans to build a new set of financial tools that will launch in 24 months. Anticipating this will be a set of products in your revenue portfolio. What are you doing now to train your sales organization on this complex new offering? Here's another example. Your company has indicated a plan to take some of your direct sales products and offer them online as well. What will this do to your direct sales revenues? How will you compensate for this lost revenue as part of your direct channel? Overall, the message here is to avoid the tendency to structure your entire sales strategy around one or two quarters but rather to develop a balanced approach to strategy that allows you to meet the immediate quarterly revenue but does not leave you with surprises 12 months out.

Lastly, make sure you have thought beyond your organization's four walls. In particular, which partners provide services that advance sales cycles? Do you rely on outsourcing your lead generation activities to another firm, perhaps in another country and if so, what risk mitigation do you have in place if their service immediately stopped? Or as another example, do you rely on key partners to manage the servicing of your products? If so, what risk mitigation plan do you have in place should your next product release prove to be riddled with product malfunctions?

Develop and Set the Strategy

Here are the basic steps you'll follow in developing and prioritizing your strategies.

Assess the environment. For Sales, it is a constant battle of managing results, resources, and time. To effectively pull off this balancing act, it is essential that you start by assessing where you are today. This assessment needs to include both internal and external factors and look not only for opportunities but identify potential risks as well. Internal factors to consider include systems to track sales performance, sales training and education resources, marketing investment in brand awareness and lead generation, call center staffing and telecosts, revenue recognition, and quota assignment. External factors include competitive offerings, shifting customer needs, economic downturns, legal or regulatory actions, shareholder relationships, and analyst and media perceptions.

Identification of the risks is not enough; you must understand the potential impact of the risk on sales, its likelihood, and the strategies you need to employ to mitigate these risks. This assessment needs to map the overall value of each opportunity in terms of revenue and complexity to implement. It also needs to address the ever-increasing number of compliance initiatives, such as Sarbanes-Oxley.

Set the mission, values, and vision. Understanding the nature of your Sales team and company is key. For example, if you are a product driven company with significant product innovations, this may require a more technically savvy sales organization. Or if you are a product company that sells a single widget that works for everything and is commoditized in the market, your Sales organization may require less experience but needs drive and stamina to manage a transactional volume-based business.

Once you have identified the type of company you are, you begin to build the profile of the best-suited sales team to drive revenue. Further, you begin to identify what sort of sales methodology will work best for your selling process. Common sales methodologies include Miller Heiman, Conceptual Selling, Solution Selling, Spin Selling, Six Sigma, and Strategic Selling. Each of these has merits and it is up to sales management to identify and implement the methodology that best aligns with your sales model.

From here you begin to define the sales mission and core values of the organization. Specifically, what are the guiding principles of the team and what bar will the organization be held to? As an example, are people seen as the cornerstone of the Sales organization's success? Is leadership what differentiates your Sales organization? If so, how do you inspire leadership throughout the organization? Remember sales is as much psychology as it is a process and therefore it is critical to have a sales mission and culture that motivates your organization and gives salespeople the confidence they need to command the revenue. Common core values center on the areas of customer focus, quality, product excellence, integrity, commitment, and passion. Beyond just the qualitative aspects, it is important to define a long-term vision and quantitatively set targets for the future (for example, we will be the market share leader in our product category within 3 years).

Set the Goals

Define your sales strategies and set business objectives using risks as a key variable for deciding which strategies to pursue. With all that contextual information in hand, set your goals and ensure alignment with corporate objectives for:

- Profitable revenue attainment
- Organizational effectiveness
- Customer satisfaction

Consider using a strategy map to display the cause and effect relationships among the objectives that make up a strategy. A good strategy map tells a story of how value is created for the business.

Assign KPIs to Goals

It is now time to define our sales KPIs and targets in order to appropriately set performance expectations and ensure that we focus on activities that will drive the most value to the organization. In Sales, the KPIs are fairly straightforward in their explanation but are extremely detailed in the

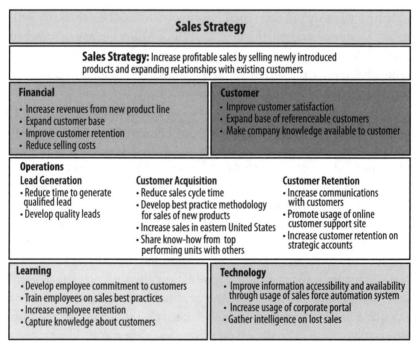

Sales Strategy

Sales Strategy: Increase profitable sales by selling newly introduced products and expanding relationships with existing customers

Financial
- Increase revenues from new product line
- Expand customer base
- Improve customer retention
- Reduce selling costs

Customer
- Improve customer satisfaction
- Expand base of referenceable customers
- Make company knowledge available to customer

Operations

Lead Generation
- Reduce time to generate qualified lead
- Develop quality leads

Customer Acquisition
- Reduce sales cycle time
- Develop best practice methodology for sales of new products
- Increase sales in eastern United States
- Share know-how from top performing units with others

Customer Retention
- Increase communications with customers
- Promote usage of online customer support site
- Increase customer retention on strategic accounts

Learning
- Develop employee commitment to customers
- Train employees on sales best practices
- Increase employee retention
- Capture knowledge about customers

Technology
- Improve information accessibility and availability through usage of sales force automation system
- Increase usage of corporate portal
- Gather intelligence on lost sales

Figure 10-4. An Example of a Sales Strategy Map

amount and frequency of data to collect, monitor, analyze and optimize. You must select KPIs that make sense for your strategy (see "KPIs for Success in Sales" earlier in this chapter for a sample list).

KPIs and metrics cannot be looked at in isolation because each has associated risks. These risks should be identified and tolerance levels established, from which a key risk indicator (KRI) can be established. This connectivity between a value driver and a relevant KPI and KRI is an important bridge from a strategic view of risk—which can have a time horizon of three or more years—to a more focused budgetary view of risk, which is often applied to a single year.

Perform Additional Risk Analysis and Set Key Risk Indicators (KRIs)

As we have discussed, KRIs are as important as KPIs; they should never exist in isolation. Let's shift our focus now onto some of the possible risks for a Sales organization and potential remedies to apply to avoid such risks, specifically the predefined risk response strategies you can employ as "plan B" if you are unable to mitigate the risk. There is no shortage of examples of how failures to properly manage sales risk can cause harm to the company, from losing a major deal because of a competitor swooping in at the last minute to providing an inaccurate forecast midway through the quarter that leads the CFO to issue the wrong guidance to the Street to wholesale fraud that results in restated earnings.

Identifying your risks is not as hard as it may seem. The easiest possible way to tackle this is to start by reviewing your goals and objectives and identifying the uncertainties that could inhibit you from meeting those goals and objectives. You can do this by mapping the process steps associated with executing your key strategies and identifying financial, operational, and strategic risks. As a Sales organization, you should be able to identify risks associated with each major goal and process step. Insight into account penetration, ownership of account, overall customer satisfaction, customer loyalty and retention, and upsell and resell opportunities all influence the level of risk in the sales practice.

Now look again at these risks and decide what your risk appetite is. Can you afford to take that risk? What's the worst-case scenario? Does taking the risk mean possibly missing revenue targets? For example, if you restructure your sales territories, what potential implications does this have for your customer satisfaction ratings? Can you afford to change

---

Examples of Risks for Sales

Here are some risks to consider for sales, but this list is not exhaustive:

- Forecast predictability—Poor forecast accuracy has dramatic downstream consequences for revenue attainment and ultimately the financial forecast, which in turn impacts stock price

- Customer satisfaction—Decreases in customer satisfaction levels are a harbinger for reduced purchasing activity

- Revenue attainment—Revenue retention and the predictability of your forecast, in terms of the sales stages and your sales conversion rates is a risk to your business and needs to be frequently monitored and optimized. Fraud is also a risk in the selling process. Selling processes occur in a variety of channels and collaborating with sales channels to eliminate fraud potential is critical

- Margin attainment—It might be possible to achieve your revenue targets but not without dramatically increasing your cost of sales

- Organizational effectiveness—Decreases in call volume and increases in T&E expense

- Pipeline visibility—Do you have full view to all the opportunities? Are sales reps sandbagging? Does the pipeline represent the full opportunity?

- Account penetration—Coverage model changes

- Compliance risk—Such as fraud, revenue recognition, and credit

---

account executives on the customer, interrupting the preexisting relationship for the opportunity for more revenue? How low can your customer satisfaction rating drop as a result of a restructuring while still meeting your revenue priority?

Set a response strategy for the risk (watch, research, transfer, delegate, mitigate). For example, you could decide that the sales team will have weekly training sessions on your new product lines to drive adoption and sales. However, you recognize this is a significant investment of the sales team's time off the road and therefore believe you may see a decrease in sales productivity—call volume, face-to-face meetings, and demos. You decide to implement the weekly training and watch the risk for now by implementing controls and alerts to let you know if sales productivity statistics drop below average. Further, you define a mitigation strategy in case you see indications that the risk has materialized, such as allocating telesales resources to secure face-to-face meetings for account executives. You also schedule weekly online demos with customers and prospects to give the account executives more time to train on the new product line.

Now that you have done it once, set a risk response strategy now for addressing each of the potential risk areas as outlined above. This may involve identifying other means for generating revenue because the risk may be too high to operate within certain channels or markets. Make sure you have set the floor for the minimum sales pipeline required to meet the existing revenue targets and then align the KRIs. These KRIs should act as early warning signals that define the threshold at which a risk could occur.

Perform Additional Compliance Analysis and Set Controls

In addition to identifying and mitigating your risks, ensure you have factored in compliance requirements. Compliance defines the boundaries within which companies must operate when achieving their strategies.

Work on the Strategic Action Plan and Initiatives

The strategic initiatives help define the exact methodology (the roadmap) for achieving the various goals. The results of this planning may require revisiting the strategy.

Controls That Are Relevant for Sales

As a sales organization, define policies, procedures, and controls that must be in place to ensure that you can meet compliance requirements and translate compliance expectations into performance. Make sure that this applies not only at the main business process level but also to all sub-processes.

Salesforce Management

- Quota management—assignments
- Opportunity management—lead assignment, pipeline management and conversion
- Incentive management—rules and regulations
- Territory/Account management—account coverage and customer satisfaction
- Cost of Sale management—total expense tracking
- Compensation management

Order Entry and Processing

Revenue Recognition Rules, Policies and Procedures

Contracts Management

- Generating all sales contracts on approved company forms
- Ensuring that all required signatures are obtained
- Maintaining files of all sales transactions
- Deal Sheet completed for every transaction

Legal Counsel

- Counsel from Legal in reviewing, structuring, documenting and negotiating deals

Credit and Underwriting

Credit standards, customer credit checks, and other underwriting policies and procedures must be established and consistently applied. The credit department should prepare a "credit memo" detailing the underwriting analysis for each customer, to be transmitted to the contracts manager and filed with the related transactional documents.

Pricing

In transactions defined by the revenue recognition rules as "multiple element arrangements," historical pricing information must be collected for the purpose of establishing vendor specific objective evidence (VSOE). When more than one item is sold in a transaction, the rules use VSOE to determine the fair value of each item. This requires the following:

- A database of the current and past prices charged for each product and service sold by the company
- A review of the pricing of all transactions to ensure consistency and flag exceptions
- Software. A necessary component of the internal controls. A general order and billing software solution should be able to maintain the pricing databases described above and determine revenues to be recognized from specific transactions
- Warranty compliance

Strategic Planning for Sales

The steps to working through strategic planning go something like this:

- Develop the roadmap (sequence of actions) for achieving Sales' piece of the strategic plan. Include performance, risk, and compliance (control activities, policies and procedures) in the roadmap

- For each initiative, define critical success and failure factors for all initiatives. Critical success factors might include effective sales training for the new product. Failure factors might be any bumps along the way in an initiative's roadmap that could derail the initiative. These "failure factors" can then be translated into metrics that serve as an early warning system so that the initiative can be put back on track in time or alternatives can be found
- Develop different risk adjusted scenarios with contingency plans should risks to achieving plans materialize

Strategic plans should be risk-adjusted, with contingency plans for as many risk scenarios as you can reasonably imagine based on past experience and the current environment. You then want to come up with risk response plans that help you address how you will handle the risks if monitoring those risks provides an alert of risks materializing. These should be included in your contingency plans.

Cascade Accountability

Each KPI, KRI, and control and its target should be owned by some department or group.

The MBOs of the staff in those groups must reflect the KPIs, KRIs, and controls you set. This sounds obvious, but frequently performance is measured at an individual level in a way that does not in fact relate directly to corporate goals and strategies. In fact in Sales, as quota carrying individuals, salespeople often do not have individual MBOs or if they do they are an insignificant part of their compensation. The challenge then becomes how you make the direct linkage between the KPIs and KRIs to a rep's probability of making their revenue number. You can do this leveraging a performance management system because salespeople respond to numbers and with a performance management framework you can demonstrate the direct linkages between their behaviors and actions to revenue. You can show them a model of the top performing rep and the magnitude of positive or negative trend implications. Reps can start to see at a granular level at what frequency and output they do each activity and its correlation to performance. This helps to build accountability and discipline into the sales force.

Further, for sales support functions, it also ensures they recognize their direct contribution to revenue, heightening the importance of their role and their ability to deliver accurate and timely information. As an example, if

Guaranteeing Accountability in Sales with Incentive Compensation Management

It goes without saying that compensation is the overriding decisive factor in influencing how salespersons do their jobs. As part of a complete sales performance management approach, sales incentive compensation management (ICM) is a critical component because it establishes the rewards for meeting and exceeding sales targets and for annual quotas as well as for ad hoc campaigns and promotions. This process entails defining, documenting, and allocating remuneration plans as well as associated rules and variances for internal and external sales personnel. The system must be flexible enough to allow rapid changes in compensation models driven by changing business conditions. The solution must be able to determine the full breadth of compensation components of individual sales reps as measured by commissions, bonuses, SPIFs, and draws, and perform what-if analysis to help sales management evaluate alternatives. It should also be possible to manage noncash rewards, such as merchandise, travel, and recognitions like plaques, which also form a key part of the incentive that drives salespeople's behavior.

As we have articulated throughout the book, performance must be looked at in the context of risk and compliance, and ICM solutions also add value in ensuring auditability and traceability of compensation plans. Many ICM solutions also tie directly to territory and quota management systems, allowing for automatic territory and quota allocation, both of which we discuss further in the next section of this chapter.

on-time delivery of the new compensation model at the annual sales kick-off is critical, make sure the people on the team benefit from putting in all those nights and weekends to make the deadline. If their individual goals do not relate to on-time delivery, they will not have the incentive to work hard to make the date.

Plan and Execute

In the plan and execute phase, you link your financial and operational planning to your strategic goals and objectives. You need to be able to answer questions like:

- How are we going to structure the salesforce?
- How many sales reps do I need to meet capacity?
- What is the optimal sales territory configuration?
- What is the quota capacity of an individual rep?

- What enablement do I need to provide in the form of training and education to certify the reps on our solution offering?

This exercise should not be in a silo—in fact, quite the opposite. Sales organizations should leverage the wider organization of supporting functions (Marketing, Service, Presales, Telesales, Support, and Contracts).

Depending on your sales model, the complexities with external partners can be small or significant. For example, if you sell your products via indirect channels, you have an extra layer of complexity in terms of understanding your channel resources, how they assign revenue, and their go to market model. Specifically, how do you ensure they are effectively representing your brand and offering in the market in a manner that is consistent with your corporate policies and guidelines?

Align Corporate Budget to Sales Budget and Link Corporate and Sales Initiatives

The budgeting process takes each of the outcomes or actions from the planning process and aligns revenues and expenses against them. Take each of the steps in the sales initiatives you've defined and put in revenues and expenses for them.

To create risk-adjusted budgets, incorporate the range of possible revenues and costs of each action into the budget at the appropriate organizational level. In a traditional sales budget, you list the individual line items (sales costs including travel costs, training costs, human capital costs, and IT systems costs as well as the high-level revenue you expect to deliver) in each row with the actuals, budgeted amounts, forecast, and actual/budget comparisons and forecast versus budget comparisons going across in columns. In a risk-adjusted sales budget, for every decision to allocate revenue to one line item versus another (like hiring more salespeople while reducing the travel budget for the group), you determine the impact and probability of the highest priority sales risks (not having enough salespeople to visit customers to sell the product that is about to be released) on those individual line items and use this to set a range of expected budget and forecasted values instead of fixed values. In this case, if the risk materializes and you suddenly have customer demand you cannot meet on your existing budget, you need a contingency plan that shows the performance and risk implications (for example, not having enough trained reps three months from now for the next new product rollout) if we removed the budget from hiring more salespeople and had to put it into getting salespeople on planes quickly.

Align Budget to Sales Operational Plans

As part of the planning process, you need not only a tight linkage to the financial plan but also to the company's operational plan. The operational planning process links the budget to operational factors. Plan each step of each initiative in terms of what will be required in terms of technology, time, and resources. Consider what risks you have in each area of the operational plan. The operational plan under this definition means looking beyond your immediate sales operational plan and working closely with other functions tightly aligned to customers. The best two examples of front office functions that need to link their operational plans with sales are marketing and service. Close coordination of marketing and services operational plans with sales plans is vital to ensuring a closed loop between corporate goals and objectives and meeting the demand of your customers and the market.

Sales effectiveness is directly tied to the implications of Marketing's plans and execution and vice versa. Nonetheless, they make plans independently. For example, suppose the Marketing team discovered in a recent market research study a new target market for an underperforming product. The Marketing organization decides to enter this new market as the best strategy for revitalizing the underperforming product. The Marketing organization reallocates a portion of its budget and operational resources to execute campaigns to this new target audience. Neither the Sales nor Service organizations are aware of this new opportunity and have not allocated budget for additional hiring and training of resources to cover the demand that Marketing will generate. Marketing activities generate a record high response rate on the campaigns but the leads go cold because there was no link in the operational plan to field readiness.

There are several kinds of sales planning. In a high-level sales plan, you enter sales targets at the level of territory, customer or customer group, product or product category, and time (monthly, quarterly, or annually). You should be able to aggregate information from the individual account or opportunity planning that your reps do as well as automatically allocate their targets to them.

Territory planning is the process of developing optimized sales territories through analysis of geographic markets and available opportunities. This is how you ensure two different reps can both make about the same quota while residing in completely different markets. You develop equivalent patches of opportunity through sizing and analysis of the territories. Territory planning capabilities allow sales managers to define territories

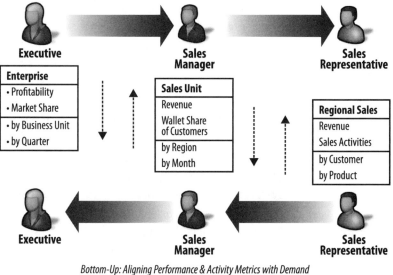

Figure 10-5. An Example of Sales Planning

based on size, revenue, geography, products, product lines, and strategic accounts. It's important to note that the dynamic nature of sales organizations requires that the territory structure have a validity period, which enables you to create territory hierarchies in the future as well as keep a history of territories for before and after analyses of territory assignment effectiveness. Sales managers should be able to easily assign sales reps for each territory as well as identify the prospects and products associated with each territory. You should be able to allocate employees permanently or for a specific time period. You should also be able to reallocate responsibilities if an employee has to fill in for another employee.

Quota planning and management is the process of ensuring that sales quotas are allocated fairly and align with corporate goals and objectives. What happens if you don't effectively manage quota allocation? You end up with missed opportunities. The quota setting process is essential to a successful execution plan. You need to be able to ensure that you mitigate risk exposure as part of the process. For example, let's say you develop a new plan. What is your risk response if you later uncover an over attainment scenario? How will you mitigate your risk to your margins because you have to pay the sales force more than expected?

Account planning enables account executives to plan revenue, volume, and trade spends by account. Reps need to be able to enter nonpromoted sales figures for an account, plan regular sales as well as regular discounts, plan account-related costs, include planned promotion volumes and costs, see the total volume forecast plus corresponding promotional and non-promotional costs, understand contribution margins, and adjust planned revenues where necessary

Opportunity planning enables detailed planning of important sales figures, particularly for long-running sales engagements. It allows you to analyze cumulated planning figures, providing an important basis for higher-level sales and production planning. The planning figures can be stored directly in the opportunity, facilitating detailed sales revenue planning for the coming weeks, months, quarters, or, if appropriate, years. Planning figures should also be created for the whole opportunity (for example, sales revenue, market share, and sales quantity) as well as for individual products (for example, sales revenue and number of pieces).

Channel planning is the process of defining how you will grow your revenues via your channels. This requires you to review your existing channels and determine if they are delivering. Further you need to consider whether or not your strategy has changed and therefore requires new channels. If, for example, you acquire a new product portfolio, how do you integrate these new products into an existing channel without creating channel conflict? Also are channels effectively communicating the brand and offering? What training do they need? What are the most effective pricing programs and incentives you can offer?

Headcount and forecast planning is a process that includes Sales, HR, Finance and compensation teams, which addresses forecasting and planning annual headcount and total compensation. This process forecasts compensation expense based on the predicted number of staff each quarter within each department. It also accounts for key expenses such as fringe benefits and variable pay.

Sales education planning is the process of assessing the skills of your organization and developing a corresponding curriculum that addresses gaps in the product offerings and/or sales development skills. What are the training requirements and what are the risks associated with a rep not receiving complete training due to unexpected budget cuts?

Sales support planning encompasses developing the support models required for pre and post sales activities and securing the appropriate service level agreements from the supporting stakeholders. For example, how many customer references will you require as part of each sales cycle? What is the total number of references you anticipate you will need and who in the organization is going to cultivate and secure these references for you? Another might be how many product demonstrations you anticipate you will need to show to close the required number of deals to meet you revenue target. Do you have a service level agreement with pre sales to deliver those demos and do you have certainty that they will be effectively trained to deliver those demos? If they do not get the training, what is your risk response to ensure you are still able to provide customers with demos?

In a risk-adjusted operational plan, for every decision to allocate resources to one set of operational activities versus another, like visiting existing customers to harvest existing leads versus pursuing net new customers for leads, versus determining the impact and probability of the highest priority operational risks (like the risk of saturating your existing accounts) on those individual line items and use this to set a range of expected and forecasted values instead of fixed values. In this case, if the risk materializes, you would want a contingency plan in place that showed what the performance (increasing footprint of your existing accounts by 10%) and risk implications would be if we then removed the budget from pursuing the existing customer opportunities and had to put it into going after new opportunities.

Taking these factors into account, adjust your plans with a range of operational outcomes and probabilities rather than an absolute number based on the various contingencies.

Forecast Performance and Risks

Nothing strikes more dread in a salesperson's heart than not knowing if deals are going to close. At a managerial and executive level, this translates into poor forecast visibility and hence inaccuracy. This is borne out by Ventana Research's 2008 Sales Performance Management Research Benchmark, where forecasting and planning were ranked the highest by far of sales applications most important to an organization. At most companies, sales forecasting is a painful process that adds little value. First, it takes an inordinate amount of time, and for a sales forecast to be valuable, it can't be stale or the reaction to the forecast may be based on a reality that has already passed you by. Second, there is a lot of gaming of the system. No individual sales rep gets positive feedback for having a low forecast, but her over-optimistic forecast can translate into getting more management attention which gets the cavalry directed toward closing the deal, despite the fact that the deal may have no chance of closing. Finally, most aggregated sales forecasts do not systematically take into account the explicit risks of achieving the forecast, like the pricing pressure of competitors or a key destabilizing event in the customer's environment that would preclude a purchase.

In order to forecast accurately, companies need to leverage statistical projections of historical demand patterns. Forecasting can be very simple; for example, add three months of your current data to nine months of your budget data. It can also be much more sophisticated, as there are a large number of statistical forecasting techniques that can be applied that are appropriate to your industry, business model, and geography, which can take into account factors like seasonality and promotional lifts for example. The forecasting process also involves creating alternative scenarios by changing the underlying business assumptions to provide a "what if" capability. Companies also need to take into account the current opportunities and the context about the market dynamics. The challenge with the sales forecasting process from a technology perspective that makes it quite inaccurate is that forecasts need to be aggregated from varying levels of forecast detail (territories, accounts, opportunities) that may not be reconciled with each other, they often come in different units of measure (is the forecast based on number and type of products or individual products or overall account revenue or opportunity revenue?). These forecasts in turn have significant impact on the collaborative business processes in the organization as well. If the sales forecast is inaccurate, by definition the finance forecast, marketing forecast, and the product-level demand forecast are inaccurate as well, which can lead to dramatic inefficiencies like wasted campaign budget, excess inventory, and even poor guidance by the CFO to the Street on what the quarter is going to look like.

In manufacturing industries, sales & operations planning solutions that we discuss in Chapter 13 can bridge the gap between the supply and demand chains of your company, by allowing account executives the ability to create a bottom-up sales forecast by product (at SKU/model level detail) and customers, containing both—revenue and units. It is also possible to track historical sales forecast accuracy and correlate this with the actual outcomes to more prescriptively guide sales reps as to the specific steps they should take to achieve their forecast.

Try creating rolling, risk-adjusted forecasts of the budget (revenues and costs) and operational plan (including number, capacity, and cost of resources necessary to achieve the plan) so that you can see trends over a rolling time horizon for those risks whose probability, consequence, and/or resiliency change over time. That way if you have to make adjustments, you can see where you've been and the direction in which things are likely to go. Predictive analytical techniques with a rich library of forecasting and machine learning algorithms can be a particular powerful tool for building risk-adjusted forecasts by modeling the impact previous risks had on previous forecasts and then using that to automatically course correct forecasts over time.

Example: In a risk-adjusted Sales forecast, you create a four-quarter rolling forecast of expected revenue and associated budget forecast of T&E, training and demos and an associated range of expected sales productivity and revenue outputs that is dependent on the key risks in the environment. When the probability or impact of a risk changes, you adjust the financial or operational forecast costs or activities accordingly. Using predictive techniques, you can learn from the impact of previous risks on previous actual (the company adjusts the pricing model, what historically has been the significance of the impact of revenue performance) to predict the impact of your current risks on your current cost or activity forecasts.

Examine Repercussions for Execution Problems

In a down economy take another look at the sales forecast and training initiatives and reevaluate if all the products are feasible to sell given the shift in the market dynamics. Readjust your forecast higher for the products that have the highest probability of selling and realign initiatives to support the revenue generation of those product lines. Planning and execution must be based in strategy and be aligned to the strategies that have been set down. Market and internal conditions will always require that you constantly monitor your strategies and adjust them according to market changes.

Also, understand how to recover from execution problems that exist within your four walls and business network, not just macro issues. As an example, if IT delays the rollout of a new sales force automation system, of which is properly aligned with corporate strategy, what are its impacts on your Sales organization? These types of impacts can be massive so you must have cross-functional coordination across and with all the business units so there are no surprises.

Execute

The keys to excellence in sales execution are predictability and performance. The reality is while there are numerous sales productivity statistics that indicate the likelihood of a sales rep's performance, at the end of the day a sales rep is mostly measured on the degree of predictability in forecasting their revenue and their ability to meet their revenue targets. Predictability is as important as revenue attainment. If a sales rep cannot accurately forecast their revenue outcome, the Sales organization sees this as a liability to the company in that it leaves Finance staff to create a gut feel cost operating model. To minimize risk on the execution side, sales staff must document any changes in the forecast and be able to hit the targets they forecast. While budget/quota attainment is ideal, forecast attainment is essential.

Monitor and Analyze

In the monitor and analyze phase of the PM lifecycle, you monitor to understand what is happening in the business, analyze to understand why it is happening, and for those things not on track, adjust to improve the situation relative to your goals.

Monitor

It is important to distinguish the different categories of monitoring in evaluating business performance.

- Event monitoring looks for a single, discrete activity or exposure event, such as the detection of a single breach in discounting practices by a sales rep
- Trend monitoring is similar to event monitoring, but looks at events over time to determine patterns, for example, the number of times a sales rep violates the discount policy in a year
- Intelligence monitoring collects information from a variety of external sources that are of interest to the company and may indicate a risk exposure, such as monitoring your most significant competitor and the timing of their new product releases and their pricing practices

The presentation of information to be monitored is also crucial in order to facilitate decision-making. Dashboards bring together in one place all the relevant pieces of information in all the major domain areas of business that need to be monitored in role-based, contextual views to get a status at a glance. Sales dashboards are typically targeted at sales executives, district or regional managers, and individual sales reps might include:

- Pipeline dashboards
- Competitive dashboards
- Up-sell and cross-sell dashboards

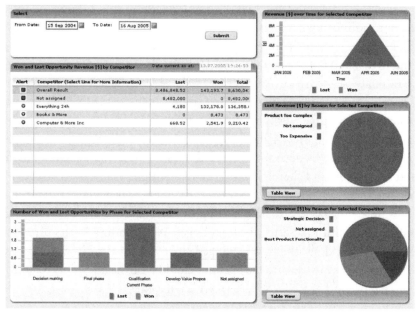

Figure 10-6. An Example of Competitive Win-Loss Dashboard

- Sales team productivity dashboards
- Customer satisfaction dashboards
- Lead conversion and coverage dashboards

The entire dashboard is designed with the same goal in mind: to systematically identify the best sales opportunities to pursue, providing fact-based decisions around resource allocation and time management. Do you really understand the key factors impacting your ability to win deals and their relative importance? By effectively monitoring these different sales-related variables via dashboards, you can analyze previously closed or lost deals, and make a better decision on how to execute current and similar deals.

As an example, you are able to quickly prioritize which opportunities to pursue based on your defined criteria. This in turn enables your sales team to be more efficient with their time through improved forecasting and focus on the deals with the most likelihood of converting to revenue.

No longer are opportunities subject to guesswork. Salespeople can understand immediately where they stand with each opportunity in the funnel, and forecasting becomes more precise. And, even when you don't win, scorecards facilitate the loss review process so you can better institutionalize learning and refine your success criteria moving forward.

Dashboards are effective ways of combining the events, trends, and intelligence monitoring patterns across all of the major facets of the business, including key business dimensions like customers, products, projects, and employees, and the related KPIs, KRIs, controls, and incidents and losses.

Evaluate performance using the KPIs you've set to identify progress made toward achievement of objectives and trends. Is the critical KPI of account penetration on target? Is it trending up or down and has the trend changed since the last time it was checked? If it has declined, why? For example, has rep coverage by account decreased because your competitor is hiring your top talent and therefore not leaving enough resources to effectively penetrate new accounts?

Evaluate initiatives that are failing or behind schedule. Is the critical KPI of organizational effectiveness at risk? Is it trending in the direction of declining and has the trend changed since the last time it was checked? What variables are causing the decline? Could it be the key initiative to roll out new product training to sales staff is delayed?

Evaluate risk. Examine KRIs to identify:

- Top risks. Are you having sales headcount and staffing issues (lost top performing sales reps or new reps are not yet ramped and therefore not fully productive)?
- Changes to risk levels. Is there an upswing in competitive risks? What types of deals show an increased loss rate and why?
- Proper assessment of risks. Are we effectively complying with SOX mandates and Vendor Specific Objective Evidence (VSOE) as part of our pricing and revenue recognition processes?
- Effectiveness of mitigation strategies. Are key quality controls effectively mitigating the risk of an incomplete or inaccurate forecast?

Evaluate internal controls. Report key control deficiencies, approvals, verifications, and reconciliations to mitigate risk. How good is the forecast accuracy? Are all the appropriate sales methodology activities being completed before an opportunity can advance to the next stage in the sales cycle? What alerts do we have in place to ensure that incomplete assessments by sales stage block a rep from advancing the opportunity in the pipeline?

Evaluate incidents and losses. What incidents or losses have occurred? If risks or losses have occurred, or external events are affecting the sales department (demo environment crashes or a natural disaster hits making it impossible to travel into that market), document this information, even if you haven't been tracking it in the system yet.

No matter how proactive you are, manual monitoring can be very inefficient. Automated monitoring can proactively identify out-of-tolerance conditions, highlighting key areas for analysis on under/over pre-defined tolerances associated with a KPI, KRI, or control, and then alert the responsible party. This should take into account forecasting, trending and modeling capabilities so that if a metric falls out of range of a trend or budget/plan, then the appropriate alert is raised, along with the workflow process to get the investigation under way.

Analyze

Assessing performance of your Sales organization logically falls into this portion of the PM lifecycle. The deeper you look at your Sales organization, the more you may want to know about why things aren't working and why. Analysis is a key step in which you not only look at where you are, but what is happening (or what has happened) and why. The techniques for analysis can range from highly manual and simple to fairly automated and complex in terms of the usage of statistical techniques.

Now you need to analyze and monitor your plan. You have to keep evaluating your organizational productivity, territory coverage, quota structure incentive plan, and sales training and education. You monitor to see if your sales plans are working.

Analyze performance. Look at the KPIs to identify progress made toward achievement of goals and objectives. For example, after analyzing the pipeline dashboard, you determine a downward trend. Analyzing further, you see this is due to your largest revenue-generating product not meeting its historical targets.

Analyze initiatives. Perform analysis on an initiative to understand why it is succeeding or failing. Say, for example, you find that the pipeline is declining for your largest revenue-generating product because unintended defects are impeding the progress on the new product release.

Analyze risk. Perform analysis on KRIs to understand why they are increasing or decreasing. Conduct a correlation analyses to identify the product deficiencies that most significantly increase risk before it reaches critical levels. Pinpoint what product bugs are inhibiting sales.

Analyze internal controls. Report key control deficiencies, approvals, verifications and reconciliations to mitigate risk. For example, you notice that a control to test for sales acceptance of marketing leads in the CRM system generates a lot of incidents and determine that the thresholds are set too low, creating a false positive. Concluding that your controls have lost their effectiveness due to a change in the lead scoring model, you reset your controls.

Analyze incidents and losses, examining the root causes and trends. You notice a significant uptick in contracts management compliance and determine that the root cause was a failure to follow the documented contracts management policy.

In all of these cases, analysis was being done with human intervention but this does not have to be the case. The volume and complexity of data in the enterprise today makes it increasingly difficult to mine through data and come to intelligent conclusions. Using data mining techniques, software can determine the most likely root causes and even suggest recommended actions. For example, a key risk indicator for account coverage is increasing. Without any manual intervention, the system does a series of correlations. When you highlight the KRI, a pop-up shows that the number one factor associated with the account coverage risk is a sudden decrease in sales coverage due to a competitive hiring attack.

Throughout the monitor and analyze phase, you constantly refine your strategy to get the best possible yield. You will be studying:

- Customer satisfaction levels
- References attainment
- Sales productivity—call volume, meetings, demos
- Pipeline by product and stage
- Revenue recognition
- Demand analysis
- Campaign and offer analysis
- Risk analysis and monitoring across sales processes
- Audit and assurance of sales compliance

Adjust

After monitoring and analyzing to know what has happened and why, for things that did not go accordingly to plan, it is time to set the business back on course by taking what you've learned and using that information to adjust the settings. Always consider the impact of your goals, risks, and compliance concerns on other business units.

Adjust KPIs. For KPIs trending in the wrong direction, it should be clear what actions to take to set things back on course. However, remember that KPIs are interlinked, and you must optimize your performance goals in the context of risk objectives and without violating your compliance objectives. For example, if only one sales region is the root cause for the poor revenue performance on the revenue KPI, you can assign more resources from other regions and increase marketing program funding. However, this can only be done if it does not increase the risk of not delivering in other regions.

Adjust initiatives. For initiatives that are not going as planned, rapidly take remedial action or cancel them. If it's clear that the initiative is not going to work, either make changes that can help save the project or cancel the project, if possible, so you can reallocate those resources. You observe that the sell through of a new product is failing and determine the root cause to be the sales incentives for the sales reps were not appealing enough. Restructure and sweeten the incentive to see if this sets the initiative back on target.

Adjust KRIs. For KRIs trending in the wrong direction, once you analyze the root causes, put the appropriate mitigating controls in place to stabilize them. However, remember that KRIs are interlinked, and you must optimize your risk goals in the context of performance objectives and without violating your compliance objectives. For example, a correlation analysis identifies product deficiencies that are most significantly increasing your revenue attainment risk before it reaches critical levels. You put a mitigating control in place to have the development team fix functionality issues and test prior to re-release. However, do this only if it does not decrease the likelihood of delivering on the goal of other new product releases and if it doesn't violate any compliance objectives, like having employees working longer than law allows them to.

Adjust controls. For controls violations, adjustment takes the form of remediation and certification. For example, after a contracts violation, you set up a remediation plan to create a more stringent training plan on your contract policies. This would include adding an online certification control for every sales rep, post training and before they can access the contracts management system.

Adjust after incidents and losses. For incidents and losses, the correct adjustments typically involve reexamining whether you are tracking the right risks and putting the appropriate controls in place to mitigate them. For example, after determining that the uptick in contracts violations is due to failure to follow appropriate procedures as outlined in the contracts management policy, put an automated risk monitoring process in place that alerts you to the first sign of increased contracts violation activity.

Model and Optimize

When you are creating a model of your operations, the goal is to be predictive—you will base your model on past and current performance, as a means to forecast future performance—in terms of creating a model of the organization's resources utilization.

Model

You now have a much better sense of territory coverage, quota structure and segmentation of accounts and you are able to run various "what-if" scenarios in order to forecast opportunities for the next few years. A sales plan ten years ago was a callsheet that looked at the number of dials and live phone conversations. Now the Sales organization is savvier in developing their account plans and opportunity plans. When a sales management executive asks for a sales forecast and a supporting territory plan, he or she expects a comprehensive view of the business that incorporates numerous factors such as target buyers, influencers, project scope, existing products, purchase price, competitive products, available spend, and timeframe to close. To fulfill those needs, your system has to help you provide an informed view of the customer and/or prospect. Further it needs to allow you to take like features and compare the propensity to buy based on certain factors so you can prioritize your territory penetration strategies.

To do so, you will be modeling Sales effectiveness and opportunity, leveraging several forms of models, including revenue, cost and profitability modeling, scenario modeling, and simulation modeling.

Revenue, Cost, and Profitability Modeling

Modeling the costs, revenue, and profitability implications of performance, risk, and compliance management activities and their drivers can be achieved at a very detailed level using activity-based costing (ABC) and associated methodologies. During this phase, when you are exploring data with a greater level of granularity than in any of the other phases, ABC is an extremely useful way of understanding all the costs of producing a sale or customer win. Say you have a sale. How much did you spend in order to get it? What was the total sales investment made to secure that order? How much activity did you undertake as a Sales organization to close that deal process? How much time and money did you absorb in T&E while closing that deal? What discounts were applied to the deal? Is your budget granular enough to answer these questions? ABC allows you to evaluate all the activities that go into acquiring and maintaining a customer, and it often reveals surprisingly jarring results. The customer, who appeared to be the company's biggest deal in sales history, was actually unprofitable to the company in that it taxed too many sales resources, making the overall cost to acquire too high.

Scenario Modeling

Another very valuable type of modeling for Sales organizations to leverage is scenario modeling, which can be applied to financial and operational modeling and which focuses on creating different business scenarios. Simple scenario modeling can include creating a base case and then high and low cases based on changes made to input variables, such as market growth rates or inflation rates. This technique is often used in modeling market and business opportunities and creating business plans. In this case, let's think about it in terms of modeling indirect channels for your new fiscal year.

By now you have a much better sense of your profitability associated with cost of sale for your direct selling model, and you are able to run various "what-if" scenarios. Now you want to model new opportunities to lower your cost of sale via indirect channels.

You want to model the implications of your selling some of your more expensive cost of sales portfolio products via indirect channels. You are now able to take historical trends from your indirect channel sales and develop what-if scenarios based on those assumptions to determine the potential outcomes of increasing your indirect channel. In your modeling, you find two competing channel partners and to avoid channel conflict, you want to isolate the better partner. You then model the performance of those two partners based on historical performance and recent sales plans you received from them which included their forecasted headcount plans and training and education budgets. You are now able to model the scenarios to understand the best channel to sell these products and the best partners within the channel to invest marketing program funds for lead generation.

Simulation Modeling

The third and equally valuable form of modeling is simulation modeling. Simulation modeling is a more-advanced modeling that includes Monte Carlo simulation, which supports creating a broad range of scenarios based on multiple iterations of input assumptions and combinations. With this technique, probabilities can be assigned to the various outcomes. These techniques allow the uncertainty associated with a given forecast to be estimated and to reduce risk by applying sensitivity analysis, correlation, and trend extrapolation. By simulating the effect of uncertainty, it becomes possible to answer questions such as, "How certain are you that sales certifications will result increase revenue?" Or, conversely, "What's the lowest rate of certification you can have while still having 100% certainty of achieving the revenue target?" Simulation also makes it possible to identify and rank the various contributors to overall uncertainty.

Optimize

The goal at this phase of the PM lifecycle is to determine the optimal way to achieve objectives by taking into account the entire context of the problem, including all relevant constraints and assessments (costs, benefits, risk, labor and time), as well as business strategies, objectives, risks, and compliance factors. Optimization can be done both through human evaluation as well as through advanced algorithmic techniques.

As part of your optimization exercise you will be evaluating the following areas:

- **Customer Profitability Optimization.** Pick the best set of operational actions to improve profitability with the customer
- **Customer Retention Optimization.** Pick the best set of operational actions to ensure customer retention based on evidence of historical successes
- **Opportunity Optimization (finding the "low hanging fruit").** Pick the best opportunities to target based on propensity to close
- **Account Targeting Optimization.** Pick the best accounts to target based on profitability and propensity to buy
- **Sales Risk Optimization.** Pick the most important actions to remediate key deal risks such as drop in customer satisfaction, drop in demand, sales retention issues—and readjust strategy as a result
- **Deal Optimization.** Pick the best price and associated deal parameters to optimize margin and reduce leakage

With all this insight, you can optimize sales incentives or territory and quota plans. If you want to change something in the lifecycle, you can be agile. You now have an integrated performance management plan. If you have only four to six weeks to hit your number, you can revise your plan, reforecast, and reallocate five salespeople to a big deal. In the PM lifecycle you have increased visibility, which in turn increases the probability of hitting your revenue targets at a lower margin.

Using a more sophisticated software-based optimization approach, you could input a goal of increasing overall sales profitability, and input all of the drivers to this goal mentioned earlier in the chapter, and have the software tell you exactly which customer to target, what products to sell them, and what revenue levels you would have to achieve at what cost of sales in order to make the initiative work and achieve the specific-level of profitability you inputted as a goal.

Deal Optimization

Pricing optimization, described in Chapter 11, uses analytical techniques to set optimal prices. This prevents unnecessary margin leakage by identifying significant attributes that define unique customer segments and then recommending the appropriate price for each segment based on overall business goals, such as market share growth or margin improvement. Pricing optimization techniques can also be applied at the deal level. Deal optimization allows a sales rep to predict and then set the optimal price a given customer might be willing to pay in the specific deal situation, improving his ability to meet margin targets and revenue goals. The individual rep can determine profit impact of different deal scenarios and view different what-if scenarios. And as we've seen throughout the book, there is a risk and compliance angle as well. Deal optimization can enforce company sales policies and management guidance in negotiations, which enables faster quote turnaround time via automated approvals.

Case Study: Performance Management in Action

Virtual Gates is a fictional cutting-edge computer manufacturer with retail outlets. This section provides an analysis of how the finance department's team at Virtual Gates closes its loop during the process of reducing the cost of sales and increasing revenue growth by focusing its limited resources on maximizing the value of the opportunities in its pipeline.

Setting the Context

Leah Broder, Chief Sales Officer at Virtual Gates, was asked by CEO Clint Hobbs to focus on maximizing the value of the opportunities in its pipeline while reducing the cost of sales. Leah must achieve this initiative such that VG's revenue grows by 3% while ensuring that her strategies and

Closed-Loop Selling

Individualized coaching for sales reps to optimize their performance while managing their risks

(Source: Birst, www.birst.com/closedloopselling)

Closed-loop selling is a process that continually improves and reinforces the sales effectiveness of an entire organization. Closed-loop selling constantly evaluates customer interactions and quickly identifies newly emerging market opportunities, sales practices, and product combinations that are producing exceptional results. These opportunities are then translated into a set of specific actions for each individual to maximize the value of their unique client base—actions which are then further assessed and refined by the system.

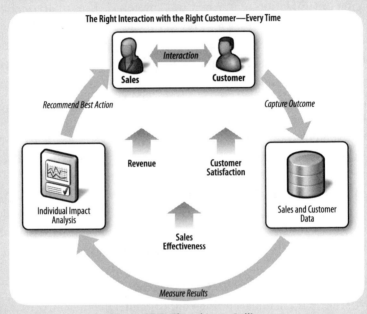

Figure 10-7. Closed Loop Selling
(Source: Birst, www.birst.com/closedloopselling)

To implement closed-loop selling, you need a system that can learn from the vast amount of sales data generated by your organization every day, and then use that information to drive optimal activity for each individual. A closed-loop selling solution provides three critical components:

- First is the efficient consolidation of customer and sales data. With this information channeled to one location from across the enterprise, the closed-loop selling system can continually measure individual and group sales performance and monitor the status of each customer relationship. By combining these capabilities, the system can measure the impact different sales strategies have on different customers in different situations

- Second is the creation of tailored strategies for each individual in the organization. For every individual, the system evaluates many different sales strategies and then selects those that are expected to generate the greatest overall business impact—those with the highest potential value and likelihood of success. The system determines this for each individual based upon the likely success and impact of each strategy for each individual based upon the success of that individual's peers—those professionals with similar levels of experience, product focus and client base

- Third is the delivery of specific recommendations that drive focused and productive action. For each individual in the organization, the system determines the specific interactions that will most drive success with each customer—and then delivers those specific recommendations to the field

Closed-loop selling enables your professionals in the field to quickly grow their business by focusing on the best interactions with the best customers. The outcomes of these high-value interactions are then captured in the sales and customer data, incorporated in the system's learning—and then replicated across the organization. Together these individual directions persistently align the entire organization's efforts toward your best new business opportunities and consistently develop deeper, more meaningful customer relationships.

plans align with Clint's larger objective, which requires all growth to be measured against Virtual Gates' net income and earnings per share growth, especially as compared with competitors Hypercell and Packingflash.

Sales, of course, are VG's make-or-break point. The quality and number of new products is irrelevant if Leah's team doesn't use every resource at its disposal to close the big deals.

At first, Leah was somewhat dismayed upon hearing Clint's request: VG is working in the midst of an economic meltdown, and sales have been anything but encouraging. However, when Clint told her about a corresponding initiative in Product Development, she had the same reaction as CFO Asha Madon. Not only is the new line of netbooks that Product Development is set to release extremely strong, but the market research conducted by CMO Samantha Curtin's team suggests that no matter how bad the market is, Leah won't have much trouble selling this product. According to Samantha's research, 21.5 million netbooks will be sold in 2009 (a growth of 189% from 2008), and those numbers are projected to increase to 50 million by 2012. Suddenly, Leah's concern shifted from whether she could sell the netbook to the percentage of market share she'll be able to capture with it!

To accomplish her ends, Leah's team will first establish their current baseline values and targets, and then concentrate on optimizing close rates, cross-sell and up-sell, and forecast accuracy.

Understand the Collaborative Impact

Leah's team is on the front line of customer-facing business processes. Salespeople engage with existing customers, convert leads into new customers, and, of course, sell products and services to existing customers, thus impacting Finance, Production, Inventory, and Service. In other words, sales activities span VG's entire value chain, and play key roles in business processes such as summary of sales, rolling sales, forecast down to sales level, pipeline coverage, and actual sales against quota.

Because Leah's decisions affect not only Sales and related VG departments but beyond company boundaries, she must carefully consider the impact on her partners when choosing a course of action. A choice that is reasonable for Sales may have a negative impact on them. For instance, Marketing, Product Development, and Service all need specific demographics about VG's customers, especially those pertaining to their age and income brackets and the products that they buy. These departments also need to know which customers that are willing to provide feedback about product functionality and suggestions to improve customer service. Since all of this data informs critical decisions in every department, and each department's decisions impact those of their partners, it's imperative that Leah remains in tight collaboration with them all. When she chooses well, her team can improve customer relationships and, ultimately, increase the company's profitability.

Establish KPIs and KRIs

Until Leah selects a set of *relevant* KPIs and KRIs, neither her department nor VG itself can accurately measure progress on their initiatives. Not only must she and her team identify the top KPIs and KRIs, but they've also got to grasp the chief risks to which they may be exposed as well as the main interfaces between their partners and their processes. They need to know the drivers behind their KPIs and KRIs, the relationships between them, and the leading indicators of performance.

Close rates, cross-sell and up-sell, and forecast accuracy are the principle metrics to watch as Leah and her team maximize the value of the opportunities in the sales pipeline and reduce their overall costs, as we said. Leah must make her partners aware of the implications. For instance, limiting headcount in Sales (as per the directive from HR) and increasing sales quota for each remaining sales rep will generate the funds that both HR and Finance have called for, as well as free up capital so that marketing can expand its campaigns to launch the new netbook. As the sales of VG's netbook is forecasted to take off, the increase in the sales quota will create even more of an incentive for Leah's team to help exceed the company's overall goals.

Establish the BI Foundation

Before KPIs and KRIs can be established, Leah and her team must harvest the data from which those KPIs and KRIs are created. This data comes from a variety of source systems, including CRM and ERP systems as well as territory management, sales methodology, and contact management systems. Information from these systems must be consolidated as Leah and her team execute sales-related business processes.

Their raw data must also be transformed and loaded into a data mart or data warehouse. This master data becomes the single version of the truth by which Sales successfully navigates toward its goals of reducing sales costs and improving the department's profit margin. Data from other systems such as PLM, SCM, and FI must be available and integrated into the team's semantic layer, too, if it is to stay abreast of how their activities affect key stakeholders.

Strategize and Prioritize

Leah's initiative to reduce the cost of her department is coinciding with multiple initiatives across VG's entire enterprise, each of them precipitated by Finance's need to free up working capital for the immediate term while leaving room for longer-term investments for growth. For instance, while HR has initiated a drive to reduce the staff by 15% in most departments, Marketing is attempting to increase the velocity with which its leads are converted to revenue, Service is reducing support to nonstrategic customers and enhancing support for top customers, and Product Development is sunsetting as many low-profit products as it can while introducing its new netbook.

Each of these campaigns has considerable bearing on the decisions Leah must make at this stage, since taking advantage of one can expose her to risk from another. She will have fewer team members working in the field, for example, and fewer reps at the call center to handle any difficulties with customer concerns related to existing products, but she expects these shortcomings to be countered by increased sales of the new netbook, as well as by the enhanced forecasting technology and training for her remaining staff, enabled with the funds freed up when she lowered her headcount.

These and other factors have been accounted for in consultation with her colleagues in each department, and now she is ready to create a scorecard by which to monitor the development of her strategy and plan. In addition to the aforementioned risks, Leah must include KRIs on the card that establishes inflexible thresholds: once crossed, contingency measures will be automatically activated. If the rolling four-quarter pipeline of opportunities drops by 25%, for example, Leah's team will respond by carving out a separate initiative for building long-term pipeline, such as working with Marketing to introduce a new upsell and cross-sell strategy for the new netbook. Again, her decisions must be aligned with VG's overall strategy. She does not want any of her salespeople to violate revenue recognition rules by pushing sales deals with promises about product capabilities that aren't yet available.

Plan and Execute

Leah's plan includes allocating funds to obtain the resources she needs to achieve her aims, including assets such as vehicles, Blackberries, headsets, laptops, desks, chairs, facilities, travel expenses, and, of course, her salespeople. She may also reassign more team members to a specific account as a means of driving more aggressive cross-sell/up-sell and close rates. That she is activating these processes with a fixed budget, however, exposes her to the risk that the execution and outputs of other initiatives may suffer. Leah may have to live with risks associated with other initiatives outside of her control and accept the remediation plan, which is not to do anything at all. If at a certain point Leah sees that any part of her plan isn't working, she must compare her planned, actual, and forecast results and then either recalculate or reallocate her resources, perhaps to a different initiative that will make up for the shortfall.

Monitor and Analyze

Once Leah and her team begin to execute their plan, they've got to record key activities such as account management, opportunity management, and quotation and order management in their CRM sales module, and then monitor and analyze the incoming results to confirm that Leah's team is hitting targets for cross-sell/upsell and close rates. Correlating the forecasted revenue to her KPIs is absolutely critical. By incorporating her risks into the equation, Leah can generate a risk-adjusted forecast that conveys the probability that her team will perform within the range of uncertainty created by the risks.

At the first sign that any of her activities are off target, Leah must find out why. Was her understanding of the relationship between cross-sell/upsell, close rates, and revenue growth incorrect? Are the cross-sell/upsell and close rates increasing at a lower rate than the costs accrued by her team's activities, leading to higher revenues but lower profitability? Does the customer size impact her teams' cross-sell/upsell opportunities or success rates? Do KRIs for pipeline percentage indicate that reps are being too aggressive? Or is the number of revenue recognition violations for this initiative increasing as salespeople step up their efforts? No matter what the results, Leah's solution must be aligned with all other departments.

Model and Optimize

To be certain that her understanding of her activities is accurate, Leah needs a detailed operational model. For example, a modeling exercise could reveal that while her campaign budget seemed appropriate, it would also show that her team was already overcommitted to the extent that her processes were unable to free up the capacity to focus on more profitable accounts and she can work hand in hand with marketing to get a dedicated resource to help execute the campaign to reduce risk of overextending her team and impacting sales profits.

With such a model, too, Leah can modify key assumptions such as the headcount devoted to her initiative and remove constraints such as the level at which the pipeline is maintained. She can also identify which customers are the lowest cost to serve or locate the range of incentive compensation her reps are receiving in different regions. Finally, after simulating various "what-if" scenarios to confirm that her strategy and resources are sound, Leah can deploy a variety of optimization techniques to achieve her goals. For instance, it may be that the best way to achieve predictable, profitable revenue growth is to take the risk of emptying out the rolling four-quarter pipeline after observing the revenue and pipeline forecasts.

Closing the Loop in an Integrated System

Leah's team has the technology to handle the circumstances described thus far. And yet that technology is in constant evolution. Before long, closed-loop systems will enable most departments to align their execution and strategy with remarkable accuracy. Once Leah can build a strategy management process that captures goals, initiatives, and metrics that she can link to her driver-based financial and operational planning process, as well as to her monitoring and analysis, modeling and optimization, and risk and control processes, a new set of circumstances will arise. Most importantly, she and her team can push the preferred activities through to their transactional processes via their goals, initiatives, plans, and risks and controls.

Leah is among the many executives to celebrate the recent availability of these very capabilities to Sales departments today. With it, she can merge her performance management and transactive capabilities for use in processes such as real-time sales force management whereby her team can enter goals such as increasing profitable revenue growth and receive a suggested course of action. To generate its recommendations, the system combines historical analytical data with contextual data from current interactions with one or more sales reps (where reps are working on four or five opportunities at once). What is more, with repeated iterations, the system's ability to accurately recommend specific actions increases. As such, the strategy to increase profitable revenue growth, the initiative to reduce sales costs, and the specific actions of the sales reps are integrated so that both efficiency—doing things right—and effectiveness—doing the right things—are substantially increased.

Aligning the Workforce

Before Leah's work is done, she must accomplish one more objective, connecting all of the previously mentioned activities with the compensation her team members receive for their efforts. There is simply no better way to reinforce desired behaviors. In fact, every department will increase their labors the moment they understand that their bonuses are linked to the speed and efficiency with which Sales attains its objectives. The lesson? Success for her collaborators is success for Leah. When CEO Clint Hobbs takes her report stating that she has attained a 5% growth in sales' overall profit with a reduced sales team as measured by Virtual Gates' net income and earnings per share growth, including a 20% increase in netbook market share capture (leaving Hypercell and Packingflash stumbling in the shadows), she can rest assured that he will replace that report with a nice bonus check.

Action Items

Performance management is a journey not a destination. It begins with steps toward monitoring sales performance, moving from ad-hoc to structured sales activities, and stepping into an integrated metrics program and finally with the ability to effectively implement predictive sales planning. The journey is iterative and dynamic and can be applied to many aspects of your Sales organization. Ventana Research's framework for sales performance management best practices across people, process, technology, and information recommends the following.

People:

- Broaden sales performance management deployment to include executive management, finance, demand planning, supply planning and marketing
- Work with sales operations team to look at educational and maturing challenges in advancing processes
- Link all business units into sales performance management to understand the potential of people's contribution to goals

Technology:

- Look for software that can help span across the sales performance management needs while providing consistent data
- Consider supporting technologies that can help integrate data and also collaborate across organization
- Examine role-based applications that can adapt to user requirements and functions

Process:

- Use Sales performance management to align operations with operational performance objectives
- Conduct ongoing formal demand and sales forecast review meetings
- Set sales plans and targets to extend 18 months across business units and brands to help understand rolling forecast changes

Information:

- Match sales metrics with financial targets and business goals

- Integrate sales performance management with scorecards and dashboards that provide actual versus forecast
- Leverage operational metrics with plans
- Generate exception-based guidance to managers and planners
- Provide integration with external information

You can select any item in the checklist or set of best practices and begin applying it to your sales performance management challenges.

Chapter 11

Performance Management for Marketing

In a flat economy, Marketing departments are at risk of getting slashed disproportionately and to the detriment of future business growth. The problem is many Marketing executives lack the capability to demonstrate Marketing's return on investment. Marketing's inability to quantify its direct contribution to the bottom line largely comes from the way many organizations have historically operated—in silos, isolated from one another, so that, even with the advent of helpful technology, such as Customer Relationship Management (CRM) software, the useful information created and stored by these applications is underused and tends not to leave the independent silos it lives within. An essential ingredient to Marketing being able to quantify its value is access to these silos of information. Marketing can truly only develop meaningful insights about customers and create compelling offers for customers that drive revenue when they have a full view to a company's customer and prospect interaction. This means a company needs to recognize the strategic value of a Marketing organization and set it sights on collective information from Marketing bigger than just the latest promotion results or the details of the latest event sponsorship. A company that misunderstands the value of its Marketing department is as hobbled as a Marketing department that does not know the profiles of its best customers, and this ultimately impacts the ability to drive the bottom line.

The means for which Marketing is able to gather meaningful information on customers and prospects to formulate demand-driven plans that contribute to the bottom line has changed significantly with the advent of Internet and Web 2.0 technologies. The days of long lead times with snail mail direct marketing campaigns where you were lucky if you had the right mailing address are of the past. Today, marketing has become focused on collecting as much information about the purchasing habits of buyers and influencers as possible—the Web plays a central role in that collection activity. The marketing mix which used to be heavily weighted on brand advertising has shifted and the budgets are now heavily weighted to 1:1 preference marketing campaigns where the level of segmentation and targeting applied is a science, not an estimate.

Performance management provides a framework to manage this information and make decisions about cutting and expanding elements elegantly to understand the decision's impact and to invest appropriately to get the right outcome.

If the CEO wants to reduce the marketing budget, how does she arrive at the amount? How do you as a marketer quantify how each dollar cut translates into pipeline reduction? How do you ensure you are making meaningful cuts and not hitting an artery? Companies often put trade and promotions on steroids as a short-term fix to lift market share and sales. But heavy promotion often lowers profitability disproportionately because it tends to over-reward loyal consumers, offering a stimulus they don't necessarily need. It's better to invest these funds in targeted loyalty or relationship programs that build, rather than destroy equity and value.[1] You set and meet those targets by implementing performance management techniques.

In this chapter, we will show you how to measure the effectiveness of your marketing programs and align these efforts with measures that truly matter to the C-suite and which will result in continued optimized performance of your organization as a whole, and will ensure the continued health and support of the Marketing department, in particular.

---

[1] Mary Beth Kemp. "Can Marketing Deliver Growth in the Downturn?" Forrester Research, December 9, 2008.

History Lesson: How Has Your Company and Your World Changed in Marketing?

In this section, we explore the context in which the contemporary Marketing department operates. With stiff competition and shrinking consumer budgets, now more than ever, Marketing must be convincing that the products and services your organization offers are absolutely essential, and if the products and services you offer are commoditized, then you must differentiate on customer experience like never before.

How the World Has Changed

Historically, Marketing departments have always been intensely interested in the success of their campaigns. They have developed numerous methods for evaluating the success of individual campaigns but have not done a great job of looking at the relationship of marketing campaigns to the sales cycle (or in other words, relating each dollar of marketing spend to each new dollar of revenue).

Now CMOs are being asked to produce this information. As more companies become specialized in areas where they truly can differentiate themselves, more outside partners are joining the sales channel to complete the business process lifecycle. Marketing can no longer afford to evaluate only its internal campaigns; it must also now evaluate the effectiveness of channel partners in bringing about the desired results. CMOs are using performance management applications, especially to understand brand and category issues. Therefore, it is ever more critical that information is shared throughout the entire business lifecycle, which starts and ends with the customer.

How Technology Has Changed

The evolution of the Web is the single biggest change in marketing technology. Its effect on marketing practices is nothing short of revolutionary. In the past, a marketing plan could consist of sponsoring events, running a few media ads, and in the case of consumer products, purchasing more advantageous product placement, such as end-caps in supermarkets. Today, if you are sitting around a conference room discussing the results of a shopping-mall focus group meeting held months ago, you are going to miss something your competitors have learned already.

Marketers still pursue these tactics, but they are increasingly shifting more of their budgets to the Web. This requires a new approach for many organizations. Relearning conventional wisdom about four-color brochures and 30-second television ads (which many consumers simply "TiVo" through) and transferring these approaches to the Web entails a learning curve. The speed and efficacy of the Web can be intimidating, and its power to collect information can potentially be overwhelming for the marketer, and compromising for the consumer's private information, resulting in unpleasantness for both. Consumers are now able to visit numerous sites and instantly voice their opinion—and not always to the benefit of your campaign (witness the frenzy around the release of the iPhone). On the other hand, the ability to overcome the lag time inherent in other forms of media and respond almost instantaneously to market events is one of the extraordinary boons of Internet marketing, especially as we move into the Web 2.0 environment.

Where once you would perform market research annually, now it is a continuous process that is constantly updated. Every customer interaction is now an opportunity to do market research; a well-crafted research strategy will extract just a little bit more information out of the customer with each interaction. The more electronic that interaction is, the easier it is to do this. Where formerly one might have said, "I am targeting 18- to 24-year-olds," now you can say, "I want to reach 18 to 24 year-olds who are on Facebook, who have purchased music online from the following three venues in the past 6 weeks." The level of information that you can customize for your strategies has increased exponentially in just a few years. You can build a much richer profile of your target audience—and you should.

To summarize, it's a new world, and the only way marketers can get a handle on it is to get a grip on their information—the information they put out to the public, the information they receive from the public, and the information they share with their organization and its channel partners.

The Evolution of Performance Management for Marketing

The old adage about marketing and advertising is that "it can't be measured." When organizations accepted this, no one made any attempt to measure it. Emerging technologies have begun to punch holes in this theory. It started with the development of individual systems that encapsulated processes within marketing, such as campaign management, data mining, profitability, and lead management. The advent of marketing resource management (MRM) and customer relationship management (CRM) software has meant that it is now possible to stitch together the metrics from these disparate, siloed systems and begin to form a complete picture of the marketing process. A true closed-loop system would mesh performance management and governance, risk, and compliance (GRC) on top of an integrated execution system. We are very nearly there.

Why You Must Do This Now

The modern business network is a global and dynamic entity. Unfortunately, so is the economic downturn in which we find ourselves. Marketing departments are under pressure to reduce costs and increase ROI, and they will have to prove it across campaigns that need to be increasingly specific and targeted not only to local markets, but to individual customers in those markets, varying the approach based on demographics, language, the overall economy in each market, and individual purchasing habits. The level of information marketers must collect in order to deliver optimal results is unprecedented, and they have to do so across an increasingly large number of channel partners. Marketers are increasingly dependent upon these partners to achieve their objectives in local markets and to report back accurately the success of the campaigns. That means rapid development cycles and clean data, with standardized identifiers and codes, are essential.

The other major transformative force in the marketplace is, of course, the Internet. This has raised the buying public's and executives' expectations that everything should happen immediately. We now live in a world where bloggers can drive public opinion. Do you have the capability to react to their comments about your new product release, or a recall, in a matter of hours, consistently, across all of your information channels? Are you able to observe, analyze and craft a marketing strategy in response to a change in purchasing trends of your product, hours after a major announcement, rather than waiting to summarize it in a quarterly report? With Marketing under this kind of microscope, performance management has never been more necessary.

Many companies encounter missed opportunities for collaboration and optimization because other business units do not communicate well with Marketing. If new product development does not have clear view of customer behavior and profile, they will not be able to respond to Marketing's intelligence with any semblance of speed. If Marketing and Service are not able to collaborate effectively, and Marketing does not have a way of providing its analytical understanding of call center representative interactions, then a key opportunity to cross-sell products is lost.

In order to perform optimally, Marketing must capitalize on every interaction every customer has with the company, for any purpose. Whenever a customer interacts with your company, you should know what they've bought, who they are, when they last had a service event, and what their complaint history has been, whether you are in Sales, Service, or Marketing.

Performance management provides the framework for the necessary tradeoffs to optimize performance under difficult conditions. Consider the downturn the world economy is in. Most companies that don't use performance management techniques have turned to flat cost-cutting (reduce all discretionary spending by 10%, cut headcount by 10%, etc.) without understanding the end-to-end impact of such a move. With performance management techniques, we have a framework to make these decisions elegantly, to understand the decision's impact, and to iterate to get the right outcome.[2]

What Kind of Company Are You?

The fundamental operational approach of your company will determine how you approach marketing, and this can vary widely. Some companies are far more concerned with marketing than others. Companies that are focused on product and service leadership, or operational excellence, usually do not differentiate themselves by making huge investments in marketing. To some extent, their marketing serves to underscore the aspects of their product or service that does not "speak for itself."

On the other hand, companies that look to differentiate based on customer experience typically do invest a lot in marketing. If you are working for a company whose value is derived from assets or its supply chain, you will be treated very differently in the Marketing organization than if long-term customer relationships are the key to your success. So you should manage your expectations accordingly. You may not get all of the resources you want, because your company may take the position that it does not sink or swim on the strength of its marketing program.

---

[2] Mary Beth Kemp. *"Can Marketing Deliver Growth In The Downturn?"* Forrester Research, December 9, 2008.

Does This Sound Familiar?

- You have multiple disparate data sources and an inefficient infrastructure and data sources.

- You have siloed applications and cumbersome tools for garnering market research and evaluating the performance of your campaigns.

- You have complex, inconsistent processes that hobble your capability to react to market changes quickly and effectively.

- You have multiple marketing systems spread across several business units.

- Once you gain customer insight, it is too little, too late to do anything about it, for too few customers.

- The alignment between your organizational goals and marketing goals seems to be off.

- Your campaign cycles are slow—you're still talking about something your competitors or consumers seem to have left behind six months ago.

- You have mismanaged "moments of truth" and bungled an opportunity to rise to the occasion, incurring risk to your reputation.

- The customer experience is fragmented; some report being "extremely satisfied," yet are not buying anything; others are turning up in droves and finding supplies are not in stock; still others complain bitterly and do not seem to be getting timely resolutions.

- Your leads fall through the cracks; something is missing from your follow-through.

- There is poor visibility into and accountability for marketing practices.

The Business Process Angle

Marketing plays a role in many cross-functional business processes, as shown in Figure 11-1.

Because of business network transformation, the processes that once might have been isolated in Marketing are now linked to processes in other business units, and indeed, span business units. Where once Marketing might have received a lump-sum budget each year, now its budget is routinely appraised and must be connected with budgets for Sales and Service, and managed by the Finance department. The short cycle times required for product development, particularly in competitive fields such as consumer

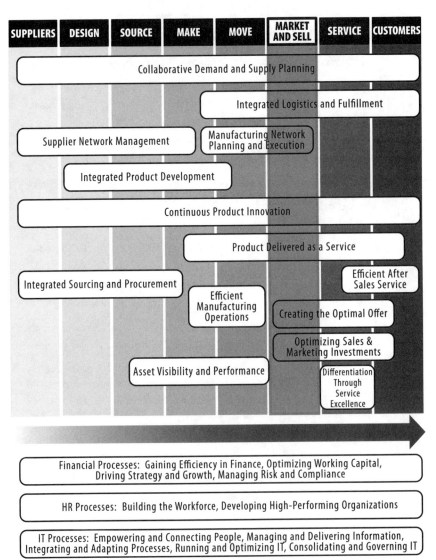

Figure 11-1. *The Integrated Business Processes That Touch Marketing*

electronics and software, means that Marketing is directly engaged with product development processes. Customer feedback and purchasing habits will increasingly be fed directly into the systems and processes of research and development, to make these cycle times even shorter and the products more competitive. In order to accomplish this, data standardization and compatibility will be paramount.

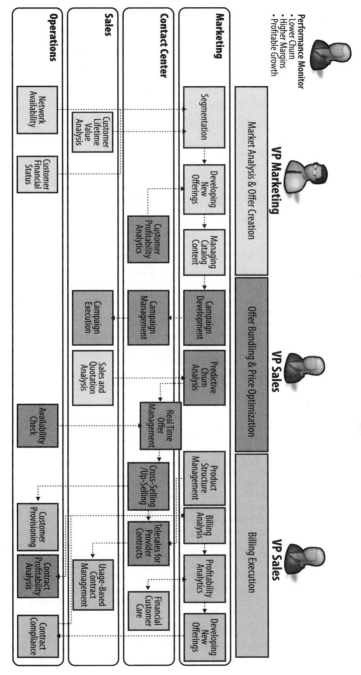

Figure 11-2. Creating the Optimal Offer

Marketing is engaged with creating the optimal offer for customers. This entails leveraging a true 360-degree view of the customer to create the optimal offer based on customer information and aligned with business goals. Marketing should maximize revenues and profits at every selling opportunity through leveraging advanced price and margin management. Marketing also determines the best recommendations to offer the customers in any channel they choose to contact the company.

Marketing's business process lifecycle includes processes such as prospecting, segmentation, and predictive modeling—these fall under the category of "database marketing," and reflect the elements necessary to develop good business intelligence (BI). You could think of this as the left or analytical side of the brain of the Marketing department. The right side of Marketing's brain is creative and covers advertising, branding, and marketing communications. These processes are more people-intensive and broadly fall into the category of "field work." Together, these processes inform one more category of work, which includes competitive intelligence, product marketing, and trade shows. Some companies are large enough

Table 11-1. Business Processes within Marketing

Segmentation & List Management	Multiple Data Source Access; High Speed Data Search; Preview Lists; Pre-Filtered Personalized Attribute Lists; Sampling and Splitting; Embedded Predictive Modeling; Personalized Filters; Quick Counts; Segment Deduplication; Suppression Filters; Target Group Optimization; Clustering; Data Mining; Decision Trees; ABC Analysis; List Mgmt—List Format Mapping; Duplicate Checks; Postal Validation; Data Cleansing; Data Enrichment; List Quality; Lead & Activity Imports
Campaign Management	Campaign Planning; Graphical Campaign Modeling; Campaign Optimization; Campaign Simulation; Marketing Calendar; Campaign-Specific Pricing; Multiwave Campaign Execution; Event-Triggered Campaign Execution; Real-Time Response Tracking; Cost/Financial Reporting; Personalized Emails; Bounce Handling; Call Lists; Campaign ROI; Interactive Scripting; Target Group Analysis; Campaign Analysis
Lead Management	Multiple Interaction Channels; Automated Qualification; Rule-Based Distribution; Lead Dispatching; Web-Based Lead Generation; Lead Partner Mgmt; Mass Generation; Response Recording; Lead Surveys; Automatic Generation of Follow-Up Activities; Lead Analysis
Real-Time Offer Management	Offer Portfolio Mgmt; Real-Time Event Detection & Recommendation; Interaction Assistance; Self-Learning & Optimization Mechanism; Offer Simulator; Data Mapping Tool; Configuration & Migration Tool; Offer Performance Analytics; Channel Performance Analytics

to split employees across these three areas; others have one or two people doing all of this.

It's important to understand the business processes that happen largely within Marketing (see Table 11-1) so that you can select some to optimize using the PM lifecycle, as described later in this chapter.

Key Roles in Marketing Performance Management

Although we will suggest that these key roles will be most intimately involved in asking the critical questions of performance management in marketing, it is worth emphasizing here that other roles in the organization need to be kept in the loop as well. Remember—we're not on a farm—no silos!

The Vice President of Marketing or Chief Marketing Officer

This role is principally concerned with optimizing marketing performance for competitive advantage. The CMO has oversight over the Marketing department and bears a responsibility to report directly to upper management. He or she makes many of the key budgeting decisions that will affect Marketing.

The key questions he or she will ask include bottom-line questions such as,

- "How is the marketing budget being consumed?"
- "What areas and programs are going to go over budget?"

The CMO will ask top-line, or revenue-related questions, such as:

- "How should I allocate the marketing budget to generate the best results?"
- "What areas have historically yielded the best results?"

The true test of the CMO will be his or her ability to synthesize the answers to these questions into a coherent marketing strategy.

The Marketing Director

The marketing director is concerned with gaining deep insights from the marketing strategy, and will be watching for indicators of the following bottom-line questions:

- Which customer segments are our most profitable and why?
- What is our most profitable acquisition method?
- Which trade shows that we have attended have generated the best ROI?

On the top line, the marketing director wants to know:

- How can we increase revenue through more effective cross-selling or up-selling?
- What can we do to increase customer satisfaction or loyalty?
- What types of promotions deliver the most revenue lift?

The Marketing Communications or Direct Marketing Manager

This role is interested in better managing customer acquisitions and the performance of campaigns. He or she is also concerned with the way that content is being used and displayed, getting materially involved in content and creative planning. He or she might ask bottom-line questions like:

- "Do purchased lists perform better than our in-house list, and if so, why?"
- "Is the sales organization picking up leads in a timely manner?"

On the top line, he or she will want to ask:

- "Which marketing campaigns generated the most qualified leads?"
- "Which programs or campaigns yielded the highest level of customer action (take rate)?"

The Marketing Operations Director

Another role that will become increasingly important as Marketing is linked more deeply to the overall business lifecycle is that of the marketing operations director, who is charged with ensuring that the links between marketing's operations and the overall organization's goals are solid and that the rest of the organization is supportive of Marketing's goals. Think of this role as an ambassador to the rest of the organization, whose sworn duty is to smooth the path for the business process.

KPIs That Matter for Your Success

It is not possible to create an exhaustive list of all the key performance indicators (KPIs) for marketing, as some vary extensively from industry to industry. Table 11-2 shows a sampling of metrics to consider.

As we mentioned earlier, customer-centricity and customer experience management (CEM) are rising trends that are increasing the centrality of Marketing's role in a company's overall performance. The most important metrics in CEM are the brand-experience dimensions at an operational

Table 11-2. Marketing Metrics

Strategic	Brand Awareness
Share of Wallet	Customer Lifetime Value (CLTV) (see sidebar)
Strategic	Net Promoter Score
Tactical	ROI—Marketing Spend: quite literally, how many dollars are you able to produce for every dollar spent on marketing?
	Analyst Ratings
	References
	Share of Voice—Reach and Tonality
Operational	Conversion Rates
	Lead Conversion—how many leads are accepted by sales and approached as prospects?
	Revenue generated by campaign
	New customer retention rate

level—where the rubber hits the road; the touch points where a company interfaces with the customer. These can be monitored daily and can be used quickly in decision-making to transform the customer experience so that the value of the customer is built up with each contact.

Brand experience dimensions should each have an owner assigned, so that when one of these dimensions is falling below customer expectations, there can be a fast analysis and reversal of the situation. This figure shows the metrics of greatest interest, or optimal ownership, by people at different levels of the organization's hierarchy.

These metrics all work best when there is a functioning feedback loop from customers, back through operations and up to strategic levels, and back down again.

Remember, metrics should not be thought of simply as a flat list. They constitute a network of relationships; many metrics are dependent on or predictive of other metrics, and there can be chain reactions between them. It's important to understand where in the value chain your metric exists. Here is an example: customer satisfaction predicts customer retention, customer retention predicts revenue, and customer revenue predicts profitability. So, research should include statistical analysis to study customer satisfaction, data mining to determine retention, revenue studies to analyze customer value, and profitability as measured by activity-based costing.

What's In It for Me?

Every organization likes to say that they wouldn't be here without the customer, and that is certainly true. But you must take steps to ensure

Customer Lifetime Value

Customer Lifetime Value (CLTV), also called Return on Relationship or RoR, is one of the single most important metrics in Marketing. As we have illustrated and will emphasize again, it is usually far less expensive, and more worthwhile, to work hard to retain the customers you have than to try to win new customers. Nevertheless, there are customers, even longtime customers, who may be costing you more than they earn you. Figuring out which is which is a major aspect of marketing performance management. CLTV, in its ideal state, represents exactly how much each customer is worth in monetary terms, and therefore exactly how much a marketing department should be willing to spend to acquire each customer. In reality it is considerably more nuanced, but, the more you measure, the less nuanced a metric becomes.

This value can be defined as the net present value of the profit that a customer will generate for you during the time he continues to buy your products.

It helps you understand the behavior of different groups of customers by providing you with:

- The profit they generate for you

- The impact of different costs (e.g. marketing costs) on their profitability

- The retention rate within each group

CLTV can be used as a basis for planning future marketing strategies and testing the effectiveness of existing ones.

Tracking the CLTV over time allows you to measure purchasing patterns, market changes, and most importantly, how well your company is performing.

It helps you estimate future retention rates, telling you how many customers will churn in each prediction period.

It will also provide you with the profit your customers are likely to generate in the future.

Based on this information, you can optimize your marketing and planning strategies.

the loyalty of customers and employees simultaneously, in order to truly capitalize on that loyalty and retain your top marketing staff and your customers. One of the best ways to make sure that the marketing staff stays motivated to serve the customer's needs is to link their compensation with customer incentive results. Stock options and profit-oriented pay are two traditional ways to link overall company performance to executive compensation, but in addition to this, the power of today's Marketing Resource Management (MRM) technology, fused with Web 2.0 marketing strategies, allows organizations to directly link compensation to the results of customer campaigns. The deeper challenge lies in personnel allocation.

One of the biggest marketing challenges organizations face today is matching their organizational structure—which not only includes compensation schemes, but the hierarchy of employees with different skill sets—to changes in customer behavior. For example, tracking customer access behavior across electronic and brick-and-mortar service channels, or across segments (such as age groups) has proven challenging for many organizations. Customer movements across segments are more dynamic than product changes in many vertical sectors. Consequently, the real challenge of segment-based resource allocation is the ability to alter resources dynamically as individual customers move among segments. Leading organizations are starting to design flexible delivery teams pulled from "communities of practice" (i.e., similar skill pools) as required.

You can think of customer experience management—the totality and efficacy of using your entire organization's body of interactions with the customer as a marketing tool—in terms of three axes. One axis is the customer's satisfaction (measured by a sense of value), the second is employee goals (measured by pay), and the third is the enterprise goal (measured by profit).

Many companies manage these goal axes completely separately—the enterprise sets profit goals, and this is managed by performance management systems. Customer relationship management is in the domain of Sales and Marketing, and is managed by CRM systems. These technologies, as well as the business processes and incentives they support, need to be much better aligned. Many compensation systems focus exclusively on financial considerations, ignoring staff and customer satisfaction. There is often no alignment between staff incentives and delivering customer value and a good experience. But with the presence of performance management, and a robust application to support it, a commission bonus could be based on customer experience, as well as sales, thus integrating customer experience fundamentally with employee and corporate goals.

Effective Collaboration

The Marketing department's role is to promote the overall organization to the public and drive sales. This demands that Marketing coordinate with nearly all the departments in the company.

Collaboration with Product Development

Marketing essentially bookends the product development process. Marketing feeds the product development process, so Marketing comes together with Product Development in two ways: at the very beginning, by feeding the marketing requirements to the product developers, and at the very end of the process, by taking the product to market once it's developed.

At the beginning of the product development process, the product developer asks the marketing manager about key trends in business or technology that apply to your field. You will be asked to provide the latest research on market trends so that they are not caught behind the curve. You will also need to have a good sense of what needs to be addressed right away and what can wait or is "nice to have." Questions you will need to be able to answer include:

- How big is the market?
- What is the revenue opportunity?

At this point, you may be asked to create a marketing requirements document (MRD) that shows the trends, specifies the relative size of the influence spheres for you and your competitors, and identifies revenue opportunities.

The biggest hazard to effective communication is the likelihood that product developers might see this as "their baby." No one wants to come in and tell someone that the baby he's been working on for ten months is "ugly"—not what the market needs. So language and diplomacy will come in handy here.

You need to prepare significant amounts of market research—customer, economic and competitive research—to reinforce your position because product developers have spent months compiling their reasons the new lever or widget is the greatest thing since sliced bread.

Collaboration with Finance

Everyone needs to play nice with Finance because they hold the purse strings of your campaigns. But there is also valuable information to be gained in your collaboration.

Finance is your friend when you are trying to determine the efficacy of your product strategy. When you are trying to set product ROI, Finance has the historical information of expenses and sales receipts. You need to be able to answer:

- What was the average cost of this product?

- What was the actual cost of sale?
- What was the fully loaded cost to the company once the product was on the market?
- What was the profitability of the product?
- What was the profitability of the product in a particular region for all 20 flavors?

You then feed the results of these dialogues into the next phase of product development and marketing strategy. You will use this information to develop pricing models, a go-to-market strategy, and sales training programs.

Collaborating with Sales

Marketing generates the sales training program in many organizations. A big part of this task consists of training the sales force on the latest products and on market trends. You need to be able to clearly understand and articulate the needs of different audiences to the sales force and educate them on the profile of different target audiences.

When you have large organizations as your clients, you must also instruct sales on account segmentation, determining how to segment products by client roles, geographies, and divisions, and then match sales strategies to those segments, to make sure Sales pursues the right people in the target organization. Your payoff, if your organization is truly structured to support performance management, is getting credit for the lead generation you are performing.

To be sure this go-to-market strategy is working, you will likely spend some time looking over the Sales department's shoulders. You will be studying the volume in the sales pipeline, constantly recalculating to determine whether the sales strategy is actually working. And you will be replenishing the sales pipeline by crafting offers that bring leads to Sales. To do this effectively you need a detailed view into sales pipeline data such as pipeline aging, average sales price, volume of units, promotional effectiveness/impact, and win/loss information to refine and strengthen competitive differentiation.

The opportunities for tension are legion here. Sales will be asking, "Why are you looking over my shoulder?" and "Why did you give me these lousy leads?" While there are many ways to obtain leads, many of them "lead" nowhere, especially if it involves a giveaway to an unqualified lead that has little or nothing to do with the product—just because someone accepted a candy bar at a trade show does not mean they need your uninterruptible power supply generator. That's why your targeted market research is so critical and so valued by Sales—when you get it right.

Collaboration with Service

For Marketing, Service typically represents a relatively untapped source for customer and prospect information. Service has a wealth of information and the valuable information that they carry is the difference between good and great marketing results. Service is a brand ambassador and therefore it is essential that Marketing make an investment in Service to ensure the department is fully versed on the company's value proposition and emulates its core values with their every customer interaction.

Service is a key ingredient in baking the next big marketing idea. Service can provide Marketing with qualitative and quantitative findings typically captured through customer surveys and even anecdotally from the notes section in the call center module in the CRM system. You feed the results into the next phase of product development and marketing strategy, and you use this customer information to improve your brand awareness and perception, increase overall customer satisfaction, refine your customer loyalty approach, and identify cross-sell and up sell opportunities to drive incremental revenue.

One of the best ways to conduct market research is to take advantage of service calls. What are people complaining about the most? What do they tell Service that they like, or would like to add to, the product? Product development will ask Service these questions, so you should too. It behooves you to meet frequently with Service and say, "Before the customer hangs up, please ask them these three market-trend questions."

Collaboration with Procurement

Procurement can effectively drive down the cost per lead and drive overall cost efficiencies throughout the Marketing organization. In Marketing, the number of vendors, contracts, and volume of invoices generated is many times that of any other department. Marketing is laden with program costs and these costs do not materialize in the same way they are communicated to the market, meaning you may execute one campaign but have hundreds of expenses associated with it. As a result, Marketing needs a business partner in Procurement to help manage the volume and complexity associated with vendor management. Simply take one activity within Marketing and think about the spending involved, such as a conference or a tradeshow. You start with the cost to sponsor the event, but you also need to think about all the logistics fees for optimizing your presence at the conference, such as booth exhibits, signage, audio visual equipment, video demonstrations, lead tracking machines, promotional giveaways, and staffing. Procurement and Marketing typically start their interaction on a project-by-project basis. We recommend a more strategic approach: communicating your goals to Procurement and having them drive cost efficiencies directly from your strategic plan. Nonetheless, when Procurement works on a project, Marketing often wants them to manage vendor selection. This starts with Procurement working closely with Marketing to spec out the requirements and the budget. From there Procurement puts out a request for proposal (RFP) to target vendors. Procurement manages the information gathering process, conducts all the background reviews, and handles the contract negotiations on price and terms once a vendor is selected. Procurement then typically stays involved to ensure vendor fulfillment on their stated products or services and that the work is performed under the guidelines of the defined service level agreement.

Collaboration with IT

IT and Marketing can be like two storm systems. While Marketing in the past consisted mainly of the creative department, today's Marketing departments house analysts whose mathematical prowess likely exceeds the training of most computer science departments. Marketing analysts need access to data so that they can slice and dice it and find the best way forward to make the right offer to the right customer and thereby get the business that will keep the company going.

You can expect IT to resent this relatively recent development in the Marketing arsenal. IT may even have a perception that business and marketing were relatively easy degrees to come by and that marketing people are not as intelligent as they are.

If there was ever room for improvement between the collaboration of two departments, it is here.

You need access to data and you need it now, and you need to impress that fact upon IT (nicely but firmly). You even need data to help analyze what data you need. So if the database folks say, "Put in your request and in a month we'll give you back the data file," and you set your pull criteria too narrow, you won't get the full-spectrum customer picture that you need to craft your strategy. IT needs to understand this, and to begin chipping away at any data silos that may have been sitting around, previously ignored.

Data quality for Marketing means data consistency. From an IT perspective, the data in various systems may be relatively clean, but Marketing needs to identify customers uniquely. You don't want to send separate offers to "John Public" and "John Q. Public" if that's really the same person.

Marketing needs to build a profile for each customer, and as they aggregate the data from various databases, it must be consistent.

Data dictionaries are often low on the priority for the IT department. It is your mission to raise that priority with IT so that you can build your BI foundation.

Collaborating with HR

HR is the conduit for providing good people with both creative and analytical skills to the Marketing organization. It's a little ironic that there is tension between Marketing and HR, because both suffer from the same criticism, which is that their work is not "measurable." But collaborate they must.

Both Sales and Marketing have tension with HR over recruiting. At many larger organizations, HR has a standard protocol for examining resumes electronically for key words that correlate with certain skill sets and job descriptions. But if this process is rote or out of date, HR will be circumvented by Sales and Marketing managers, who will write outlandishly inflated job descriptions so that HR's calculators return an appropriately competitive salary. Rather than game the system, it would be much more productive for both parties to change the game. That starts with aligning your goals.

Orchestrating the Business Network

Marketing's business network is massive. The study and execution of Marketing requires an in-depth understanding of the available market and your target audience at every step of the awareness and buying cycle. A very important aspect of the business network is the channel. Depending on your sales model, you may have enormous reliance on channels to ensure profitable revenue growth. The term marketing channel is often used interchangeably with "sales channel" or "distribution channel," referring to any individual or company used in making the company's products or services available to customers. The channel is an extension of your company; keep it in the forefront of your mind in all phases of marketing strategy development and execution. Specifically, you need to direct the promotional efforts at specific links or levels (distributor, wholesaler, retailer) in a channel of distribution. You need to ensure that different channels are trained on your value proposition and can represent your brand effectively.

Establishing Your BI Foundation in Marketing

A successful Marketing department relies heavily on accurate data from all points on the value chain. Marketing is a very analytically rich organization.

This includes, but is not limited to, customer-facing data, marketplace data, and supply chain data from upstream. It is this data mart, or repository of business data, from which you will build your models and analysis.

The Business Intelligence foundation should provide Marketing with:

- **Relevant visualizations.** BI provides visualizations like decision trees, which are very effective for visually depicting the appropriate segments in a campaign. Marketing also uses the funnel or waterfall diagram to depict the states of awareness, interest, consideration, close, and resell
- **Relevant event-capture and alerting.** The ability to gather information from event sources, such as RSS feeds from blogs and press announcements, and the ability to define alerts for critical events ("our key competitor launched a new product") and inform the right person in the Marketing organization to take action
- **A unified semantic layer, data integration and data quality across departmental and application silos.** BI allows the marketing users to bridge the silos when they do not have access to a single integrated transactional system, but instead have many point systems (such as a lead system, an events system, a list management system, a campaign system), or multiple CRM systems. Use BI to create common definitions and business rules of the key dimensions in marketing (how we define customers, channels, products, leads) and metrics and their relationships
- **Trusted, cleansed master data.** BI allows Marketing to create a protocol for how a customer is defined as well as standard definitions of the individual customers themselves ("AT&T" is the same customer as "ATT" and "AT and T") as well as key attributes, such as addresses
- **Structured and unstructured data.** BI handles structured and unstructured data such as social media. The perceptions of customers and information about organizations are discussed at length in blogs, podcasts, and message boards. For example, survey information from trade shows and customer preferences information is typically not entered into systems and is often stored separately in PDF or email. This valuable information can be captured in BI
- **Reports,** including:
  - Publication-quality reports such as the monthly campaign budget for an entire division

- Dashboards to visualize total budget and spend breakdown by category for marketing campaigns
- Queries such as the types of campaigns executed last year, the number of new leads generated, and spending on different types of campaigns

BI can help you disambiguate addresses, match and link customer information, assign a persistent ID so that it is represented consistently, and enrich data with demographic data and business statistics. This strong foundation of clean and rich data will inform the data models you need to measure and optimize performance.

Assessing Performance Management Maturity and Setting Your Course

Assessing the maturity of your performance management efforts in marketing requires reflection. In part, the question is deceptively simple: are you making the right offer to the right customer at the right time using the right channel? If you examine that question in more detail, the implications for the data behind it are varied and substantial (see "Establishing Your BI Foundation" earlier in this chapter for an idea of what you will need to answer any single piece of that question). However, you may want to examine particular aspects in a great deal more detail, including how well you are doing in the area of interactive marketing via new media. Forrester offers an interactive marketing maturity model in which you can classify your firm as a skeptic, experimenter, practitioner, or conductor, the most accomplished level that orchestrates online interactivity.

The PM Lifecycle for Marketing

Your business is dependent on customers. We have structured this performance management lifecycle for marketing to reflect that emphasis. This customer centricity affects all players in the marketing value chain. It also incorporates channel partners, with whom marketers must coordinate and plan and share information to an increasing degree as the business network expands.

It is important to be aware that the PM lifecycle is not necessarily linear, in which you complete one phase and move sequentially to the next. You might create a model and go directly back to the planning phase because until you plan and execute, there will be nothing to monitor. Each step of the process is iterative and informs the others. For instance, you would not be asking,

"Who are my most profitable customers?" if you had no customers, and you must have had a strategy for obtaining those customers at some point, or you would not have them. Each implementation of the PM lifecycle needs to be taken in the context of your business strategy, and can be entered at any point in the cycle, as long as each phase is eventually explored.

While marketing may appear to be a simple process where you conduct a situation assessment, develop assumptions, and from there set your strategy, objectives, tactics, metrics and budget, the reality is that a number of contextual issues must be factored in and considered throughout. For example, simply checking that you have set metrics is meaningless without a full view into the interdependencies and connection points throughout the organization for effectively tracking those metrics. Further, having a budget is not good enough. You need to understand the drivers of the budget and what moves the budget up or down. What will be your risk mitigation plan for budget fluctuations?

If you are not sure what areas to focus on, take a look at "The Business Process Angle," which lists both cross-functional business processes as well as business processes that occur largely within Marketing. Our advice is to start small and build on that success.

Strategize and Prioritize

When setting your strategy for marketing performance management, it's important to take into account the risks inherent in setting up a strategy, which could lead to a poorly executed marketing lifecycle. In this section, we provide a framework for evaluating and refining your Marketing performance management process step by step.

A word of caution: ensure you start by developing your strategic plan and put the development of your operational plan as a separate activity. It is critical that you first cement your key strategies based on sound quantitative and qualitative market and company data. All too often marketers jump to the tactics of the operational plan and are left later unable to defend why some programs are executed and how they are providing value toward the corporate initiatives.

Understand the Context

Review the corporate strategic goals, strategic plans, initiatives, and metrics that track progress against them and understand them. Contextualize them to the implications they have for Marketing and use this context to drive the PM lifecycle.

Before you go about setting your strategies for Marketing, ensure you have a common understanding of the definition of marketing and its purpose in the organization. Given how all-encompassing the discipline of marketing is, it runs the risk of being misunderstood and subject to false expectations of what Marketing should or should not deliver. Is Marketing expected to generate customer demand based on market insights or simply to sell whatever product or service has been developed? Ideally, it is a marriage of the two but often this connection is not made.

Take time to create a culture that understands and is receptive to Marketing. This means educating the wider organization on Marketing's role. By setting expectations up front of what Marketing is setting out to do, its role and the key intersection points and requirements of each participating organization, you are already halfway there. Every function needs to understand its role from a marketing perspective; for example, Service should provide feedback to Marketing and get help with how Marketing would answer relevant client questions. Make sure the appropriate mechanisms are put in place up front to capture the level of detailed information required and that there is a process for circulating this information real-time so that Marketing can adjust plans as needed.

Make sure you have a 360-degree view of your company and are clear on what the company's strengths are and its business drivers. Are you a product company that centers every investment on the product? Or are you a customer-focused company, in which everything centers on customer interaction and customer experience? It is critical that you understand the overall strengths of the organization and develop your strategy to capitalize on it, enhancing your strengths and not resisting them. In addition, are you clear on the strategic long-term direction of the company versus today's burning issues? Avoid the tendency to structure your entire marketing strategy around a short-term initiative; instead, develop a balanced strategy that addresses short- and long-term goals.

Finally, make sure you have looked beyond your organization's four walls. What is the macro market environment? Is an economic downturn affecting overall spending? Are there larger issues related to legislation or the environment that will inhibit your success, again, regardless of a well-formulated plan?

Develop and Set the Strategy

Crafting an effective marketing strategy uses particular techniques that we will outline next.

Conduct a Market Overview

What is the market? Is the market shrinking or growing? Where are you positioned within the market? What are the key market trends? Who are the key target audiences and what is the segment size of each? What are the markets that are most suitable for your organization's strengths? In setting your strategy, bring together a collective mix of both qualitative and quantitative data, a mix of science and art. This is most easily accomplished through a formal market research process that includes SWOT analyses and gap analysis.

Conduct Market Research

For key target segments, understand the size, growth and trends of the markets by geography and by industry. Further, find out the demographics and buying behaviors of those segments. This includes developing a detailed analysis of the market including products and product descriptions, packaging, pricing, and add-ons and distribution. One best practice we suggest is developing a customer advisory board (CAB), consisting of key, high-spend customers who directly engage with Marketing on a regular basis. From meetings with this group, you can begin to instruct Sales and Service on "buyer personas," which are detailed profiles of typical customers, so that they have a very good sense of what to expect from and ask for when they encounter these personas in the field.

Perform SWOT Analysis

Analyze your strengths, weaknesses, opportunities and threats (SWOT), both at a summary level as well as by individual target audience. In conducting your SWOT analysis, include both qualitative and quantitative information about you and your competition from various stakeholders and influencers, including customers, analysts, prospects, partners, and channels. Be sure to show clear connections between your strengths, opportunities, weaknesses and threats by showing how one is addressed or capitalized on by another. For example, a strength should not be that the company is headquartered in Norway unless you know that the prime geographic market for your product is Norway and that Norwegians prefer local vendors.

Perform Gap Analysis and Develop Assumptions

With an internal and external view of the market in hand, you now need to develop your gap analysis. This is a great opportunity to have a realistic discussion within Marketing and with the wider organization about what is truly feasible. Gap analysis is truth serum. You take all the information gathered so far, critically evaluate it, and expose your risks. It is important to maintain objectivity and to educate the wider team on the gaps because otherwise there will be a lack of understanding of why one strategy was selected over another. As an example, if you do not have the sales capacity to cover the sell through of a new product line, you run the risk of another manager running around showing everyone outrageous forecasted growth rates with no reality check on how much of that revenue can realistically be captured.

In terms of strategy setting, you might have a premier product line with excess inventory and should consider strategies for increasing demand and reducing overall inventory.

Further, throughout the strategy-setting process, identify risks. Assign a risk assessment and put risk mitigations in your planning process. As you try to quantify the likelihood of something happening (we can sell 30% more of product A), there are always unknowns (a competitor coming out with a like product at half the price). Place some focus on managing the uncertainty of those risks.

Risks include brand risks, in which you need to assess the overall risk of the product being perceived as available to everyone. An example may be severely discounting a product line that had been historically valued as high-end in the market. Do you dilute the overall brand value through overly aggressive discounting practices?

Compliance challenges might include complying with email spam and privacy laws, particularly for certain geographies in your communications strategy. It also might include how best to handle revenue recognition of certain discount trade promotions you want to offer in the market.

Set the Mission, Vision, and Values

Develop a statement of purpose that supports your corporate mission. This statement should have factored in our earlier points in this chapter of what type of company you are. What is the macro market climate? What is the company's appetite for marketing? What resources and requirements are needed from other business units to support your mission?

This often seems like a simple task but can be quite challenging if the company is in a state of flux and does not have clear alignment of overall corporate objectives. A perfect example is a company caught in a struggle between being focused on product innovation and being revenue driven.

In this type of organization, there is a divide between the part of the organization focusing on having the most new and innovative products in the market while another part of the organization focuses on market trends and needs, countering with questions like, "Who cares if we have the best widgets if they have no perceived value and therefore no market?"

Avoid the tendency to be tactical in the mission statement. Think big, and beyond the immediate term. Your mission statement should include the goals of the next fiscal year but lay the groundwork for 3- to 5-years. It should include the nature of the opportunity, Marketing's competencies, what Marketing will do to seize the opportunity (the how), and what the outcome will be (desired result). Be specific; otherwise, it will be seen as Marketing fluff with no real meaning or value.

Here are some specifics. The mission is the fundamental purpose of the entity, especially what it provides to customers and clients. For example, provide valuable market insights to all areas of the business to deliver products and services best oriented to market needs.

The core values are the attitude, behavior, and character of the organization. For example, act as the voice of the customer throughout the organization, putting individual biases aside and ensuring both qualitative and quantitative findings are provided in a consistent and accurate fashion. Define the level of detail Marketing will provide across target segments, for instance, buying behavior, spending trends, and individual preference data

The vision is a concise statement that defines the 3- to 5-year goals of the organization. Say, for example, by 2012, we improve our customer satisfaction rating by 15% and improve new customer acquisition by 10%.

With your market review and your mission statement in hand, you are ready to begin your goal and objective setting with the larger organization.

Define objectives (what you want to do). Examples of objectives include:

- Motivate, empower, and enable field sales
- Increase consideration through positioning, programs, and pricing strategies
- Evaluate, prioritize and communicate market requirements
- Guide overall business strategy

Then define strategy: how you will do it. For example, drive market leadership by positioning our offerings and translating customer and market insights into actionable marketing campaigns, relevant sales tools, and clear market requirements.

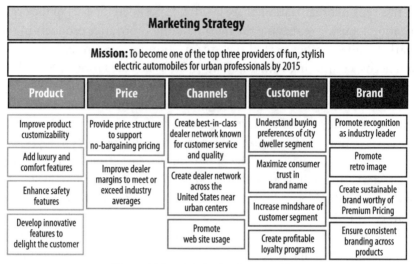

Figure 11-3. A Marketing Strategy Map

Consider using a strategy map to display the cause-and-effect relationships among the objectives that make up a strategy. A good strategy map tells a story of how value is created for the business.

Assign KPIs to Goals and Set the Right Targets

Detailed goals for your marketing objectives and strategies are essential to setting appropriate expectations and effectively managing your efforts. You cannot manage what you cannot measure. With that, have you developed agreed upon goals and targets related to the following areas with key stakeholders?

Brand Awareness

How well recognized is your brand? For example, do you say you want a soda or a Coke? Do you say I want a new pair of tennis shoes of a new pair of Nikes? What is your brand personality and attributes? How are the company's reputation and brand perceived in the marketplace? Most importantly, are you conducting aided and unaided brand studies and setting goals and setting targets for unaided brand awareness? Unaided brand awareness measures the percentage of respondents who, without prompting, indicate that they would consider your company when in the market for your category of offerings.

Here is an example of the value of tracking brand awareness when growing your business: your company has historically been associated with

---

Strategy Setting in an Economic Downturn— Consider Customer Retention

In a tight economy, something has got to give. If the marketing strategy is "all over the place," it will be cut indiscriminately. Your program must be perceived as proactive and dynamic. But before fanning out into the darkness with flashlights, searching for new customers, consider the value of the customers you already have. It takes much less time and money to draw increased share from customers who already understand and have embraced the brand than it does to increase market share. Customer retention and upselling are the name of the game as we progress forward into murky waters. Your strategy and priorities should reflect this.

Research indicates that marketers tend to overspend on traditional media and promotions and trade, but underemphasize direct sales, customer experience, and customer service.[3] When crafting your strategy, consider the effect of direct sales: take the example of Nike's customized sports shoes, which are created with direct customer input. This brings savvy sales experience into retail outlets throughout Nike's value chain.

Consider the customer experience: many companies cut customer service, considering it a cost center. But limiting interactions with live human beings is one of the surest ways to start corroding your customer base. Use customer interaction opportunities to cross- and upsell, and really listen to customer needs and complaints. The customer who feels he is not only taken care of but is actually involved in the crafting of future iterations of your product will become a brand advocate and spend more.

All of this should go into the research for and creation of the business case that drives your marketing strategy.

---

low cost and efficiency and you are now trying to enter a new high-end, premier market in which you will need to establish a new brand. You will need to design a brand awareness campaign to adjust perception and set targets and monitor them. The perception of your brand will be significant in determining the success of your new high-end offering. Regardless of how good the offering is from a quality perspective, if buyers perceive your brand as the low cost leader, they won't look to you for a higher price luxury purchase.

---

[3] Mary Beth Kemp. "Can Marketing Deliver Growth in the Downturn?" Forrester Research, December 9, 2008.

Customer Loyalty

What metrics do have in place to measure your company's ability to grow? A common management tool used is net promoter score (NPS). NPS is used to gauge the loyalty of a company's customer relationships. It serves as an alternative to traditional customer satisfaction research. NPS posits that the "likely to recommend" question is a better predictor of business growth compared to other customer loyalty questions (such as overall satisfaction or likely to purchase again). Whether you use NPS or not, put defined practices and metrics in place for understanding customer loyalty and the likelihood of your customers to recommend you to others, which are key indicators of your company's ability to grow.

Product Mix

What products will be marketed and in what capacity? Is marketing done only for new product introductions? Track the contribution of revenue by product from marketing campaigns. This is a leading indicator for product line performance and helps ensure there is not an imbalance in marketing investment that favors one product over another.

Target Audience Reach

Assess whether you are reaching the right people. High campaign response rates are no longer enough; you need to demonstrate interest of the defined target profile. What is the target number of customers to reach? Prospects? For example, perhaps you set a goal to increase net-new sales by 10%. Additionally, you set a goal to increase purchases coming from Finance versus IT by 10%. Target audience reach is a leading indicator of potential throughput to sales and customer growth.

Market Awareness Tracking

Market awareness tracking measures the impact of thought leadership, messaging, and positioning by tracking responses in the analyst community as well as press and media relative to your competition. What sort of analyst ratings are expected to be competitive as well as what targets are you setting for media mentions and share of voice?

Marketing Leads Generated

Marketing leads generated isolates and measures demand generation performance. It measures the number of sales-accepted leads generated through marketing campaigns and entered most typically into a CRM system. It indicates how well you are turning opportunity into the pipeline.

Marketing Contribution to Pipeline Revenue

How many leads does Marketing need to contribute to the pipeline to meet sales revenue objectives? Tracking Marketing's pipeline contribution provides a leading indicator of the ability to meet revenue targets.

Field Sales Enablement

Field sales enablement measures the value of market insights, marketing content, and sales support activities by capturing the value and impact of deliverables as assessed by key internal stakeholders. It indicates the possibility of increasing the market opportunity and winning more deals in the pipeline.

After considering all these elements, you align your strategies with meeting these goals.

Perform Additional Risk Analysis and Set KRIs

Now look again at risks to see what could keep you from meeting your goals. For each risk, decide what your risk appetite is. Can you afford to take that risk? What's the worst-case scenario? Does taking the risk have the potential to wipe out important projects or a high-flying reputation?

So what is your contingency plan if you are not meeting your objectives? How will you know when you are failing and what will be the procedure for remediation and reducing risks of problems happening again? What's the worst-case scenario? This needs to be examined for each strategy at the most granular levels by dissecting the processes associated with each key strategy and creating a risk assessment that applies weighted scores to each risk based on your judgment. A mechanism then needs to be put in place to monitor the risk and provide alerts to flag potential risks before they happen. Select a risk response for each risk. For example, if you reinvest the marketing programs budget into the introduction of a new product line, what are the implications for existing products? Can you quantify the impact and understand to what extent you can reduce the budget on existing products while maintaining a solid revenue stream?

Set a risk response strategy for addressing reduced spending on existing products. This may involve identifying other means for generating customer repurchase and upsell. Set the minimum pipeline required to meet

---

Examples of Risks for Marketing

Demand Risk. Fluctuations in supply and demand

Privacy Risk. Data security and privacy violations

Fraud Risk. Sampling, free goods and product trial/evaluation violations

Vendor Risk. Ensuring vendors adhere to guidelines on corporate brand use, messaging and positioning, and quality standards

Competitive Risk. Pricing offers, acquisitions, and new product introduction

Brand Risk. Loss of reputation in industry and/or buyer communities—negative press

Promotional Risk. Ensuring that you meet all legal obligations and offer commitments

Intellectual Property Risk. Copyright and trademark issues

---

existing product targets and then define KRIs. These KRIs should act as early warning signals that define the threshold at which a risk could occur.

Perform Additional Compliance Analysis and Set Controls

Analyze compliance requirements. Compliance defines the boundaries within which companies must operate while achieving their strategies. For example, you must observe customer privacy laws. While they can be limiting, the good news is that compliance requirements tend to be precise, so you will know if you are bumping up against trouble.

Define policies, procedures, and controls that must be in place to ensure that you can meet the compliance requirements. Make sure that this applies not only at the main business process level but to all subprocesses including and perhaps especially those related to partners. For example, what does the law require? Can software help you ensure that your incorporation of customer privacy is within the boundaries of the law? You could designate someone to supervise customer privacy. You could also designate someone to investigate available software solutions for improved controls that don't require as much manual monitoring.

Define controls that translate compliance expectations into performance expectations. For example, set up a system of alerts that notifies you whenever an apparent compliance violation has occurred. At the very least, your organization can then be seen as responsive to violations when they occur.

Controls That Are Relevant for Marketing

Market Spending. Key controls for monitoring marketing spend

Contracting. Background checks, SOW (statements of work), receipt of deliverables, competitive bids

Expense Reporting. Limits, approvals, receipts

Administrative Check Requests. Limits, authorizations, segregation of duties (SoD)

Gifts and Gratuities. Notification, limits and documentation

Privacy. Meet privacy and spam laws, incorporate appropriate messaging into privacy notices, establish controls for protection of data

Brand. Controls for monitoring and auditing the usage of the brand and ensuring it complies with brand identity standards

Competitive. Controls for tracking and monitoring competitive programs

Vendor management. Centralize vendor data, manage relationships, assess vendor risk—financial and operational, and ensure compliance with your policies and controls

---

Work on the Strategic Action Plan and Initiatives

The strategic initiatives help define the exact methodology (the roadmap) for achieving various goals. The results of this planning may require revisiting the strategy.

Marketing should have a strong and clear supporting role in the strategic plans of the organization. The strategy is here broken down into strategic initiatives. The steps to strategic planning go something like this:

- Develop the marketing plan for achieving Marketing's piece of the strategic plan. Include performance, risk, and compliance (control activities, policies and procedures) in the roadmap
- For each initiative, define critical success and failure factors. Critical success factors might be something like converting 75% of all marketing leads into qualified sales leads in a quarter. Failure factors might be any of the dominos along the way in that initiative's plan that could derail its on time delivery. These failure factors can then be translated into metrics that serve as an early warning system so that the initiative can be gotten back on track or alternatives found
- Develop different risk-adjusted scenarios with contingency plans at the ready, should risks to achieving plans occur

Strategic plans should be risk-adjusted, with contingency plans for as many risk scenarios as you can reasonably imagine based on past experience and the current environment. You then develop risk response plans that help you address how you will handle the risks if monitoring those risks provides an alert of the risks materializing. These should be included in your contingency plans.

Cascade Accountability

Each KPI, KRI, and control and its target or threshold should be owned by some department or group.

The MBOs of the staff in those groups must reflect the KPIs, KRIs, and controls you set. This sounds obvious, but frequently performance is measured at an individual level in a way that does not in fact relate directly to corporate goals and strategies. For example, if sales lead conversion is a primary goal, make sure that everyone involved can take proper credit for it and can see clearly how their contribution assists the overall corporate-level goals. It might be the kind of process that can be automated or enhanced by a system of awards and recognitions.

Plan and Execute

In the strategize and prioritize phase, you made the business case justification to upper management. Now it's time to start writing the market plans, essentially a list of things you need to do. You need to be able to answer questions like, "How are we going to build and execute?" and "What are the key milestones?" You will need to define your business network of partners, suppliers and influencers. Specifically, you will need to be able to answer questions such as which channel partners sell what, what sort of promotions do they run, and how performance is measured for each of the channels. What is the distribution method for the content you have developed?

If you are not a direct sales organization, you have an extra layer of complexity in terms of channel training. You must develop sales tools and scripts so that your channel partners can effectively pitch on your behalf.

One of the best ways to synthesize your market strategies into effective marketing plans is to use marketing resource management (MRM) software. MRM helps you conduct strategic planning and financial management of your campaigns; manage creative production cycles for marketing programs (such as working with advertising agencies); build a repository of marketing assets, content and collateral; support global brand management; and measure performance. The MRM tool can also help you improve that elusive marketing program ROI that management is always trying to grasp.

If you only want to improve accountability, the emphasis is in MRM is on financial management. If you need to manage a complex marketing process, the requirement becomes more robust and incorporates fulfillment as well as creative asset management and budgeting.

Using MRM, you can create a global marketing calendar and set objectives, populating the calendar with these objectives. You can align your marketing programs with strategy, and with corporate goals and objectives. You gain visibility into marketing programs and what you are spending on them, tracking and managing your costs in real time. You can strategically manage resources across marketing programs and make sure no one is stretched too thin or doing too little. You can also make financial decisions in real time, with real-time information—an increasingly significant requirement of marketing strategy. You can reallocate funds and resources to higher per-forming campaigns and channels or support new initiatives as well as limit your spending to an authorized set of vendors to hold down vendor costs.

Align Corporate Budget with Marketing Budget and Link Corporate and Marketing Initiatives

One of the major flaws of marketing planning and budgeting is the way that budgets are usually set by management using a top-down approach. Typically, managers set a budget at a percentage of the revenue they expect from the campaign that year—for example, an $800 million revenue generation goal results in an $80 million marketing budget.

Such an approach is arbitrary and does not consider the customer perspective. Marketing spend should be tied to the amount of growth desired, measured from the bottom up. The marketing budget should be based on finding the right drivers, focusing on the brand that is going to show the most growth, according to the Marketing department's research, not based on a top-down allocation that has no correlation with existing facts or growth potential. The moral: spend money where the key growth opportunities exist. Financial budgeting is useless if it is not tied to your operational drivers, and it is also useless if it is not tied to your strategy.

As you plan and execute, the pressure is on to tie spend and revenue to overall organizational goals, which provides even more impetus for measurement. If you cannot develop these links for some objectives, they are likely nonstrategic and may be cut. The more comprehensive your model, the easier it is to link changes in the budget to the strategy and to the value you're delivering.

CRM Marketing Plan Top Down Planning

Page1
[Save] [Exit] [Refresh]

Marketing Projects			
▼ M/1 001	Global Plan 2006	800.000.000,00	USD
M/1 001	Global Plan 2006	100.000.000,00	USD
▼ M/1 001-1	Direct Marketing	100.000.000,00	USD
M/1 001-1	Direct Marketing	15.000.000,00	USD
M/1 001-1-1	Retention Programs	10.000.000,00	USD
▼ M/1 001-1-2	Customer and Prospect Events	50.000.000,00	USD
M/1 001-1-2	Customer and Prospect Events	30.000.000,00	USD
C/1 001-45	Global customer council	20.000.000,00	USD
▼ M/1 001-1-3	New Customer Acquisition	25.000.000,00	USD
M/1 001-1-3	New Customer Acquisition	20.000.000,00	USD
▶ C/1 001-35	Winter new customer program	5.000.000,00	USD
▼ M/1 001-2	Brand and Advertising	300.000.000,00	USD
M/1 001-2	Brand and Advertising	75.000.000,00	USD
▼ M/1 001-2-1	Sponsoring	50.000.000,00	USD
M/1 001-2-1	Sponsoring	0,00	USD
C/1 001-1	US-Super Bowl	15.000.000,00	USD
C/1 001-2	Germany - World Cup	35.000.000,00	USD
		0,00	

Figure 11-4. A Marketing Budget with Major Categories of Expenses

Planning and financial management enables Marketing to improve planning and budgeting processes. For example, you can make better decisions about when to give more money to campaigns that drive growth or retain profitable customers. It also helps you manage financials, such as expected income and committed vs. actual income, and make real-time decisions on spending for different marketing programs (such as reallocations or whether or not to halt a campaign). This capability enables the Marketing organization to:

- Cut costs for programs that don't drive strong returns
- Reduce unnecessary spending to avoid "losing" funds (for example, save 1–10% of the total marketing budget by avoiding rash end-of-year spending)
- Reduce spending for programs that aren't aligned with corporate goals. MRM software can help you achieve 60–90% reduction of misaligned programs

The key metric you are pursuing is program ROI, which looks at revenue attributed to the program minus the costs of the program.[4]

---

[4] Kimberly Collis. "Use Marketing Resource Management During Economic Uncertainty to Cut Costs and Manage Resources," Garner Research, ID number G00155143. February 22, 2008.

Align Budget to Marketing Operational Plans

The operational planning process links the budget to operational factors. Plan each step of each initiative in terms of technology, time, and resources. Consider the risks for each area of the operational plan.

Marketing Calendaring

Different types of marketing campaigns in the marketing mix, such as consumer promotions, media campaigns, advertisements, and public relations activities, while managed by different organizational units, should be aligned with and strengthen each other.

Marketing calendaring applications are operational planning applications that provide an overview of all running and planned marketing activities shown by different dimensions, such as the planning timeframe, the activity type (product launch, customer retention, newsletter, and so on), the brand and product, and the customers.

Planning capabilities of marketing calendaring applications are highly interactive and allow you to create new marketing projects, determine time dependencies—with other marketing activities of the company, and reschedule any planned marketing activity.

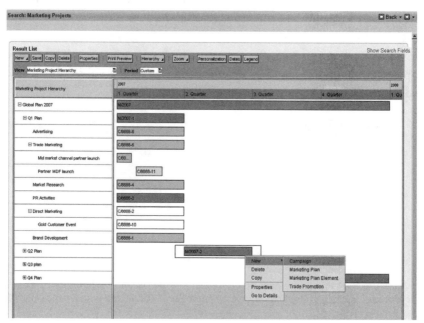

Figure 11-5. An Operational Marketing Calendaring Application Connecting Marketing Plans and Campaigns and Financial Outcomes

Campaign Planning

Campaign planning allows for allocation of nonfinancial resources across multiple planning dimensions along with the ability to tie these to the marketing budget, such as:

- Products: plan expected sales quota, product costs per unit, marketing costs, sales price, expected revenue, and expected profit
- Responses: activities, responses, leads, opportunities, marketing costs, expected revenue

Given the critical nature of how marketing campaigns evolve over different time periods and are status-dependent, plan "snapshots" to track plan changes over time are critical to assuring accurate campaign planning.

For example, in a risk-adjusted operational plan, for every decision to allocate resources to one set of operational activities versus another (to attempt to convert leads for one campaign for car radios versus another for boom boxes), you determine the impact and probability of the highest priority operational risks (like the possibility that the pipeline for boom boxes will be suboptimal) and use this to set a range of expected and forecasted values instead of fixed values. In this case, if the risk materializes, you need contingency plan that shows the performance (the goal to generate a 3X pipeline for car radios) and risk implications if we remove the budget from lead conversion activities for car radios and put it into lead conversion activities for boom boxes.

Taking these factors into account, adjust your plans with a range of operational outcomes and probabilities rather than an absolute number based on the various contingencies.

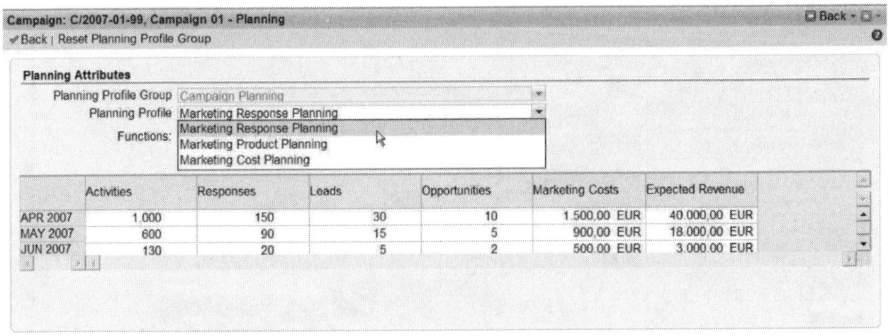

Figure 11-6. An Operational Response Planning Application Where Activities, Responses, Leads, and Opportunities Are Planned and Connected with Financial Results

Forecast Performance and Risks

Create rolling, risk-adjusted forecasts of the budget (revenues and program costs) and operational plan (including headcount and contract resources as well as discretionary program-related costs required to achieve the plan) so that you can see trends over a rolling time horizon for those risks whose probability, consequence, or resiliency change over time. That way if you have to make adjustments, you can see where you've been and the direction in which things are likely to go. Predictive analytic techniques can be a powerful tool for building risk-adjusted forecasts by modeling the impact previous risks had on previous forecasts.

From a financial perspective, marketing forecasting should support a detailed cost planning for current or planned marketing programs and a basis for improved accrual process of marketing expenses.

Suppose that you create a rolling forecast with a six- to twelve-month window and incorporate a range of resource and campaign related costs and an associated range of expected activity outputs such as response rates, lead attainment, and conversion to pipeline revenue that are dependent on key risks. When the probability or impact of a risk changes, you adjust the financial or operational forecast costs or activities accordingly. Using predictive techniques, you can learn from the impact of previous risks on previous actuals (the shortfall of leads attained with a 10, 20, or 30% budget reduction) to predict the impact of your current risks on your current cost or activity forecasts.

Examine Repercussions for Execution Problems

In a tight economy, another look is in order before beginning to execute your plan. Planning and execution must be based in strategy and be aligned with the strategies that have been set down. If Marketing delays a campaign that is properly aligned with corporate strategy, its impact across the company can be profound. Coordination across the business is critical so that there are no surprises.

Execute

In the Execute phase, the goals, risks, and compliance objectives you have set in your strategy and the resources you have allocated in your plans now drive the end-to-end business processes discussed earlier in "The Business Process Angle."

Once the plan is developed and approved, we can begin executing the operational elements of the plan, including individual projects and tasks. It typically involves solid project management capabilities such as managing timelines, assigning roles and responsibilities, maintaining program budgets, developing an associated bill of materials, providing progress updates and tracking actions to be taken.

Now, your thought leadership message is out in the marketplace, and you are training your sales team on their messages. Using tactics such as customer loyalty programs based on the buyer personas, you can now speak effectively to your current and new customer base.

As you execute, the pressure will be on to tie spend and revenue to overall organizational goals, which makes even more of an impetus for measurement. If there are objectives for which you cannot develop these links, these are likely to be considered non-strategic, and in difficult times will be cut or receive reduced funding. The more comprehensive your model is, the easier it will be to link changes in the budget to the strategy and to the value from execution you're delivering.

Monitor and Analyze

In the monitor and analyze phase of the PM lifecycle, you monitor to understand what is happening in the business, analyze to understand why it is happening, and for those things not on track, adjust to improve the situation relative to your goals.

Monitor

It is important to distinguish the different categories of monitoring in evaluating business performance.

Event monitoring looks for a single, discrete activity or exposure event, such as a competitor announcing a new product in the market.

Trend monitoring is similar to event monitoring, but looks at events over time to determine patterns, for example, how frequently that event occurred, and if that frequency was more or less common than in the past. An example of trend monitoring is monitoring the frequency with which competitors bring new products to market.

Intelligence monitoring collects information from a variety of external sources that are of interest to the company and may indicate a risk exposure. One example is the activities of our top competitor. This is effectively competitive intelligence to help predict a competitor's next move in the market and employ marketing strategies to minimize the impact of that release in the market with counter activities.

The presentation of information to be monitored is also crucial in order to facilitate decision-making. Dashboards bring together all the relevant pieces of information in the all the major domain areas of business that need to be monitored in role-based, contextual views to get a status at a glance. For example, here are some possible marketing dashboards:

- Market share dashboards
- Competitive dashboards
- Campaign management and effectiveness dashboards
- Lead generation dashboards
- Sales pipeline dashboards
- Marketing spend dashboards

Dashboards combine events, trends, and intelligence monitoring across major facets of the business. They can include key business dimensions such as customers, products, projects, and employees and related KPIs, KRIs, controls, and incidents and losses.

Evaluate performance. Look at the KPIs to identify progress made toward objectives. Is a critical KPI to measure the share of voice you have in the

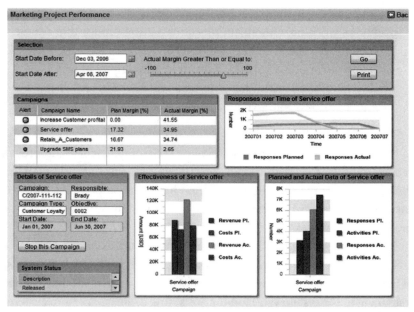

Figure 11-7. A Marketing Analytics Dashboard

market versus your competitors? A competitive dashboard can show how frequently you are mentioned in the media versus your competitor and the tone of the coverage.

Evaluate initiatives. Are any failing or behind schedule? Is your 30-day price discount offer not achieving the expected response rates?

Evaluate risk. Data is monitored from source systems that provide transactional data for the KRI. Dashboards can help identify and manage key risks versus overall risks (being able to prioritize them based on exposure through quantitative and qualitative assessment to thresholds). Look at the KRIs to identify:

- **Top risks.** Was the sales force effectively trained on the 30-day discount offer? Was the ad completed in time to promote the offer in target publications? Did a competitor launch a deeper discount offer at the same time?
- **Changes to risk levels.** Are there an increasing number of instances where the ad team did not complete creative development in time and missed the promotional window? Or are you seeing an increase of Sales promoting offers? Why? Did a new Sales training program get rolled out?
- **Assessment procedures.** Are risks being assessed in accordance with company policy or according to industry best practices? Is the ad team working with an approved marketing vendor that adheres to deadlines specified in service-level agreements?
- **Effectiveness of mitigation.** Are our vendor approval processes being monitored and adhered to on a regular basis? At what frequency do we audit vendors about whether they comply with service level agreements?

Evaluate internal controls. Report key control deficiencies, approvals, verifications, and reconciliations to mitigate risk. Do the right people in the Marketing organization have access to vendor approvals? Have you ensured the person who selects the vendor is not on the same list to approve the vendor's invoices?

Evaluate incidents and losses. If incidents or losses have occurred, or external events are affecting the Marketing department (consistent losses of data, for example), document this information, even if you haven't been tracking it in the system yet. Monitor marketing database access to customer and prospect information.

No matter how proactive you are, manual monitoring is inefficient. Automated monitoring can proactively identify out-of-tolerance conditions, highlighting when a KPI, KRI, or control goes over or under defined tolerances and then alerting the responsible party. This should take into account forecasting, trending, and modeling capabilities so that if a metric falls out of range of a trend or budget/plan, the appropriate alert is raised, along with a workflow process to get the investigation under way.

Analyze

Assessing performance of the Marketing organization is a key step in which not only do you look at where you are, but what is happening (or what has happened) and why. You conduct both qualitative and quantitative market analysis, determining factors such as the size of your market, win and loss information from your competitors, and past product performance, for example. Look first at the internal and external quantitative factors (which are easier to measure) and then overlay these with internal and external qualitative factors (which have historically been harder to measure). The overall condition of the economy is a good example of an external qualitative factor.

During this phase, weed out activities that do not play to your core strengths as an organization—wherever you find that one of your activities or strategies is not a core differentiator, that is a key aspect to outsource to a channel partner.

All of these aspects should be taken into consideration as you continue to refine the business case. You want to be able to show the C-suite that your narrowed-down strategy has a revenue impact. In particular, you will be watching the progress of the campaigns and procedures you have created closely. You will leverage various types of marketing analytics ranging from campaign, media, customer, and sales analytics to understand overall marketing performance.

Analyze KPIs to understand why they are increasing or decreasing. You see that a marketing campaign response rate on the campaign effectiveness dashboard is trending downward and find out that it is because one of the offers is performing significantly worse than the others.

Analyze initiatives to understand why they are succeeding or failing. In understanding why offer A is performing so poorly, you learn that the cause is not the offer, but rather an incorrect target list. The people most likely to respond to this specific offer did not receive it.

Analyze KRIs to understand why they are increasing or decreasing. You conduct a correlation analyses to identify the most significant elements impacting your campaign response rates (creative development, segmentation and list development, offer strategy, media mix, and telemarketing) and conclude that your offer strategy is the reason your campaign responses are not as high as they should be.

Analyze controls to see if they are effective. For example, you notice that a control to test for proper list segmentation seems to generate a lot of incidents and determine that the thresholds are set too high. You need to adjust your controls to ensure the accuracy of database pulls and list segmentation.

Analyze incidents and losses to determine root causes and trends of incidents and losses. You notice a significant uptick in the number of complaints tied to privacy laws being broken with poor emailing practices and determine that the root cause is violations of the privacy policy, which is supposed to provide an easy automated opt-out for all campaign respondents.

In all of these cases, analysis was being done with human intervention but this does not necessarily have to be the case. The volume and complexity of data today makes it increasingly difficult to mine data and arrive at intelligent conclusions. Using data mining techniques, software can determine likely root causes much quicker and suggest recommended actions. For example, you observe that a KRI for service delivery is increasing. Without manual intervention, the system does a series of correlations. When you highlight the KRI, a popup shows that the number one factor associated with the service delivery risk is the sudden decrease in capacity due to a reorganization.

The problem is that marketers perform these analytics without tying them to their plans or to the company strategy, and they don't optimize their use of analytics.

The opportunities to mesh governance and risk control with performance management in marketing are endless—imagine a sales force automation application that maps the performance management and governance, risk, and compliance (GRC) lifecycles on top of each other (see Chapter 6 for further details). Once you model your marketing strategy, the system could actually tell you which customers you should attempt to close this quarter, reinforcing its argument with historical data and displaying the probability of success based on the success rate of peers attempted to close similar accounts in the past.

Throughout the monitor and analyze phase, you constantly refine your strategy to get the best possible yield. You analyze areas such as:

- **Expected versus committed versus actual costs of your program, campaign, and product category.** You can use the results of this analysis to reallocate funds and resources to higher performing campaigns and channels and away from expensive media that don't return results
- **Competitive analysis.** What are the price points that move your competition's products? What kinds of new approaches are they using? Can you rapidly adjust your program to meet and exceed those approaches?
- **Market analysis.** What are the buying trends? What is "hot" right now? Can you anticipate major economic events and their impact on your customer base?
- **Cycle time analysis.** How long does it take customers to respond to your campaigns? How vigorously do they adopt your offers? How quickly can you develop another offer that builds upon the success of the previous offer or is equally successful with a different target group?

Table 11-3. Types of Packaged Marketing Analytics

Analytic Type	Description
Campaign Performance	Provides campaign results and effectiveness data by offer, segment, agent performance, and time. Manager can monitor a campaign scorecard and identify root causes for shortfalls in meeting predicated goals. Integrates with data from financials, order management, and supply
Customer Insight	Provides product affinity, market basket, and next product purchases analysis. Provides demographic information and information on impact of customer behavior due to marketing activities
Marketing Event Analytics	Provides analytics related to trade shows and customer events and their ROI. Analyzes event registrations and expenses and supplies by vendor, region, and event
Lead Analytics	Provides analytics to assess number of leads with the status of open, In process, won, or lost. Analyze duration of leads until won or lost, changes in qualification level, number of leads won (transformed into opportunity or contract), expected order quantity per lead, and activities per lead

Web Analytics

The explosive growth of Web usage in the last decade has led to a host of analytics specifically targeted at capturing value through the web channel using techniques that are unique to this segment. Spending for online marketing is growing at a much faster rate than for offline channels, and tools are required to optimize and account for the spending. Given the increasing complexity of web sites, tools are needed to truly understand visitor behavior. Web analytics are tools for answering questions on how well online content, channels, partners, and campaigns are influencing customer behavior. The primary mechanism for capturing customer behavior is through visitor traffic information. Web analytics can allow you to:

- Obtain complete views of online and offline customer profiles

- Improve channel performance for attributing revenue contribution as well as marketing and sales funnel for visibility from lead acquisition to revenue

- Get visibility into online customer behavior surrounding purchase intent

- Tie purchase intent to actual transactions, which enables closing the marketing performance management loop

- Identify new customer segments

- Uncover the largest site conversion improvement opportunities

- Optimize search, email, and online campaign performance and content placement

- Optimize site design and navigation

- Analyze using marketing-specific techniques like funnel reports and real-time segmentation

For example, web analytics can tell marketing managers that users are clicking through and responding to campaigns, indicating their interest in your offering, but then abandoning the interaction on the site after a few minutes because it takes too many clicks for them to find what they want. Web analytics is an important component of a multichannel marketing strategy. Tie web analytics data into your overall marketing strategy, plans, monitoring, and optimization processes.

Marketers have long been one of the savviest groups in exploiting advanced analytic techniques. It is critical to leverage these techniques as part of risk-aware marketing performance management. Some of the relevant techniques for marketers are mentioned in the following sections.

Data Mining

Data mining techniques include:

- **Clustering.** A technique for data analysis that partitions a data set into subsets whose elements share common traits. In marketing, clustering allows you to separate massive lists of customers based on common characteristics
- **Association analysis.** Otherwise known as market-basket analysis, association analysis helps determine items people buy together. For example shoppers often buy cameras with batteries or cartridges with printers
- **Weighted scoring tables.** A holistic index based on attributes such as age, gender, and income to show the combined effect on a dependent variable that cannot be observed by looking at any one variable alone

Predictive Analytics

Predictive analytics techniques include the following:

- **Regression analysis.** A collective name for techniques for the modeling and analysis of numerical data consisting of dependent values and independent variables (predictors). Regression can be used to predict price sensitivity for consumers for a new product based on previous data capturing the relationship between price and independent variables like quality and attractiveness
- **Decision trees.** A diagram that shows the sequence of variables that narrow down choices to make a decision. In determining the propensity to buy something, decision trees might show that the most important factor is the number of previous complaints they have made, the second is their gender, and the third is income

It should be noted that analytics might require talents you don't currently possess. You may need help with the way you are evaluating metrics. Ensuring that your analysis is statistically sound may mean hiring an analyst with these qualifications or consulting with one.

Adjust

After monitoring to know what has happened and analyzing to understand why it happened, for those things not going accordingly to plan, set things back on course by taking what you've learned and using that information to make adjustments. Always consider the impact of your goals, risks, and compliance concerns on other business units.

The good news is, with performance management, adjusting the results of your campaigns is much easier than in the past. No longer is it common practice to send out 100,000 pieces of direct mail, only to find out four months later that the mailing had a poor response rate. Now, you can send out a B2B email blast and learn that in 48 hours you reached 86% of your potential respondents. In today's fast-moving climate, B2B marketing has a "long tail" of response, which means your initial blast of responses constitute the majority and then gradual tapering off. So the bad news is, if you have not met your campaign response rates in the first 48 hours, you need to adjust your plan. You will need to quickly pursue alternate approaches without making massive new investments. You will need to be able to anticipate which levers to pull and then pull those levers to make changes and observe the results quickly.

For example, with web-based marketing you can alter the text copy, the graphics, and the navigation with relative ease (at least compared to brainstorming, commissioning and printing a whole new run of brochures). And it's likely that you will issue several different "looks and feels" of the same strategy, to see what "sticks."

Adjust KPIs. For KPIs trending in the wrong direction, set things back on course. However, remember that KPIs are interlinked, and you must optimize your performance goals in the context of risk objectives and without violating your compliance objectives. For example, if lack of adherence to the email privacy policy is the root cause for the poor response rates on your campaign effectiveness KPI, you can assign more resources and quality checks to monitor adherence. However, this can only be done if it does not increase the risk of not delivering on other key projects. If it requires the database marketing and web team to check for opt outs from online respondents, it backs them up on other campaigns.

Adjust initiatives. For initiatives that are not going as planned, rapidly take remedial action or cancel them. If it's clear that the initiative is not going to work, either make changes that can help save the project or cancel it, if possible, so you can reallocate those resources. Now that you understand that offer A is performing so poorly because of an incorrect target list, you stop the current offer, apply the correct target list, and then restart the offer.

Adjust KRIs. For KRIs trending in the wrong direction, once you have analyzed the root causes, put the appropriate mitigating controls in place to stabilize them. However, remember that KRIs are interlinked, and you must optimize your risk goals in the context of performance objectives and without violating your compliance objectives. For example, you identify the most significant steps that impact your campaign response rates and conclude that your offer strategy is the reason your campaign responses are not as high as they should be. You put a mitigating control in place to have the web team conduct multiple trial runs before making the offer available to everyone. However, this can only be done if it does not decrease the likelihood of delivering on the goal of delivering the campaign on time (since now your team is testing the responses before full implementation) and if it doesn't violate any compliance objectives like having employees working longer than allowed by law. For each risk, you can decide to treat it, tolerate it (since a mitigating control is in place), transfer it, or terminate the activity that is producing the risk.

Adjust controls. For controls violations, adjustment takes the form of remediation and certification. After the list segmentation control is violated, set up a remediation plan to create a more stringent set of policies for all of your database marketers to follow.

Adjust after incidents and losses. For incidents and losses, the correct adjustments typically involve reexamining whether you are tracking the right risks and have the appropriate controls in place to mitigate them. After noticing the significant uptick in the number of complaints tied to poor emailing practices and analyzing that the root cause is the opt out policy not being adhered to, put an automated risk monitoring process in place that alerts you to the first sign of complaints from email campaign respondents.

Model and Optimize

When you are creating a model of your operations, the goal is to be predictive—you will base your model on past and current performance, as a means to forecast future performance—in terms of creating a model of the organization's resources utilization.

In this phase, you are perfecting your model and becoming more aggressively predictive about leads and potential strategies, which will be based on an increasingly accurate and sophisticated information supply.

Model

Modeling in Marketing takes several forms, including revenue, cost, and profitability modeling; scenario modeling; and simulation modeling.

Revenue, Cost, and Profitability Modeling

Modeling the costs, revenue, and profitability implications of performance management, risk management, and compliance management activities and their drivers can be achieved at a very detailed level using activity-based costing (ABC). ABC is an extremely useful way of understanding all the costs of producing a sale or customer win. Say you have a sale. How much did you spend in order to get it? What was the total Marketing investment made to secure that order? Is your budget granular enough to answer this question? Activity-based costing allows you to evaluate all the activities that go into acquiring and maintaining a customer, and it often reveals surprisingly jarring results (see Table 11-4). The customer, who appeared in a traditional profit & loss analysis, to be extremely valuable, when subjected to ABC, may turn out to be a money-loser.

Table 11-4. An Activity-Based Costing Reality Check

Customer P&L Based on Apportioned Overheads			Customer P&L Based on Activity Based Costing		
	Customer A	Customer B		Customer A	Customer B
Revenue	$10,000	$11,000	Revenue	$10,000	$11,000
Cost of Sales	$7,000	$7,000	Cost of Sales	$7,000	$7,000
Contribution	$3,000	$4,000	Contribution	$3,000	$4,000
			Sales Calls @ $50	(6) $300	(12) $600
			Order Processing @$ 10	(12) $120	(52) $520
			Pick and Pack @ $15	(12) $180	(52) $780
			Shipping @ $40	(12) $480	(52) $2,080
			Credit Control Calls @$25	(0) $0	(12) $300
Overhead (30% Cost of Sales)	$2,100	$2,100	Cost to Serve	$1,080	$4,280
Profit / Loss	$900	$1,900	Profit / Loss	$1,920	($280)

ABC is an extremely valuable activity for Marketing since all too often marketers discover the volume game of generating awareness, interest, and opportunities by throwing the net wide across large target segments is far less effective than reinvesting the Marketing budget in developing tighter target audience profiles. With ABC modeling capabilities, you can develop a much more sophisticated view of your ideal target audience. You can analyze the total cost to acquire the customer as well as spending behaviors in terms of frequency and time to purchase. These allow you to yield a target group with a much higher probability of profitable purchases and repurchase. By now you have a much better sense of your target profile leveraging profitability modeling, and you are able to run various "what-if" scenarios. Now you want to model your lead forecast for these target audiences. A marketing plan ten years ago was a tactical list of trade shows for the team to attend in a year. Now, marketing is understood as a quantifiable science. When a C-suite executive gives you a dollar, she really wants to know how many dollars to expect back in revenue. To answer that question, your systems must be able to track the initial outreach, first customer response, result of a sales call, through proof of concept and close of the sale. Your system must also correctly allocate credit where it is due in the sales cycle, especially as more channel partners join your campaign. The answer to "who gets what?" must be as scientifically determined as the answer to "what percentage of customers took us up on that offer?"

In other words, you will be tracking your department's direct contribution to revenue, via two metrics:

- **Sales-accepted leads.** The number of marketing-generated leads that result in a closed sale
- **Influence revenue.** The percentage of marketing's contribution to sales that did not result directly from a marketing-generated lead

The first metric is an industry standard and relatively straightforward. The second is less straightforward but no less valuable. Here's an example. If there were 100 closed deals in a period and 30 came from sales-accepted leads, a marketer would look at the other 70 instances and scour the customer data—what ads they responded to, what kinds of interactions they had with customer service, and soon. It is important for Marketing to quantify the successes in which it created an environment (a tutorial web page, an online offer to chat with a salesperson, a promotion, or customer forum) that facilitated the sale. But it is counterproductive and hazardous to pit Marketing and Sales against each other for a share of credit. The more metrics you have, and the more accurate and detailed they are in their accounting of the sales cycle, the fewer the number of misunderstandings with Sales. These departments exist to complement each other, and no marketing strategy should run counter to that maxim.

And while we are speaking about stepping on toes, don't forget the most important set of toes: the customer's. While it may seem as if we are advocating marketing saturation at every customer touch point, that is not the case. The information extraction we are advocating must be woven subtly into service calls, opinion boards, sales calls, and the like. Organizations that tend to abuse their customer interactions tend to fail. Instead, you must be increasingly sophisticated and pursue multiple paths to the customer, tracking statistics such as:

- Click-through rates on banner ads
- Download rates for white papers
- Click-throughs during webinars to sign up for live seminars
- Attendance of seminars and webinars
- Responses to and utilization of loyalty programs
- Customer satisfaction ratings with each interaction. Avoid the tendency to do one annual survey and assume customer satisfaction using that score. That is a snapshot and does not consider the granularity of each interaction and the varying expectations of different customer segments by interaction
- Customer feedback through both quantitative and qualitative data. Avoid the temptation to rely only on quantitative data. Ensure you are also capturing qualitative data and have a means for factoring the information when modeling and optimizing business scenarios. Ensure that your performance management capabilities can leverage both structured and unstructured data so that you can incorporate information such as the notes and comments from customers provided in text fields when placing orders and interacting with your Service organization

The more you are able to model the possible scenarios for meeting your lead generation targets and develop a solid understanding of the most efficient and profitable lead sources, the better off your campaign execution will be.

Scenario Modeling

Another very valuable type of modeling for Marketers to leverage is scenario modeling. Simple scenario modeling can include creating a base case and then high and low cases based on changes made to input variables, such as market growth rates or inflation rates. This technique is often used in modeling market and business opportunities and creating business plans. In marketing scenario planning, you can model a number of different marketing scenarios by varying the marketing spending, segment, and response rate to test the expected results for different types of campaigns. By changing marketing spending or any of the parameters, you can determine what the high-end (optimistic) and low-end (pessimistic) forecasted results are for each scenario. The scenarios can be used in what-if analyses to compare alternatives. You can run reports on the scenarios and evaluate and analyze the related metrics such as budget, cost, resources, expected ROI, and so on. The scenario that will most likely achieve the goals becomes the operative scenario. All other scenarios are alternative scenarios. Alternative scenarios or parts of them can be set to inactive and are ignored in reporting and in operative processes.

Simulation Modeling

The third and equally valuable form of modeling is simulation modeling. Simulation modeling is a more advanced modeling technique that includes Monte Carlo simulation. Monte Carlo simulations support creating a range of scenarios based on multiple iterations of input assumptions and combinations. With this technique, probabilities can be assigned to various outcomes. These techniques allow the uncertainty associated with a given forecast to be estimated and to reduce risk by applying sensitivity analysis, correlation, and trend extrapolation. By simulating the effect of uncertainty, it becomes possible to answer questions such as, "How certain are we that this customer loyalty program will result in a certain net promoter score?" Or, conversely, "What's the lowest net promoter score we can have while maintaining a 90% certainty of achieving customer growth goals?" Simulation also makes it possible to identify and rank the various contributors to overall uncertainty.

Optimize

The goal at this phase of the PM lifecycle is to determine the optimal way to achieve objectives by taking into account the entire context of the problem, including all relevant constraints and assessments (costs, benefits, risk, labor and time) as well as business strategies, objectives, risks, and compliance factors. Optimization can be done both through human evaluation as well as through advanced algorithmic techniques. Some common types of Marketing optimization are media mix optimization to support media planning and buying and resource optimization of all marketing programs and campaigns.

Here's a simple example of human-led optimization: Say you send out an email campaign to 1,000 targeted customers of your technology product. The email contained a survey, to which 40% responded. Of those respondents, you determine that all were on an earlier version of your product. It makes sense to return to those customers and focus on up-selling them to the newest version, and not to bother people who have not responded, until the next campaign.

By contrast, a non-optimal (even abusive) approach to customer capture would be running cunningly disguised advertorials in trade publications or blasting a customer forum intended for open-ended discussions of your product with a banner ad. Transparency is as important in customer relations as it is in sharing your data with the rest of the organization.

Marketing Optimization and Refinement

A marketing-specific analytical optimization approach that you should consider is marketing optimization and refinement (MORE). This process allows you to perform analysis on existing transactional processes, using constraints as a control factor. MORE can help you determine which campaigns to offer when, based on your models of targets, channel choices, and the overall profitability level you are seeking. MORE also allows you to improve efficiency of direct marketing campaigns. By building models that look at historical response rates, it suggests how to best address the individual customers of a given target group to maximize profitability.

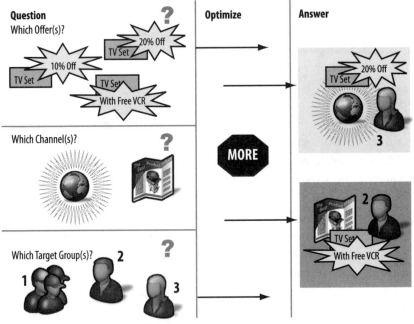

Figure 11-8. MORE Overview

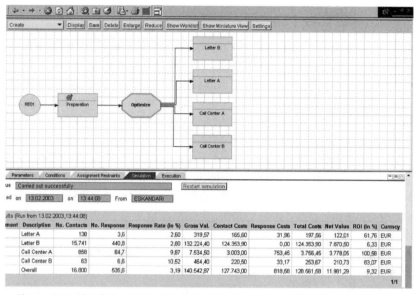

Figure 11-9. Simulation Using Marketing Optimization and Refinement (MORE)

Using MORE, you can apply constraints such as budget, channel capacity, and offer availability. The methodology is also useful for predicting key success figures, such as response rates, costs, profits, and marketing ROI. You can also incorporate multiple channels and offers into the model simultaneously, which is increasingly important as the business network expands and multiple channels become a matter of course. The ultimate goal is to select the best offer, segment, and channel combinations to achieve maximum profitability.

Pricing Optimization

Pricing optimization leverages analytical techniques to set optimal prices. It can help prevent unnecessary margin leakage by identifying significant attributes that define unique customer segments and then recommending the appropriate price for each segment based on overall business goals, like market share growth or margin improvement. Predictive capabilities can determine the maximum that customers can be charged and how much they will buy at that price. Price lists can be set from this information. Segmentation capabilities can automatically determine discrete groups of customers by their price sensitivities.

A particularly powerful analytic manifestation of pricing and profitability that marketing managers can relate to is the price waterfall. The price waterfall is a framework for organizing and analyzing all of the elements that impact margin. Graphical representations show these elements as a series of price points and adjustments that move from a list price on the left to a net or "pocket margin" on the right. (Pocket margin is what you actually put in your pocket after making allowances for all of the on-invoice and off-invoice discounts, costs, and other adjustments.) Moving left to right, the impression is that of a waterfall.

Leading analysts predict that pricing and profitability optimization solutions will integrate with demand management systems whereby pricing applications determine optimal pricing based on expected demand while simultaneously shaping channel demand. Conversely, by taking into account sell-side price projections, the pricing and profitability optimization application can be used to make profitable capacity planning and sourcing decisions.[5] As we have highlighted throughout the book, from our perspective, risk variables (such as customer satisfaction sensitivity to price manipulations) as well as compliance factors (such as the need to publish price books in certain countries and not manipulate prices afterward) need to become part of the overall pricing optimization equation in order to truly optimize performance in the full context of your business landscape.

Case Study: Performance Management in Action

Virtual Gates is a fictional cutting-edge computer manufacturer with retail outlets. This section will describe how the Marketing team at Virtual Gates will positively impact VG's corporate goal of driving profitable growth as measured by Virtual Gates' net income and earnings per share growth. The Marketing group has assessed that a key strategy for driving profitable growth is through the successful launch of their new product line. The team will leverage performance management to ensure a closed loop process between their key strategy, launching the new product line to market, and execution.

Setting the Context

The foremost subject on Chief Marketing Officer Samantha Curtin's mind these days is the smartest, most efficient way to drive profitable revenue growth of the new product within the coming fiscal year. Her focus is set on developing a compelling GTM positioning strategy against their

[5] Noha Tohamy, "The SAP-Vendavo Partnership: The Progress, Future, and Effect on the Pricing Applications Market," AMR Research, 2007.

most formidable competitors, Hypercell and Packingflash. She needs an awareness plan that will create enough air cover to prime the funnel for lead generation. She will also need an aggressive lead generation strategy that can drive both volume and velocity through the sales funnel. Lastly and most importantly, she will need to ensure that the Sales organization is effectively trained on key messages and selling strategies so that the interest generated converts to revenue.

Samantha knows what achieving this goal entails, and it is no small feat. First, she must clearly communicate her goals within the Marketing department. Second, and just as importantly, she must ensure that her message extends to all the other business units and beyond to the customer, analyst, and partner community.

The success of the new product development and launch (NPDL) process rests primarily on the shoulders of Marketing. If Marketing cannot create ways to sell as many new products as possible, at the best price, the organization as a whole will suffer, particularly if its competitors are successful.

Samantha's team is able to accurately define market requirements that fuel new product direction and development, the go-to-market strategies and execution for new production introductions, and the ongoing enablement of direct and indirect sales channels. Market share data, analyst ratings, media share of voice and tonality statistics, unaided purchase consideration statistics and profiling information are just a few of the things that Samantha's department feeds to the entire organization as a means of continuously refining strategy and plans.

Market research conducted under Samantha's direction showed CEO Clint Hobbs that in 2009, 21.5 million netbooks are expected to be sold (a growth of 189% from 2008), and that, by 2012, sales are projected at 50 million. To capture the largest portion of that market, Clint's strategy is to develop a new line of netbooks that isn't merely smaller and faster than VG's competitors, but one whose look and feel is customizable on demand, much the way that companies such as Scion and Nike allow buyers to customize their products.

Every marketing executive knows that there is a correlation between leads and revenue. In general, consumers move through four phases in the buying process. Awareness leads to interest, interest to consideration, and consideration to purchase. Therefore, while the plan that Marketing has developed to achieve Clint's strategy is dynamic, two of its foremost goals are to increase qualified leads in the sales funnel and the velocity with which qualified leads are converted to closed revenue. To meet these objectives, Samantha's team must focus on aspects of the sales funnel such as target audience, segmentation, marketing program mix, offer strategy, and field readiness.

Understand the Collaborative Impact

Every decision in the Marketing department must be made in light of affected stakeholders. Given that the Field Marketing organization, for instance, is on the front lines, it must be able to clearly articulate VG's value proposition to the market. Product Development, in turn, must create products that reflect that value proposition. The new netbook that Clint intends to launch is an example of this. With it, the customer-facing departments such as Sales, Telesales, Service, and Support will function effectively because the new netbook's benefits and capabilities are aligned to create a unified message that ultimately converts to greater sales.

Samantha's dilemma when confronted with these concerns is how to determine the most effective way to draw consumers into the buyer model (of awareness, interest, consideration, and purchase). At her disposal are the Corporate Marketing, Product Marketing, Partner Marketing, Field Marketing, and Sales organizations.

At VG, as at all major companies, Corporate Marketing is the brand steward, nurturing a brand that reaps a high level of positive, unaided awareness in as wide a geographic and virtual space as possible. The focus of Field Marketing, on the other hand, is narrower. It is brought to bear on creating interest, opportunity, understanding, and qualification for Sales. Its primary concern is to acquire qualified leads and deliver them to Sales. As for Sales, its charge is to move customers from the awareness and interest phase of the buyer model into the phase where they are considering and then purchasing as many of the new VG netbooks as possible. All three of these groups must collaborate to ensure an integrated marketing approach that cultivates customers and prospects at various stages.

Establish KPIs and KRIs

No team can achieve goals without a benchmarking system that accurately measures progress. Samantha and her team must identify their primary KPIs and KRIs, the foremost risks to which their decisions expose them, and the significant interfaces between their partners and their processes that need instrumentation. They must also ascertain the drivers behind their KPIs and KRIs, the relationships between them, and the leading indicators of performance.

Samantha will garner vital data about her teams' progress using two critical documents: the Program Plan Report and the Opportunity Report. The Program Plan Report provides data pertaining to the number responses, the number of net, qualified responses, and, the number of leads generated through each campaign. Samantha will also want to know how those leads break down by geographic, title, and interest areas. The Opportunity Report provides insight into the number of leads that were passed to Sales in a given timeframe and then subdivides that number into leads accepted by Sales and leads converted to the forecasted pipeline. In the campaign for VG's forthcoming netbook, it is also imperative to ascertain the extent to which those leads support the netbook itself (as opposed to other VG products). As well, both reports will note those factors that could hinder Samantha's team in the campaign to market the new netbook, including slow lead velocity, murky qualification and compensation models, and faulty sales training.

Establish the BI Foundation

A metric as expressed in a KPI or KRI does not spontaneously manifest, regardless of the quality of your technological platform. To get their metrics, Samantha and her teams must harvest data from a host of various source systems such as CRM, ERP, SCM, PLM, and others. Once in hand, the raw data must be aligned and loaded it into a data mart or data warehouse.

Virtual Gates' Marketing organization must also translate the numbers into terms that are meaningful to BI and PM applications. These activities are not executed for themselves. Without them, neither Samantha nor VG's C-suite, to whom she reports, can access a single source of truth about the progress of the campaign to market the new netbook. As the campaign proceeds, Samantha and her teams will manage the data via various Web sites, blogs, forums, and social networks, as well as through direct interaction with customers.

Strategize and Prioritize

Samantha must implement the required cuts without comprising corporate value. If that were not enough, Clint has personally directed her to shift the Marketing department's focus to highly targeted direct marketing programs that continue to increase lead volume and lead velocity, measured according to a scorecard. With this goal in mind, Samantha and her team employ a strategy of reverse-engineering the Sales targets systematically back into the required number of campaign responses and qualified leads they need to generate to provide 4X pipeline coverage to the Sales organization. From this exercise, the team now has in hand a very aggressive set of response and lead targets and realizes they need to generate 135% more qualified leads than the prior year. This is a challenge since their budget is the same. They will need to generate more responses and to improve the response to lead conversion rate by 65% to pull through more to revenue. They simply cannot afford to just generate more responses to meet the increased revenue target. The quality must improve too.

To boost the volume of leads related to the new netbook, Samantha has decided to increase the number of campaigns and offers by buying segment. As with any strategy, this one does not come without risks, namely that the quality of leads will suffer when Marketing managers around the globe begin to focus exclusively on lead volume. She knows, too, that this strategy could also result in sharp rises in offer costs when Marketing makes more generous offers as a way to meet its lead-volume targets.

To account for these risks, Samantha has implemented a KRI that establishes a minimum threshold and consequent response: once the average cost per lead increases by 25%, her teams must act to mitigate the risk by capping the budgeted offer spending. Ensuring that this offer-spending cap process complies with her strategy will also require Samantha's team to document, test, monitor, and certify her proposed control mechanism.

Another possible risk that the marketing strategy might be exposed to is a decline in customer satisfaction—there is a fine line between strong offers and antagonistic bombardment. Should the risk begin to manifest, Samantha's team must be ready to modify its approach to increasing leads.

Plan and Execute

The economic downturn will also force Samantha to tie Marketing's budget to specific operational activities. Most of the budget must be allocated to strategic objectives while all other spending is reduced, including that for advertising and executive events. Because of the strength of the new netbook, however, combined with the market demand for such a product, this is not necessarily a bad thing—the targeted direct marketing programs Samantha has implemented will likely produce extraordinary buzz.

Samantha's financial plan allocates funds to her lead-volume and lead conversion campaign initiatives. Her team will use these funds to pursue the offers budget, campaign collateral, and telemarketing qualification needed to drive her percentage of lead conversions. The risk at this juncture lies in the reduction of funding for other initiatives. Should the campaign falter, Samantha would modify her budget once again to jumpstart projects that have been temporarily benched. To generate her target lists, send customers the appropriate offer, and so forth, Samantha's teams will rely heavily on their CRM marketing module.

Monitor and Analyze

As customers respond to the offers disseminated by the CRM module, the marketing teams will monitor and analyze the incoming results to find out whether lead volume and velocity are meeting their targets, while a close eye is kept on the aforementioned KRIs.

Further analysis includes scrutiny of brand awareness and customer reference integrity. It is critical that these are still in place despite cuts to advertising budget and customer loyalty programs. Should the results not meet expectations, quick action should be taken. For instance, should Samantha see that she's not going to hit one or more of her planned KPIs, she must decide whether it would be better to allocate resources elsewhere. It may be that a different initiative can make up for the shortfall in the plan. For example, if Samantha sees that they simply are not going to make the response volume target, she may determine that it is best for her to reallocate some of this budget to more lead conversion activities. Any number of conditions may prevail. In all cases, Samantha and her team will continuously examine key points in both their strategy and plan to determine the best course of action.

Model and Optimize

By now it is clear to Samantha that she needs a more detailed operational model to help her see where her resources are being leveraged. For instance, modeling the operational resource consumption of people, time, and materials will enable her to see whether she lacks the capacity or the appropriate skill-set in the call center to execute on her campaigns, despite what initially appeared to be sufficient funding. After changing key assumptions and simulating different scenarios using "what-if" scenarios to ascertain that her strategy and resources are sound, Samantha deploys a variety of optimization techniques to achieve her goals. She determines from her modeling exercise that she should in fact reallocate a portion of the lead volume budget tied to net new campaigns to the call center. By doing so, she can add 20% more call time, which yields a 40% increase in lead conversion. Since she is focused on meeting the immediate revenue targets while staying within budget, she knows she needs to reset her team's focus to getting more leads out of the responses they have already generated.

Close the Loop in an Integrated System

By now, Marketing is using Marketing Resource Management applications and a CRM system that combine performance management and transactive capabilities to effect real-time offer management. When the Marketing team enters the goals that pertain to up-selling or cross-selling additional products to a select group of customers, for instance, the system combines historical analytical data with contextual data from the current interaction with the customer to make a recommendation. By continually monitoring its offers, the system can see which is most successful. In this way, the strategy to increase penetration of the installed base, the campaign to offer up-sell or cross-sell, and the real act of offering are thoroughly integrated such that both efficiency—doing things right—and effectiveness—doing the right things—are greatly enhanced.

Align the Workforce

Samantha's final goal is to link all of the aforementioned activities with her teams' objectives and compensation, which will further reinforce desired behaviors not just in Marketing, but also across the company. For example, any time a marketer sees that a campaign successfully executed as per corporate strategy results in a bonus, she will almost certainly do what it takes to meet her targets. The same holds true for other functional areas. When bonuses are tied to the effectiveness with which Marketing reaches its goals, staff will strive that much harder. The success of Samantha's partners is her own success. At the end of the year, after she has reported a 5% growth in overall profit as measured by Virtual Gates' net income and earnings per share growth, including a 20% increase in netbook market share capture (leaving Hypercell and Packingflash in the far distance), Samantha is sure to receive her own nice bonus package from CEO Clint Hobbs.

Action Items
- Align marketing goals with those of the broader organization by:
  - Linking employee compensation with customer satisfaction
  - Establishing a BI infrastructure for sharing data with other business units and channel partners

- o Learning to speak the language of your collaborators, particularly Finance, so that marketing KPIs are aligned with other departments
- Invest in marketing resource management (MRM) software
- Incorporate Web 2.0 and social media into customer interaction and marketing research as much as possible
- Maintain customer centricity by considering every interaction from the customer point of view and as a marketing and data collection tool
- Focus your marketing efforts:
  - o Plan and understand the impact of marketing programs and campaigns
  - o Link marketing budgeting and planning processes to strategic customer goals
  - o Continuously refine customer segments to achieve specific revenue or ROI goals
  - o Analyze campaigns to understand the drivers of success
- Perform customer analytics:
  - o Understand the complete customer history, including purchases and transactions
  - o Identify typical patterns of customer behavior—what do they buy, when and why?
  - o Calculate profitability at the customer level
  - o Calculate customer lifetime value (CLTV)

Chapter 12

Performance Management for Service

Service professionals must listen to customers and resolve their problems. It takes time to listen and time is money. Service teams are on the front lines of the business, handling the complex challenges of a sophisticated customer whose expectations are on the rise. Isn't the customer always right? Only when it doesn't cost too much.

Company executives understand that while the service team resolves problems and satisfies the customers, the service team can also contribute to company profit. Service teams need to empathize with the customer, and manage service costs while selling additional services to meet revenue goals. A tension exists for service professionals: satisfy customers, protect the company brand, keep customer service costs to a minimum and extract revenue from customers when you can. It's a tall order but now is the time for Service organizations that have been traditionally overlooked as a "necessary evil" to move to the forefront of business strategy. In today's competitive landscape, maintaining growth and customer loyalty is mission-critical and as a result companies are now recognizing the need to improve Service capabilities. Performance management can provide the kind of visibility needed in today's increasingly complex and competitive service environment.

Looking Back: How Life Has Changed in Service

In today's world, companies can't do business without a service model. Service has become strategic. More than in any other department, Service is where we find out what is working well and what needs improvement from the standpoint of the customer. We find out where the problems are with the product. We find out where the problems are with delivery. We also find out which customers are high maintenance and will take all our time if we let them, despite being of marginal value to the company. In any case, what you learn in Service is of the highest value for the rest of the company and must be made actionable. Some organizations don't recognize the value of customer input and for those that do the challenge of accessing and using the information to manage the business effectively continues to escape even the savviest organizations.

A combination of a globalized workforce, technological changes and an evolving performance management landscape demand a renewed inspection of the services function. Performance management and its emphasis on collaboration can generate some short and long term financial improvements for the service team and can maximize service activities so that company goals and customer needs are truly aligned.

In the last thirty years, the U.S. economy has shifted from manufacturing toward a highly service intense economy. Today, approximately 60–70% of the U.S. Gross Domestic Product (GDP) is generated by services and not by products.

Some companies are actually delivering their product as a service, so that's a big change in the market, which heightens the need for a services model.

Years ago, customer feedback didn't carry the weight that it currently does. Today, more than ever the customer feedback that flows into the organization via the services function is part of a company's secret sauce. It's not only about how you collect information and feed it back into your strategy development but how you use it as a way to strategically gain more information about your customers.

In the last ten years, the contact center has become more important due to trends in the post sales world. After a sale is made with a customer, marketing data reveals the long-term customer relationship is infinitely more profitable than trying to set up a new relationship with a new customer. With improved analytical capabilities, companies understand their most valuable customers. The value of service has shifted from being a cost center to a potential profit center.

In this context it is crucial for companies to embrace service excellence and to ensure they're optimizing the value of the information they're getting from the service channels and feeding it into the other areas of the business.

How Business Network Transformation Affects Service

The Service arm of many companies is managed outside its four walls, beyond its boundaries, in the tentacles of business network transformation. During the 1990s, the service function in many companies was outsourced; companies gave up significant pieces of their value chain and let somebody else run Service. The contact center was viewed as a cost center, not a revenue-generating arm of the company. Today companies have started to rethink outsourcing customer service activities, including Dell, which now offers onshore customer service as a premium option. Over the last couple of decades, many companies have gone through an entire cycle of people saying, you know what, service is a cost center. I'm going to give my entire customer responsive value chain to a company in India. Companies went bargain hunting for the lowest price customer service solutions. Efficiency was the predominant business strategy here.

Today, the customer is more involved in shaping product direction. And this is another example of how the business network no longer exists only within the four walls of your organization. Companies and service professionals are collaborating with customers to innovate and shape product direction and innovation.

Does This Sound Familiar?

– Customers call customer support multiple times to get product returns and replacements resolved, which jacks up the cost of service and decreases customer satisfaction.

– Our service leakage continues to exceed acceptable targets. Customer service agents don't have an easy and reliable way of verifying service entitlements and warranties.

– Our service technicians make multiple customer calls due to lack of reliable and accurate part information.

– Our customers are flooding call centers with unanticipated service problems and we don't have enough staff or knowledge to effectively diagnose and resolve customer complaints.

How Technology Has Changed in Service

Technological changes for Service have automated service activities and have opened communication channels so that service professionals and customers can use the Web to resolve problems.

Companies are also integrating a rich set of diagnostic capabilities into products, such as vehicle communication capabilities like Onstar, to proactively manage service activities. From a technology perspective, companies are instrumenting products and services to provide better customer value and reduce the cost of service.

Service departments have also evolved technologies to reduce costs. It costs a lot more money to have a person answer a phone call than it does to have the customer use some kind of automated tool. But it can cost even less for companies to eliminate the problem completely. The investment in diagnostics can minimize some service costs. Some companies are also investing more in quality and compliance requirements to reduce service costs.

Additionally, technologies for contact centers support unified communication, a trend in business to simplify and integrate all forms of communications. Unified communications allow customers to interact with you through a variety of mediums: via web forms, discussion groups, and live chat. The new set of communication mediums that customers are using benefits sales, marketing, and service. It also raises customer expectations that the person they are speaking with knows about all their other interactions with the company, regardless of the channel through which that interaction came.

As a result of these changes, Service is being pressed to grow revenue by:

- Understanding who the most valuable customers are and how to retain them

---

Gaining Visibility into Business Partner Data

At Whirlpool a few years ago, outsourcing was not visible to the company. Whirlpool used Sears or other vendors to execute the distribution and used their service personnel. Whirlpool did not have access to the outsourced service data. Whirlpool initiated a project to provide Sears personnel with mobile devices so that Sears service personnel could then flow data back to Whirlpool. This level of coordination allowed Whirlpool to gain insight about the volume of service tickets for specific products.

- Satisfying changing customer expectations
- Leveraging customer data for targeting and upsell

And as these pressures mount, service leaders are being forced to shift their focus, or at least increase their focus on activities such as:

- Cost Reduction
  - Controlling labor costs
  - Decreasing use of high-cost service channels
- Increased Service Effectiveness
  - Increasing speed to access customer and product data
  - Strengthening historical knowledge regarding issue resolution

This all adds up to the need for service organizations to become more performance focused.

The Evolution of Performance Management for Service

It is an old adage: "What gets measured gets done," and the service organization is no exception. Without strategies or processes in place for measuring and tracking the success of service, it becomes difficult to improve overall performance and increase shareholder value. With this in mind, service organizations are beginning to awaken to the notion that value can be achieved by running service as a profit center and, as such, taking a more targeted approach to measuring, monitoring, and improving service performance.

The increasing strategic importance of post-sales service, coupled with the need for a more standardized approach to service performance management, has raised questions regarding best practices for realizing the full potential of an effective service operation.

Most service organizations use CRM to manage and analyze service activities. The service organization needs to reconcile its performance-based activities with other business units and the entire company to link rich customer data, staffing costs, and profit targets with corporate goals.

Performance management involves financial measures, but it is also typically driven by the finance function that is oriented toward that view. CRM functions are driven by a desire to meet the financial goals of the enterprise, but most of their metrics and performance are oriented to the processes they undertake or support. Reconciling these two views so that business functions understand the real business impact of their activity and finance understands the value and use of corporate resources associated with the service functions is key for effective service performance management.

The essence of CRM is to provide a satisfactory customer experience while delivering value (generally in the form of profits) to the enterprise. CRM-level metrics should focus on these two issues: satisfaction with the customer experience and the impact it has on profitability. Assessing satisfaction is not just a matter of collecting customer feedback about their latest complaint; it is about understanding what drives customer behavior and how every aspect of the enterprise is aligned (or not) to deliver what the customer wants and needs. Profitability analysis is about understanding what the provision of satisfaction costs the enterprise and how the experience of satisfaction drives a relationship that will enhance profitability.

As part of successful performance management, service organizations should evaluate the following service processes and their impact on profitability:

- Plan costs and revenues for service offerings
- Track and manage compliance to service level agreements
- Understand the root causes behind complaints and returns
- Review service cases to identify accelerators for resolution
- Understand the customer's importance to the business
- Develop collaborative decision-making to resolve issues
- Establish metrics for successful customer service

Why You Must Do This Now

Service departments are contributing more and more to the profit margin of companies. In the ongoing battle to retain customers and win new business, as well as develop new revenue streams, service itself is becoming increasingly important to the bottom line.

Service-related activities are trending toward becoming a bigger piece of the profitability mix in best-in-class companies (45% for services versus 55% for products). Profit margins from service increasingly approach profit margins for products. In fact, more than 20 years ago, in 1987, services surpassed goods in terms of their contribution to the U.S. economy (see Figure 12-1).

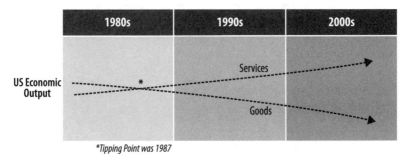

*Tipping Point was 1987

Figure 12-1. Macroeconomic Shift to Services
(Source: "Seizing the White Space: Innovative Service Concepts in the
United States," Peer Insight in conjunction with Tekes, 2007)

For these reasons, it is imperative that companies focus on improving
their service processes, both to stay competitive and to help improve
bottom-line results.

Service Pain Points

At the same time service is becoming increasingly critical to revenue,
pain points are being felt more acutely than ever. Table 12-1 breaks down
pain points by business area.

Table 12-1. Service Pain Points

Area	Pain Points
Contact Center	• Lack of visibility into customer history, products purchased, and repair histories • Service leakage can occur without adequate visibility, so customer support may be giving away service to a customer who is not entitled to it • Lack of systems to effectively schedule and dispatch third party field service technicians can lead to unsatisfied customers
Sales/Marketing	• Lack of integration with sales and marketing systems makes it difficult to staff for increased service demands from new promotions • Missed opportunities for creating cross-sell/upsell during a service call
Supply Chain/ Operations	• Lack of coordinated systems makes execution of service parts management and the logistics of returns, in-house repairs, and replacements a nightmare
Finance	• Lack of integration causes billing errors • Late payment for service parts and components • Poor handling of warranties

Issues That Service Currently Faces

Flawed Execution
- Hard to manage logistics for returns and replacements
- Difficult to ensure service parts availability
- Excessive spare parts inventory
- Suboptimal service parts pricing
- Global trade compliance issues

Inadequate Data Tracking
- Sarbanes-Oxley compliance issues
- Increased warranty claim leakage

Long Resolution Times
- Inability to efficiently diagnose root cause of product issues

Service Leakage
- Difficult to verify contracts, entitlements, and warranties

Customer Inconvenience
- Difficult to process returns, exchanges in single call

No Partner Support
- Unable to schedule/dispatch third-party service providers

Lost Revenues
- Difficult to coordinate cross-sell/upsell campaigns

On further examination, these pain points highlight areas of weakness both within service and across the company. While the goal is to increase revenue and share of wallet and increase customer satisfaction, the current state of many Service departments does not support these goals in any effective way.

Further, providing excellent customer service is more difficult today. Factors that exacerbate service pain points include the following complexities.

- The complexity of how products are manufactured. Global supply networks and volatility in the supply chain may mean that tracing a faulty component in a product is difficult and perhaps impossible with current systems
- The complexity of how products are sold. The resulting networks of relationships between business partners complicate issues such as returns and who is obliged to service equipment. How much visibility is there into the reasons for customers returning the product?

- The complexity of service delivery. Service may be delivered by internal staff or may be outsourced. In many cases, service organizations have outsourced parts of their work to partners, and as a result may have limited visibility into the activities of those partners, including how well they are representing the company's policies and goals for providing customer service. Companies may sell and provide service directly to customers or they may rely on channel partners to sell to their own customers. They may also perform service or may direct customers back to the Original Equipment Manufacturer (OEM)

Customers struggle with service due to the lack of integration and coordination between different parts of a company. Performance management can help you identify and work toward closing the gaps that lead to unsatisfied customers.

If you add up all the pain points that impact service staff and customers, you have the potential to lose revenue. Let's face it. You are probably losing revenue now, losing customers, and leaving money on the table through not maximizing service profits through making the right service offerings. Furthermore, it's highly unlikely that all the wisdom is being reaped from the rich stream of detailed data that should flow from Service and right back into improving the product and the customer experience.

Lack of Integration Leads to Customer Alienation

A durable white goods manufacturer produces washing machines and dryers and conducts sales through retailers. You recently purchased a washing machine and it stopped working. With a warranty in hand, you call the 800 number for service. What is the likelihood that the call center agent is going to have a record of your purchase and know whether it is under warranty?

After being on hold for minutes and bounced to a tech support agent, it is determined that you need to have a service technician diagnose and fix the issue. You're bounced back to a different call center agent who schedules a service appointment. Unfortunately, the service representative misses the scheduled appointment, so you have to call back in and reschedule.

Once the representative shows up, he doesn't have the right part. So, you wait for a return visit—and still can't do the laundry. Eventually the machine is repaired. You receive a bill for the service, despite the fact that it is under warranty. You go back to the phone to dispute the bill.

The service team must embrace performance management to begin tackling all the touch points that affect the customer and the ability to provide excellent service.

What Kind of Company Are You?

How to maximize service effectiveness depends largely on aligning your goals with the type of company you work at. What is the core of your business, versus the context, the tasks that someone else can handle for you?

For this discussion, we will focus on two main alternatives: whether you provide service at a product company or at a company whose main goal is increasing customer satisfaction.

Chief Goal: Making Great Products

Are you working at a product company? Then service is important, but the main goal is to create great products and provide a level of service that effectively lets those products penetrate the market.

A product company that markets to consumers wants to move more products and keep creating great products. Service is important, but secondary to that primary goal. Brand protection is important and customers must be kept happy. However, the lessons learned from service will be taken back to the product group to ensure that the next version of the product is even better and more compelling than the last one was.

If you're at a product company functioning within business network transformation the way in which you bring product to market is more distributed, which adds complexity. And maintaining or having competitive edge is about the ability to incorporate real-time voice of customer feedback into your design and product development lifecycle.

Customers have access to a plethora of choices and have input into how products should be customized. As a product company you have a mandate to collaborate with your customers. And services within a product company have an opportunity to share valuable customer stories with the rest of the company. You should get more respect for your services arm and leverage it as a strategic advantage. And you should also ask yourself how you are using your services arm to get more revenue with your spare parts.

Chief Goal: Increasing Customer Satisfaction

Are you working at a company that is primarily focused on increasing customer satisfaction and managing the customer experience? In this case,

---

Service Business Drivers

– Products are quickly commoditized.

– Interaction channels continue to proliferate.

– Customers are empowered and have instant access to information.

– Differentiation through superior customer service is key for growth.

---

providing excellent service is of primary importance in keeping customers and increasing your share of wallet. Further, you may want to expand service offerings to provide additional revenue streams by finding out what your customers want and need from you.

A company primarily focused on increasing customer satisfaction will work hard at understanding the customers, especially those that are most valuable, and finding out what is working and what isn't.

As a service company you are focused on superior customer value and marketing, service, and sales must collaborate to achieve service excellence. The goal of a service-oriented company is to maximize the "return on relationship" by enhancing the share of wallet or by providing partners with access to the customer.

Customer relationships are strategic assets. A customer-centric business strategy is focused on creating customer value, developing profitable long-term relationships with customers, and delivering an exceptional customer experience across all customer touch points, thus maximizing customer lifetime value (return on relationship), a topic covered in more depth in Chapter 11.

For a company whose number one value generation lever is maximizing the return on relationship, service is very important, and if you're the head of service in this context, you are pretty high on the business value food chain.

The Business Process Angle

Companies rely on business processes to efficiently execute critical, repetitive and interdependent tasks so the company engine purrs smoothly and efficiently. Business processes are cross-functional animals. Collaboration within the Service department and outside the boundaries of the Service department is necessary for efficient delivery. Hopefully your company has invested in automating many of the processes required to effectively complete your work. You should have a library of established core transactional processes that help you to set up efficient collaborative relationships with various business units to deliver value. Service plays a role in many cross-functional business processes, as illustrated in Figure 12-2.

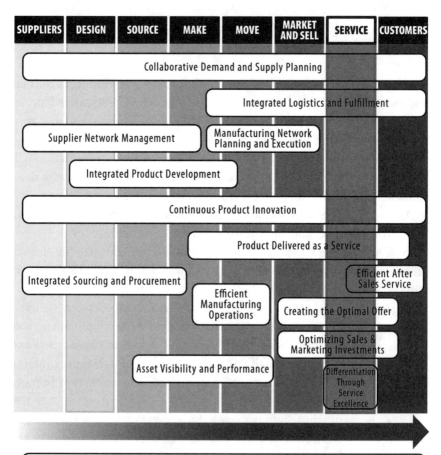

Figure 12-2. Business Processes That Involve Service

Service is a key function in the end-to-end processes in the areas of product and service leadership as well as playing a key role in developing responsive supply networks. It is the main driver of superior customer value.

Performance management offers the methodology and tools to pull back the covers of the organization to provide visibility into the interconnected nature of these end-to-end processes. These processes include collaborative demand and supply planning, integrated logistics and fulfillment, continuous product innovation, and delivering products as a service. Service takes the lead in owning efficient after-sales service and differentiation through service excellence.

The definition of differentiation through service excellence is as follows: reduce service costs and increase customer satisfaction/retention by resolving customer problems at first contact, leveraging appropriate resources; help transform Service operation from a cost center to a profit center through identifying most valuable customers and providing relevant cross-sell and upsell product and service offerings; manage the entire warranty and claims process—from return materials authorization (RMA) to receipt and inspection.

In summary, a classic service process for customer support includes service contact management and service request management. But billings and payment management is also a huge part of Finance and requires the Service team to collaborate with the Finance department. When you're doing warranty returns, you need to interface with operations, through supply chain and billing and crediting. Business processes for Service require constant collaboration and fall under two main categories: cross-functional business processes and internal business processes (those that occur primarily within service itself).

Internal Service Business Processes

It's important to understand the Service business processes over which you have direct influence. They tie to the collaborative business processes and you can use performance management to improve their effectiveness.

Key Roles in Service

Understanding the people and the roles within the Service department can not only be beneficial to staff within the Service department but can benefit other departments such as Marketing, Sales, Finance and HR who

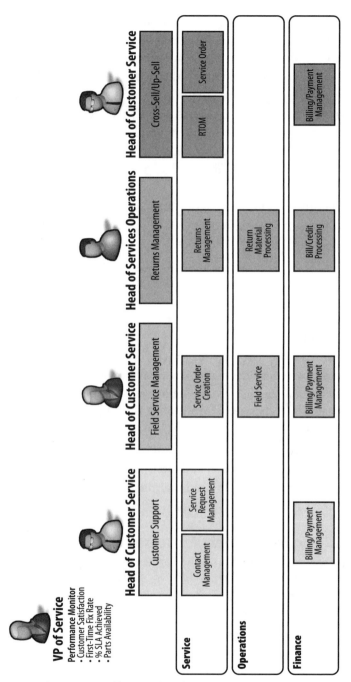

Figure 12-3. Differentiation through Service Excellence

Table 12-2. Business Processes within Service

Service Order Management	Service Order Quotation; Service Order Processes; 3rd Party Integration; Service Employee Resource Planning; Service Confirmation Processing; Product Service Letter Processing; Logistics Integration Processes; Financial Integration; Service Order Analytics
Service Contract	Service Agreement; Service Contract Quotation Processing; Service Contract Processing; Usage Based Contract Mgmt; Service Level Mgmt; Value and Quantity Contracts; Contract Determination; Service Plan Processing; Financial Integration; Service Contract Analysis
Complaints and Returns	Knowledge Mgmt; Complaints Processing; Follow-Up Processes; Recall Mgmt; Warehouse Mgmt Integration; Logistics Integration; Financial Integration; In-House Repair Analytics
In-House Repair	Inventory Mgmt; In-House Repair Processing; Loaner Mgmt; Service Confirmation Processing; Logistics Integration; Quality Mgmt Integration; Financial Integration; In-House Analytics
Case Management	Case Processing; Change Request Mgmt; Service Confirmation Processing; Activity Processing; Supporting Processes; Case Mgmt Analytics
Installed Base Management	Installed Base Processing; Component Hierarchy; Object Fact Sheet; Backend Integration; Installed Base Analytics
Warranty Management	Customer and Vendor Warranty; Product and Warranty; Registration; Warranty Determination; Warranty Claim Processing; Warranty Analysis
Resource Planning	Service Resource Planning; Resource Master Data; Assignment Mgmt; Absences/Attendances Maintenance; Appointment Scheduling; Communication Integration; Rule-Based Synchronization for Mobile Devices; Integration to Third Party Scheduling Engines

must collaborate with the Service department to truly realize various aspects of performance management. Familiarity with the motivations and roles of service staff supports effective collaboration. Also roles within the Service department operate at different levels of granularity so that a VP of Service probably has an idea about the responsibilities of the call center manager and the field service technician but the reverse is not necessarily true. So the motivations and goals that people have as you move up the service food chain are not necessarily as transparent as when you move down the food chain. Part of digging into performance management requires you to know the key players and the concerns of each player. Each role in the service hierarchy is measured differently. If you're the VP of Service, you're going to view performance management in a different way than a field technician would. Performance management can help to align unique goals across the organization.

As a VP of Service, you care about customer satisfaction levels, propensity for customer defection and contact and warranty profitability, which lines up with service strategic key performance indicators or KPIs (see "KPIs for Success in Service" later in this chapter).

As a call center manager, you care about average time to resolution and SLA compliance numbers. As a field technician, you care about field service repair rates. Each role needs to understand or visualize the context for another service professional's role, especially as you move up the chain. Marketing and Sales teams also need to ask, "You know what? We've done nothing about getting feedback from Service," or, "We don't even trace whether our campaigns are working correctly. Let me go read what Service is up to." Service, Marketing, and Sales organizations must collaborate to effectively reap the benefits of performance management. Understanding a Service organization's roles and pain points allows a company to begin the process of interacting in meaningful ways.

As the head of Service, you have something to offer other business units such as rich marketing data to evaluate whether campaigns work or not and rich data for Product Development to understand product defects. And as a service manager who has an ongoing dialogue with Product Development, you can plan staff numbers for your call center and predict service issues for the next three months if you know when products are coming online and what quality criteria is being used to release a product. Companies don't always release high-quality products, but a known and visible risk allows the service team to optimize staff and service-related activities to adequately support a company's business decision.

KPIs for Success in Service

Selecting metrics that matter to benchmark your service activities requires a disciplined approach. And within Service, different KPIs apply to different roles. Service goals will influence the KPIs you emphasize. You need to establish a causal link between a set of KPIs and financial outcomes. Select a KPI that you believe links to your role, a strategic goal and a financial outcome. Then validate your KPI assumptions.

In the past decade, increasing numbers of companies have been measuring customer loyalty, employee satisfaction, and other performance areas that are not financial but that they believe ultimately affect profitability. Doing so can offer several benefits. Managers can get a glimpse of the business's progress well before a financial verdict is pronounced and the soundness of their investment allocations has become moot. Employees can receive better information on the specific actions needed to achieve strategic objectives. And investors can have a better sense of the company's overall performance, since nonfinancial indicators usually reflect realms of intangible value, such as R&D productivity, that accounting rules refuse to recognize as assets.

—Christopher D. Ittner and David F. Larcker, "Coming Up Short on Nonfinancial Performance Measurement," *Harvard Business Review, November 2003.*

Table 12-3. Service Roles and KPIs

KPI Type	Service Roles	Service KPIs
Strategic	VP of Service	Customer Satisfaction; First-time Fix Rate; % SLA Achieved; Parts Availability; Service contract win ratio; Percentage of service renewals
	Head of Customer Service (Customer Support)	1st call resolution rate; Contract profitability; Service leakage; Cost per contact
	Head of Customer Service (Field Service Management)	1st time fix rate; Labor utilization; SLA compliance
	Head of Customer Service (Cross Sell/ Up Sell)	Customer Satisfaction and Customer Retention; Margin Contribution
Operational	Head of Service Operations	Product Quality; Warranty Claims; Processing Efficiencies; Number of service calls ; Average number of service defects
	Call Center Manager	Customers Service Satisfaction; Staff and Customer Contact Ratios; Staff retention and training; Call duration; Wait times; Number of calls handled by agent
Tactical	Call Center Representative	Average handle time; One-and-done rates; Customer profitability; Product/services offers; Abandoned call rate
	Field Service Technician	Field service repair time; Average number of service calls per day; Average time to resolution

What's in It for Me?

It doesn't matter where you are in the Service department; you are always managing your activities to satisfy your customers, reduce service related costs, and add incremental revenue based on the services you sell. For you, it's all about customer satisfaction and so at the end of the day, you are measured on your ability to meet service cost targets without compromising the customer relationship, your company's brand reputation, or the company coffers.

So if you and your entire Service organization have greater visibility into service staff planning, service-related issues, customer complaints, warranty compliance issues, partner support and customer selling opportunities and you have the levers to help increase the likelihood of managing cost and contributing to company profitability, you are going to find performance management highly appealing. At each level of the Service organization, you want to collaborate with Marketing, Sales, Finance, Product Development, and service partners, and you want to have an understanding of the health of your customers so you can deliver superior customer service. If you can get that information accurately and quickly, you have a much greater chance of succeeding.

Effective Collaboration

Effective collaboration can't be underscored enough when you are looking to optimize performance. It's time to break down the barriers.

Service, Sales and Marketing processes and metrics all touch the customer. All three of these groups are blending together. If you optimize a process in Marketing, you need to look at the impact in Sales and in Service. Why? You may hurt the customer.

If you look at what happens in the call center today, you have an opportunity for getting feedback on your current products, which can feed back to Product Development and to the Marketing team. Customer service data is a great place for harvesting stories about what's working and not working from a Marketing perspective. You are the first line of defense and an extra pair of eyes for the organization. You have the single most intimate relationship with the customer. And it's great because that means you have a perfect opportunity to sell more products and services to the customer. Imagine a picture with a bubble, and the customer is on the outside of a bubble, and within the bubble you have Sales, Marketing, and Service. These functions are all touching the customer, which is why all of those individual point solutions that were created for each department eventually aggregated into customer relationship management (CRM).

So, once you see Sales, Marketing and Service as one single touch point for the customer, you begin to recognize that they all need to interact in order to get the full picture of the customer. If you don't have a full picture of the customer, you will not be able to optimize their customer lifetime value (CLTV). And you need to optimize customer lifetime value in your PM lifecycle.

The customer lifecycle is another example of how Sales, Marketing and Service all touch the customer. The customer lifecycle is a term used to describe the progression of steps a customer goes through when considering, purchasing, using, and maintaining loyalty to a product or service.

In layman's terms, the customer lifecycle entails getting a potential customer's attention, teaching them what you have to offer, turning them into paying customers, and then keeping them as loyal customers, whose satisfaction with the product or service urges other customers to join the cycle.

Collaboration with Marketing

The Service department can provide a reality check for Marketing. Marketing is often populated with optimists and Service is often staffed by hardened realists, if not pessimists. A little collaboration can bring needed balance to both groups.

Marketing might want to ask the following questions of Service:

- Are the products meeting the customer's needs?
- Do the customers understand the products?
- Are we reaching the right customers?
- What do you hear are our greatest strengths from our customers? Weaknesses? Opportunities? Competitive threats?
- What do they say about our pricing relative to the competition?
- What is their overall propensity to buy?
- What are the key influencing factors in making their purchase decision?

Collaboration with Sales

Sales can find out a lot from Service and use it to make happy clients even happier and work on relationships with unhappy clients. But you probably won't know unless you ask Service questions like the following:

- Who are my happiest clients?
- Who is unhappy and at risk?
- What do my clients say is their single biggest pain?
- Do customers mention the competition and if so what do they say?
- Do they mention the timeframe in which they are likely to make their next purchase? What are they considering?
- Do they mention the support of our partners? If so, which ones and how do they rate them?

Collaboration with IT

Service needs the support of IT to get all the customer touch points as integrated as possible and to have control over tactical issues such as call center routing. IT should ask Service the following types of questions:

- What type of call center are you running? What do your systems need to optimize for? Are you all about creating the ultimate customer experience or are you focused on high volume, low touch interactions that drive efficiency?
- Specifically, what are your contact management requirements? What fields of information do you need to be able to gather about the customer and in what views do you need to see the data?
- What sort of controls do you need put in place to ensure coordination among callers and to protect customers' personal information?
- What are your requirements for order management?
- What means do you want the customers to have for placing orders, whether phone, fax, email or the Web?
- What sort of controls do you need in place to ensure each step of the order process is completed in a compliant manner?

Collaboration with Procurement

When it comes to Procurement, Service has questions to ask, including the following:

- What is the best possible rate you can get me on my service vehicles?
- What sort of maintenance and repair agreements can you secure for my service technician equipment?
- What sort of training is available from the equipment supplier to train the service technicians? Can it be included in the cost of the equipment?

- What payment terms can be negotiated on the equipment given I need to amortize the cost over the lifetime value it provides?

Collaboration with HR

As is the case with nearly every other department, Service will have a give-and-take, love-hate relationship with human resources. It is in your best interest to help them help you.

HR determines the direction of and administers the training programs for your organization. They are primarily interested in the length of time it takes to bring a new employee up to speed on how things are done. They will be focused on the training cost per employee and the total cost of bringing new products to market. Service is a big part of that.

Let's take the example of training the call center staff to support a new product. HR must coordinate the training schedule and take one group off the phones to train while the other group provides skeletal staffing. HR will then help validate the progress of your employees on the training and certify them based on their retention of key points. Obviously, there are opportunities for tension in such interactions because half your staff will be overburdened, handling twice their usual call volume while the other half will feel oppressed because they are having to go "back to school" and be "tested." That's why it's worth having a continuous dialogue with HR so that you can manage expectations of your staff for this and for similar situations.

HR is also charged with evaluating your routine operations. They will be focused on your employees' productivity: "How many dials does this service person make? What's the average time a service person's on the line? Does this person have a high drop rate? What's the customer satisfaction rating on this person? Are customers responding to incentives? Does the service staff have the right incentives to upsell the customer?" HR writes the script where the service employee asks the customer, "Do you mind staying on the line and telling me how I did today?" A certain amount of preparation can make your employees more amenable to this valuable evaluation scheme and will make the training process go much more smoothly when HR walks in the door. You can also be a hero to your staff if you can accurately describe to HR the incentives that will truly motivate your people to keep the customer on the line just for a little bit longer and entice them into an upsell or responding to a satisfaction survey. That means you will need to be as good a listener as your staff are to the customers, and your communications skills will be needed when you talk to HR about incentives programs.

Collaboration with Product Development

Whether they know it or not, Product Development needs your help, and the more knowledge transfer about the good, bad, and ugly points of the current product line, the more you both will benefit. (Fewer problems mean fewer calls.)

Service tends to get a lot more feedback about what's wrong than about product strengths. Nonetheless, this is an excellent opportunity for Service to communicate this information back to Product Development. Product Development should ask questions such as "What is the demand for the product? What's the perceived quality of the product? What complaints do you hear? What makes the product difficult to use or maintain?"

All of these questions focus on existing products. In a second round of questions, Product Development might be more inclined to ask Service more open-ended questions that would feed future product development. Those questions might include: "How do our customers perceive their needs in three or five years? What are some wish lists or gaps in our offering that they would like to see filled?"

Your job, then, is to canvass the customer base during service calls and collect information on behalf of your organization. There are few market research methodologies more effective than collecting information from customers who are proactively contacting you.

Collaboration with Supply Chain

If Supply Chain fulfills the perfect order, Service doesn't hear about it. If they don't, service costs increase. You'll get plenty of calls and you will begin to be seen as more of a cost to the organization. So it's worthwhile to proactively notify Supply Chain when you encounter a broken process. It will lead to greater customer satisfaction and a much easier time of it overall for you.

If I'm building a house, fixing a car, or creating my production plan, I need parts. So if you tell me that, "Within the next three to five business days I can get you parts", that won't help me. I will purchase from the vendor who can tell me, "You'll have it tomorrow" or "You'll have it Friday afternoon." Being able to make such a commitment and deliver on your promise requires an end-to-end view across different organizational departments and different systems.

Orchestrating the Business Network

The service organization can play a strategic role in the orchestration of the business network. Customer service and call centers have been outsourced beyond the boundaries of the company since the '90s. The distribution and servicing of products is typically owned by third parties. What roles can Service play to further extend and orchestrate the business network? Service has a unique function in the organization: listening to the customer. Customer intelligence and customer relationship management will continue to grow in value. Customers are a critical part of the service and company business network. With the adoption of performance management, Service can leverage customer relationships and stories to drive profits and to innovate products. With the ability to analyze data from many data sources, Service is poised to strategically impact the business network.

Establishing Your BI Foundation

Increasing customer demand for faster and more efficient service performance and rising resource costs centered on workforce, parts, and fleet management are challenging Service executives to make faster and more accurate decisions related to service operations. To meet this challenge, post-sale service organizations are leveraging business intelligence platforms (BI) to provide better access to critical service data. Service executives are also using data analysis tools and centralized knowledge bases to better forecast service trends and requirements, ensure service financial performance is on track with corporate goals, and validate service expansion initiatives.

In Service, you will be able to use BI as the source of information about the customer experience, as well as a source of intelligence about how well products and services are performing for your best customers. The BI foundation should provide:

- **Relevant visualizations.** Service managers often use geographically oriented heat maps to understand visually which regions have "hot spots" in terms of customer outages. Utilization rates and many other service metrics can be visualized as well
- **Relevant event-capture and alerting.** The ability to gather information from event sources such as key customer-facing touch points like the supply chain, billing, and ordering and the ability to define alerts for critical events (our Midwest factory is out of

inventory; the customer service lines are going to be flooded) and inform the right person in the service organization to take action

- **A unified semantic layer, data integration and data quality across departmental and application silos.** BI allows service users to bridge silos when they do not have a single, integrated transactional system, but many point systems (service contract systems, warranty management systems, case management systems), or multiple CRM systems. Use BI to establish definitions and business rules of key dimensions in service (how we define customers, contracts, service requests, field territories) and metrics and their relationships. Data integration for service is even more important when third parties are involved

- **Trusted, cleansed master data.** BI platforms allow Service to consolidate on standard data (such as contract 123 is the same contract as 1-2-3 is the same contract as 1.2.3) and key attributes such as service level agreements. Sears may store a Maytag washer as Maytag washer 123 while Maytag identifies the same unit as Maytag washer ABC. In passing product information between the two companies, clean master data and a mapping between the two material codes are crucial

- **Structured and unstructured data.** BI platforms can generate insights from both structured as well as unstructured data. Unstructured data can provide tremendous additional value to Service. Insight is available in service request logs (everyone is frustrated by the battery life of the new product), voice mining (what is the sentiment of everyone who has called about the new product), as well as contracts. Additional unstructured information from Service includes manuals, product sheets, and product defect updates. Information can also be integrated from outside the organization if an urgent situation arises that presents real logistical challenges (getting supplies to an area hit by a hurricane, for example)

Assessing Performance Management Maturity and Setting Your Course

How mature is your approach to Service performance management? Where do you start? Start with the basics. Don't try to boil the ocean. What is the one issue that requires you to collaborate either within or outside of your department? To assess your maturity, run the issue through the PM lifecycle and once you see improvement then start on another one.

The Case for Customer-Centric Business Processes

A customer bought a bedside table and about a year later she had an issue with it, so she called the store and said, "I'm having this problem. Something's happening with the wood." The store rep said, "Oh, no worries. We're going to replace it." A couple of days later, a store technician replaced the old table with a new one. She was a happy and satisfied customer. But then the nightmare began, because the store was not able to handle an exchange in their system. The financial system created a new order and a return. One process from a customer perspective became two separate internal processes. An end to business process should have been designed before the system was implemented. The system imposed constraints on the business processes. The customer received a new charge on her credit card because the system generated a new shipment and the second process, which should have been a credit memo, failed.

When the customer realized she had been charged she phoned the call center and they apologized and said, "It's basically our system that dictates the internal process." She said, "Okay, I don't really care about your internal processes—I want my money back." The call center promised to fix the problem. The customer waited a few days and checked her credit card and noticed that she had been charged again.

The customer called the contact center and was routed to the customer escalation manager. The customer escalation manager apologized and said "Yeah, they're going to fix it," and the customer asked, "Can't you fix it right now?" And she said, "No, I don't have access to the correct systems. I can see the mistake, but I will need to send a memo to finance to properly process this issue." So the customer waited a few more days and checked her credit statement online and she had been charged a third time.

So she called the store manager and said "I bought this at your place. I want the money back from you now. Cut me a check. I want my money back." And he said, "I can't." And she said, "Why?" He said, "Well, I can see your record, but I have no authorization to give you a check. Even though I would like to I have no way to enter it in the system." After many weeks the issue was finally resolved.

Internal processes were efficient and logical from a finance department perspective. The payment process was managed on the finance side. But the accounts receivable team was managed through a different process in the system. From a customer experience perspective the business process failed. Getting a snapshot of your service business process from both within and outside of the Service department and collaborating with your customer to design an effective process can improve customer satisfaction and reduce service costs.

As an example, if customer satisfaction is the number one issue for you, let's start there with your performance management techniques and then assign risk and some controls to customer satisfaction activities. Once customer satisfaction improves then you can move on.

Although few maturity models are available for Service in particular, the movement generally goes from reactive (putting out fires) to proactive (calling customers when you know something might go wrong for them). It moves from siloed (a customer contacts you in five ways and no one can see that) to integrated (all touch points are aligned and visible to everyone). One more dimension moves from helpless to empowered. If customer service reps cannot help customers because they do not have the power to do so—or access to someone who can help customers who truly need help—customer dissatisfaction is the sure result.

If you examine service horror stories, you can learn a lot about service immaturity. As described in "The Case for Customer-Centric Business Processes," Service maturity isn't really just about service at all. The integration between Service and Billing is absolutely key to driving customer satisfaction or driving customers away.

We would also like to add using a risk-aware PM lifecycle to drive improvements as a point to consider as a gauge of maturity, as well as strong collaboration across the entire organization.

The PM Lifecycle for Service

The service performance management lifecycle sits on top of the transactional collaborative business processes. Understanding the interdependent nature of business processes allows you to apply the performance management lifecycle in a way that is relevant to your service model.

Performance management involves the routine, and sometimes non-routine, measurement of key aspects of service performance, and making this information available to decision-makers. In this section, we will walk you through the performance management lifecycle, highlighting the factors and evaluation methods that your peers have found useful. Before you begin, keep in mind that to manage your performance successfully, you have to enrich your notion of service performance management with service risks and the appropriate controls. Some of these risks will be financial in nature, while others like customer loyalty and satisfaction and company brand reputation are equally important and will also need to be managed. Service professionals can play a strategic role in proactively managing these risks. Customers talk and service people listen. Service staff is on the front lines of the business, talking to customers on a minute-by-minute basis. As an incredible source of information, the service team can provide details about product returns and malfunctions. It's important for companies to pay attention to customer feedback coming from the service function.

In the following discussion, we weave consideration of risks in with the performance management lifecycle.

Strategize and Prioritize

Service team executives can align service and customer support with corporate goals as a first step in the service PM lifecycle. The question service executives need to answer as part of the strategy setting process is "How can I transform the service function from a cost center to a profit center?"

Once the performance management strategy is been articulated, service leaders can begin defining a plan and execute activities that align with transforming the service team from a cost to a profit center.

Understand the Context

Review the corporate strategic goals, strategic plans, initiatives, and metrics that track progress against them and understand them. Contextualize them to the implications they have for Service and use this context to drive the Service PM lifecycle.

Develop and Set the Strategy

Strategy for Service, as for any other department, is not an independent exercise. It should cascade down from the corporate level and provide you with detailed guidance about what to do and how to measure success. See "The Business Process Angle" earlier in this chapter to understand all of the collaborative processes that intersect with the Service organization, some of which you are the lead for, like differentiation through service excellence. You should also understand the levers that you yourself are in complete control of and directly accountable for, which are business processes like complaints and returns and case management.

Review the Environment

What are you good at or well-positioned for? You might be excellent at providing very high quality service, but at a pretty significant overall cost.

What are the main problems you face? What risks do you have? Your risks might include customer-facing issues related to service quality, overall customer satisfaction, number of product returns, and number of warranty claims. You also have people-related risks associated with occupational health and safety. As an example, if you have field service technicians, what are your risks and liabilities associate with on the job work related injuries? Are you tracking the number of work-related injuries and do you have mitigation and remediation response plans?

What compliance requirements must you meet? Your compliance challenges might include complying with regulation related to employee work practices, specifically the work environment standards for call centers. Another example is a minimum standard of health and safety standards for field service technicians, including training and certification.

Set the Mission, Values, and Vision

Define the mission, which is the fundamental purpose of the entity, especially what it provides to customers and clients. For example, make every asset in the company add value to every customer service interaction. Make sure that customer service is a companywide initiative and not simply owned by the call center. Research shows that companies that put their money where their mouth is and execute on an enterprise wide initiative to increase the level of customer service and convert the information they receive from customers into actionable business intelligence are more profitable and have higher stock evaluations. This is because the information they gather serves to better inform them about which are the most strategic initiatives to impact revenue. According to research by Claes Fornell, a professor at the University of Michigan and the developer of the American Customer Satisfaction Index (ACSI), "A typical $1 billion business could add $40 million in profit by increasing its customer-facing capabilities by 10%." In a nutshell, companies that do not invest in customer service are taking away from the overall long-term profitability of their organization.

Define the core values, which are the attitude, behavior, and character of the organization. We are willing to do whatever it takes to help our customers succeed through providing superior customer service. This will translate into the customer service organization shifting into a front and center leadership role internally within the organization where they are evangelizing a change in culture that puts the focus on linking corporate goals and objectives to customer service KPIs. To do this effectively customer service leaders will need to drive cross-functional initiatives, in addition to their own department's activities and seek direct accountability and commitment from all levels of the organization. These programs will need to track performance at a departmental level using dashboards and aggregate the overall performance into executive dashboards to demonstrate that customer service can actually fuel important revenue decisions. Further, externally it will mean customer service taking greater accountability for its role as brand ambassadors of the company.

Define the vision, which is a concise statement that defines the 3- to 5-year goals of the organization. For example, by 2012, be consistently ranked in the top 10% of all companies in customer satisfaction as rated by the leading third-party assessor for our industry.

Set the Goals

With all that contextual information in hand, set a strategy or strategies to follow (of course, you'll collaborate with the CEO and other top execs). Here are some sample strategies:

- To be able to track and quantify Service revenue contribution and demonstrate that 5% of revenue was directly attributed to new opportunities uncovered through initiatives orchestrated by customer service
- To shift the focus of customer service from only contributing to the bottom line and to managing the overall customer experience. In the new world, this means shifting away from traditional KPIs such as call volume and incenting call center representatives to focus on customer loyalty and customer lifetime value, both of which have a direct effect on the bottom line

Consider using a strategy map to display the cause-and-effect relationships among the objectives that make up a strategy. A good strategy map tells a story of how value is created for the business.

Assign KPIs to Goals and Set the Right Targets

In a customer service oriented organization, something transpires much differently than at companies that place customer service low on the corporate priority list. Leading customer service organizations create KPIs that are focused on overall customer experience as opposed to KPIs that focus on solely on conducting each interaction step in the most efficient manner. Companies that do not fully understand the power of customer lifetime value and the fact that it is actually far cheaper in most cases to keep a customer than to create a new one tend to rely on traditional service KPIs (such as calls per day and duration of call). This volume approach does not typically yield

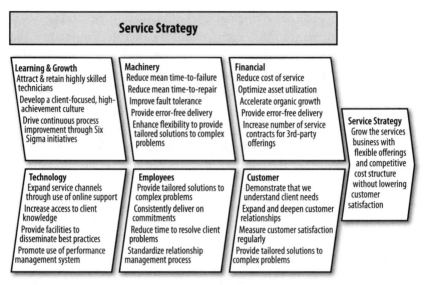

Figure 12-4. A Service Strategy Map

high customer value and certainly does not leave the rep time to explore or fully understand the needs of the customers. While this approach may actually be tied to a corporate level initiative (such as reducing costs by 30%), it is shortsighted because it does not account for the ever-increasing demands of customers and certainly does not show the true cost for saving 30%.

Another example could be a leading premier airline that reduces the number of agents staffing its premier reservations line by 30%. While the airline can document immediate savings in headcount, what has it done to the average wait time? Has the abandon call rate increased? Did they potentially hurt longer-term revenue growth by alienating their most profitable customers?

Leading services organizations structure KPIs to link to corporate goals that address the bottom line. In "KPIs for Success in Service," we talk about a broad spectrum of KPIs for Service. Within the PM lifecycle we choose relevant KPIs for the strategy we are trying to implement. Given the strategy to increase Service revenue through upsell opportunities and move the Service organization to focusing on overall customer experience, we might choose KPIs like the following:

- Revenue driven from opportunities captured by the call center
- Customer satisfaction levels as measured by customer experience surveys

Perform Additional Risk Analysis and Set Key Risk Indicators (KRIs)

Now look again at risks to see what could keep you from meeting your goals. For each risk, decide what your risk appetite is. Can you afford to take that risk? What's the worst-case scenario? Does taking the risk have the potential to wipe out important projects?

Say, for example, you are a cable company and you put your best field technicians supporting the installation of a new digital box that provides premier HDTV service. You decide to reallocate your resources to this new digital box because Marketing is currently running a limited time price discount and you expect an uptick in installations. The offer is released and the installation requests go through the roof, but meanwhile you have an outage in a key market coverage area and do not have technicians to address the outage. Customers in this market have paid for premium maintenance and are unhappy that the 24-hour service-level agreement is not being met. As a result, customers go without service for an extended period of time and the company sees a 15% decrease in maintenance renewal revenue for the year.

For each risk, set a response strategy for the risk (such as watch, research, transfer, delegate, or mitigate). In the previous example, when deciding to send your best technicians into the field for the cable box installations, you may not have been aware of the risk of not having capable staff on hand for a Service outage. Given your resources, you decide to send the technicians into the field and to watch the risk (for now) by implementing controls that alert you if a major outage happens in a market with a high percentage of premier maintenance customers. Further, you define a mitigation strategy in case you see indications that the risk has actually materialized. For example, you tell the Marketing organization to offer a slightly higher discount for customers willing to wait an extra week for installation to reduce demand on your field technicians.

Decide whether you can afford the worst-case scenario presented by that risk from a performance management perspective. Could it bring down some critical value-generating mechanism for the company? For example, say you determine your risk appetite is very low for disrupting maintenance renewals because this is the bread and butter of the organization and you need to establish KRIs associated with maintenance renewals and administer controls to ensure that resource allocation is effectively managed.

Examples of Risks for Service

Service Quality. Customer Satisfaction, Complaint Ratio, Product Returns, Warranty Costs, and Warranty Claims

Occupational Health and Safety (Field Service personnel). Number of accidents, number of injuries, energy and emissions

Maintenance and Reliability Risks. Overdue maintenance orders, Maintenance orders—Planned/Actual Cost Deviation, Maintenance tasks—Adherence to Deadlines, Product Returns, Mean Time To Repair (MTTR) and Mean Time Between Repair (MTBR)

Physical Assets. Telephony system, computers

HR Risks. Working conditions, overtime rate, utilization rate

Job Satisfaction risks. Departure rate, Employee initiated leaving rate due to resignation, Percentage Breakdown of Leavers, Illness Rate, Average length of service, Employer-initiated leaving rate (dismissal)

Skills Development/Training. Training Hours per Employee, Training Costs per Employee

Privacy Risk. Data security and privacy violations

Services Vendor Risk. Ensuring your vendors adhere to your guidelines on corporate brand use, messaging and positioning, and quality standards

Brand Risk. Loss of reputation in industry and/or buyer communities—negative press

Promotional Risk. Ensure you meet all legal obligations and offer commitments

---

Define KRIs and targets for those risks. Key risk indicators are the early warning signals that define the threshold at which a risk could occur. Let's say that you set a cap on the number of technicians that can be reallocated to support Marketing promotions. You set the cap to ensure you have ample staff to support unexpected outages and can preserve your maintenance renewals.

Perform Additional Compliance Analysis and Set Controls

Define your compliance requirements. Compliance defines the boundaries within which companies must operate when achieving their strategies. A large number of compliance mandates impact Service, especially customer data privacy, which places many restrictions around the disclosure and sharing of customer information. Also, Section 404 of the Sarbanes-Oxley Act prescribes the evaluation and remediation of controls for service-related areas such as customer order fulfillment.

Define policies, procedures, and controls that must be in place to ensure that you can meet compliance requirements. Make sure that this applies not only at the main business process level but to all subprocesses including and perhaps especially those related to partners. Establishing both a customer-facing and internal set of policies about your data privacy practices is mandatory along with the procedures that employees within your company must follow to adhere to those policies. You then put a control in place, a procedure that ensures that risk responses are being effectively carried out, such as performing random customer data archive audits and testing them against the privacy policies.

Work on the Strategic Action Plan and Initiatives

The strategic initiatives help define the exact methodology (the roadmap) for achieving the various goals. The results of this planning may require revisiting the strategy.

Controls That Are Relevant for Service

Occupational Health and Safety

Global trade compliance controls

Sarbanes-Oxley compliance controls

Service order processing

Service order quotations

Data access controls

Order quality controls

Returns controls

Service parts inventory controls

Pricing controls

Warranty redemption controls

Wait time controls

Utilization controls

3rd party integration controls

Strategic Planning for Service

In developing your strategic plan for Service, you need to factor in the culture of your organization and incorporate the cultural changes required to create a customer-centric culture. Your strategic plan needs to address both financial and operational aspects of the service business and demonstrate a direct linkage to your company's strategic plan. This means addressing both the immediate fiscal year goals (within 12 months) and longer term goals (3 years or more).

The strategic planning process is an exciting opportunity for customer service leaders because they have the opportunity to accomplish goals they had not previously had enterprisewide support for. The single biggest reason that past goals typically did not gain enterprisewide adoption was that they were costly and did not demonstrate ROI. Strategic plans for leading service groups today will tie to revenue and shift from being associated with high cost to high value and contribution to revenue. It could not be a better time for customer service to take center stage in the organization with external drivers such as increased corporate regulation, rising demands of customers, greater complexity of products, and highly decentralized distribution. Service has the opportunity to act as the voice of the customer.

Start by developing your Service roadmap, specifically the sequence of actions for achieving Service's piece of the corporate strategic plan. Be sure to address performance, risk, and compliance activities in the strategic roadmap.

For each initiative, define critical success and failure factors. Critical success factors might include customer service return on investment and customer satisfaction ratings. Failure factors might be any of the dominos along the way in that initiative's roadmap that could derail the one-time delivery of the initiative. Another example is service technician recruitment and hiring. If this is not executed successfully, the implications are massive. These "failure factors" can then be translated into metrics that serve as an early warning system so that the initiative can be gotten back on track in time or alternatives can be found. For example, are we meeting our hiring and ramp-up certification goals for technicians? If not, what are the implications downstream in our time to repair KPI and customer satisfaction evaluations?

Further, if controls send out alerts that hiring and training goals are not being met at certain levels, what contingency plans have we defined to respond to these alerts before risks to achieving our plans materialize?

What is plan B and plan C for ensuring coverage if you have a headcount freeze or if the training budget is cut?

Strategic plans should therefore be risk-adjusted, with contingency plans for as many risk scenarios as you can reasonably imagine based on past experience and the current environment. You then want to come up with risk response plans that help you address how you will handle the risks if they occur. These risk responses should be included in contingency plans.

Cascade Accountability

Each KPI, KRI, and control should be owned by some department or group. The MBOs of the staff in those groups must reflect the KPIs, KRIs, and controls you set. This sounds obvious, but frequently performance is measured at an individual level in a way that does not directly relate to corporate goals and strategies.

If customer satisfaction is a primary goal, make sure that everyone who interacts with the customer has accountability and can also see clearly how the interaction supports or hurts the overall brand reputation and profitability of the company. How can you motivate a Sales team to do the proper hand off to Service? Ideally, their compensation is tied to successful implementation and usage of the product, not just closing the sale. This ensures that the Sales organization remains honest about product capabilities does not set false expectations and then leave the Service department to clean up the mess.

Plan and Execute

The planning phase gets into the details of planning strategic initiatives both from a financial and operational standpoint. The next sections outline the steps to take in planning.

Now that you have aligned Service with the corporate strategic plan, you now have a seat at the table called "the bottom line." You effectively sold your organization on its value toward revenue and shifted its thinking that you are just a cost center. Now you need to ensure that your plan and execution are flawless and deliver on that promise.

Align Corporate Budget to Service Budget

The budgeting process takes each of the outcomes or actions from the planning process and aligns revenues and expenses against them. Decisions regarding investment priorities and resource allocations define how the company will operate and set the bar for measuring performance. Take each of the steps in the initiatives you've defined and put in revenues and expenses for them.

To create risk-adjusted budgets, incorporate the range of possible revenues and costs of each action into the budget at the appropriate organizational level. A risk-adjusted budget responds to changing circumstances, providing the financial capability to react to events in a planned, proactive manner. Develop different risk-adjusted budgets with contingency plans should risks to achieving budgets materialize.

For example, in a traditional budget, you list the individual line items (such as headcount expense, training expense, CAPEX expenses such as laptops, telephony, service mobiles, and the like) in each row with the actuals, budgeted amounts, forecast, and actual/budget comparisons and forecast versus budget comparisons going across in columns. In a risk-adjusted budget, for every decision to allocate revenue to one line item versus another (like the decision to invest in purchasing a call center telephony module instead of a promotional campaign with Marketing), you determine the impact and probability of the highest priority risks (such as the telephony system not working effectively, resulting in a significant decrease in caller productivity, which hinders campaign response rates regardless of how good the offer is) on those individual line items and use them to set a range of expected budget and forecasted values instead of fixed values. In this case, if the risk materializes and your telephony upgrade does not occur and your phone system locks up, you need a contingency plan in place that shows the performance and risk implications (of the telephony upgrade going awry for example) if we outsource inbound and outbound calling to a third-party call center.

Align Budget to Service Operational Plans

The operational planning process links the budget to operational factors. Plan each step of each initiative in terms of what will be required in terms of technology, time, and resources. Consider the risks in each area of the operational plan.

As you identify the key milestones within your planning process, you focus on the core operational areas of Service:

- Service resource planning
- Services portfolio planning
- Service order planning
- Service contract planning

- Case planning
- Warranty planning
- Productivity planning—training and enablement
- Partner and channel planning
- Campaign and promotional planning

Service resource planning is an operational planning application that allows resource planners to schedule and dispatch, giving the resource planner the ability to find the most suitable resource for a selected service order and the most fitting service order for a selected resource.

In a risk-adjusted operational plan, for every decision to allocate resources to one set of operational activities versus another, for example, service order management versus installed base management, you determine what the

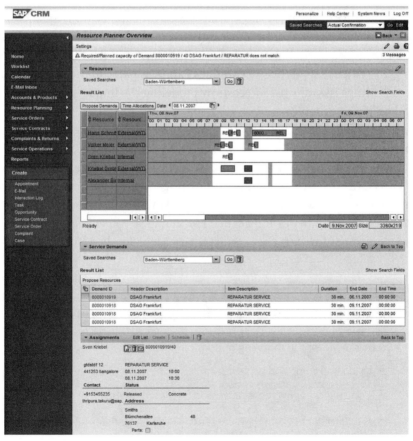

Figure 12-5. Service Resource Planning

impact and probability of the highest priority operational risks are on those individual line items and use this to set a range of expected and forecasted values instead of fixed values. In this case, if the risk materializes, you need a contingency plan that shows what the performance and risk implications would be if we then removed the budget from service order management and had to put it into installed base management.

Taking these factors into account, adjust your plans with a range of operational outcomes and probabilities rather than an absolute number based on the contingencies.

Forecast Performance and Risks

Create rolling, risk-adjusted forecasts of the budget (revenues and costs) and operational plan (including the number, capacity, and cost of resources necessary to achieve that plan) so that you can see trends over a rolling time horizon for those risks whose probability, consequence, or resiliency change over time. That way if you need to make adjustments, you can see where you've been and the direction in which things are likely to go. Predictive analytical techniques can be a particular powerful tool for building risk-adjusted forecasts by modeling the impact previous risks had on previous forecasts.

In a risk-adjusted Service forecast, you create a rolling forecast over a six month to one year window of a range of headcount and resource related costs (such as technology and promotions) and an associated range of expected activity outputs such as certain labor utilization rates, parts availability and repair time, which are dependent on key risks in the environment. When the probability or impact of a risk changes, you adjust the financial or operational forecast costs or activities accordingly. Using predictive

---

For call center staff planning, you might need five more people, but you don't have that budgeted. How would you add staff? So you sit down and say I am undertaking more work than I negotiated in the budget. I am taking an additional 400 calls a day for the following reasons:

- Marketing campaign was successful

- Compliance requirements increased agent script time

- Complexity of products sold increased sales value of customer contact

techniques, you can learn from the impact of previous risks on previous actuals (for example, the impact on repair time when parts are not available) to predict the impact of current risks on current cost or activity forecasts.

Examine Repercussions for Execution Problems

In a tight economy, another look at the strategy is in order before beginning to execute it. Planning and execution must be aligned with all the strategies that have been set down. If Finance decides to delay capital expenditures that are properly aligned with corporate strategy, the impact across the company can be profound. For Service, this may translate into no new service trucks purchased. This could have huge downstream impacts on repair fix time if the technicians are driving old trucks that break down. Further, it could create violations of health and safety regulations. Specifically, is it a safe working environment for the employee? Coordination across and with all departments is critical so that there are no surprises.

The key to excellence in execution is visibility. For Service, you need a view not only in execution-related activities that you directly manage (such as daily call center representative productivity) but also to those beyond your four walls. For Service, you need visibility to all touch points within the organization to understand the implications of their actions on your ability to serve the customer.

Execute

In the Execute phase, the goals, risks, and compliance objectives you have set in your strategy and the resources you have allocated in your plans now drive the end-to-end business processes discussed earlier in "The Business Process Angle."

For example, you begin to implement a strategy for increasing maintenance renewal rates by increasing the number of customer notifications for the six months prior to the customer's renewal date. To do this effectively, you need to review transactive processes and identify the steps in those processes that are best suited for communicating the value of your maintenance offerings and providing reminders. You start by going into your CRM system and modifying the follow up process for customers, and you put a change in the outbound calling process to put customers with near term maintenance expiration dates at the top of the list.

Monitor and Analyze

Once the Service performance management planning activities have been set into motion, it's time to start monitoring and analyzing. In the monitor and analyze phase of the PM lifecycle, you monitor to understand what is happening in the business, analyze to understand why it is happening, and for those things not on track, adjust to improve the situation relative to your goals. A robust set of service analytics can give you the power to monitor and analyze your Service organization. These analytical capabilities can also be shared with departments such as Marketing and Sales to support intelligent and insightful collaboration. Where are your pain points and where are you succeeding? Did your call center staff planning and forecasting produce the projected upsell targets? As you monitor and analyze, you can learn and then adjust, improving and realigning any aspect of the service function.

Monitor

It is important to distinguish the different categories of monitoring in evaluating business performance.

Event monitoring looks for a single, discrete activity or exposure event. An example of event monitoring is a data privacy violation where an agent shares customer-sensitive information without prior permission.

Trend monitoring is similar to event monitoring, but looks at events over time to determine patterns, for example, how frequently the event occurred, and if the frequency was more or less than in the past. One example of trend monitoring is call abandon rate. Seeing a call drop a handful of times in a high volume call center is one thing but to see a consistent trend where the abandon rate skyrockets on the same day of the week and time of day begs the question of what is driving the trend. After investigation, you discover call center training is run at this time every week and call wait times triple because of a lean staff during training.

Intelligence monitoring collects information from a variety of external sources that are of interest to the company and may indicate a risk exposure. For example, perhaps every time the FDA releases public service announcements on child safety and safe plastics, there is an uptick in returns despite the fact that our plastic bottles are compliant with FDA child safety regulations.

The presentation of information to be monitored is also crucial in order to facilitate decision-making. Dashboards bring together in one place all the relevant pieces of information that need to be monitored in role-based, contextual views to get a status at a glance.

In Service, typical dashboards for monitoring might be organized as follows:

- Service Requests Dashboard
- Agent Utilization and Productivity Dashboard
- Maintenance Renewals Dashboard
- Product /Portfolio Performance Dashboard (defects, returns)
- Campaign Effectiveness Dashboard
- Customer Satisfaction Dashboard

Dashboards are effective ways of combining events, trends, and intelligence monitoring patterns across all of the major facets of the organization, including key business dimensions like customers, products, projects, and employees, and related KPIs, KRIs, controls, and incidents and losses.

Evaluate performance. Look at KPIs to identify progress made toward achievement of goals. Is the KPI of increasing the maintenance renewal

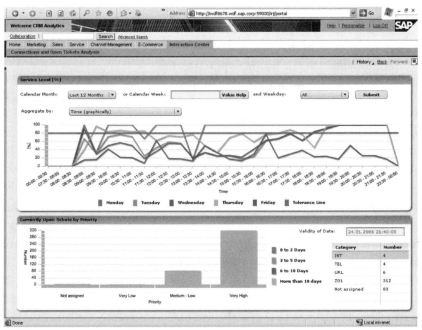

Figure 12-6. A Service Dashboard

rates by 10% on target? Is there progress on the outbound call campaign that results in a more effective renewal rate?

Evaluate initiatives. Is your system of increasing renewal rates meeting its timeline?

Evaluate risk. Data is monitored from source systems that provide transactional data for KRIs. Dashboards can help identify and manage key risks versus overall risks (being able to prioritize based on exposure through quantitative and qualitative assessment to thresholds). Look at the KRIs to identify:

- Top risks. Is your account information accurate? If not, you may not be able to reach the decision maker for maintenance renewal agreements. One risk is that the renewal expires prior to reaching the appropriate contact in the organization
- Changes to risk levels for key activities and opportunities. Is there an increase in the number of instances where the call center did not extend the renewal offer and missed the expiration date? Was there a significant increase in the number of calls where the representative made the offer? If so, why? Did the call center run a caller incentive for the month that increased the offer rate?
- Assessment procedures. Are risks being assessed in accordance with company policy or according to industry best practices? Are promotions that your call center representatives are offering compliant with fair business practices?
- Effectiveness of mitigation. Are mitigation strategies effective in reducing the likelihood or impact of risk? Is there a step in the process that requires legal counsel's review of all promotions prior to disclosure? At what frequency do you audit your promotional offers to ensure they are compliant with corporate and legal policies?

Evaluate internal controls. Report key control deficiencies, approvals, verifications, and reconciliations to mitigate risk. How clean is our access control? Have there been major organizational shifts requiring that we reexamine our roles? Do the right people in the organization have access to maintenance contacts and are they appropriately engaging these contacts to ensure renewals?

Evaluate incidents and losses. For example, an economic crisis hits and your client decides not to renew the maintenance agreement because they do not see a perceived value for your product in their overall priorities. How do you learn from the implications of the economic downturn and safeguard your organization to minimize the impact of incidences beyond your immediate control?

No matter how proactive you are, manual monitoring can be very inefficient. Automated monitoring can proactively identify out-of-tolerance

When Performance Monitoring in the Call Center Really Needs to be in "Real-Time"

The latency associated with performance management processes can vary quite dramatically. Despite the rapid changes in the business environment and the interconnectivity between enterprises as a result of business network transformation, many performance management processes require fresh, but not up-to-the minute data by any means. For strategic goals and their execution processes, data can be collected at fairly infrequent, but regular intervals, such as on a quarterly basis. As goals and execution processes cascade into the tactical realm, monthly or even weekly monitoring is more appropriate. However, as the front-line toward the customer, the call center is one of the most reactive and dynamic mechanisms for allowing you to perceive the needs of customers, and as such, is often worthy of more precise, up-to-the minute instrumentation to manage its performance.

Business Activity Monitoring is a set of capabilities that provides truly real-time, to the second, instrumentation of key business processes like those in the call center. Important business KPIs, like call volume and queue length, as well as relevant business KRIs, can be displayed on dashboards and continually updated using a steady stream of data flowing in from operational systems. By dramatically reducing the latency in converting data to insight, BAM allows you to manage potentially damaging situations proactively before they do real harm. Of course, few managers or executives in the call center have the time to sit in front of a monitor all day, and BAM can provide contextual alerts to notify them on their pagers or any other device of their choosing so that they are proactively notified. When a significant event, such as a massive spike in the call queue, is detected and evaluated against a specific rule, managers can be immediately notified. However, individual events themselves are not always interesting, but a pattern of events (like a rapid and steady increase in call volume over the course of two hours) makes them worthy of note, and BAM capabilities frequently include correlation, filtering, and predictive capabilities to make sense of these patterns.

Although this will increase over time, truly real-time monitoring may not be relevant for most business processes in the enterprise, but the service organization is one place where this technology can be highly valuable today. The key to making BAM work is to align it with the strategic and tactical goals in your broader performance management initiatives.

conditions, highlighting key areas for analysis of violations of predefined tolerances associated with a KPI, KRI, or control, and then alerting the responsible party. This should take into account forecasting, trending and modeling capabilities so that if a metric falls out of range of a trend or plan, the appropriate alert is raised, along with a workflow process to get the investigation under way.

Analyze

Assessing performance of your Service organization logically falls into this portion of the PM lifecycle. The deeper you look at your Service organization, the more you may want to know about what things aren't working and why. Analysis is a key step in which you not only look at where you are, but what is happening (or what has happened) and why. The techniques for analysis can range from highly manual and simple to fairly automated and complex in terms of the usage of statistical techniques. Some of the key questions to analyze in Service include:

- Who are the most effective service reps?
- What is the service contract profitability?
- How satisfied are customers with our service and what is their propensity to churn based on their service interactions?
- What service order quotation revenue can I expect?
- Which customers are my most profitable or unprofitable based on warranty costs?
- Which cases are being escalated and why?
- How long did it take for a service complaint or service order to be resolved? Are we meeting our SLAs?

Throughout the monitor and analyze phase, you constantly refine your strategy to get the best possible yield. Analyze KPIs to understand why they are increasing or decreasing. For example, you find that the case management close time KPI is trending downward and drill down to find out that it is happening because of a break in your logistics fulfillment process.

Analyze initiatives. For example, you can drill down to understand why case management close time is down and determine that the break is in the warehouse in the fulfillment of lost orders. You discover that a different delivery transportation vendor is used for lost product cases. The transportation vendor is not meeting their stated SLAs and is acting in a fraudulent manner, stealing merchandise. You terminate the relationship with the transportation vendor. In the meantime, what has this done to your customer satisfaction levels?

Analyze risk. Analyze KRIs to understand why they are increasing or decreasing. For example, you conduct a correlation analysis to identify the process steps that are the most significant in impacting your case management close time (call resources to log cases, resources to troubleshoot a case, product defect rates, and logistics fulfillment issues).

Analyze the effectiveness of internal controls. For example, you notice that a control to test for proper case management close time seems to generate a lot of incidents and analyze that the thresholds are set too high. You conclude from your analysis that your controls are ineffective and that you need additional controls to ensure product quality and vendor compliance with SLAs.

Analyze incidents and losses. For example, you notice a significant uptick in the number of cases tied to not receiving the product. You determine the root cause is the transportation vendor not adhering to agreed-upon delivery times.

In the cases above, analysis was done with human intervention but this does not have to be the case. The volume and complexity of data today makes it increasingly difficult to mine through data and arrive at intelligent conclusions. Using data mining techniques, software can determine the most likely root causes and even suggest recommended actions. For example, you observe that a KRI for service delivery is increasing. Without any manual intervention, the system does a series of correlations. When you highlight the KRI, a popup shows that the number one factor associated with service delivery risk is the sudden decrease in capacity due to a reorganization.

It should be noted that analysis may require talents that you don't currently possess and that not all changes will be minor. Some may require a full scale restructuring of your service model to optimize for changing market dynamics (such as globalization). Table 12-4 describes relevant service analytics.

Adjust

After monitoring and analyzing to discover what happened and why it happened, it is time to set the business back on course by taking what you've learned and using that information to adjust the settings across the enterprise. Always consider the impact of your goals, risks, and compliance concerns on other business units when adjusting your actions.

Table 12-4. Examples of Service Analytics

Analytic Category	Analytic	What the Analytic Shows
Service Order Quotation Analytics	Service Order Quotation Success Analysis	Shows the percentage of service order quotations that were created within a defined period and accepted by the customer
	Service Order Quotation Expiration Analysis	Shows which service order quotations are going to expire within a defined period, but which have not yet been accepted or rejected by the customer
	Service Order Quotation Pipeline Analysis	Shows the expected net value of service order quotation items. The calculation is based on the net value of all open (but not expired) and all accepted service order quotation items in Service Order Quotations for a defined time span, multiplied by the probability percentage
Warranty Analytics	Warranty Usage List	Shows for a particular reference object, which individual objects are covered by valid time-based warranties
	Warranty Expiration Analysis	Shows which time-based warranties are going to expire in a specific time period per product, product group, object family, customer, or region
	Warranty Entitlement Analysis	Shows the percentage of service order items containing reference to a warranty per characteristic (for example, per product, product group, object family, customer, or region)
Service Workforce Analytics	Employee Availability	Shows the availability of service employees within a defined timeframe and how many hours they have planned for productive and unproductive (non-billable) work
	Employee Utilization	Shows how unproductive time is being spent by service employees, and enables revenue to be forecast per employee/employee group
	Qualification/Skill/Job Function Requirement Frequency	Shows which qualifications, skills, or job functions are required most/least frequently, or which job functions are held most/least frequently by service employees
	Qualification Requirement Completeness Analysis	Shows whether all mandatory qualification or project role requirements have been fulfilled within a service demand (for example, in a service or project order)

Adjust performance. For KPIs trending in the wrong direction, analyze the root causes and it should be clear what actions will set things back on course. However, because KPIs are interlinked, you must optimize performance goals in the context of risk objectives without violating your compliance objectives. For example, if lack of adherence to the transportation SLA is the root cause for longer close times on the case management KPI, you can assign more quality checks to monitor the transportation vendor's performance. However, this can only be done if it does not increase the risk of not delivering on other key projects such as creating additional steps in your order confirmation process or has implications for your order rate KPI.

Adjust initiatives. For initiatives that are not going as planned, rapidly take action or cancel them. If it's clear the initiative is not going to work, either make changes to save the project or cancel it, if possible, to reallocate those resources. For example, you observe that a key initiative is failing and determine the root cause is tied to the MBOs for the service technicians who are staffing the initiative. Currently they are compensated on repair time rate, meaning their incentive is to fix the problem and move onto the next customer. These incentives do not leverage the time with the customer to explore additional needs or upsell additional services. The simplest thing to do would be to change the MBOs to see if this sets the initiative back on target.

Adjust risk. For each risk, you can decide to treat it, tolerate it (since a mitigating control is in place), transfer it, or terminate the activity that is producing the risk. For KRIs trending in the wrong direction, once you have analyzed the root cause, put mitigating controls in place to stabilize them. However, remember that KRIs are interlinked, and you must optimize risk goals in the context of performance objectives without violating compliance objectives. For example, a correlation analysis identifies the most significant process deficiencies in increasing risk before it reaches critical levels. You put a mitigating control in place to have the asset maintenance team more frequently service technician's vehicles to ensure customer repair times are not in jeopardy. However, do this only if it does not decrease the likelihood of the asset maintenance team delivering properly operating phone systems to the call center (since now your asset maintenance team is investing more time in servicing vehicles), and if it doesn't violate compliance objectives such as having employees working longer than they are allowed to by law to meet daily call volume goals.

Adjust controls. For controls violations, adjustment takes the form of remediation and certification. For example, after the vehicle maintenance control is violated, set up a remediation plan to create a more stringent set of policies for the certification of service vehicles for repair service use.

Adjust after incidents and losses. For incidents and losses, the correct adjustments typically involve reexamining whether you are tracking the right risks and have put the appropriate controls in place to mitigate them. For example, after determining that the increase in repair time rates is due to the failure to follow appropriate procedures for vehicle maintenance, impose an automated risk monitoring process that alerts you to the first sign of a missed deadline for regularly scheduled vehicle maintenance.

Be on the lookout for variances between actual and planned performance. You can use this knowledge to optimize activities that are falling short or to replicate those that are succeeding beyond expectations.

Monitoring is key to providing project visibility to key stakeholders. Identify projects that are behind schedule and thus at risk. Investigate why customer satisfaction levels are falling short of expectations. Address the cause of the problem and formulate corrective actions that put customer satisfaction ratings back on course, and incorporate what you have learned into better results for your organization.

Model and Optimize

When you are creating a model of your operations, the goal is to be predictive—you will base your model on past and current performance, as a means to forecast future performance—in terms of creating a model of the organization's resources utilization.

For example, is your management complaining about spiraling call center costs? Are you facing challenges of trying to hire and keep skilled call center personnel? Would you like some better techniques for justifying call center equipment to your senior management? Would you like to know what drives the number of calls and how to reduce the number of unnecessary calls? All of these issues can be addressed by leveraging modeling capabilities to evaluate what-if scenarios.

Model

In order to create value for an organization, a call center must know the cost and length of each type of call. A call center must understand which products/services, customers, and internal departments are driving call volume. They must communicate findings to the appropriate people so that call volume can be reduced. They must focus on process improvement by understanding which types of calls create the greatest cost in their call center. Finally, they must continue their efforts to improve productivity in the call center while focusing on reducing call volume. Activity-based costing (ABC) and activity-based management (ABM) are critical to effectively managing a call center today.

Revenue, Cost, and Profitability Modeling

Modeling the costs, revenue, and profitability implications of performance management, risk management, and compliance management activities and their drivers can be achieved at a very detailed levels, yielding massive return on profit to organizations. Modeling takes several forms, including revenue, cost, and profitability modeling, scenario modeling, and simulation modeling.

Let's say your company closes a sale. This analysis starts with asking a lot of questions about your business, which we discussed in the analyze phase of the lifecycle. For example, how much did you spend in customer service and order management to get the sale? What was the total Service investment made to secure that order? How much activity did you undertake to process the order? How much time and money did your call center absorb in dealing with customer returns associated with the original sale? Is your budget granular enough to answer these questions? activity-based costing allows you to evaluate all the activities that go into acquiring and maintaining a customer, and it often reveals surprisingly jarring results. For example, the customer service representative, who appeared in a traditional productivity analysis to be extremely efficient may prove, when evaluated with an activity-based costing analysis, to be your worst performer.

Most call center managers are completely occupied with the details of managing their call center or team. This leaves little time to embrace:

- Cost reduction
- Process improvement
- Product improvement
- Output costing

> You cannot do it in every instance, for every industry, in every department, or for every line item but there are large elements of controllable costs, most of them people-related, in areas where there's highly repetitive activities like call centers and processing, claims management, selling, and manufacturing and shop floor operations. In these cases, you can actually build dynamic models of resource requirements, which are important for testing assumptions and for what-if analysis.

Yet the value of availing yourself of these techniques is significant. After conducting an ABC analysis of your call center operations, you will be able to truly understand what is driving the cost of your call center. You will have at your fingertips:

- The time and cost of each category of call your service organization handles and the unit rate cost for each category of call
- The products and services that are most responsible for driving call volume
- The types of customers that are driving call volume and how much capacity they really require in order to be served at their contractual SLAs

As an example, one organization found that they completed anywhere from 15 to 35 major types of calls in most call centers per day. These calls represented the call center's highest costs as a portion of the total call center cost and were 75% higher in cost than the average cost per call. By having views to this information, it was possible for the call center to improve its processes for these types of calls and create significant savings.

Scenario Modeling

Scenario modeling can be applied to financial and operational modeling and focuses on creating different business scenarios. Simple scenario modeling can include creating a base case and then high and low cases based on changes made to input variables, such as market growth rates or inflation rates. This technique is often used when developing resource models to optimize staff levels. You can also create scenario models to look at various "what-if" scenarios by modeling your Service engagements in an attempt to understand macro factors such as shifts in the demographics of your customer base that would drive poor customer satisfaction levels and hence erode revenue.

Simulation Modeling

More advanced modeling including Monte Carlo simulation supports creating a broad range of scenarios based on multiple iterations of input assumptions and combinations. With this technique, probabilities can be assigned to the various outcomes. These techniques allow the uncertainty associated with a given forecast to be estimated and to reduce risk by applying sensitivity analysis, correlation, and trend extrapolation.

For example by simulating the effect of uncertainty, it becomes possible to answer questions such as, "How certain are we that a power outage will result in a loss of order volume?" or, conversely, "What's the minimum number of orders we can process and still achieve our customer satisfaction target?" Simulation also makes it possible to identify and rank the various contributors to overall uncertainty.

Optimize

The goal at this phase of the PM lifecycle is to determine the optimal way to achieve objectives by taking into account the entire context of the problem, including all relevant constraints and assessments (costs, benefits, labor, and time), as well as business strategies, objectives, risks, and compliance factors. Optimization can be done both through human evaluation as well as through advanced algorithmic techniques.

The most important assets in the Service organization are the people who form the front-line interface to your customers. As such, the number one place where optimization adds value in the call center environment is around what is commonly referred to as workforce optimization. You need to find a way to make your contact center agents as successful and valuable as possible. Consider the following questions:

- Are we motivating and incentivizing people appropriately?
- Are we collaborating with HR and Finance to communicate staffing gaps and training costs?
- What type of people do we need working in the contact center to support the corporate and service strategy?
- Can contact center staff skills adequately meet the challenge of both satisfying customers and up selling new services?

In a workforce optimization framework, you deploy agents and put them on the phone and start monitoring to see how well they are doing. Are they polite to customers? How quickly are they able to understand the root cause of customer's issues? How well are they able to control the flow of the call? Once you have this data and can turn it into insight, you can motivate the correct behaviors. Workforce optimization can even take into account constraints such as an individual call center representative's preferences for the way they like to work and the availability of existing resources to generate the optimal staffing plans to maximize goals like response time and customer satisfaction.

Coaching—The Fine Art of Adjusting the Performance of Your Agents

Since call center agents are the most valuable resource in a service organization, improving their performance correlates with improved service delivery capability more than any other factor. Coaching has become an important topic in Service operations. It can lead to significant gains in agent productivity, customer satisfaction, and ultimately revenue. Yet it is surprising how many service organizations do not consider the value of coaching. Here are three considerations to help you take a more critical look at your operation's current coaching practices.

First, all performance management initiatives start with the organization's underlying culture, and by extension, coaching is part of this. For coaching to be successful, agents need to be comfortable that coaching is intended for improvement, not reprimand, and the culture of the organization needs to be one that embraces improvement based on data. Coaching someone with real data in hand about their performance allows you to give them specific actions for improvement. When done right, coaching allows you to adjust or tune service agents' goals to better align them to the Service organization's goals and ultimately the company's goals by making agents accountable for the linkage and incenting them for it. When both managers and employees comply with standard coaching practices and coaching sessions happen in a regular rhythm, progress can be accurately measured so that credit can be given where it is due.

Second, where you invest your coaching resources is also a critical consideration for making coaching successful. Most agents by definition are middle-of-the-road performers when their effectiveness is plotted against a traditional bell curve, and they are the ones who have the largest chance of improving to become excellent performers and who should reap the greatest benefits from coaching. On the other hand, spending a disproportionate amount of time coaching the lowest performers in the hopes of getting them to mediocrity is not the most effective use of a coach's time, and yet instinctually it is natural that managers want to focus their coaching efforts on these agents.

Finally, make sure you provide the appropriate resources and infrastructure for the coaches themselves. Coaches need timely access to agent performance information and a set of best practices that are specific to the culture of your organization and the types of customers you serve in order to be truly effective. While feedback about agent performance is critical, coaches need feedback on the impact of their own performance.

Workforce optimization in the service organization also needs to tie very closely with the other customer-facing processes in the organization orchestrated by Sales and Marketing. Explicitly optimizing the scheduling training, and incentives of representatives, as well as the activity metrics against marketing campaign goals can lead to much better campaign response and conversion rates than when these are not aligned.

Since workforce optimization is directly linked to the human capital of the service organization, these processes also touch underlying HR processes within the company. Workforce optimization allows you to assess if you have the right talent and the appropriate skills to best satisfy the needs of your customers, which then ties into your talent management processes. For more information about working with your HR department to optimize your workforce, see Chapter 8.

Case Study: Performance Management in Action

Virtual Gates is a fictional cutting-edge computer manufacturer with retail outlets. This section provides an analysis of how the Service department's team at Virtual Gates closes its loop during the process of enhancing support for top customers while reducing service levels for customers who are no longer strategically viable.

Real-Time Offer Management—Turning the Call Center into a Profit Center

There is never a better time to upsell or cross-sell a customer than when you are on the phone with them in your call center. You have the context of your existing relationship with them and can make use of information you already have about the customer. Real-time offer management systems identify best offers for a customer in real time based on the customer's intent of interaction (for example, interest in a new product, paying an invoice online, or making a complaint). Based on their response, the system can learn from the interaction and immediately optimize the offer for the next customer. The system can recommend the best product based on the customer's expressed needs and preferences and can even adapt to seasonal effects and changes in taste. And like other optimization technologies we've discussed throughout the book, real-time offer management can make the best decision under the relevant constraints, such as priority and sales quotas for each offer.

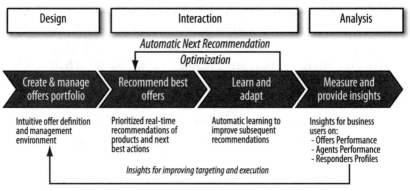

Figure 12-7. The Real-Time Offer Management Process

Setting the Context

Virtual Gates' CEO, Clint Hobbs, has just directed Madison Rice, VP of Service, to focus her limited resources on her most profitable customers. Specifically, he wants her to establish hard metrics to measure the improved satisfaction of their top customers by offering them instant access to the call center's in-person agents. Of course, the shift will mean a reduction in the service level for Madison's remaining customers, who, without additional fees, will only be eligible for web site and interactive voice response (IVR) support.

Another important consideration for Madison is Clint's demand that she achieve her initiative such that VG's revenue grows by 3% while ensuring that her strategies and plans align with his bigger objective, which requires all growth to be measured against Virtual Gates' net income and earnings per share growth, especially as they compare to Hypercell and Packingflash, VG's main competitors.

After Madison and her team have established their baseline values and targets, they'll monitor their progress against the key metrics of first call resolution rate, contract profitability, service leakage, and customer satisfaction. Madison will need to articulate the main activities required to meet her aims, particularly improved training for her service representatives, without which they won't be able to increase their call-resolution rate or meet stipulations in their new service-level agreements (SLAs). In addition, to accommodate its non-premium customers, Service must enhance both its IVR system and its web site.

Madison has to communicate her goal and its implications to her team. And just as her team must understand all of the initiative's touch points, so, too, must collaborative in-house departments, especially Finance, Product, Marketing, and Sales.

Understand the Collaborative Impact

Madison has her work cut out for her. The Service organization owns the key processes of supporting customers and leveraging customer relationships to help Sales, Marketing, and Product Development maintain high satisfaction levels to upsell and cross-sell into their existing customer base. Madison must also consider the impact on other departments. For instance, other than the staff reduction, the extra-departmental initiative that will affect her most is Product Development's drive to sunset low-profit products while simultaneously introducing a new netbook. Retiring old products could upset existing customers, and Madison's team is likely to receive an influx of new, high-level customers for the netbook. These conditions along with the changes in the self-service model for customers will place considerable stress on her team.

If Service cannot provide support to new and existing strategic customers, that will only compound dissatisfaction from less strategically important customers. If Service fails to satisfy, the effect on consumers could quickly reach epidemic proportions. If word gets out that VG's service leaves a lot to be desired, both Marketing and Sales teams will be forced to work harder to turn that impression around. And what was once an aggressive but personable promotion could be perceived as an advertising bombardment, creating a downward cycle with no easy solution. At its end loom the specters of lost brand value and shrinking profit margins. On the other hand, if Madison's team can smoothly and efficiently manage their processes and maintain strong collaboration with their partners, VG's prospects are much better.

Establish KPIs and KRIs

A moment ago we mentioned the importance of metrics to the progress of Madison's initiatives. Without a benchmarking system by which to measure growth efficiently and accurately—one that is built via the shrewd selection and implementation of *relevant* KPIs and KRIs—she and her team will almost surely fail.

Not only is it imperative that Madison's team identify the primary KPIs and KRIs, but it must also grasp its foremost risks, the chief lines between its partners and its processes, the drivers behind its KPIs and KRIs, the relationships between them, and, finally, the leading indicators of performance. For example, Madison will need to understand the impact of the new self-service support for non-premium customers on the risk of losing additional sales from this customer base.

Madison must also convey the impact of these metrics to her partners. For instance, improving customer satisfaction will result in increased sales to both new and existing customers. Failure to deliver on the new SLAs could result in penalties for VG.

Establish the BI Foundation

Madison and her team must build the metrics foundation for their KPIs and KRIs. Once Madison understands the key business dimensions and relevant KPIs and KRIs that matter, Service needs to obtain the data from various source systems, cleanse it, and load it into a data mart or data warehouse. Data should be harvested from a host of source systems, including their transactional customer service, help desk, CRM, and ERP systems, all of which pull from SCM and other data sources such as web tracking, click-through rates, and time spent viewing. CRM is connected to the call center, which culls data pertaining to all service support and telemarketing activities, including the number of inbound calls and outbound dials. The service team must consolidate these systems, too, as they execute their various processes.

Madison's team must also verify that the company's BI and PM applications can consume this data. This foundation is a prerequisite for obtaining a single version of the truth to support VG's spectrum of related activities. For example, Madison needs to be able to see the impact of headcount reduction on the number of service calls that her team can handle from the premium customer segment.

Strategize and Prioritize

Service is not the only department at Virtual Gates that is in the midst of flux. In fact, Madison's initiatives are a function of the enterprise-wide transformation initiated by CEO Clint Hobbs in concert with CFO Asha Madon: given the country's deepening economic rut, VG needs to free up working capital for the immediate term while leaving room for longer-term investments for growth. To accomplish this aim, Clint has directed the heads of each department to reduce staff. Beyond this, however, each department must work to capitalize on its strengths.

Madison's initiative to strengthen support for VG's strategic customers while reducing service for low-value customers has been validated by both VG's larger objective and by her peer departments, but even so, there are risks. Overall service profitability could drop because Madison's investment in additional time for customers is more costly than anticipated. Further, Service's enhanced support for top customers could anger second- and third-tier customers. After all, without additional fees, they're no longer eligible to speak with agents.

The Service team needs a scorecard for monitoring progress toward its goals. In addition to listing the aforementioned risks, it must also include the KRIs and contingency measures that Madison has recommended. For instance, if customer satisfaction drops by 10% or more, Service would immediately look for ways to modify the initiative and, if satisfaction for the non-premium customers falls too low, perhaps even suspend it. Finally, Madison documents, tests, monitors, and certifies a control to ensure that the customer service process is proceeding in an effective manner to ensure that the response time is tied correctly to legally binding contract arrangements with customers.

Plan and Execute

Madison will spend funds on the resources she needs to accomplish her goal, including call center facilities, employee training, laptops, desks, chairs, and miscellaneous supplies. Working with a fixed budget, however, exposes her to the risk that the execution and outputs of other initiatives may suffer. If so, Madison must immediately compare her planned, actual, and forecast results. Depending on the outcome of her investigation, she'll need to recalculate her numbers and then modify her plan accordingly, or reallocate her resources in the hope that another initiative will make up for the shortfall.

She has also been asked by VP of HR Chad Fuller to reduce headcount in her department by 15%. Madison will need to understand the impact of the headcount reduction and build a contingency plan to handle the increased volume of calls due to service questions on phased out products. In addition, Madison will need to work closely with Sales to get more customers to sign up for the additional terms for the SLAs and transition non-premium to premium customers. The execution of this plan will help Madison review all her alternatives and offer options in executing Clint's corporate goals.

Monitor and Analyze

Now that Madison's team is executing her plan, it must monitor its CRM system to see whether its targets for first call resolution rate, contract profitability, service leakage, and customer satisfaction are in line with its strategy and plan.

If Madison notices that one or more of her metrics might not be met, she must act immediately to see if her understanding of their relationship was correct. If that is not the problem, she needs to look elsewhere. Are rising customer satisfaction levels being dwarfed by dissatisfied customers who are not eligible for support? Are the KRIs for overall service profitability falling? Or perhaps the number of contract violations for SLAs is increasing? No matter what the result, any solution Madison creates must be aligned with all other departments.

Model and Optimize

If Madison wants to be certain that she properly understands her activities, she needs a detailed operational model. For example, a modeling exercise could reveal that though her campaign budget seemed appropriate, the existing SLAs had already absorbed too much capacity such that there isn't enough manpower to execute on the new initiative nor enough budget to hire additional staff.

With an operational model, Madison could also alter key assumptions such as the number of needed service reps and remove constraints such as the requirement to maintain all of the department's existing SLAs. Finally, after simulating "what-if" scenarios to confirm that her strategy and resources are sound, Madison can deploy optimization techniques to achieve their goals. She may allow the software to examine the constraints and assumptions for the KPIs and KRIs and then recommend the best way to maximize a KPI that is at the lowest risk and within the tolerance of her contingency measures.

Closing the Loop in an Integrated System

Madison doesn't need more technology to manage the scenario described to this point. Very shortly, however, closed-loop systems will enable most departments to align their execution and strategy with amazing precision. No sooner will Madison be able to create a strategy management process that captures goals, initiatives, and metrics that she can link it to her driver-based financial and operational planning process, as well as to her monitoring and analysis, modeling and optimization, and risk and control processes. With this development, new possibilities emerge, including the ability to use goals, initiatives, plans, and risks and controls to push the desired activities out to transactional processes.

Fortunately for Madison and others like her, these very capabilities are presently available to Service departments. Such a system can enable her to merge her performance management and transactive capabilities for use in processes such as real-time call center management. Her team can enter goals such as improving customer satisfaction by optimizing SLAs for the most profitable customers and receive a suggested course of action for the call center agent. To generate its recommendations, the system combines historical analytical data with contextual data from current interactions with customers. What is more, with repeated iterations, the system's ability to accurately recommend specific actions increases. Thus, the strategy to increase the satisfaction of premium customers, the initiatives to create new support offerings, and the real act of the customer/agent interaction are integrated so that both efficiency—doing things right—and effectiveness—doing the right things—are substantially increased.

Aligning the Workforce

Madison's final goal is to link all of the aforementioned activities with the compensation her team members receive for their efforts. The moment a customer service manager receives a bonus for contributing to the successful achievement of the department's initiatives, you can lay odds that he'll take pains to increase his efforts. In fact, Madison knows that every department will step up its labors when they see that their bonuses are linked to the speed and efficiency with which Service surmounts its obstacles. The moral of this story is clear: Madison's success is the success of her peers. When CEO Clint Hobbs receives a report that shows him how Madison has attained a 5% growth in Service's overall profit as measured by Virtual Gates' net income and earnings per share growth, he'll be more than happy to hand her a bonus of her own.

Action Items

- Measure how the customer experience is driven by behavior across the enterprise
- Evaluate sales, service and marketing data to get an overall picture of your customer
- Define performance expectations to track at-risk customers
- Before implementing a system to measure the performance of the organization in delivering the customer experience, perform a segment-by-segment analysis of the key elements and the necessary level of performance

- Organizations need to validate agent call topic assignments through quality management evaluations or even speech analytics once contextual performance management is deployed

Chapter 13

Performance Management for the Supply Chain

Supply chain may be the department most in need of an effective performance management (PM) program. The techniques outlined in this chapter will enable you to view supply chain performance using models of increasing granularity, and execute your processes more effectively. You will then be able to measure, monitor, and optimize strategy and performance.

We begin by explaining why you need performance management in the supply chain and the best way to implement its techniques into your operations. You'll find specific directives for each phase of the performance management lifecycle as it applies to the supply chain, along with ways to evaluate your progress.

We will then look at must-have metrics for profitability, how to harvest, measure, and analyze essential data and how to put what you've learned into practice—closing the loop. Along the way, we'll touch on the most effective ways to integrate risk and compliance into performance management, and what it all means in terms of collaboration with other business units as well as with suppliers.

We will conclude with a summary, a checklist of actions, and recommended practices to take supply chain performance management to the next level.

History Lesson: How Have Supply Chain Practices Changed?

Modern business ecosystems are not what they were ten years ago. At that time, traditional supply chains involved only factories, suppliers, distributors, carriers, and customers. For better or worse, this relatively simple model no longer exists for most companies. Processes that were once linear are now dispersed; multiple parties with whom you deal—to purchase materials, manufacture, and deliver products to market—are no longer as much a "chain" as they are networks. These networks are expensive to manage and difficult to oversee in terms of risk and compliance.

The challenges you face in supply chain are daunting. To meet or exceed your current corporate goals, you and your team must respond to supply and demand with greater speed and efficiency. Your operations must be visible and most important, flexible enough to respond to network needs while controlling cost and risk.

How Business Network Transformation Affects Today's Supply Chains

As we learned in Chapter 1, business network transformation has impacted the way companies do business. Corporations no longer own and operate all of their own departments or divisions. As a result, supply chain managers control and orchestrate a vast array of partners.

When the success of your business depends on strict deadlines, you need to guarantee that your partners will deliver. The most effective way to achieve this is through collaboration and transparency, two core principles of business network transformation.

How Technology Has Changed Supply Chains

Chapter 5 describes how Business Intelligence (BI) technology enables companies to collect, aggregate, transform, and manage data culled from

According to a recent McKinsey Global Survey, the greatest challenge now facing supply chain managers in their efforts to reduce costs, improve customer service, and more rapidly deliver product to market is three-fold:

- The sheer number of resources required

- The recruitment and retention of sufficient talent

- Integrating and standardizing the IT of companies and vendors

enterprise systems. Without BI, performance management is more difficult and laborious.

Until recently, spreadsheets were the technology that supported supply chain performance management efforts (and let's face it—they are still widely used). The biggest problem with spreadsheets is that they cannot provide a single version of the truth. You cannot integrate and reconcile spreadsheets with the processes that underlie supply chain performance management nor use them to gain real-time data or business process guidance.

Technology such as radio-frequency identification (RFID) and wireless sensor networks (WSNs) has brought voluminous data to the supply chain, allowing you to identify and track your products using radio waves. The received data can be transmitted to your ERP and SCM systems, where it can be collected, manipulated, and managed by BI, just like any other data.

RFID and WSN can detect, aggregate, correlate, and track events at every level of your operations. These technologies allow you to monitor and control your supply networks at a level of granularity that was previously impossible to imagine. The benefits of this are obvious. Should a product recall be necessary, for example, you have a clear record of the source and its current location. Instead of recalling an entire production batch, you can recall just the defective units.

With RFID and WSN, manually created traceability logs are relics. Instead, quality control personnel, armed with RFID scanners, read product data at every stage of its lifecycle. Not only can you learn who examined each product, but also when and where.

Many other technological improvements can be suggested for the supply chain. However, you must work with your IT department to ensure proper governance. In a survey of 22 manufacturers, Forrester found that only 41% of supply chain improvements generated a positive ROI. This means you must carefully consider IT deployments and align them with the most critical corporate strategy.

The Evolution of Performance Management for Supply Chains

Performance management was sparked by the need for increased visibility. The ability to see how each component of your supply chain functions at a detailed level enables you to make smarter, more efficient decisions, optimizing both your distributive functionality and flexibility. In today's globally distributed environment, companies have fluctuating demand and high product complexity. To run a truly responsive supply network, you must examine and analyze your operations in real time. Adapting to this changing market means:

- Improving customer service to increase revenue and market share
- Reducing capital lockup to invest in other strategic areas
- Reducing total delivered costs to compete effectively

Why You Must Do This Now

The fact is, a quarterly snapshot of your supply chain activities just won't cut it anymore. With each passing day, your need for modern modeling and optimization processes becomes greater. If you don't have a detailed, real-time view of your supply chain, you will simply be unable to compete in today's marketplace. This limited view will also prevent you from aligning your supply chain strategy with your corporate goals.

The prescriptions we offer will help you to:

- Manage an extended, globally dispersed, responsive supply network
- Use models to view the performance of your network
- Execute based on visibility gained by closing the loop
- Link strategy to execution
- Systematically measure, monitor, and optimize strategy and performance

Business Drivers Behind Modern Supply Networks

For responsive supply networks, there are four primary business drivers: globalization, complexity, rising costs, and customer focus.

Globalization. Increasing globalization has fueled progressive volatility and risk in customer supply and demand. Today, it is not feasible for you to monitor your supply network's performance by merely analyzing people and processes; you must also account for risk. An organization can be aggressive and highly profitable while engaging in very high-risk

---

Does This Sound Familiar?

– Are you carrying too much inventory?

– Are your manufacturing costs so high that you don't have the opportunity to invest in innovation?

– Are your on-time delivery capabilities way off from where they should be?

activities. C-suite, stakeholders, investors, and regulatory agencies are demanding that organizations disclose verifiable data about both their rate of returns and their level of risk exposure. Expanding too quickly into too many markets without dominating a specific market first creates risks on the globalization front.

Complexity. Understanding the complexity of modern supply networks is another critical business driver. You must be able to track the resources assigned to deliver a single objective—such as verifying the total delivered cost of your overall operations, or the specific power to hone in on the location of a batch of motherboards.

Rising costs. Yet another driver behind your supply networks is the relationship between rising overall costs and shrinking margins. A typical issue for supply chains is the problem of too much inventory. You need to keep it in check by knowing not just how much you have, but where inventory is stored, how much that storage costs, and how much insurance costs to secure it.

Customer focus. If you are not providing superior customer service, you are not competing, period. According to Forrester, some 92% of supply chain professionals are focused on cutting costs as a top priority but only 54% aim at improving customer service. The payback is substantial; when transforming its supply chain, IBM found that for each point increase in customer satisfaction, its annual revenue went up by about $3 billion. You must balance customer expectations of faster service with the impact of profitability and margins.

What Kind of Company Are You?

Supply chain may be the department most impacted by business network transformation because there are so many different players. A typical product lifecycle begins with designers and proceeds through a matrix of suppliers, manufacturers, distributors, sales, and service before finally reaching customers. At any point along the way, operations can be outsourced, causing the process to begin anew, further complicating what is already a finely nuanced chain.

To harmonize these processes, you must clearly define and articulate the kind of company that you are. If you're Wal-Mart, for example, you don't meet your profit margins by moving product; rather than build your own distribution network, you outsource it. UPS, on the other hand, has defined itself as logistics experts for outsourcing operations.

Knowing what drives your company is key to improving performance.

The Business Process Angle

Figure 13-1 shows key processes related to the supply chain. These processes are described in the following sections.

Collaborative Demand and Supply Planning

Organizations must be able to continuously sense and respond to changing customer demands, supplier delivery volatility, and operational disruptions across the entire network. Companies looking to optimize this process internally must focus on bringing together multiple departments to come up with an aligned sales and operations plan. To derive benefits across the business network, you must establish an integrated, collaborative, end-to-end planning process to drive supply strategies and tactics, synchronize supply activities, and mitigate supply risks. Doing so will improve demand visibility and forecast accuracy and increase customer satisfaction.

Manufacturing Network Planning and Execution

In today's global environment where many companies have outsourced part or even all of their manufacturing capabilities, it is critical to have visibility and control across your network of manufacturing locations.

By delivering planning and execution functionality across all manufacturing facilities, both internal and outsourced, you can combine global coordination with local execution across the manufacturing network to ensure that your production plans are based on the latest demand data available. The result is fast, cost-effective response to network demand changes, disruptions, or unanticipated economic events.

Integrated Logistics and Fulfillment Processes

Ensuring integrated, end-to-end logistics and fulfillment processes allows companies to effectively and profitably source, store, and move goods to deliver the right product, in the right quantity, at the right time. The goal of delivering the perfect order, however, has to be balanced with the common goals of reducing network-wide inventory and logistics costs, improving asset utilization, and improving customer service levels.

Thus, logistics and fulfillment are not just about working individually as the warehouse, transportation, or sales department—it's about how the three of them can work together and communicate to better serve the customer and deliver the perfect order.

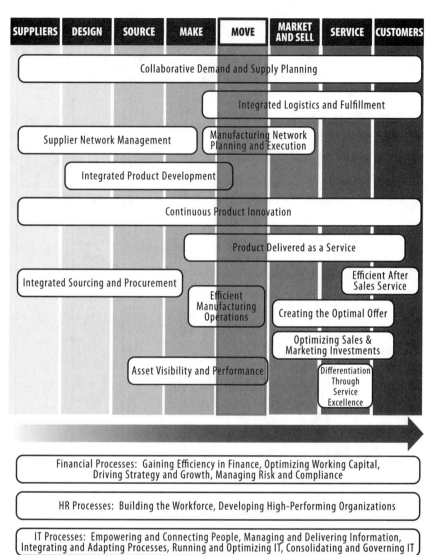

| SUPPLIERS | DESIGN | SOURCE | MAKE | MOVE | MARKET AND SELL | SERVICE | CUSTOMERS |

Collaborative Demand and Supply Planning

Integrated Logistics and Fulfillment

Supplier Network Management

Manufacturing Network Planning and Execution

Integrated Product Development

Continuous Product Innovation

Product Delivered as a Service

Integrated Sourcing and Procurement

Efficient After Sales Service

Efficient Manufacturing Operations

Creating the Optimal Offer

Optimizing Sales & Marketing Investments

Asset Visibility and Performance

Differentiation Through Service Excellence

Financial Processes: Gaining Efficiency in Finance, Optimizing Working Capital, Driving Strategy and Growth, Managing Risk and Compliance

HR Processes: Building the Workforce, Developing High-Performing Organizations

IT Processes: Empowering and Connecting People, Managing and Delivering Information, Integrating and Adapting Processes, Running and Optimizing IT, Consolidating and Governing IT

Figure 13-1. Key Processes for the Supply Chain

Service Parts Management

Across multiple industries, organizations are looking for ways to boost profits, reduce the cost of service and repair, avoid equipment downtime, and optimize the use of their assets. Achieving these goals requires integrated processes including order management, planning, and execution to ensure that you deliver the right parts to the right places in the network as soon

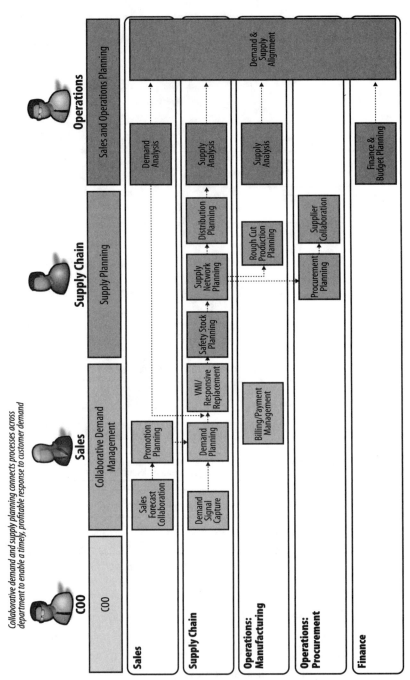

Collaborative demand and supply planning connects processes across department to enable a timely, profitable response to customer demand

Figure 13-2. Collaborative Demand and Supply Planning

as, or even before, they are needed. This reduces service and maintenance costs and increases reliability, availability, and return on network assets while improving customer service.

Supplier Network Management

To drive improved interaction and visibility across the supply network, it is critical to enhance collaboration across the entire procure-to-pay cycle, from purchasing execution, receiving, and invoicing through to payment status follow-up. Optimizing this process also involves setting up network-wide supplier performance metrics and KPIs regarding delivery performance, quality, and price compliance. Once you have identified the business process most critical to your company's role in the supply network, the next step is to look for technology that will support it.

Table 13-1. Within Supply Chain Processes

Demand & Supply Planning	
Demand Planning & Forecasting	Statistical Forecasting; Causal Forecasting; Composite Forecasting; Lifecycle Planning; Promotion Planning; Data Handling; Collaborative Demand Planning; Macro Calculation; Planning with Bill of Materials; Characteristics-Based Forecasting; Transfer of Demand Plan
Safety Stock Planning	Basic Safety Stock Planning; Advanced Safety Stock Planning
Supply Network Planning	Heuristics; Capacity Leveling; Optimization; Multilevel Supply & Demand Matching; Subcontracting; Scheduling Agreement; Aggregated Supply Network Planning
Distribution Planning	Distribution Planning; Responsive Replenishment
Service Parts Planning	Strategic Supply Chain Design; Parts Demand Planning; Parts Inventory Planning; Parts Supply Planning; Parts Distribution Planning; Parts Monitoring
Procurement	
Strategic Sourcing	Long-term Planning; Bid Mgmt; Contract Mgmt; Catalog Mgmt; Source Determination
Purchase Order Processing	Conversion of Demands to Purchase Orders; Confirmation and Monitoring Purchase Activities; Procurement Visibility
Invoicing	Receiving an Incoming Invoice; Verifying an Incoming Invoice; Release of Blocked Invoices
Manufacturing	
Production Planning & Detailed Scheduling	Production Planning; Detailed Scheduling; Multilevel Supply and Demand Matching; Materials Requirements Planning
Mfg Visibility & Execution & Collaboration	Make to Order; Repetitive Mfg; Flow Mfg; Shop Floor Mfg; Lean Mfg; Process Mfg; Batch Management; Mfg Intelligence Dashboard; Mfg Visibility
MRP Based Detailed Scheduling	Production Planning; Detailed Scheduling

Warehousing	
Inbound Processing & Receipt Confirmation	Determination of External Demands; Acknowledge of Receipt within Logistics; Advanced Shipping Notification; Value-Added Services; Yard Mgmt; Delivery Monitoring; Goods Receipt; Material Valuation
Outbound Processing	Delivery Processing & Distribution; Delivery Monitoring; Value-Added Services; Yard Mgmt; Goods Issue; Proof of Delivery; Fulfillment Visibility
Cross Docking	Planned Cross Docking; Opportunistic (unplanned) Cross Docking
Warehousing & Storage	Strategies; Slotting/Warehouse Optimization; Native Radio Frequency Processing; Task Interleaving & Resource Mgmt; Multiple Handling Units; Inventory Mgmt; Storage and Stock Mgmt; Quality Mgmt Integration; Production Supply; Visibility of Warehouse Activities; Decentralized Warehouse
Physical Inventory	Planning Phase of Physical Inventory; Counting Phase of Physical Inventory; Monitoring of the Physical Inventory Activities
Order Fulfillment	
Sales Order Processing	Rules-based Available-to-Promise (ATP); Multilevel ATP Check; Capable-to-Promise (CTP); Product Allocation; Backorder Processing
Billing	Creation and Cancellations of Invoices; Transfer Billing Data to Financial Acctg
Service Parts Order Fulfillment	Parts Marketing & Campaign Mgmt; Parts Order Processing; Complaints Processing
Transportation	
Freight Mgmt	Capture Transportation Requests; Dynamic Route Determination; Credit Limit Check; Send Confirmation; Distance Determination Service
Planning & Dispatching	Load Consolidation; Mode and Route Optimization; TSP Selection; Transportation Visibility; Shipping
Rating & Billing & Settlement	Supplier Transportation Charges; Customer Transportation Charges; Transportation Charge Rates; Integrate Invoice Request to Financials System
Driver & Asset Mgmt	Asset Maintenance; Driver Maintenance
Network Collaboration	Collaboration Shipment Tendering; Seamless Integration
Real World Awareness	
Supply Chain Event Mgmt	Procurement Visibility; Fulfillment Visibility; Transportation Visibility; Mfg Visibility; Supply Network Visibility; Outbound/Inbound RFID; Railcar Mgmt; Container Track/Trace
Auto ID / RFID Sensor Integration	Serialization Data Mgmt; Hardware & Device Management

Supply Network Collaboration	
Supplier Collaboration	Release Process; SMI Process; Purchase Order Process; Dynamic Replenishment Process; Kanban Process; Delivery Control Monitor Process; Invoice Process; Self-Billing Invoice Process
Customer Collaboration	Responsive Demand Planning; Responsive Replenishment Planning
Outsourced Mfg	Contract Mfg Purchasing; Supply Network Inventory; Work Order Process

Key Roles in Performance Management for the Supply Chain

Each department has its own prime movers. For supply chain, this includes members of the C-suite, the VP of Supply Chain, and supply chain managers and analysts. Other key personnel include plant, manufacturing, production, inventory, and procurement managers.

Ceos and Cfos

Members of the C-suite are responsible for achieving the growth demanded by shareholders and board members as well as increasing the company's margins and ensuring brand protection in the face of mounting risk. For example, recent problems with melamine in milk and contamination of peanut products in the U.S. have impacted numerous brands. The supply chain must confront issues such as imperfect orders, escalating transportation costs, purchasing failures, and product recalls.

The stakes are high. When companies report supply chain problems, their market cap drops about 25%, according to research from Prof. Vinod Singhal of the Georgia Institute of Technology (see Figure 13-3).

VP or Head of Supply Chain

As the VP or Head of Supply Chain, you bridge the territory between higher level strategic concerns and hands-on operations. (Your title may not reflect how important you are; according to research from Ohio State Professor Bud La Londe, fewer than 20% of supply chain executives have a title of Vice President or Director.) You ensure that objectives from the C-suite are communicated through the chain of command and that concerns from operations management are transmitted back to the top. You are also responsible for guaranteeing that your team is fulfilling customer

Figure 13-3: Impact of Supply Chain Glitch on Market Cap
(Source: Vinod Singhal, Georgia Institute of Technology)

demands through efficient use of their distribution capacity, inventory, and labor. For instance, you may work with the plant, production, engineering, supply chain, and maintenance managers to optimize flow of product from the plant floor to transportation.

SC Managers and Analysts

As a supply chain manager or analyst, you need to balance ever-shifting demand and supply, calls for improved network efficiency, and more complex compliance requirements (for example, in the area of global trade). Depending on the organization, you may oversee warehouse and expediting functions involving up to 50,000 materials. You must make sure there is a proper supply of equipment, raw materials, and parts. You manage the logistics of shipments and transportation. You grapple with inventory levels that are either too low or too high, one-off spending, and regulatory and border obstacles. You collaborate and communicate with other departments, keeping production, maintenance and quality assurance on track.

KPIs That Matter for Your Success

Standard business practice dictates the need for clearly articulated metrics in finance. Unfortunately, that practice has not been applied to most organizations' supply chain management programs. If businesses are to compete in the 21st century, they must find the right metrics system for their supply chains. You must have the tools to set targets, monitor operations, and collect, examine, and analyze data to ascertain the relationships between the numbers, the processes from which those numbers are being taken, and the target values defined by the organization's mission.

KPIs for Responsive Supply Networks

At any given time, there are hundreds of KPIs that could fit into your metrics framework. Make sure you select KPIs with an eye toward the necessary granularity for your level and role. Recognize which KPIs best serve your needs in a specific context. Once you have achieved your goals, you can move on to the next problem, and the next set of KPIs you need to solve it.

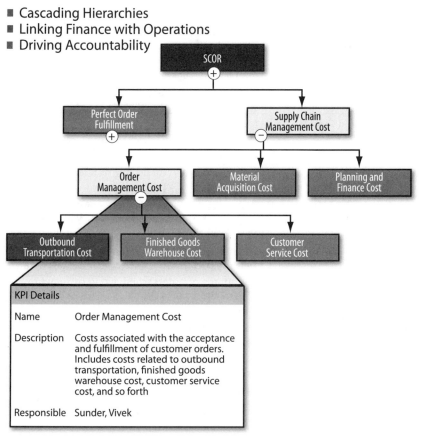

- Cascading Hierarchies
- Linking Finance with Operations
- Driving Accountability

How does sourcing affect my supply chain cost?

Figure 13-4. How Metrics Cascade

SCOR

The Supply-Chain Operations Reference-model (SCOR®) is a process reference model developed by the management consulting firm PRTM and AMR Research and endorsed by the Supply-Chain Council (SCC) as the cross-industry de facto standard diagnostic tool for supply chain management. SCOR enables users to address, improve, and communicate supply chain management practices within and between all interested parties in the extended enterprise.

From our experience, the following metrics derived from the SCOR model can be very valuable for managing instrumenting the supply chain at the strategic, tactical, and operational levels:

Table 13-2. KPIs for the Supply Chain

Strategic Focus	KPI
Customer Service (to increase revenue and market share)	Forecast accuracy
	Perfect order rating / service levels
	Production delivery to due dates
	Order cycle time (number of days between customer order and shipment)
Total Delivered Costs (to compete effectively)	Manufacturing costs
	Distribution/logistics costs
	Material costs
Reduce Capital lock-up (to invest in other strategic areas)	Inventory levels
	Supply chain cycle time
	Cash-to-cash cycles (the number of days between when you buy from a supplier until you receive payment from a customer)
Delivery Performance	Delivery performance to scheduled commit date
	Delivery performance to customer request date
	Percentage of orders scheduled to customer request date
	Order fulfillment lead time
Manufacturing	Capacity utilization
	Yield
	Production plan adherence
	Build cycle time
	Make cycle time
Inventory Control	Inventory obsolescence as a % of total inventory
	Inventory days of supply
	Raw material or product days of supply
Product Costing	Unit cost
	Overhead costs

While the metrics themselves are important, it is the relationship among the metrics that describes the causal flow from operational activities to value delivered. AMR Research has developed a hierarchy of supply chain metrics, illustrated in Figure 13-5, to help companies prioritize what they measure depending on their strategic focus. The top tier assesses a company's supply chain health while the two tiers underneath can help determine the root cause of problems and provide insight for corrective action, as follows:

- Top tier: The supply chain health assessment helps executives assess, at 50,000 feet, the overall health of the supply chain and the high-level tradeoffs they might be making
- Mid-level: The supply chain diagnostic level of detail is the 25,000-foot view. This level uses a composite cash flow metric to provide an initial diagnostic tool
- Ground level: The bottom level, supply chain effectiveness, uses a variety of metrics that support effective root cause analysis and allow surgical, highly efficient corrective action, as follows:

The beauty of the AMR model is that having benchmarked over 70 supply chains in detail, AMR has come to the conclusion that companies can assess their supply chain health using just three key metrics: demand forecast accuracy, perfect order fulfillment, and supply chain cost.

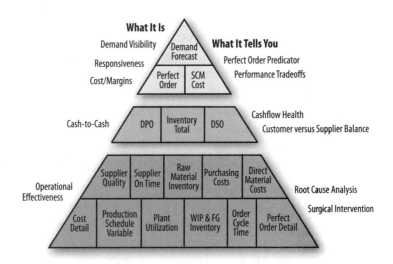

Figure 13-5. AMR's Hierarchy of Supply Chain Metrics
(Source: AMR Research, 2008, "The Hierarchy of Supply Chain Metrics—
Diagnosing Your Supply Chain Health")

Table 13-3. Three Metrics for Measuring Supply Chain Health
(Adapted from AMR Research, 2004, "The Hierarchy of Supply Chain Metrics:
Diagnosing Your Supply Chain Health")

Metric	Definition
Perfect Order	An order that is complete, accurate, on time, and in perfect condition The conditions that prevent a perfect order include: • Orders not delivered on time • Orders not meeting customer requirements
Demand Forecast Accuracy (DFA)	The difference between forecasted and actual demand
Supply Chain Management Cost	Total supply chain operating costs, including all fixed and variable costs, taken as a percent of revenue SCM cost includes the following operating costs: direct purchasing, manufacturing, transportation, warehouse/distribution, inventory holding, and customer service

What's In It for Me?

The big answer is that performance management will enable you to do your job more effectively by dealing with obstacles in the chain: When you learn you can't convert your raw material to the product you've been tasked with shipping a week later, or despite your efforts, your costs have been driven up because your inventory team always has too much stock in the warehouse, performance management provides the immediate data that you need to solve these problems.

With this data, the inventory stock is now in line with your metrics and the warehouse team is aligned to the same goals as your manufacturing and logistics teams. Instead of lacking the raw material needed to manufacture, your procurement team found another source for the material when they learned that the first source could not deliver. Performance management also facilitates your collaboration with other business units, helping you to deliver on promises and forecast more accurately.

If this all seems somewhat obvious—simply good business practice— you're right. However many companies do not align corporate, departmental, and individual goals on a single, clear trajectory. If you're the inventory manager, the job of building your quarterly inventory plan would be much easier, for example, if you collaborated with the head of manufacturing. However, if your personal MBOs prioritize other goals, most likely you won't focus on collaboratively managing inventory.

So what's in performance management for you? In a word—success.

Effective Collaboration

The importance of achieving meaningful collaboration across the organization cannot be overstated. Here are some key points to consider with regard to collaboration across the company:

- A cross-functional approach to supply chain performance management will be effective only if you align resource allocation and workforce incentives to match your business unit strategy
- Talk to the business unit most closely linked to the areas you want to optimize and get them to synchronize with your strategies, initiatives, and plans. You'll both benefit
- Set up a scorecard with those business unit leaders and yourself
- Feed the supply chain planning model into their planning model
- Provide management reports and statutory reports specific to that department that shows how your language translates to theirs. For example, 500 widgets in supply chain terms equals $1,000,000 in COGS for the Finance department

More specifically, these are some of the issues and tensions you will encounter when collaborating with the other business units.

Collaboration with Product Development

Your collaboration with the Product Development department ensures that your company has a product to sell. The analysis, modeling, and business experience you have accumulated is invaluable to them. Product Development will want to know if suppliers are reliable, whether you can get the best possible price, and whether you are getting the best raw materials and parts to turn their dreams into a commercial reality. You will need to have the answers.

You can formulate the tastiest candy bar in the universe—but if you trust the ingredients to someone who subcontracts to a third party, it may not taste as it was intended because the ingredients are inferior. That blame will be laid at your door, by Product Development, and the rest of the company.

Collaboration with Procurement

The supply chain can break down in a hurry if Procurement and the Supply Chain are not collaborating well. You can whittle costs as low as possible, but you can't do it at the expense of a quality product. That's where clear communications with Procurement is vital. They must be advised of the minimum quality that you will accept. They must also collaborate with you to make sure your network is chaos-tolerant. In other words, you don't want to consolidate all your supply of a critical binding agent or semiconductor in one supplier. At the very least, you need to have one backup on the "red phone" just in case. Procurement is your friend when it comes to determining who to call.

Collaboration with IT

The IT department is critical to helping the supply chain get visibility into "where everything is all the time." You need:

- Automation of all your shipments
- Help with compliance activities related to those shipments. Regulations and documents differ from one country to another and one industry to another
- Visibility into this complex process. Every single "touch" of the shipment: the bill of lading, the signoffs, customs, border control, and more must be automated so that supply chain executives can look from beginning to end. Customers or suppliers will call and ask if something has shipped. But if you do not have adequate visibility, even though it was shipped, it could be anywhere along the way and there could be additional charges, such as penalties or fees, associated with getting the shipment to the customer
- Help with managing (and preventing) supply chain horror stories. What if a truck gets turned around at customs and it's got to go back to the warehouse? Then there's the cost of that return trip, the driver, and the implication for the other shipments it throws off, the cost to check everything back into inventory, and finally, the cost of reprocessing the order

Collaboration with Finance

The supply chain is about the careful balance of supply and demand to minimize stock outages and inventory. Outages mean lost revenue opportunities and inventory represents costs, so Finance is invested in understanding and supporting the supply chain. The conversation between these two groups centers around which products are actually profitable. What are the highest costs (for example, transportation or inventory storage) and how can we manage them most efficiently? Finance and the Supply Chain also work closely to ensure days sales outstanding (DSO) and inventory totals remain manageable through effective demand forecasting.

Collaboration with HR

Increasing globalization has changed the game of talent management within the supply chain. The complexity associated with hiring and retaining top talent has expanded. HR needs to assist supply chain executives with navigating the hiring processes and employee regulations of a given country. When you look at the numbers of interactions within a supply chain, they often cut across countries and geographies, each with a different code of conduct for hiring and managing human resources. In order to eliminate risks and to be competitive in hiring practices across geography, HR must be savvy on these changing practices and regulations. Further HR must help Supply Chain develop retention strategies since commodization has not just impacted product pricing but also employment. Workers, whether employees or contract workers, tend to shop for the best possible pay, and as a result there may not be a lot of loyalty to the organization.

Collaboration with Sales

The supply chain relies on Sales to help achieve operational excellence. Sales can provide meaningful insight into the operational effectiveness of the supply chain. This then allows Supply Chain to conduct a root cause analysis. For example, supply chain analysts might explore which manufacturing processes need to be improved based on customer feedback. Supply Chain also looks to Sales to help determine which products offer the greatest up-sell opportunity. In general, the primary touch point between Supply Chain and Sales is the forecast. Supply chain executives rely on Sales to provide forecast accuracy so that they can manage demand and supply.

Collaboration with Marketing

With customer expectations growing, supply chain executives recognize that cost alone cannot measure effectiveness. Insight about the customer is essential. Marketing is a great resource for such information. Supply chain executives look to Marketing to provide key insights on market trends including customer needs, buying patterns, and competitive threats.

Collaboration with Service

The Supply Chain relies on the Service department for visibility into order management and fulfillment as well guidance into the process of service parts planning and logistics. Supply Chain will typically ask Service questions related to forecast accuracy, service levels, and order rate fulfillment, all with a goal of optimizing supply chain performance.

Orchestrating the Business Network

Not only is it important to have predictability in your own company, but also you must have predictability in your partner companies, and you must be predictable to them. Your program should reflect the philosophy that all operations constitute a single global network, a supply chain of one. In this light, everything is interrelated. Without data from your partners, you can't achieve the truly holistic view required to see the big or little picture. To gain this view, you must be able to pull data from any system within or beyond your company's boundaries, and your partners must be able to do the same.

From 2000 to 2005, supply chain management was focused on making the right tradeoffs between make, buy, source, return, and deliver processes within the four walls of the enterprise.[1] This new focus on cross-functional coordination gave rise to supply chain planning (SCP). During this shift, demand processes were passive, focused primarily on improving manufacturing forecasting. As companies matured, these flows widened to include not only product information, but also intelligence on cash-to-cash cycles, inventory management, embedded product innovation, and channel demand sensing. As companies began this journey, the most mature processes were extended past the four walls of the company to focus on external, customer-focused networks.

Three primary networks emerged:

- **Demand networks.** Sensing demand and translating customer insights into actual channel demand to maximize selling opportunities
- **Design networks.** Focused on external collaboration with design partners and suppliers to drive open innovation processes with a broader base of partners
- **Supply networks.** Networks of suppliers focused on providing services and products against buy-side contracts and purchase orders

The world has slowly shifted to the concept of a value network. Traditional supply chain processes are shifting from a supply-based focus on transactions and inward-focused metrics to an external focus on the design and management of relationship, or to put it succinctly, supply networks are

---

[1] AMR Research, "How Do I Drive Value Through a Value Network," November 2007.

morphing into value networks. These "demand-driven value networks" are holistically designed to maximize value across a set of processes and technologies that senses and orchestrates demand based on a near real-time, zero-latency demand signal across multiple networks of employees, suppliers, and customers.

There are three primary differences between a supply network and a value network:

- **Focus.** Supply networks focus on supply, while value networks focus on delivering value
- **Primary technologies.** Supply networks are based on transactional technology, while value networks are based on relationship enablement
- **Metrics and reward systems.** Supply networks are inward and inside-out focused. Value networks work from the outside in

Establishing Your BI Foundation

Establishing your BI foundation involves a multiphase process, including:

- Finding a solid metrics framework
- Eliminating your dependence on spreadsheets
- Reconciling data from multiple sources, including warehouse, inventory, and transportation management systems

Your supply chain team alone cannot meet the challenge posed by these objectives, which is why it's important to bring in Finance, IT, and Procurement. The right systems are meaningless without the right people to run them. You will find it difficult to grasp the nuanced ways that finance metrics, for instance, decompose into operational metrics. It's only after all these resources are in place that optimization in end-to-end processes can take place.

Once your data is pulled and integrated, you'll need to reconcile it with other business units and provide consistent translation layers.

Next comes your master data. Quality is critical, and to ensure it you'll likely need a supply master list. Supply master lists are frequently in disarray, especially those from companies that haven't yet reconciled them. Until you consolidate your suppliers and reflect that consolidation on your supply master list, you'll be hard pressed to develop an elegant supply network.

Finally, you must gather all unstructured data, such as tariff bills, customs papers, and so forth, then reconcile them with the master data created in the previous steps.

Supply chain needs the following capabilities from BI:

- **Relevant visualizations.** Supply chain-specific visualizations should supplement standard tables and graphs. For example, many supply chain professionals are used to visualizing the flow of goods in the supply chain as a network diagram. Additional visualization for supply chain includes production sourcing, inventory optimization, transportation planning, production planning, and detailed scheduling

- **Relevant event-capture and alerting.** The ability to gather information from event sources, such as from transportation and logistics systems, along with external sources such as key suppliers, and the ability to define alerts for critical events (the shipping capacity of our Malaysian operations just went down 33%) and inform the right person to take action

- **A unified semantic layer and data integration and data quality across departmental and application silos.** BI allows supply chain users to bridge applications when they do not have access to a single, integrated transactional system, but instead many point systems (transportation management, inventory management, warehouse management, etc.), or multiple SCM systems. Use BI to define business rules of key dimensions (definitions of locations, routes, distribution mechanisms) and metrics (definitions and relationships)

- **Trusted, cleansed master data.** BI platforms give supply chain analysts standard definitions of assets as well as standard definitions of individual products themselves (for example that "Chocolate Delight" = "Yummy Chocolate Treats" = "Chocoholics R Us") and their key attributes such as batch numbers, individual RFID tags, etc.

- **Structured and unstructured data.** BI platforms can provide insight from both structured and unstructured data, such as invoices, cargo manifests, and more, which can provide tremendous additional value

- **Reports including dashboards for visualizing supply chain information.** Examples include product line analysis by region to determine finished good inventory by warehouse, sales by product line versus actual product inventory, and optimal routing for transportation planning. BI can also provide queries of supply data and intuitive analytics capabilities for end users. Examples of supply chain query and analysis include enabling suppliers to check their inventory to replenish materials or allowing customers to track the location of their order.

Assessing Performance Management Maturity and Setting Your Course

In its nascent stages, the typical organization monitors its supply chain performance using reporting and dashboards, only to find itself overwhelmed by a sea of chaotic data. The key to solving this problem lies in an integrated metrics framework. With it, you can build consolidated views of performance metrics. However, even though you may understand how your critical metrics are functioning (at this level) in relation to your past SC operations and, perhaps, to the whole enterprise, it is unlikely that you have harnessed this metric power to drive your business value. Your highest performance level is the integration of smart decision-making, business plans, and process workflow. To achieve this, you'll use data from day-to-day operations to deliver product according to demand on a near real-time basis.

The AMR Supply Chain Maturity Model

This maturity model, developed by AMR, shows five levels of maturity: the static supply chain, functional excellence, horizontal integration, external collaboration, and on-demand responsive supply networks.

Supply chain maturity matters; according to PRTM management consultants, companies with best-in-class supply chains are 1.65 times more profitable than those with immature supply chains.

Table 13-4. Levels of Supply Chain Maturity

Level	Characteristics
Level 1: Static Focus: Transactions, production, supply to customers	Quarterly generated plans
	Frequent overstock and understock conditions
	Different approaches to logistics and fulfillment by business unit
	No formal supplier relationships or centralized management of suppliers
Level 2: Functional Excellence Focus: Increased process efficiency	System generated demand/supply plans
	High inventory levels
	Centralized and consolidated management of suppliers
	Common logistics network and infrastructure
	Key customers receive additional services
	Online ordering and/or EDI

Level 3: Horizontal Integration Focus: Working more closely with other business units and sharing info with key suppliers	Supply and demand plans are automated and integrated across functional areas Plans set weekly Department managers set planning objectives Key suppliers now have service-level agreements Visibility into orders and inventory across the enterprise Planning for and identifying new sources of supply Customers receive differentiated service based on segmentation Context activities are outsourced
Level 4: External Collaboration Focus: Work with multiple partners and share assets	All non-core activities are outsourced Dashboards provide monitoring capability and alerts Visibility to supplier inventory, orders, forecasts, and shipments Visibility to entire order to cash process Commitments are demand-driven with responsive replenishment
Level 5: On-Demand Responsive Supply Network Focus: Full visibility across supply network	Result: 15% less inventory, 17% better perfect order performance, 35% shorter cash-to-cash cycle

Responsive supply networks are the result of a careful balance of supply and demand to minimize stock outages and inventory. Visibility across the supply network to sense early demand and supply fluctuations is essential. Responsive supply networks allow companies with fluctuating demand and high product complexity to sense and respond faster to dynamics across a globally distributed environment. The ability to predict and intelligently adapt to changing market conditions is key to reinventing relationships, containing cost, and supporting new markets, channels, mergers and acquisitions.

The PM Lifecycle for Supply Chain

As we have noted, ad hoc methods and processes can no longer manage the complexity of today's intricate supply networks. Without the certainty that a single source of truth provides, your team will be unable to get the necessary data to formalize a reliable metrics program. The absence of data ownership is an obstacle to accountability. Any KPIs and metrics you manage to establish will be so slow in development that by the time you can use them, they'll be obsolete.

If you want to survive in today's economy, you must implement performance management for your supply networks whose stages—strategize, plan, monitor, and optimize—create a formalized and reproducible cycle. This will enable you to manage numerous, complex activities with clarity.

Earlier in this chapter, "The Business Process Angle" lists both the business processes within the supply chain, as well as end-to-end business processes that touch the supply chain. You may want to consider optimizing these processes using the PM lifecycle.

Strategize and Prioritize

The following sections outline basic steps you'll follow in developing and prioritizing your strategies.

Understand the Context

Strategy is not an independent exercise. It should cascade down from the corporate level and provide you with detailed guidance about what to do and how to measure success.

Review the corporate strategic goals, strategic plans, initiatives, and metrics that track progress against them and understand them. Contextualize them for the supply chain and use this context to drive the supply chain PM lifecycle.

Develop and Set the Strategy

Review the environment. What are you good at? For example, you might have good control of inventory relative to your competitors. What are the main problems you face? What risks do you have? Your risks might include fraying relations between two nations in your resource chain. What compliance requirements must you meet? Your compliance challenges might include complying with trade regulations such as REACH. You may be overwhelmed with the unprecedented number of documents needed for cross-border shipments to different countries.

Set the mission, values and vision. Define the mission, which is the fundamental purpose of the entity, especially what it provides to customers and clients. For example, by leveraging the supplier base, we improve our processes and better serve our customers through improvement in purchasing, manufacturing, and distributing products and services to our customers.

Next, define the core values, the attitude, behavior, and character of the organization. We are willing, for example, to leverage our partner ecosystem to help our customers succeed.

Define the vision, a concise statement that defines the 3- to 5-year goals of the organization. Say, for example, that by 2015, we will be consistently ranked in the top 10% of customer satisfaction as a value-added partner for every business unit in the company.

Set the goals. With all that contextual information in hand, set a strategy or strategies to follow. Consider using a strategy map to display the cause-and-effect relationships among the objectives that make up a strategy. A good strategy map tells a story of how value is created for the business.

Assign KPIs to Goals and Set the Right Targets

Define KPIs and targets associated with your strategy. See "KPIs That Matter for Your Success" earlier in this chapter for details. Two that you might want to consider include Cost-to-Serve (or Total Delivered Cost) and Level of Customer Satisfaction.

As you set your strategy, remember not to lose sight of the balance between KPIs—all too often supply chain optimization focuses exclusively on cutting costs and not on enhancing customer satisfaction. The KPIs you select will depend on your strategy.

Perform Additional Risk Analysis

Now look again at risks to see what could keep you from meeting your goals. Figure 13-7 shows potential threats to the supply chain identified in AMR's research.

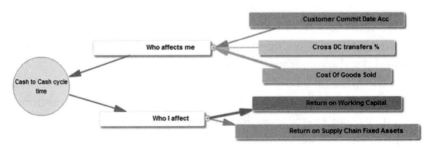

Figure 13-6. KPI Relationship Insight

Q: In your opinion, which category of risk poses the most potential threat to your organization? Percentage of responses, n = 89

Figure 13-7. Risk Factors—Most Potential Threat
(Source: AMR Research, "Managing Risk in the Supply Chain—A Quantitative Study," 2007)

For each risk, decide what your risk appetite is. Can you afford to take that risk? What's the worst-case scenario? Does taking the risk have the potential to wipe out important projects or compromise the level of performance that you currently enjoy? For example, if you put your best operations managers to work on supporting a new Lean manufacturing initiative, what will happen to the other projects?

Set a response strategy for the risk (watch, research, transfer, delegate, mitigate). You could decide that the new Lean initiative has such great potential that you want to put the key team all on that initiative to help it gain traction. You decide to watch the risk for now, implementing a mitigation strategy if you see indications that the risk has materialized.

Decide whether you can afford the worst-case scenario presented by that risk from a performance management perspective. Could it bring down some critical value-generating mechanism for the company? If you are implementing Lean manufacturing at all your plants simultaneously, it might be efficient, but if there are hitches in the implementation, all the plants might produce below their capacity during the transition. A pilot in one area of one plant is obviously less risky.

Define KRIs and thresholds for those risks. KRIs, like KPIs, are the early warning signals that define the point at which you want to be alerted about an impending risk. For example, by monitoring inventory against sales revenue in real-time, setting a threshold of more than 1% will create an early warning signal for you.

Examples of Risks for the Supply Chain

Reliability. To measure risk in terms of reliability, you will be concerned with tracking key risk indicators (KRIs) such as:

- Overall equipment effectiveness
- Machine malfunctions per production order
- Purchase order quantities delivered complete

Demand-Supply Mismatch. To catch mismatches in demand and supply early, focus on the following KRIs:

- Inventory (days) above maximum
- Inventory (days) below minimum
- Sales forecast accuracy
- Demand/Supply Match—Order Lead Time
- Demand/Supply Match—Inventory Values

Supplier. You are probably dealing with an ever-larger network of suppliers. To keep your performance optimal, focus on:

- Fulfillment rate for deliveries
- Price trends over the last three months
- Vendor assessment total score over time
- Purchase order quantity confirmed as requested
- Supplier performance

Quality. To mitigate quality risks, carefully watch the following KRIs:

- Supplier performance
- Finished product inspections passed
- Quality of service provision

Perform Additional Compliance Analysis and Set Controls

Define your compliance requirements. Compliance defines the boundaries within which companies must operate when achieving their strategies.

Maybe you've ignored the area of global trade compliance to date, but the increase in shipments to countries like Brazil means that you must pay attention to automating compliance with new laws such as Nota Fiscal Eletronica, an electronic invoicing mandate from the Brazilian government.

Define policies, procedures, and controls that must be in place to ensure that you can meet the compliance requirements. Make sure that this applies not only at the main business process level but to all subprocesses including

Table 13-5. Risk Management Technologies for the Supply Chain
(Source: AMR Research, 2008, "Revamping SCM Technologies to Manage Supply Chain Risk")

Risk Categories	Examples	Functionality Needed	Applications
Catastrophic	Pandemic, earthquake, geopolitical unrest	Some of these risks can be predicted and some can't. Applications here must focus on quick recovery of the supply chain resources, like production and transportation, enabling customer and employee self-service, and providing visibility	Response Management Inventory Management Supply chain visibility and event management Transportation Management
Strategic	Unprofitable new product introduction, quality risks associated with low-cost countries, supplier rationalization, tax and financial impact of a market expansion, environmental risks	For strategic planning, simulation, optimization and what-if analysis, applications are needed to quantify the strategic risk, compare options, and analyze possible tradeoffs	Strategic Business Planning Carbon Emission Management Network Design Tools Sourcing and Supplier Management
Periodic Incident	Recurring supplier failure, recurring customer service failure, technology failure because of upgrades or migration	To manage these risks, there is a need for applications that identify the pattern of a recurring risk, assess the implications of that risk on the supply chain, and help the user make tactical tradeoffs, as well as outline long-term strategies to eliminate those risks	Demand forecasting with pattern recognition Supplier collaboration Supply Chain Performance Management Order Fulfillment
Daily Surprise	Plan shutdowns, unanticipated fluctuations in demand, unanticipated transpiration shortages	What's needed are tools that can escalate the risk to the right user and help respond to the surprise in real-time	Supply Chain visibility and event management Real-time inventory repositioning Real time forecasting Real-time S&OP

those related to partners. For example, what does Nota Fiscal Eletronica require? Can software help you generate those documents consistently? Designate someone to work closely with IT and sales to monitor global trade activities. What countries are in scope? Designate someone in IT to investigate available software solutions for automating this ever-changing area for compliance, with a supply chain manager corresponding directly with that person. Is there a difference for Nota Fiscal Eletronica for inbound versus outbound shipments? Is the requirement different for Europe versus Asia for doing business with Brazil?

Define control targets that translate compliance expectations into performance expectations. If you make one shipment to a different country, handling the paperwork by hand is not problematic. But if you begin shipping components to multiple suppliers in that country, not only will the paperwork be overwhelming, but without strict compliance, you'll probably have delays in getting those components each time you add a new supplier. Working with IT and Sales, set controls that allow you to monitor global shipping trends to help you see where global trade compliance may need to be automated to ensure the speedy execution of key business processes.

Table 13-6. Key Controls for the Supply Chain

Control Area	Controls
Invoice Verification	Individual Inventory postings other than system date, Org Level Inventory postings other than system date
Inventory Valuation	Material Valuation changes at standard price, Material Valuation changes at Moving Average price
Receive Goods	Payments without Good Receipts (GR), Org Level Payments without GR, Purchase orders created thru GR
Manage Inventory	Document Level Physical Inventory Tolerance, Item Level Physical Inventory Tolerance, Changes to Physical Inventory Tolerances, Physical Inventory Differences at Document Level, Physical Inventory Differences at Item Level

Managing Global Trade

Companies today must deal with four major areas in global trade, including higher volumes of import and export transactions, increased regulatory pressures, government mandates for electronic communication, and increased complexity coupled with less time to deal with these issues.

Companies are increasingly sourcing, manufacturing, and distributing goods on a global basis. According to the World Trade Organization, approximately 30% of world trade crosses borders, and this proportion is increasing. Overall, global trade volume is growing by about 10% annually. In particular, more and more companies are doing business in China and in the entire Asia-Pacific region.

At the same time the business landscape is becoming more global, companies need to comply with more regulations. The threat of global terrorism has brought export and import processes are under closer scrutiny. Post 9/11, the topic of trade security has taken on new dimensions.

Companies need to strictly adhere to various regulations, including the U.S. Export Administration Regulations (EAR), Chemical Weapon Convention Regulations (CWCR), International Traffic in Arms Regulations (ITAR), dual-use regulations, and many others.

In addition, many antiterrorist regulations have been introduced in recent years. For example, one legal requirement imposed by regulatory authorities requires companies to check their business partners against prohibited party lists published by governments around the world. These lists contain the names of thousands of individuals, companies, and organizations that are

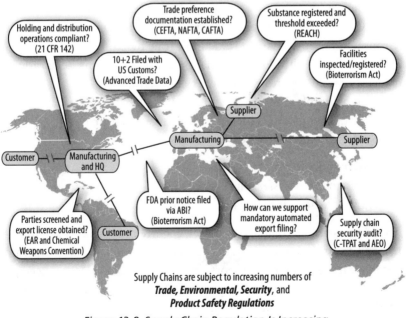

Figure 13-8. Supply Chain Regulation Is Increasing

prohibited from cross-border trade. It is the legal responsibility of exporters, importers, and financial institutions to know the identities of their business partners. Failure to comply with such regulations can result in hefty fines and a revocation of trading privileges. Those found to be responsible for the failure may even face imprisonment.

Goods that used to pass borders easily might get stopped at the border just because of compliance failures. Companies that fail to comply risk fines and penalties as well as brand image and supply chain disruptions. As a result, ensuring compliance with import and export regulations is essential.

Another area that has undergone significant changes in recent years is the interaction between companies and customs authorities, an area of global trade that had been very much paper-dominated to date. With the increase in global trade, more and more governments are upgrading and standardizing their IT systems and introducing new, simplified procedures. They then expect the trade community to modernize its systems.

The U.S. government, for example, intends to amend regulations mandating that all U.S. exporters electronically file export declarations via the Automated Export System (AES). Historically, U.S. exporters could file export shipments paper-based or electronically.

Furthermore, electronic systems are currently implemented in other parts of the world. The European Union launched its eCustoms Initiative in 2004. Over a seven-year span, its main vision is to implement a paperless environment for customs and trade in Europe by 2010. The participating economies should ultimately be able to submit a customs declaration in any member state, regardless of country of origin.

Although complexity is increasing, there is less time available to deal with the details of global trade. According to analyst firm ARC, a typical cross-border shipment involves:

- More than 25 parties
- Generating or transferring 35 documents
- Taking into account 600 laws and 500 trade agreements

Companies need to manage these new requirements while keeping costs down and ensuring fast movement of goods. This can be a major dilemma, especially when a company's import and export processes do not keep pace with the increased complexity in global trade. As a result, more companies are automating this area because manual processes are not only inefficient and costly, but also do not provide the kind of support needed to master the manifold challenges of international trade. Software solutions can help automate this difficult and changing area.

Work on the Strategic Action Plan and Initiatives

The strategic plan helps define the exact methodology for achieving the goals of the various initiatives. The results of this planning may require revisiting the strategy with key stakeholders at predetermined times, as well as by necessity.

Strategic Planning for the Supply Chain

Here are the steps to working through strategic planning. Develop the supply chain strategic plan, including risk and control management, specifically, automating the process, workflow, and guidance for conducting risk and control assessments.

For each initiative, define critical success and failure factors. Critical success factors might include the finalization of trade agreements with a key supplier or locking in rates before an expected government treasury move adjusts exchange rates unfavorably. Failure factors can be anything that might derail the initiative. Translate failure factors into KRIs that provide an early warning system to get the initiative back on track in time or find alternatives.

Develop different risk-adjusted scenarios, with contingency plans for as many risk scenarios as you can reasonably imagine based on past experience and the current environment. You then come up with risk response plans that help you address how you will handle the risks if they materialize. These risk responses should be included in your contingency plans.

Cascade Accountability

Each KPI, KRI, and control and its target should be owned by some department or group. The MBOs of the staff in those groups must reflect the KPIs, KRIs, and controls you set. This sounds obvious, but frequently performance is measured at an individual level in a way that does not in fact relate directly to corporate goals and strategies. For example, if Lean Manufacturing is a key strategy for the company, incentives to measure each of the seven waste areas must be tied to each group. For example, reducing time on the transportation front is an important aspect of Lean Manufacturing; therefore, even the truck drivers must own Lean Manufacturing KPIs as part of their MBOs.

Plan and Execute

In the strategize and prioritize phase of the PM Lifecycle, we put together strategic action plans and initiatives. The planning phase gets into the details of planning the strategic initiatives both from a financial and operational standpoint.

Align Corporate Budget to Supply Chain Budget

The budgeting process takes each of the outcomes or actions from the planning process and aligns revenues and expenses against them. Decisions regarding investment priorities and resource allocations define how the company will operate and set the bar for measuring performance. Take each of the steps in the initiatives you've defined and put in revenues and expenses for them.

To create risk-adjusted budgets, incorporate the range of possible revenues and costs of each action into the budget at the appropriate organizational level. A risk-adjusted budget responds to changing circumstances, providing the financial capability to react to events in a planned, proactive manner. Develop different risk-adjusted budgets with contingency plans should risks to achieving budgets materialize.

In a traditional budget, you list the individual line items (raw material, transportation, and production assets) in each row with the actuals, budgeted amounts, forecast, and actual/budget comparisons, and forecast versus budget comparisons going across in the columns. In a risk-adjusted budget, for every decision to allocate revenue to one line item versus another (like purchasing an additional piece of equipment for production versus expanding the plant size), you determine the impact and probability of the highest priority risks (like not being able to keep up with the production plan) on those individual line items and use this to set a range of expected budget and forecasted values instead of fixed values. In this case, if the risk materializes and you run out of capacity, you need a contingency plan that shows the performance and risk implications (the risk of not moving forward with the plant expansion) if we then purchase the additional equipment for the plant.

Align Budget with Supply Chain Operational Plans

The operational planning process links the budget to operational factors. Plan out each step of each initiative in terms of what will be required in terms of technology, time, and resources. Consider what risks you have in each area of the operational plan.

In a risk-adjusted operational plan, for every decision to allocate resources to one set of operational activities versus another (from keeping an existing work center setup versus doubling the capacity by upgrading the equipment in your current work center configuration), you determine the impact and probability of the highest priority operational risks (production downtime) on those individual line items and use this to set a range of expected and forecasted values instead of fixed values. In this case, if the risk materializes, you need a contingency plan that shows the performance (the goal of production capacity on your current work center versus the new capacity with the new work center layout) and risk implications if you move the budget from the existing work center to the new work center layout.

Taking these factors into account, adjust your plans with a range of operational outcomes and probabilities rather than an absolute number based on various contingencies.

Supply Chain Planning

Supply chain planning is multifaceted, including demand planning, supply network planning, production planning and detailed production scheduling, global available to promise, and transportation planning.

Demand planning allows you to calculate future demand to improve demand quality and accuracy. Demand planning solutions typically have comprehensive forecasting toolsets with causal and time-series models, the ability to select the best-fit model, support complex aggregation and disaggregation logic, and support lifecycle and seasonal planning. This generates a consolidated demand plan across different regions, countries, and departments.

Supply network planning calculates quantities to be produced and delivered to the locations to match customer demand and maintain desired service levels. Supply network planning solutions integrate data across purchasing, manufacturing, distribution, and transportation; consider constraints and penalties to plan the product flow along the supply chain; provide advanced safety stock methods considering multilevel supply chain networks and demand variability; and enable heuristic, rule, or optimization-based algorithms.

Production planning delivers a short-term plan that matches overall supply to demand, given available resources and production methodology. Using multilevel techniques and order pegging, production planning determines how, when, and where resources and materials should be deployed to accomplish production goals.

Detailed production scheduling determines the optimal production sequence for execution to meet delivery commitments based on actual constraints on the shop floor.

Global available to promise (ATP) provides online information about whether orders can be filled. These solutions allow for rule-based and multilevel ATP, the ability to manage backorders, and integration with the production planning and detailed scheduling systems to check the production plan and consider capacity constraints.

Transportation planning helps plan and optimize shipments for orders (sales orders, purchase orders, returns, and stock transport orders) and deliveries. This helps reduce transportation costs by optimizing shipments.

Sales and Operations Planning

Sales and operations planning (S&OP) is a powerful, integrated business management process to help achieve focus, alignment, and synchronization across business units. A typical S&OP plan is a monthly document that includes such things as a sales plan, an inventory plan, and a production plan, along with several other plans that help the executive leadership reach its desired goals.

Early S&OP models involved the basic concept of a single factory serving a single market, and usually involved a simple coordination process that consisted of a basic staff meeting in which staff members went over data and reports. With the advent of globalization, which caused the supply chain to become much more complex, companies found that they needed to make the transition from traditional S&OP to strategic alignment with corporate goals by incorporating integrated business planning (IBP).

To successfully incorporate IBP, companies need the following additional capabilities: strategic supply chain modeling, financial planning and modeling, and analytics. By making this transition to IBP, S&OP becomes much more than a staff meeting; it becomes a strategic business process, where the company can show a direct correlation with top-line metrics.

In most older S&OP scenarios, executives made certain supply and demand decisions and engaged in changing capacity, pricing, promotion, and inventories. But these decisions are not typically shared across all levels of business and with supply chain partners, nor are they given what is referred to as metric relief, which is the ability to understand overall business goals and produce a compensation metric based on the tradeoff decision made by the S&OP team.

One outcome of such executive planning could be that decisions could be made that don't ultimately result in an optimal financial plan. One way to avoid this is to link executive compensation with S&OP forecasts. Also, coordination and cooperation with HR, Sales and Marketing departments is essential. Each department should be accountable for its own forecasts, which results in better enforcement of the compensation scheme.

Here are several recommendations to achieve this kind of enforcement:

- Align compensation metrics of each S&OP member with the tradeoff decisions made
- Include Finance on the S&OP agenda and have each tradeoff decision mapped against the financial plan
- Develop a roadmap of S&OP membership six to nine months out. Include future acquisitions, new business partners, personnel movements, plant and product changes, and movement within the corporate decision-making politics
- Communicate the tradeoff decisions and assumptions agreed on in the S&OP meeting to the operational teams

Although each department has its own responsibility to achieve this new approach, by partnering and collaborating with the other departments involved, the company will greatly benefit.

Forecast Performance and Risks

Create rolling, risk-adjusted forecasts of the budget (revenues and costs) and operational plan (including number, capacity, and cost of resources necessary to achieve plan) so that you can see trends over a rolling time horizon for those risks whose probability, consequence, or resiliency change over time. That way if you have to make adjustments, you can see where you've been and the direction in which things are likely to go. Predictive analytical techniques can be a particular powerful tool for building risk-adjusted forecasts by modeling the impact previous risks had on previous forecasts.

For example, in a risk-adjusted supply chain forecast, you create a rolling forecast over a six-month to one-year window of a range of expected costs (the line items in your budget like new equipment or maintenance on existing machines) and an associated range of expected activity outputs (installation and maintenance activities) that are dependent on the key risks in the environment. When the probability or impact of a risk changes, you adjust the financial or operational forecast costs or activities accordingly.

Using predictive techniques, you can learn from the impact of previous risks on previous actuals (the cost of maintenance on a machine from last year versus the investment in a new machine) to predict the impact of your current risks on your current cost or activity forecasts.

Examine Repercussions for Execution Problems

In a tight economy, another look at the cost of maintenance on an existing machine is in order. Planning and execution must be based in strategy and be aligned to the strategies that have been set down. If Sales misses its revenue targets from the previous quarter that is properly aligned with corporate strategy, its impact across the company can be profound. Minimizing the risk of a surplus of inventory in the warehouse must be factored in from a cost perspective before making a decision to buy new machines or perform costly maintenance on existing machines. Coordination across and with all business units is critical so that there are no surprises.

The key to excellence in execution is visibility. The impact of sales to production capacity to inventory management to fulfillment of raw materials by suppliers shows the dependency of each area to communicate in order for your company to maximize the bottom line.

To minimize risk on the execution side, supply chain dependencies such as sales and operation plans must be well documented, and any changes in resources and requirements accompanied with documentation.

Execute

In the execute phase, the goals, risks, and compliance objectives you have set in your strategy and the resources you have allocated in your plans now drive the end-to-end business processes discussed earlier in "The Business Process Angle."

As an example, once the plan is understood, we can install new equipment and retire old assets, open new plants and close old ones down, and develop or retire products based on the transactive business processes we have established.

Monitor and Analyze

Now that you've executed your supply chain plans, it's time to find out what's working by monitoring the performance of your operations against your planned performance using the KPIs and metrics established earlier. In the monitor and analyze phase of the PM lifecycle, you watch what is

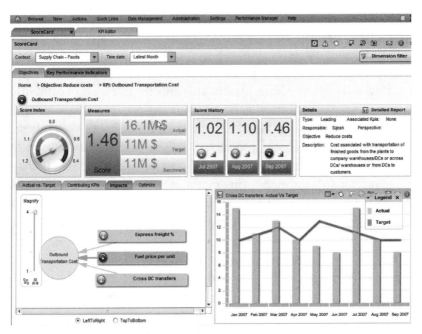

Figure 13-9. A Supply Chain Dashboard

happening (monitor), analyze why, and decide what can be done differently to improve the situation relative to your goals.

This requires analytics related to your initiative. Types of analytics to consider include contract analytics, spend analytics (see Chapter 14), supplier analytics, pricing analytics, supply and demand analytics, manufacturing analytics, inventory analytics, and logistics and fulfillment analytics.

Monitor

It is important to distinguish the different categories of monitoring in evaluating business performance. Event monitoring looks for a single, discrete activity or exposure event. In supply chain, a theft in a specific warehouse or location can create exposure for the company.

Trend monitoring is similar to event monitoring, but looks at events over time to determine patterns, for example, how frequently that event occurred and if the frequency is increasing. In supply chain, product defects for a specific product line can determine whether a pattern is related to a specific raw material, packaging, or handling.

Intelligence monitoring collects information from a variety of external sources that are of interest to the company and may indicate a risk exposure.

One example is watching the business wire reports for news on an international trade agreement that may affect tariffs. Better yet, have a lobbyist near the floor for the vote, reporting back to you before the news hits the wires.

The presentation of information to be monitored is also crucial in order to facilitate decision-making. Dashboards are effective ways of combining the events, trends, and intelligence monitoring patterns across all of the major facets of the business to be monitored, including the key business dimensions like customers, products, projects, and employees, and the related KPI, KRIs, controls, and incidents and losses. For the supply chain, typical dashboards for monitoring might include dashboards for production, procurement, inventory, accounts payable, quality, logistics, and assets. Using dashboards, you can evaluate performance, initiatives, risks, controls, and incidents and losses.

To evaluate performance, look at the KPIs to identify progress made toward achievement of objectives and trends. Is the KPI on delivery to the promise-date above the tolerance set? How is it trending and has the trend changed since the last time it was checked?

Next, evaluate initiatives. Are any failing or behind schedule? Is the capacity on the new equipment or machines on target? Is the trend improving or declining and how has it changed since the last time it was checked?

To evaluate risk, review KRIs to identify:

- Top risks. Are you having fulfillment issues such as lost capacity due to machine downtime, supplier on-time delivery ratings, or inventory turnover pace at the warehouse?
- Changes to risk levels for key activities. Do you need to extend the promise date to your customers? Or shrink the order cycle time of your suppliers?
- Assessment procedures. Are risks being assessed in accordance with company policy or according to best practices? Should you perform inventory counts on a weekly basis or monthly?
- Effectiveness of mitigation. Are mitigation strategies reducing the likelihood or impact of a risk? Are you doing detailed security checks for plant personnel?

Evaluate internal controls. Report key control deficiencies, approvals, verifications, and reconciliations to mitigate risk. Do receiving personnel in the warehouse have access to vendor master records?

Evaluate incidents and losses. If risks or losses have occurred, or external events are affecting the company (an economic downturn, for example), document this information, even if you haven't been tracking it in the system yet. For example, you can track all thefts of inventory and implement a new security procedure for searching bags and belongings if warranted.

No matter how proactive you are, manual monitoring is very inefficient. Automated monitoring can proactively identify out-of-tolerance conditions, highlighting when a KPI, KRI, or control goes over thresholds and then alerting the responsible party. This should take into account forecasting, trending, and modeling capabilities so that if a metric falls out of range of a trend, budget, or plan, the appropriate alert is raised, along with a workflow to get an investigation underway.

Analyze

Analysis is a key step in which you not only look at where you are, but what is happening (or what has happened) and why. The techniques for analysis can range from highly manual and simple to fairly automated and complex in terms of statistical techniques.

Analyze KPIs to understand why they are increasing or decreasing. For example, you review the margins KPI and drill down to the production dashboard to find that one of the machines is constantly down and is producing at 20% capacity.

Analyze initiatives to understand why they are succeeding or failing. If the manufacturing team has implemented Lean Manufacturing with a limited amount of training at the plant, the initiative would eventually fail.

Analyze KRIs to understand why they are increasing or decreasing. You conduct a correlation analyses to identify the need for training and implement a training and awareness program.

Analyze controls to see if they are effective. For example, employees must go through a certification process for the Lean Manufacturing rollout and earn an official certification and sign-off from their managers within the next month.

Analyze incidents and losses to determine root causes and trends of incidents and losses. You notice, for example, that inventory theft is increasing across the warehouses. You do an analysis to determine if there is a trend in the products that are missing or for specific shifts of workers.

In all of these cases, analysis was done with human intervention, but this does not have to be the case. The volume and complexity of data in the enterprise today makes it is increasingly difficult to mine data and come to intelligent conclusions. Using data mining techniques, software can determine likely root causes and suggest recommended actions. For example, you observe that a KRI for overpayment to a supplier is increasing. Without any manual intervention, the system does a series of correlations. When you highlight the KRI, a popup shows that the number one factor associated with the supply chain is the sudden decrease in capacity due to a reorganization.

Supply Chain Analytics

Supply chain analytics refers to the methodologies, metrics, processes and systems that are used to monitor and manage (usually at an operational level) the performance of a distinct aspect of the supply chain (for example, demand planning or warehouse execution). The issue with this approach is how to analyze performance across end-to-end business processes that span several departments (which is what we have been advocating throughout this book). For example, a collaborative supply and demand process would require pulling data from supply chain planning, supply chain execution, CRM, accounts payable, and order management applications, all of which could effectively have separate analytical solutions monitoring performance at a functional level.

Adjust

After monitoring and analyzing to know what has happened and why things not going according to plan, set things back on course by taking what you've learned and using that information to adjust the settings. Always consider the impact of your goals, risks, and compliance concerns on other business units.

Adjust KPIs. For KPIs trending in the wrong direction, analyze the root causes, and it should be clear what actions will set things back on course. However, remember that KPIs are interlinked, and you must optimize your performance goals in the context of risk objectives and without violating your compliance objectives.

For example, in Supply Chain, a shipment held at customs will impact the delivery promise date to the customer which will, in turn, impact customer satisfaction. By working with trade managers to ensure that all the paperwork is filled out, the risk of missing the promise date to the customer is reduced.

Adjust initiatives. For initiatives that are not going as planned, rapidly take remedial action or cancel them. If it's clear that the initiative is not going to work, either make changes that can help save the project or cancel it, if possible, so that you can reallocate those resources.

For example, in rolling out a new transportation plan to balance transport and freight costs, you find that there are not enough resources to optimize the plan. The budget must then allocate additional resources to execute the new transportation plan.

Adjust KRIs. For KRIs trending in the wrong direction, once you have analyzed the root causes, put mitigating controls in place to stabilize them. However, it is critical to remember that KRIs are interlinked, and you must optimize your risk goals in the context of performance objectives and without violating your compliance objectives.

Say you conduct correlation analyses to understand how the number of distribution centers impacts the speed of delivering spare parts. You put a mitigating control in place to monitor distribution centers that have the longest cycle time in fulfilling orders. However, do this only if it does not decrease the likelihood of delivering on the goal of delivering within a customer's requirements and if it doesn't violate any compliance objectives like increasing safety incidents at the warehouses due to overworking employees.

Adjust controls. For control violations, adjustment takes the form of remediation and certification. For example, after discovering that a licensable product without the correct paperwork control was shipped and the control was violated, you set up a remediation plan to have a trade manager approve every licensable product that is shipped out of the warehouse.

Adjust after incidents or losses. For incidents and losses, the correct adjustments typically involve reexamining whether you are tracking the right risks and have put the appropriate controls in place to mitigate them. For example, finding an uptick in last-minute costs on overnight freight shipments, an automated risk monitoring process could be put in place that alerts you to the first sign of increased cost per shipment. The alert is automatically triggered if the freight cost is higher than the cost of the product.

You want to search for and identify variances between actual and planned performance. You can use this knowledge to optimize activities that are falling short and to replicate those th.at are succeeding.

Monitoring is essential to project visibility. Identify and monitor projects that are behind schedule because they run a higher risk of failure. Investigate why production is not at capacity. Address the cause of the problem and formulate corrective actions that should be taken to put production at optimal capacity or at the very least to help future production plans succeed (in other words, put lessons learned into action).

Analysis can move beyond just tracking KPIs to more sophisticated types such as:

- **Simulation.** This technique is used to see how changes in one area might affect others. It is a form of modeling that enables what-if analysis. For example, what if a lower duty shipping method is used for lower volume orders?
- **Trend analysis.** This type of monitoring takes a longer view. If you find a problem when monitoring, it's helpful to review trends in that particular area. Is the current problem an anomaly or indicative of a need for a more serious process improvement? For example, what is the average profit margin of make-to-order versus make-to-stock orders? This can help determine whether to keep the make-to-order business
- **Performance audits or reviews.** Are the resources currently allocated adequate to achieve the business goals? How often are manufacturing practices such as Six Sigma reviewed for effectiveness? This can point out areas for potential improvement

Model and Optimize

When creating a model of your operations, the goal is to be predictive— you will base your model on past and current performance as a means to forecast future performance—creating a model of the organization's resources utilization.

Taking the corporate forecast and modeling it down to the account level has particular advantages for sales as well as for the supply chain. Modeling at this level effectively cuts across departmental boundaries and gives visibility into efforts such as vendor-managed inventory (VMI). According to AMR, VMI programs, which represent 30–40% of demand, often exist in isolation without such modeling. Modeling to the account level is a leading-edge practice, with only 22% of companies that AMR surveyed modeling at this level.

Furthermore, this type of practice improves forecasts, and companies with the most accurate forecasts were also most on top of their game, according to AMR Benchmark Analytix, indicated by:

- Carrying 15% less inventory
- Demonstrating 17% stronger order fulfillment
- Enjoying 35% shorter cash-to-cash cycle times

Model

Financial modeling takes several forms, including revenue, cost, and profitability modeling, scenario modeling, and simulation modeling.

Revenue, Cost, and Profitability Modeling

Modeling the costs, revenue, and profitability implications of performance management, risk management, and compliance management activities and their drivers can be achieved at a very detailed level using activity-based costing (ABC) and associated methodologies. If, for example, the Supply Chain organization is pursuing cost reductions, it must understand the root causes that influence significant cost drivers in its business sector. Other business units surrounding the Supply Chain team will need visibility of their cost-to-serve at least at a product group level, but sometimes down to the item level, which modern ABC systems with transactional costing capabilities can support.

Scenario Modeling

Scenario modeling can be applied to financial and operational modeling and focuses on creating different business scenarios. Simple scenario modeling can include creating a base case and then high and low cases based on changes made to input variables, such as market growth rates or inflation rates. This technique is often used in modeling market and business opportunities and creating business plans. In the supply chain, scenario modeling is beneficial for optimizing transportation schedules and reviewing different options for utilizing resources and meeting delivery deadlines.

Simulation Modeling

More advanced modeling including Monte Carlo simulation supports creating a broad range of scenarios based on multiple iterations of input assumptions and combinations. With this technique, probabilities can be assigned to various outcomes. These techniques allow uncertainty associated with a given forecast to be estimated and to reduce risk by applying sensitivity analysis, correlation, and trend extrapolation. By simulating the effect of uncertainty, it becomes possible to answer questions such as "What's the minimum outcome that we can be 90% certain of achieving?" Simulation also makes it possible to rank various contributors to overall uncertainty.

For example, an optimized solution that may take account of various business conditions with probabilities (stochastic optimization) might model the entire year's planned inventory and service demands, which leads to decisions regarding what inventory should be placed where and when. The output is a single set of instructions based on the assumptions and probabilities. The data is loaded, the optimization engine run, and the output interrogated by the user. With simulation, the user can play dynamic what-if games with the data to find out where and, more importantly, when the optimized thresholds are under strain.

Optimize

The goal at this phase of the PM lifecycle is to determine the optimal way to achieve objectives by taking into account the entire context of the problem, including all relevant constraints and assessments (costs, benefits, risk, labor and time), as well as business strategies, objectives, risks, and compliance factors. Optimization can be done both through human evaluation as well as through advanced algorithmic techniques. At its essence, supply chain optimization can be distilled to balancing the cost-to-serve, which includes all costs associated with serving the customer, and the level of customer satisfaction and loyalty in the relevant market.

The supply chain exists in a chaotic world. Lean manufacturing and other industry initiatives have led to a collective assumption that every business process in the supply chain can be explicitly defined and controlled. Not surprisingly, this has not been a resoundingly successful thought paradigm because so much of the supply chain is out of your direct control.

You should not try to design for every conceivable fail-safe scenario, but instead design for capability and resilience or chaos-tolerant business processes. The need to model and simulate more of the supply chain in a holistic fashion and to take account of more of this chaotic world with management guardrails and responses led to the development of solutions with a holistic and dynamic view of the real world that is beyond traditional optimization routines. A new breed of supply chain planning software solutions covering ISO standards has emerged and is beginning to address this reality. ISO solutions extend supply chain analysis by looking at network dynamics further across the entire supply chain to develop responses and policies and to include customer and supplier locations, in a manner that seeks to create scenario responses prebuilt by the enterprise.

These ISO solutions are at the forefront of the convergence of business intelligence, analysis, optimization, simulation, and decision-making technology and represent the kind of "chaos-ready" thinking that is needed.

Inventory Optimization

Inventory planning is typically done at a very high degree of granularity, which is not nearly as effective as it should be since it does not allow for accurate forecasting. Managing inventory effectively requires modeling the uncertainties, constraints, and complexities across the global supply chain on a continuous basis, which allows for greatly improved inventory forecasting ability and the ability to set inventory targets accurately. Inventory optimization software models inventory and the associated processes around inventory at a much finer granularity to determine optimal time-varying inventory targets for every item at every location throughout your supply chain. This allows you to significantly reduce inventory without adversely affecting service levels.

However, it is important to realize that while inventory optimization is a legitimate problem in its own right, higher-than-necessary inventory can also be a symptom of a more pervasive problem. Many other problems in the supply chain drive a company to hold inventory, such as poor forecast accuracy, lack of visibility in production, poor supply chain design, functional silos, demand variability, and procurement bonus programs. This may call for even broader modeling capabilities like supply chain network optimization.

Case Study: Performance Management in Action

Virtual Gates is a fictional cutting-edge computer manufacturer with retail outlets. This section provides an analysis of how the supply chain department's team at Virtual Gates closes its loop during the process of reducing its overall supply chain cost to create working capital.

Setting the Context

Having just left the CEO Clint Hobbs' office at Virtual Gates with the directive to reduce the overall cost of the supply as a means of generating working capital, George Martin, VP of Supply Chain, knows his hands will be full this year. After all, this wasn't Clint's only request. To accomplish his task, George needs to lower the department's working inventory levels and establish firm metrics to measure the health of supply chain's demand forecast accuracy, cash-to-cash cycle time, perfect order fulfillment, and supply chain management costs.

Moreover, Clint wants George's success to parlay into a 3% revenue growth for VG as his strategies and plans align with Clint's bigger objective, which requires all growth to be measured against Virtual Gates' net income and earnings per share growth, especially as they compare to VG's main competitors, Hypercell and Packingflash.

George must also implement his initiatives during HR's campaign to reduce VG's workforce by 15% and drive Product Development's goal to release a new netbook while retiring products that are no longer profitable.

George must first make sure that everyone in the Supply Chain department clearly grasps both the goal and its implications. Further, all of the initiative's touch points must be conveyed to every department with which Supply Chain collaborates, especially Finance, Product, Procurement, and Sales.

Understand the Collaborative Impact

A technical product company like VG (to which brand value is everything) tackles its activities with a single, concentrated intention: bringing new products to market as quickly as possible. Anything outside its window of expertise is left to partners that can do it better; therefore, everything that goes into VG's products comes from partner companies. Along with Procurement, Supply Chain is the link between VG and the world of suppliers. Consequently, it plays a critical role in nearly all of VG's business processes, including integrated product development, integrated logistics and fulfillment, asset visibility and performance, manufacturing network planning and execution, to say nothing of Finance, HR, and IT processes. As such, supply chain owns the collaborative demand and supply planning business process, which touches all of VG's suppliers and most of its customers.

Procurement and Product depend most on Supply Chain's success. The product lifecycle management process is long and complex, moving from market assessment and conceptual design to product launch and aftermarket support and service. As the new netbook makes its way through this maze, it is at the mercy of Procurement's assurance that suppliers can meet their obligations and Supply Chain's ability to deliver materials, equipment, and parts to their destinations on time.

A lot is riding on George and his team. If they are out of joint with Procurement on one side, or their suppliers on the other, then production schedules can be disrupted. In turn, the collaborative demand and supply plan would be affected, resulting in budget fractures that would distress Finance, HR, and IT and that might lead to disastrous consequences. For instance, if VG knows that Hypercell is developing a similar netbook, George must make sure that each of VG's production stage deadlines is met so that the netbook launches within its anticipated window. Should VG miss this window because of Supply Chain's failure to deliver needed parts, materials, or equipment, Hypercell could release its netbook first. Then, to meet Clint's goals, VG would have to invest more in marketing and sales that could verge from aggressive promotions to an advertising bombardment with more customer dissatisfaction, loss of brand value, and shrinking profit margins.

Just as Procurement's margin for error is slim under ordinary conditions, so too is Supply Chain's. In the current economic downturn, with all departments working harder due to newly imposed staff and IT service reductions, the margin is virtually nonexistent—George and his team must be at peak performance every day. Product Development is dependent on Procurement, Procurement on Supply Chain, and so forth. If George stays connected to his partners, his processes should run smoothly.

Establish KPIs and KRIs

Until George and his team establish a system by which to benchmark their growth efficiently and accurately, success is next to impossible.

George must select and implement a set of relevant KPIs and KRIs and identify the foremost risks to which his decisions expose him and his team, the main interfaces between its partners and its processes, and the drivers behind his KPIs and KRIs. He must also note their relationships as well as leading indicators of performance.

George realizes how important it is to convey the impact of his metrics to his partners. For instance, when his team decreases cash-to-cash cycle times, more working capital will be available for Finance. Increasing perfect order fulfillment will increase customer satisfaction, benefits, no doubt, that Sales, Marketing, and Service will all be happy to reap.

Establish the BI Foundation

George could have the best technology on the planet, but it will not magically generate the metrics foundation for his KPIs and KRIs. To get them, he and his team must harvest raw data from source systems, including their SCM and ERP systems as well as from individual warehousing, inventory management, and transportation management systems. All of these systems pull from PLM, CRM, and other data sources such as web tracking, click-through rates, and time spent viewing. As they execute various processes, the Supply Chain team must consolidate information from all these systems to ensure continuous visibility.

Once they've got their raw data, the team must transform it and then load it into a data mart or data warehouse. After that, the team needs to verify that the data can be consumed by the company's BI and PM applications. Without such functionality, neither George nor any other department head can access a single source of truth for VG's activities.

Strategize and Prioritize

George and his team must ensure an unobstructed flow of materials, supplies, and equipment to and from affiliate manufacturers. In theory, this sounds elemental, but in practice pitfalls are many. Angela Washington's team in Procurement has been charged with consolidating suppliers as a means of increasing Procurement's percentage of on contract spend and spend under management while simultaneously shedding members of her team per HR's directive. And yet George has also been asked to decrease his inventory, a directive that could be at odds with Angela's. If one or more of Angela's suppliers fails to deliver on its obligations, for example, she would call upon George's inventory to fill any shortage of materials, supplies, or equipment. However, if George reduced his inventory too much, he would not be able to supply Procurement's need, thus setting off a chain reaction of difficulties. George's task, then, is to reduce his inventory enough to deliver the savings Clint Hobbs has demanded from him while he maintains enough to guarantee that nothing will prevent Product Development from launching its new netbook within the forecast window. All of this requires that George and his team work in tight proximity with the various teams in both Procurement and Product Development, among others.

The scorecard George creates to monitor his activities must include all of his risks. As we just noted, lowering his inventory too much could create a scenario in which George's team fails to achieve perfect order fulfillment, which in turn could result in a drop of customer satisfaction. Accounting for these risks entails that George establish KRIs and related contingency measures. Once he sees that his perfect order fulfillment or customer satisfaction drops by 10% or more, George would immediately initiate a plan to segment his customers into high profitability and lower profitability groups, keeping just enough inventory on hand to satisfy only his most valuable customers. George also needs to build a plan with Sales for the top customers and their shipment priorities. His activities must be compliant with VG's overall strategy, particularly as they pertain to existing contracts with suppliers.

Plan and Execute

When George's inventory levels reach the desired level, costs for procurement work, warehouse management, and transportation activities should lower accordingly, too. George's fixed budget, however, carries the risk that other initiatives may not produce the needed outputs as a result of inappropriate funding.

The same risks and mitigating steps described in the strategy phase apply here, so George's team must keep a close watch on them. And while George will maintain clear visibility into his operations, he needs his partners to do the same. To ensure that they do, he could allocate a portion of his budget to processes such as integrated sourcing and procurement, integrated product development, or collaborative demand and supply planning before they go to the Procurement department and individual suppliers. Eliminating the possibility that other business units have initiatives that compete with Supply Chain can only help George's cause.

Monitor and Analyze

Now that George's team has begun to reduce its inventory and tighten its manufacturing, transportation, warehousing, and logistics activities, it needs to observe the results of its labors in all of its transactional systems, and especially in SCM. The acid test is whether George's inventory reduction, perfect order fulfillment, and supply chain costs are in line with his strategy and plan. George must also watch to see that raw materials are not being held up between procurement and manufacturing because his team has reduced its inventory. An eye must be kept out for increased complaints in the Service department because orders are not being fulfilled on time. Other concerns include the efficiency with which the manufacturing network is working to keep inventory levels down and the freeing up of working capital from the supply chain to increase its value relative to costs. Finally, George's reduced inventory cannot impact the performance of his suppliers and customers, nor can he permit a supply-demand mismatch or poor product quality.

The moment George senses that any part of his plan has gone awry, he must investigate. Is the capital he freed up by reducing inventory levels enough to impact the bottom line as expected? Is customer dissatisfaction with stockouts caused by low inventory now affecting his top line revenue performance from sales? No matter what the concern, George's main priority once he creates a possible solution is to check that it does not throw his partner activities or corporate's larger objectives out of sync.

Model and Optimize

To see exactly where his resources are being leveraged, George needs a detailed operational model. For instance, from it, he could learn that while his reduced budget seemed appropriate for his inventory reduction initiative, the existing pressures on the supply chain from his demand forecast, manufacturing capacity, or the service level agreements demanded by suppliers are preventing the reduction of his inventory levels. A costing analysis could reveal those products in the supply chain that give George's team the most value per resources such as transportation and warehousing. The products that appeared to be most profitable might actually be liabilities when all costs are factored in.

Simulating different scenarios via what-if analyses will also enable George to change key assumptions, such as the capacity of his warehouses, and to remove constraints, such as the number of employees needed to stock the warehouses. To optimize his activities, George could enter the goal of reducing his inventory to increase available cash while minimizing the key risk of decreasing customer satisfaction. The model would then make recommendations. For instance, it could suggest which products to keep in inventory for specific customers and which products to eliminate.

Closing the Loop in an Integrated System

George's team has the technology to handle the circumstances described to this point. However, very shortly it will require a holistic, closed-loop system to consistently align execution and strategy. Once his team can build a strategy management process that captures goals, initiatives, and metrics that can be linked to their driver-based financial and operational planning process, as well as to their monitoring and analysis, modeling and optimization, and risk and control processes, a new set of scenarios will develop. His team will be able to drive the desired behavior out to its transactional processes via its goals, initiatives, plans, and risks and controls.

George and many others in his position are happy to know that such a system is available to them now. Integrated supply chain performance management and transactional supply chain management solutions can enable George and his team to define supply chain strategy and align it with corporate strategy, set and cascade metrics targets, assign accountability for metrics, define and visualize relationships between metrics, and perform root cause analyses. Of course the supply chain management system provides needed data, but so do the procurement execution and financial systems. If George sees that asset inventory levels are off target, or that perfect order fulfillment is trending unfavorably, he can move directly to the transactional supply chain management application and change the inventory levels or increase resources for transportation and warehousing. In this way, the strategy to free working capital from the supply chain, the initiative to reduce inventory, and the real act of altering inventory levels and manipulating operational order fulfillment processes are seamlessly integrated such that both efficiency—doing things right—and effectiveness—doing the right things—are significantly enhanced.

Align the Workforce

George's final goal is to connect all of the aforementioned activities with his team's compensation. Whenever a warehouse manager understands that his bonus is the result of his contribution to the successful execution of George's inventory reduction initiative as per corporate strategy, that manager will work harder and smarter. This logic applies enterprisewide. Any time personnel in other departments are shown that they will receive bonuses for contributing to the successful attainment of Supply Chain's goals, George knows they will work hard at it, too. There is a message here: George's success is a function of his partners' success. No sooner will he hand CEO Clint Hobbs a report detailing supply chain's 5% growth in overall profit as measured by Virtual Gates' net income and earnings per share growth than Clint will hand George a bonus package of his own.

Action Items

By now, the benefits of implementing performance management for your supply network should be plain. The following list recaps action items to consider while on the road to formalizing your program:

- Engage in what-if analysis to understand risks across the supply chain
- Leverage all existing BI infrastructure and metrics

- Implement a single user interface for all strategic and operational systems

The PM lifecycle for your supply network can help promote compliance and hedge risk. Toward this end, you should:

- Automate filings and controls for global trade and emissions control
- Monitor and report compliance-sensitive actions
- Account for supply chain risk and plan for measured responses

Chapter 14

Performance Management for Procurement

As a Procurement professional, you are being pressed to do more than ever before. Rather than simply act to fulfill purchasing requests from the other areas of the company, executives are demanding that you play a far more strategic role. They want your work to be closely aligned with the strategic goals of the company as well as demonstrating a better understanding of how to manage spend across the organization to find new opportunities for savings while at the same time assuring continuity and on-time delivery of needed supplies.

However, your efforts are continuously frustrated by your inability to quickly gain visibility into corporate spend and supplier relationships. Data resides in multiple systems making it difficult and time consuming to collect; you cannot exert discipline over the other areas of the company to control unplanned and off-contract spend; and you are not able to fully understand the sourcing leverage you have in order to negotiate better contracts, not to mention a thorough comprehension of what each supplier provides and costs. For example, could you quickly—with a click rather than over a few days or weeks with IT intermediation—provide detailed answers to the following questions?

- How much spend do you have under management companywide?
- At what rate is that percentage growing?

- Can you confidently say that you have visibility into and are comprehensively mitigating supplier risks?
- How much do you spend with your top suppliers?
- How much do you spend on your top purchasing categories?
- How often are you buying the same materials from multiple suppliers at different prices?
- Are you effectively and in a compliant manner managing all of the company's supplier contracts?
- How do you determine your supply source, for example, global versus local?
- How do you quantify savings achieved for your senior management?
- Do you know if spend is within the budget or plan for a particular department or project?
- What percentage of your spend data is appropriately classified?
- How long does it take to get the information you need?

The answer for many of these questions is probably no. Without visibility into spend across the company, you are at a dead end. How can you optimize your company's procurement performance if you can't see it and measure it?

Research has shown that companies with outdated procurement models are being surpassed by companies using modern techniques and systems. It's the difference between a manual assembly line versus an automated and integrated manufacturing solution—one is a reflection of the other, but vastly superior in performance.

Money Left on the Table

According to a recent benchmark, a company with annual revenues of $1 billion would add $28 million to its bottom line by decreasing external spend by 5%.

A study from the Aberdeen Group[1] reports that inadequate spend analysis capabilities causes businesses to leave approximately $260 billion on the table in lost savings opportunities annually.

The fact is, more than any other area of the company, improved performance within procurement functions will have the single most significant net effect on financial performance.

---

[1] The Aberdeen Group, "The Spending Analysis Benchmark: Dissecting a Corporate Epidemic."

> ### *Does This Sound Familiar?*
>
> - "I am being asked to find more savings for the company, but by the time I find the data I need, cleanse it, and prepare it for analysis, it is out of date and all but useless."
>
> - "The number of suppliers and partners our company relies on has exploded to the point where I can barely manage the contracts much less the risks inherent in having so many relationships."
>
> - "There is a significant gap between my ability to find savings opportunities and turn them into realized savings. And even when I can orchestrate it, it is difficult to fully quantify the savings to Finance and corporate executives."
>
> - "I know we have unused sourcing leverage. I just can't find it."
>
> - "I spent days trying to track down why we spent so much on 'spanners' only to find out that the U.K. division uses that term to mean 'wrench.' Why can't we classify things in a standard way?"

Performance management can provide the visibility you need to manage procurement processes and activities. Using these methods and systems, you will begin the process of transforming Procurement into an effective and strategic agent that enhances the company's profitability.

Looking Back: How Your World Has Changed in Procurement

Activist stockholders, globalization, business network transformation, intense competition, and economic conditions mean that companies must increase profitability while controlling and lowering costs.

Procurement offers the largest and most direct lever to control and reduce costs. Purchased products and services represent the biggest expense for most companies and cost savings here translates directly—dollar-for-dollar—into improved financial performance for your company.

Because procurement represents the greatest opportunity for corporate savings, CEOs across the business world are turning to you and asking for more. According to the Aberdeen Group, procurement professionals are being pressed to:[2]

---

[2] Andrew Bartolini and William Browning III, "Spend Analysis: Working Too Hard for the Money," Aberdeen Group, August 2007.

- Identify savings opportunities across spend categories
- Prioritize spend categories
- Increase the percentage of spend under management
- Improve negotiation leverage through better understanding the value of supplier relationships

Furthermore, you are also likely being asked to:[3]

- Set up Lean operations that can support dynamic compliance requirements
- Be the enabler and owner of spend management as well as the primary procurement process, procure to pay, which encompasses spend analysis, strategic sourcing, contract negotiation, purchasing, settlement, and contract/supplier relationship management
- Rapidly expand the role of Procurement to act as a strategic partner to the other business units
- Participate in strategic activities such as new product introduction and product design, mergers and acquisitions, supply chain transformation, and so on

All this translates into is an unprecedented transformation on a performance level. Whether you're the CPO, a category manager, or a member of the sourcing group, you must become more performance-focused because your role is increasingly strategic. All departments should be engaged with you to help discover new savings opportunities.

Lack of Formalized Procurement

For many organizations, Procurement represents a frontier for savings and automation. Approximately 60% of companies rely on manual processes to collect and analyze procurement-related data.[4] Furthermore, rather than leveraged centralized sourcing, procurement—or much of it—is largely managed at the department level. This means you don't have visibility into how most of the purchased supplies are sourced and then how the money is spent (perhaps on duplicate supplies from multiple suppliers or multiple contracts with a single supplier). The result is that you can't leverage the aggregate spend with suppliers. You are also unable to identify where money

---

[3] Ibid
[4] Ibid

is being leached and how to stop that loss of funds. These issues combined mean you are leaving significant savings opportunities—the low-hanging fruit—on the table.

The business units may not be organizationally motivated to allow you to handle spend on their behalf. Are policies, KPIs, and MBOs aligned to drive behavior as well as allow you to discipline across the organization?

Business Network Transformation and Procurement

Procurement—and all that it encompasses—is one of the areas most affected by business network transformation. Managing procurement across an extensive business network of suppliers and the suppliers of those suppliers is increasingly difficult, both from an economic perspective as well as from a risk perspective. Business network transformation offers a number of opportunities while at the same time creating numerous challenges, including:

- A much larger system of suppliers that must be orchestrated to maximum effect. Your suppliers have suppliers, creating a chain in which problems occur if one link fails. When that happens, it can affect the whole chain of suppliers
- Complex business network relationships. You now have direct partnerships, outsourced supply chain, and subcontractors with their own network of suppliers. It is your job to determine the optimal relationships that can deliver at the lowest possible cost
- Corporate expectations. Executives are leaning on you for far more than a stable supply chain. They are also demanding that you not only negotiate the best prices but that you continue to realize savings to drive profitability. The problem is that you are reaching the limit of where simple price negotiations can get you in terms of annual costs savings. It is likely that yearly contract negotiations with suppliers are becoming tenser as each side faces significant pressure to grow the value of their respective businesses

You have to be innovative. You have to find opportunities for mutual value creation with suppliers and partners and new ways to leverage the business network, while continuously optimizing and reconfiguring your company's ability to extract profits.

The problem is that in order to sustain this level of optimization and innovation you need visibility not just into the immediately identifiable

Procurement Challenges

At most companies, procurement-related data is held in multiple locations and source systems making a consolidated and multidimensional view impossible. This in turn leads to a number of issues related to procurement's ability to deliver costs savings and properly manage procurement processes. The following is a sampling of challenges that a pervasive practice of performance management could help overcome:

- Limited spend visibility
- Multiple data sources and systems lead to a lack of trust in the data
- Inability to identify savings opportunities
- Difficulty measuring spend under management
- Inability to quantify procurement's contribution to the organization
- Inability to track spend patterns and trends to identify off-contract and maverick spend leading to a gap between identified savings and actual savings
- Inability to predict options for optimizing spend

— Ineffective Contract Management
  - Leads to savings leakage
  - Difficult to ensure compliance to contracts, SLAs and regulations
  - Difficult to track captured cost savings

— Difficulty Delivering Identified Cost Savings
  - Lack of formalized sourcing practices
  - Limited and siloed supplier data and management capability
  - Longer cycle times

— Higher Transaction Costs
  - Non-standardized processes
  - Poor user adoption
  - Non-compliance with government regulations and internal policies

savings opportunities but also into cross-organizational savings opportunities. To act as a partner to the business units and advisor on corporate spend, you need a granular understanding of costs and profitability across the network so that you can accurately provide guidance when a supplier relationship does not make sense. When is a $10 item less expensive than an $8 item? The answer is when the cost to integrate the supplier, transport the items, and the risks associated with the $8 per-item supplier are greater. We should add too that the cost would be greater when the $8 item causes you to miss out on sourcing and negotiating leverage that could lead to an overall cheaper, yet more effective deal for your company even if the per product cost is higher. In addition, driving costs into the ground sometimes leads to supplier bankruptcies and subsequent supply disruptions.

Identify What Type of Company You Work For

Though every company has its own unique way of viewing and approaching its core value proposition, there are generally five approaches taken to value creation:

- Superior customer value
- Operational excellence
- Responsive supply networks
- Product and service leadership
- Collaborative innovation

Each approach has distinct implications. For example, responsive supply networks require a different focus as compared with differentiating based on operational excellence or superior customer value.

No matter the approach, though, it is more important than ever to collaborate with the other business units to understand where they touch the company's core value proposition and how you can best support their unique procurement needs. This means that your procurement strategy needs to match the company's approach to generating wealth, which requires greater understanding of spend across the organization and business network, increased understanding of business processes for each department, and strong companywide collaboration.

The Business Process Angle

Enterprise applications have made business more efficient, but this efficiency is no longer enough. A focus on business process is needed to effectively drive value.

Your competitors have implemented the same systems and automated the same processes. As a result, companies are using one or two of the five approaches to business network transformation to improve effectiveness and look at business processes in a new way. They are taking all the individual transactive processes—in Supply Chain, Sales, Marketing, Service and Finance—and placing them within a larger end-to-end process that spans the multiple parts of the organization. And all of consolidation must be done within the business network context.

Performance management offers the methodology and tools to pull back the covers of the organization to provide visibility into the interconnected nature of these end-to-end processes. Broadly speaking, these processes

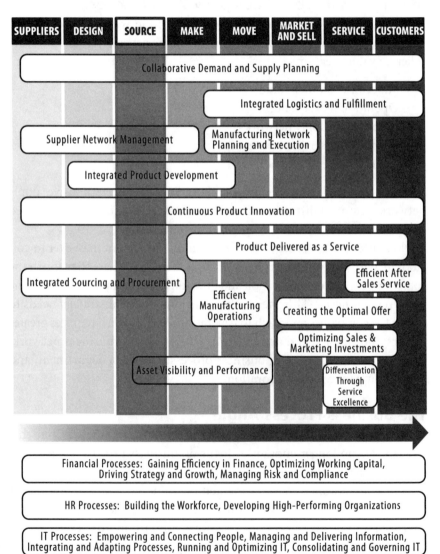

Figure 14-1. Cross-Functional Business Processes Affecting Procurement

include collaborative demand and supply planning, supplier network management, integrated product development, and asset visibility and performance. Procurement takes the lead in owning the integrated sourcing and procurement business process.

For the CPO, sustainable savings can only be achieved by closing the loop between the strategic sourcing cycle and the procurement order cycle. The integrated sourcing and procurement business process includes strategic sourcing, contract lifecycle management, operational procurement, and spend analytics.

Tying together the integrated sourcing and procurement process with finance business processes creates a larger process known as procure-to-pay. Procure-to-pay involves the process of strategic sourcing in which you determine whom you are going to buy from. Acting on the results of that process, you negotiate with suppliers for the best price and terms, make the transactions, and receive the items. You manage the contracts and supplier relationships to ensure that the consumer of the items in your company is buying within the contracts and that the supplier is living up to the terms of the contracts.

In the past, this process was enough to meet your job requirements—make sure we have what we need, when we need it, at the best price. However, you are now being asked to play a more strategic role, which requires not only providing needed supplies, but doing so in a manner that supports strategic goals of the organization and its many operational units. Your department must operate like a business in which you establish strategy (which is aligned with and driven by corporate strategy), create initiatives, plan their execution, monitor results, and then optimize activities and processes. This is the performance management lifecycle explained in detail in Chapter 3 and later in this chapter in the context of procurement.

Because the procure-to-pay process touches all of the other areas of the company (after all, every other area of your company needs to make purchases to accomplish its own objectives), you must have the visibility that can be provided using performance management technologies. And in order to use the information gained from these technologies, you must also view yourself as an enabler of business processes in other business units.

Let's step back for a moment. Without performance management, the high-level goals of the company are decomposed down to, say, the CPO's requirement to reduce spend by some percentage in order to achieve the company's overall revenue goal of 3% growth.

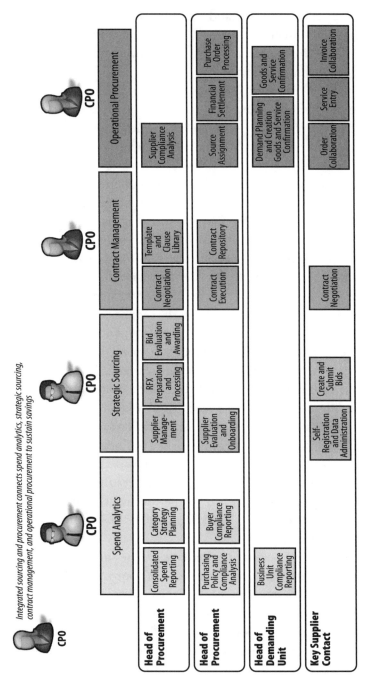

Figure 14-2. Integrated Sourcing and Procurement

Under current conditions, this probably causes some chaos because the CPO dictates that category managers must find their own way to cut costs. So if you're a category manager you know the drill: develop plans to try and meet some measure of what you are being directed to do. The problem is that your plans may be at odds with those of another manager or may in turn unwittingly undermine the ability to manufacture the company's widgets.

A CPO or category manager will run into problems without a consolidated and holistic view of spend as well as a methodology to analyze and find the most effective means and opportunities to cut costs. Performance management provides a methodology (the performance management lifecycle) and the tools (business intelligence, analytics and various performance management and GRC applications) to ensure that the procure-to-pay process as well as KPIs for the other business units that rely upon you support the goals of the company as well as the goals of the operational areas.

In addition to cross-functional processes, Procurement is in charge of the business processes listed in Table 14-1.

Table 14-1. Business Processes within Procurement

Purchasing Governance	Global Spend Analysis; Category Mgmt; Compliance Mgmt
Sourcing	Central Sourcing Hub; RFx / Auctioning; Bid Evaluation & Awarding
Contract Management	Legal Contract Repository; Contract Authoring; Contract Negotiation; Contract Execution; Contract Monitoring
Collaborative Procurement	Self-Service Procurement ; Service Procurement ; Direct / Plan-Driven Procurement ; Catalog Content Mgmt
Supplier Collaboration	Web-based Supplier Interaction; Direct Document Exchange; Supplier Network
Supply Base Management	Supplier Identification & Onboarding; Supplier Development & Performance Mgmt; Supplier Portfolio Mgmt

Why You Must Do This Now

To meet the kinds of strategic and cost-cutting demands executives and managers are placing upon you necessitates a continuous system of measurement and optimization, which is the foundation of performance management.

Why performance management right now? According to numerous studies, companies are losing billions in the form of squandered savings opportunities because of a lack of organized data. If you can't see it, you can't measure and optimize it. Performance management integrated with a Business Intelligence platform provides a closed loop methodology to locate savings opportunities, create a plan of action, monitor performance, and then create a model to optimize execution of the plan while feeding this insight back into your strategy and planning efforts.

In addition, risk and compliance are very important issues for you. A performance management solution integrated with your company's governance, risk and compliance efforts enables you to remove a significant amount of risk from the supply chain while improving compliance across the organization as well as your own compliance to numerous regulatory

---

Business Drivers

While there are numerous business drivers behind the need for procurement performance management, four general areas include:

Competitive pressure. Companies must be agile and able to create and sustain competitive advantage. Critical to that is continually optimizing the performance of procurement in order to control and reduce costs. This has become all the more difficult as globalization and business network transformation add complexity and volatility to markets.

Operational pressure. Business leaders are asking more from you in terms of being a strategic asset to the company. This means placing more spend under management as well as aligning procurement initiatives to overall strategic objectives. There is also the issue of managing supplier performance as these relationships are becoming more numerous and complex.

Risk and compliance pressure. Risk is ever present within the world of Procurement as the actions and activities of suppliers can play havoc with the reputation, brand, and profitability of your company. It is also necessary to become more proactive in terms of understanding the risks and the methods and means to prevent or mitigate them.

Change pressure. At the core of this change mandate is the need for a more effective and efficient stream of analytical data. However, most companies continue to operate with profoundly inefficient data collection, aggregation, and transformation capabilities.

regimes. Maintaining the status quo only heightens your chances of incurring increased risk and leaving more money on the table.

According to research by the Aberdeen Group,[5] each dollar brought under management by procurement can yield between 5–20% in cost savings. However, identifying maverick spend requires a system in place that provides visibility into spend corporatewide. You must have the means to bring identified areas under management, enforce necessary governance, monitor and measure actual savings versus planned savings, and then model and optimize performance.

Visibility and management by data rather than gut instinct is at the heart of performance management—it turns on the lights and provides the means to take action and make improvements in order to develop and sustain competitive advantage.

Key Roles in Procurement

To help you begin your performance management journey, this section covers the key roles in Procurement and how each one can benefit from performance management.

Chief Procurement Officer (CPO)

You are in charge of managing the funds used for external spending for the company, including ensuring that funds are not being spent off-contract or outside of a formalized management process. You are also charged with managing the largest spend items in the company as well as setting budgetary priorities for the department. You need performance management to establish a closed loop strategic lifecycle to drive departmental alignment with the overarching strategic goals of the organization—identifying and acting on new opportunities and strategies for saving money. You also must facilitate the transformation of procurement from a relatively benign function to the driver of strategic costs savings. Your job also includes a significant risk component. You not only have to understand supplier risk, but the myriad regulatory compliance issues the company needs to constantly monitor in order to mitigate the risk of fines and other forms of noncompliance loss. You are also in many ways the holder of the company's brand and reputation in that recent scandals have shown that problems with suppliers—product

---

[5] Tim Minahan and Kevin Fitzgerald, "Procurement's Goal: Intelligent Supply Management," Aberdeen Group, August 19, 2005.

contamination, improper business practices, poor sustainability management, and the like—can have severe consequences. You need information at your fingertips presented in a language that can be understood by your peers as well as management including the CFO, CEO, and COO.

Category Managers

Whether you are an indirect or direct spend manager, you hold the most prevalent role in the department. As such, you are concerned with the core needs of the company, understanding and ensuring the effectiveness of your piece of the global supply chain, garnering volume deals, reducing maverick spend within your relative category, and finding new savings opportunities through whatever means available. You need performance management to gain visibility across the supply chain and into partner and supplier organizations, to see where sourcing leverage is being wasted, to understand the true value of a supplier relationship in order to optimize supplier performance within your category, and to see how you are performing against your KPIs and MBOs.

Strategic Sourcing Group

Although not all companies have a group dedicated to strategic sourcing, this trend is on the rise as businesses see the benefits of having a group dedicated to optimizing various purchasing activities. Your job is to understand the global supply chain of your company and its many supplier relationships in order to assure that specific goals of the company in the areas of cost savings, low-cost country suppliers, diversity suppliers, sustainability, tax optimization, efficient transport, and so forth, are achieved and continually being improved and updated. You need performance management to gain a consolidated view into the company's sourcing efforts to fully understand the interconnected nature of these many relationships. If one should wane, what would be the net effect on cost, tax breaks for diversity suppliers, sustainability efforts and so on. You also care about risks that could disrupt the smooth flow of materials and items necessary for the company's continued functioning, which means you need to have access to continuous data on supplier performance.

KPIs That Matter for Your Success

KPIs are key to understanding procurement performance—are we achieving the goals of the organization and department—is the use of well-targeted KPIs. For Procurement these KPIs include:

- Spend
  - Percentage of total spend under management
  - Amount and percentage of identified/implemented/negotiated/realized cost reduction savings
  - Total spend to number of suppliers

- Strategic Sourcing
  - Percentage of sourcing projects captured in the system
  - Amount and percentage of negotiated savings
  - Sourcing cycle-time
  - Percentage of sourcing from low-cost-countries
  - Cost savings from sourcing efforts
  - Diversity of suppliers

- Contract Management
  - Amount and percentage of captured cost savings in contracts
  - Percentage of compliant transactions with contracts
  - Contract creation cycle-time
  - Contract leakage

- Operational Procurement
  - Procurement operating cost as % of revenue
  - Amount and percentage of savings realized
  - Percentage of compliant transactions with contracts
  - Procurement productivity

What's in It for Me?

No matter what your role is in Procurement, performance management can provide a number of benefits such as:

- The ability to make fact-based intelligent decisions via analytic capabilities integrated into the system rather than a mix of questionable data and gut instinct
- The ability to track your performance against personal KPIs, MBOs and corporate incentive packages
- The tools you need to find savings opportunities, establish a plan of action and then implement the plan to assure savings are realized
- The ability to understand, monitor and mitigate risk within a personalized dashboard
- The ability to quantify the value of procurement and its many activities to the company

- A cleansed and consolidated data management platform powered by Business Intelligence, which will enable you to view spend-related data across the organization

Many companies rely on a number of siloed and manual processes that are primarily spreadsheet-based, making an enterprise-wide view of spend all but impossible because the data resides in a number of disconnected systems and databases. Most organizations operate with a number of ERP and SRM systems, homegrown applications, and databases as well as legacy systems rather than a holistic and integrated performance solution. Retrieving and aggregating data from an amalgamation of systems is not only inexact and laborious; it makes it very difficult to evaluate the company's overall procurement processes.

Performance management with an integrated data management platform enables you to create multidimensional databases that allow you to pinpoint the source of data as well as any issues you may be encountering. Remember the infamous story of the company that wondered why it was spending so much money on fruit until they discovered that Blackberry handhelds were being improperly classified. Access to a wealth of trusted data that can be easily manipulated by business users without intermediation from IT will enable you to do far more for the company as a department than ever before.

Performance management can help you find untapped savings opportunities. Access to cleansed data that can be intuitively applied to analytic capabilities will allow you to see where money is escaping through the cracks. This might include fragmented contracts, multiple contracts with a single supplier, inefficiencies between direct and indirect spend, and more.

Effective Collaboration

Although obvious, it cannot be overemphasized: collaboration and communication is the core of any successful organization. Efforts to bring more spend under management will be useless if the other business functions are engaging in volumes of off-contract spend because they are paying scant attention to the guidance and governance you have established.

It is also important for you to understand the business processes, strategies, and initiatives being employed by these other areas of the business. You are no longer a point person for making purchases in a silo of sourcing and procurement activities. You are no longer an isolated entity, making

Bridging the Gap Between Identified and Realized Savings

Perhaps one of the greatest frustrations for any Procurement professional is to identify savings opportunities and establish cost reduction measures only to find a gap between identified opportunities and actually achieving savings. This represents a strategy-to-execution gap specific to Procurement.

Maverick spend in the IT department is an excellent example because in many companies, IT is a difficult place to exert spend discipline. However, using a consolidated view into procurement-related data you should be able to gain visibility into spending across the organization, which will provide insight into IT spend that is occurring outside a managed process.

If IT purchases contracts for laptops for a single division, without realizing that six divisions need laptops, you can see this and set in motion activities to leverage the entire volume needed into a greater discount than could be gained from a contract for a single division.

There is also a direct connection here with compliance to organizational governance, which should establish criteria for purchases that should be managed by Procurement. This data should also be included with the company's GRC (governance, risk and compliance) systems, which should be integrated with your performance management solution for Procurement. In all, spend should only be considered under management when strategic sourcing methods and standardized compliance methods are both applied to a specific spend category or instance. Being able to see when these are out of alignment, and close the gap, is an important performance management capability.

Further, given that there is a compliance and financial component to this activity, Finance will also have an interest in collaborating with you to reduce off-contract spend. What's good for Procurement is good for Finance.

purchases in an organizational void. Your responsibilities affect every person in every business unit.

The following sections provide tips on collaborating with some of the business units closest to you.

Collaboration with Supply Chain

Supply Chain needs to understand the totality of your relationship with suppliers and needs to coordinate the product numbers of supplies with those of finished products. This means that tightly coordinated documentation must be delivered to your department and by your department.

You don't have to look very far through the headlines to find a company whose fortunes have fallen on the failure of their Procurement division to perform due diligence. The food and children's toy industries represent two salient examples from the recent past.

The more tightly integrated your notification system is, the better off your entire organization will be. If you are in the food industry, for example, and you have a delivery issue with your plastic packaging supplier, your perishables are immediately at risk. If there is no backup supplier, an alarm system that rings all the way through Supply Chain to Service will be extraordinarily valuable. The Service department will need to know about any interruptions or problems because soon customers will be calling wondering when their deliveries will arrive.

Your other major goal (and pressure) from the supply chain will be reconciling compliance, quality, and cost control. Your mission is to reconcile the best-cost (not necessarily lowest-cost) suppliers with the needs of the supply chain. As pressures mount to outsource to ever-cheaper providers, be aware that the brunt of that responsibility will fall on your shoulders. Supply Chain and the C-suite may need to be reminded that your hesitance to select a noncompliant or shady provider is an attempt to protect the entire organization. The egg on the face of the organization will be flung from your barnyard.

You can take additional responsibility for quality by staying in close contact with Supply Chain and by making sure you understand what minimum quality standards they will accept.

You must also take steps to make sure your network is chaos-tolerant. In other words, you don't want to consolidate all your supply of a critical binding agent or semiconductor in one supplier. At the very least, you need to have at least one backup on the "red phone," just in case. Supply Chain will be looking to you for an understanding of whom to call.

Collaboration with Product Development

Essentially, you gather together the constituent parts of the products that Product Development invents. You are a fundamental player in this process. Your interaction with (and pressure from) Product Development rests on a single key point: getting things done at the lowest possible overall price. Do not confuse the lowest overall price, however, with the lowest cost of materials. The overall price includes the cost of materials and goods, of course, but it also considers returns, failures, malfunctions, and service and repairs.

Your company should never skimp on product quality just because you think it will translate to greater profit margins. In the long run, that will not prove to be the case. Consider how NASA felt when the space shuttle was destroyed because of a faulty O-ring. Consider how the supplier of that O-ring felt. The next worst thing to hear is that you have just received a warehouse full of fraudulent or stolen goods. Mutually open lines of communication, as well as supplier and quality evaluations, can help prevent such problems.

Collaboration with HR and IT

Today's organizations are fluid. People come and go, especially as wages are under pressure and it's ever more difficult to remain competitive. From an internal standpoint, that means that as people change, begin, or leave roles, you will be hearing a lot from the HR department about what they are and are not allowed to purchase. Standardization of data formats between employee requisitioning systems, HR systems, and your purchasing system will be very helpful in this regard. In an unlinked, siloed organization, it's typical to get batch feed updates from HR regarding changes in employment and purchasing privileges. In an optimized organization, these updates happen automatically. Even if optimization is a major organizational goal and is in the pipeline, in the meantime, some proactive vigilance will probably be called for, whether that takes the form of weekly meetings or teleconferences, or some other kind of routine update system. Coordination with IT will also be essential so that technology is not inhibiting cost control. Links will need to be made between accounts payable, requisitioning, and HR systems so that "shadow vendors" and other suspicious entities do not start appearing.

Collaboration with Marketing

Procurement sees Marketing as a big source of company spending and therefore looks to actively engage with Marketing to ensure the volume of spending they incur is efficient and compliant. Procurement will typically ask Marketing not to make verbal or written vendor commitments without Procurement's prior review. Further, Procurement expects Marketing to develop a business case for each program expenditure to ensure that there is a revenue justification to substantiate the purchase. Procurement also expects Marketing to leverage existing vendors identified under the corporate purchasing preferred vendor program. When there is not a suitable vendor for the services of products required under the preferred program, Procurement will typically ask Marketing to submit at least three vendors to bid on the work and get a quote. This is to ensure fair practices in vendor evaluations so that preference is not given unfairly to friends at vendors and that the cost being quoted is commensurate with the going rate.

Collaboration with Sales and Service

Sales and Service are both customer-intensive roles. They both spend the majority of their time interacting with customers and have the least amount of time to focus on the back office tasks of securing products and resources to help them successfully deliver on the customer's expectations. They rely on Procurement to help them secure the resources they need at the best possible price and at the right time, all while ensuring that they meet customer expectations. A good Procurement group will study and understand the customer buying cycle and competitive differentiation of the company in order to make intelligent purchase decisions that support company differentiation and not erode it. For example, if a high level of customer service is a differentiator for the company, Procurement should consider this when making any purchases that directly impact customer satisfaction.

Collaboration with Finance

Procurement looks to Finance for spending guidance by department as well as information on compliance requirements and regulations tied to statutory and management reporting. Procurement also looks to Finance to provide visibility into department-level budgets as well as updated budget forecasts to ensure that Procurement can effectively support the organization within the financial guidance and policies of the company. This involves constant interaction and dialogue between Finance and Procurement around the financial exposure related to supplier contracts and visibility into total spending across all cost centers.

Effective Collaboration Across the Business Network

Of course, it is important not to focus solely on internal activities, but also to manage spend across external organizational boundaries. This is a two-way street because, just as you want your suppliers to be predictable to you, they want you to be predictable to them. Therefore, working collaboratively should be a shared goal, supported by technologies capable of pulling data from source systems to create as complete a model of corporate spend as is possible.

You need to think about being responsible for the series of partners, suppliers and subcontractors that comprise a significant piece of your company's value chain. Consider implementing initiatives such as remote bidding for reverse auctions, improved planning and forecasting with external entities, supplier scorecarding, and more.

Establishing Your BI Foundation

Visibility into procurement data companywide is the goal. BI is a critical element of establishing that visibility. You need BI to provide:

- **Relevant visualizations.** For example, procurement managers often visualize the products in their categories as items in a catalog
- **Relevant event-capture and alerting.** The ability to gather information from event sources, such as the supply chains of key suppliers and the ability to define alerts for critical events, such as the price of an important raw material jumping 20% worldwide, and informing the right person in the Procurement organization to take action
- **A unified semantic layer, data integration, and data quality across departmental and application silos.** BI allows Procurement users to bridge silos when they do not have access to a single, integrated transactional system, but instead many point systems (sourcing, contract management, category management), or multiple SRM systems. Use BI to establish common definitions and business rules of the key dimensions in procurement (such as suppliers, categories, and contracts) and metrics and their relationships
- **Trusted, cleansed master data.** BI platforms allow Procurement to consolidate on standard definitions a supplier but also standard definitions of the individual suppliers themselves in a process called supplier normalization. For example, supplier normalization can identify that "Vic's" is the same supplier as "Vic's Office Supply" is the same supplier as "Vic's House of Staples" and can standardize the suppliers' key attributes such as location, ownership, and standard discounts. Spend classification is also a critical aspect of having clean master data. With the number of fragmented source systems that have spend data, significant issues arise with orphaned records, client material key transformations, and code inconsistencies. Spend classification technologies use predictive analytical techniques to analyze who made the buy, what source system the data came from, system keys, the supplier names, the purchasers' roles, the transaction size, and the description

to correctly identify the item the purchaser procured. Spend classification techniques can also map spend to industry standards like The United Nations Standard Products and Services Code® (UNSPSC®), which provides an open, global multi-sector standard for efficient, accurate classification of products and services

- **Structured and unstructured data.** BI platforms can generate insights from both structured as well as unstructured data. Unstructured data from contract management systems (how many contracts do we explicitly state that we must purchase at a certain discount percentage), procurement catalogs, RFQs, and other sources can provide additional insight
- **Reporting.** BI reporting capabilities include:
  - Publication-quality reports such as open purchase orders by business unit
  - Visualizations such as supplier rating compared with the company's top 5 suppliers
  - Query and analysis such as average pricing of raw materials by supplier and average spend per department on direct and indirect goods

Assessing Performance Management Maturity

Where you are, in terms of being able to achieve an advanced state of performance management maturity will depend on the idiosyncratic nature of the organization and its existent capabilities, as well as a number of related factors.

Here are a few sample questions to consider:

- What is the percentage of non-payroll spend under management?
- Do I have procurement-specific analytics and management capabilities?
- Do we utilize spend analysis reports that provide detail at the transactional level?
- Do we have a Business Intelligence infrastructure that can act as a data management platform?
- What is our rate of compliance with contracts?
- Is spend management handled by a dedicated group or is it performed on an ad hoc basis?
- Is there strong executive support for procurement management initiatives?

Figure 14-3 will help you gain insight into your organization's sourcing and procurement maturity and decide where you should be headed.

The overall sourcing and procurement maturity model contains within it a model for assessing the maturity of Procurement performance management, as shown in Figure 14-4.

AMR Research describes these stages as follows:

- **Stage 1.** Scorecards tend to include the traditional metrics of cost, quality, and reliability. Scorecard usage and format are not consistent across the organization and are implemented ad hoc
- **Stage 2.** The use and format of a scorecard becomes standardized globally, with a focus on strategic suppliers. Scorecard metrics evolve and start to include key performance indicators (KPIs) for responsiveness
- **Stage 3.** Companies start to look for further flexibility in their supply relationships. Contracts that are negotiated and follow-up scorecards need to address this requirement. For example, can a supplier provide a shorter lead time when necessary or, through product or process innovation, add more value? Besides a more globally consistent

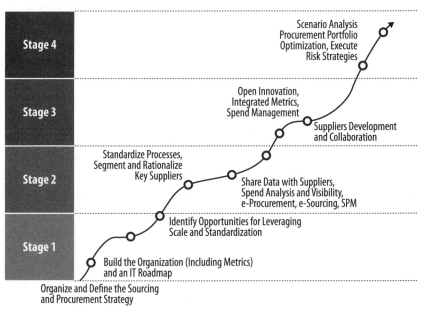

Figure 14-3. The Sourcing and Procurement Journey
(Source: AMR Research, 2007, "Advanced Sourcing and Procurement:
The Demand-Driven Transformation to Strategic Supply Management")

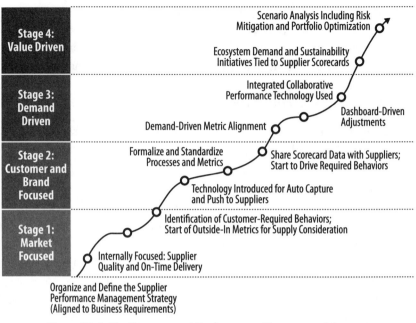

Figure 14-4. *The Procurement Performance Management Journey*
(Source: AMR Research, 2008, "Supplier Performance Management:
It's More Than a Scorecard—It's a Strategy")

process and format, the scorecard at this stage now becomes more frequently used, automated, and bidirectional through effective use of technology

- **Stage 4.** The greatest benefits are realized once the partnership becomes value-driven, with a focus on multienterprise collaboration, sensing and responding, and open innovation

The PM Lifecycle for Procurement

Performance management involves the routine, and sometimes non-routine, measurement of key aspects of financial performance, and making this information available to decision-makers. In this section, we will walk you through the performance management lifecycle for Procurement, highlighting the factors and evaluation methods that your peers have found useful.

When considering what to optimize using the PM lifecycle, refer to "The Business Process Angle" earlier in this chapter, which includes both cross-functional and departmental business processes that may be worthy of optimization.

Strategize and Prioritize

Your first priority as a procurement manager is to ensure that the strategic goals being established for Procurement align with corporate goals. The overall organization strategic goal is to improve margins and Procurement can contribute to the strategic goal by negotiating better prices for raw materials and increasing production margins.

You then develop goals and initiatives that can be communicated in a way that is meaningful to each team. These could include:

- Defining pricing goals and initiatives for all purchased materials including direct and indirect spend
- Rationalizing and optimizing supplier relationships by identifying key partners in the ecosystem, increasing the percentage of diversity supplier spend,[6] improving contract management, or increasing low-cost-country sourcing
- Reducing maverick spend and increasing the percentage of spend under management
- Improving management of spend across the business network by optimizing planning and forecasting in collaboration with suppliers and partners

A strategy management capability can be leveraged to help set the objectives that should be met within Procurement, the initiatives to meet them, and the high-level KPIs to measure performance.

Here are the basic steps you'll follow in developing and prioritizing your strategies.

Understand the Context

Strategy for Procurement is not an independent exercise. It should cascade down from the corporate level and provide you with detailed guidance about what to do and how to measure success.

Develop and Set the Strategy

Review the corporate strategic goals, strategic plans, initiatives, and metrics that track progress against them and understand them. Contextualize

---

[6] Diversity supplier spend is a trend worth noting. It refers to spending with suppliers that meet criteria such as minority-owned. Maintaining a certain percentage of diversity spend is not only socially responsible, but can provide tax breaks.

them to the implications they have for Procurement and use this context to drive the Procurement PM lifecycle.

Review the Environment

What are you good at or well-positioned for? What are the main problems you face? What risks do you have? Your strategic risks may include volatility in commodity or raw material prices. More tactical risks may include your supplier's ability to keep up with fulfillment for high-demand products.

What compliance requirements must you meet? Compliance challenges include vendor compliance, contract compliance, and ensuring segregation of duties for internal procurement processes such as invoice verification and inventory valuation.

Set the Mission, Values, and Vision

Define Procurement's mission. For example, make Procurement a strategic weapon in both reducing costs and driving value in every relevant business process.

Define Procurement's core values, including attitude, behavior, and character. For example, we value our internal business partners' reliance on us to provide excellent procurement skills to meet their objectives and we treat them with appropriate respect at all times.

Define Procurement's vision, a concise statement of the 3- to 5-year goals of the organization. By 2012, our department will be ranked in the top 20% of all companies in our peer group benchmark for managing spend effectively.

Set the Goals

Now set a strategy or strategies to follow (of course, you'll collaborate with the CEO and other top execs). Here are some sample strategies:

- Increase visibility into spend across the enterprise
- Increase savings and improve margins with a disciplined procurement process
- Improve procurement efficiency by rationalizing the supplier base

Consider using a strategy map to display cause-and-effect relationships among strategic objectives. A good strategy map tells a story of how value is created.

Assign KPIs to Goals and Set Targets

Define KPIs and targets that translate strategy into performance expectations. Identify value drivers. Value drivers and KPIs have risks associated with their achievement. Identify these risks and establish tolerance levels to set key risk indicators (KRIs). This connectivity between a value driver and a relevant KPI and KRI is an important bridge from a strategic view of risk—which can have a time horizon of three or more years—to a more focused budgetary view of risk, which is often applied to a single year. See "KPIs That Matter for Success in Procurement" earlier in this chapter for details.

- How does creating visibility into spend impact the other departments?
- Will identified savings be pushed back to each budget owner?
- By optimizing the procurement process, can we improve the time to benefit such as contributing to the production process?
- With better supplier relationships, can sourcing cycle time be reduced?
- Does the reduction in the supplier base get us better pricing?

Risk-Adjusting Supplier Performance

As business networks increase in size, scope, and complexity, supplier scorecards are highly useful for the understanding the goals, initiatives, metrics, and targets of key suppliers and setting the tone for a collaborative value-added relationship. Figure 14-5 shows a framework for developing supplier scorecards.

Perform Additional Risk Analysis and Set KRIs

Now look again at risks. For each risk, decide what your risk appetite is. Can you afford to take that risk? What's the worst-case scenario? For example, consider single-supplier items. Are they mission-critical? Diversify sources for those items. Find out whether a supplier's manufacturing base is diverse enough to provide items even if a specific factory goes offline.

There is also the issue of market and economic volatility. If you are a home building company, it is critical that your suppliers can manage through tough times (supply shortages or gluts in the market). You need contingency plans for supplier failures, including not only the same materials, but also similar pricing. Procurement is responsible for making Finance aware of potential supply disruptions and for managing their impact on financial forecasts.

You also need to establish governance, such as requiring an additional signature for purchase requisitions over $10,000. In addition, credit checks

A Framework for Developing Supplier Scorecards

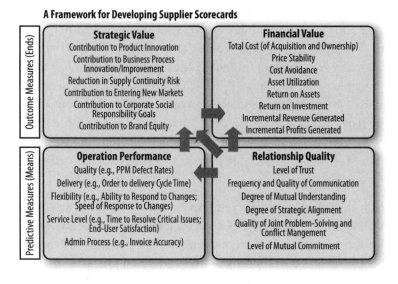

Illustrative Metrics for Measuring and Managing Supplier Collaboration in New Product Development

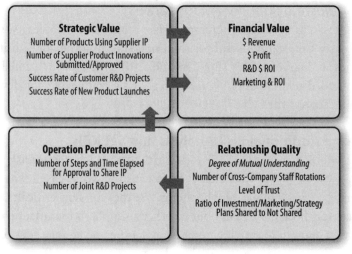

Figure 14-5. A Framework for Supplier Metrics

and ratings should be validated for vendors at least quarterly to ensure that key vendors are not going out of business or having credit problems.

It is also important to leverage technology in order to automate as much as possible. It is one thing to enact governance and attempt to track compliance as an after-the-fact exercise. It is another to use technology to your advantage in order to further guide and impel people toward the right behavior. For example, computers and other tech devices represent a significant amount of indirect spend and are typically rife with off-contract spend. By making it easy to order a device directly from a contracted supplier, employees get what they need in a compliant way. Make it more difficult to purchase outside the approved system, thereby making the right path effectively the path of least resistance.

Set a response strategy for the risk (watch, research, transfer, delegate, mitigate). For example, you put in a new system to streamline IT procurement, but find that employees are still charging IT expenses under office supplies. To prevent this, notify managers that there will be a random audit for all purchase outside the new IT procurement system.

Decide whether you can afford the worst-case scenario for a risk. Could it bring down some critical value-generating mechanism for the company? For example, if you make any exceptions for any maverick spending for IT, you risk that additional rollout to optimize procurement processes in areas such as production sourcing, facility management, and other key areas will be impacted.

Define KRIs and targets for those risks. KRIs are early warning signals that define the threshold at which a risk could occur, such as employees not using the IT procurement system. Requisitions outside the IT procurement system should trigger a risk alert.

Example of Risks for Procurement

Vendor Monitoring. Quality of Service Provision, Fulfillment rate—Deliveries, Vendor Assessment Total Score Overtime, PO Quality Confirmed as Requested, Supplier Performance, PO Quantities Delivered Completed, Vendor Analysis—defective quantity, Vendor Evaluation: Problem Deficiencies

Demand-Supply Mismatch. Inventory (days) above maximum, Inventory (days) below minimum, Sales forecast accuracy, Demand/Supply Match—Order Lead Time, Demand/Supply Match—Inventory Values

Supplier. Fulfillment Rate—Deliveries, Price Trends Over the Last Three Months, Vendor Assessment Total Score Over Time, Purchase Order Quantity Confirmed as Requested, Supplier Performance, Purchase Order Quantities Delivered Complete, Machine Malfunctions per Production Order), Supplier Concentration, Supplier Credit, Single-source Supplier, Supplier Risk Profile, Geography

Finance. Commodity prices, Currency, Raw Material Prices, Subcontracting prices for key materials, Overdue Payments

Perform Compliance Analysis and Set Controls

Define your compliance requirements. Compliance defines the boundaries within which companies must operate when achieving their strategies. Compliance issues pertaining to Procurement typically arise in contracts, purchase orders, invoice and payment, and capital expenditures, which can all impact financial statements.

Define policies, procedures, and controls that must be in place to ensure that you can meet the compliance requirements. Make sure that this applies not only at the main business process level but to all subprocesses including and perhaps especially those related to partners. In transactional processing such as entering an invoice and payment within an ERP system, the control is segregation of duties, limiting payment up to a certain dollar amount, and reviewing duplicate payments. These controls in the Procurement process will minimize the financial reporting to the balance sheet.

Define control targets that translate compliance expectations into performance expectations.

Work on the Strategic Action Plan and Initiatives

The strategic initiatives help define the exact methodology (the roadmap) for achieving various goals. The results of this planning may require revisiting the strategy.

Develop the roadmap (sequence of actions) for achieving Procurement's piece of the strategic plan. Include performance, risk, and compliance (control activities, policies and procedures) in the roadmap. For example,

---

Example Procurement Controls

Vendor Payments. Check all system records and report on posted invoices that has resulted in overpayment

Invoice Verification. Inventory postings that override system date

External Procurement. Incorrect approval procedures, including missing approval limit or amount

Receive Goods. Payments without good receipts or purchase orders created from goods receipts

Vendor Payment. Changes to vendor master double invoice check settings

Procurement Data. Changes to source list records and users who made such changes

a detailed alternative supplier plan is created as part of the contingency plan for raw material sourcing in case a key supplier cannot provide the needed volume.

For each initiative, define critical success and failure factors. Critical success factors might include having a system that automatically suggests alternative suppliers based on price and availability. Failure factors include anything that could derail the initiative. Failure factors can then be translated into risks.

Develop risk-adjusted scenarios along with contingency plans. For example, understanding demand and supplier mismatch risks and putting appropriate controls in place might be appropriate especially because it provides visibility into the concerns of the Supply Chain department. Risk mitigation could include reserving money for spot procurement during the supplier rationalization process.

Strategic plans should be risk-adjusted with contingency plans for as many risk scenarios as you can reasonably imagine based on past experience and the current environment. You then develop risk response plans that detail how you will handle the risks if alerts show that they are materializing and include the risk response plans in your contingency plans.

Cascade Accountability

Each KPI, KRI, and control and its target should be owned by a department or group. The MBOs of the staff in those groups must reflect the KPIs, KRIs, and controls you set. This sounds obvious, but frequently individual performance metrics are not aligned in this way. If reducing maverick spending is important, a daily dashboard can show purchases made using the IT procurement system along with savings realized to highlight the reasons for using the system.

Plan and Execute

In the strategize and prioritize phase, we put together strategic action plans and initiatives. The planning phase gets into the details of planning the strategic initiatives both from a financial and operational standpoint.

Most organizations have some planning processes, but they are often too informal and inconsistent to be effective. Planning must be aligned with corporate objectives to take into account factors such as green supply chain initiatives, diversity supplier spend, and corporate responsibility goals. To engage in a more formalized process, it is important to be supported by capabilities such as negotiation planning, spend planning, and supplier planning. These plans and targets should be integrated with your strategy management solution.

Since one of your key responsibilities is to control costs, you must work collaboratively with Finance, operational areas, and IT in order to gather the necessary data to indicate financial outcomes such as budget returned, impact to working capital, and contributions to EBIT or net income. These efforts must be supported by available technologies.

As described in Chapter 6, it is also critical to factor in risk scenarios and develop appropriate prevention, mitigation, and response strategies.

Align Corporate Budget to Procurement Budget

The budgeting process takes each of the outcomes or actions from the planning process and aligns revenues and expenses against them. Decisions regarding investment priorities and resource allocations define how the company will operate and set the bar for measuring performance. Take each of the steps in the initiatives you've defined and put in revenues and expenses for them.

To create risk-adjusted budgets, incorporate the range of possible revenues and costs of each action into the budget at the appropriate organizational level. A risk-adjusted budget responds to changing circumstances, providing the financial capability to react to events in a planned, proactive manner. Develop different risk-adjusted budgets with contingency plans should risks to achieving budgets materialize.

For example, in a traditional procurement budget, you list individual line items such as office supplies, contracted services, building supplies, building maintenance, and capital expenditures in each row with actuals, budgeted amounts, forecast, and actual versus budget comparisons, and forecast versus budget comparisons going across in the columns. In a risk-adjusted procurement budget, for every decision to allocate revenue to one line item versus another (like increasing the amount spent on contracted services and adding a new supplier), you determine the impact and probability of the highest priority procurement risks (such as not having enough procurement managers to negotiate and process purchase orders, especially for capital expenditure items) on individual line items and set a range of expected budget and forecasted values instead of fixed values. In this case, if the risk materializes and you no longer have enough skilled staff, you need a contingency plan showing the performance and risk implications if you halt negotiations with suppliers.

Align Budget to Operational Plans

The operational planning process links the budget to operational factors in your core business processes (sourcing, contracts, and operational procurement, for example). Plan each step of each initiative in terms of technology, time, and resources. Consider risks for each area of the operational plan. Negotiation planning, spend planning, and supplier planning are all crucial operational planning processes be linked with the budget.

For example, in a risk-adjusted operational plan, for every decision to allocate resources to one set of operational activities versus another (putting all of your best contract negotiators to work on one strategic contract for a single strategic vendor to supply all raw materials), you determine the impact and probability of the highest priority operational risks (such as the risk that contracts for nonstrategic suppliers will be processed slowly or negotiated poorly) on those individual line items and use this to set a range of expected and forecasted values instead of fixed values. In this case, if the risk materializes, you need a contingency plan in place that shows implications for performance (the goal to move to a single strategic supplier for all raw materials) and risk. Risk implications show what could happen if operational budget is removed from sending your best contract negotiators to your primary supplier and instead put into securing an ad-hoc supplier that may cost more for the one-time transaction while still not securing the best possible deal with the strategic supplier.

Taking these factors into account, adjust plans with a range of operational outcomes and probabilities rather than an absolute number based on the various contingencies.

Forecast Performance and Risks

Create rolling, risk-adjusted forecasts of the budget (revenues and costs) and operational plan (including number, capacity, and cost of resources necessary to achieve the plan) so that you can see trends over a rolling time horizon for risks whose probability, consequence, or resiliency change over time. If you have to make adjustments, you can see where you've been and the direction in which things are likely to go. Predictive analytical techniques can be powerful for building risk-adjusted forecasts by modeling the impact previous risks had on previous forecasts.

In a risk-adjusted procurement forecast, create a rolling forecast with a one-year window for expected costs such as asset/equipment costs, raw materials, and facilities costs to cover production planning and an associated range of expected activity outputs (supplier interactions, contract nego-tiations, and sourcing activities) that are dependent on key risks in the environment. When the probability or impact of a risk changes, adjust the financial or operational forecast costs or activities accordingly. Using predictive techniques, you can learn from the impact of previous risks on previous actuals (the number of products sold, previous negotiated pricing as a benchmark, commodity pricing in the last year) to predict the impact of your current risks on your current cost or activity forecasts.

Examine Repercussions for Execution Problems

In a tight economy, another look at the commodity pricing against existing supplier contracts for raw materials is in order. Planning must be aligned with strategy. If Production delays manufacturing because they do not have enough components, its impact across the company can be profound. Coordination across departments is critical so that there are no surprises.

The key to excellence in execution is visibility. Being able to see spend across the entire organization gives managers the ability to cut wasteful spending such as paying for ad-hoc office supplies when an employee decides to go to Staples instead purchasing from an approved vendor.

To minimize risk on the execution side, alerts must be set up when pro-curement thresholds are exceeded, such as maverick spending over a certain amount or contracts that need to be renegotiated ending within a month.

Monitor and Analyze

In the monitor and analyze phase of the PM lifecycle, you monitor to understand what is happening, analyze to understand why it is happening, and, for those things that are not on track, adjust to improve the situation relative to your goals.

Just as Finance performs regular consolidations for reporting the com-pany's financial performance, you too must establish an effective consoli-dation model for spend-related data.

Analytic capabilities for Procurement include including contract ana-lytics, spend analytics, supplier analytics, and pricing analytics. Analytics are used to monitor, track, and report on procurement-related KPIs and KRIs (ongoing versus planned performance).

Monitor

It is important to distinguish the different categories of monitoring in evaluating business performance.

Event monitoring looks for a single, discrete activity or exposure event. An example of an event is vendor selection without competitive bidding. Trend monitoring looks at events over time to find patterns. In Procurement, a trend worth monitoring is a control that compares employee bank account numbers with those listed on vendor records once per quarter.

Intelligence monitoring collects information from a variety of external sources that are of interest to the company and may indicate a risk exposure. Collecting commodity pricing and competitive product pricing can help Procurement negotiate competitive rates.

Dashboards facilitate decision-making, bringing together information that needs to be monitored, providing status at a glance. Procurement dashboards might include dashboards for contracts, direct and indirect spend, supplier analytics, and pricing analytics.

Dashboards are effective ways of combining the events, trends, and intelligence monitoring patterns across all of the major facets of the business to be monitored.

Next, evaluate performance. Look at KPIs to identify progress made toward achieving objectives. How much money has been saved to date with the procurement system? Is it increasing on a monthly basis?

Evaluate initiatives that are failing or behind schedule. Is the number of employees using the procurement self-service application increasing or

Figure 14-6. A Procurement Dashboard

decreasing? What are peak periods for usage of the application? Is usage increasing or decreasing?

Evaluate risk. Look at the KRIs to identify:

- **Top risks.** As sales peak, will suppliers be able to keep up with demand? Has there been an issue with quarterly vendor evaluations? What is the impact of commodity pricing on margins?
- **Changes to risk levels for key activities.** Have any supplier services or fulfillment rates declined? Has pricing on raw materials increased by more than 10%?
- **Assessment procedures.** Are risks being assessed in accordance with company policy or industry best practices? Are quarterly vendor evaluations documented and signed off?
- **Effectiveness of mitigation.** Are mitigation strategies reducing the likelihood or impact of a risk? For example, when business owners rate suppliers poorly, are those suppliers taken off the preferred supplier list?

Evaluate internal controls. Report key control deficiencies, approvals, verifications, and reconciliations to mitigate risk. How many duplicate payments have occurred in the last month? To remediate the process, double-check the settings that should flag such payments before they are processed.

Evaluate incidents and losses. If incidents or losses have occurred or external events affect the company (an economic downturn, for example), document this information, even if you haven't been tracking it in the system yet. For example, if one of the suppliers appears on the denied party list, it must be flagged since receiving goods from this vendor could result in a fine.

No matter how proactive you are, manual monitoring is inefficient. Automated monitoring proactively identifies out-of-tolerance conditions, highlighting key areas when a KPI, KRI, or control goes over or under defined tolerances and then alerting the responsible party. This should take into account forecasting, trending, and modeling capabilities so that if a metric falls out of range of a trend or budget, or plan, the appropriate alert is raised, along with a workflow to begin an investigation. For example, if you want to increase a certain percentage of low-cost country spend, these systems will track relevant suppliers' spend and alert you when that trend is dipping. This knowledge of ongoing performance can be used to optimize activities that are falling short and replicate successes.

Analyze

The deeper you look at your Procurement organization, the more you may want to know about why things aren't working and why. Analytics might require talents you don't currently possess. You may need help with the way you are evaluating metrics. Ensuring that your analysis is statistically sound may mean hiring an analyst with these qualifications or consulting with one. Analysis is a key step in which you not only look at where you are, but what is happening (or what has happened) and why. Techniques for analysis can range from manual and simple to automated and statistically sophisticated.

The next step is to analyze performance. Understand why KPIs are increasing or decreasing. For example, when reviewing lead time for delivery for raw materials from a key supplier, you notice that other suppliers have been late, causing your company to miss last month's production forecast, which eventually impacts sales.

Analyze initiatives to understand why they are succeeding or failing. After seeing that the Procurement self-service initiative is heading in the wrong direction, you determine that it is happening because the HR self-service system is behind schedule.

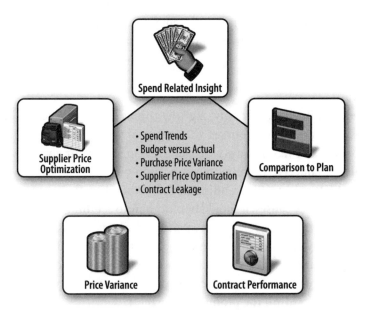

Figure 14-7. Elements of a Spend Analytics Solution

Analyze risk to understand why KRIs are increasing or decreasing. You conduct a sensitivity analysis to identify process deficiencies or other trends that are increasing the price of raw materials before it reaches critical levels.

Analyze controls to see if they are effective. You notice that a control to test for effective administration of your vendor payment policies generates a lot of incidents and find that the thresholds are set too low, creating a false positive. You discover that some controls have lost their effectiveness due to changing business conditions or organizational structures and you need to analyze why.

Analyze incidents and losses to determine root causes and trends. You notice more inventory is missing after cycle counts at the warehouse. After reviewing the goods receipt transactions, you review what type of products are missing and see if there is a trend.

In all of these cases, analysis was done with human intervention but this does not have to be the case. The volume and complexity of data in the enterprise today makes it increasingly difficult to mine data and come to intelligent conclusions. Using data mining techniques, software can determine the most likely root causes and suggest recommended actions. For example, you observe that a KRI for forecasted fulfillment rate is increasing. Without any manual intervention, the system does a series of correlations. When you highlight the KRI, a popup shows that the number one factor associated with the change in fulfillment rate is the sudden decrease in raw materials availability in the supply chain because of unforeseen weather disruptions.

Adjust

After monitoring and analyzing why things did not go accordingly to plan, set things back on course by taking what you've learned and using it to adjust the settings. Always consider the impact of your goals, risks, and compliance concerns on other business units.

Adjust KPIs. For KPIs trending in the wrong direction, once you have analyzed the root causes, it should be clear how to set things back on course. However, remember that KPIs are interlinked, and you must optimize your performance in the context of risk objectives and without violating your compliance objectives. If suppliers continue to miss delivery dates, it can impact sales revenue. You can increase order volumes to have more inventory on hand to fulfill the production forecast.

Adjust initiatives. For initiatives that are not going as planned, rapidly take remedial action or cancel them. If it's clear that the initiative is not going to work, either make changes that can help save the project or cancel it if possible so that you can reallocate those resources. For example, if a preferred vendor continues to miss delivery dates, you find a more reliable vendor.

Adjust KRIs. For KRIs trending in the wrong direction, analyze the root cause. It should be clear what actions to take will set things back on course, often by putting appropriate mitigating controls in place. However, it is critical to remember that KRIs are interlinked and you must optimize your risks in the context of performance objectives and without violating your compliance objectives. For example, after conducting a correlation analysis of vendor assessment scores and on-time delivery percentages, you put in a mitigating control to automatically order from another vendor if the original vendor misses the delivery date. However, do this only if it does not decrease the likelihood of delivering on the goal of holding vendors accountable for promised dates and if it doesn't violate any compliance objectives such as not paying the vendor on time.

Adjust controls. For controls violations, adjustment takes the form of remediation and certification. After contracts are violated, you set up a remediation plan to prevent such violations by requesting detailed reports for services and purchases to help your company with reconciliations.

Adjust after incidents and losses. For incidents and losses, the correct adjustments typically involve reexamining whether you are tracking the right risks and have put appropriate controls in place to mitigate them. For example, after noting an uptick in contract violations, add an automated risk monitoring process to alert you to the first sign of increases beyond the contract budget.

You want to search for variances between actual and planned performance. Use this knowledge to optimize activities that are falling short and to replicate those that are succeeding.

Model and Optimize

Creating a model of the organization's spend and procurement allows you to be predictive, based on past and current behavior. This model should have the capability to analyze and determine the best methods of optimizing activities and processes from contract negotiation to spend management to supplier and pricing options.

You should be working toward gaining a consolidated view of spend. However, modeling is not enough. It is necessary to capture the knowledge gained and use it to optimize processes and activities.

Model

Modeling takes several forms, including revenue, cost, and profitability modeling, scenario modeling, and simulation modeling.

Revenue, cost, and profitability modeling. The revenue, cost, and profitability implications of performance management, risk management, and compliance management activities and their drivers can be modeled at a very detailed level using activity-based costing (ABC). ABC can be very useful for breaking down costs of the individual activities people perform to get a much more detailed sense of where purchasing manager's time is being spent to find efficiencies. For example, using ABC, you can model the time purchasing managers spend on the phone negotiating and working with suppliers and the costs of each unit of activity.

There is also a need to understand an item's direct and indirect procurement costs. For example, to monitor the cost of a component to an air conditioner manufacturer requires understanding not just the price per unit, but transport costs, warehousing expenses, duties, taxes, drawbacks, fees, handling, transportation and global logistics costs, as well as any other activity or resource consumed in the provision of that item. By identifying and monitoring these ancillary costs, you will be developing an ABC model for the company's spend. You will also be better able to identify heretofore unseen cost variances as well as the actual cost/benefit ratio for specific suppliers and items. This can also translate into profitability ratios, providing critical decision support for balancing risk with performance or risk with cost.

Scenario modeling. This type of modeling can be applied to financial and operational modeling and focuses on creating different business scenarios. Simple scenario modeling includes creating a base case and then high and low cases based on changes made to input variables, such as market growth rates or inflation rates. This technique is often used in modeling market and business opportunities and creating business plans. For example, you might build a set of scenario models to understand how critical macro variables such as the price of commodities impact supplier management strategies in a growth market.

Simulation modeling. More advanced modeling including Monte Carlo simulation supports a broad range of scenarios based on multiple iterations of input assumptions and combinations. With this technique, probabilities are assigned to various outcomes. These techniques allow the uncertainty associated with a given forecast to be estimated and to reduce risk by applying sensitivity analysis, correlation, and trend extrapolation. By simulating the effect of uncertainty, it becomes possible to answer questions such as, "How certain are we that increasing spend under management by an additional 10% will result in a minimum decrease in overall spend of 5%?" Or, conversely, "What's the minimum decrease in overall spend that we can be, for example, 90% certain of achieving given a 10% increase in spend under management?" Simulation also makes it possible to identify and rank the various contributors to overall uncertainty.

Optimize

The goal at this phase of the PM lifecycle is to determine the optimal way to achieve objectives by taking into account the entire context of the problem, including all relevant constraints and assessments (costs, benefits, risk, labor and time), as well as business strategies, objectives, risks, and compliance factors. Optimization can be done both through human evaluation as well as through advanced algorithmic techniques.

If we are clear on our strategy and resources, we could use optimization techniques to tell us the best way to achieve our goals by letting the software examine the constraints and assumptions and suggesting the correct actions to reach the goal. For example, we could input a goal of reducing the number of suppliers and increasing the spend under management, and input all of the drivers to this goal mentioned earlier, and have the software tell us exactly which suppliers to keep, which to remove, and what they would have to produce in order to make the initiative work.

Case Study: Performance Management in Action

Virtual Gates is a fictional cutting-edge computer manufacturer with retail outlets. This section describes how the Procurement department's team at Virtual Gates closes its loop during the process of increasing its control spend to realize measurable savings and free up working capital.

Setting the Context

Virtual Gates' Chief Procurement Officer, Angela Washington, has just received a set of high-level directives from her immediate superior, CEO Clint Hobbs. At the top of the list is the task of increasing Procurement's control of spend to realize a 3% savings and free up working capital.

In a typical year, this might not present such a challenge, but VG is working in an economy in which the market is wreaking daily havoc on industries across the board with commodity prices and cost of doing business increasing to better serve the customers. Moreover, Clint wants Angela to align these savings with his bigger goal of driving profitable growth as measured by VG's net income and earnings per share growth, especially as they compare to the company's principal competitors, Hypercell and Packingflash. Last, but certainly not least, Angela must implement her initiatives during HR's campaign to reduce VG's workforce by 15% and Product Development's drive to release a new netbook while retiring products that are no longer profitable.

To start, Angela will need to consider increasing her on contract spend and spend under management by consolidating suppliers. To succeed, Angela must clearly communicate her goal throughout the entire organization and then beyond, to her supplier network.

Understand the Collaborative Impact

No modern organization, nor the departments within it, function in isolated silos. Virtual Gates is no exception, nor is its Procurement department.

VG is a technological product company to which brand value is everything. VG tackles the market with a single, concentrated intention—conceiving of and bringing new products to market as quickly as possible—leaving anything outside its window of expertise to partners that can do it better. At VG, everything that goes into the products it makes comes from partner companies. Because Procurement is the link between VG and its world of suppliers, it plays a critical role in nearly all of VG's key business processes, including collaborative demand and supply planning, supplier network management, integrated product development, continuous product innovation, asset visibility and performance, Finance, HR, and IT. It owns the integrated sourcing and procurement process, which is linked to VG's network of suppliers.

All of these departments lean on Procurement, but Product Development depends on it most. The product lifecycle management business process is long and complex, moving from market assessment, conceptual design, engineering and detailed design to change management, sourcing and supplier collaboration, and production process planning, and concluding with product launch, aftermarket support and service, and product portfolio management. As the netbook under development at VG makes its way through this maze, it is continually at the mercy of Procurement's ability to ensure that its supply needs are met consistently and on time and that raw materials are purchased at the lowest rate.

Imagine how critical a responsibility Angela and her team in Procurement have. If they are out of joint with the supplier network, production schedules can be disrupted. In turn, collaborative demand and supply plan would be affected, resulting in budget fractures that would distress Finance, HR, and IT processes. Ultimately, these slips could have serious consequences. For instance, if VG knows that its competitor Packingflash is developing a similar netbook, it is imperative that each of VG's production stages reach completion on or before deadline so that VG can launch its netbook on time. Should VG miss this window because Angela's team failed to acquire needed parts, materials, or equipment, Packingflash could release its netbook first, an unwanted outcome with far-reaching consequences. Virtual Gates, for example, might have to invest more in Marketing and Sales than it had intended to reach the number of consumers it needs to meet Clint Hobbs' demand to achieve a minimum of 2% overall growth.

Under ordinary conditions, Angela's margin for error is slim. In the current climate, where the economy has gone south and her team is being asked to work harder as a result of newly imposed staff and IT service reductions, the margin is virtually nonexistent—she and her team must be firing on all pistons at every turn of the road. Just as Procurement is dependent on the departments with which they it is working, so too are those departments dependent on others. As long as Angela remains in close collaboration with all concerned parties, her processes should run smoothly and outcomes result as planned.

Establish KPIs and KRIs

For Angela to measure her progress toward goals with efficiency and accuracy, she must select and implement KPIs and KRIs that are most relevant to her processes. Without them, she and her team are essentially helpless. Before taking any action, it's critical that they identify the top KPIs and KRIs, the principle risks to which they could be exposed as a result of their choices, and the main interfaces between their partners and their processes that require monitoring. It is also important to understand drivers behind KPIs and KRIs, along with the relationships between them and to identify leading indicators of performance.

A moment ago, we said that the metrics with which Angela should be most concerned as she and her team work toward achieving their initiatives are percentage of on contract spend and spend under management. The Procurement team may well be clear about these criteria, but Angela needs to know that the impact is clear to her partner departments as well.

For instance, once increasing Procurement's on contract spend and spend under management frees up the anticipated working capital, Finance will be able to loosen some of its budget restraints. Contingency measures for any potential difficulties can be rapidly initiated because of the clear inter-departmental visibility Angela is working to maintain.

Establish the BI Foundation

The metrics for your KPIs or KRIs are the product of hard work. Once Angela understands the key business dimensions and the relevant KPIs and KRIs, she needs to obtain the data for them from various source systems, cleanse the data, align the master data, and load it into a data mart or data warehouse. Source systems will include SRM and ERP systems, to say nothing of their miscellaneous sourcing, contracting, and operational procurement systems. She must also cull data from such systems as PLM, CRM, and SCM.

BI becomes a single source of truth upon which Angela's team will rely as they continue to eliminate spend and help maximize production investments while VG develops and launches its latest netbook.

Strategize and Prioritize

We have emphasized the intensity of the relationship that Angela and her Procurement team has with the other departments at VG. Particularly important is Procurement's affiliation with Paul Burton's Product Development department. What is at stake during Product Development's drive to release its new netbook even as it sunsets unprofitable products is a continuous free-flow of materials, supplies, and equipment to its affiliate manufacturers. Procurement, as you know, is the point department here. Angela was selected from a field of highly talented candidates because of her ability to consistently find solutions where others could not. However, now that Clint Hobbs has asked her to consolidate suppliers as a means to increase procurement's percentage of on contract spend and spend under management while simultaneously shedding members of her team per HR's directive, the potential for lapses in supply increase substantially, at least until contracts are signed and the dust has cleared. To cover her bases in the meantime, Angela will need to work with George Martin in Supply Chain to ensure that inventory levels are substantial enough to tide them over should a lapse occur while suppliers are being consolidated. At the same time, she and her team must also work in extra close proximity to the various teams in Product Development.

Monitoring her team's progress toward their goals will require Angela to create a scorecard that lists, among other things, the risks inherent to her initiative. Heading the list is the possibility that procurement could be rendered vulnerable not merely to suppliers' inability to fulfill their obligations, but also to those that may attempt to leverage their sudden opportunity and raise prices, too. To account for them, Angela must introduce KRIs and related mitigating actions. Finally, she must document, test, monitor, and certify a control to ensure that the supplier rationalization process is proceeding in an effective way that is compliant with the strategy and with legal contracts with suppliers.

Plan and Execute

Angela's plan entails spending the funds for her supplier rationalization initiative on the operational resources needed to consolidate her key suppliers and divest her department of all others. This should produce reduced costs for the contract work, sourcing initiatives, and operational procurement activities. Another risk associated with this initiative lies in the limited budget to achieve it. If other initiatives don't receive the appropriate funding, they might not be able to execute sufficiently.

As a means of coaxing her peer departments into collaborating with her more closely, Angela might consider allocating funds directly to processes such as integrated sourcing and procurement, integrated product development, increased budget for product promotion or collaborative demand and supply planning.

Monitor and Analyze

Once her plan to reduce the number of suppliers, contracts, and operational procurement activities is set, Angela will focus primarily on whether her percentage of on contract spend and spend under management are matching the numbers forecast in the strategizing and planning phases. This, of course, will require her team to maintain a keen eye on their established KPIs and KRIs. For example, as she consolidates her suppliers and divests from others, is Manufacturing still getting materials in a timely fashion? Is Product Development still on track to launch the new netbook? Has the Procurement initiative freed up working capital through smarter sourcing?

The team must immediately discover the source of any discrepancy between the anticipated and actual results of her department's initiative and develop a contingency plan in case any of the KPIs go below the threshold. It could be that the amount of spend Angela's team has gotten under management is not enough to make the impact she expected on the bottom line. Or perhaps the suppliers she chose keep using their leverage to increase their own margins at VG's expense. Regardless of the issue, Angela's chief priority after deciding upon a possible solution is to ensure that it's in line with all partner activities and with corporate strategy.

Model and Optimize

By this phase in the performance management process, Angela sees that her team needs a more detailed operational model to understand where resources are being leveraged. For example, by modeling the consumption of people, time, and materials, she could learn that her budget to fund the supplier rationalization initiative is not big enough: the existing suppliers have already absorbed too much capacity, leaving a headcount that was too low to execute the campaign. Angela's costing analysis could also show her which suppliers give her the most value for the amount of operational resources they consume. It's not unusual during such analyses to find that those suppliers that had been thought to reduce costs most are actually more expensive than others because of factors such as higher freight costs.

By simulating various "what-if" scenarios, Angela can change key assumptions in the model and remove various constraints. For example, she could modify an assumption such as the talent that Procurement must hire and remove a constraint such as the requirement to keep suppliers with whom VG has had historical relationships.

Optimizing her initiative would require Angela to enter the goal of reducing the number of suppliers and increasing the spend under management, along with the affiliated drivers. Thereafter, she would let the model make recommendations. For example, it could suggest not only which suppliers to keep, but also the results they must produce to ensure the initiative's success.

Closing the Loop in an Integrated System

The circumstances described to this point are manageable with current technology. But technology is always moving forward, and soon holistic, closed-loop systems will enable most departments to align their execution and strategy more easily. Angela's ability to produce a strategy management method that captures goals, initiatives, and metrics that can be linked to her driver-based financial and operational planning process, as well as to her monitoring and analysis, modeling and optimization, and risk and control processes, will precipitate an entirely new set of circumstances. Moreover,

Angela's team can steer preferred behavior toward transactional processes with their goals, initiatives, plans, and risks and controls.

Fortunately for Angela, Procurement has at its disposal just this type of closed-loop system. Integrated spend performance management and transactional sourcing solutions equipped with analyses for budget vs. actual, purchase price variance, supplier price optimization, and contract leakage can enable her to establish the goals and measures of her spend performance and monitor her spend trends. She can also use these same functionalities to pull data from all of the systems in which her partners work, including supply chain and financial systems. Once Angela has identified the right suppliers based on the rationalization goals and the analysis, she can send aggregate spend data directly from the transactional sourcing application to the sourcing system and instantly create a sourcing project, RFx, and auction. In this way, the strategy to increase spend under management, the initiatives to consolidate suppliers, and the real act of eliminating suppliers and hiring new ones are integrated such that both efficiency—doing things right—and effectiveness—doing the right things—are significantly improved.

Align the Workforce

Angela has one further consideration in her bid to meet Clint Hobbs' directives and that is to link the objectives of all of the aforementioned activities with her team's compensation. Whenever one of her buyers sees that a successful execution of the supplier rationalization initiative brings her a bonus, she will surely work very hard indeed. Any time departments see that their bonuses are linked to the successful attainment of Procurement's goals, you can rest assured that they'll be working to support them. Angela's success, then, is contingent on the success of her partners, and vice versa. Clint Hobbs is sure to reward her with her own significant bonus package when he learns that she has achieved a 5% growth in Procurement's overall profit as measured by Virtual Gates' net income and earnings per share growth.

Action Items

In this chapter you have seen how performance management benefits your company, department, and you professionally. We also cannot over-stress the point that performance management is a journey not a destination. It begins with very simple and small initiatives that lead to a larger and more comprehensive solution.

The following provide a starting point:

- Audit existing spend data management capabilities
- Garner executive support by showing the ROI of an initial investment in the tools that will help you begin to build-out the performance management lifecycle
- Create a baseline procurement analysis capability
- Develop commodity[7] expertise within your procurement organization (gathering more data and visibility into spend will provide limited benefits unless it is matched with the expertise to understand and utilize the data)
- Create and/or enhance reporting capabilities to support multiple views and dimensionality
- Adopt and publish a common classification scheme for the organization
- Integrate spend management tools with sourcing, GRC, contract, and other related solutions to build a more consolidated view
- Establish where you are in terms of amount of spend under management
- Evaluate your analysis capabilities (do you have spend, contract, price, and other analytic capabilities?)
- Evaluate your performance management maturity in order to create a baseline from which to build your efforts
- Consider automating global trade management procedures

---

[7] Ibid: This is an important trend that should garner some significant consideration. According to Aberdeen's research, companies that underperform in terms of performance management and spend analysis are 35% less likely than best-in-class companies to possess commodity expertise.

Chapter 15

Performance Management for Product Development

In today's global market, it doesn't matter whether your product is raw materials, finished goods, merchandise, or services. Your products are developed, created, and delivered as a collaborative effort of business networks that include brand owners, suppliers, and partners, all of which are undergoing a process of constant transformation in response to customer needs and market demands. Make no mistake—to compete in such an environment, you must employ cutting-edge performance management (PM) techniques as you orchestrate and grow your products across their lifecycle, from the earlier innovation, design, and source stages, to the later phases, where your product is made, sold, and moved.

Looking Back: How Life Has Changed in Product Development

The size and complexity of managing the product development lifecycle is so great, in fact, that it would be difficult to overstate the cooperation, sensitivity, and flexibility required to profitably accomplish it month after month, year after year.

This was not always the case. Despite the quality revolution of the 1980s, and the adaptation in the 1990s of quality principles for application to white-collar processes in the form of business process reengineering, product development was still considerably less complex than it is today.

Most phases in the product lifecycle were siloed much as the other business units once were. Design was not concerned with the extent to which engineering became Lean any more than engineering wasted time considering how lean manufacturing, quality control, or marketing had grown. To make matters simpler still, products were driven by engineering and design—pushed upon the market—rather than driven by customer demand—pulled into the market—the prime mover behind all current major business activities.

Today, on the other hand, innovation is the business discipline that leads to profitable transformation. Innovating with the required speed and agility is no longer a matter of ensuring that Lean techniques are efficiently implemented at each phase of the product lifecycle. Product development organizations have recognized that increasing growth and profit margins depends on how well each phase in the product lifecycle coordinates with the others. Silos across the lifecycle must be eliminated so that the work of every phase is collaborative and mutually interdependent. Universal data management and efficiently coordinated distributed processes are the rule now, not the exception. Manufacturing can't wait until design and engineering have completed their work any more than marketing and launch can wait for manufacturing and distribution.

In short, you must imagine the product lifecycle end-to-end, from designing the virtual factory where your product will be made (understanding the ways and means by which all of its processes can be optimized), to standardizing your bills of materials, to creating suites of electronic assets that allow truly distributed product engineering, to receiving accurate market feedback about customer requirements for your product. Moreover, you must guarantee that your product moves smoothly through its lifecycle, in compliance with all specifications, regulations, tariff controls, and the like. Finally, when one lifecycle is complete, you must be able to recycle everything it used in its next iteration. Add to this mix frequent design changes, incompatible data from multiple systems, new regulatory compliance, and globally distributed supply networks, and you can quickly see the magnitude of the challenge.

Performance management for product development is the framework you need to establish strategy for your products, projects, and resources. You also need performance management to plan the allocation of resources to meet that strategy and to know that you're progressing along the right path by monitoring your execution activities via the KPIs that your business intelligence infrastructure has collected from your transactional systems. Lastly, performance management for product development will enable you to see where and when you are not performing according to plan. As such, you can adjust routings, work centers, and resources to produce the specified finished goods.

How Business Network Transformation Affects Product Development

We just noted the magnitude of the task of product development. It begins with market assessment, conceptual design, engineering and detailed design. From there it transitions to change management, sourcing and supplier collaboration, and production process planning, and then concludes with product launch, aftermarket support and service, and product portfolio management. The success of each of these phases depends upon many factors, none of which can be managed successfully if others are competing for your attention at the same time.

To cite just one example, selling as much product at the best price requires your sales division to thoroughly understand the final cost of your product, including the overhead related to its production and the cost required to ship, store, and monitor it as stocked inventory. Gaining this insight requires that you capture activity data and then deploy analytics that can correlate the data with financial results and valuation throughout the process. In turn, this enables you to meet your objectives by controlling your risks and optimizing advantages and thus to capitalize on opportunities while avoiding potential market barriers. Service, on the other hand, is tasked with the single but difficult goal of achieving 100% customer satisfaction. To meet this requirement, you must deploy proven metrics to shape intermediary goals and activities, along with the resources you need to make those happen.

In the face of these related but discrete endeavors, however, you are confronted with the first law of business network transformation—that of specialization. Every company must concentrate solely on its core competency—the thing it does best—while outsourcing every other task to trusted partners. Because most of today's companies focus all of their energy on mastering a single phase or subphase of the business process, it is rare to find one that is capable of successfully navigating the demands of both Sales and Service within its own four walls, much less of any other stage in the product development lifecycle.

The core competency of successful product-centric companies such as Nestle, Nike, or Apple, therefore, resides in their products and their brands. These corporations have not become industry leaders by happenstance. Rather than struggling to be great at all of the possible value-generating mechanisms, they attack the market with a single, concentrated focus—conceiving of and bringing new products to market as quickly as possible—leaving anything outside their window of expertise to partners that can do it better. Apple, for instance, conducts sales through its stores and web site, as well as via third parties. And while the company provides service through its store, too, customers can also request onsite service through any number of third parties. Delivering its products, service, and support through its own store enables Apple to sharpen its product focus, ensuring that both established and potential customers can interact with the company's latest products. Ensuring customers continued access to its products in its own store provides Apple with still more benefits, though. The company recognizes the value of customer feedback and knowledge, which is why it never relegates distribution of its productions to suppliers alone. Yet another means of staying in touch with its customer base is through the on-site, hands-on classes that Apple offers, after which participants are surveyed about product usage. The results of these surveys help to feed future enhancements and new product development.

How Technology Has Changed

It was not long ago that most stages of the product development process were conducted manually. Consider, for instance, processing product releases and changes. Without automation, this phase demanded extensive document collection and copying efforts and repetitive, error-prone, change-order creations. It was also at the mercy of time-consuming interoffice mail. At times it might even have required an engineer or analyst to deliver packages by hand. When supply chain partners were involved, other time-wasting activities entered the fray, as well, from shipping parcels via mail services (whereupon the risk of insufficient security and loss arose) to email containing unrelated or erroneous file attachments.

Later, with the introduction of ERP, a single, standardized platform used in concert with ad hoc methodologies was sufficient to coordinate the resources, information, and activities needed to complete most business processes.

Today, ERP still provides the basis for managing the shared services for Finance, HR and IT, but if you are a product-based company, you need more. For instance, you own a standardized way of executing detailed conceptual design. You also own a standardized means of engineering your designs, planning your production process, and launching products.

Product lifecycle management (PLM) systems help to automate many additional areas, including the ability to:

- Build and manage product structure records
- Manage documents for design and process
- Enable workflow and process management for approving changes
- Control secured access for multiple users
- Import and export data to and from ERP systems
- Create reports for environmental compliance
- Store electronic files
- Effectively manage product launches and introduction

PLM is often supplemented by systems like supply chain management (SCM), supplier relationship management (SRM), and, to manage sales, customer relationship management (CRM).

The Evolution of Performance Management for Product Development

The current business environment has evolved from no automation whatsoever, to individual applications per discrete sector to rough product development processes within the four walls of a single company, to the current plug-and-play product development process functionality across networks. Performance management techniques have evolved to greater levels of sophistication in tandem.

In the beginning, static, Excel-based reports were the best companies had to work with. From there, siloed reporting tools emerged to run on top of siloed process tools. Finally, business intelligence systems were developed, which in turn gave rise to the performance management systems that provide the agility and comprehensive visibility needed to connect and consolidate the entire business process map, both within and beyond the network.

PLM was sparked by a need for the enhanced visibility that is required to increase profits and grow, and yet applying performance management to product development poses an especially difficult challenge. While PLM provides you with a central data source from which to execute all of your processes, you must nevertheless apply performance management across a spectrum of concerns that, taken together, constitute a vast network, each of which usually have networks of their own. For instance, a company whose core competency lies in sourcing and supplier collaboration may coordinate its production process planning with 10 other companies. Each of these companies must provide visibility into their own processes, since without it, the parent company has no assurance that it is engaging companies whose business practices are compliant with current regulations and, just as importantly, that it will receive the materials it needs. Because the parent company does not own all of its processes, this level of collaboration from each of its partners is vital.

The same holds true if you are a company that owns market assessment, conceptual design, or product portfolio management. Any process that you do not own will be outsourced to a partner. To deliver on your revenue plan and growth objectives, you must have confidence in them via service level agreements that enable you to communicate information from one partner in the process to the next. When the engineers to which you've outsourced the design of your MP3 player announce that they will be three weeks late, you must be able to quickly inform your sourcing partner so that they don't order materials that would have to sit in inventory.

Without performance management, neither of the above scenarios would be possible, because neither company would be able to align their strategies to their plans. In turn, execution would suffer, as would the monitoring, analyzing, and optimizing activities that are vital to viewing operations at progressively granular levels, and, more importantly, in

---

A recent AMR benchmarking study showed that concern about product, process, and systems complexity in extended value chains is on the rise.

Higher complexity product portfolios, for example, can translate to as much as:

- 80% higher direct supply chain cost
- 53% increase in forecast error
- 40% greater manufacturing schedule variance

real time. Finally, governance over your key processes would be weakened or perhaps even absent, allowing for the emergence of numerous potential risks.

Why You Must Do This Now

As we have said, the cardinal rule at the heart of business network transformation is specialization. You must decide on your core competency and then put all of your efforts toward becoming the best you can be, outsourcing operations beyond the scope of your specialty to partners. As you continue to do everything yourself, you will almost certainly succumb to market competition.

Value chains in the product lifecycle are no longer fixed. Process stages from concept to product launch and everything in between, are more fluid than ever. Monthly or even weekly assessments cannot provide the data you need for an accurate view of each stage in your product lifecycle. To get that, you must manage performance in real time.

Performance management enables you to align all functions in your company and in your extended business network with your corporate goals. In turn, this alignment strengthens the balance between your goals and initiatives for innovation, design, quality, project and resource, and component and task sourcing activities, and prevents you from missing or unintentionally working against corporate goals. This same balance also works toward the continuous creation of strong plans. Monitoring activities for products, design, quality, and so forth, will also be stable, resulting in accurate analysis. Finally, the modeling and optimization activities that are vital to effective performance management will be effective and lasting, available for use across multiple product lifecycle iterations.

The research suggests just how dire the need is for a strong integration of performance management for product development. For example, where the majority of retailers state that their concept testing and research and development would benefit from effective performance management, 42% feel that effective calendaring and line planning using performance management techniques will enable stronger product portfolio management. Across all industry sectors, respondents reported that product launches fail when products don't meet customer needs. For retailers, 68% report they look to improve idea generation within the next 12 months, and 74% indicate that customer-needs assessments should be included.

Does This Sound Familiar?

- The security you once felt under the market's protection has vanished—where you could once count on a guaranteed customer base, you must now struggle to attract and maintain your customers in a market characterized by a myriad of providers offering increasingly lower prices.

- You face a growing range of new obstructions that challenge your ability to gather, examine, analyze, and transform your data.

- You have too many data sources and no standardized processes, resulting in inferior data quality.

- Confronted with ever-rising regulations and compliance standards, you cannot maintain the overall cost of bringing your product to market.

- You lack the technology required to create meaningful reports.

- Your system automation is nonexistent, or, if operational, substandard.

- To shrink your production costs and increase your margins, you can no longer manage a simple network; you must now orchestrate an entire value chain that includes multiple partners around the world, thus decreasing your visibility and increasing your risks.

- You lack a fundamental methodology to achieve the objectives required to successfully manage your product lifecycle from beginning to end.

- You have no reliable means of measuring your supplier content.

Product Development Business Drivers

Beyond the need to differentiate across markets, shorten product life-cycles, and comply with increasing global and local regulations, the key factor driving growth and profitability in Product Development is the pressure to innovate.

From 1991 to 2002, new product launches nearly doubled, rising from 17,000 per year to 32,000. The last two decades of the 20th century saw new product complexity double, as well, and, in the years from 1998 to 2007, revenues from new products rose by nearly 40%, proving that at the end of the day, more launches of more complex products contribute to more revenue. In this light, it's no wonder that new product launches continue to increase and the pressure to reduce time-to-market is mounting. A company with limited resources must increase efficiency to stay competitive. Making sound decisions about how to invest R&D dollars is one way to start, as is improving the new product development and launch (NPDL) process. Current benchmark data from AMR shows that industry leaders bring products to market twice as fast as their competition and invest more time in the early stages of development.

These last concerns have been especially critical. According to AMR, the NPDL process has suffered greatly from a lack of investment in outdated engineering systems, in part a function of failing to persuade investors that new product growth plans are valid. Whereas best practice in functional silos is good, say company leaders, a full 90% improvement of NPDL processes is still possible. This should come as no surprise, given that only 69% of companies believe their NPDL to be under financial and strategic control. The last and best reason to support the need for improved NPDL, however, should sound loudly across the C suite: those executives that can't guarantee demonstrably effective product innovation will continue to experience backlashes from shareholders.

And yet a simple increase in product innovation and launches is not enough to stay on top. In fact, across most of the industry, new product launches are failing, as the numbers show. To cite just a few widespread examples from AMR, 75% of new launches in consumer goods have failed, while food retailers have spent an average of $975,000 per store on failed product introductions.

Typically, the inability to align strategy and plans is a result of entrenched silos across an organization. Each silo can work toward goals that appear to be reasonable but which in the bigger picture are not aligned. Manufacturing may have created a gorgeous new product, but if Marketing has not accounted for the product in its budget, or there's no capacity in the supply chain to deliver it, or you experience a shortage of trained salespeople, then the chances of the product successfully reaching the open market are slim.

The right technology for the right job is critical to discerning the degree to which your strategies, plans, and means of executing them are present and aligned. Intelligent innovation processes, for example, require a sustainable structure to cultivate and nurture a means of strong open innovation, including decision support and product, service, and market insights. You must design and manufacture your products on a global scale, activities requiring powerful collaboration and IP protection. Increasing product complexity—more and more products are digital, with embedded software—demands that you bundle products and services, and these, in turn, require the wherewithal to create performance-based business models. Further, you must design compliance into your products, just as you actively consider ways to make them as green as possible.

What Kind of Company Are You?

A product-centric company such as BMW, Sony, or the GAP follows the value-generating model of product and service leadership, in which you optimize the return on your product and brand over its lifecycle. Knowing the exact nature of your company's strengths and weaknesses can inform strategies and plans. A product and service leadership company doesn't cut costs by slowing down the R&D cycle. Every division and role across the corporate ecosystem must base its thinking, decisions, and activities on this single fact. The head of Product Development in a company that focuses on its supply chain will behave quite differently than the head of Product Development in a company that focuses on the products themselves. When a budget needs cutting, it shouldn't be cut evenly. Instead, cuts should be directed toward areas of the company that drive the least revenue.

Table 15-1 lists the core competencies of a few leading product-centric organizations.

Table 15-1. A Sampling of Product and Service Innovators

GOOGLE	APPLE	PEPSI	BOEING	STARBUCKS
Platforms and networking	Solutions and customers	Value capture, channel, presence, and brand	Organization	Experience and presence
Hire entrepreneurs Invest heavily in core platform	Strong focus on solution design Develop competency in outsourcing everything else	Incorporate ideas from anywhere; translate them to your systems Proliferate business units	Sophisticated project and personnel management Systems engineering focus	Local customization and prototyping

The Business Process Angle

The product development process is actually a series of multiple, connected processes—some related, others entirely distinct, some merging one into the next, others simply overlapping—all running along a trajectory spanning multiple business units as well as connecting the larger business network. As such, it is a super process whose success demands continuous collaboration both within and across departments.

Operational excellence in today's hyper-competitive environment demands that you execute in the present and innovate for the future. To manage innovation is to manage variation—variation in business processes, variation in products, and variation in capabilities. Doing so will enable you to address the challenges created by your blind spots, whether they pertain to globalization (enabling data communication and collaboration and IP protection), compliance (limiting risk posed by local and global regulations), or responsiveness (building adaptive, service-enabled, end-to-end business processes that enable real-time action in a constantly transforming business network).

Figure 15-1 shows the integrated business processes that touch product development.

Here are some details on particular product development business processes:

- Continuous product innovation. Managing innovation is more than tracking a portfolio of projects. Companies must actively manage corporate strategy, product road mapping, idea and concept management, feasibility assessment, a phase-gated new product development process, and market launch to drive success
- Integrated product development. Integrated product development is the core product definition and production ramp up process, when the product design and structure is defined, tested, and validated
- Product delivered as a service. Many manufacturers of classical products have started to make the benefits of their products available to the end customer through a service agreement
- Embedded product compliance. Regulations about safety, environmental or other aspects of products are gaining increasing importance. In order to comply with these regulations, companies must take them into account during design, manufacturing, shipment, servicing, and end-of-life of their products

Figure 15-2 takes a deeper look at the process of continuous product innovation.

Companies that make the most new products and bring them to market fastest succeed. In this light, the prime mover behind all product-centric

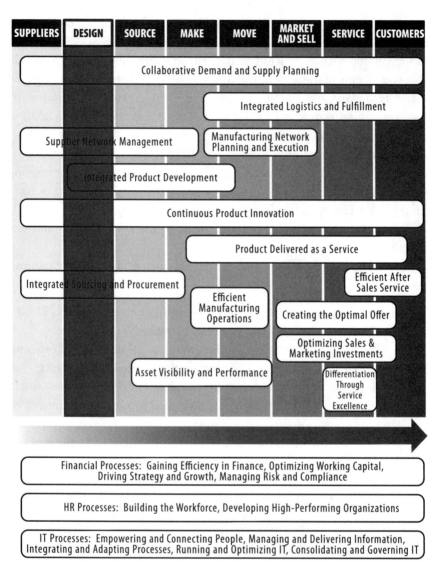

Figure 15-1. The Integrated Business Processes That Touch Product Development

organizations today is the drive to innovate. This is why the idea-to-product process is so important.

As you can see, continuous product innovation is an end-to-end transactional process involving not just Product Development, but also Manufacturing, Supply Chain, Marketing, Sales, Service, Finance, HR, and the Legal department. Table 15-2 shows business processes that by contrast occur primarily within the Product Development organization.

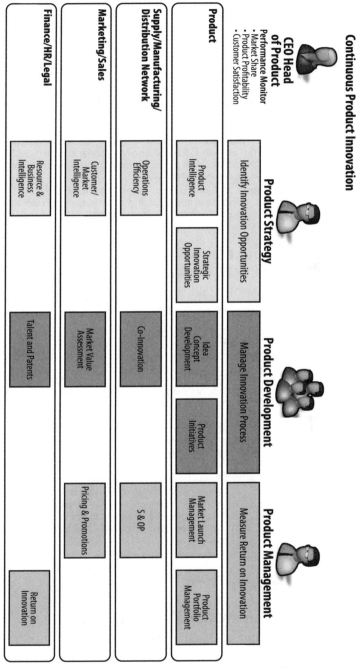

Figure 15-2. The Continuous Product Innovation Process

Table 15-2. Business Processes within Product Development

Product Management	Product Strategy and Planning; Product Portfolio Mgmt; Innovation Mgmt; Requirements Mgmt; Market Launch Mgmt
Product Development and Collaboration	Engineering, R&D Collaboration; Supplier Collaboration; Manufacturing Collaboration; Service and Maintenance Collaboration; Product Quality Mgmt; Product Change Mgmt
Product Data Management	Product Master and Structure Mgmt; Specification and Recipe Mgmt; Service and Maintenance Structure Mgmt; Visualization and Publications; Configuration Mgmt
PLM Foundation	Product Compliance; Product Intelligence; Product Costing; Tool and Workgroup Integration; Project and Resource Mgmt; Document Mgmt

Key Roles in Product Development

Table 15-3 outlines the key roles in product development and their responsibilities. Please note that the Chief Procurement Officer is also heavily involved in product development; see Chapter 14 for more information.

Table 15-3. Key Roles in Product Development

Role	Bottom Line Responsibility
VP of Product Development	Ensures the health and well-being of the company's project and product portfolios
Production Manager	Identifies market demands and prioritizes the order in which the company's development team fulfills them
VP of R&D	Directs the overall development lifecycle of the company's portfolio of products
VP of Quality Control	Ensures that the products made by the company meet both functional and non-functional specifications
VP of Manufacturing	Oversees the actual creation of the company's product

KPIs for Success in Product Development

The ultimate objective of establishing a solid metrics program with consistently dependable KPIs is to learn the specifics of your product profitability. Figure 15-3 shows a metrics hierarchy from AMR.

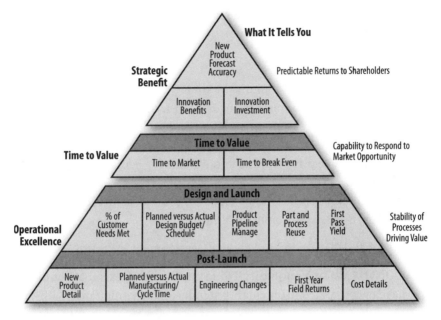

Figure 15-3. Hierarchy of Product Metrics
(Source: AMR Research, 2008, "Product Launch Dashboards,
Part 1: The Hierarchy of Product Metrics")

Strategic KPIs include:

- **New product forecast accuracy.** Identifies how well a business can predict the impact of new products on future revenue and resource requirements
- **Innovation benefits.** Defines total value of new products over a defined period
- **Product profitability.** Determines which products are actually generating value
- **Percentage of revenue from new products (< 1yr on market).** Determines which new products are most relevant in terms of revenue percentage
- **Innovation investment.** Captures the cost of developing and launching new products

Time to value KPIs include:

- **Time to market (TTM).** The time required to make new products formally available for sale

- **Time to break even.** The time required to recoup financial investment from a new product

Operational KPIs include:

- **New product detail.** Monitors the strategic health of the new product opportunity and readiness to ensure long-term competitiveness
- **New product development and launch.** Provides visibility to the status of the new products underway in the development pipeline
- **Cost detail.** Details planning and monitoring across a product's lifecycle
- **Post-launch.** Identifies how well a new product achieved predefined market success and supply capability

Additional KPIs relevant to Product Development include:

- **CONQ (Cost of Nonquality/Noncompliance).** Costs that could have been avoided using quality standards and compliance with regulations
- **Production Setup Times.** Generating your product with speed and efficiency is key to its success

Mapping KPIs to Roles

Another important consideration when building a metrics framework is the roles that will be accountable for satisfying the individual KPIs that comprise it. Your KPIs exist at different levels of granularity. Those that matter to the VP of Product Development, therefore, will not be the same as those that matter to the VP of Quality. The key to making performance management work is to set up the relationships between your metrics such that different roles take responsibility for different KPIs even as everyone understands the model of how they all work together. If you're the VP of Quality, for example, it makes no sense to hold you accountable for new product forecast accuracy, since you are not paid to innovate. Instead, the VP of Product Development would be more suitable for that obligation. In turn, the VP of Product Development understands that the VP of Quality is accountable for CONQ, and takes that into consideration when making decisions. A pyramid representing the hierarchy of product metrics could be superimposed on a pyramid of key roles. Whereas the VP of Quality, for instance, would be at the bottom of that triangle, next to the VP of Procurement, the VP of Product Development would be sitting at the pyramid's top.

Table 15-4. Product Development Roles and KPIs

Product Development Roles	Product Development KPIs
VP of Product Development	New Product Forecast Accuracy; Innovation Investment; Time to Market; Time to Break Even; Percentage of Customer Needs Met
Production Manager	Percentage of Customer Needs Met; Planned vs. Actual Design Budget Schedule; Product Pipeline Manage; Part and Process Reuse; First Pass Yield
VP of R&D	Innovation Benefit; Innovation Investment; Time to Market; Percentage of Customer Needs Met
VP of Manufacturing	Percentage of Customer Needs Met; Planned vs. Actual Design Budget Schedule; Product Pipeline Manage; Part and Process Reuse; First Pass Yield
VP of Quality Control	CONQ; Percentage of Customer Needs Met; New Product Detail
VP of Procurement/CPO	Cost Details; Spend under Mgmt; Visibility of Spend across the Organization; Identified Savings Versus Realized Savings; Rate of Compliance with Contractual Agreements; Sourcing Cycle Times; Cost Savings from Sourcing Efforts; Diversity of Suppliers; Low-Cost-Country Sourcing

What's in It for Me?

Performance management will enable you to do your job better and to consistently deliver on your promises. Performance management, underpinned by BI, can provide visibility to your stakeholders about what you're producing and not producing. If your strategy was to introduce three new products, but you dropped one to introduce the others after having learned it would be more profitable to pool your resources, you can show how you came to that conclusion.

Your improved understanding of how to run your business gives partners the incentive to make their own operations increasingly transparent. The benefits take on a synergistic effect: the greater your mutual transparency, and the more you collaborate, the more effective you will be. Instead of flying blind, producing 50,000 widgets while sending out 3 million fliers, your partner can tell you the precise number of widgets to make based on known demand and marketing goals.

As logical as it appears, corporate, business unit, and individual goals are not always aligned to achieve the same results. For example, as the VP of Product Development, your life would be easier if you collaborated with the VP of Marketing to ensure that production is aligned with the advertising and PR budget. Even so, your personal MBOs may not show working with marketing at the top of your priority list. The lesson? Compensation must be tied to desired behavior. You can have brilliant strategy and brilliant processes, but if personal incentives don't line up, progress will be elusive.

Effective Collaboration

By now the idea that any product-centric company can achieve success in the 21st century without steady collaboration across the enterprise and beyond should be gone with the wind. Throughout this book we have repeatedly stressed the importance of building long-lasting, transparent processes via open lines of communication, whereby a single version of truth is available to one and all.

To illustrate this concept, we noted the interdependence of Sales on numerous other business units. Sales must have visibility into Finance to understand the results of its effort to sell as much product as possible at the best price. The company's ability to control risk, optimize advantages, and capitalize on opportunities is affected in this endeavor, too, as is Service, which is striving to achieve 100% customer satisfaction by deploying metrics that will shape the necessary goals, activities, and resources. The Marketing team comes into play as well since their ultimate assessments will affect the next phase of product innovation. At this point, the cycle begins anew. The Product Development department must work with R&D, Development, Procurement, Manufacturing, and Supply Chain. These in turn work with Sales and Service. The process is continuous, feeding on itself, as it were, to gain progressively higher levels of operational excellence. Always at the heart of these processes is collaboration and the deep visibility that results from it, without which business network transformation would be impossible.

Here are some key points to consider when collaborating across business units:

- A cross-functional approach to performance management for product development will not work if you don't align resource allocation and workforce incentives to match your strategy
- Stay connected to the business unit most closely linked to the key levers you want to optimize. Let them know that you'll both benefit if they synchronize with your strategies, initiatives, and plans
- Create a scorecard that reflects the activities of all related business units
- Feed the product planning model into their planning model
- Provide management reports and statutory reports specific to that business unit; you want to show how their language translates

to yours. For example, 500 widgets in supply chain terms equals $1,000,000 in COGS for the Finance department

Collaboration with Marketing

The relationship between Product Development and Marketing is integral to the ultimate success of any new or existing product. This, of course, stands to reason. Without strong marketing, your products would be hard pressed to pass muster on the open market.

There are two stages of product development in which marketing plays a vital role—at the beginning of the product lifecycle, where new ideas are generated and developed according to market requirements, and at the end of the cycle, where products are introduced and sold.

The product lifecycle begins with a conversation between Product Development and Marketing, in which Product Development asks Marketing a series of questions about current market trends in the areas of business, finance, technology, and culture. Product Development always wants to know, based on research and forecasts, two things: what is happening in the market now, and, more importantly, what is going to happen.

For example, if you're a technology company, you may want to know whether a demand exists among your customers for on-demand and subscription-based solutions. If Marketing determines that the demand is high, Product Development will request that Marketing conduct a series of focus groups to substantiate the degree of the demand. Depending on the results, Product Development will adjust its budget so that R&D can initiate research into such solutions or, if the demand is not as high as had been expected, it will earmark funds for other projects. In either case, Product Development must always be able to justify its development resources and R&D dollars based on market pricing information that specifies the exact size of the market and its potential revenue opportunity. As ever, clear, open, empathetic communication at this stage is paramount. With it, clarity of trends, requirements, sizing, and competitive functionality generally prevail. Without it, ambiguity and confusion are sure to cloud the field, opening the way for failure.

Collaboration with Service

Whereas the relationship between Product Development and Marketing is a dynamic one, based on the beginning and end of the business process map, the typical relationship between Product Development and Service is founded only on existing products. Simply put, Product Development needs to know in specific terms what the demand is for an existing product at any time. What, Product Development will ask Service, is the perceived quality of the product? Has it received complaints, and, if so, to what extent? What is the nature of the complaints? How easy or difficult is it to implement a solution that satisfies the customer?

If your PLM program is especially proactive, you can also submit more open-ended questions to Service, with the goal of gaining knowledge that will aid future development. As well, you can insist that Service add to its protocol a query at the end of each customer call. Over the next three to five years, for instance, what are the top three things you as a customer would like to see improved in our product or added to our product line?

Collaboration with Procurement

Like its collaboration with Service, Product Development's interaction with Procurement rests on a single key point: getting things done at the lowest possible overall price. Do not confuse the lowest overall price, however, with merely the lowest cost of materials. The overall price includes the cost of materials and goods, of course, but it also considers returns, failures, malfunctions, services and repairs, and the like.

Your company should never skimp on product quality just because you think it will translate to greater profit margins. In the long run, that will not prove to be the case. Consider how NASA felt when the space shuttle was destroyed in consequence of a faulty O-ring. You can avoid such dilemmas and risk by ensuring that the hallmark of your collaboration with Procurement is mutually open lines communication.

Collaboration with Supply Chain

Given the number of concerns that are at stake, Product Development's involvement with Supply Chain is somewhat more complex than with other departments. Product quality, delivery SLAs, inventory, time to market, material quality, supplier performance, and manufacturing cycle time are all KPIs that Product Development needs to be regularly fed.

Discussions about product quality will concern the dependability of the manufacturer or manufacturers to which the work has been outsourced, as well as whether they are providing the best possible product or product parts at the best possible price. For instance, if you're a candy maker outsourcing the production of one of your latest candy bars, it doesn't matter how high the quality of your prototype bar is if your supplier uses inferior ingredients in the bar that goes to market.

If you are a company selling sensitive food products such a pre-made sushi or fine deserts, time to market is another KPI with which there is little leeway for error. Your product gets to market on or before the established date, or it goes bad, in which case you and your partners are in for serious difficulties. There are myriad ways that such a calamity could arise. For instance, you may have your product ready to ship, but if your packaging supplier has not delivered on time because it had a fire in one of its warehouses, and you have no backup, you will have no containers in which to ship your product. Straightaway, you'll find yourself in the midst of a ripple effect, whereby your inability to deliver in consequence of your supplier's disaster translates to trouble for your partners downstream. Supplier performance, manufacturing time, and other KPIs are subsidiary to time to market, because they are all factors that make or break it. As you can see, the dependability of your supply chain is priceless, contingent on a host of factors so delicate that ensuring they dovetail successfully nearly amounts to an act of alchemy.

Collaboration with Finance

Unless Product Development and Finance collaborate well, it will be impossible for your organization to reach its highest-level objectives. To begin, the relationship here is not so much one between two discrete entities as it is a triangle whose third side is Marketing. Data pertaining to product ROI, for instance, and market trends and requirements must be bolstered with substantial historical financial data from existing products. To get it, Marketing must interface with finance and, often enough, with HR, as well.

What, for example, was the average cost for a given product line, and what was the actual cost of sale associated with it? What was the total cost to the company to get the line out the door and on the market? How much profit did the line garner, and how much did individual products within it make, settle, or lose? Were there specific regions where it did better or worse? It may have turned out that of the 10 colors of jersey in your line, red was the only one to profit in the east while blue and gold were the only two to win in the west. In every case, you must consider these matters as you decide whether to move forward with a product or to sunset it in favor of developing something new.

Collaboration with HR

Product Development works closely with HR on talent management. As the quest for technical resources has grown in complexity with globalization, HR needs to have an in-depth understanding of the technical skills required, how to hire to those expertise as well as provide an environment for further training and learning to maintain such skills. Further, as Product Development needs to literally interact with the entire organization and beyond, including external partners and suppliers, the HR group often is tasked with helping this technical and analytical bunch with leadership and collaboration skills.

Collaboration with IT

The product team relies on IT to enable the product lifecycle processes via technology automation. IT interacts with Product Development on several aspects of the product development process from design and engineering, to providing data consistency and transparency, to driving process efficiency by automating workflows and project monitoring and lastly and very importantly, ensuring product compliance thru documentation and controls. As Product Development interacts with a wide variety of internal and external stakeholders such as partners, suppliers, and Marketing, Service and Support to fuel the product development process, data access and accuracy requires careful attention. While the conversation starts with an effective PLM system to manage aspects like design and engineering, it continues with leading Product Development groups asking for a performance management system that brings together the varying sources of information required to deliver on product innovation.

Collaboration with Sales

While the Product Development team primarily focuses on the design, engineering, manufacturing, and production of the product, they recognize that this represents only a portion of the entire product lifecycle. They know that for a product to be successful they need to coordinate with Sales, Marketing and Services on the launch and maintenance of the product in the market. Since time to value is a KPI for Product Development, they need to think beyond just time to launch but also how quickly their products can provide value to the customers. In particular the Production Manager works closely with Sales to identify market demands and to prioritize the order in which the company's development team fulfills them. As Sales has the day-to-day interaction with the customers and the most holistic view of their product needs across the organization. Production managers will leverage this knowledge Sales has by requesting specific use cases of products and product functionality from them. Further they will ask Sales for information related to product bundling to determine the best configuration of products.

Collaboration with the Business Network

Add to these potential impediments the reality and importance of outsourcing in a business network transformation world, and the difficulty with which you are faced when managing your product lifecycle multiplies exponentially. Design, Engineering, Manufacturing, Marketing, Sales, and Service divisions all outsource every aspect of business that does not pertain to their core competence. Where outsourcing prevails, you must know with certainty that your strategy is aligned with your partner's strategy. If it's hard to reconcile your budget and forecast within Finance, imagine how difficult it will be to manage your partner's activities, too. Imagine the consequences when they are unable to deliver promised goods, or, conversely, when they deliver too much. In the first case, you would not have a sufficient mitigation strategy in place. In the second, your warehouse would not have the capacity to hold the excess inventory. These and many more unwanted scenarios, when stacked one atop the other, can quickly spell ruin.

Establishing Your BI Foundation

Building a strong base from which to deploy your BI necessitates an infrastructure agile enough to generate the cleansed, high-quality data that your PLM and performance management programs require to set strategy, make and execute plans, monitor and analyze your activities, and then, finally, optimize them. Before you can execute your extract, transform, and load (ETL) process, whereby you transform data into a harmonized set of metrics and dimensions, you must first ensure that have a coherent BI platform running beneath your PM applications and that all systems are properly mapped.

Once these are in place, you can perform the various cross-process analysis, prediction and optimization tasks that produce your single source of truth. Of course, you can't have a single strategy and single execution system without a single PLM system. Most companies need to work toward this ideal by building a performance management landscape incrementally.

Building a powerful BI system first is the gateway through which you set on this path.

The following sections articulate the benefits with which your BI foundation should provide your PLM and performance management processes.

Relevant Visualizations

You need product-specific visualizations to supplement your standard tables and graphs. For example, product-engineering managers often use statistical process control charts to understand the variability in the quality of products as they come off the manufacturing line.

Relevant Event-Capture and Alerting

Another must-have is the ability to gather information from event sources and product-related touch points like procurement, supply chain, and marketing, along with the ability to define alerts for critical events (for instance, when you learn that product quality for last week's batches are 10% below average) and inform the right person in the organization to take action.

Data Integration and Data Quality Across Departmental and Application Silos

At times, product users only have access to numerous discrete point systems (e.g., product portfolio management systems, recipe management systems, CAD systems) or multiple PLM systems, and yet they must still be able to bridge the silos. Business intelligence enables you to create common definitions and business rules for the key dimensions in products and metrics. For instance, you must be able to define not only your products, but also your bills of material and your quality criteria. In the same way, you must define the key metrics and their relationship to one another, as well.

Trusted, Cleansed Master Data

Master Data Management for Products is a crucial capability for managing complex products and their hierarchies and taxonomies. A solid BI foundation with MDM enables you to consolidate on standard definitions of how a product is defined and of the individual products themselves, including key attributes such color, size, and shape. For example, without BI, you might not know that product 123 is the same as products 1-2-3 and 1.2.3. We recommend looking for the following capabilities in a product

MDM solution to serve as the backbone of your performance management needs. First, look for a centralized repository. The solution should enable a flexible repository schema, complete with taxonomy editing; the ability to manage rich parametric data, product relationships, and images; and the ability to search single-style and seamlessly—with a simple search, a partial string search, or searches by dimension. The checklist should also include the ability to aggregate and normalize data coming from different sources. You should also have a means to publish the data internally or externally through different channels such as the Web or in print. You must be able to syndicate and synchronize your information, as well as have high-performance workflows and a validation engine through which you can define valid data types stored within your master data management application. Finally, you would also want to have the ability to manage reusable product information for either the sell or buy side of your business processes (for example, for either the CRM e-commerce or the procurement side).

Structured and Unstructured Data

Business Intelligence platforms can generate insights from both structured and unstructured data. The potential for unstructured data to provide additional value to your PLM processes is vast. For instance, idea management systems are rife with data that you can mine via strong BI to gain further insight into prediction markets, product IP management, parts descriptions, and the like.

Business Intelligence Reports

You must be able to publish quality reports and distribute them to large numbers of users for products. For instance, if you can't publish and distribute reports juxtaposing your sales forecast verses production forecast on at least a weekly basis, you will soon find yourself in a compromised position.

You must also have the ability to create dashboards that feature rich, high impact graphics revealing product information. Examples of such dashboard capabilities include those that display product line analyses by region to determine your finished goods inventories by warehouse, and sales by product line versus actual product inventory.

Lastly, you need query product data and simple, intuitive analytics capabilities for end users. For instance, how quickly is the inventory turning over by warehouse? What is the capacity of each work center?

Assessing Performance Management Maturity and Setting Your Course

In its nascent stages, the typical organization monitors the performance of its product lifecycle using reporting and dashboards, only to find themselves overwhelmed by a sea of chaotic data. The key to solving this problem lies in an integrated metrics framework. Once you have acquired it, you can build consolidated views of performance metrics. At this level, however, even though you may understand how your critical metrics are functioning in relation to your past operations and, perhaps, to the whole enterprise, it's likely that you have yet to harness this metric power to actually drive your future business value. To reach this level of performance, you need data from your current actual performance to create future plans and predict future performance. At the highest performance level you can reach, your performance management initiative is to integrate your decision-making, business plans, and process workflow. Here, you'll be using data from your day-to-day operations to make decisions—delivering product according to demand on a near real-time basis.

If the 50,000-foot flyover view of your approach to performance management looks something like this, you can feel confident that you're on the right track:

- Strategies and goals are strictly aligned with the organization's overall goals
- Metrics monitor results from the outside in; your numbers must consider the customer's needs and concerns first
- Your program is cross-functional
- Your program is multidimensional, giving equal consideration to service, assets, cost, and time
- Performance management flows like a waterfall, with its objectives and behavior disaggregated and cascading
- True performance is ascertained via real-time measurements and analytics
- Accountability is clearly defined (important because performance management seeks to render accountability actionable)

The following maturity model was developed by AMR and displays five curves of increasing sophistication when comparing business value to resource investment (time, money, and credibility).

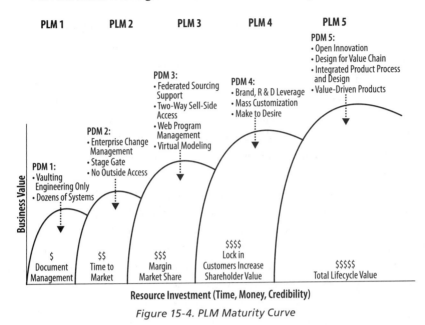

Figure 15-4. PLM Maturity Curve

At level 1, you're operating in isolation, so you aren't collaborating, and your visibility into your own operations is still quite limited. Your resources are catch as catch can. Because your outsourcing capabilities are so brittle, a result of you inventory levels are high and experience frequent stock-outs. Engineering is vaulted only.

You have dozens of systems, but most of your processes are still manual, driven by documents, spreadsheets, and email. An IT analyst extracts data from your systems, manipulates and refines it, then loads it to your spreadsheets. You lack a common metrics definition, and are not yet accounting for risk in your operations.

When you reach level 2, you have deployed automated systems to increase process efficiency. Though you have deployed ERP, you are still at the stage gate, and your visibility remains within your four walls. You're cataloging now, too, so a basic budget system is in place. Your primary KPI is time to market, but you have others, as well, which enable you to capture data pertaining to the number of products in your pipeline, your first pass yield, and your planned versus actual manufacturing cycle times. While you are now aware of risk, you haven't yet been able to account for it in your processes.

Once you've reached level 3, you've begun to collaborate with other departments, so you now have two-way, sell-side access to key data, including schedules and forecasts. Your sourcing support is federated, and your programming is online and virtual. Consequently, the strategy and plan data from performance management system is part of your class enterprise system, and you're able to predict risk accurately. Dashboards now aid your processes, providing you with increased visibility. You have common metric definitions, too, so that you can monitor your margin market share. Rather than relying on the old lagging measures, you've advanced to leading measures, which enable you to identify your progress in near real time and make necessary adjustments on the fly.

At level 4, you're working with multiple partners and sharing assets, common outsourced logistics and contract manufacturing providers. Your processes are fluid, transparent, and collaborative, and your Procurement, Operations, and Marketing divisions are aligned strategically and your plans executed in tandem. You enjoy visibility across your idea-to-product and plan-to-manufacture cycles. Importantly, you're now also systematically identifying risks, prioritizing actions, assessing exposure, and reusing technology for multiple purposes. Your dashboards are more intelligent because you've added analytics to evaluate trends and support tradeoff decisions such as portfolio prioritization. All non-core activities are outsourced, and production is demand-driven. As a result of having locked in more customers, your shareholder value has increased, giving you serious brand R&D leverage.

Level 5 is the level of operational excellence that generates a total lifecycle value. Because you collaborate with all relevant business units, you are at the peak of maturity, able to see across your entire supply network and sense and react to conditions as they develop. You've also integrated your PLM dashboard into the flow of operations to leverage Web forms, workflow, and other capabilities, all of which improves data and eliminates redundancy.

In short, your total business process map is now optimized to top performance. As a result, product process and design is integrated, and products are strictly value-driven. You've differentiated product across markets and shortened your product lifecycles. You're able, as well, to comply with increasing global and local regulation, execute in the present, and innovate for the future. Finally, your risk prediction capability is excellent, so that the tradeoffs you make between your various risks and controls are smart, accurate, and timely.

The PM Lifecycle for Product Development

In this section we will define and examine best practices and options for executing the performance management lifecycle for Product Development.

By the end of this section, you should have a basic working knowledge of the critical elements of a performance management strategy for Product Development.

Strategize and Prioritize

We have emphasized that today's number one business driver for Product Development is the pressure to innovate. As such, it should stand to reason that every company's chief priority is to accelerate their New Product Development and Launch (NPDL) capability, and that their strategy reflects this. Interestingly enough, however, this has not been the case. When asked what their company's current top focus was, 75% of executives stated that it was top-line product growth. And yet when asked about the current focus of their company's operational initiatives, 82% said that it was cost reduction.

Clearly, executives understand that they can't reduce their way to profitable growth. But the vast discrepancy between the stated and actual priorities of most companies suggests that there has been an obstacle to growing simultaneously along the two crucial axes—that of efficiency, on the one hand, and innovation, on the other.

Review the Environment

Review your environment with an eye toward ascertaining your current strengths, needs, compliance requirements, challenges, and risks. For example, are you faced with intensifying pressure to reduce the cost of your product lifecycle? Which products in the portfolio are no longer profitable? What is the cost of producing these products? What is the impact to resources and cost of assets associated with eliminating these products? Can the production resources be reallocated to another product line?

Do your risks include a host of NPDL obstacles precipitated by the market itself, such as more product variants and smaller windows of new product introduction? What are the risks, such as the threat to customer satisfaction, of eliminating products in your portfolio? Will the customer substitute or purchase another product? Or will they go to a competitor?

Have you successfully achieved wider outsourcing to dynamic, responsive supply networks even as you stumble before rapidly globalizing product development and M&A, and increasing quality and regulatory compliance? Have you been focusing more on cost and compliance than on your most successful new products?

Do you have an excellent product portfolio but a sudden lack of talent in your R&D department?

Set the Mission, Values, and Vision

Define the mission, which is the fundamental purpose of the entity, especially what it provides to customers and clients. Here's an example: To become the recognized world leader in producing innovative consumer electronic products.

Define the core values, which are the attitude, behavior, and character of the organization. For example, "we value the innovative ideas of every colleague, partner, and customer who we work with."

Define the vision, which is a concise statement that defines the 3- to 5-year goals of the organization, such as: By 2012, be ranked in the top 10 of Business Week's Most Innovative Companies list because of our products.

Set the Goals

With all that contextual information in hand, define the goals and set business objectives using risks as a key variable for deciding which strategies to pursue. For example:

- Increase revenue of existing products
- Improve operational efficiencies in production
- Maintain or improve overall customer satisfaction with our products
- Reduce the overall number of product defects

Consider using a strategy map to display the cause-and-effect relationships among the objectives that make up a strategy. A good strategy map tells a story of how value is created for the business.

Figure 15-5 shows a sample strategy map interlinking the objectives in different perspectives.

Assign KPIs to Goals and Set the Right Targets

Define KPIs and targets that translate strategy and into performance expectations. As we discussed earlier, the key metrics relevant to products include product profitability, innovation benefits, innovation investment, time to market, and time to break even, along with more operational metrics like first pass yield, planned versus actual design budget/schedule, etc.

One way to help answer your initial queries and thus ensure the successful negotiation of the performance management strategy phase is to deploy the performance measurement system of balanced scorecards for both your products and your product innovation processes. These scorecards are not mere lists of measures, but rather descriptions of your product and product innovation objectives, measures, and targets.

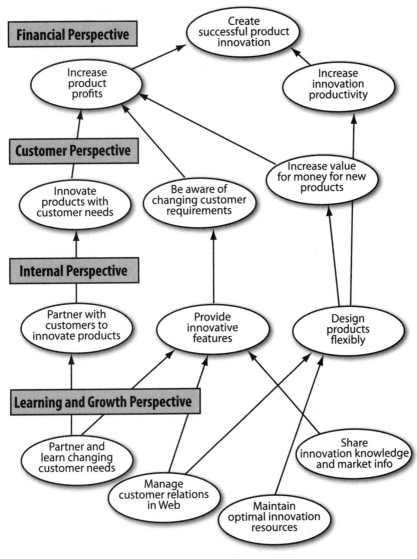

Figure 15-5. Sample Strategy Map
(Source: *http://lifelong.engr.utexas.edu/emc/pdf/score.pdf*)

The product scorecard's main strength lies in its ability to sharpen your view of product performances by looking at several perspectives at once, from financial, customer, and internal processes perspectives to mission, stakeholders, and learning and growth. As such, you can see where you are at any time, whether you're evaluating, adopting, positioning, or managing the product lifecycle and its growth.

Table 15-5. Example of Product Scorecard Adaptable for Product Innovation

Perspectives	Objectives	Measures	Targets	Initiatives
Financial	• Increase revenue from product • Attract and retain high-value corporate customers	• Annual increase in revenue • Percentage of revenue from product • Percentage of revenue for the corporate customers	50% 70% 70%	• Product innovation program
Customer	• Meet customer requirements • Provide superior product support service	• Change in customer retention rate • Returning product support customer ration	50% 80%	• Needs capture program
Internal	• Accelerate innovative product development • Understand customer requirements • Cross-sell with other products	• First-to-market and time-to-market • Customer survey of requirements • Cross-sell ratio	• 80% and 6 months • 90% • 50%	• Product acceleration program • Customers survey • Cross-sell program
Learning and growth	• Develop and retain strategic skilled resources	• Specialized availability • Key resource retention ratio	• 90% • 80%	• Strategic training program • Strategic hiring program

Like the product scorecard, the product innovation scorecard enables you to see your product innovation processes from multiple perspectives simultaneously. As a result, you can link your strategic objectives to metrics KPIs, engage in high-level metric reporting, and establish a foundation from which to trigger your metrics, KPIs, and data normalization.

The product innovation scorecard is accompanied by a strategy-focused innovation process. It suggests that you:

• Accelerate product innovation through specific leadership initiatives
• Translate your innovation strategy into product development
• Align product design and development process to the product innovation strategy
• Ensure that every engineer implements your strategy for product innovation
• Transform product innovation strategy into a continuous process

Of course both product and product innovation strategies must be of high quality for you to achieve success. But the quality of your strategies, no matter how high, will be irrelevant if you cannot execute them. Building and honing your strategies across a continuous process will go a long way toward your success in later stages of your performance management implementation.

Perform Additional Risk Analysis and Set KRIs

Now look again at risks to see what could keep you from meeting your goals. For each risk, decide what your risk appetite is. Can you afford to take that risk? What's the worst-case scenario? Does taking the risk have the potential to wipe out important projects? For example, if you discontinue an unprofitable product, will you lose a strategic customer or a strategic supplier who is also providing raw materials for other finished goods? For example, suppose R&D has laid three cutting-edge product ideas on the table, each of which has potential the change the market game. You would like to bring all three to market simultaneously, but getting the resources to do so would require you to significantly reduce the budget on a project that is already in progress. Can one or two products wait while the best idea advances, or is it necessary to move on all three?

Set a response strategy for the risk (watch, research, transfer, delegate, mitigate). For example, you mitigate the risk of losing the customer by offering a discount for a product substitution for orders in the first three months or working with the customer to create a new profitable product. For the strategic suppliers, you research prices to renegotiate contracts to ensure that the volume levels are maintained to minimize the purchase of raw materials for the other product lines.

Decide whether you can afford the worst-case scenario presented by that risk from a performance management perspective. Could it bring down some critical value-generating mechanism for the company? For example, your decision to discontinue the unprofitable products could cause levels of customer satisfaction to drop or even to lose a customer to a competitor. You could put the bulk of your energies into your three new product ideas, knowing they are guaranteed to bear fruit once on the market. If, however, you experience an unexpected interruption in both your new developments and the key product in progress, everything would come to a halt. Developing just one or two of the products would be a good hedge.

Define KRIs and thresholds for those risks. KRIs, like KPIs, are the early warning signals that define the threshold at which a risk could occur. For examples, if the customer satisfaction levels decrease by 10%, this signals an unhappy customer due to the discontinuation of the product. If the revenue by customer decreases by 15%, this is also an indicator of the impact of the end-of-life of the product. If the raw material costs increase by more than 5%, this is an indicator that volumes need to be increase to get better prices from the strategic supplier or you need to evaluate the supplier base and start to consolidate the purchasing efforts of all raw materials across the entire product portfolio.

Risks in Product Development

The top risks faced by today's product-centric companies are those that threaten product quality, quality suppliers, security, brand equity, and time to market. Here are some categories of risks that affect Product Development.

Product Quality

Given the larger business network, attaining successful open innovation requires you to share your products and associated data with partners, suppliers, and customers to facilitate the development process. Since you can't guarantee quality from them, you must take precautions to ensure that your planned and actual products are aligned. It's also strongly recommended that a CAPA mechanism be established.

Supplier Qualification

Your suppliers' knowledge of the trends, needs, and laws of their region does not guarantee that they will provide you with high-quality products or materials. In fact, the record shows that without a sufficient qualification process to help you find approved and compliant vendors and to monitor your manufacturing capabilities you stand the chance of receiving substandard and, in some cases, even dangerous products or product elements.

People

The huge rise in offshoring leads to serious risks around the types of people who intersect with your global product development practices. Local, specialized, and independent contractors combined with your own staff have to be managed very carefully to ensure the value of lower-cost operations more than exceeds the potential concerns.

Security

Firewalls may do the job to ensure security for basic processes, but they are certainly no longer enough to protect the intellectual property of Product Development. Sensitive data must be limited to key roles only.

Brand Equity

Jeopardizing your reputation to save a few dollars on labor or supplies is simply not worth it—poor quality materials or a security breach are all it would take. Make sure you've got the processes to reduce or eliminate exposure to this risk, along with due diligence, just in case.

Slow Time To Market

Securing resources at or near the point of your product's consumption and bringing products to market faster are the benefits of global product development. On the other hand, working across multiple time zones increases the risk of critical data getting lost in translation. To ensure that your new time to market target date or product launch remain steady, take steps to establish transparency via a single version of the truth.

Geopolitical

Political unrest and stability as well as lack of government regulation are wild cards to be aware of in global product development.

Perform Additional Compliance Analysis and Set Controls

Define your compliance requirements. Compliance defines the boundaries within which companies must operate when achieving their strategies.

KRIs in Product Development

Quality. Number of Quality Notifications

Maintainability. % Overdue Maintenance Orders, % Maintenance Orders—Planned/Actual Cost Deviation, % Maintenance Tasks—Adherence to Deadlines

Reliability. % Mean Time To Repair (MTTR), % Mean Time Between Repair (MTBR)

Environmental. Energy consumption, Substances that have not been registered for REACH, Substances that have not been registered for TSCA 12B, Volume of greenhouse gases emissions in tons, Emissions of ozone-depleting substances in tons, NO, SO, and other significant emissions to air in tons, Total water discharge by quality and destination in tons, Total weight of waste by type and disposal method in tons, Total number and volume of significant spills in tons, Amount of hazardous emissions in tons, Number Emissions permit violations (air/water/waste)

There are myriad regulations like ROHS and WEEE for discrete industries, REACH for the chemical industry, and EuP (Eco Design of Energy Using Products) that are relevant to product development.

All products must be classified for trade compliance. Any products with chemicals going into Europe must be registered under REACH compliance regulations.

All products must be shipped with the correct documentation, such as electronic invoicing into Brazil.

Additions of customers and vendors must be screened for denied parties. You should also designate someone to:

- Work closely with supply chain and sales to monitor global trade activities. What countries are in scope?
- Investigate available software solutions for automating this ever-changing area for compliance

Environment Health & Safety Compliance Management

In order to protect people and the environment against chemical and physical hazards caused by manufacturing, products and transport, a huge and rapidly growing number of Environment, Health and Safety (EH&S) regulations are in force worldwide.

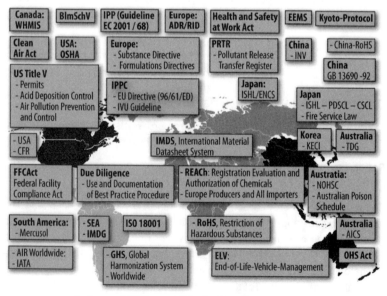

Environmental **Process** and **Product** Compliance

Figure 15-6. The Plethora of Environmental Legislations that Affect Product Development

Complying with these EH&S regulations is always the responsibility of C-level management in all enterprises and across all industries. Typically, management enables a set of business experts to assure compliance on operational level resulting in diverse local solution approaches characterised by a low level of transparency.

Globalization of business drives globalization of regulations significantly, thus demanding a strategic approach to mitigate business risks arising from compliance failure. Noncompliance can expose business to serious financial threat.

Since EH&S regulations affect nearly all business core processes, the resulting risk spectrum is broad and requires an integrated approach, able to perform with the same excellence both on a corporate as well as on a local level.

EH&S solutions provide best practice processes for managing product safety including specification management and global label management, Hazardous Substance Management, Dangerous Goods Management, Waste Management, Industrial Hygiene and Safety, and Occupational Health. EH&S compliance business processes interface with the core business process throughout the enterprise, including the following:

- **Compliant product development.** There are region and even country specific legal restriction lists for the use of hazardous materials (and defined limits) in products and goods. Lack of dedicated up-to-date information what is allowed actually or, in planning could lead to the development of products that may not be sold later on in certain regions
- **Fulfill customer requirements.** More and more often customers specify their own substance restriction list for suppliers in order to make sure that deliveries comply with legal and even with stricter corporate rules. Failures here can result in loss of customers or, even worse, in litigation
- **Meet legal regulations.** Keeping up to date with the impacts of amount and changing legal issues on a global scale is a big challenge for the entire organization. To recover from non-compliance events is always costly and resources extensive
- **Assure compliant and safe production.** All manufacturing processes are legally regulated by an operating permit clearly defining monitoring and reporting rules (e.g. for emissions, water quality, or waste management). Deviation here can impact

productivity (countermeasures, audits, and so forth) and, in extreme cases may lead to production stops. Furthermore, companies have to ensure safety for their employees, the community, and the environment

- **Manage supplier collaboration.** Lack of powerful control mechanisms to avoid the use of non-compliant supplier deliveries can impose business to many risks such as sales and delivery stop, compensation funding and brand damage

Work on the Strategic Action Plan and Initiatives

The strategic initiatives help define the exact methodology (the roadmap) for achieving the various goals. The results of this planning may require revisiting the strategy.

Develop the roadmap (sequence of actions) for achieving performance, risk, and compliance (control activities, policies and procedures) expectations). For example, a strategic product rationalization initiative in the product development organization may look like the following:

- Evaluate the competitive landscape to understand competitor's market share and put together a strategy for customer retention
- Communicate and work with customers on end-of-life strategy and suggest alternatives for customers
- Create customer council to collect requirements to create substitute product (invest in R&D) or enhance an existing product
- Monitor customer satisfaction levels

Define critical success and failure factors for all initiatives. Critical success factors might include ensuring that the end-of-life strategy has been verified as being legal before your next major new product launch. Failure factors might be any issue that could derail the product's on-time delivery. You can then translate these into early-warning metrics that enable you to get your project back on track in time or, if that's not possible, to find an alternative.

Develop different risk-adjusted scenarios with contingency plans for imminent or materialized risks. Create plans for as many risk scenarios as you can reasonably imagine based on past experience and the current environment.

Further considerations when setting priorities and creating strategy for your product lifecycle include the use of a phase-gate methodology, the means by which you manage your portfolio of projects, and the degree to which this process is integrated with your innovation management practices. You should also take into account whether your supply chain is integrated into the product development process, as well as the accuracy of your resource management practices and product development costs.

Cascade Accountability

Each KPI, KRI, and control should be owned by some department or group. The MBOs of the staff in those groups must reflect the KPIs, KRIs, and controls you set. This sounds obvious, but frequently performance is measured at an individual level in a way that does not in fact relate directly to corporate goals and strategies. Furthermore, these must be synchronized across all departments. Here are some examples:

- **Sales.** Maintain revenue stream from unprofitable products. For example, if the discontinuing of the product results in a decrease of 10M of the portfolio, Sales should make up for the 10M by selling existing customers the remaining product lines
- **R&D.** Reallocation of R&D budget into existing products. If the budget for R&D is 30M for the discontinued products, then a committee must decide on how the budget will be reallocated (either to existing products innovation of a new product)
- **Service.** Maintain customer satisfaction levels for the customers who will be impacting by the discontinuation of these products

Plan and Execute

In the strategize and prioritize phase of the PM lifecycle, we put together strategic actions and initiatives. The planning phase gets into the details of planning the strategic initiatives both from a financial and operational standpoint.

Align Corporate Budget to Product Development Budget

The budgeting process takes each of the outcomes or actions from the planning process and aligns revenues and expenses against them. Decisions regarding investment priorities and resource allocations define how the company will operate and set the bar for measuring performance. Take each of the steps in the initiatives you've defined and put in revenues and expenses for them.

Industry leaders demonstrate their firm grasps on the importance of operational excellence and high-level innovation by limiting the ratio of incremental launches to new product launches by a nearly 2:1 margin, regardless of their industry cycle. Moreover, advanced innovators always remain faithful to their strategy by allocating nearly 25% of their R&D budget to breakthrough projects, while spending considerably less on those that are next-generation. None of this would be possible without a PM system whose formalized methodology ensures that all of its stages are mutually aligned, as the research shows.

To create risk-adjusted budgets, incorporate the range of possible revenues and costs of each action into the budget at the appropriate organizational level. A risk-adjusted budget is one that responds to changing circumstances, providing the financial capability to react to events in a planned, proactive manner. Develop different risk adjusted budgets with contingency plans should risks to achieving budgets materialize.

For example, in a traditional Product Development budget, you list the individual line items (product development costs including innovation costs, development costs, quality costs, human capital costs, and IT systems costs) in each row with the actuals, budgeted amounts, forecast, and actual/budget comparisons and forecast versus budget comparisons going across in the columns. In a risk-adjusted Product Development budget, for every decision to allocate revenue to one line item versus another (like hiring more quality engineers while reducing development engineers), you determine the impact and probability of the highest priority Product Development risks (like not having enough development engineers to release your new products on time) on those individual line items and use this to set a range of expected budget and forecasted values instead of fixed values. In this case, if the risk materializes and you run out of development engineering capacity, you would want a contingency plan in place that showed what the performance and risk implications would be if we then removed the budget from acquiring new quality engineers and had to put it into getting more development engineers quickly.

Align Budget to Operational Plans

The operational planning process links the financial budget for the Product Development organization to operational factors that the Product Development organization manages (innovation, design, production, and projects) specific to running the Product Development organization and the costs and capacity for providing them. It is important to plan out each step of each initiative in terms of what will be required in terms of technology, time, and resources and consider what risks you have in each area of the operational plan.

For instance, in a risk-adjusted Product Development operational plan, for every decision to allocate resources to one set of operational activities versus another (from developing a new product to reengineering an existing product), you determine the impact and probability of the highest priority Product Development operational risks (like the new product being delayed in its release) on those individual line items and use this to set a range of expected and forecasted values instead of fixed values. In this case, if the risk materializes and you are alerted to the fact that the product development process is proceeding more slowly than you expected, you would want a contingency plan in place that showed what the performance (the goal to release product) and risk implications would be if we then removed the budget from reengineering the old product and had to put it into investing much more heavily in developing the new product.

Forecast Performance and Risks

Although the exact nature of each company's plan depends on the nature of its business, customers, and products, the general goal of each is essentially the same—to ensure that you can you can manufacture your designs and launch your products in a predictable manner.

Being able to forecast product development outcomes is much more difficult than it might appear to be on the surface. Globalization and outsourcing, as we've noted, have resulted in stretched supply chains and increased risk. Without the benefits of combining the performance management lifecycle with your product development execution processes, you'll lack the required collaboration, synchronization, and visibility into your partners' operations necessary to forecast the impact to you accurately. In turn, timely analysis, response, and resolution of procurement and distribution issues to get the forecast back on track are all but impossible, and resources will likely be wasted. Rapid fluctuations in energy and fuel costs, too, translate to increased challenges for your ability to forecast product development related costs accurately. Lacking the ability to understand customers can result in the inability to sense and respond to real-time demand signals, and delayed feedback from trading partners can produce excess inventory. All of these complications tend to create unexpected delays and other assorted hot spots that make forecasts highly time consuming and yet still frustratingly inaccurate.

To combat these challenges, we recommend creating rolling, risk-adjusted forecasts of the budget (revenues and costs) and operational plan (including number, capacity, and cost of resources necessary to achieve plan) so that you can see trends over a rolling time horizon for those risks whose probability, consequence, and/or resiliency change over time. That way if you have to make adjustments, you can see where you've been and the direction in which things are likely to go. Predictive analytical techniques can be a particular powerful tool for building risk-adjusted forecasts by modeling the impact previous risks had on previous forecasts.

For example, in a risk-adjusted Product Development forecast, you create a rolling forecast over a six-month to one-year window of a range of expected costs (the line items in your budget like development costs and human capital costs) and an associated range of expected activity outputs (innovation, development, and quality activities) that is dependent on the key risks in the environment. When the probability or impact of a risk changes, you adjust the financial or operational forecast costs or activities accordingly. Using predictive techniques, you can learn from the impact of previous risks on previous actuals (the number of upgrades that you were actually able to perform last year when applications unexpectedly needed to be maintained) to predict the impact of your current risks on your current cost or activity forecasts.

Examine Repercussions for Execution Problems

As enormous as the above litany of planning protocol may seem, there is more. For instance, in a tight economy, we recommend that you double and triple examine your product project portfolio before executing any plans for it. Planning and execution must be based on and aligned with the strategy you defined in the previous phase. If you delay a project that is aligned with corporate strategy, its impact across the company can be profound.

Your plans must also consider the extent to which your adaptive fulfillment processes are able to sense and respond in real time. You or your partners must be able to manage all warehouse activities to maximize process efficiencies, preferably via RFID technology that enables sense-and-respond processes. You also need to ensure that you can plan, optimize, and execute an end-to-end transportation process. Finally, your plans must account for the ways and means by which you track and monitor the entire fulfillment process, ensuring that you can oblige your promises based on known availability of product in production, distribution centers, warehouses, and transit. To avoid unwanted surprises, coordination across and with all business units is critical.

The key to excellence in execution is visibility. At all times you must know the current status of your project down to the least detail. Visibility at such a granular level means that it must extend throughout your PLM business process map and beyond. Early warning of project delays can help other departments adapt to those delays or provide additional resources, if possible, to accelerate progress toward strategic goals.

It is imperative to your success that you address each of the areas we've discussed in this section with a critical eye. Some may take precedent over others, but until you've understood their place in your operations, you won't be able to judge.

Monitor and Analyze

In the monitor and analyze phase of the PM lifecycle, you watch what is happening (monitor) and then analyze why it happened and what, perhaps, could be done differently to improve the situation relative to your goals.

Monitor

Once we begin execution, we now monitor and analyze the incoming results from the product lifecycle management and other transactional systems as the product rationalization initiative begins to take hold and observe whether our product profitability, innovation investment, and time to break even targets begin to fall in line with our plan and strategy.

It is important to distinguish the different categories of monitoring in evaluating business performance.

- **Event monitoring** looks for a single, discrete activity or exposure event. In Product Development, an example of an event might be notification of a single product having an important consumer safety-related defect
- **Trend monitoring** is similar to event monitoring, but looks at events over time to determine patterns. For example, how frequently that event occurred, and if that frequency was more or less common than in the past. In Product Development, an example of trend monitoring might be to review product defects to see if it is consistent across product lines
- **Intelligence monitoring** collects information from a variety of external sources that are of interest to the company and may indicate a risk exposure. In Product Development, an example of intelligence monitoring might be monitoring competitive product pricing

The presentation of information to be monitored is also crucial in order to facilitate decision making. Dashboards bring together in one place all the relevant pieces of information in all the major domain areas of business that need to be monitored in role-based, contextual views to get a status at a glance.

For example, in Product Development, typical dashboards for monitoring might be organized like this:

- Product Dashboard
- Project and Resource Dashboards
- Design Dashboards
- Quality Dashboards
- Innovation Dashboards
- Component and Task Dashboards

Dashboards are effective ways of combining the events, trends, and intelligence monitoring patterns across all of the major facets of the business to be monitored, including the key business dimensions like customers, products, projects, and employees, and the related KPIs, KRIs, controls, and incidents and losses. Using dashboards, you can evaluate all of these elements.

Evaluate the KPIs you've set to identify progress made toward achievement of objectives and trends. Is the critical KPI of Percentage of Revenue from New Products on target? Is it trending in the direction of improving or declining and has the trend changed since the last time it was checked?

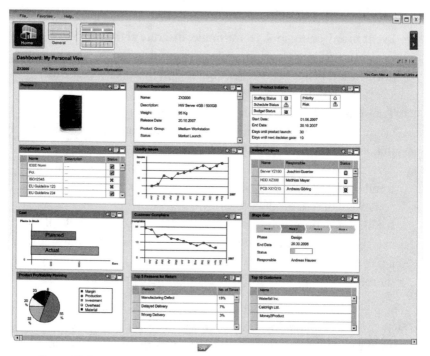

Figure 15-7. An Example of a Product Development Analytics Dashboard

Evaluate the initiatives that are failing or behind schedule. Is the critical initiative to roll out five new products this year on target? Is it trending in the direction of improving or declining and has the trend changed since the last time it was checked?

Monitor the key risk indicators you've set.

- What and where are our top risks? For example, what is the risk on customer satisfaction if we start discontinuing unprofitable products?
- How have risk levels changed for key activities/opportunities? For example, are you seeing an upswing in product quality defects?
- Have incidents or losses occurred? For example, are you being threatened with legal action due to our decision to discontinue products that are not profitable?
- Are risks being assessed in accordance with company policy or according to industry best practices? For example, are we ensuring we are following our sustainability practices with respect to environmental safety in our product development processes?
- Are our mitigation strategies effective in reducing the likelihood or impact of a risk? For example, are our daily inspections of our integrated product development process mitigating the potential losses due to regulatory non-compliance?

Evaluate internal controls. Report key control deficiencies, approvals, verifications, and reconciliations to mitigate risk. For example, are we randomly sampling and testing our products for defects? Are quality inspections occurring in all stages?

Evaluate incidents and losses. Are losses starting to mount as a few product returns starts to foreshadow the need to do a full-blown product recall?

No matter how proactive you are, manual monitoring can be very inefficient. Automated monitoring can proactively identify out-of-tolerance conditions, highlighting key areas for analysis on under/over pre-defined tolerances associated with a KPI, KRI, or control, and then alert the responsible party. This should take into account forecasting, trending and modeling capabilities so that if a metric falls out of range of a trend or budget/plan, then the appropriate alert is raised, along with the workflow process to get the investigation under way.

Analyze

Analysis is a key step in which you not only look at where you are, but what is happening (or what has happened) and why. The techniques for analysis can range from highly manual and simple to fairly automated and complex in terms of the usage of statistical techniques.

Table 15-6. Enabling Questions

	Planning	Post Launch	Data Integration Points
Product	• Is there similar product sales history you can learn from and lessons learned you can apply?	• Did you meet time-to-market goals? • How are your marketing programs performing? • Is your product meeting sales and revenue goals?	• PLM, MES, QM, ERP
Employees	• What has been employee's performance overall and on like projects? • Have they demonstrated the skill set and drive that would add value to the new product development and launch process?	• Are your employees meeting their deadlines? • Are your employees producing quality work? • Do I have the right people on the right teams?	• HCM, PLM, ERP
Partners	• Whether a co-development, selling, or marketing relationship, you need to know how responsive your partners have been to opportunities and deadlines, is your relationship worth your while?	• Continually evaluate performance and requalify partners. How did my partners perform in support of my product launch? • Are your partners meeting their Service Level Agreements?	• SRM, BPM
Suppliers	• Do your suppliers deliver you compliant and quality materials on time, so you can launch your products on time and meet market demand?	• Continually evaluate performance and requalify suppliers. How did my suppliers perform in support of my new product launch?	• DMS, SRM, ERP
Manufacturing	• Have I digitally validated my product ensuring optimal manufacturing process and tooling path, based on manufacturing history?	• What was the actual performance against specs (to ensure quality and manufacturing process ability)?	• MES, PLM
Process	• Do you have the optimal processes in place from design to manufacturing to recycling and back to design?	• Were your processes followed? • Did they enable/impede time-to-market goals?	• BPM, MES
Infrastructure	• Is the necessary infrastructure (portals, data and application integration, storage, security, and BPM) in place to enable rapid product development and launch?	• Did you meet time-to-market goals? • Was development or launch impeded by the lack of robust infrastructure?	• BPM, PLM

Analyze performance. Perform analysis on KPIs to understand why they are increasing or decreasing. For example, you analyze that the percentage of revenue from new products (< 1yr on Market) KPI on the products dashboard is trending downward will not hit its target and drill down to find out that this is because one of the new products is having significant quality problems that is preventing it from being successful with customers.

Analyze initiatives. Perform analysis on an initiative to understand why it is succeeding or failing. For example, you analyze that the critical initiative to roll out five new products this year is heading down the wrong direction and determine that this is due to the unintended effects of the new "quality development processes" initiative which is grinding innovation to a halt.

Analyze risk. Perform analysis on KRIs to understand why they are increasing or decreasing. For example, you conduct a correlation analysis to identify the relationship between number of defects per product line and quality per product line to ascertain the process deficiencies or other trends that are the most significant in increasing your customer satisfaction risk before it reaches critical levels.

Analyze controls. Perform analysis on the effectiveness of internal controls. For example, you notice that a control to randomly sample and test your products for defects seems to generate a lot of incidents and analyze that the thresholds are set too low creating a false positive. You conclude from your analysis that your controls have lost their effectiveness due to the newly improved quality processes you've rolled out and recognize the need to adjust the thresholds to be far more sensitive.

Analyze incidents and losses. Perform analysis on the root causes and trends of incidents and losses. For example, if incidents or losses have occurred due to the failure or absence of controls, such as shipments of defective products due to failure to follow quality steps.

In all of the cases above, analysis was being done with human intervention. However, it is important to note that this does not necessarily have to be the case. With the volume and complexity of data in the enterprise today, it is becoming increasingly difficult for humans to mine through the data and come to intelligent conclusions. Using data mining techniques, it is possible to have software determine the highest likely root causes for you, often much quicker than you could on your own, and even suggest recommended actions to remediate.

For example, you observe that a key KRI for number of quality incidents has been increasing. Without any manual intervention, the system does a series of correlations or more sophisticated statistical analyses in the background. When you highlight the KRI, a pop-up shows that the number one factor associated with the quality incidents is the sudden increase in machine downtime due to equipment failure.

It should be noted that analysis might require talents you don't currently possess. You may need help with the way you are evaluating metrics. Ensuring that your analysis is statistically sound may mean hiring an analyst with these qualifications or consulting with one.

Adjust

After monitoring to know what has happened and analyzing to understand why it happened, for those things not going accordingly to plan, it becomes time to set the business back on course by taking what you've learned and using that information to adjust the settings across the enterprise. However, you must always consider the impact of your goals, risks, and compliance concerns when making decisions to adjust your actions.

Adjust KPIs. For KPIs trending in the wrong direction, once you have analyzed the root causes, it should be clear what actions to take to set things back on course. However, it is critical to remember that KPIs are interlinked with each other, and you must optimize your performance goals in the context of risk objectives and without violating your compliance objectives. For example, you analyze that the Percentage of Revenue from New Products (< 1yr on Market) KPI on the products dashboard is trending downward because one of the new products is having significant quality problems that is preventing it from being successful with customers. You should invest resources in getting this product's quality back to an acceptable level. However, this can only be done if it does not increase the risk of jeopardizing the other key product's quality and if it doesn't violate any compliance objectives like having employees working longer than they are allowed to by law.

Analyze initiatives. For initiatives that are not going as planned, it becomes essential to rapidly take remedial action or cancel them. If it's clear that the initiative is not going to work, either make changes that can help save the project or cancel the project altogether if it is not critical so you can reallocate those resources. For example, you analyze that the critical initiative to roll out five new products this year is heading down the wrong direction due to the unintended effects of the new "quality development processes" initiative. You make the decision to streamline the quality development process initiative to get the new products rollout initiative back on track.

Analyze risk. For KRIs trending in the wrong direction, once you have analyzed the root causes, it should be clear what actions to take to set things back on course, often by putting the appropriate mitigating controls in place to stabilize them. However, it is critical to remember that KRIs are interlinked with each other, and you must optimize your risk goals in the context of performance objectives and without violating your compliance objectives. For example, with customers logging in more defects and numbers rising on a weekly basis, you increase the random sampling of batches in the production. You identify that you need to scratch the entire week's worth of production and double the production rate for the week. You need to also closely monitor resource overtime and ensure that you pay the hourly workers the correct labor rates that will impact other KPIs such as budget and product profitability.

Analyze controls. For controls violations, adjustment takes the form of remediation and certification. For example, after the product defect control is violated, you set up a remediation plan to include two signatures in the sign-off process from the supervising production and quality manager.

Analyze incidents and losses. For incidents and losses, the correct adjustments typically involve reexamining if we are tracking the right risks and have put the appropriate controls in place to mitigate them. For example, after determining that the uptick in product returns is due to the root cause of the failure to follow the appropriate procedures for an established quality monitoring policy, it would be appropriate to put an automated risk monitoring process in place that alerted you to the first sign of increased quality defects.

At the end of the day, your monitoring, analyses, and adjustments reveal where your strategy is working and the degree to which you are executing your plans. The results become the input to the next stage in the PM lifecycle, modeling and optimizing.

Model and Optimize

When you are creating a model of your operations, the goal is to be predictive—you will base your model on past and current performance, as a means to forecast future performance.

Model

Modeling takes several forms, including revenue, cost, and profitability modeling, scenario modeling, and simulation modeling.

Revenue, Cost, and Profitability Modeling

Modeling the costs, revenue, and profitability implications of performance management, risk management, and compliance management activities and their drivers can be achieved at a very detailed level using activity-based costing and associated methodologies. For the Product Development organization, ABC can be very useful for breaking down the costs of the individual activities people perform to get a much more detailed sense of where the various people who touch the integrated product development process are spending their time in order to find efficiencies. For example, using ABC, you can model the amount of time quality engineers are running tests, product managers are prototyping with customers, and development engineers are designing chip assemblies along with the costs of each unit of activity.

Scenario Modeling

Scenario modeling can be applied to financial and operational modeling and focuses on creating different business scenarios. Simple scenario modeling can include creating a base case and then high and low cases based on changes made to input variables, such as market growth rates or inflation rates. This technique is often used in modeling market and business opportunities and creating business plans.

For example, you might build a set of scenario models in Product Development to understand how critical macro variables such as consumer spending levels will impact your new product introduction strategies in a growth market.

Simulation Modeling

More advanced modeling including Monte Carlo simulation supports creating a broad range of scenarios based on multiple iterations of input assumptions and combinations. With this technique, probabilities can be assigned to the various outcomes. These techniques allow the uncertainty associated with a given forecast to be estimated and to reduce risk by applying sensitivity analysis, correlation, and trend extrapolation. By simulating the effect of uncertainty, it becomes possible to answer questions such as, "How certain are we that a given product will increase our overall product portfolio net profitability by a minimum of 5%?" Or, conversely, "What's the minimum increase in our overall product portfolio net profitability that we can be, for example, 90% certain of achieving?" Simulation also makes it possible to identify and rank the various contributors to overall uncertainty, proving yet another way that risk and performance interact.

Optimize

The goal at this phase of the PM lifecycle is to determine the optimal way to achieve objectives by taking into account the entire context of the problem, including all relevant constraints and assessments (costs, benefits, risk, labor and time), as well as business strategies, objectives, risks, and compliance factors. Optimization can be done both through human evaluation as well as through advanced algorithmic techniques.

It is now possible with the latest technologies to build very sophisticated models that incorporate activity-based costing, constraint-oriented process modeling, and comprehensive financial modeling to provide a single model for operational and financial metrics that ultimately results in seeking out the best solution to a given problem for a given set of business constraints. These systems have the ability to quickly change assumptions, variables, and the interdependencies between them, which make for much more dynamic models. Ultimately, these solutions can identify the best strategic and tactical actions to take for a given scenario, using financial and operational metrics as the objective function.

For example, we could input a goal of reducing the number of products and increasing the product ROI, and input all of the drivers to this goal mentioned earlier, and have the software tell us exactly which products to keep, which to remove, and what revenue levels they would have to produce and at what costs in order to make the initiative work.

Case Study: Performance Management in Action

Virtual Gates is a fictional cutting-edge computer manufacturer with retail outlets. This section describes how the Product Development department's team at Virtual Gates closes its loop during the process of creating a new product line while retiring products that are no longer profitable.

Setting the Context

Clint Hobbs, CEO of Virtual Gates, has asked his VP of Product Development, Paul Burton, to find the smartest, most efficient way of increasing the net profitability of his product portfolio. This would be a challenge of itself, but that's not all Clint wants. Paul must enhance VG's portfolio such that it also aligns with VG's larger goal of driving profitable growth as measured by Virtual Gates' net income and earnings per share growth, especially as they are compared to VG's competitors, Hypercell and Packingflash.

To begin, Paul must create a product rationalization initiative that introduces a new key product while reducing the number of unprofitable ones, a result that will be expressed in the key metrics of innovation investment and time to break even. Next, he needs to communicate the goal and all of its touch points to the Product Development department itself. Paul must ensure that his message extends to departments with which Product Development collaborates in-house and, finally, beyond, to the customer, analyst, and partner community as appropriate.

The key factor driving growth and profitability in Product Development is the pressure to innovate. Industry leaders bring products to market twice as fast as their competition and invest more time in the early stages of development. Critical to reaching operational excellence is the new product development and launch (NPDL) process. Once Paul's department has made its decisions about the products it will sunset (based on assessment of the market demand and fluctuations), its success in the early phase of the NPDL process rests primarily on the shoulders of its R&D house, where concepts are generated and brought to life through sharp designs and even sharper engineering. After all, without strong product ideas, VG would have nothing on which to base its reputation.

As it turns out, good ideas are the least of Paul's worries. His teams at VG achieves continuous success for numerous reasons. Working closely in tandem with Product Development, the Marketing team, run by Samantha Curtin, continually and accurately defines market requirements that fuel new product direction and development, the go-to-market strategies and execution for new production introductions, and the ongoing enablement of direct and indirect sales channels. Market share data, analyst ratings, media share of voice and tonality statistics, unaided purchase consideration statistics and profiling information are just a few of the things that Samantha's department feeds to product and other departments as a means of continuously refining its strategy and plans. But more than this, once Paul's teams have been armed with data from Marketing, they have consistently conceived of and developed one game-changing product after the other.

Market research conducted under Samantha's direction determined that in 2009, 21.5 million netbooks are expected to be sold (a growth of 189% from 2008) and that by 2012, sales are projected to increase up to 50 million. After consulting with Paul, Samantha, and CSO Leah Broder, CEO Clint Hobbs has decided that the best strategy to capture the largest possible portion of the market is to develop a new line of netbooks that isn't merely smaller and faster than VG's competitors, but one whose look and feel is customizable on demand, much the way that companies such as Scion and Nike allow buyers to customize their products.

Understand the Collaborative Impact

By now it's clear that none of the stages in a product's lifecycle are executed in a vacuum. Paul and his teams in Product Development own the integrated product development and continuous product innovation business processes, both of which span VG's entire value chain, including its suppliers and customers.

As the netbook under development progresses from design to engineering, engineering to manufacture, and manufacture to marketing, distribution, sales, and service, Paul's chief priority is to ensure that each of these processes remain in strict alignment. This is critical. For instance, if integrated sourcing and procurement is out of joint with the supplier network management, production schedules can be disrupted. In turn, the collaborative demand and supply plan would be affected, resulting in budget fractures that would distress Finance, HR, and IT processes.

Ultimately, these slips could have serious consequences. For instance, if VG is knows that its competitor Packingflash is developing a similar netbook, it is imperative that each of VG's production stages reaches completion on or before deadline so that VG can launch its netbook on time. Should VG miss this window, Packingflash could release its netbook first, an unwanted outcome with far-reaching consequences. Virtual Gates, for example, might have to invest more in Marketing and Sales than it had intended to reach the number of consumers it needs to meet Clint Hobbs' demand to achieve a minimum of 2% overall growth. If, on the other hand, each of these processes run smoothly and in strong collaboration, the outcome is likely to be positive: the entire organism that is Virtual Gates would remain in a state of steady and vigorous growth that encourages enhanced loyalty in existing customers as well as attracting new ones.

Establish KPIs and KRIs

No team can achieve goals without a benchmarking system that efficiently and accurately measures progress. As we have said, the means by which every company and every department does this is through the shrewd selection and implementation of relevant KPIs and KRIs. As Paul and his teams set out to achieve their respective goals, it is crucial that they first identify the primary KPIs and KRIs, the foremost risks to which their decisions expose them, and the significant interfaces between their partners and their processes that need instrumentation. They must also ascertain the drivers behind their KPIs and KRIs, the relationships between them, and the leading indicators of performance. They must sell the strategy to upper management and help to get it pushed down to every employee.

Communicating the impact of these metrics to product's partners is also crucial. For instance, decreasing investment in innovation by reducing the budget to create multiple products in favor of one or two game-changers such as the new netbook will result in more working capital for the entire company. In turn, Finance will benefit, as will Procurement and Supply Chain. More working capital means that time to break can loosen somewhat. With less stress on these operational processes, they can focus more on the quality of the job rather than solely on its speed.

Establish the BI Foundation

A metric expressed in a KPI or KRI does not spontaneously manifest. Once Paul understands the key business dimensions and relevant KPIs and KRIs that matter, Product Development needs to obtain the data from various source systems, cleanse it, align the master data, and load it into a data mart or data warehouse. Paul and his teams must harvest data from a host of source systems, beginning with PLM, which, in turn, pulls from CRM, ERP, SCM, as well as from other data sources both structured and unstructured.

Virtual Gates' Product Development department must also translate its data into terms that are meaningful to the company's BI and PM applications. All this can't happen by itself, but without these efforts, neither Paul nor VG's CEO, to whom he reports, can access a single source of truth about the new netbook's development progress.

Strategize and Prioritize

Now that the rationale behind VG's cutting most of its unprofitable products has been established—the enhanced brand recognition and value that VG's new netbook will generate, along with the correlative fattened profit margins—Paul will direct his teams to create a scorecard by which to monitor the netbook's development. The scorecard must also take into account the risk inherent to reducing the product portfolio, namely that the cuts could upset customers who are still using those products, which ultimately could result in dissatisfaction and injury to VG's brand equity.

Given that VG is operating in an economic downturn, this could be tricky. Samantha Curtin, the head of marketing, has reiterated to Paul that the harvest opportunities with existing customers when their products are being retired are quite sensitive. The KRI for such a possibility should have a threshold of a 10% decrease in customer satisfaction, and the mitigation strategy would be to segment VG's customers into strategic and non-strategic groups. Those products that have been identified as critical to the strategic group of customers could be kept in production and perhaps increased in price to protect the company's overall profit margin from further damage. Products related to non-strategic groups would be retired as planned.

Finally, Paul will document, test, monitor, and certify a control to ensure that the product rationalization process is proceeding in a way that is compliant with existing contracts with customers as well as with suppliers who provide the raw materials for these products. Sunsetting a product that the company is contractually obligated to produce could be a disaster.

Plan and Execute

Having chosen which products to keep and which to sunset makes Paul's planning job considerably easier. To begin, the portion of the budget that had been allocated to those products slated for retirement can now be split between the remaining products, the new netbook, and other projects in development. Engineers, designers, product managers and others will now have more availability, too, and increasing numbers of resources can be redeployed across Procurement, Supply Chain, Marketing, Sales, and Service as unprofitable products are retired. Innovation investments should reflect more profit, while time to break even for remaining products improves.

The plan, of course, must account for all of the aforementioned risks, from the opportunity costs of removing the non-profitable products, to potential customer satisfaction, to loss of brand equity. This concern is especially important to understand in light of other departments and stakeholders since they may have competing initiatives and different expectations. Paul will need his teams to put KRIs and mitigating controls in place to understand this tradeoff.

Monitor and Analyze

Now that old products have been retired and others developed while the new netbook goes to market, Paul and his teams must ensure that his product profitability, innovation investment, and time to break even metrics are on target. It is also important to monitor the dependent KPIs in the other departments. For instance, is Procurement accumulating raw materials for the products that are being retired? Is Service receiving increased complaints about the product retirement program? Have more resources actually been freed up? Has the remaining product portfolio increased in value relative to costs and thus contributed to profitable revenue growth? How is the current product portfolio impacting the performance of VG's suppliers and customers?

If the results are not satisfactory, Paul and his teams must take quick action to determine the reason and the solution. For instance, it may be that the portfolio's profitable products are so low in volume that they can't make up for higher volume but less profitable products. On the other hand, perhaps Supply Chain, Procurement, or Sales has a competing initiative that is counteracting the effect of Product Development's plan. It is also possible that the problem lies in an unreasonable strategy. Does the formula to increase working capital by removing unprofitable products need adjusting? Whatever the results of the analysis are, any solution must be aligned with all the other departments.

Model and Optimize

Paul and his teams need a detailed operational cost model to understand which products are profitable and to what degree. Modeling the resource consumption to focus on the use of people, time, and materials will enable them to see whether they lack the capacity or the appropriate skill-set to bring the aforementioned strategy and plan to successful fruition.

A costing analysis model shows them which products provide the most value per planning, product design, and portfolio management resource. In some cases, the products that seem to be generating the greatest top line growth may in fact be liabilities. The costing model will reveal whether they have been consuming more resources and assets than originally thought.

After changing key assumptions and simulating different "what-if" scenarios to confirm that their strategy and resources are sound, they can deploy a variety of optimization techniques to achieve their goals.

Closing the Loop in an Integrated System

The scenario described to this point is one that current technology can manage. However, the industry is evolving toward a holistic, closed-loop system that consistently aligns execution with strategy. Paul's ultimate goal is to create a strategy management process that captures goals, initiatives, and the appropriate metrics that can be linked to his driver-based financial and operational planning process, as well as to his monitoring and analysis, modeling and optimization, and risk and control processes. With this alignment, a whole new set of scenarios emerges: Paul and his teams can use goals, initiatives, plans, and risks and controls to push the desired behavior out to their transactional processes.

For example, Paul wants to deploy integrated PLM and performance management solutions to achieve instant visibility into product and project status by quickly drilling into a central product information repository at any assembly level or project step tailored to individual reporting requirements. He and his teams can pull data from the PLM system and those deployed by Supply Chain, Procurement, and Finance. If a product or project is behind schedule or trending in the wrong direction, users can work within a single interface to send that performance management context into the PLM system, and modify such variables as the number of designers assigned to a project or resources assigned to product management. In this way, multiple objectives are achieved. The strategy to improve profitable growth in Product Development, the initiative to rationalize shifts in the product portfolio, and the real act of sunsetting unprofitable products while introducing products like the new netbook are thoroughly integrated. Moreover, both efficiency—doing things right—and effectiveness—doing the right things—are greatly enhanced.

Align the Workforce

Paul's last aim is to link all of the aforementioned activities with his teams' objectives and compensation. For example, any time a product development professional is shown that his contribution to the successful restructuring of the product portfolio according to corporate strategy will result in a bonus, he will almost certainly do what it takes to meet his targets. When departments see that their bonuses are tied to the effectiveness with which Product Development reaches its goals, they will strive that much harder. The success of Paul's partners is his own success. At the end of the year, after he has reported a 5% growth in product's overall profit as measured by Virtual Gates' net income and earnings per share growth, including a 20% increase in netbook market share capture (leaving Hypercell and Packingflash in the far distance), Paul is sure to receive his own nice bonus package from CEO Clint Hobbs.

Action Items

We have shown how implementing performance management for Product Development can benefit your business across the enterprise. Once your program is in place, your strategies and goals will be aligned with the organization's overall goals, and your metrics will monitor results from the outside in, considering the customer's needs and concerns first. Your program will be cross-functional and multidimensional, considering service, assets, cost, and time with the same keen eye. Finally, you'll have clearly defined, and hence actionable, accountability.

The following list includes a recap of action items to consider when setting out to formalize your program:

- Know what kind of company you are, define your company's needs, and base your thinking, decisions, and activities on these key facts
- Envision managing your product from end-to-end—from ideation to manufacture to sales and service
- Break down organizational barriers
- Reduce ad-hoc reporting capabilities to the lowest level of available information
- Use technology systems to move away from spreadsheet-based systems
- Engage in "what-if" analysis to understand cause-and-effect across the product development business process
- Drive your progress through innovation
- Outsource all non-core processes and operations. Building supplier trust is key to mitigate risk
- Leverage all existing BI infrastructure and metrics
- Implement a single user interface for all strategic and operational systems

Advice and Best Practices

Along with the top best practices for your performance management program for supply networks, the following list includes advice to ensure that your program remains effective and competitive.

- Nobody can track more than seven KPIs at a time, so pick the ones that make the most difference in a given context, and get them under control before you move to others

- Leverage cutting-edge communication technologies to encourage end-users to collaborate: wikis, blogs, and tagging are all useful; instant messaging can provide a new level of immediacy to cross-functional collaboration
- Always consider leading indicators that predict performance instead of lagging indicators that reconcile the past
- Integrate product development and sourcing so that you can respond to customer needs faster and more efficiently
- Provide the central language of the organization by translating the key objectives that the other business units care about (service requests, number of new product introduced, etc.) into the key financial objectives that measure shareholder value
- Always align your supply network goals to HR goals. MBOs and incentives should be structured to reward desired behavior

Chapter 16

Conclusion

The mission of this book is to help people working in business learn how to implement better forms of performance management. As we said right from the start, the right way forward is different for each company. The challenge of performance management is to understand what is possible, discover what processes others have used, find out what technology may be helpful, and learn how to apply performance management to specific situations. The authors hope that this book has moved you forward in obtaining answers to these questions.

Some of the people reading this volume will be in positions of authority and will be able to hand this book to the teams under their control and ask someone to make a plan for improving performance management. But most people will not be in that situation. Most of us reside somewhere in the middle of an organization. To prove the value of performance management in our own jobs, we just need to implement the performance management lifecycle as best we can, using the information and tools available. Nothing is as persuasive as a tangible demonstration of success based on application of performance management in the context of the everyday struggle in a business. Our success as individuals provides a platform to promote performance management to a wider audience. To effect change on a companywide basis, we have to convince others that we have discovered the right way forward. It is time then, for us to review some of the main points discussed in the previous pages and to analyze how best to make a case for improving performance management.

The Role of Risk

Perhaps the most useful point of this book for companies that are seeking to get the most value from performance management is to include analysis of risk at every stage of the lifecycle. Adding the dimension of risk forces companies to ask deeper questions about their strategy, methods of execution, skill portfolio, partner relationships, compliance issues, and other business issues. By attempting to find ways to measure and monitor risk, an early warning system is put in place.

Performing a risk analysis means two important things happen. First, the context in which a business activity is taking place is analyzed for potential threats. A risk analysis by definition considers not just the happy path but what sort of nightmares might occur and what the early warning signs of those nightmares might be. Second, the potential reward from an activity is balanced by the recognition that some sort of risk is involved. Two equal rewards can now be compared based on the level or risk each entails.

Finally, performing a risk analysis is a collaborative process. Everyone involved in planning and execution must be consulted. In performing a risk analysis, the awareness of risk is propagated throughout a company so that when potential problems arise, people know what to do to make sure those issues are analyzed, monitored, tracked, and managed proactively.

The Expanding Scope of Performance Management

The domain of performance management has steadily increased in scope and shows no signs of stopping. From the field's beginnings in business intelligence dashboards and financial consolidation to the expansion to spend analytics, activity-based costing, and strategy management, as one layer of challenges were discovered and met, new ones appeared.

There are three ways that performance management seems to be expanding and each offers the promise of a significant payoff. The first mode of expansion is that performance management is increasingly stretched across the boundaries of a company into the extended business network. Partners are being asked to participate in providing large amounts of data about their internal processes so that the orchestrating companies can adjust the flow of production, control quality, ensure compliance, and spot problems early.

The second area of expansion is the growth of performance management beyond financial and operational measures to a broader set of indicators related to sustainability and environmental impact. As performance management grew from a sole focus on financial metrics to encompass operational metrics, the models of business activity started to cover new forms of processes and deepen the understanding of what drives the performance of the business. Now, a new set of stakeholders, a group that demands accountability, has emerged alongside investors, who seek profitable growth. As more metrics related to sustainability and the environment are tracked, the scope of models will grow further and the drivers will also be discovered.

A third area of growth in the scope of performance management is the way that companies are increasingly seeking deeper and more specific benchmarks. At a high level, companies have always compared their financial and certain types of operational indicators, such as days sales outstanding or inventory levels, to those of their industry peers. Now that the operational models of the business are becoming more detailed, the scope for benchmarking has increased.

This latest wave of expansion in performance management is occurring for the same reasons that drove the previous trends: there is significant value to be gained from tracking these additional dimensions of business activity.

How Performance Management Could Change the World

Even though performance management practices have come a long way, it is important to recognize that in many ways, we are still in the early days. The information has started to flow and companies are now run with an increasing awareness of many things that were left unexamined, but there is much room for more to be done.

Imagine a board meeting five years from now. It is easy to imagine a meeting, for example, to discuss a downward trend in profits. Instead of having to discuss what questions should be studied and brought back for later review, it should be possible to ask and answer questions right then, using a performance management system that allows drilldown into all the relevant areas. For example, the CFO should be able to look at the trends in all of the components of net income. Perhaps the CFO discovers the most obvious cause of the declining income is increased costs in a particular product line. The VP of Supply Chain looks up the product line and identifies increased costs in a category (such as feedstock or oil). Then the VP of Procurement looks up that category and identifies spend breakdown and determines to identify alternate sources of supply. It is not hard to imagine that alternate sources are presented on the dashboard. One could be chosen and submitted for a risk review. The Chief Risk Officer can pull up a dashboard and start to determine if there are unacceptable risks. The head of customer service can report on any quality problems that may have had an effect on the market. The VP of Sales can look for other contributing factors reported from the field that may have dampened sales. The VP of marketing can analyze how to reshuffle resources to prop up demand in the desired area. During all this, the CIO and CTO can both beam happily now that everyone is speaking the same language. At the next board meeting, it would be just as simple to see if the adjustment worked. The VP of Procurement could show the costs from the new supplier. The VP of Supply Chain's dashboard shows that costs have gone down and so the product line margin is looking good again. The CFO agrees and indicates to the CEO that the revenue on the dashboard is trending back up.

It is possible to imagine an even more advanced integration of performance management, risk and compliance management, and business process management. In a world in which a company is run according to explicitly defined end-to-end processes, it will be possible to look at a goal that the company is trying to achieve in an integrated fashion. One side of the goal will be the business process used to achieve that goal, another side will be the performance management metrics that are used to track the progress of the execution of the process, and the third side would be the risk indicators and compliance processes that must be performed as part of that processes. Any goal in business involves all three of these dimensions, but now they are treated more separately than they should be. Any attempt at optimization involves all three as well. The end result of this kind of strategy-driven execution is the ability to rapidly reconfigure your business with confidence that no important issues are being ignored.

What Then Must We Do?

Success in business is a combination of many things. Performance management is a way to ensure that as little as possible gets in the way. Performance management does not create the strategy, but it can make sure the strategy is created with adequate information and is carried out according to plan so the various business owners are accountable. Performance management does not eliminate risk, but it does help determine when a company is going off track. Performance management started out as an enabler of success, and in today's increasingly complex businesses, it has become a necessity, for individuals, for departments, for divisons, and for entire companies.

High quality performance management is mandatory to give a company the best chance of surviving and thriving in today's world.

We have encountered many people in many companies in our careers and in our research for this book, and a pattern has emerged in those who have succeeded in becoming masters of performance management. The following playbook has emerged from their experience:

- Take action. Start immediately. Think big, but start small. The strongest players pick the highest value processes, the two most important metrics, the highest priority decisions, and apply the performance management lifecycle to the fullest extent possible
- Apply performance management locally. We have tried to make this easy. Go back to the chapter most applicable to you and your area of the business and take up the mantle. Don't attempt to tackle more than is practical at first. Use the local victory to get a shot at the global challenges
- Be a leader in the transformation of culture. Be the person who always brings up risk and who always asks for more data and more ways to understand it. Don't wait for perfection but do the best you can with what you have

We have dedicated our careers to helping advance the practice of performance management. We hope that after reading this book, you will find it as compelling an endeavor as we have and put it to work to enhance your success and that of your organization. To dialogue with us, please visit:

- www.driventoperform.net